W9-CON-496

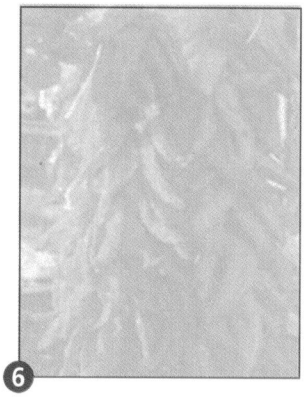

1 **Dominican Republic** Girl in festival costume with gold braid and bells
2 **Miami Beach, Florida** The Art Deco district at night
3 **Argentina** Gaucho on a cattle drive in Patagonia
4 **Mexico** Serpent head from the Pyramid of Quetzalcóatl in Teotihuacán
5 **Spain** Plaza Mayor, Madrid
6 **Texas** A string of red chile peppers, El Paso
7 **Chile** Central market in the town of Antofagasta
8 **Peru** Market in the town of Pisaq
9 **Puerto Rico** Colonial architecture in Old San Juan
10 **Costa Rica** Red macaw in the Jardín Zoológico, San José

(Back cover: **Peru** Teens in traditional costume)

HOLT SPANISH 1

TEXAS EDITION

¡Exprésate!®

Nancy Humbach

Sylvia Madrigal Velasco

Ana Beatriz Chiquito

Stuart Smith

John McMinn

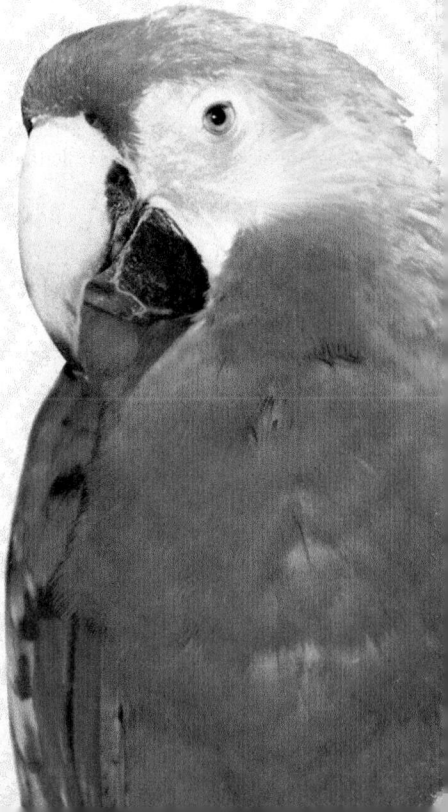

HOLT, RINEHART AND WINSTON

A Harcourt Education Company

Orlando • Austin • New York • San Diego • Toronto • London

Holt Teacher Advisory Panel

As members of the **Holt World Languages Advisory Panel,** the following teachers made a unique and invaluable contribution to the ***¡Exprésate!*** Spanish program. They generously shared their experience and expertise in a collaborative group setting and helped refine early materials into the program design represented in this book. We wish to thank them for the many hours of work they put into the development of this program and for the many ideas they shared.

¡Muchísimas gracias a todos!

Erick Ekker
Bob Miller Middle School
Henderson, NV

Dulce Goldenberg
Miami Senior High School
Miami, FL

Beckie Gurnish
Ellet High School
Akron, OH

Bill Heller
Perry High School
Perry, NY

MilyBett Llanos
Westwood High School
Austin, TX

Rosanna Perez
Communications Arts
High School
San Antonio, TX

Jo Schuler
Central Bucks High School East
Doylestown, PA

Leticia Schweigert
Science Academy
Mercedes, TX

Claudia Sloan
Lake Park High School
Roselle, IL

Judy Smock
Gilbert High School
Gilbert, AZ

Catriona Stavropoulos
West Springfield High School
Springfield, VA

Nina Wilson
Burnet Middle School
Austin, TX

Janet Wohlers
Weston Middle School
Weston, MA

Copyright © 2006 by Holt, Rinehart and Winston

All rights reserved. No part of this publication may be reproduced or transmitted in any form or by any means, electronic or mechanical, including photocopy, recording, or any information storage and retrieval system, without permission in writing from the publisher.

Requests for permission to make copies of any part of the work should be mailed to the following address: Permissions Department, Holt, Rinehart and Winston, 10801 N. MoPac Expressway, Building 3, Austin, Texas 78759.

COVER PHOTOGRAPHY CREDITS

FRONT COVER (from top left to bottom right): John Langford/HRW; ©Royalty-Free/CORBIS; © Kit Houghton/CORBIS; ©Royalty Free/CORBIS; Don Couch/HRW; Gary Russ/HRW; Gaston Oyarzun; © Mario Corvetto/Evergreen Photo Alliance; John Langford/HRW; ©Philip Coblentz, Brand X Pictures.

BACK COVER: Don Couch/HRW.
Acknowledgments appear on page R54, which is an extension of the copyright page.

HOLT, ¡EXPRÉSATE!, and the "Owl Design" are trademarks licensed to Holt, Rinehart and Winston, registered in the United States of America and/or other jurisdictions.

ExpresaVisión and **GramaVisión** are trademarks of Holt, Rinehart and Winston. **TEKS** and **Texas Essential Knowledge and Skills** are trademarks of the Texas Education Agency, which does not endorse this product.

Printed in the United States of America

ISBN-13: 978-0-03-073687-2
ISBN-10: 0-03-073687-0
9 10 11 2266 13 12 4500374245

Authors

Nancy Humbach

Nancy Humbach is Associate Professor and Coordinator of Languages Education at Miami University, Oxford, Ohio. She has authored or co-authored over a dozen textbooks in Spanish. A former Fulbright-Hayes Scholar, she has lived and studied in Colombia and Mexico and has traveled and conducted research throughout the Spanish-speaking world. She is a recipient of many honors, including the Florence Steiner Award for Leadership in the Foreign Language Profession and the Nelson Brooks Award for the Teaching of Culture.

Sylvia Madrigal Velasco

Sylvia Madrigal Velasco was born in San Benito, Texas. The youngest of four siblings, she grew up in the Rio Grande Valley, between two cultures and languages. Her lifelong fascination with Spanish has led her to travel in many Spanish-speaking countries. She graduated from Yale University in 1979 and has worked for over 20 years as a textbook editor and author at various publishing companies. She has written bilingual materials, video scripts, workbooks, CD-ROMs, and readers.

Ana Beatriz Chiquito

Professor Ana Beatriz Chiquito is a native of Colombia. She teaches Spanish linguistics and Latin American culture at the University of Bergen, Norway, and conducts research and develops applications for language learning at the Center for Educational Computing Initiatives at the Massachusetts Institute of Technology. She has taught Spanish for more than thirty years and has authored numerous textbooks, CD-ROMs, videos, and on-line materials for college and high school students of Spanish.

Stuart Smith

Stuart Smith began her teaching career at the University of Texas at Austin from where she received her degrees. She has been a professor of foreign languages at Austin Community College, Austin, Texas, for over 20 years and has been writing textbook and teaching materials for almost as long. She has given presentations on language teaching methodology at ACTFL, SWCOLT, and TCCTA.

John McMinn

John McMinn is Professor of Spanish and French at Austin Community College, where he has taught since 1986. After completing his M.A. in Romance Linguistics at the University of Texas at Austin, he also taught Spanish and French at the secondary level and was a Senior Editor of World Languages at Holt, Rinehart and Winston. He is co-author of both Spanish and French textbooks at the college level.

Contributing Writers

Jeff Cole
Tucson, AZ
Mr. Cole developed activities for **Taller del escritor.**

Jabier Elorrieta
The University of Texas at Austin
Mr. Elorrieta wrote **Letra y sonido.**

Karin Fajardo
Englewood, CO
Ms. Fajardo wrote vocabulary activities and material for **También se puede decir.**

Catherine Gavin
New York City, NY
Ms. Gavin wrote material for **Geocultura** and **Cultura.**

Kathy Hoyt
Olympia, WA
Ms. Hoyt wrote additional material for the **Comunidad** feature.

Pablo Muirhead
Shorewood High School
Shorewood, WI
Mr. Muirhead wrote suggestions for the story sequence art.

Gloria Munguía
Austin, TX
Ms. Munguía wrote activities for **Integración.**

Marci Reed
Ms. Reed contributed to the selection of and wrote material for **Literatura y variedades.**

Mayanne Wright
Austin, TX
Ms. Wright contributed to the selection of and wrote material for **Leamos** and wrote the **Comunidad** features.

Reviewers

These educators reviewed one or more chapters of the Student Edition.

Elizabeth Baird
Independence High School
Independence, OH

Paula Camardella Twomey
Ithaca High School
Ithaca, NY

Johnnie Eng
Alamo Heights High School
San Antonio, TX

Patricia Gander
Berkeley High School
Moncks Corner, SC

Laura Grable
Riverhead Central School District
Riverhead, NY

Mani Hernández
Presentation High School
San Jose, CA

Yoscelina Hernández
Montwood High School
El Paso, TX

Jessica Shrader
Charlotte High School
Punta Gorda, FL

Sharlene Soto
D.C. Everest Jr. and Sr. High Schools
Wausau, WI

Nancy Walker de Llanas
George C. Marshall High School
Falls Church, VA

Thomasina I. White
Lead Academic Coach
World Language Education
Philadelphia, PA

Field Test Participants

We thank the teachers and students who participated in the field test of *¡Exprésate!* Levels 1–6.

Heather Beaty
Mt. Vernon High School
Mt. Vernon, OH

Tom Burel
West Middle School
Rockford, IL

Anita Gibbs
Robert E. Lee High School
San Antonio, TX

Alicia Granto
Bennett High School
Buffalo, NY

Francois Jackson
Bryan Station Senior High School
Lexington, KY

Rebekah Lindsey
Campbell Middle School
Daytona Beach, FL

Yamilette Osuna
St. Vincent Ferrer High School
New York, NY

Mary Ann Seward
Central VP High School
St. Louis, MO

Sarah Taylor
Richland Middle School
Richmond, VA

Carmen Truax
Lincoln College Prep
Kansas City, MO

Contenido en breve

Table of Contents vi
El español, ¿por qué? xvi
En la clase de español xx
Nombres comunes xxi
Instrucciones xxii
Texas Essential Knowledge and Skills xxiii

España
Geocultura xxiv
Capítulo 1 4
Integración Capítulo 1 36

Puerto Rico
Geocultura 38
Capítulo 2 42
Integración Capítulos 1–2 74

Texas
Geocultura 76
Capítulo 3 80
Integración Capítulos 1–3 112

Costa Rica
Geocultura 114
Capítulo 4 118
Integración Capítulos 1–4 150

Chile
Geocultura 152
Capítulo 5 156
Integración Capítulos 1–5 188

México
Geocultura 190
Capítulo 6 194
Integración Capítulos 1–6 226

Argentina
Geocultura 228
Capítulo 7 232
Integración Capítulos 1–7 264

Florida
Geocultura 266
Capítulo 8 270
Integración Capítulos 1–8 302

La República Dominicana
Geocultura 304
Capítulo 9 308
Integración Capítulos 1–9 340

Perú
Geocultura 342
Capítulo 10 346
Integración Capítulos 1–10 378

Literatura y variedades
España 382
Puerto Rico 384
Texas 386
Costa Rica 388
Chile 390
México 392
Argentina 394
Florida 396
La República Dominicana 398
Perú 400

Mapas
La Península Ibérica R2
México R3
Estados Unidos de América R4
América Central y las Antillas R5
América del Sur R6

Vocabulario adicional R7
Expresiones de ¡Exprésate! R12
Síntesis gramatical R16
Vocabulario español-inglés R24
Vocabulario inglés-español R42
Índice gramatical R50
Agradecimientos R54

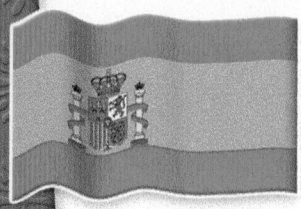

España

Capítulo 1 ¡Empecemos! 4

Vocabulario en acción 1 6
- Asking someone's name
- Asking how someone is
- Introducing others
- Saying where you and others are from

Gramática en acción 1 12
- Using subjects and verbs in sentences
- Using subject pronouns

Cultura 16
- **Comparaciones**
- **Comunidad**

Vocabulario en acción 2 18
- Giving phone numbers
- Saying the time, day, and date
- Spelling words and giving e-mail addresses

Gramática en acción 2 24
- Using the verb **ser**
- Punctuation marks and written accents

Novela 28
¿Quién será? Episodio 1

Leamos y escribamos 30
Participa en el club de español (Leamos)
La página Web del club de español (Escribamos)

Repaso 32

Integración Capítulo 1 36

Literatura y variedades
El Museo del Prado (folleto) 382

Geocultura

Mapas de España ..... xxv, R2
Almanaque xxiv
A conocer España 2

En video

Geocultura	GeoVisión
Vocabulario 1 y 2	ExpresaVisión
Gramática 1 y 2	GramaVisión
Cultura	VideoCultura
VideoNovela	¿Quién será?
	Variedades

Visit Holt Online
go.hrw.com
KEYWORD: EXP1 CH1
Online Edition

Puerto Rico

Capítulo 2 A conocernos 42

Vocabulario en acción 1 44
- Asking what someone is like
- Describing someone
- Asking someone's age and birthday

Gramática en acción 1 48
- Using **ser** with adjectives
- Gender and adjective agreement
- Forming questions

Cultura 54
- **Comparaciones**
- **Comunidad**

Vocabulario en acción 2 56
- Talking about what you and others like
- Describing things
- Descriptive adjectives

Gramática en acción 2 60
- Using nouns with definite articles
- Using **gustar**, **¿por qué?**, and **porque**
- Using the preposition **de**

Novela 66
¿Quién será? Episodio 2

Leamos y escribamos 68
¿Qué color prefieres? (Leamos)
Mi personalidad (Escribamos)

Repaso 70

Integración Capítulos 1–2 74

Literatura y variedades
El coquí (artículo) 384

Geocultura

Mapas de Puerto Rico ... 38, R5
Almanaque 38
A conocer Puerto Rico 40

En video

Geocultura	GeoVisión
Vocabulario 1 y 2	ExpresaVisión
Gramática 1 y 2	GramaVisión
Cultura	VideoCultura
VideoNovela	¿Quién será?
	Variedades

Visit Holt Online
go.hrw.com
KEYWORD: EXP1 CH2
Online Edition

Texas

Capítulo 3 ¿Qué te gusta hacer? 80

Vocabulario en acción 1 82
- Talking about what you and others like to do
- Talking about what you want to do
- Pastimes and sports

Gramática en acción 1 86
- Using **gustar** with infinitives
- Using pronouns after prepositions
- Using **querer** with infinitives

Cultura 92
- **Comparaciones**
- **Comunidad**

Vocabulario en acción 2 94
- Talking about everyday activities
- Saying where you go and how often
- Places and activities

Gramática en acción 2 98
- Using regular **-ar** verbs
- Using **ir** and **jugar**
- Using weather expressions

Novela 104
¿Quién será? Episodio 3

Leamos y escribamos 106
Los cuatro elementos (Leamos)
Horario de actividades (Escribamos)

Repaso 108

Integración Capítulos 1–3 112

Literatura y variedades
Obras de Carmen Lomas Garza (comentarios) 386

Geocultura

Mapas de Texas 76, R4
Almanaque 76
A conocer Texas 78

En video

Geocultura	GeoVisión
Vocabulario 1 y 2	ExpresaVisión
Gramática 1 y 2	GramaVisión
Cultura	VideoCultura
VideoNovela	¿Quién será?
	Variedades

Costa Rica

Capítulo 4 La vida escolar 118

Vocabulario en acción 1 120
- Saying what you have and what you need
- Talking about classes
- Naming school supplies and school subjects

Gramática en acción 1 124
- Using indefinite articles, **¿cuánto?, mucho,** and **poco**
- Using **tener** and **tener** idioms
- Using **venir** and **a la/las** with time

Cultura 130
- **Comparaciones**
- **Comunidad**

Vocabulario en acción 2 132
- Talking about plans
- Inviting others to do things
- Naming school events and places

Gramática en acción 2 136
- Using **ir a** with infinitives
- Regular **-er** and **-ir** verbs and tag questions
- Some **-er** and **-ir** verbs with irregular **yo** forms

Novela 142
¿Quién será? Episodio 4

Leamos y escribamos 144
Pepito, el niño precoz (Leamos)
Un recorrido con nuevos estudiantes (Escribamos)

Repaso 146

Integración Capítulos 1–4 150

Literatura y variedades
La artesanía chorotega (entrevista) 388

Geocultura

Mapas de Costa Rica ... 114, R5
Almanaque 114
A conocer Costa Rica 116

En video

Geocultura **GeoVisión**
Vocabulario 1 y 2 **ExpresaVisión**
Gramática 1 y 2 **GramaVisión**
Cultura **VideoCultura**
VideoNovela **¿Quién será?**
Variedades

Visit Holt Online
go.hrw.com
KEYWORD: EXP1 CH4
Online Edition

Chile

Capítulo 5 En casa con la familia 156

Vocabulario en acción 1 158
- Describing people and family relationships
- Family members
- Physical characteristics

Gramática en acción 1 162
- Possessive adjectives
- Stem-changing verbs **o → ue**
- Stem-changing verbs **e → ie**

Cultura 168
- **Comparaciones**
- **Comunidad**

Vocabulario en acción 2 170
- Talking about where people live
- Talking about responsibilities
- Naming chores, parts of the house, and furniture

Gramática en acción 2 174
- Using **estar** with prepositions
- Negation with **nunca, tampoco, nadie,** and **nada**
- Using **tocar** and **parecer**

Novela 180
¿Quién será? Episodio 5

Leamos y escribamos 182
Casas y apartamentos (Leamos)
¿Qué les toca hacer? (Escribamos)

Repaso 184

Integración Capítulos 1–5 ..... **188**

Literatura y variedades

Las novelas de Isabel Allende (comentario y fragmento) .. **390**

Geocultura

Mapas de Chile **152, R6**

Almanaque **152**

A conocer Chile **154**

En video

Geocultura	GeoVisión
Vocabulario 1 y 2	ExpresaVisión
Gramática 1 y 2	GramaVisión
Cultura	VideoCultura
VideoNovela	¿Quién será?
	Variedades

Visit Holt Online
go.hrw.com
KEYWORD: EXP1 CH5
Online Edition

México

Capítulo 6 ¡A comer! 194

Vocabulario en acción 1 196
- Commenting on food
- Making polite requests
- Naming foods and table settings

Gramática en acción 1 200
- Using **ser** and **estar**
- Using **pedir** and **servir**
- Using **preferir, poder,** and **probar**

Cultura 206
- **Comparaciones**
- **Comunidad**

Vocabulario en acción 2 208
- Talking about meals
- Offering help and giving instructions
- Naming more foods

Gramática en acción 2 212
- Using direct objects and direct object pronouns
- Affirmative informal commands
- Using affirmative informal commands with pronouns

Novela 218
¿Quién será? Episodio 6

Leamos y escribamos 220
La montaña del alimento (Leamos)
¿Cómo lo preparas? (Escribamos)

Repaso 222

Integración Capítulos 1–6 226

Literatura y variedades
La comida de dos continentes (artículo) 392

Geocultura

Mapas de México 190, R3
Almanaque 190
A conocer México 192

En video

Geocultura	GeoVisión
Vocabulario 1 y 2	ExpresaVisión
Gramática 1 y 2	GramaVisión
Cultura	VideoCultura
VideoNovela	¿Quién será?
	Variedades

Visit Holt Online
go.hrw.com
KEYWORD: EXP1 CH6
Online Edition

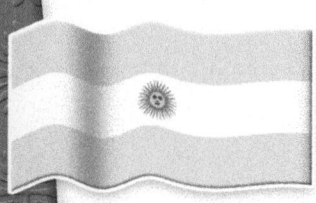

Argentina

Capítulo 7 Cuerpo sano, mente sana 232

Vocabulario en acción 1 234
- Talking about your daily routine
- Talking about staying fit and healthy
- Naming parts of the body

Gramática en acción 1 238
- Using verbs with reflexive pronouns
- Using infinitives
- Review of stem-changing verbs

Cultura 244
- **Comparaciones**
- **Comunidad**

Vocabulario en acción 2 246
- Talking about how you feel
- Giving advice
- Naming more parts of the body

Gramática en acción 2 250
- Using **estar**, **sentirse**, and **tener**
- Negative informal commands
- Using object pronouns and reflexive pronouns with commands

Novela 256
¿Quién será? Episodio 7

Leamos y escribamos 258
¡En buena salud! (Leamos)
El doctor te aconseja... (Escribamos)

Repaso 260

Integración Capítulos 1–7 264

Literatura y variedades

Juegos de palabras (adivinanzas) 394

Geocultura

Mapas de Argentina ...229, R6

Almanaque 228

A conocer Argentina 230

En video

Geocultura	GeoVisión
Vocabulario 1 y 2	ExpresaVisión
Gramática 1 y 2	GramaVisión
Cultura	VideoCultura
VideoNovela	¿Quién será?
	Variedades

Visit Holt Online
go.hrw.com
KEYWORD: EXP1 CH7
Online Edition

Florida

Capítulo 8 Vamos de compras 270

Vocabulario en acción 1 272
- Identifying clothing
- Asking for and giving opinions
- Asking for and offering help in a store

Gramática en acción 1 276
- Using **costar** and numbers to 1 million
- Using demonstrative adjectives and comparisons with adjectives
- Using **quedar**

Cultura 282
- **Comparaciones**
- **Comunidad**

Vocabulario en acción 2 284
- Saying where you went and what you did
- Talking on the phone
- Naming stores and saying what you buy there

Gramática en acción 2 288
- The preterite of **-ar** verbs
- The preterite of **ir**
- Review of the preterite of **-ar** verbs with reflexive pronouns

Novela 294
¿Quién será? Episodio 8

Leamos y escribamos 296
Una moneda de ¡Ay! (Leamos)
A mí me parece perfecto... (Escribamos)

Repaso 298

Integración Capítulos 1–8 302

Literatura y variedades
El amor a la poesía (poemas) 396

Geocultura

Mapas de Florida 266, R4
Almanaque 266
A conocer Florida 268

En video

Geocultura	GeoVisión
Vocabulario 1 y 2	ExpresaVisión
Gramática 1 y 2	GramaVisión
Cultura	VideoCultura
VideoNovela	¿Quién será?

Variedades

Visit Holt Online
go.hrw.com
KEYWORD: EXP1 CH8
Online Edition

La República Dominicana

Capítulo 9 ¡Festejemos! 308

Vocabulario en acción 1 310
- Talking about your plans
- Talking about past holidays
- Naming holidays

Gramática en acción 1 314
- Preterite of **-er** and **-ir** verbs
- Review of the preterite
- Using **pensar que** and **pensar** with infinitives

Cultura 320
- **Comparaciones**
- **Comunidad**

Vocabulario en acción 2 322
- Talking about preparing for a party
- Greeting and introducing others
- Saying goodbye

Gramática en acción 2 326
- Using direct object pronouns
- Using **conocer** and the personal **a**
- Using present progressive

Novela 332
¿Quién será? Episodio 9

Leamos y escribamos 334
Las mañanitas and **Canción de cumpleaños** (Leamos)
¡Juy, qué desastre! (Escribamos)

Repaso 336

Integración Capítulos 1–9 340

Literatura y variedades
El regalo de cumpleaños (cuento) 398

Geocultura

Mapas de la República Dominicana 304, R5

Almanaque 304

A conocer la República Dominicana 306

En video

Geocultura	GeoVisión
Vocabulario 1 y 2	ExpresaVisión
Gramática 1 y 2	GramaVisión
Cultura	VideoCultura
VideoNovela	¿Quién será?
	Variedades

Visit Holt Online
go.hrw.com
KEYWORD: EXP1 CH9
Online Edition

Perú

Capítulo 10 ¡A viajar! 346

Vocabulario en acción 1 348
- Asking for information
- Reminding and reassuring
- Naming places in the airport

Gramática en acción 1 352
- Review of the preterite
- Preterite of spelling change verbs **-car, -gar, -zar**
- Preterite of **hacer**

Cultura 358
- **Comparaciones**
- **Comunidad**

Vocabulario en acción 2 360
- Talking about a trip
- Expressing hopes and wishes
- Naming places and things to do around town

Gramática en acción 2 364
- Informal commands: spelling-change and irregular verbs
- Review of direct object pronouns
- Review of verbs followed by infinitives

Novela 370
¿Quién será? Episodio 10

Leamos y escribamos 372
¡Bienvenidos a la ciudad de Lima! (Leamos)
Cartas del extranjero (Escribamos)

Repaso 374

Integración Capítulos 1–10 378

Literatura y variedades
Ollantaytambo (leyenda) 400

Geocultura

Mapas de Perú 342, R6
Almanaque 342
A conocer Perú 344

En video

Geocultura	GeoVisión
Vocabulario 1 y 2	ExpresaVisión
Gramática 1 y 2	GramaVisión
Cultura	VideoCultura
VideoNovela	¿Quién será?
	Variedades

Visit Holt Online
go.hrw.com
KEYWORD: EXP1 CH10
Online Edition

El español, ¿por qué?

Why Study Spanish?

Por lo mundial *Because it's worldwide*

Spanish is the fourth most commonly spoken language in the world. You can visit any one of 21 countries in the world that speak Spanish and feel at home. Even in the United States, knowing Spanish can open doors to you.

So whether you're in Europe, North, Central, or South America, or even Africa, as a Spanish speaker you won't have to rely on someone else to watch television or read a newspaper. You'll learn things on your own. You'll truly be a citizen of the world.

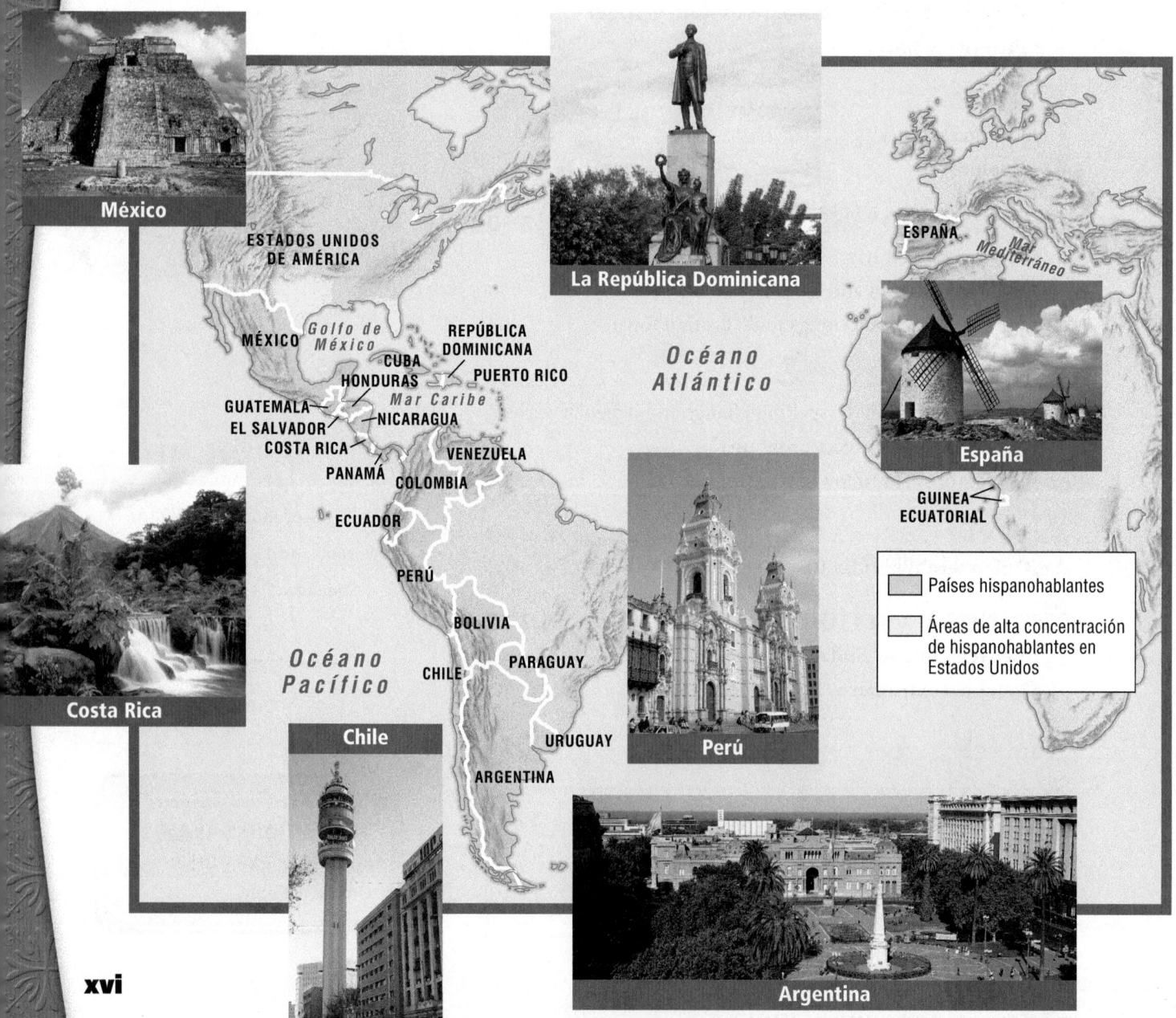

Por lo bello *Because it's beautiful*

You'll be amazed to discover how rich the Spanish-speaking world is in works of music, literature, science, religion, and art. The novels of Miguel de Cervantes or Isabel Allende, the paintings of Fernando Botero or Frida Kahlo, the poetry of Gabriela Mistral or Pablo Neruda: all these treasures and many more await you as you explore the Spanish-speaking world.

Ceramic tiles form this mural by Dominican artist Said Musa.

This popular folk dance is often called the Mexican hat dance.

Traditional painted carts in Costa Rica are a part of **El Festival de las Carretas.**

The fountain of Cibeles, named after the goddess Cybele, is one of Madrid's best-known landmarks.

Por lo práctico *Because it's practical*

You're living in the country with the fifth-largest Hispanic population in the world, more than 33 million people. And whether they're originally from Mexico, Puerto Rico, or Cuba—or from any other part of Latin America or Spain—almost nine out of ten are Spanish speakers.

Businesses, government agencies, educational institutions, and other employers will be looking for more bilingual employees every year. Give yourself an edge in the job market with Spanish!

Bilingual doctors, nurses, and others in the field of medicine provide care for Spanish-speaking patients.

Patricia Janiot is a popular anchor at the Spanish language news department of CNN en Español.

Miami is an international center and a multicultural hub for Latin American trade.

¡Porque puedes! *Because you can do it!*

Applying your learning skills to a new language will be challenging at first. But you have the tools you need to do the job. And you're lucky to be living at a time when there are almost no limits to your opportunities to practice Spanish. You can interact with Spanish speakers not just in your community but all over the world, via pen pal organizations, the library, or a multitude of resources and online networks.

Bicyclists stop at a spot overlooking the historic city of Toledo, Spain.

En fin, porque sí *Finally, just because...*

The best reason of all to study Spanish is because you want to! You know better than anyone what motivated you to enroll for Spanish class. It might be one of the reasons given here, such as getting a job, learning about world issues, or enjoying works of art. Or it might be something more personal, like wanting to communicate with Spanish-speaking friends and family, or travel. So pat yourself on the back and **¡Exprésate!**

Young people in Segovia, Spain, enjoy a walk after classes.

En la clase de español

In Spanish class

Here are some phrases you'll probably hear in your classroom, along with some responses.

Phrases:	Responses:
Tengo una pregunta. *I have a question . . .*	**¿Sí? Dime.** *Yes? What is it?*
¿Cómo se dice...? *How do you say . . .?*	**Se dice...** *You say . . .*
¿Cómo se escribe...? *How do you spell . . .?*	**Se escribe...** *It's spelled . . .*
No entiendo. ¿Puede repetir? *I don't understand. Could you repeat that?* **Más despacio, por favor.** *More slowly, please.*	**Claro que sí.** *Yes, of course.*
¿Sabes qué significa (quiere decir)...? *Do you know what . . . means?*	**No, no sé.** *No, I don't know.* **Sí, significa (quiere decir)...** *Yes, it means . . .*
Gracias. *Thank you.*	**De nada.** *You're welcome.*
Perdón. *I'm sorry.*	**Está bien.** *It's okay.*

Here are some things your teacher might ask you to do.

Levanten la mano.
Raise your hand.

Escuchen.
Listen.

¡Su atención, por favor!
Attention, please.

Silencio, por favor.
Silence, please.

Abran sus libros en la página...
Open your books to page . . .

Cierren los libros.
Close your books.

Estamos en la página...
We're on page . . .

Miren la pizarra (la transparencia).
Look at the board (transparency).

Saquen una hoja de papel.
Take out a sheet of paper.

Pasen la tarea (los papeles) al frente.
Pass the homework (the papers) to the front.

Levántense, por favor.
Stand up, please.

Siéntense, por favor.
Sit down, please.

Repitan después de mí.
Repeat after me.

Nombres comunes
Common Names

Here are some common names from Spanish-speaking countries.

Nombres de muchachas

Ana	Inés	Patricia
Bárbara	Irene	Pilar
Beatriz	Isabel	Rosalía
Cecilia	Josefina	Rosario
Cristina	Lourdes	Sonia
Dolores	María	Susana
Elena	Maribel	Tamara
Elisa	Marisol	Teresa
Emilia	Nuria	Vanesa
Fátima	Olga	Yolanda

Nombres de muchachos

Alfredo	Francisco	Óscar
Antonio	Gilberto	Pablo
Arturo	Héctor	Pedro
Bruno	Javier	Rafael
Carlos	Julio	Ramón
Daniel	Lorenzo	Roberto
Eduardo	Luis	Sergio
Enrique	Manuel	Tomás
Esteban	Marcos	Vicente
Fernando	Miguel	Víctor

Instrucciones
Directions

Throughout the book, many activities will have directions in Spanish. Here are some of the directions you'll see, along with their English translations.

Completa... con una palabra del cuadro.
Complete . . . with a word from the box.

Completa el párrafo con...
Complete the paragraph with . . .

Completa las oraciones con la forma correcta del verbo.
Complete the sentences with the correct form of the verb.

Con base en..., contesta cierto o falso. Corrige las oraciones falsas.
Based on . . ., respond to these statements with true or false. If they're false, correct them.

Con un(a) compañero(a), dramatiza...
With a classmate, act out . . .

Contesta las preguntas usando...
Answer the questions, using . . .

Contesta (Completa) las siguientes preguntas (oraciones)...
Answer (Complete) the following questions (sentences) . . .

En parejas (grupos de tres), dramaticen...
In pairs (groups of three), act out . . .

Escoge el dibujo (la respuesta) que corresponde (mejor completa)...
Choose the drawing (the answer) that goes with (best completes) . . .

Escribe..., usando el vocabulario de la página...
Write . . ., using the vocabulary on page . . .

Escucha las conversaciones. Decide qué conversación (diálogo) corresponde a cada dibujo (foto).
Listen to the conversations. Decide which conversation (dialog) corresponds to each drawing (photo).

Mira las fotos (los dibujos) y decide (di, indica)...
Look at the photos (drawings) and decide (say, indicate) . . .

Pon en orden...
Put . . . in order.

Pregúntale a tu compañero(a)...
Ask your partner...

Sigue el modelo.
Follow the model.

Túrnense para...
Take turns . . .

Usa el vocabulario de... para completar...
Use the vocabulary from . . . to complete . . .

Usa una palabra o expresión de cada columna para escribir...
Use one word or expression from each column to write . . .

Usa los dibujos para decir lo que pasa.
Use the drawings to say what is happening.

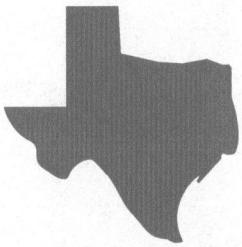

Texas Essential Knowledge and Skills for Languages Other Than English

The activities in ***¡Exprésate!*** will help you develop the skills necessary to reach the novice progress checkpoint outlined in the Texas Essential Knowledge and Skills. Each activity in your book is referenced to the appropriate TEKS.

Levels I and II—Novice Progress Checkpoint

Knowledge and skills

1. Communication The student communicates in a language other than English using the skills of listening, speaking, reading, and writing.

The student is expected to:

A. engage in oral and written exchanges of learned material to socialize and to provide and obtain information;

B. demonstrate understanding of simple, clearly spoken, and written language such as simple stories, high-frequency commands, and brief instructions when dealing with familiar topics; and

C. present information using familiar words, phrases, and sentences to listeners and readers.

2. Cultures The student gains knowledge and understanding of other cultures.

The student is expected to:

A. demonstrate an understanding of the practices (what people do) and how they are related to the perspectives (how people perceive things) of the cultures studied; and

B. demonstrate an understanding of the products (what people create) and how they are related to the perspectives (how people perceive things) of the cultures studied.

3. Connections The student uses the language to make connections with other subject areas and to acquire information.

The student is expected to:

A. use resources (that may include technology) in the language and cultures being studied to gain access to information; and

B. use the language to obtain, reinforce, or expand knowledge of other subject areas.

4. Comparisons The student develops insight into the nature of language and culture by comparing the student's own language and culture to another.

The student is expected to:

A. demonstrate an understanding of the nature of language through comparisons of the student's own language and the language studied;

B. demonstrate an understanding of the concept of culture through comparisons of the student's own culture and the cultures studied; and

C. demonstrate an understanding of the influence of one language and culture on another.

5. Communities The student participates in communities at home and around the world by using languages other than English.

The student is expected to:

A. use the language both within and beyond the school setting through activities such as participating in cultural events and using technology to communicate; and

B. show evidence of becoming a lifelong learner by using the language for personal enrichment and career development.

From Texas Education Agency http://www.tea.state.tx.us/rules/tac/chapter114/ch114c.htmlg

GeoVisión

Geocultura España

▲ **Los Picos de Europa** con su pico más alto, Torre Cerredo, a 2.648 metros.

▲ **Andalucía** es una región que exporta aceite de oliva a muchas partes del mundo.

▼ **En Sevilla** se celebra la Feria de Abril con vestidos tradicionales.

Almanaque

Población
40.037.995

Capital
Madrid

Gobierno
monarquía parlamentaria

Idiomas
castellano, gallego, vasco, catalán

Moneda
euro

Código Internet
www.[ ].es

¿Sabías que...?

Did you know that Texas was a Spanish colony from 1716 to 1821? The Spanish flag flew over missions and settlements around San Antonio.

◀ **Los Pirineos** separan España y Francia.

▲ **Tossa de Mar** es una playa bonita que atrae a turistas de todo el mundo.

▲ **Madrid** Este monumento, en la Plaza de España, es un homenaje a Miguel de Cervantes y a sus personajes ficticios, Don Quijote y Sancho Panza.

▶ **La Mancha** todavía inspira sueños con sus molinos, tanto hoy como en el tiempo de Don Quijote.

3B

¿Qué tanto sabes?

Which countries border Spain? Where in Spain would you go skiing?

A conocer España

Las celebraciones

▲ **La gente de Barcelona** se reúne enfrente de la Catedral para bailar «la sardana».

▲ **Galicia** muestra sus raíces celtas en sus festivales musicales.

▲ **La Feria de Abril en Sevilla** se celebra con colores brillantes, flores y trajes de flamenco.

▶ **Las castañuelas** marcan el compás de los cantos y danzas populares.

La comida

▼ **La paella** es el plato más reconocido de España.

▲ **La Plaza Mayor** de Madrid es un lugar muy frecuentado a la hora del almuerzo.

▲ **La tortilla** se hace con huevos, cebolla y patatas.

La arquitectura

Interactive TUTOR

Visit Holt Online
go.hrw.com
KEYWORD: EXP1 CH1
Photo Tour

▶ **El Museo de Guggenheim** en Bilbao es un edificio muy contemporáneo.

¿Sabías que...?

Did you know that the Mezquita in Córdoba is so large that a cathedral was built inside of it?

▲ **Ávila** está rodeada de murallas medievales.

◀ **La Mezquita** refleja la influencia árabe en Córdoba.

El arte

▶ **Las cuevas de Altamira** en Santillana tienen arte prehistórico.

◀ ***La Infanta Margarita,*** un retrato por Diego Velázquez (1599-1660), se encuentra en el Museo del Prado en Madrid.

Conexión Arte

1B

▲ ***Personnages Oiseaux*** *(Personajes pájaros)*

The Spanish painter Joan Miró (1893-1983) often painted dreamlike images. He frequently used the colors blue, red, yellow, green and black. Using the color chart below, identify the colors used in this painting.

Joan Miró

rojo **azul** **verde** **amarillo** **morado**

blanco **negro** **anaranjado** **gris** **café**

Capítulo 1

¡Empecemos!

OBJETIVOS

In this chapter you will learn to

- ask someone's name and say yours
- ask how someone is and say how you are
- introduce people and say where they are from
- give phone numbers, the time, the date, and the day
- spell words and give e-mail addresses

And you will use

- subjects, verbs, and subject pronouns
- numbers 0–31
- the alphabet
- the verb **ser**
- punctuation marks and written accents

¿Qué ves en la foto?

- **How are these teenagers greeting each other?**
- **Where in this plaza would you try to meet a friend?**
- **Based on the photo, what do you think Madrid is like?**

Texas

TEKS Look for the ★ next to each activity to learn how it can help you achieve the goals of the **Texas Essential Knowledge and Skills,** found on page xxiii.

La Puerta del Sol, Madrid

Visit Holt Online
go.hrw.com
KEYWORD: EXP1 CH1
Online Edition

Objetivos

Asking someone's name, asking how someone is, introducing others, saying where you and others are from

Vocabulario en acción 1

ExpresaVisión

¡Exprésate!

To ask a classmate or other young person's name *(familiar)*	To ask an adult's name *(formal)*	To give your name
¿Cómo te llamas? *What's your name?*	**¿Cómo se llama usted?** *What's your name?*	**Me llamo...** *My name is . . .* **Soy...** *I'm . . .*

Interactive TUTOR

To ask who someone is	To say who someone is
¿Quién es...? *Who is . . .?*	**(Él/Ella) es...** *He/She is . . .*
¿Cómo se llama (él/ella)? *What is his/her name?*	**(Él/Ella) se llama...** *His/Her name is . . .*

Online
Vocabulario y gramática, pp. 1–3

▶ **Vocabulario adicional** — Palabras descriptivas, p. R10

Visit Holt Online
go.hrw.com
KEYWORD: EXP1 CH1
Vocabulario 1 practice

1 ¿Qué hacen? 1B

Escuchemos As you listen, decide whether the people speaking are **a**) asking someone's name or **b**) giving a name.

2 ¿Cómo te llamas? 1B

Leamos Decide if you would hear these phrases in scene **a, b, c,** or **d.**

1. ¿Cómo te llamas?
2. Me llamo Margarita.
3. ¿Cómo se llama usted?
4. ¿Cómo se llama él?

3 Pareo 1B

Leamos Match each question to the correct response. There may be more than one correct answer.

1. ¿Cómo se llama él?
2. ¿Cómo se llama ella?
3. ¿Cómo se llama usted?
4. ¿Cómo te llamas?

a. Me llamo Gustavo.
b. Se llama Pablo.
c. Soy Elena Rodríguez.
d. Se llama Josefina.

TEKS Focus

1B Demonstrate understanding of simple, clearly spoken, and written language when dealing with familiar topics

Nota cultural

Family members, friends, and teachers may add an ending such as **-ito** or **-ita** to a person's name to show affection. Rosa becomes **Rosita,** Teresa, **Teresita,** Juan becomes **Juanito,** and Miguel becomes **Miguelito.** There are nicknames, **apodos,** associated with names that may be an abbreviation or part of a name. For example, Pilar, a very common girl's name in Spain, becomes **Pili,** and Santiago, a boy's name, becomes **Santi.** Do we have similar nicknames in English? 2A, 4A

Comunicación

4 Nombres y más nombres 1A, 1C

Hablemos Get together with three classmates and ask them their names in Spanish. Then report their names to the class.

Hola, ¿cómo estás?

Más o menos. ¿Y tú?

Más vocabulario...

Greetings and Goodbyes

Buenos días, señor.	*Good morning, sir.*
Buenas tardes, señorita.	*Good afternoon, miss.*
Buenas noches, señora.	*Good evening, ma'am.*
Adiós.	*Goodbye.*
Buenas noches.	*Good night.*
Hasta luego.	*See you later.*
Hasta mañana.	*See you tomorrow.*
Hasta pronto.	*See you soon.*
Nos vemos.	*See you.*
Tengo que irme.	*I have to go.*

¡Exprésate!

To ask how a friend is	To ask how an adult is	To respond
Hola, ¿cómo estás? *Hi, how are you?*	**¿Cómo está usted?** *How are you?*	**Estoy bien/regular/mal.** *I'm fine/all right/not so good.*
¿Qué tal? *How's it going?*		**Más o menos.** *So-so.*

Interactive TUTOR

Online
Vocabulario y gramática, pp. 1–3

5 ¿Qué dicen? 1B

Escuchemos Are the people you hear **a**) greeting each other or **b**) asking each other how they are?

6 Adiós 1C

Hablemos How would you say goodbye to someone . . .

MODELO **you will see tomorrow?**
Hasta mañana.

1. you will see again soon?
2. you will see tomorrow in class?
3. when you don't know when you will see them next?
4. you will see in a few days?
5. wishing them a good night?
6. when you have to go?

Comunicación

7 Estoy bien, gracias. 1A

TEKS Focus
1A Engage in oral and written exchanges of learned material to socialize and to provide and obtain information

Hablemos Work with a partner. Decide how you would greet these people and ask how they are. How would they respond? Base your answers on the cues given by the pictures and times. Take turns asking and answering the questions.

MODELO **—Buenos días, señor Garza. ¿Cómo está usted?**
—Estoy bien, gracias.

8:00 A.M.
el señor Garza

11:00 A.M.
Teresa

2:00 P.M.
Santi

9:00 P.M.
Maribel

8 Conversación 1A

Hablemos Create a short conversation with a classmate. Greet each other, find out each other's name, ask and say how you are, and then say goodbye.

¡Exprésate!

To introduce someone	To respond	To say that you are also pleased to meet someone
Éste es Juan. (Él) es un compañero de clase. *This is Juan. He is a classmate.*	**Encantado(a). / Mucho gusto.** *Pleased/Nice to meet you.*	**Igualmente.** *Likewise.*
Éste es el señor Vega. (Él) es mi profesor de español. *This is Mr. Vega. He is my Spanish teacher.*		
Ésta es Rosa. (Ella) es una compañera de clase. *This is Rosa. She is a classmate.*		
Ésta es la señora (la señorita) Talavera. (Ella) es mi profesora de ciencias. *This is Mrs. (Miss) Talavera. She is my science teacher.*		

Interactive TUTOR

Online
Vocabulario y gramática, pp. 1–3

Más vocabulario...

¿Quién es el muchacho?
Who is the boy?
(Él) es mi mejor amigo.
He is my best friend.
(Él) es estudiante.
He is a student.
¿Quién es la muchacha?
Who is the girl?
(Ella) es mi mejor amiga.
She is my best friend.
(Ella) es estudiante.
She is a student.

9 Tus amigos 1C

Hablemos/Escribamos How would you introduce these people?

MODELO **your classmate Antonio**
Éste es Antonio. Él es mi compañero de clase.

1. your best friend Ana
2. your best friend Juan
3. your classmate Enrique
4. your classmate Luisa
5. your Spanish teacher
6. yourself

¡Exprésate!

To ask where someone is from	To say where you and others are from
¿De dónde eres? *Where are you from? (familiar)*	**Soy de Estados Unidos.** *I'm from the United States.*
¿De dónde es usted? *Where are you from? (formal)*	**Soy de España.** *I'm from Spain.*
¿De dónde es...? *Where is . . . from?*	**Es de Cuba.** *He (She) is from Cuba.*

Interactive TUTOR

Online
Vocabulario y gramática, pp. 1–3

10 ¿De dónde son? 1B

Escuchemos As you listen, match the name of the person with the place he or she is from.

1. Javier
2. Angélica
3. la profesora Gutiérrez
4. Rafael
5. Fernando

a. Es de Cuba.
b. Es de México.
c. Es de España.
d. Es de Estados Unidos.
e. Es de Puerto Rico.

TEKS Focus
1B Demonstrate understanding of simple, clearly spoken, and written language when dealing with familiar topics

11 Es de... 1C

Hablemos Using the pictures, introduce these people and tell where they are from.

MODELO **Ésta es mi amiga Carolina. Ella es de España.**

Carolina, España

1. Juan José
la República Dominicana

2. María
Cuba

3. Blas
Puerto Rico

4. Irma
México

5. Alberto
Estados Unidos

Comunicación

12 El club de español 1A, 1C

Hablemos Imagine that you and your partner have both just joined the Spanish Club at your school. Greet each other, find out each other's name and where each other is from. Then introduce one another to a classmate.

Objetivos
Using subjects and verbs in sentences, using subject pronouns

Gramática en acción 1

GramaVisión

Subjects and verbs in sentences

Interactive TUTOR

1 In English, sentences have a **subject** and a **verb**. The **subject** is the person or thing that is being described or is doing something. The **verb** is the action word like **run** or **sing**, or a word like **am**, **is**, or **are** that links the subject to a description.

subject *verb*

Mrs. Pérez is my teacher.
She is from Madrid.

2 In Spanish, sentences also have a subject and a verb.

subject *verb*

La señora Pérez es mi profesora.
Ella es de Madrid.

3 Both English and Spanish use nouns as subjects. Nouns can be replaced with **pronouns**. Some examples of Spanish **pronouns** you have seen are **él**, **ella**, **tú** and **usted**.

él stands for Juan

Juan es un compañero de clase.
Juan is a classmate.

Él es mi mejor amigo.
He is my best friend.

4 English sentences always have a subject or a subject pronoun. But in Spanish the **subject** or the **subject pronoun** can be left out if everyone knows who you're talking about.

María is my friend.
She is from Spain.

María es mi amiga.
Es de España. *Ella can be left out.*

Online
Vocabulario y gramática, pp. 4–6 | Actividades, pp. 1–3

Nota cultural

Students in Spanish-speaking countries address teachers in several ways. Women may be called by their title and first name **(señorita Rosa)** or by title and last name **(señorita García)**. If the teacher is older, she may be addressed as **doña** with her first name, such as **doña Josefina.** Men may be addressed as **don Pablo** (title and first name) or **señor Gómez** (title and last name). Compare this to the way you address your teachers. 4B

La Plaza de Cibeles, Madrid

13 Mis amigos de Madrid 1B, 4A

Leamos Identify the subjects and verbs in the following dialogs.

1. —Susana is my friend.
   —She is from Spain.
   —Mrs. García is my teacher.
   —She is from Madrid.

2. —Susana es mi amiga.
   —Es de España.
   —La señora García es mi profesora.
   —Es de Madrid.

Visit Holt Online
go.hrw.com
KEYWORD: EXP 1 CH 1
Gramática 1 practice

14 ¿Quién es quién? 1B

Leamos Identify the subjects and the verbs in the following sentences. Then say whether you would use **él** or **ella** in place of each subject.

1. Laura es de Toledo. Es una compañera de clase.
2. Juan es mi mejor amigo. Es estudiante.
3. La señora Ayala es mi profesora de ciencias. Es de Perú.
4. El señor Garza es mi profesor de español. Es de España.
5. El muchacho es un compañero de clase. Es de Estados Unidos.
6. La señorita Jiménez es de la República Dominicana. Es mi profesora de matemáticas.
7. Ramiro es un compañero de clase. Es de Cuba.
8. Don Pablo es profesor. Es de México.
9. Doña Lourdes es de Panamá. Es profesora.

Unos amigos en la Plaza de Zocodover

TEKS Focus
1C Present information using familiar words, phrases, and sentences

Comunicación

15 ¿De quién hablas? 1A, 1C

Leamos/Hablemos Use at least three phrases from the word box to write a description of one of the people pictured below. Read your description aloud to your partner. He or she will guess which person you have just described. Then switch roles.

Éste es el señor Madero.	Ella es mi profesora de español.
Él es mi mejor amigo.	Es de Estados Unidos.
Es de España.	Ella es mi mejor amiga.
Ésta es Rosaura.	Él es un compañero de clase.
Éste es Mario.	Ella es una compañera de clase.
Él es mi profesor de ciencias.	Ésta es la señora Matute.

A

B

C

D

Subject pronouns

1 These are the **subject pronouns** in Spanish.

yo *I*		**nosotros**	*we*
		nosotras	*we (all female)*
tú *you*		**vosotros**	*you*
		vosotras	*you (all female)*
usted *you*		**ustedes**	*you*
él *he*		**ellos**	*they*
ella *she*		**ellas**	*they (all female)*

2 The subject pronouns **tú** and **usted** both mean *you* when you're talking to one person. However, they are used in different situations.

friend
relative
someone your age
} **Familiar** **tú**

Formal **usted** { *teacher*
adult you've just met
someone you show respect to

Although subject pronouns are often left out, the pronoun **usted** is commonly stated when addressing someone to show respect.

¿Cómo está **usted**? *How are you?*

3 The subject pronouns **ustedes** and **vosotros** mean *you* when talking to more than one person. They are also used in different situations.

friends
relatives
people your age
} **Familiar (in Spain)** **vosotros**

Formal and Familiar **ustedes** { *any group*

4 The pronouns **nosotros**, **vosotros**, and **ellos** have feminine forms.

	Masculine	Feminine	
group of all males *group of males and females*	**nosotros**	**nosotras**	*group of all females*
	vosotros (Spain)	**vosotras** (Spain)	
	ellos	**ellas**	

Online
Vocabulario y gramática, pp. 4–6 | Actividades, pp. 1–3

En inglés

In English, the subject pronoun *you* is used with anyone, no matter their age or relationship to you.

In Spanish, the pronoun you use (**tú** or **usted**) is based on your relationship to the person.

TEKS Focus
2A Demonstrate understanding of practices (what people do) and how they relate to perspectives (how people perceive things) of the cultures studied

16 ¿Cómo le(s) dices? 2A, 4A

Hablemos What pronouns would you use to speak to these people?

1. two or more teachers
2. a group of female students (in Spain)
3. your best friend
4. a school principal
5. two or more males
6. a group of male and female students (in Spain)

17 ¿Con quién habla Javier? ←1B, 2A

Escuchemos Listen as Javier, a teenager from Spain, talks to his friends and teachers. Match each statement with the correct picture. Remember that Javier uses **vosotros** and **vosotras.**

A

B

C

D

E

F

18 Nuevos amigos ←1B

Leamos/Escribamos Complete this conversation using the correct subject pronouns.

—Hola. __1__ *(I)* soy Rosalinda Chávez. Y __2__ *(he)* es mi amigo Juan. ¿Cómo te llamas __3__ *(you)?*

—__4__ *(I)* me llamo Antonia. Y __5__ *(she)* es mi amiga Talía. __6__ *(We–Talía and I)* somos de Estados Unidos. Juan y tú, ¿de dónde son __7__ *(you, plural)?*

Comunicación

19 Eres reportero(a) ←1A

Hablemos Imagine that you are a reporter interviewing new students and teachers for the school paper. With a partner, role-play one interview with a student and one with a teacher. In each interview:

1. Greet the person you are interviewing
2. Ask what his or her name is
3. Ask where he or she is from
4. Say goodbye

Cultura

VideoCultura

Comparaciones

Buenos amigos, Madrid

¿Cómo saludas a tus amigos, familiares y profesores? ➔2A, 4B

Spanish speakers usually greet each other with a handshake or kiss, depending on the situation. Here, you will see several people greet each other in different situations. See if you can find any similarities to the greetings and goodbyes you use with your friends, family, and teachers.

Saludos informales

In Spain, friends and family members may greet each other with two kisses, one on each cheek. In Latin America, friends and family members kiss each other on only one cheek. Men and boys greet each other with a hug, a pat on the back, or a handshake. In some Latin American countries, men who have not seen each other in a long time greet with a handshake, followed by a hug, followed by a second handshake.

—Hola, madrina, ¿cómo estás?

—¡Hola amigo! ¡Tanto tiempo!

—¿Cómo estás?

Visit Holt Online
go.hrw.com
KEYWORD: EXP1 CH1
Online Edition

—Mucho gusto.
—Igualmente.

Saludos formales

In professional or school settings, or when meeting someone for the first time, the usual greeting in Spain and Latin America is a handshake.

—Es un compañero de clase.
—Encantado.

Para comprender ✦2A

1. How would a young girl greet her grandparents in Spain?
2. How would a young girl greet her grandparents in Latin America?
3. How would a businessman and a businesswoman greet each other in Spain or Latin America?
4. In Latin America, how might a boy greet his uncle if they haven't seen each other in a long time?

Para pensar y hablar ✦4B

Among family and close friends, hugs and kisses are common greetings throughout the Spanish-speaking world. Do family and close friends in your community greet each other with hugs, kisses, or handshakes?

Cuaderno para hispanohablantes, pp. 1–12

Texas

Comunidad

Famous Hispanic Texans

Texas is proud of its talented Hispanics and their many interesting accomplishments. A good example is Robert Rodríguez, a San Antonio native and the director of *Spy Kids, Spy Kids 2,* and other movies. Some other well-known Hispanics in the art world include artist Carmen Lomas Garza and writer Sandra Cisneros. Others are Texas Republic heroes like General Lorenzo de Zavala and Juan Nepomuceno Seguín. Using your library or the Internet, find three other well-known Hispanic Texans, write down their major accomplishments, and tell the class about them. ✦3A

Robert Rodríguez

Objetivos
Giving phone numbers, the time, the date, and the day, spelling words and giving e-mail addresses

Vocabulario en acción 2

ExpresaVisión

Los números

0	1	2	3	4
cero	uno	dos	tres	cuatro

5	6	7	8	9	10
cinco	seis	siete	ocho	nueve	diez

Más vocabulario...

11	once
12	doce
13	trece
14	catorce
15	quince
16	dieciséis
17	diecisiete
18	dieciocho
19	diecinueve
20	veinte
21	veintiuno
22	veintidós
23	veintitrés
24	veinticuatro
25	veinticinco
26	veintiséis
27	veintisiete
28	veintiocho
29	veintinueve
30	treinta
31	treinta y uno

20 Contando ➜1C

Hablemos What numbers do you think of for the following things? Say the number in Spanish.

1. hours in a day
2. a rectangle
3. the English alphabet
4. a volleyball team
5. a spider
6. a quarter
7. a lucky clover
8. a carton of eggs
9. a trio
10. days in a week

21 ¿Qué números faltan? ➜1C

Hablemos Complete these series of numbers logically. Then read them aloud.

1. 1, 3, ____, 7, 9, ____, 13, 15
2. 2, 4, ____, 8, ____, 12, ____
3. 16, 17, ____, 19, ____, ____
4. 30, 25, ____, ____, ____, 5
5. 19, 18, ____, 16, 15, ____, 13, 12
6. 20, 22, ____, 26, ____, 30
7. 3, 6, ____, 12, ____
8. 5, 10, ____, 20, ____, ____

Visit Holt Online
go.hrw.com
KEYWORD: EXP1 CH1
Vocabulario 2 practice

¡Exprésate!

To ask for phone numbers	To give phone numbers
¿Cuál es tu teléfono? *What's your telephone number?*	**Es tres-dos-cinco-uno-dos-tres-uno.** *It's 3-2-5-1-2-3-1.*
¿Cuál es el teléfono de Rosita? *What's Rosita's telephone number?*	**Es seis-uno-nueve-uno-cinco-dos-ocho.** *It's 6-1-9-1-5-2-8.*

Interactive TUTOR

Online
Vocabulario y gramática, pp. 7–9

22 Números de teléfono 1B

Escuchemos You and your friend Elena are double-checking phone numbers for some of the students in your class. Listen to what Elena says and fill in the missing numbers.

1. Beatriz 3-____-____-1-9-____-____
2. Jorge 2-____-____-____-____-2-8
3. Rosaura ____-1-3-____-____-3-1
4. Ángel 7-1-8-____-____-____-____
5. Gladys ____-2-8-1-5-____-____

Comunicación

23 Directorio telefónico 1A

Leamos/Hablemos Pick a person from the school directory and ask a classmate if you have the right number for him or her. When you give the number, get one digit wrong. Your partner should correct the number.

MODELO **—¿El teléfono de Teresa Benavides es uno-uno-cuatro-siete-ocho-dos-dos?**
—No, es uno-uno-cuatro-uno-ocho-dos-dos.

28

BENAVIDES, Teresa Núñez de Cáceres 11 ..... **1-14-18-22**
GÓMEZ, Emilia Santo Tomás de Aquino 27 ..... **2-13-25-17**
GONZÁLEZ, Rocío Avenida Juárez 18 ..... **6-15-29-17**
MARTÍNEZ, Elena Camino Real 25 ..... **4-11-16-28**
ORTEGA, Jaime Avenida Mella 31 ..... **3-31-13-27**
RODRÍGUEZ, Alberto Calle Constitución 12 ..... **6-27-19-12**
TORRES, Federico Carretera Simón Bolívar 13 ..... **9-21-15-10**

TEKS Focus
1A Engage in oral and written exchanges of learned material to socialize and to provide and obtain information

24 Número secreto 1A

Hablemos Try to guess the secret number between 0 and 31 that your partner has written down. If you are wrong, your partner will point up or down to indicate a higher or lower number. Keep trying until you guess right. Then switch roles and play again.

25 ¿Son las dos? 1B

Leamos Choose the correct time.

1. 3:00
   a. Son las tres en punto.
   b. Son las tres y media.
2. 9:15
   a. Son las nueve menos cuarto.
   b. Son las nueve y cuarto.
3. 7:25
   a. Son las siete y media.
   b. Son las siete y veinticinco.
4. 1:30
   a. Es la una y cuarto.
   b. Es la una y media.
5. 11:40
   a. Son las doce menos veinte.
   b. Son las once y veinte.
6. 8:10
   a. Son las ocho en punto.
   b. Son las ocho y diez.
7. 2:50
   a. Son las tres menos diez.
   b. Son las tres y diez.
8. 4:05
   a. Son las cuatro y cinco.
   b. Son las cuatro y cuarto.

TEKS Focus
1C Present information using familiar words, phrases, and sentences

26 ¿Qué hora es? 1C

Hablemos/Escribamos Say what time it is.

1. 4:00 P.M.
2. 6:10 A.M.
3. 12:00 P.M.
4. 9:05 A.M.
5. 4:45 A.M.
6. 1:15 P.M.

¡Exprésate!

To ask someone the date and day of the week	To respond
¿Qué fecha es hoy? *What's today's date?*	**Es el primero (dos, tres...) de enero.** *It's the first (second, third . . .) of January.*
¿Qué día es hoy? *What day is today?*	**Hoy es lunes.** *Today is Monday.*

Interactive TUTOR

Online
Vocabulario y gramática, pp. 7–9

Los días de la semana

Los meses del año

Las estaciones

la primavera	*spring*	**el otoño**	*fall*
el verano	*summer*	**el invierno**	*winter*

27 ¿Sabes? ➤1B

Escribamos/Hablemos Complete each series logically.

1. lunes, _____, miércoles, _____
2. viernes, _____, _____, lunes
3. enero, _____, marzo, _____
4. mayo, junio, _____, _____
5. primavera, _____, otoño, _____
6. invierno, _____, _____, otoño

Comunicación

28 ¿Cuándo es tu cumpleaños? ➤1A

Hablemos Work in groups of three to guess one another's birthday. Guide your classmates by saying **antes** *(before)* or **después** *(after)* until they guess correctly. Guess the month first, then try for the date.

El alfabeto

a *(a)* árbol	b *(be)* bebé	c *(ce)* ciclismo	d *(de)* dinosaurio	e *(e)* elefante
f *(efe)* flores	g *(ge)* geografía	h *(hache)* hipopótamo	i *(i)* iguana	j *(jota)* jirafa
k *(ka)* kárate	l *(ele)* león	m *(eme)* manzana	n *(ene)* nido	ñ *(eñe)* piñata
o *(o)* oso	p *(pe)* pez	q *(cu)* queso	r *(ere)* pera	s *(ese)* salvavidas
t *(te)* tortuga	u *(u)* uvas	v *(ve or uve)* violín	w *(uve doble)* Wilfredo	x *(equis)* examen
y *(i griega)* yoyo	z *(zeta)* zanahorias	**Dos letras, un sonido**		
		ch *(che)* chimpancé	ll *(elle)* llama	rr *(erre)* burro

¡Exprésate!

To ask how words are spelled and give e-mail addresses

Interactive TUTOR

¿Cómo se escribe...? *How do you spell . . . ?*	**Se escribe...** *It's spelled . . .*
¿Cuál es el correo electrónico de Marisa? *What is Marisa's e-mail address?*	**Es eme punto ge-o-ene-zeta-a-ele-o arroba ere-e-de punto hache-ere-uve doble punto a-ere.** *It's m.gonzalo@red.hrw.ar*
¿Cuál es tu correo electrónico? *What's your e-mail address?*	**Es...** *It's . . .*

Online
Vocabulario y gramática, pp. 7–9

29 Dictado 1B

Escuchemos/Escribamos Listen as several speakers say and spell out the Spanish words for some animals. On a separate sheet of paper, write the words in Spanish as you hear them.

TEKS Focus
1B Demonstrate understanding of simple, clearly spoken, and written language when dealing with familiar topics

Comunicación

30 ¿Cómo se escribe...? 1B, 1C

Hablemos/Escribamos Spell each item below aloud in Spanish while your classmate writes it out.

MODELO **eme-e-ere-ce-e-de-e-ese (Mercedes)**

1. your name
2. your e-mail address
3. the name of the city or town where you were born
4. your best friend's full name
5. your best friend's e-mail address
6. your favorite actor's name

31 El proyecto 1A

Hablemos You and several classmates have to finish a project outside of class. Work with three partners to create a conversation in which you ask for one another's names (spell them out if you have to), phone numbers, and e-mail addresses.

Objetivos

Using the verb **ser**, punctuation marks, and written accents

Gramática en acción 2

GramaVisión

The present tense of the verb ser

Interactive TUTOR

1 In Spanish, a verb has different forms to tell you who the subject is. Changing a verb form so that it matches its subject is called **conjugating.** This is the conjugation of the verb **ser** *(to be)*.

yo	**soy**	*I am*	nosotros(as)	**somos**	*we are*
tú	**eres**	*you are*	vosotros(as)	**sois**	*you are*
usted	**es**	*you are*	ustedes	**son**	*you are*
él	**es**	*he is*	ellos	**son**	*they are*
ella	**es**	*she is*	ellas	**son**	*they are*

With nouns and names of people, use the same form of the verb as for **él/ella** or **ellos/ellas.**

Mi profesora es de Cuba. **Juan y Carlos son de España.**

2 To make a sentence negative, place **no** in front of the verb.

Mi profesora no es de México. Es de España.

Online

Vocabulario y gramática, pp. 10–12 | Actividades, pp. 5–7

¿Te acuerdas?

You've used forms of the verb **ser** to say who someone is or where you or others are from, to give your telephone number, and to say the date, the day, and the time.

Éste **es** un compañero de clase.
Yo **soy** de Perú.
Mi teléfono **es** 555-5555.
Hoy **es** el diez de febrero.
Hoy **es** jueves.
Son las tres de la tarde.

32 Presentaciones ← 1B

Leamos What is Maribel saying? Complete her statements by matching elements from the two columns.

1. Hola. Yo	**a.** son de España.
2. Y ella	**b.** somos de México.
3. Nosotras	**c.** eres?
4. Y tú, ¿de dónde	**d.** son ustedes?
5. Juan y tú, ¿de dónde	**e.** es mi amiga Carla.
6. Jorge y Carlos	**f.** soy Maribel Gómez.
7. Juan, ¿cuál	**g.** es?
8. Carla, ¿qué hora	**h.** son las dos.
9. No, Carla, no es la una,	**i.** es tu teléfono?

33 Nuestro club 1B

Leamos/Escribamos Miguel has written a description of the International Spanish Club. Complete the paragraph with the correct forms of the verb **ser.**

Nosotros __1__ estudiantes y profesores del club internacional de español. Yo __2__ de Puerto Rico. Juan Emilio __3__ de la República Dominicana. Lisa y Rebeca __4__ de Estados Unidos. El teléfono del club __5__ 5-24-11-21. El correo electrónico del club __6__ clubinternacionaldeespañol@school.org. Nosotros __7__ el club internacional. ¡Hasta pronto!

34 Combinaciones 1B

Escribamos/Hablemos Form sentences using the words from the boxes and the correct forms of **ser.** You may also use other names and dates to make up sentences of your own.

MODELO **Yo soy Raquel.**

Yo	de Estados Unidos	el ____ de ____
Mi mejor amigo(a) y yo	lunes	el señor ____
Mi profesor(a) de español	el diez de mayo	miércoles
Él/Ella	la señora ____	Juana
Ellos/Ellas	compañeros de clase	de ____
Hoy	de México	Pablo
Mañana	estudiantes	viernes

Comunicación

35 No es correcto 1A, 1C

TEKS Focus
1A Engage in oral and written exchanges of learned material to socialize and to provide and obtain information

Hablemos Take turns with a partner giving information about the people in the pictures, but include at least one detail that is not correct. Your partner should use **no** to disagree and then provide the correct information.

MODELO **—Ana es de Guatemala. El teléfono de Ana es 3-20-16-04.**
—No, el teléfono de Ana no es 3-20-16-04. Es 3-29-16-04.

Ana, Guatemala
3-29-16-04

Juan, Puerto Rico
5-14-07-21

Lupe, México
7-20-11-05

Ricardo, España
2-23-01-16

Punctuation marks and written accents

Interactive TUTOR

1 In Spanish, upside-down **punctuation marks** such as **(¿)** and **(¡)** are placed at the beginning of a phrase to signal a question or an exclamation. These are used along with those that come at the end of phrases.

¡Hasta luego!
¿Cómo se llama ella?

2 In Spanish, some words have written **accent marks**. An accent mark is a tilted line **(´)** placed over a vowel. Putting accent marks over vowels is part of spelling words correctly. When learning new words, memorize where the accent marks are.

Adiós.
¿Cuál?

3 The wavy line in the letter **ñ** is called a **tilde**. The **ñ** is pronounced similar to the *ny* in the word *canyon.*

señor
compañero

Online
Vocabulario y gramática, pp. 10–12 | Actividades, pp. 5–7

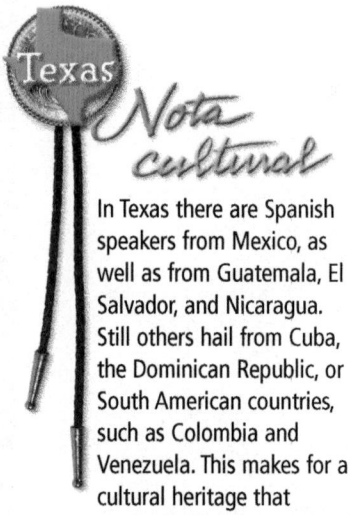

In Texas there are Spanish speakers from Mexico, as well as from Guatemala, El Salvador, and Nicaragua. Still others hail from Cuba, the Dominican Republic, or South American countries, such as Colombia and Venezuela. This makes for a cultural heritage that reflects the divesity of the Spanish-speaking world. Contact your local Chamber of Commerce and ask where Spanish speakers in your city or area come from. Are there cultural events you might attend? 5A

TEKS Focus
5A Use the language both within and beyond the school setting by participating in cultural events and using technology to communicate

36 ¡Cuidado con los acentos! 1B

Leamos/Escribamos On a separate sheet of paper, rewrite each sentence, placing accents and punctuation marks where needed.

1. Buenos dias, senorita
2. Como esta usted senor
3. Que tal
4. Mucho gusto
5. Que hora es
6. De donde eres
7. Cual es tu telefono
8. Me llamo Pedro
9. Hola Como te llamas
10. El es un companero de clase
11. Quien es la profesora de ciencias
12. Como estas
13. Que fecha es hoy
14. Estoy bien gracias

Una carnicería *(butcher shop)* en Segovia, España

37 En contacto ➤4A

Leamos/Escribamos Accents can be difficult to put in an e-mail. On another sheet of paper, rewrite these two messages by including the missing accent marks, tildes, and punctuation marks.

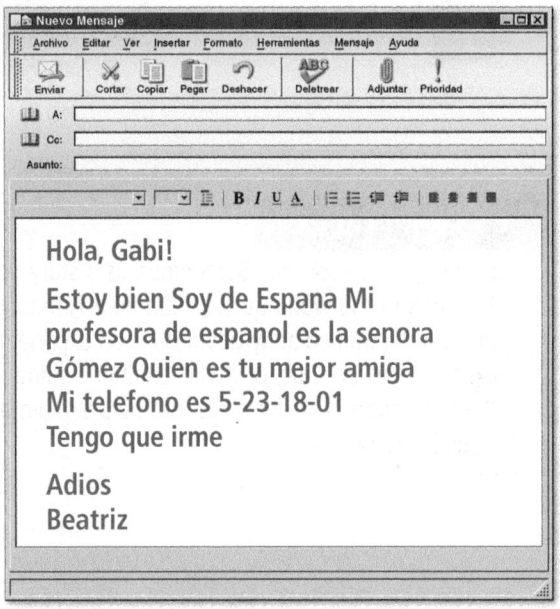

Comunicación

38 En la clase ➤1A, 1B

Hablemos Today is the first day of school. With a partner, create brief conversations for each scene. Then perform a scene for the class and have your classmates guess which scene it is.

Novela en video

¿Quién será?

Episodio 1

ESTRATEGIA

Making Connections Sometimes, as a story unfolds on screen, things happen in different parts of the world at the same time. Although the connection between those events may not be immediately obvious, as an experienced viewer, you know that one probably exists. In this episode, you will see things going on in Spain, Mexico, and Puerto Rico at the same time. Look for clues that help explain the connection among the events in all three locations. 3B

En España

In Madrid, Spain, a woman is studying the files of a Mexican student and a Puerto Rican student. She calls her assistant, Marcos, and makes an appointment to meet with him.

1

La profesora Y tú, Sofía Corona Ramírez, eres de México, ¿no es así? Hmmm... Nicolás Ortega García, el artista puertorriqueño.

2

La profesora Sí, Marcos. Necesito hablar contigo. Sí, pronto. Es urgente. A ver, mañana es domingo. Bien, el lunes, en mi casa. Sí, a las diez de la mañana.
Oye, ¿cuál es tu e-mail? Te quiero enviar unos documentos. Bien. Nos vemos el lunes.

Visit Holt Online
go.hrw.com
KEYWORD: EXP1 CH1
Online Edition

En México

In Mexico City, Mexico, a girl named Sofía is having breakfast before going to school. Both her father and her little brother interrupt her.

3

Sr. Corona Buenos días, Sofía... Hola, Sofía, buenos días...

4

Quique Sofía, Sofía, ¡cara de tortilla!

En Puerto Rico

In San Juan, Puerto Rico, a boy named Nicolás is in a rush on his way home from school. He bumps into some of his neighbors.

5

Sra. Ortiz ¡Buenas tardes, Nico!

Nicolás ¡Buenas tardes, señora Ortiz!

6

Nicolás ¡Uy, perdone, don Pablo! ¿Cómo está usted?

Don Pablo Estoy bien, gracias, Nico. ¿Y tú? ¿Cómo estás tú?

¿COMPRENDES?

1. Why does the professor need to talk to Marcos? Could it have something to do with the students in the files? On what day will she meet with him?
2. What is Sofía doing while she eats breakfast? Does this tell you anything about her?
3. What is Nicolás holding under his arm? What can you tell about him from this? Does anything else in this episode support your conclusion?
4. Are the Sofía and Nicolás you see in Mexico and Puerto Rico the same students the professor talks about? Why do you think so? 1B, 3A

Próximo episodio

Marcos goes to visit la profesora. Can you predict what she might ask him to do?

PÁGINAS 66–67

Leamos y escribamos

TEKS Focus
4A Demonstrate understanding of the nature of language through comparisons

ESTRATEGIA

para leer Recognizing cognates
Cognates are words that look alike and have similar meanings in two languages. Recognizing these words will help you get a general idea of what a reading passage is about.

A Antes de leer 1B, 4A

Look at the homepage for one school's Spanish Club. To get an idea of what the club has to offer, write all the cognates you can find on a separate sheet of paper. Compare your list with a classmate's and try to guess what each word means. If you are not sure, look the word up in a dictionary.

Archivo Editar Ver Herramientas Ayuda

Atrás Adelante Actualizar Detener Página Inicial Buscar Favoritos Correo Imprimir

Dirección:

Participa en el club de español

¿Interesante? ¡Claro que sí!
Programas de inmersión en Cádiz, España. Clases de español, excursiones turísticas y mucho más. Del 26 de mayo al 10 de junio y del 22 de julio al 6 de agosto. Más información en http://www.spprogramsabroad.hrw.com

¡Y divertido[2]! Ritmos del momento
Escuchen la música favorita de muchos estudiantes hispanos y diviértanse bailando[3]. Clases de salsa y merengue. Martes y jueves en el gimnasio. Hora: 4:30 a 5:30 Más música en http://morelatinmusic.hrw.com

Eventos deportivos
Gran partido[4] de fútbol. Viernes 19 de septiembre. En el estadio local. Hora: 7:00 p.m. Más información en el teléfono 2-17-22-08 o en http://schoolevents.hrw.edu

Nuevo Mensaje

Correspondencia con estudiantes de España y Latinoamérica

To: clubesp@exchange.hrw.com
From: Camim@exchange.hrw.com

Hola, ¿qué tal? Me llamo Camilo Medina. Soy de Guanajuato, México. Soy estudiante del Colegio Benito Juárez y participo en el Club de español. Escríbanme[1].

1 write to me **2** fun **3** have fun dancing **4** game

Visit Holt Online
go.hrw.com
KEYWORD: EXP1 CH1
Online Edition

B Comprensión ✦1B, 3B

Based on the reading, say if the following statements are true (**cierto**) or false (**falso**). Correct the false statements.

1. The Spanish Club offers a variety of fun and interesting activities.
2. The club sponsors summer trips to Spanish-speaking countries.
3. If you join the club, you will be able to correspond with students from Asia.
4. The club offers **salsa** and **merengue** classes on Fridays.
5. The club homepage provides you with links to other sites.

C Después de leer ✦1B

Would you like to become a member of this club? Why or why not? Which activity seems the most interesting to you? What other activities would you suggest if you were a member?

Taller del escritor

Nombre
Número de teléfono
Correo electrónico
Soy de ...

ESTRATEGIA

para escribir You can often get ideas for writing by making a list of everything that you want to include in your work. List all your ideas even if you don't know how to say something in Spanish. You can get help later from the dictionary if you need to find a specific word or phrase.

La página Web del club de español ✦1C, 5A

You have joined the Spanish Club. The club asks all new members to write a short paragraph about themselves to be posted on the club's Web site. In your paragraph, be sure to include your name, where you are from, and your e-mail address.

1 Antes de escribir

Make a list of the information you will need for the Web site. You may use English or Spanish for this step.

2 Escribir un borrador

Write your information in complete sentences in Spanish.

3 Revisar

Read your sentences at least twice. Make sure you have included all the information you want to post on the Web site. Then check your spelling and punctuation.

4 Publicar

Post your completed paragraph on the bulletin board or your class Web site.

Cuaderno para hispanohablantes, pp. 1–12

Prepárate para el examen

Repaso capítulo 1

Interactive TUTOR

1 Vocabulario 1
- asking someone's name
- asking how someone is and saying how you are
- introducing others
- saying where you and others are from

pp. 6–11

2 Gramática 1
- subjects and verbs in sentences

pp. 12–13

3 Gramática 1
- subject pronouns

pp. 14–15

4 Vocabulario 2
- numbers 0–31
- asking for and giving phone numbers
- telling time
- giving the date and the day of the week
- the alphabet
- spelling words and giving e-mail addresses

pp. 18–23

1 Pretend you are introducing the following people to a classmate. Greet your classmate and ask how he or she is, then introduce each person, and say where he or she is from. **1C**

Beatriz, México

el señor Huang, Estados Unidos

Antonio, España

2 For each pair of sentences, identify the subject and verb in the first sentence. Then choose the correct subject pronoun in the second sentence. **1B**

1. Rosa es mi mejor amiga. (Ella/Él) es de Segovia, España.
2. La señora Cortez es mi profesora de español. (Ellos/Ella) es de Estados Unidos.
3. El muchacho es de México. (Él/Ustedes) es un compañero de clase.
4. El profesor Muñoz es de la República Dominicana. (Nosotros/Él) es mi profesor de ciencias.

3 Choose the correct subject pronoun to complete the following short conversations. **1B**

1. —Alicia y Laura, ¿de dónde son _____ *(you, plural)*?
   —_____ *(We)* somos de Costa Rica.
2. —Hola, señor Martínez. ¿Cómo está _____ *(you, formal)*?
   —Bien, gracias, Jorge. ¿Y _____ *(you, familiar)*?
3. —¿De dónde son Juan y Susana?
   —_____ *(They)* son de Bolivia.

4 Answer the following questions. **1B, 1C**

1. ¿Cuál es tu correo electrónico?
2. ¿Cuál es tu teléfono?
3. ¿Qué fecha es hoy?
4. ¿Qué hora es?
5. ¿Qué día es hoy?

Visit Holt Online
go.hrw.com
KEYWORD: EXP1 CH1
Chapter Self-test

5 On a separate sheet of paper, rewrite the following conversation between two students at a high school in Miami. Use the correct form of **ser** and add the correct punctuation and accent marks. 1B

—Hola Me llamo Pilar (Yo) ____ tu companera de clase
—Mucho gusto Me llamo Luis
—Mucho gusto
— De donde ____ (tú)
—(Yo) ____ de Espana Y tú, ____ de Miami
—Si, (yo) ____ de Miami. Que hora ____
— ____ las dos en punto

6 Answer the following questions. 2A

1. How do Spanish speakers change their friends' names to show affection for them? Give at least two examples.
2. Name four ways that a teacher might be addressed in a Spanish-speaking country.

7 Listen to the following conversations. For each one, decide whether the speakers are **a**) telling time, **b**) greeting each other, **c**) introducing someone, or **d**) exchanging phone numbers. 1B

8 Use the drawings to create a conversation for what is happening. Give as many details as you can. 1C

5 Gramática 2
- the present tense of **ser**
- punctuation marks and written accents
pp. 24–27

6 Cultura
- **Comparaciones** **pp. 16–17**
- **Notas culturales** **pp. 7, 12**
- **Geocultura** **pp. xxiv–3**

TEKS Focus
2A Demonstrate understanding of practices (what people do) and how they relate to perspectives (how people perceive things) of the cultures studied

Gramática 1
- subjects and verbs in sentences **pp. 12–13**
- subject pronouns **pp. 14–15**

Repaso de Gramática 1

Every sentence has a **subject** and a **verb.** The verb tells what the **subject** does or links the **subject** to a description.

La señora Pérez es mi profesora.

The **subject pronouns** in Spanish are:

yo	nosotros(as)
tú	vosotros(as)
usted/él/ella	ustedes/ellos/ellas

The subject pronouns **tú** and **usted** both mean *you.* Use **tú** when you're talking to a friend. Use **usted** to show respect towards elders and professors. When talking to a group of people, use **ustedes** to say *you.* In Spain only, use **vosotros(as)** to say *you* to a group of friends, family, or children.

¿De dónde es usted? ¿De dónde eres tú?

Gramática 2
- the verb **ser** **pp. 24–25**
- punctuation marks and written accents **pp. 26–27**

Repaso de Gramática 2

This is the conjugation of **ser** *(to be).*

yo **soy**	*I am*	nosotros(as) **somos**	*we are*
tú **eres**	*you are*	vosotros(as) **sois**	*you are*
usted/él/ella **es**	*you are/ he/she is*	ustedes/ellos/ellas **son**	*you/they are*

TEKS Focus
1B Demonstrate understanding of simple, clearly spoken, and written language when dealing with familiar topics

Question marks	**Exclamation points**	**Accent marks**
¿ ... ?	**¡ ... !**	**á, é, í, ó, ú, ñ**
¿Cuál es tu teléfono?	¡Hola!	cuál, qué, sí, cómo, tú, mañana

Letra y sonido a e i o u

Las vocales *(The Vowels)*

The five vowels in Spanish are always pronounced clearly and fully no matter where they are in a word.

- **a:** between the **a** of *cat* and *father*: amigo, hola
- **e:** as in *they,* but shorter: enero, correo
- **i:** as in *police,* but shorter: igualmente, abril
- **o:** as in *low,* but shorter: once, cómo
- **u:** as in *sue,* but shorter: uno, estudiante

Trabalenguas

La a, la e, la i—son fáciles para mí.
La a, la e, la i—las puedo hacer así.
A, e, i, o, u—¡aprende a hacerlas tú!

Dictado 1B

Escribe las oraciones de la grabación.

Repaso de Vocabulario 1

Asking someone's name and saying yours

¿Cómo se llama él (ella)?	*What's his (her) name?*
¿Cómo se llama usted?	*What's your name? (formal)*
¿Cómo te llamas?	*What's your name? (familiar)*
Él (Ella) es...	*He (She) is . . .*
Él (Ella) se llama...	*His (Her) name is . . .*
Me llamo...	*My name is . . .*
¿Quién es...?	*Who is . . .?*
Soy...	*I'm . . .*

Asking and saying how you are

Adiós.	*Goodbye.*
Buenas noches.	*Good evening, good night.*
Buenas tardes.	*Good afternoon.*
Buenos días.	*Good morning.*
¿Cómo está usted?	*How are you?*
Estoy bien, gracias.	*I'm fine, thanks.*
Estoy regular/mal.	*I'm all right/not so good.*
Hasta luego.	*See you later.*
Hasta mañana.	*See you tomorrow.*
Hasta pronto.	*See you soon.*
Hola, ¿cómo estás?	*Hi, how are you?*
Más o menos.	*So-so.*
Nos vemos.	*See you.*
¿Qué tal?	*How's it going?*
señor	*sir, Mr.*
señora	*ma'am, Mrs.*
señorita	*Miss*
Tengo que irme.	*I have to go.*

Introducing others

Encantado(a).	*Pleased/Nice to meet you.*
Ésta es Rosa/la señora...	*This is Rosa/Mrs. . . .*
Éste es Juan/el señor...	*This is Juan/Mr. . . .*
estudiante	*student (male or female)*
Igualmente.	*Likewise.*
mi mejor amiga	*my best friend (female)*
mi mejor amigo	*my best friend (male)*
mi profesora	*my teacher (female)*
mi profesor	*my teacher (male)*
...de ciencias	*science . . .*
...de español	*Spanish . . .*
la muchacha	*the girl*
el muchacho	*the boy*
Mucho gusto.	*Pleased/Nice to meet you.*
una compañera de clase	*a (female) classmate*
un compañero de clase	*a (male) classmate*

Saying where you and others are from

¿De dónde eres?	*Where are you from? (familiar)*
¿De dónde es...?	*Where is . . . from?*
¿De dónde es usted?	*Where are you from? (formal)*
Es de...	*He (She) is from . . .*
ser	*to be*
Soy de...	*I'm from . . .*

Subject pronouns . . . . . *See p. 14.*

Repaso de Vocabulario 2

Exchanging phone numbers

¿Cuál es el teléfono de...?	*What's . . . telephone number?*
¿Cuál es tu teléfono?	*What's your telephone number?*

Los números 0–31 . . . . . *See p. 18.*

Telling time

de la mañana	*in the morning A.M.*
de la noche	*at night P.M.*
de la tarde	*in the afternoon P.M.*
en punto	*on the dot*
Es la una.	*It's one o'clock.*
medianoche	*midnight*
mediodía	*midday, noon*
menos cuarto	*a quarter to*
¿Qué hora es?	*What time is it?*
Son las...	*It's . . . o'clock.*
y cuarto	*a quarter past*
y media	*half past*

Giving the date and the day

Es el primero (dos, tres) de...	*It's the first (second, third) of . . .*
Hoy es lunes.	*Today is Monday.*
¿Qué día es hoy?	*What day is today?*
¿Qué fecha es hoy?	*What's today's date?*

Los días de la semana . . . . . *See p. 21.*
Los meses y las estaciones del año . . . . . *See p. 21.*
El alfabeto . . . . . *See p. 22.*
Spelling words and giving e-mail addresses . . . . . *See p. 23.*

Integración

capítulo 1

1 Listen to each conversation and match it with the appropriate picture. 1B

A

B

C

D

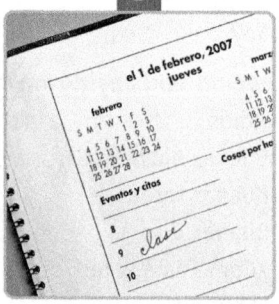

2 Read the following conversation between Marisa and Marta and decide if the statements are **cierto** or **falso.** 1B

MARISA Hola, Marta. ¿Cómo estás?

MARTA Bien. ¿Y tú?

MARISA Más o menos. Dime, ¿cuál es el correo electrónico de Pilar, Alicia y Jorge?

MARTA No sé el correo electrónico de Pilar. El correo electrónico de Alicia es a-ele-i arroba be-ese-te punto hache-ere-uve doble punto ce-o-eme y el correo electrónico de Jorge es jota-uno-tres-seis arroba a-te-ene punto hache-ere-uve doble punto ce-o-eme.

MARISA ¿Cuál es el teléfono de Pilar?

MARTA Es dos-treinta y uno-veintinueve-doce.

MARISA Gracias. ¿Sabes *(do you know)* qué hora es?

MARTA Sí, son las dos menos cuarto de la tarde.

MARISA Uy, tengo que irme. Hasta luego.

MARTA Adiós.

1. Marisa y Marta son amigas.
2. Marisa está mal.
3. El correo electrónico de Alicia es ali@bst.hrw.com.
4. El correo electrónico de Jorge es j136@atn.hrw.com.
5. El teléfono de Pilar es 2-31-19-12.
6. Son las 2:15.

Visit Holt Online
go.hrw.com
KEYWORD: EXP1 CH1
Cumulative Self-test

3 Work with a partner and imagine that you are the student body president and vice-president. It is your job to make the morning announcements over the intercom the first day of class. Greet your fellow classmates and teachers, introduce yourselves, and give everyone the day, date, and time. 1C

4 Look at the painting and compare it to the painting by Joan Miró on page 3. Using the color chart, write the Spanish names of the colors the two painters like to use. Then write (in Spanish) the time on each clock. Do you think this painting is more or less abstract than the painting by Miró? What do you think this painting is about? 2B

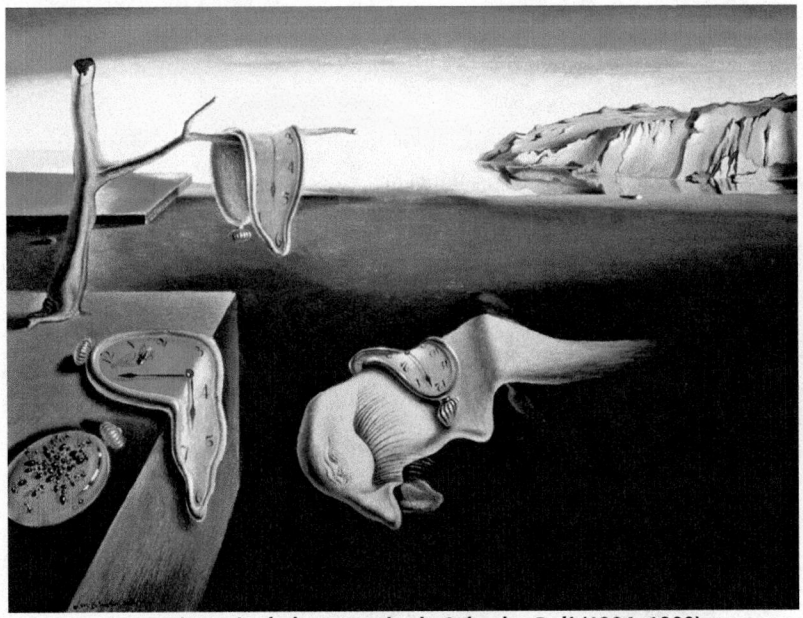

Dalí, Salvador. *The Persistence of Memory (Persistence de la mémoire).* 1931 Oil on canvas, 9 1/2 x 13" (24.1 x 33 cm). The Museum of Modern Art, New York. Given anonymously. Photograph © 1999 The Museum of Modern Art, New York.; ©2003 Salvador Dalí, Gala-Salvador Dalí Foundation/ Artists Rights Society (ARS), New York; Digital Image © The Museum of Modern Art/Licensed by SCALA/Art Resource, NY.

La persistencia de la memoria, **de Salvador Dalí (1904–1989)**

TEKS Focus

2B Demonstrate understanding of products (what people create) and how they relate to perspectives (how people perceive things) of the cultures studied

5 You're sending a letter to a new pen pal in Spain. Introduce yourself and say where you're from, give him or her your phone number and e-mail address, and ask two questions you'd like him or her to answer. Check for correct punctuation and accent marks. 1C

6 **Situación**

The Spanish Club is meeting for the first time to get to know new members. Introduce yourself to one person, tell him or her where you are from, and ask how he or she is doing. Then introduce this person to someone else. Try to speak to four people before you finish. 1A, 1C

GeoVisión

Geocultura
Puerto Rico

▲ **El Viejo San Juan** Las calles reflejan la época colonial.

▼ **San Juan** La capital de Puerto Rico está en el noreste de la isla.

Almanaque

Población
3.937.316

Capital
San Juan

Gobierno
estado libre asociado de Estados Unidos

Idiomas oficiales
español e inglés

Moneda
dólar estadounidense

Código Internet
www.[ ].pr

¿Sabías que...?

Did you know that the Galveston hurricane of 1900, the deadliest weather disaster ever to strike the United States, also affected Puerto Rico? The storm passed over Puerto Rico on September 6, then strengthened in the Gulf of Mexico before hitting Galveston, Texas, on September 8.

◄ **El béisbol,** o para mujeres el sóftbol, es el deporte nacional del país. Reúne a puertorriqueños de todas las edades.

▲ **Isabela** Las bellas playas son muy conocidas por sus olas grandes.

▲ **El Yunque** Con 113 km², el Bosque Nacional del Caribe, o el Yunque, es el área forestal más grande de Puerto Rico. Es conocido por sus numerosas especies de plantas y animales.

OCÉANO ATLÁNTICO

SAN JUAN

Arecibo

Río Grande de Arecibo

avernas del
ío Camuy

Río Grande de Manatí

Río de la Plata

Carolina

Bayamón

Río Grande de Loíza

ISLA DE CULEBRA

PLAYA SARDINERA

Parque Nacional El Yunque

Lago Dos Bocas

Embalse Río Grande de Loíza

El Toro (1070m)

Lago Caonillas

Caguas

Sierra de Luquillo

ISLA DE VIEQUES

PUERTO RICO

Cordillera Central

Coamo

Río Coamo

Ponce

BAHÍA DE RINCÓN

ISLA CAJA DE MUERTOS

MAR CARIBE

▲ **El coquí,** llamado así por el sonido que produce, es el anfibio más famoso de Puerto Rico.

3B

▼ **La Cordillera Central** Aquí crece el flamboyán, el árbol de flores rojas.

¿Qué tanto sabes?

What is **El Yunque,** and what is it known for?

A conocer Puerto Rico

La comida

▲ **Las habichuelas** son frijoles y se comen con arroz y pollo o carne.

▲ **Turistas y sanjuaneros** disfrutan de la deliciosa comida puertorriqueña y de las temperaturas templadas.

▲ **El pollo frito con tostones** es un plato típico de Puerto Rico.

El arte

▼ **En el Museo de Arte de Ponce** se encuentra el *Retrato de un Oficial del Regimento Fijo* (1790), pintado por José Campeche, uno de los pintores más famosos de Puerto Rico.

► **Las máscaras de vejigante** se hacen con la mitad de un coco seco. Con frecuencia son pintadas en negro y rojo y tienen cuernos.

► **La cultura taína** fue la cultura dominante en Puerto Rico antes de la llegada de Colón en 1493. El arte taíno conserva la tradición precolombina.

Visit Holt Online
go.hrw.com
KEYWORD: EXP1 CH2
Photo Tour

Interactive TUTOR

Las celebraciones

▶ **La Fiesta de Santiago** se celebra en Loíza Aldea por una semana con música tradicional, como la bomba y la plena.

◀ **El Festival Casals,** creado por Pablo Casals hace más de 40 años, se dedica a la música clásica.

¿Sabías que...?

Did you know that on his second voyage, Christopher Columbus landed on the island of Puerto Rico by accident when trying to reach Hispaniola, today's Dominican Republic and Haiti?

La arquitectura

◀ **El Parque de Bombas** en Ponce es un museo dedicado a la historia del famoso cuerpo de bomberos de Ponce.

▲ **Ponce,** o la *Perla del Sur*, se conoce por la fina arquitectura de sus casas.

Conexión Historia

TEKS Focus

4B Demonstrate understanding of the concept of culture through comparisons

El Morro

Construction of this Spanish fortress began in 1539. Six-meter-thick outer walls and its strategic position made it the most important Spanish fortress in the Caribbean. Circular sentry boxes, or **garitas**, provided shelter for guards and have become the architectural symbol of Puerto Rico. What do you think the role of **El Morro** was in the 1500s and 1600s? What type of structures in the U.S. have towers like **garitas**? What are some similarities and differences? **2B, 4B**

Capítulo 2

A conocernos

OBJETIVOS

In this chapter you will learn to

- describe people
- ask someone's age and birthday
- talk about what you and others like
- describe things

And you will use

- **ser** with adjectives
- gender and adjective agreement
- questions
- nouns and definite articles
- **gustar, ¿por qué?** and **porque**
- the preposition **de**

¿Qué ves en la foto?

- ¿De dónde son estas personas?
- ¿Quiénes son?
- ¿Qué hora es?

Texas

TEKS Look for the ✦ next to each activity to learn how it can help you achieve the goals of the **Texas Essential Knowledge and Skills,** found on page xxiii.

Visit Holt Online
go.hrw.com
KEYWORD: EXP1 CH2
Online Edition

Unos estudiantes al lado de las murallas del Viejo San Juan

Objetivos
Describing people, asking someone's age and birthday

Vocabulario en acción 1

ExpresaVisión

Mi amigo es...

Más vocabulario...

aburrido	*boring*
activo	*active*
antipático	*unfriendly*
extrovertido	*outgoing*
inteligente	*intelligent*
simpático	*friendly*
tonto	*silly, foolish*
trabajador	*hard-working*

▶ **Vocabulario adicional** — Palabras descriptivas, p. R10

Visit Holt Online
go.hrw.com
KEYWORD: EXP1 CH2
Vocabulario 1 practice

Mi amiga es...

pelirroja | morena | morena | morena | rubia

bonita

perezosa

intelectual | baja | alta | atlética

seria | romántica | tímida | graciosa

Más vocabulario...

aburrida	*boring*
activa	*active*
antipática	*unfriendly*
extrovertida	*outgoing*
inteligente	*intelligent*
simpática	*friendly*
tonta	*silly, foolish*
trabajadora	*hard-working*

¡Exprésate!

Interactive TUTOR

To ask what someone is like	To describe someone
¿Cómo es Paco? *What's Paco like?*	**Paco es moreno. También es inteligente y un poco tímido.** *Paco has dark hair/a dark complexion. He's also intelligent and a little shy.*
¿Cómo eres? ¿Eres cómico(a)? *What are you like? Are you funny?*	**Sí, soy bastante cómico(a).** *Yes, I'm pretty funny.*

Online
Vocabulario y gramática, pp. 13–15

Nota cultural

In many Latin American countries, someone with dark hair and skin that goes from very light brown to darker shades of brown is described as **moreno(a)** or **trigueño(a)**. The word **rubio(a)** in most Spanish-speaking countries, or **güero(a)** in Mexico, may be used to describe someone with fairly light skin and blond to light brown hair. How are these descriptions similar to or different from ones used in English?

4A, 4B

TEKS Focus

4A Demonstrate understanding of the nature of language through comparisons

1 Luis y Marta son... 1B

Leamos/Hablemos Complete each description with the most logical choice.

1. Luis no es moreno. Es...
   a. bajo **b.** rubio **c.** perezoso
2. Marta no es antipática. Es...
   a. tímida **b.** activa **c.** simpática
3. Luis no es perezoso. Es...
   a. trabajador **b.** inteligente **c.** pelirrojo
4. Marta no es tímida. Es...
   a. extrovertida **b.** morena **c.** atlética
5. Luis no es bajo. Es...
   a. romántico **b.** gracioso **c.** alto
6. Marta no es pelirroja. Es...
   a. morena **b.** perezosa **c.** bonita

2 Jimena y Daniel 1B

Leamos Jimena and Daniel are complete opposites. Based on Jimena's description, choose the word in parentheses that best describes Daniel.

MODELO **Jimena es perezosa. Daniel es _____.**
(antipático/trabajador)
Daniel es trabajador.

1. Jimena es tímida. Daniel es _____. (extrovertido/guapo)
2. Jimena es morena. Daniel es _____. (alto/rubio)
3. Jimena es graciosa. Daniel es _____. (atlético/serio)
4. Jimena es baja. Daniel es _____. (alto/pelirrojo)
5. Jimena es atlética. Daniel es _____. (moreno/intelectual)

3 ¿Cómo es cada uno? 1C

Escuchemos For each picture, you will hear two descriptions. Write the letter of the description that best matches the picture.

1. Roberto

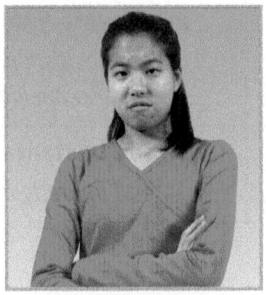

2. Magda

3. Geraldo

4. Julieta

¡Exprésate!

To ask someone's age and birthday	To respond
¿Cuántos años tienes? *How old are you?*	**Tengo quince años.** *I'm 15 years old.*
¿Cuántos años tiene María? *How old is Maria?*	**Ella tiene veintiún años.** *She's 21 years old.*
¿Cuándo es tu cumpleaños? *When is your birthday?*	**Es el 6 de mayo.** *It's May 6th.*
¿Cuándo es el cumpleaños de Ana? *When is Ana's birthday?*	**Es el 24 de noviembre.** *It's November 24th.*

Interactive TUTOR

Online
Vocabulario y gramática, pp. 13–15

Más vocabulario...

32	treinta y dos
33	treinta y tres...
40	cuarenta
50	cincuenta
60	sesenta
70	setenta
80	ochenta
90	noventa
100	cien

4 Respuesta lógica 1B

Leamos Choose the best response to each question.

1. ¿Cuántos años tienes?
2. ¿Cómo eres?
3. ¿Cuándo es tu cumpleaños?
4. ¿Quién es tu mejor amigo?
5. ¿Cómo es?
6. ¿Cuántos años tiene?

a. Es Juan.
b. Mi cumpleaños es el dos de mayo.
c. Es bajo y un poco perezoso.
d. Soy tímido y serio.
e. Tengo dieciséis años.
f. Tiene quince años.

TEKS Focus
1B Demonstrate understanding of simple, clearly spoken, and written language when dealing with familiar topics

Comunicación

5 ¿Y tú? 1A

Hablemos Working in pairs, ask each other the questions from Activity 4.

6 ¿Quién es? 1A, 1B

Escribamos/Hablemos Ask four classmates where they're from, what they're like, when their birthdays are, and how old they are. Pick two and write a description of each one. Present your descriptions to the class and have everyone guess who you're describing.

Objetivos

Using **ser** with adjectives, gender and adjective agreement, forming questions

Gramática en acción 1

GramaVisión

Ser with adjectives

1 **Adjectives** are words that describe people or things. You can use the verb **ser** with **adjectives** to describe what someone is like.

Carlos **es simpático**. Pedro **es pelirrojo**.

Ana **es simpática**. Rosa y Julio **son inteligentes**.

2 In Spanish, you don't usually need the subject pronoun if it's clear who the subject is.

¿Cómo **es** el profesor? **Es** bajo y gracioso.

¿Cómo **son** Leticia y Diego? **Son** simpáticos.

3 To say what someone is not like, put **no** in front of the verb.

No soy tonto. Soy inteligente.

Online

Vocabulario y gramática, pp. 16–18 | Actividades, pp. 11–13

¿Te acuerdas?

Remember that **ser** means *to be.*

yo	**soy**	nosotros(as)	**somos**
tú	**eres**	vosotros(as)	**sois**
usted	**es**	ustedes	**son**
él/ella	**es**	ellos/ellas	**son**

7 ¿Cómo son...? 1B

Leamos Complete these sentences about your classmates, your friends, your teacher, and yourself.

1. Yo ____ muy alto(a).
   a. soy **b.** no soy
2. Profesor(a), usted ____ moreno(a).
   a. es **b.** no es
3. *(The person next to you)* Tú ____ tímido(a).
   a. eres **b.** no eres
4. Mi mejor amigo ____ cómico.
   a. es **b.** no es
5. Mis amigos(as) y yo ____ serios(as).
   a. somos **b.** no somos
6. Los estudiantes ____ tontos.
   a. son **b.** no son
7. Mis compañeros de clase ____ perezosos.
   a. son **b.** no son

Visit Holt Online
go.hrw.com
KEYWORD: EXP1 CH2
Gramática 1 practice

8 Una persona simpática 1B

Escribamos/Hablemos Roberto always says good things about everyone. What does he say about the following people?

MODELO **yo/guapo → Soy guapo.**
tú/tonta → No eres tonta.

1. yo/perezoso
2. tú/bonita
3. mi amigo Carlos/inteligente
4. Profesor Garza, usted/aburrido
5. nosotros/simpáticos
6. Mari y Gisela/graciosas
7. mis compañeras de clase/antipáticas
8. ustedes/activos

TEKS Focus
1B Demonstrate understanding of simple, clearly spoken, and written language when dealing with familiar topics

9 ¿Quién es...? 1B

Escribamos/Hablemos Look at the photos below, and say which person each adjective describes.

MODELO **activo**
Felipe es activo.

Felipe

Gladys

Juan

Rebeca

1. rubia
2. atlética
3. morena
4. seria
5. intelectual
6. tímido
7. moreno
8. pelirrojo
9. extrovertido

Comunicación

10 Yo soy... ¿Y tú? 1B, 1C

Hablemos Write down three adjectives that describe you. If you're male, use the words on page 44. If you're female, use the words on page 45. Then get together in groups of four. Record how many students in your group used the same adjectives that you used.

MODELO **atlético**
—¿Eres atlético?
—Sí, soy atlético./—No, no soy atlético.

Gender and adjective agreement

Interactive TUTOR

1 Nouns and pronouns in Spanish are divided into genders. Nouns for men and boys are **masculine**. Nouns for women and girls are **feminine**.

Masculine: amigo, él, Juan **Feminine:** amiga, ella, María

2 Adjectives describe nouns. They have different forms that match, or agree with, the noun or pronoun in gender. The **masculine** form of most adjectives ends in **-o**, while the **feminine** form ends in **-a**.

Raúl es romántic**o**. **Mari** es romántic**a**.

Adjectives that end in **-e** have the same **masculine** and **feminine** forms.

Rafael es inteligent**e**. **Carmen** es inteligent**e**.

Adjectives ending in consonants do not add an **-a**, unless they end in **-or** or are adjectives of nationality.

Lorenzo es intelectual y trabajad**or**. **Gloria** es intelectual y trabajad**ora**.
Sergio es españ**ol**. Sara es españ**ola**.

3 Adjectives also agree with nouns in number. An adjective that describes one person or thing is in **singular** form. When it describes more than one person or thing, its form is **plural**. If the singular form ends in a vowel, add **-s** to make it plural. If it ends in a consonant, add **-es**.

Joaquín es alt**o**. Paco y Luis son alto**s**.
Rosa es intelectua**l**. Mis amigos son intelectual**es**.

To describe a mixed group of men and women, or boys and girls, use the **masculine plural** form of the adjective:

Carlos y **Ana** son romántic**os**.

TEKS Focus
1B Demonstrate understanding of simple, clearly spoken, and written language when dealing with familiar topics

Online
Vocabulario y gramática, pp. 16–18 | Actividades, pp. 11–13

En las calles del Viejo San Juan

11 ¿Cómo son los mellizos? 1B

Escribamos Mario and María are twins. Say what María is like based on Mario's description. Then, describe Gabriel and Gabriela as the opposite of Mario and María, using plural adjectives.

MODELO **Mario es moreno.**
María es morena también.
Gabriel y Gabriela son rubios.

1. Mario es bajo.
2. Mario es intelectual.
3. Mario es perezoso.
4. Mario es simpático.
5. Mario es tímido.
6. Mario es serio.

12 Mi clase preferida ➜1B

Leamos/Escribamos A student has only good things to say about her favorite class. Complete her description with the correct forms of the most logical adjective in parentheses.

La clase es muy interesante y la profesora es __1__ (simpático, antipático). Los estudiantes son __2__ (perezoso, trabajador). Mis amigas Marta y Gabi son muy __3__ (tonto, intelectual) y mi amigo Ricardo es muy __4__ (gracioso, aburrido). ¿Y yo? Soy __5__ (tonto, inteligente) y __6__ (activo, perezoso).

13 ¿Cómo son? ➜1B, 1C

Escribamos/Hablemos Describe yourself and people you know by combining words from each column. Use the correct forms of the verb **ser** and the adjectives listed.

MODELO **Mis amigas y yo somos graciosas.**

1	2	3	
yo	eres	simpático	activo
mi mejor amigo(a)	es	inteligente	perezoso
mis amigos y yo	son	atlético	interesante
los estudiantes	somos	gracioso	tímido
tú (una compañera de clase)	soy	trabajador	serio
Profesor(a), usted			
ustedes (tus amigos)			

Comunicación

14 Nuestros compañeros ➜1A, 1B

Hablemos With a partner, take turns describing someone from the picture below and guessing who is being described.

Sócrates Romeo Azucena Linda Paco Luis Jimena

Question formation

Interactive TUTOR

1 To ask a question that may be answered **sí** or **no,** just raise the pitch of your voice at the end of the question. The subject, if included, can go before or after the **verb**.

¿**Eres** extrovertido?	*Are you outgoing?*
¿La profesora es simpática?	*Is the teacher nice?*
¿**Es** simpática **la profesora?**	*Is the teacher nice?*

2 You can answer a question like this with **sí** or **no.** You say the word **no** twice in your answer: once to mean ***no*** and another time to mean ***not***.

—¿Eres atlético?	*—Are you athletic?*
—**Sí**, soy atlético.	*—Yes, I'm athletic.*
(—**No**, **no** soy atlético.)	*(—No, I'm not athletic.)*

3 You can ask for more information by using **question words**. Notice that all question words are written with an accent mark.

¿**Cómo** es Paco?	*What's Paco like?*
¿**Cuándo** es tu cumpleaños?	*When is your birthday?*
¿**Quién** es?	*Who is he (she)?*
¿**Quiénes** son?	*Who are they?*
¿**Qué** día es hoy?	*What day is today?*
¿**De dónde** eres?	*Where are you from?*
¿**Cuál** es tu teléfono?	*What's your phone number?*

Online

Vocabulario y gramática, pp. 16–18 | Actividades, pp. 11–13

¿Te acuerdas?

Remember that **¿Cómo está?** is asking how someone is feeling. To ask what someone is like say **¿Cómo es?**

¿Cómo está usted?

Estoy bien, gracias.

¿Cómo es tu amigo?

Él es guapo.

15 ¿Pregunta o no? ✦1B

Escuchemos Decide if what you hear is a question or statement.

16 ¡Muchas preguntas!

Hablemos Mari is full of questions for her new neighbor, Jorge. Fill in her questions with the best question word. Use Jorge's answers as cues.

1. ¿ ____ estás? (Estoy bien, gracias.)
2. ¿ ____ te llamas? (Me llamo Jorge.)
3. ¿ ____ eres? (Soy de Puerto Rico.)
4. ¿ ____ es tu cumpleaños? (Es el 10 de enero.)
5. ¿ ____ eres? (Soy un poco serio y bastante activo.)
6. ¿ ____ son ellos? (Son mis amigos Luisa y Óscar.)
7. ¿ ____ es? (Son las tres. Tengo que irme.)

17 ¿Qué tal? 1B

Leamos/Escribamos Read the e-mail and then answer the questions.

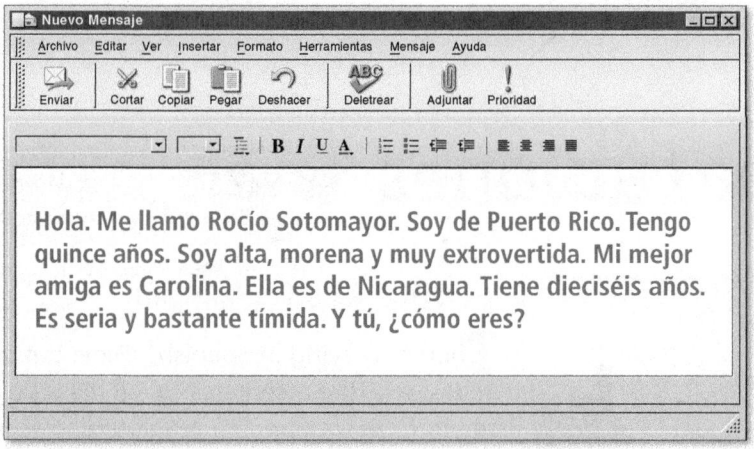

Rocío y Carolina

1. ¿De dónde es Rocío?
2. ¿Cuántos años tiene?
3. ¿Es rubia o morena?
4. ¿Cómo es Rocío?
5. ¿De dónde es Carolina?
6. ¿Cómo es ella?

Nota cultural

In most Spanish-speaking countries, the legal driving and voting age is 18. Since Puerto Ricans are U.S. citizens, they can vote when they are 18 years old. They can get their driver's license at age 18, although some people can get a learner's permit at 16 with parental consent. How would your 18th birthday be different if you lived in Puerto Rico?

2A, 4B

18 Entrevistan a Gisela 1B

Hablemos/Escribamos On a separate piece of paper, write the missing questions to complete the interview.

MODELO **—¿Cómo estás?**
—Muy bien, gracias.

1. —¿ _____ ? —Me llamo Gisela Ríos Perales.
2. —¿ _____ ? —Soy de Burgos, España.
3. —¿ _____ ? —No, no soy tímida. Soy extrovertida.
4. —¿ _____ ? —Son inteligentes, simpáticos y atléticos.
5. —¿ _____ ? —Tengo catorce años.
6. —¿ _____ ? —Mi cumpleaños es el quince de marzo.

Comunicación

19 Veinte preguntas 1A, 1B

Hablemos Ask your partner to think of a classmate. Guess who he or she is by asking questions that can be answered with **sí** or **no.** Switch roles.

MODELO **—¿Es una compañera?**
—No, no es una compañera. Es un compañero.

TEKS Focus
1A Engage in oral and written exchanges of learned material to socialize and to provide and obtain information

Cultura

VideoCultura

Comparaciones

Un grupo de amigos, San Juan

¿Cómo eres? 2A, 4B

There's a saying in Spanish, **"Dime con quién andas, y te diré quién eres."** *(Tell me who you spend time with and I'll tell you who you are.)* This saying is like the English expressions "Birds of a feather flock together" and "You're known by the company you keep." These sayings stem from the belief that we choose as friends those who are much like ourselves. Why do you think both English and Spanish have these sayings? Do you think they are true? Why or why not?

Luis
San Juan, Puerto Rico

Dime, ¿cómo eres tú?

Bueno, pues, yo me considero una persona simpática, gracioso, alegre, un buen amigo y una buena persona.

¿Y qué cosas te gustan?

Me gusta el deporte, me gusta la música. Me gusta la escuela.

¿Tú tienes un mejor amigo?

Sí.

¿Bueno, cómo es tu mejor amigo?

Pues, es una persona que es simpática también, amigable, alegre, atleta. Él es moreno. Es bien activo. Me gusta ser amigo de él.

¿Qué cosas le gustan a él?

Le gusta también la música, el deporte. Le gusta la escuela. Y como es una persona alegre, pues no le gusta estar aburrido.

¿Cómo son ustedes?

Pues, tenemos muchos gustos como lo de la música y pues además nos llevamos bien y nos comprendemos en todo.

¿Qué significa la expresión "Dime con quién andas, y te diré quién eres"?

Yo pienso que, que es con quien tú te pasas, según esa persona, pues, va a ser tu personalidad.

Okay, muchas gracias, Luis.

Visit Holt Online
go.hrw.com
KEYWORD: EXP1 CH2
Online Edition

Andrea
Ciudad de México, México

¿Cómo eres tú?

Soy alegre, soy inteligente, soy muy divertida.

¿Qué cosas te gustan a ti?

Me gusta el cine, los libros, el cantar, bailar.

¿Cómo es tu mejor amigo o tu mejor amiga?

Es alegre también, es inteligente y divertida.

¿Qué cosas le gustan a ella?

Le gusta el cine, los libros, bailar.

¿Cómo son ustedes?

Somos muy parecidas.

¿Qué cosas les gustan?

Nos gusta el cine, bailar.

Para comprender 1B, 1C

1. ¿Cuáles son tres cosas que le gustan a Luis?
2. ¿Cuáles son tres cosas que le gustan a Andrea?
3. ¿A quién le gustan las películas?
4. ¿El amigo de Luis es atlético?
5. ¿Quiénes son alegres?
6. ¿Luis y Andrea son más serios o son más extrovertidos?

Para pensar y hablar 1B

Based on how Luis and Andrea describe themselves and their friends, do you think the expression **"Dime con quién andas, y te diré quién eres"** applies to them? How alike are you and your friends? What are two advantages of being exactly like your friends? What are two disadvantages?

Cuaderno para hispanohablantes, pp. 13–20

Texas

Comunidad

Tejano Music 3A, 5B

Tejano (or **Conjunto**) music is popular in Texas and other states where Mexican Americans live. This musical style, developed from **música norteña** (music from Northern Mexico), features the **bajo sexto**—a 12-string guitar from Mexico—and the accordion, brought to Texas and northern Mexico by German, Czech, or Polish immigrants in the 19th century. Some famous Tejano artists are Eva Ybarra, Santiago Jiménez, Jr., and Flaco Jiménez. Search the Internet or the library to find out more information in Spanish about Tejano artists and their music.

Santiago Jiménez, Jr., reconocido acordeonista tejano

Objetivos
Talking about what you and others like, describing things

Vocabulario en acción 2

ExpresaVisión

Me gusta...

el ajedrez

el helado

la comida italiana

la pizza

la música

la música de Puerto Rico

la comida china

la comida mexicana

▶ **Vocabulario adicional** — Comida, p. R7

Visit Holt Online
go.hrw.com
KEYWORD: EXP1 CH2
Vocabulario 2 practice

Me gustan...

los libros (de aventuras, de amor)

las películas (de ciencia ficción, de terror, de misterio)

los carros

las fiestas

las hamburguesas

las verduras

las frutas

los deportes

los videojuegos

los animales

¡Exprésate!

To ask someone what he or she likes	To respond
¿Te gusta(n)...? *Do you like . . . ?*	**Sí, me gusta(n) mucho...** *Yes, I like . . . a lot.* **No, no me gusta(n)...** *No, I don't like . . .*
¿Te gusta(n) más...o...? *Do you like . . . or . . . more?*	**Me gusta(n) más...** *I like . . . more.* **Me da igual.** *It's all the same to me.*

Interactive TUTOR

Online
Vocabulario y gramática, pp. 19–21

▶ **Vocabulario adicional** — Deportes y pasatiempos, p. R8

Nota cultural

In Puerto Rico, music is very popular, and there are several musicians who trace their roots to the island. Tito Puente made **salsa** music famous by using instruments like the **güiro** and **maracas** to add Afro-Caribbean rhythms to Big Band jazz sounds. Thanks to Tito Puente, Willie Colón and Marc Anthony, among others, **salsa** continues to gain world-wide popularity.

20 Dime cómo eres... ←1B

Leamos/Hablemos Based on the descriptions, which item would these people say they like or don't like?

MODELO **Me llamo Carlos. Soy muy atlético. Me gustan ═══ (los libros, los deportes).**
Me gustan los deportes.

1. ¿Qué tal? Soy Marta y soy muy extrovertida. Me gustan ═══ (las fiestas/los libros).
2. Soy Juan y me gusta la pizza. Me gusta ═══ (la comida mexicana/la comida italiana).
3. Buenas tardes. Me llamo Javier y soy muy romántico. Me gustan ═══ (las películas de ciencia ficción/las películas de amor).
4. Hola. Yo soy Samuel y soy intelectual. Me gustan ═══ (los videojuegos/los libros).
5. Soy Carlota y no soy muy activa. Me gustan ═══ (los videojuegos/los deportes).
6. Hola, me llamo Celia. No soy muy atlética. No me gustan ═══ (los deportes/las fiestas).

21 ¿Quiénes hablan? ←1B

Escuchemos You will hear four conversations. Decide which conversation goes with each photo.

A

B

C

D

¡Exprésate!

To describe something

¿Cómo es...?
What's . . . like?

Es pésimo(a)/fenomenal/formidable.
It's awful/awesome/great.

Es (muy) delicioso(a)/horrible.
It's (really) delicious/horrible.

Es algo divertido(a)/interesante.
It's kind of fun/interesting.

Es bastante bueno(a)/malo(a).
It's pretty good/bad.

Online
Vocabulario y gramática, pp. 19–21

22 ¿Qué dice? 1B

Leamos Match each sentence with the picture it describes. Then choose the word that best completes each sentence.

a. b. c. d.

1. Los videojuegos son pésimos/fenomenales.
2. Los libros de amor son muy románticos/no son interesantes.
3. La música es aburrida/divertida.
4. Las verduras son deliciosas/horribles.

23 En tu opinión 1C

TEKS Focus
1C Present information using familiar words, phrases, and sentences

Hablemos Say whether you think each description is correct. Make sure adjectives agree with the nouns they modify.

MODELO **la pizza/bueno**
Sí, la pizza es buena./No, la pizza no es buena.

1. las películas de aventuras/fenomenal
2. los libros de misterio/pésimo
3. el helado/horrible
4. los libros de amor/tonto
5. las películas de terror/formidable
6. la comida china/malo
7. las verduras/delicioso
8. los deportes/divertido

Comunicación

24 ¿Te gustan o no? 1A

Hablemos Work with a partner. Find out whether your classmate likes the things listed below. Take turns.

MODELO **—¿Te gustan los videojuegos?**
—Sí, me gustan. Son bastante divertidos.

1. los videojuegos
2. los libros de amor
3. los animales
4. los deportes
5. las películas de aventuras
6. las fiestas

Objetivos

Using nouns and definite articles, **gustar, ¿por qué?** and **porque,** the preposition **de**

Gramática en acción 2

GramaVisión

Nouns and definite articles

1 In Spanish, all nouns belong to one of two gender categories: **masculine** or **feminine**. Masculine nouns usually end in **-o** (carr**o**). Feminine nouns usually end in **-a** (frut**a**).

2 Singular nouns name one of something. Plural nouns name more than one of something. If a singular noun ends in a **vowel**, add **-s** to make it plural. If a singular noun ends in a **consonant**, add **-es** to make it plural.

estudiante *student*	estudiante**s** *students*
animal *animal*	animal**es** *animals*

3 The **definite articles** in Spanish can be used to say *the* with a specific noun. They have different forms that agree with their noun in gender and number.

	Masculine	Feminine
SINGULAR	**el**	**la**
PLURAL	**los**	**las**

—¿Cómo es **la** profesora?
What is the teacher like?

—**La** profesora es simpática.
The teacher is friendly.

—¿Quiénes son **los** muchachos allí?
Who are the boys over there?

—Son **los** compañeros de clase de Rafael.
They are Rafael's classmates.

4 Use **definite articles** to talk about a noun as a general category or when saying what you like with **gustar.**

—¿Cómo es **la** pizza?
What's pizza (in general) like?

—Es deliciosa. Me gusta **la** pizza.
It's delicious. I like pizza.

Online

Vocabulario y gramática, pp. 22–24 | Actividades, pp. 15–17

En inglés

In English, people and animals are masculine or feminine, but things are always neuter in gender.

The book? It's interesting.
Ana? She's pretty.

In Spanish, all nouns, including things, are masculine or feminine. With some exceptions, nouns ending in **-o** are **masculine**, and nouns ending in **-a** are **feminine**.

el libro
la pizza

25 Son así... 1B, 1C

Escribamos/Hablemos Write sentences about these things, using words from each column. The articles and adjectives must agree.

MODELO **La música mexicana es fenomenal.**

TEKS Focus
1C Present information using familiar words, phrases, and sentences

1	2	3	4	
El	estudiantes de español	es	serio	aburrido
La	deportes	son	interesante	divertido
Los	helado	somos	bueno	fenomenal
Las	música mexicana		malo	delicioso
	fiestas		romántico	gracioso

26 En mi opinión 1B, 1C

Escribamos Write a sentence saying what you think each item pictured is like.

MODELO **Las frutas son muy deliciosas.**

1.

2.

3.

4.

5.

6.

7.

8.

Comunicación

27 Entrevista 1A, 1B, 1C

Hablemos Ask three classmates their opinions about the things in Activity 26. Are their opinions the same as yours?

MODELO **—¿Cómo son los libros?**
—Los libros son horribles/divertidos.

The verb gustar, ¿por qué?, and porque

Interactive TUTOR

1 Use the verb **gustar** to say what people like. If the thing they like is singular, use **gusta**. If it's plural, use **gustan**. Use **¿qué?** with **gusta** to ask what someone likes.

—¿Te **gusta** la pizza?
Do you like pizza?

—Sí, y me **gustan** las verduras.
Yes, and I like vegetables.

—¿**Qué** te **gusta**?
What do you like?

—Me **gustan** los carros.
I like cars.

2 Put one of these **pronouns** before **gustar** to say who likes something.

me gusta(n)	*I like*	**nos** gusta(n)	*we like*
te gusta(n)	*you* (tú) *like*	**os** gusta(n)	*you* (vosotros) *like*
le gusta(n)	*you* (usted) *like, he, she, it likes*	**les** gusta(n)	*you* (ustedes) *like, they like*

3 Notice that **le** can stand for *you* **(usted),** *he, she or it;* and **les** can stand for *you* **(ustedes)** or *they.* To ask who is being talked about, use **a quién** or **a quiénes**. To clarify who is being talked about, use **a** + **name(s)**.

—¿**A quién** **le** gusta la pizza?
—Who likes pizza?

—**A Juan** **le** gusta la pizza.
—Juan likes pizza.

—¿**A quiénes** **les** gusta la pizza?
—Who likes pizza?

—**A Juan** y **a Sara** **les** gusta la pizza.
—Juan and Sara like pizza.

4 Put the word **no** before the pronoun to say *don't* or *doesn't.*

—¿Te gusta la fruta?

—No, **no** **me** gusta la fruta.

5 To ask *why,* use **¿Por qué?** Answer with **porque** *(because).*

—¿**Por qué** te gusta el helado?

—Me gusta **porque** es delicioso.

Online

Vocabulario y gramática, pp. 22–24 | Actividades, pp. 15–17

En inglés

In English, the definite article *the* is not used when talking about general likes and dislikes.

I like pizza.

In Spanish, the definite articles **el, la, los,** and **las** are always used when talking about things you like or dislike.

Me gusta *la* pizza.

El festival de Ponce

28 El festival de Ponce ↳1B

Escuchemos Listen to Mari and Josué as they talk about the festival. Decide if the following statements are **cierto** or **falso.**

1. A Mari y a Josué les gusta la fiesta.
2. A Juan no le gusta la fiesta porque no le gusta la comida.
3. A Ana y a Silvia no les gusta la música.
4. A los amigos de Mari les gusta la música.

29 ¿Qué les gusta más? 1C

Escribamos Based on the following people's personalities, which things do they like more?

MODELO **Somos muy románticos. (películas de amor/películas de terror)**
Nos gustan más las películas de amor.

1. Eres muy intelectual. (libros/videojuegos)
2. Mis amigos Juan y Beti son atléticos. (música/deportes)
3. Teresa es muy extrovertida. (fiestas/libros)
4. Soy un poco perezoso. (videojuegos/deportes)
5. Ustedes son bastante serias. (películas de amor/libros de misterio)
6. No somos muy activos. (deportes/películas de aventuras)

Comunicación

30 La fiesta 1A, 1C

TEKS Focus
1A Engage in oral and written exchanges of learned material to socialize and to provide and obtain information

Hablemos You're throwing a party and you want to find out what your guests like. Ask four classmates if they like each of these things. Report your findings to the class.

1. ice cream
2. Italian food
3. fruit
4. videogames
5. hamburgers
6. music by . . .

31 ¿Por qué te gusta(n)? 1A, 1B

Hablemos With a partner take turns asking each other if you like the things pictured. Then tell why you like them or not.

MODELO **¿Te gustan los deportes?**
No, no me gustan los deportes porque son aburridos.

The preposition de

Interactive TUTOR

1 **De** is used to show possession or relationship.

Es el carro **de** Ernesto.	*It's Ernesto's car.*
Son los amigos **de** la profesora.	*They're the teacher's friends.*

2 In addition, **de** can be used to indicate what type of thing you're describing.

los libros **de** aventuras	*adventure books*
las películas **de** misterio	*mystery movies*

3 The word **de** is also used to say where someone is from.

Julio es **de** Costa Rica.	*Julio is from Costa Rica.*

4 The preposition **de** followed by **el** makes the contraction **del**.

el correo electrónico **del** profesor	*the teacher's e-mail address*

Online
Vocabulario y gramática, pp. 22–24 | Actividades, pp. 15–17

En inglés

In English, we add **'s** or just an apostrophe **(')** to show ownership.

Charles' class
the teacher's book

In Spanish, use **de** to show possession.

la clase de Juan
los libros de la profesora

32 ¿Cómo son? 1B

Escribamos/Hablemos Complete the statements with **de, del, de la, de los,** or **de las.** Then decide whether or not each statement is **cierto** or **falso.**

MODELO **Los animales de Rafael son malos.**
Falso. Los animales de Rafael son buenos.

1. El carro ____ profesora es fenomenal.

2. La pizza ____ Roberto es deliciosa.

3. La fiesta ____ amiga de Ana es pésima.

4. El carro ____ profesor es bueno.

5. Los videojuegos ____ amigas son divertidos.

6. El libro ____ profesor es horrible.

33 ¿Hoy es el cumpleaños del profesor? 1B

Leamos/Hablemos Complete each question with **de, del, de la, de los** or **de las.** Then answer the questions.

MODELO ¿Tu mejor amigo(a) es de Miami?
No, mi mejor amiga es de Denver.

1. ¿El(La) profesor(a) ____ español es ____ Puerto Rico?
2. ¿Hoy es el cumpleaños ____ profesor(a)?
3. ¿Cómo se llama el libro ____ español?
4. ¿Te gustan más los libros ____ amor o ____ aventuras?
5. ¿Las películas ____ ciencia ficción son interesantes?
6. ¿Te gusta la música ____ Tito Puente?
7. ¿Las fiestas ____ estudiantes son divertidas o aburridas?

In Texas, many Mexican-American girls celebrate their fifteenth birthday with a **quinceañera.** This involves a church ceremony and a dance with family and friends in attendance. **Quinceañeras** are an important milestone in the lives of many Mexican-American girls. Do research at your library or on the Internet to find out if there are similar celebrations in Spain and other Latin American countries. 3A, 3B

34 La preposición de 1B

Escuchemos As you listen to each sentence, decide how the preposition **de** is being used.

a) to ask about ownership
b) to tell ownership
c) to ask where someone is from
d) to tell where someone is from
e) to describe something

Comunicación

TEKS Focus
1A Engage in oral and written exchanges of learned material to socialize and to provide and obtain information

35 Gustos 1A, 1C

Hablemos Working with a partner, use the drawings to describe Alicia and Rodrigo and to tell what they like and dislike.

Novela en video

¿Quién será?

Episodio 2

ESTRATEGIA

Drawing Conclusions Drawing logical conclusions based on information you've gathered is an important skill. Even if things turn out differently than you thought, that does not mean that your conclusion was illogical. Maybe you did not have all the information. As you read the Novela or watch the video, gather all the information you can so that you can draw conclusions about the story and the characters as events unfold. 3B

En España

Marcos meets with the professor in her office. He reviews Nicolás's file. She describes Nicolás to him, and gives him an assignment in Puerto Rico.

1

La profesora Nicolás Ortega García. Le gusta el arte. Es un chico muy simpático. Es de San Juan, Puerto Rico.

2

Visit Holt Online
go.hrw.com
KEYWORD: EXP1 CH2
Online Edition

En Puerto Rico

An art professor and a gym coach compare notes about a student they each have in their class.

3

Profesora de arte ¿Tienes buenos estudiantes este año?

Entrenador Sí, tengo unos estudiantes muy atléticos este año, y unos que son un poco perezosos.

4

Profesora de arte Yo tengo un estudiante que es muy trabajador. Siempre hace las tareas a tiempo. Es un poco serio y también un poco tímido. Pero creo que va a ser muy buen artista.

Entrenador ¿Quién es?

Profesora de arte Se llama Nicolás Ortega García.

5

Entrenador ¿Nicolás? Dime, ¿cómo es?

Profesora de arte Es alto y rubio.

Entrenador ¿Cuántos años tiene?

Profesora de arte Tiene quince años.

6

Entrenador Yo también tengo un Nicolás Ortega García en mi clase de educación física.

Profesora de arte ¿Ah, sí?

Entrenador Sí, pero este Nicolás no es trabajador. Es perezoso.

7

Entrenador No, este Nicolás no es serio. Es cómico.

8

Profesora de arte No es el mismo Nicolás.

Entrenador No, es verdad. Hay dos Nicolás de apellido Ortega García en este colegio, ¿no crees?

Profesora de arte Sí. Así es.

¿COMPRENDES?

1. What information does la profesora give Marcos about Nicolás?
2. What do you think Marcos's assignment is? Why do you think that?
3. How do the art professor and the coach describe the student in their two classes?
4. What conclusion do they draw about the student? Was the conclusion logical? Was it correct?
5. What is your conclusion about Nicolás? Which class does he like better? Why does he act so differently in the two classes? 1B, 3A

Próximo episodio
Can you predict whether Marcos might be going to Puerto Rico? Why?
PÁGINAS 104–105

Leamos y escribamos

ESTRATEGIA

para leer Inferring is drawing conclusions based on evidence that is only hinted at, or implied, in what you read. To make inferences, think of the information provided by the author, connect it with your own knowledge and experience, and then draw conclusions based on a combination of the two.

A Antes de leer 1C

Did you know that there is a relationship between someone's personality and the colors he or she likes? On a separate sheet of paper, write two personality traits in Spanish that you would associate with each of the colors blue, red, green, yellow, orange, and black.

¿QUÉ COLOR PREFIERES?

Mi color favorito es el verde.

Si te gusta el color verde, eres una persona muy inteligente, inventiva y lógica. No eres muy extrovertido(a) y no te gusta la rutina. Para ti[1], la naturaleza[2] es importante. Personas famosas: Sócrates, Sherlock Holmes y Thomas Edison.

Mi color preferido es el ANARANJADO.

Si te gusta el anaranjado, eres una persona simpática, graciosa y espontánea. Tienes mucha energía y te fascinan las cosas nuevas, interesantes y diferentes. Para ti, la acción y la diversión[3] son muy importantes. Personas famosas: Winston Churchill y Lucille Ball.

¿Te gusta el color AZUL?

Si te gusta el azul, eres una persona creativa y artística. Eres romántico(a) y sincero(a). Para ti, la armonía entre[4] las personas es muy importante. Personas famosas: Mozart, Indira Gandhi y Thomas Jefferson.

Me fascina el color negro.

Si te gusta el negro, eres una persona seria, elegante y algo misteriosa. También[5] eres disciplinado(a), eficiente y muy independiente. No eres muy extrovertido(a) y no te gustan las personas expresivas. Personas famosas: Cervantes y Abraham Lincoln.

Me gusta el rojo.

Si te gusta el color rojo, eres una persona apasionada, enérgica y activa. Eres muy extrovertido(a) y sociable. Te fascina ser[7] el centro de atención. Personas famosas: Ernest Hemingway, Elizabeth Peña y F. Scott Fitzgerald.

A mí me encanta el color amarillo.

Si te gusta el amarillo, eres intelectual, metódico(a) y analítico(a). Eres tímido(a) y tienes pocos[6] pero buenos amigos. Eres un líder formidable, organizado, eficiente y puntual. Para ti, la familia y las tradiciones son muy importantes. Personas famosas: George Washington y la Madre Teresa.

1 for you **2** nature **3** fun **4** harmony between **5** also **6** few **7** you love being

Visit Holt Online
go.hrw.com
KEYWORD: EXP1 CH2
Online Edition

B Comprensión 1B, 3A

Based on the reading, match the colors from Column A with the personality types from Column B. Then draw your own inferences and say what someone might like or dislike based on his or her personality.

A	B	Te gusta(n)…/No te gusta(n)…
1. el azul	a. Eres tímido(a).	las personas
2. el amarillo	b. Eres muy inteligente.	los videojuegos
3. el anaranjado	c. Eres romántico(a).	los animales
4. el rojo	d. Eres extrovertido(a).	los libros
5. el verde	e. Eres serio(a).	las fiestas
6. el negro	f. Eres simpático(a).	la música

C Después de leer 1B, 3A

1. Did the personality traits you listed for the various colors in **Antes de leer** agree with the reading?
2. Does your favorite color match your own personality? Explain why or why not.

TEKS Focus
3A Use resources in the language and cultures being studied to gain access to information

Taller del escritor

ESTRATEGIA

para escribir Cluster diagrams can help you organize and see how your ideas are related.

Mi personalidad 1C

Write a paragraph in which you describe yourself and say what you like and don't like. Tell which "personality color" comes closest to your description of yourself.

1 Antes de escribir

Draw four circles. Label the first one **Yo soy**..., the second **Yo no soy**..., the third **Me gusta(n)**..., and the fourth **No me gusta(n)**... Connect other circles to these four and label the new circles with words that describe you, words that do not describe you, things you like, and things you don't like.

2 Escribir un borrador

Use your cluster diagram to organize the information for your paragraph. Include information from each part of the diagram.

3 Revisar

Read your sentences at least twice. Make sure the paragraph describes you well. Then check spelling and punctuation.

4 Publicar

Get together with three or four classmates. Each member of the group takes someone else's paragraph from the stack and reads it aloud without telling who wrote it. See if the group can guess who wrote each paragraph.

Cuaderno para hispanohablantes, pp. 13–20

Repaso capítulo 2

Interactive TUTOR

1 Vocabulario 1
- describing people
- asking how old someone is

pp. 44–47

2 Gramática 1
- using **ser** with adjectives
- gender and adjective agreement
- question formation

pp. 48–53

3 Vocabulario 2
- talking about what you and others like
- describing things

pp. 56–59

1 Write descriptions of each person. Give each person's age and say something about his or her appearance. **1C**

2 Complete the following conversations using adjectives, **ser,** and question words. Remember to use the correct adjective and verb forms. **1B**

1. —¿_____ es tu mejor amigo(a)?
   —_____ Paco.
2. —¿_____ día es hoy?
   —_____ sábado.
3. —¿Cómo _____ tu mejor amigo(a)?
   —Es _____. No es _____.
4. —¿_____ eres tú?
   — _____ _____.
5. —¿_____ es tu cumpleaños?
   —_____ el _____.

3 Ask your partner if he or she likes the following things and why. Then ask which things he or she likes more. Switch roles. **1A, 1B**

1.

2.

3.

4.

Visit Holt Online
go.hrw.com
KEYWORD: EXP1 CH2
Chapter Self-test

4 Complete the paragraph, using the correct word in parentheses. ➤1B

___1___ (El/La) cumpleaños ___2___ (de/del) Fernando y Maribel es ___3___ (el/la) catorce de diciembre. A ellos ___4___ (les gusta/les gustan) mucho las fiestas ___5___ (de/del) cumpleaños. A Maribel ___6___ (le gustan/les gustan) los libros ___7___ (de/de las) aventuras más que ___8___ (los/las) películas. A Fernando ___9___ (le gusta/le gustan) los videojuegos más que ___10___ (el/la) música de Los Hidalgos.

5 Answer the following questions. ➤2A

1. How do Latin Americans describe someone with dark or light-brown hair and skin?
2. Why are ages sixteen and eighteen important to young people in Puerto Rico?

6 Listen as Patricia reads the e-mail message from Yoli. Then say whether the statements that follow are **cierto** or **falso.** ➤1B

1. A Yoli no le gustan las clases porque son aburridas.
2. Los compañeros de clase son antipáticos.
3. El cumpleaños de Yoli es el 16 de agosto.
4. A Yoli le gusta la comida china.

7 Describe Alicia and her friends and tell what they like. ➤1C

4 Gramática 2
- nouns and definite articles
- **gustar, ¿por qué?,** and **porque**
- uses of the preposition **de**

pp. 60–65

5 Cultura
- **Comparaciones** **pp. 54–55**
- **Notas culturales** **pp. 46, 53, 58**
- **Geocultura** **pp. 38–41**

TEKS Focus
2A Demonstrate understanding of practices (what people do) and how they relate to perspectives (how people perceive things) of the cultures studied

Gramática 1
- **ser** with adjectives **pp. 48–49**
- gender and adjective agreement **pp. 50–51**
- question formation **pp. 52–53**

Gramática 2
- nouns and definite articles **pp. 60–61**
- the verb **gustar**, **¿por qué?** and **porque** **pp. 62–63**
- uses of the preposition **de** **pp. 64–65**

TEKS Focus
1B Demonstrate understanding of simple, clearly spoken, and written language when dealing with familiar topics

Repaso de Gramática 1

You can use adjectives with the verb **ser** to describe people. Adjectives should agree with the nouns they describe in number and gender. Adjectives are either singular or plural, masculine or feminine.

Carlos es alto. **Lupe es alta.** **Carlos y Lupe son altos.**

Form questions by changing your tone of voice or using question words such as **qué, cómo, cuándo, quién, quiénes, cuál** and **de dónde.**

Repaso de Gramática 2

Nouns can be singular or plural, masculine or feminine.

	Masculine	Feminine
SINGULAR	carro	fiesta
PLURAL	carros	fiestas

Use definite articles to say *the* or use them to talk about a noun used as a general category. Definite articles agree with the nouns they describe in gender and number.

	Masculine	Feminine
SINGULAR	el libro	la pizza
PLURAL	los libros	las pizzas

The verb gustar is used to talk about likes and dislikes.

Me gusta la comida italiana. No te gustan los deportes.

The preposition de is used to indicate possession, relationship, or where someone is from. It can also describe a type of thing.

Es el libro de Juan. **Es un libro de misterio.**

Letra y sonido

La sílaba tónica

- Words ending in a vowel, **-n**, or **-s** are normally stressed on the next-to-last syllable: **in-te-li-GEN-te, mo-RE-nos, bas-TAN-te**
- Words ending in a consonant other than **-n** or **-s** are normally stressed on the last syllable: **us-TED, se-ÑOR, es-TOY**
- All words whose pronunciation doesn't follow these rules are written with an accent mark over the vowel that is stressed: **ca-FÉ, pe-LÍ-cu-la, a-ten-CIÓN**

Trabalenguas

Tres tristes tigres tragaban trigo en un trigal en tres tristes trastos.

Dictado 1B

Escribe las oraciones de la grabación.

Repaso de Vocabulario 1

Describing people

aburrido(a)	*boring*
activo(a)	*active*
alto(a)	*tall*
antipático(a)	*unfriendly*
atlético(a)	*athletic*
bajo(a)	*short*
bastante	*quite, pretty*
bonito(a)	*pretty*
cómico(a)	*funny*
¿Cómo eres?	*What are you like?*
¿Cómo es...?	*What's . . . like?*
¿Eres...?	*Are you . . .?*
Es...	*He (She, It) is . . .*
extrovertido(a)	*outgoing*
gracioso(a)	*witty*
guapo(a)	*good-looking*
intelectual	*intellectual*
inteligente	*intelligent*
moreno(a)	*dark-haired; dark-skinned*
muy	*very*
pelirrojo(a)	*red-headed*
perezoso(a)	*lazy*
romántico(a)	*romantic*
rubio(a)	*blond*
serio(a)	*serious*
simpático(a)	*friendly*
Soy...	*I'm . . .*
también	*also*
tímido(a)	*shy*
tonto(a)	*silly, foolish*
trabajador(a)	*hard-working*
un poco	*a little*

Asking and saying how old someone is

¿Cuándo es el cumpleaños de...?	*When is . . . 's birthday?*
¿Cuándo es tu cumpleaños?	*When is your birthday?*
¿Cuántos años tiene...?	*How old is . . .?*
¿Cuántos años tienes?	*How old are you?*
Él (Ella) tiene... años.	*He (She) is . . . years old.*
Es el... de...	*It's the . . . of . . .*
Tengo... años.	*I'm . . . years old.*

Numbers 32–100 . . . . . *See p. 47.*

Repaso de Vocabulario 2

Describing things

el ajedrez	*chess*
los animales	*animals*
los carros	*cars*
la comida china (italiana, mexicana)	*Chinese (Italian, Mexican) food*
los deportes	*sports*
Es algo divertido(a).	*It's kind of fun.*
Es bastante bueno(a).	*It's pretty good.*
Es delicioso(a).	*It's delicious.*
Es pésimo(a).	*It's awful.*
fenomenal	*awesome*
las fiestas	*parties*
formidable	*great*
las frutas	*fruit*
las hamburguesas	*hamburgers*
el helado	*ice cream*
horrible	*horrible*
interesante	*interesting*
los libros (de aventuras, de amor)	*(adventure, romance) books*
malo(a)	*bad*
la música (de...)	*music (of/by . . .)*
las películas (de ciencia ficción, de terror, de misterio)	*(science fiction, horror, mystery) movies*
la pizza	*pizza*
las verduras	*vegetables*
los videojuegos	*videogames*

Talking about what you and others like

Me da igual.	*It's all the same to me.*
Me gusta(n)... mucho.	*I like . . . a lot.*
Me gusta(n) más...	*I like . . . more.*
No, no me gusta(n)...	*No, I don't like . . .*
¿Te gusta(n)...?	*Do you like . . . ?*
¿Te gusta(n) más... o...?	*Do you like . . . or . . . more?*

Integración

capítulos 1-2

1 Listen to these statements and match them with the appropriate picture. 1B

A

B

C

D

2 You want to find an Internet pen pal. Read the ads for **Ciber-amigos,** and then answer the questions that follow. 1B, 1C

Andrés Vallejo
14 años
avall123@mailmex.hrw.com
Soy cómico y activo. Me gustan las computadoras y las películas de terror. No me gusta la comida italiana. Me gustan las hamburguesas.

Yasmín Herrera
15 años
yazz@telecom.hrw.com.es
¿Qué tal? Soy inteligente y extrovertida. No me gusta la televisión, pero sí me gustan los libros de aventuras y las fiestas.

Liliana Caraval
13 años
lilcar@correo.hrw.com.pr
¡Hola! Soy simpática y seria. No soy aburrida. Me gustan los videojuegos y la música rock. No me gusta la pizza.

1. ¿Quién es inteligente? ¿simpático(a)? ¿activo(a)?
2. Según *(according to)* el correo electrónico, ¿de dónde es Liliana? ¿Yasmín?
3. ¿Cuántos años tiene Andrés?
4. ¿Qué le gusta a Liliana? ¿Qué no le gusta?
5. ¿A quién le gustan las hamburguesas? ¿los libros de aventuras?

Visit Holt Online
go.hrw.com
KEYWORD: EXP1 CH2
Cumulative Self-test

3 Write a **Ciberamigos** message that describes you and tells how old you are, where you're from, what your e-mail address is, and what you like and don't like. **1C**

4 In groups of three, take turns playing one of the three **Ciberamigos** in Activity 2. The first person "sends" his or her own description to one of the **amigos,** along with two questions asking for more information. The **amigo** writes back, answering the questions, and then asking two questions in return. The first person answers. The second person then picks an **amigo** and "sends" an e-mail. Continue until everyone has had a turn writing and answering. **1A, 1B, 1C**

5 Imagine that you are writing a short story in Spanish based on what you see in the painting. Who are these people and how old are they? What do they look like and what do they like to do? Where do they come from? Write your story in Spanish. **1C, 2B**

TEKS Focus
2B Demonstrate understanding of products (what people create) and how they relate to perspectives (how people perceive things) of the cultures studied

Día lluvioso en El Viejo San Juan *(Rainy Day in Old San Juan)* by Orlando Santiago Correa courtesy of Patrick Santiago

Día lluvioso en El Viejo San Juan, de Orlando Santiago Correa

6 **1B, 1C**

Situación This year the student council wants to sponsor a film festival and the homecoming dance. In order to sponsor these events, the council needs information from the students about what they like and don't like. In groups of three, create a survey asking about movies, music, and foods people like, and then ask your classmates to fill it in. Afterward, tally the results to see what the student council needs to do.

GeoVisión

Geocultura Texas

▼ **En el Valle de Texas** se cultiva la fruta del estado: la toronja roja.

▼ **El Parque Nacional Big Bend** El nombre Big Bend se refiere a la gran curva en forma de U del Río Grande.

Almanaque

Población
20.851.820

Capital Austin

Área
266.807 millas cuadradas (691.030 km^2)

Moneda
dólar estadounidense

Economía
productos químicos, comestibles, equipos de transporte, productos petroleros, computadoras, ganado, frutas

El Paso
La tradición vaquera continúa fuerte en Texas.

¿Sabías que...?

Did you know that the Rio Grande forms the entire length of the Texas-Mexico border, a total of close to 1,200 miles (1,931 km)?

◀ **Dallas** es un centro de comercio internacional.

▲ **San Antonio** es una ciudad multicultural y es hogar del famoso Paseo del Río.

OKLAHOMA

Red

Llano Estacado

Lubbock

Escarpe de Caprock

Fort Worth

Dallas

Trinity

TEXAS

Neches

LOUISIANA

Pecos

Brazos

ontañas
Rocosas

Meseta
de Edwards

AUSTIN

Houston

Colorado

Guadalupe

Río Bravo del Norte

Escarpe Balcones

BAHÍA
GALVESTON

Parque
Nacional
Big Bend

San Antonio

Río Grande

Nueces

Corpus
Christi

MÉXICO

Laredo

ISLA DEL
PADRE

GOLFO
DE
MÉXICO

El Valle
de Texas

LAGUNA MADRE

▲ **Houston** El puerto de Houston tiene la mayor cantidad de comercio marítimo internacional de Estados Unidos.

▼ **La Isla del Padre** La costa de Texas tiene bonitas regiones como esta isla que se extiende por 113 millas (182 kilómetros).

3B

¿Qué tanto sabes?

What is the name of the Rio Grande in Mexico? Where is the state fruit of Texas grown?

A conocer Texas

La arquitectura

▲ **La biblioteca central de San Antonio** fue diseñada por el famoso arquitecto mexicano Ricardo Legorreta.

▲ **La capilla de San Elceario** en El Paso es un buen ejemplo del estilo de misiones españolas en Texas.

▲ **El convento de la Misión de San José** en San Antonio originalmente fue construido en 1770. Hoy, solamente quedan las ruinas del convento.

El arte

▲ ***Tamalada*** fue pintada por Carmen Lomas Garza, una artista chicana que pinta la vida diaria de los mexicanoamericanos.

◀ **Carmen Lomas Garza** (1948–) con su pintura al óleo, *Una tarde*

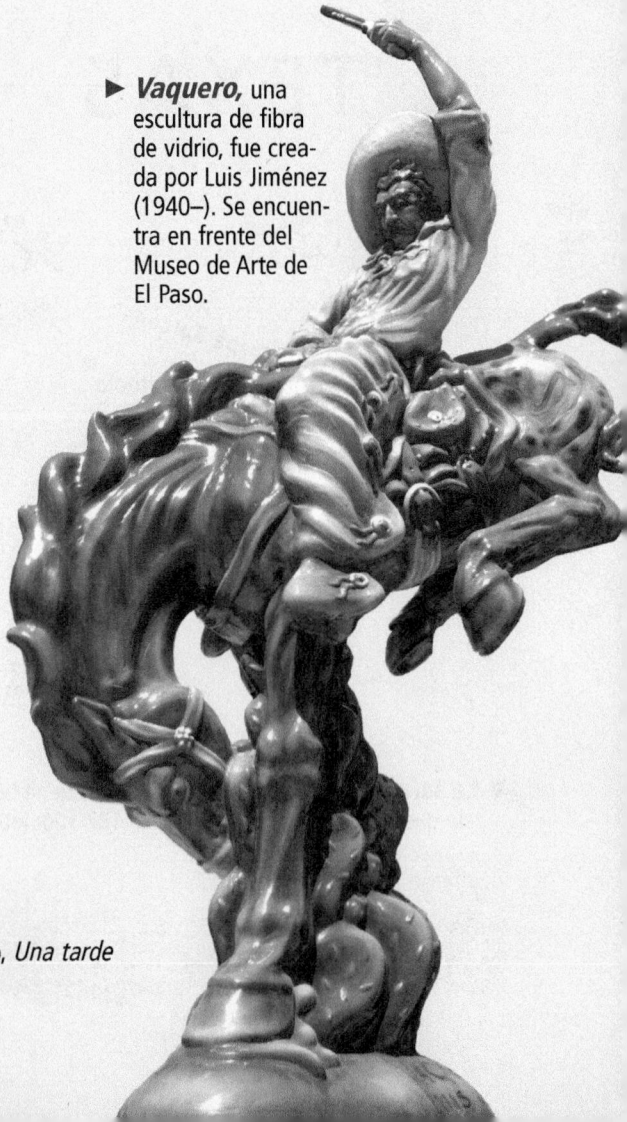

▶ ***Vaquero,*** una escultura de fibra de vidrio, fue creada por Luis Jiménez (1940–). Se encuentra en frente del Museo de Arte de El Paso.

La comida

▶ **Las quesadillas**
La comida mexicana influye mucho en la comida tejana.

Interactive TUTOR

Visit Holt Online
go.hrw.com
KEYWORD: EXP1 CH3
Photo Tour

¿Sabías que...?

Did you know that over the course of history, Texas has been ruled by six different governments: France, Spain, Mexico, the Republic of Texas, the Confederate States, and the United States of America?

▲ **Tostaditas con salsa** es el tentempié oficial de Texas.

◀ **La barbacoa al estilo tejano** es la comida más típica de Texas.

Las celebraciones

◀ **El Cinco de Mayo** se celebra cada año con festivales tanto en Texas como en México. Conmemora la Batalla de Puebla, símbolo de la unidad mexicana.

▶ **El rodeo**
Los tejanos son famosos por su cultura vaquera. En los rodeos se practica el arte de montar a caballo y controlar el ganado.

Conexión Música

Conjunto music is popular dance music from northern Mexico and southern Texas. It sprang to life in the late nineteenth century. The German and Eastern European settlers along the Texas and Mexico border brought their accordions, waltzes, and polkas to the region. The music-loving Mexican and Tejano populations adapted this music to their own style, which continues to evolve today.

Look for **conjunto** music on the Internet or at the library. Can you find a sample of the music to listen to? How is the **conjunto** accordion music different from the European styles that it is adapted from? **3B, 4C**

Capítulo 3

¿Qué te gusta hacer?

OBJETIVOS

In this chapter you will learn to

- talk about what you and others like to do
- talk about what you want to do
- talk about everyday activities
- say how often you do things

And you will use

- **gustar** with infinitives
- pronouns after prepositions
- **querer** with infinitives
- regular **-ar** verbs
- **ir** and **jugar**
- weather expressions

¿Qué ves en la foto?

- ¿Son activos o perezosos los amigos?
- ¿Cómo son las muchachas?
- ¿Cómo es el muchacho? ¿Qué le gusta?

Texas

TEKS Look for the ★ next to each activity to learn how it can help you achieve the goals of the **Texas Essential Knowledge and Skills,** found on page xxiii.

Visit Holt Online
go.hrw.com
KEYWORD: EXP1 CH3
Online Edition

Unos amigos cerca de Hueco Tanks, Texas

Objetivos

Talking about what you and others like to do, talking about what you want to do

Vocabulario en acción 1

ExpresaVisión

A mis amigos y a mí nos gusta...

montar en bicicleta

correr

hacer ejercicio

leer revistas y novelas

escuchar música

dibujar

pasear

patinar

Más vocabulario...

alquilar videos	*to rent videos*	ir al cine	*to go to the movies*
cantar	*to sing*	nadar	*to swim*
comer	*to eat*	navegar por Internet	*to surf the Internet*
escribir cartas	*to write letters*	pasar el rato solo(a)	*to spend time alone*
hacer la tarea	*to do homework*	ver televisión	*to watch television*

Visit Holt Online
go.hrw.com
KEYWORD: EXP1 CH3
Vocabulario 1 practice

Me gusta jugar...

al básquetbol

al béisbol

al fútbol americano

a juegos de mesa

al volibol

al fútbol

al tenis

Más vocabulario...

¿Con quién?	***With whom?***
conmigo	*with me*
contigo	*with you*
con mis amigos(as)	*with también*
con mi familia	*with my family*

También se puede decir...

Spanish speakers in Mexico say **el baloncesto** instead of **el básquetbol,** and **andar en bicicleta** instead of **montar en bicicleta.** In Texas, **básquetbol** is often shortened to **básquet,** and **bicicleta** is shortened to **bici.**

¡Exprésate!

To ask what others like to do	To respond
¿Qué te gusta hacer? *What do you like to do?*	**A mí me gusta salir con amigos.** *I like to go out with friends.*
¿A Juan y a Pablo les gusta ir al centro comercial? *Do Juan and Pablo like to go to the mall?*	**Sí, porque les gusta ir de compras.** *Yes, because they like to go shopping.*

Interactive TUTOR

Online
Vocabulario y gramática, pp. 25–27

▶ **Vocabulario adicional** — Deportes y pasatiempos, p. R8

Nota cultural

Latin American high schools typically do not sponsor organized sports teams. Students who may want to take a more active part in sports can do so by joining clubs and associations outside of school. How is this similar to or different from your school sports program? 4B

1 Les gusta... 1B

Escuchemos/Leamos Choose the most logical description based on the sentences you hear.

1. Es (extrovertida/tímida).
2. Es (muy activo/perezoso).
3. Es (trabajador/perezoso).
4. Son (atléticos/intelectuales).
5. Es (activa/seria).
6. Son (divertidas/serias).

2 A mí me gusta... 1C

Hablemos Say whether or not you like to do the things pictured.

MODELO **Me gusta jugar al béisbol. (No me gusta jugar al béisbol.)**

3 ¿Qué les gusta hacer? 4B

Escribamos/Hablemos Completa las oraciones.

¿Se te olvidó? Gustar, p. 62

1. Me gusta...
2. No me gusta...
3. Me gusta salir con...
4. Me gusta ir al cine con...
5. A mi mejor amigo(a) le gusta...
6. A mi familia y a mí nos gusta...
7. A mis amigos les gusta...
8. A mis amigos y a mí nos gusta...

¡Exprésate!

To ask what a friend wants to do	To answer
¿Qué quieres hacer hoy? *What do you want to do today?*	**Ni idea.** *I have no idea.*
¿Quieres ir al cine conmigo? *Do you want to go to the movies with me?*	**Está bien.** *All right.* **No, gracias. No quiero ir al cine hoy.** *No, thanks. I don't want to go to the movies today.*

Interactive TUTOR

Online
Vocabulario y gramática, pp. 25–27

4 Una conversación 1B

Leamos/Escribamos Completa la conversación.

montar	jugar	gustar	ir	alquilar	hacer

GERARDO ¿Quieres __1__ al centro comercial?
MARÍA No, no quiero. ¿Quieres __2__ videos?
GERARDO No, no quiero. Quiero __3__ ejercicio.
MARÍA ¿Quieres __4__ al básquetbol?
GERARDO No, no me gusta el básquetbol. ¿Quieres __5__ en bicicleta?
MARÍA Está bien. Buena idea.

TEKS Focus
1B Demonstrate understanding of simple, clearly spoken, and written language when dealing with familiar topics

5 ¿Qué quieres hacer hoy? 1B

Hablemos/Escribamos Ana loves sports, and she doesn't like to do things indoors. How does she respond to these invitations?

MODELO **—¿Quieres patinar? —Sí, quiero patinar contigo.**

1. ¿Quieres leer revistas?
2. ¿Quieres jugar al béisbol?
3. ¿Quieres ver televisión?
4. ¿Quieres dibujar?
5. ¿Quieres jugar al ajedrez?
6. ¿Quieres correr?

Comunicación

6 Entrevista 1A

Hablemos Interview three classmates to learn what they want to do this Saturday.

MODELO **—Roberto, ¿qué quieres hacer este sábado?**
—Quiero ir al centro comercial con...

Objetivos

Using **gustar** with infinitives, using pronouns after prepositions, using **querer** with infinitives

Gramática en acción 1

GramaVisión

Gustar with infinitives

Interactive TUTOR

1 An **infinitive** tells the meaning of the verb without naming any subject or tense. There are three kinds of **infinitives** in Spanish: those ending in **-ar**, those ending in **-er**, and those ending in **-ir**.

-ar infinitives	**-er** infinitives	**-ir** infinitives
cantar *to sing*	**com**er *to eat*	**escrib**ir *to write*

2 Just like **nouns, infinitives** can be used after a verb like **gustar** to say what you and others like *to do.*

follows gustar

Me gusta **la música.**
I like music.

Me gusta **cantar.**
I like to sing.

3 Always use **gusta** (not **gustan**) with **infinitives.**

Me **gustan los deportes.**
I like sports.

Me **gusta jugar al tenis.**
I like to play tennis.

Online

Vocabulario y gramática, pp. 28–30 | Actividades, pp. 21–23

En inglés

In English, infinitives do not have any special endings, but they almost always have the word **to** in front of them.

to play **to run** **to write**

In Spanish, infinitives always end in **-ar**, **-er**, or **-ir**.

jugar **correr** **escribir**

7 Gustos 1B

Hablemos/Escribamos Based on the things Carlos and his friends like, what activities do you think they like to do?

¿Se te olvidó? Gustar, p. 62

MODELO **A Roberto le gustan las películas.**
Le gusta ir al cine.

ir al cine	**ver televisión**	**escuchar música**
jugar al tenis	**comer comida italiana**	**jugar a los videojuegos**

1. A mis amigos les gustan los deportes.
2. Me gusta la televisión.
3. A Paco le gusta la música.
4. A mi familia y a mí nos gusta la pizza.
5. Te gustan las películas.
6. A mis amigos y a mí nos gustan los videojuegos.

8 Más gustos 1B

Hablemos/Escribamos Based on their personalities, which activity do you think these people would like more?

MODELO **Raúl es muy activo. (patinar/ver televisión)**
Le gusta más patinar.

1. Diego es perezoso. (hacer ejercicio/ver televisión)
2. Mis amigos son atléticos. (nadar y correr/alquilar videos)
3. Elena es trabajadora. (hacer la tarea/escuchar música)
4. Mario es tímido. (ir a fiestas/pasar el rato solo)
5. Lili es romántica. (leer novelas de amor/novelas de terror)
6. Soy muy seria. (hacer la tarea/ir a fiestas)
7. Eres muy extrovertido. (salir con amigos/pasar el rato solo)

9 Preguntas y respuestas 1B

Leamos/Escribamos Read the answers that Andrés gave during his interview. Then write the missing questions.

¿Se te olvidó? Question words, p. 52

MODELO **¿ ═══ ? Me gusta leer revistas.**
¿Qué te gusta hacer?

1. ¿═══? Soy de Chile.
2. ¿═══? Tengo dieciséis años.
3. ¿═══? Soy extrovertido y gracioso.
4. ¿═══? Me gusta ir al cine y hacer deportes.
5. ¿═══? Me gusta ir al cine con mis amigos.

Comunicación

10 Preferencias 1A, 1C

Hablemos Ask whether your partner likes to do each of the following things. Switch roles. Then tell the class what you found out.

TEKS Focus
1C Present information using familiar words, phrases, and sentences

Pronouns after prepositions

Interactive TUTOR

1 Pronouns can stand for the same noun yet still have different forms, depending on how they're being used in the sentence.

Both stand for Javier

Yo soy Javier. Tengo quince años y **me** gusta dibujar.

2 You already know subject pronouns and the pronouns used with **gustar.** **Pronouns** have a different form when they come after prepositions, such as **a** *(to),* **de** *(of, from, about),* **con** *(with)* and **en** *(in, on, at).*

Subject	With **gustar**	After **preposition**
yo	me	**mí**
tú	te	**ti**
usted, él, ella	le	**usted, él, ella**
nosotros(as)	nos	**nosotros(as)**
vosotros(as)	os	**vosotros(as)**
ustedes, ellos, ellas	les	**ustedes, ellos, ellas**

3 The pronouns **mí** and **ti** combine with **con** to make the special forms **conmigo** and **contigo**.

4 With **gustar,** the phrase formed by **a** and a pronoun can be added to a sentence to clarify or emphasize who likes something.

adds emphasis — ¿**A ti** te gusta dibujar?

adds emphasis — **A mí** no me gusta. *clarifies* — **A ella** le gusta.

Online
Vocabulario y gramática, pp. 28–30 | Actividades, pp. 21–23

¿Te acuerdas?

Pronouns take the place of nouns. They can stand for the person talking, the person being talked to, or someone or something that has already been named.

—¿Cuántos años tienes **tú**?
—¿**Yo**? Tengo catorce años.

Juan es mi amigo. **Él** tiene quince años.

11 María y los amigos 1B

Leamos Complete María's letter choosing the correct prepositions and pronouns.

Soy extrovertida. **1.** (A mí/A ellos) me gusta pasar el rato con amigos. Mis amigos son muy divertidos. Me gusta mucho salir **2.** (a ellos/con ellos). Mi amigo Jorge es muy activo. **3.** (A él/A mí) no le gusta ver televisión. Mi amiga Laura es muy tímida. **4.** (A ti/A ella) no le gusta ir a fiestas. **5.** (A ellas/A nosotras) nos gusta ir al cine. Juan y Carlos son mis amigos también. **6.** (A ellos/A mí) les gusta jugar a los videojuegos. Y **7.** (a nosotras/a ti), ¿qué te gusta hacer?

12 ¿Te gusta...? 1B

Hablemos Look at the pictures and say whether you like to do those activities. Also say what friends you do each activity with.

MODELO **Me gusta ir de compras con mi amiga, Mari.**

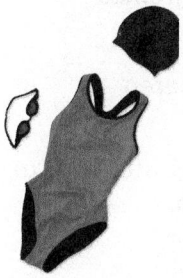

1.

2.

3.

4.

5.

13 ¿Qué les gusta? 1B

Leamos/Escribamos Read each description and tell what these people like and don't like to do. Use pronouns whenever posssible.

MODELO **Juan es muy activo. Le gustan los deportes.**
A él le gusta jugar al béisbol.
A él no le gusta jugar a los videojuegos.

1. Sara es muy intelectual. Le gustan los juegos de mesa.
2. Pablo es muy gracioso. Le gustan las fiestas.
3. Lupe es muy extrovertida. No le gustan los videojuegos.
4. Alonso es serio y tímido. Le gustan los libros de aventuras.
5. A Cristina le gustan las películas. No le gusta salir. Es tímida.
6. Carlos es extrovertido. A él y a sus amigos les gustan las películas.
7. Alicia es atlética. A ella y a sus compañeras les gusta el tenis.
8. Miguel es muy inteligente y trabajador. Le gustan los libros.

TEKS Focus

1B Demonstrate understanding of simple, clearly spoken, and written language when dealing with familiar topics

Comunicación

14 Los sábados y los domingos 1A

Escribamos/Hablemos First, write a list of three things you like to do on weekends. Then discuss what you like to do with a small group of classmates and find out what you have in common.

MODELO
ROBERTO **Me gusta jugar al fútbol. No me gusta jugar a los videojuegos.**
FELIPE **A mí me gusta jugar a los videojuegos. También me gusta escuchar música.**
CARLA **Me gusta ir a las fiestas. ¿Les gusta ir?**
ROBERTO Y FELIPE **Sí, nos gusta ir a fiestas.**

Present tense of querer with infinitives

Interactive TUTOR

1 To say what you or others *want,* use a form of the verb **querer**. The form you use depends on the subject.

yo quiero	nosotros(as) queremos
tú quieres	vosotros(as) queréis
Ud., él, ella quiere	Uds., ellos, ellas quieren

2 Just as with **gustar,** you can use a **noun** or an **infinitive** after a form of **querer** to say what you and others *want* or *want to do.*

Quiero fruta.
I want some fruit.

—¿Qué **quieres hacer**?
What do you want to do?

Quiero comer.
I want to eat.

—**Quiero escuchar** música.
I want to listen to music.

Online
Vocabulario y gramática, pp. 28–30 | Actividades, pp. 21–23

Nota cultural

In Latin America many teens must introduce their friends to their parents before they go out with them. When inviting a friend out, teens are often expected to tell the friend's parents where they are going and when they will return. While this custom may be changing, it is still common in many places. Is this similar to or different from your parents' rules?

2A, 4B

15 ¿Quién quiere? 1B

Leamos/Escribamos Choose the correct form of **querer** to complete the sentences.

1. Marta y yo (quieren/queremos) comer.
2. Yo (quieres/quiero) salir.
3. Pablo (queremos/quiere) hacer ejercicio.
4. ¿Tú (quieres/quieren) ir al centro comercial?
5. Marco y Felipe (quieren/quiero) navegar por Internet.
6. ¿Ustedes (quieren/queremos) jugar al béisbol?
7. (¿Quiero/Quiere) usted pasar el rato solo?
8. Juan y Sandra (quiere/quieren) pasear.
9. Eres trabajadora. (Quieres/Queremos) hacer la tarea.

16 Queremos ir 1B

Leamos/Escribamos Complete the conversation with the correct forms of **querer.**

—Hola, Carla. ¿Qué __1__ hacer hoy?
—Ni idea. ¿Qué __2__ hacer tú?
—Bueno, mi familia y yo __3__ ir al cine.
—¿Y tu amigo Paco no __4__ ir al cine con ustedes?
—No, Paco y unos amigos __5__ ir de compras y __6__ alquilar videos. ¿Y tú? ¿ __7__ ir al cine con mi familia?
—Sí, gracias. Yo __8__ ver una película con ustedes.

17 ¿Qué quieren hacer? 1B

Leamos/Escribamos Say what Juanita and her friends want to do this weekend based on what they like. Use the expressions in the box.

MODELO **A mis amigos les gusta la televisión.**
Quieren ver televisión.

nadar	ver televisión	jugar al ajedrez
comer pizza	leer	comer comida china
alquilar videos	jugar al tenis	escuchar música

1. A mis amigos les gusta la comida china.
2. A ti te gustan los deportes.
3. A mi mejor amigo le gusta la comida italiana.
4. A mí me gustan las novelas.
5. A nosotros nos gustan los juegos de mesa.
6. A mi amiga le gustan las películas.

18 Vamos al centro comercial 1B

Escuchemos Listen to the conversation between Juan and Sofía and decide which photos show what they both want to do.

A

B

C

D

E

Comunicación

19 Actividades 1A, 1C

Hablemos/Escribamos Using the activities listed in Activity 17, ask three classmates what they would like to do at a class party. Then, make a list of the activities that you agree on and a list of activities that you don't want to do.

MODELO **—¿Qué quieres hacer en la fiesta?**
—Quiero escuchar música pero no quiero nadar.

TEKS Focus
1A Engage in oral and written exchanges of learned material to socialize and to provide and obtain information

Cultura

VideoCultura

Comparaciones

Friends on the River Walk, San Antonio, Texas

¿Qué les gusta hacer a ti y a tus amigos los fines de semana? 2A, 4B

It is common in Spain and Latin America for young people to get together and do things in large groups. Often they will meet up with their friends in a plaza, park or café to hang out and eat before going shopping or dancing. Many young people also spend a fair amount of time with their families, especially on Sundays, when it is typical to eat a large family meal together. What do you like to do on the weekends, and how is it different from what these people do?

Celina
El Paso, Texas

Dime, ¿adónde vas cuando hace buen tiempo?

Me gusta salir al parque.

¿Vas sola o vas con amigos?

Me gusta ir con amigos.

¿Qué les gusta hacer en el parque?

Nos gusta ir a correr o jugar fútbol; si no, a platicar.

¿Qué no te gusta hacer?

No me gusta pasar el tiempo sola.

¿Por qué no te gusta?

Porque me gusta estar acompañada... con familia y amigos.

Visit Holt Online
go.hrw.com
KEYWORD: EXP1 CH3
Online Edition

Rita
Lima, Perú

Dime, ¿adónde vas cuando hace buen tiempo?
Cuando hace buen tiempo voy a la playa, al cine o a acampar.

¿Vas sola o vas con amigos?
Voy con amigos.

¿Qué les gusta hacer en esos lugares?
Cuando vamos a la playa, nos gusta nadar y jugar; cuando vamos al cine, ver películas; y cuando vamos a acampar, hacer fogatas.

¿Qué cosas no te gusta hacer?
No me gusta ir a clases de matemáticas.

¿Por qué no te gusta?
No me gusta porque es aburrido y a veces no entiendo.

Para comprender 1B

1. ¿A quién le gusta hacer ejercicio?
2. ¿Qué le gusta hacer a Rita cuando hace buen tiempo?
3. ¿Qué les gusta hacer a Rita y a sus amigos cuando van a la playa?
4. ¿Quién juega al fútbol con sus amigos? ¿Dónde juegan?
5. A Celina no le gusta pasar el rato sola. ¿Con quién quiere pasar el rato?

Para pensar y hablar 2A, 4B

When asked where they go when the weather is good, both Celina and Rita say that they like to spend time outdoors with a group of friends. Many other Spanish-speaking young people would have given a similar answer. How would you have answered the question? Do you like to be outside or would you rather do something indoors? Would you rather do things in a group or with just one friend? Do you like spending time alone?

Cuaderno para hispanohablantes, pp. 21–28

Texas

Comunidad

Cinco de Mayo in Texas 2A, 5B

Cinco de Mayo *(May 5th)* festivals are even bigger in Texas and other areas in the U.S., where many Mexican Americans live, than they are in parts of Mexico. Not to be confused with Mexican independence day, which is September 16th, **Cinco de Mayo** is a great opportunity to immerse yourself in Mexican culture in Texas. You'll experience authentic food, music, folk dancing and costumes. Don't be surprised if you hear a lot of Spanish! If so, write down a few words or phrases that you think are interesting. Also, see if you can find out why Cinco de Mayo is important.

Cinco de Mayo festival in Goliad, Texas

Objetivos
Talking about everyday activities, saying how often you do things

Vocabulario en acción 2

ExpresaVisión

Los fines de semana me gusta...

estudiar

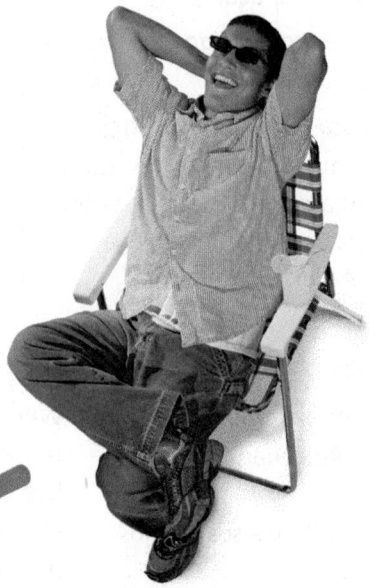
descansar

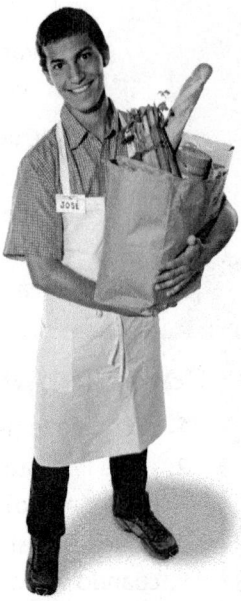
trabajar

practicar deportes

tocar el piano

hablar por teléfono

bailar

Visit Holt Online
go.hrw.com
KEYWORD: EXP1 CH3
Vocabulario 2 practice

a la piscina

a la iglesia

al gimnasio

a la playa

Más vocabulario...

al baile	*to the dance*
a la casa de...	*to . . . 's house*
al colegio	*to school*
al ensayo	*to rehearsal*
al entrenamiento	*to (sports) practice*
a la reunión	*to the meeting*
al trabajo	*to work*

También se puede decir...

In Mexico, a swimming pool is called **la alberca.** In Texas, you will also hear Spanish speakers use the word **alberca.** In Argentina, they call it **la pileta.**

¡Exprésate!

To ask about everyday activities	To respond
¿Qué haces los fines de semana? *What do you do on weekends?*	**Los sábados, cuando hace buen tiempo, voy con mis amigos al parque.** *On Saturdays, when the weather is nice, I go with my friends to the park.*
¿Qué hace Luis cuando hace mal tiempo? *What does Luis do when the weather is bad?*	**Le gusta escuchar música. No va a ninguna parte.** *He likes to listen to music.* *He doesn't go anywhere.*

Interactive TUTOR

Online
Vocabulario y gramática, pp. 31–33

▶ **Vocabulario adicional** — Deportes y pasatiempos, p. R8

20 ¿Qué planes tienes? 1B

Hablemos/Escribamos Using the pictures, complete these sentences.

MODELO **Hoy quiero ir a la piscina.**

Hoy quiero ir...

1. Me gusta...

2. Quiero...

3. Mañana voy...

4. Cuando hace buen tiempo, quiero ir...

5. ¿Te gusta ir...?

6. Cuando hace mal tiempo, ¿te gusta...?

21 ¿Adónde vas los fines de semana? 1B, 1C

Hablemos Say whether you go to these places on weekends and why or why not.

MODELO **al parque**
Sí, voy al parque porque quiero correr.
(No, no voy al parque porque quiero descansar.)

1. a la playa
2. al gimnasio
3. al baile
4. al colegio
5. al trabajo
6. al cine
7. a la casa de...
8. al entrenamiento
9. a la piscina

Nota cultural

In Spanish-speaking countries, the person who invites friends to go out with him or her will usually pay for everything. If the person inviting wants everyone to pay their own way, then he or she invites **a la americana.** Young people may also pool all their money and split the expenses evenly. Who pays when you invite friends to go out? 4B

TEKS Focus

4B Demonstrate understanding of the concept of culture through comparisons

¡Exprésate!

To ask how often	To respond
¿Con qué frecuencia vas a la playa? *How often do you go to the beach?*	**Casi nunca. No me gusta nadar.** *Hardly ever. I don't like to swim.*
¿Te gusta salir con amigos? *Do you like to go out with friends?*	**Sí. Después de clases, casi siempre vamos al parque. A veces vamos también a la piscina.** *Yes. After classes, we almost always go to the park. Sometimes we also go to the swimming pool.*

Interactive TUTOR

Online
Vocabulario y gramática, pp. 31–33

22 A mí me gusta... 1B

Escribamos Write about what you like to do. Replace the activities in italics with ones that apply to you.

1. Todos los días me gusta *ir al parque.*
2. Nunca quiero *trabajar* los viernes.
3. Los fines de semana me gusta *salir con amigos.*
4. Los domingos quiero *descansar.*
5. No me gusta *salir* los martes.
6. Los sábados me gusta *ir al centro comercial.*

Más vocabulario...

los lunes	*on Mondays*
los martes	*on Tuesdays*
los miércoles	*on Wednesdays*
los jueves	*on Thursdays*
los viernes	*on Fridays*
los sábados	*on Saturdays*
los domingos	*on Sundays*
todos los días	*every day*
nunca	*never*

23 Después de clases 1B, 1C

Leamos/Escribamos Imagine that this is your schedule. Write at least five sentences telling what you like to do and when.

MODELO **Me gusta ver videos los jueves.**

lunes	martes	miércoles	jueves	viernes
1 nadar escuchar música	2 ir al ensayo escuchar música	3 nadar escuchar música	4 ver videos escuchar música	5 salir con amigos escuchar música
8 nadar escuchar música	9 ir al ensayo escuchar música	10 nadar escuchar música	11 pasear escuchar música	12 salir con amigos escuchar música

24 Un programa de radio 1B

Escuchemos Complete the sentences based on what you hear.

1. La estudiante se llama (Susana Parra/Alicia Hernández).
2. Los jueves le gusta (ir a la casa de amigas/trabajar).
3. Susana va al cine (los sábados y domingos/los lunes).
4. Los sábados, Susana va a (nadar/patinar).
5. Los domingos, a Susana le gusta (leer/tocar el piano).
6. A Susana (le gusta/no le gusta) bailar.

TEKS Focus

1B Demonstrate understanding of simple, clearly spoken, and written language when dealing with familiar topics

Comunicación

25 ¿Qué te gusta hacer los fines de semana? 1A, 1B

Hablemos Ask three classmates what they like to do on weekends. They should say what they like to do when the weather is good and what they like to do when it's bad.

MODELO **—¿Qué te gusta hacer los fines de semana?**
—Cuando hace buen/mal tiempo me gusta...

Objetivos

Using regular **-ar** verbs, using **ir** and **jugar**, using weather expressions

Gramática en acción 2

GramaVisión

Present tense of regular -ar verbs

Interactive TUTOR

1 Every verb has a **stem** followed by an ending. The stem tells the verb's meaning. An **infinitive ending** doesn't name a subject.

verb stems	*infinitive endings*
habl	**-ar**
com	**-er**
escrib	**-ir**

2 To give the verb a subject, you **conjugate** it. To conjugate a regular **-ar** verb in the present tense, drop the **-ar** ending of the infinitive and add these **endings**. Each ending goes with a particular subject.

yo	cant**o**	nosotros(as)	cant**amos**
tú	cant**as**	vosotros(as)	cant**áis**
Ud., él, ella	cant**a**	Uds., ellos, ellas	cant**an**

—**¿Cantan** ustedes mucho?
Do you sing a lot?

—No, casi nunca **cantamos**.
No, we hardly ever sing.

3 Since the ending of the verb usually tells the subject, the **subject pronoun** is normally left out. Use **subject pronouns** to add emphasis, or when it wouldn't otherwise be clear who the subject is.

—¿Patinan **ustedes** mucho?
Do you skate a lot?

—**Ellos** patinan. **Yo** nunca patino.
They skate. I never skate.

Online

Vocabulario y gramática, pp. 34–36 | Actividades, pp. 25–27

En inglés

In English, most verbs have only two forms in the present tense so subject pronouns can't be left out.

I sing	**we** sing
you sing	**you** sing
he sing**s**	**they** sing

In Spanish, the verb ending tells you who the subject is.

Cant**o**
Cant**as**
Cant**a**

Unos amigos montan en bicicleta en un parque en Texas.

26 En el parque ➔1B

Leamos Complete the sentences that Marcos wrote.

1. Los sábados yo (paso/pasas) el rato con amigos.
2. Nosotros (practicas/practicamos) deportes.
3. Javi (nadan/nada) en la piscina.
4. A veces nosotros (montas/montamos) en bicicleta.
5. Yo (patinan/patino) en el parque con mi amigo José.
6. Maribel y Florencia (patinan/patinas) con nosotros.
7. Y tú, ¿cómo (pasas/pasa) el rato con amigos?

27 Los fines de semana 1B

Hablemos/Escribamos Based on the pictures, say what each person does on weekends.

MODELO **Escucho música y descanso.**

yo

1. nosotros

2. Juan

3. ellas

4. mi mejor amiga

28 ¿Cuándo? 1B

Leamos/Hablemos Choose words from each column to tell what you and your friends do or don't do at certain times during the week.

MODELO **Mi mejor amigo (no) descansa los sábados.**

TEKS Focus
1B Demonstrate understanding of simple, clearly spoken, and written language when dealing with familiar topics

mi mejor amigo(a)	practicar deportes	los lunes
mis amigos	pasear	los jueves
ustedes (dos compañeros de clase)	tocar el piano	los viernes
mis amigos y yo	escuchar música	los sábados
yo	estudiar	los fines de semana
tú (un compañero)	trabajar	todos los días
	navegar por Internet	después de clases
	hablar por teléfono	

Comunicación

29 ¿Con qué frecuencia vas al cine? 1A, 1B

Hablemos Take turns with a partner talking about how often each of you does the activities mentioned in Activity 28. Make a chart that summarizes the results.

MODELO **—¿Con qué frecuencia practicas deportes?**
—Practico deportes todos los fines de semana. ¿Y tú?

Present tense of ir and jugar

Interactive TUTOR

1 The **-ar** verbs you have learned are called regular verbs because their conjugations all follow a predictable pattern. Some verbs such as **ir** *(to go)* are called irregular, because they do not follow a clear pattern.

yo	**voy**	nosotros(as)	**vamos**
tú	**vas**	vosotros(as)	**vais**
Ud., él, ella	**va**	Uds., ellos, ellas	**van**

—¿Adónde **vas** los sábados? —**Voy** a la piscina.

2 The verb **jugar** *(to play a sport or game)* has regular **-ar** endings, but the vowel **u** in the stem changes to **ue** in all but the **nosotros** and **vosotros** forms.

yo	j**ue**go	nosotros(as)	jugamos
tú	j**ue**gas	vosotros(as)	jugáis
Ud., él, ella	j**ue**ga	Uds., ellos, ellas	j**ue**gan

—¿**Juegan** ustedes en el colegio? —No, no **jugamos** mucho.

3 The preposition **a** is used after **ir** to mean *to.* **A** is also used after **jugar** with a sport. When **a** is followed by **el**, the two words combine to form the contraction **al**. Use **¿adónde?** to ask *where to.*

—¿**Adónde van** los domingos? —**Vamos al** gimnasio.
Jugamos al básquetbol.

Online
Vocabulario y gramática, pp. 34–36 | Actividades, pp. 25–27

¿Te acuerdas?

When **de** is followed by **el**, the two words combine to form the contraction **del**.

el teléfono del profesor

30 Sitios 1B

Hablemos Complete the phrases with the correct word or words from the box. Then say whether or not you like the activity and when or how often you do it. *¿Se te olvidó?* Definite articles, p. 60

MODELO **Me gusta ir a la playa los sábados.**
(No me gusta ir a la playa. Nunca voy a la playa.)

al	a los	a las	a la

1. ir _____ piscina
2. jugar _____ béisbol
3. ir _____ cine
4. ir _____ iglesia
5. ir _____ entrenamiento
6. ir _____ casas de mis amigos
7. jugar _____ ajedrez
8. jugar _____ videojuegos

31 Pasatiempos 1B

Escribamos/Hablemos Based on the pictures, say where these people go in their free time and what game they play there. Use the verbs **ir** and **jugar.**

MODELO **Sonia va al parque. Juega al tenis.**

Sonia

TEKS Focus
1C Present information using familiar words, phrases, and sentences

1. yo

2. tú

3. mi mejor amigo(a)

4. nosotros

5. ellos

32 ¿Con qué frecuencia? 1C

Leamos/Escribamos How often do you, your family, and your friends go to the following places on weekends: **siempre, a veces,** or **(casi) nunca?**

MODELO **yo/playa**
Casi nunca voy a la playa los fines de semana.

1. mi familia y yo/cine
2. mis amigos/piscina
3. mi mejor amigo(a)/iglesia
4. mi mejor amigo(a)/trabajo
5. mis amigos y yo/fiestas
6. yo/clase de español
7. los profesores/colegio
8. yo/parque

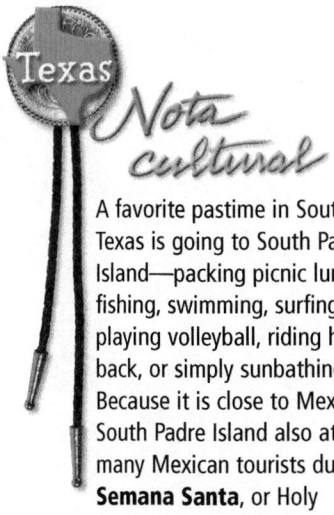

A favorite pastime in South Texas is going to South Padre Island—packing picnic lunches, fishing, swimming, surfing, playing volleyball, riding horseback, or simply sunbathing. Because it is close to Mexico, South Padre Island also attracts many Mexican tourists during **Semana Santa**, or Holy Week—the week before Easter. Call the Chamber of Commerce in your town and ask if there are local events that attract international tourists. 4B

Comunicación

33 ¿Qué haces? 1A, 1B

Escribamos/Hablemos Complete the following questions with the correct form of the verb. Then, use them to interview a partner.

1. ¿A qué deportes _____ (jugar) tú?
2. ¿Quién _____ (jugar) contigo?
3. ¿Tu mejor amigo y tú _____ (jugar) al ajedrez?
4. ¿Adónde _____ (ir) tú los sábados?
5. ¿Tu mejor amigo(a) y tú _____ (ir) de compras?
6. ¿Adónde _____ (ir) ustedes de compras?

Weather expressions

1 Many expressions for the weather begin with the word **hace,** a form of the verb **hacer.**

¿Qué tiempo **hace**?	*What's the weather like?*
Hace buen/mal tiempo.	*The weather is nice/bad.*
Hace fresco.	*It's cool.*

Hace calor.

Hace frío.

Hace sol.

Hace viento.

2 The verb **llover** means *to rain* and the verb **nevar** means *to snow*. Use **llueve** to say *it rains* and **nieva** to say *it snows*.

Llueve.

Nieva.

¿Adónde vas cuando **llueve**?	Cuando **llueve**, no voy a ninguna parte.
¿Qué haces cuando **nieva**?	Cuando **nieva**, juego con los amigos.

Online

Vocabulario y gramática, pp. 34–36 | Actividades, pp. 25–27

34 ¿Qué tiempo hace? ➜1B

Leamos/Hablemos Look at the photo. For each set of expressions, choose the one that better describes the photo.

1. **a.** Nieva. **b.** No nieva.
2. **a.** Hace calor. **b.** Hace fresco.
3. **a.** Llueve. **b.** No llueve.
4. **a.** Hace viento. **b.** Nieva.
5. **a.** Hace sol. **b.** No hace sol.
6. **a.** Hace buen tiempo. **b.** Hace mal tiempo.

35 ¿Cuál? 1B

Escuchemos Listen to six descriptions of the weather. Decide if each one describes picture A, picture B, or neither picture.

A

B

36 ¿Qué haces? 1B

Hablemos Say what the weather is usually like in these places during the given months.

MODELO **en Texas en abril**
En Texas en abril hace muy buen tiempo.

1. en Alaska en enero
2. en Florida en julio
3. en Arizona en agosto
4. en Seattle en febrero
5. en California en mayo
6. en Illinois en diciembre
7. en Texas en agosto
8. en Louisiana en noviembre
9. en Nueva York en abril
10. en Colorado en octubre

Comunicación

TEKS Focus
1A Engage in oral and written exchanges of learned material to socialize and to provide and obtain information

37 ¿Adónde van? 1A, 1C

Hablemos With a partner, use the drawings to say what Miguel and Alicia do on the weekends. Give as many details as you can.

Novela en vídeo

¿Quién será?

Episodio 3

ESTRATEGIA

Understanding Subtext People do not always say what they mean. When someone asks, "How are you?," the **text** (what you say) of your answer might be, "I'm just fine." But your **subtext** (what you really mean) may be, "I feel awful, but I don't want to talk about it." When watching or reading, figuring out if there is a subtext in people's statements will help you understand things better. If there is, what could be the reason for it? Listen for Sra. Corona's and Sofía's subtexts as they go through their day.

3B

En México

En casa de Sofía

Sofía and her mother have a conversation about Sofía's interests.

1

Sra. Corona Sofía, a ti te gusta mucho la música, ¿verdad, hija?

Sofía Claro, mamá.

Sra. Corona Y te gusta bailar, ¿no es así, hija?

Sofía Claro, mamá, me gusta mucho bailar.

2

Sra. Corona Vas a tomar clases de ballet los lunes y los viernes en la Academia de Danza Clásica.

Sofía Pero, mamá, ¡no quiero tomar clases de ballet!

Sra. Corona El ballet es música y es baile, hija, las dos cosas que más te gustan en todo el mundo.

3

Sofía ¿Viernes? Mamá, ¡hoy es viernes!

Sra. Corona Sí, hija. Hoy vas a la clase de ballet a las cinco en punto, después del colegio. ¡Adiós, cariño!

4

Sofía ¿Ballet? ¿Yo? ¿Bailarina? ¡Nunca!

Visit Holt Online
go.hrw.com
KEYWORD: EXP1 CH3
Online Edition

En el colegio... *Roque and Celeste, Sofía's classmates, want to figure out what they're going to do tonight, since it's Friday and they always do something together on Friday nights.*

5

Roque Hace muy buen tiempo hoy. ¿Por qué no vamos a la piscina a nadar?

Celeste No, no quiero nadar. Quiero ir al cine. Hay una película formidable en el Cineplex que quiero ver.

Sofía Pero, no quiero ir a la piscina. Y tampoco quiero ir al cine.

6

Roque ¡Pero, Sofía! ¡Es viernes! ¡Siempre hacemos algo juntos los viernes!

Sofía Ya lo sé. Pero hoy no quiero hacer nada. Voy a casa a estudiar.

Celeste ¿Qué te pasa, Sofía? ¡Tú casi nunca estudias los viernes por la noche!

7

Celeste Hay algo muy raro aquí.

Roque Sí, muy raro. Es viernes y ¡no quiere salir con sus amigos!

En España

The professor calls Marcos in Puerto Rico to tell him where he's going next.

8

La profesora Tengo otra candidata. Es una chica de Texas. Después de Puerto Rico, vas a Texas. A El Paso, Texas. Cuatro candidatos... Sólo nos faltan seis.

En Puerto Rico

¿COMPRENDES?

1. What does Sofía's mother want her to do? How does she try to convince Sofía to do it?
2. Sra. Corona's text is, "you like music and dancing." What do you think her subtext is? Why?
3. Sofía's text is, "I don't want to take ballet classes!" Is there a subtext?
4. What does Roque suggest that they do? What are Sofía's text and subtext in scenes 5–7? Why are Roque and Celeste surprised?
5. La profesora uses the word **candidata**. What does that mean? How many **candidatos** will she review?

1B, 3A

Próximo episodio
Can you predict what Marcos will find out about Nicolás?
PÁGINAS 142–143

Leamos y escribamos

ESTRATEGIA

para leer Predicting what will happen in a story is a helpful strategy. You will be able to read a story more quickly and easily if you focus your attention on what you expect to happen.

A Antes de leer 1B, 3A, 3B

The following story is a myth from the southwestern United States. Read the title and the first paragraph of the text and use what you know about myths to predict what will happen in this one.

Los cuatro elementos

Existen cuatro elementos en el mundo[1]: el agua[2], el fuego[3], el viento y el honor. Son amigos inseparables. Son inteligentes, divertidos y graciosos. Siempre pasan el rato juntos y les gusta hablar por horas y horas. Pero un día, el día de la creación, los amigos saben que tendrán que separarse[4]. En una reunión, en la casa del agua, se dicen adiós[5].

El agua dice así: —Vamos a lugares diferentes. En el futuro, si me quieren encontrar[6], búsquenme[7] en los lugares[8] donde llueve. ¡Nado con los océanos!

El fuego dice así: —Ustedes son mis mejores amigos. En el futuro, si me quieren encontrar, búsquenme en los lugares donde hace calor. ¡Paseo con el sol!

El viento dice así: —¡Amigos! No quiero separarme de ustedes. En el futuro, si me quieren encontrar, búsquenme en el aire, en los lugares donde hace mal tiempo. ¡Corro con los tornados y los huracanes!

El honor, el último[9] en hablar, dice así: —Compañeros. ¡Escuchen con atención! En el futuro, si me pierden[10] a mí, ¡no me busquen! ¡No me van a encontrar!

1 world **2** water **3** fire **4** will have to part **5** say goodbye **6** if you want to find me **7** look for me **8** places **9** the last one **10** if you lose me

B Comprensión 1B

Complete the following sentences.

1. Los cuatro elementos en el mundo son...
2. Los elementos son amigos inseparables y les gusta...
3. El día de la creación, los amigos se dicen adiós en...
4. En el futuro el agua, el fuego y el viento se pueden encontrar en los lugares donde...
5. El último elemento dice: "...no me busquen" porque...

C Después de leer 2A, 2B, 4B

What is the moral of the story? What does this myth tell you about the cultural values of people in the Southwest? Do the people in your community share similar values?

TEKS Focus

2A Demonstrate understanding of practices (what people do) and how they relate to perspectives (how people perceive things) of the cultures studied

Taller del escritor

ESTRATEGIA

para escribir When describing sequential events or scheduling activities, it helps first to arrange your ideas chronologically. You can use lists, timelines, or charts.

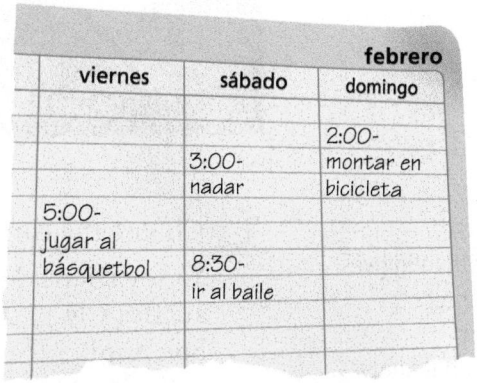

febrero

viernes	sábado	domingo
		2:00- montar en bicicleta
	3:00- nadar	
5:00- jugar al básquetbol		
	8:30- ir al baile	

Horario de actividades 1A, 1B, 1C, 3B

A friend is visiting and you need to plan activities for a week. Write your friend a letter explaining your plans and asking what he or she wants to do.

1 Antes de escribir

Divide a sheet of paper into seven columns, one for each day of the week. Decide what you want to do with your friend and arrange the activities on the chart with a description of each.

2 Escribir un borrador

Using your chart, write a letter to your friend explaining your plans. Include when and where the activities will take place and some details. Tell your friend why you like these activities. Ask what he or she wants to do.

3 Revisar

Read your draft at least two times, comparing it with your chart. Check spelling and punctuation.

4 Publicar

Exchange your letter with a classmate. Answer each other in writing by saying whether you want to do each activity, and respond after reading your classmate's letter. You might display your letters on a bulletin board.

Cuaderno para hispanohablantes, pp. 21–28

Repaso capítulo 3

Interactive TUTOR

1 Vocabulario 1
- talking about what you and others like to do
- talking about what you want to do

pp. 82-85

1 Using the pictures below to guide you, say what you like or what you want to do. 1A

A

B

C

D

E

F

2 Gramática 1
- **gustar** with infinitives
- pronouns after prepositions
- **querer** with infinitives

pp. 86-91

2 Choose the correct word in parentheses. 1B

Yo soy Diana. Mi mejor amiga se llama Maribel. Ella es muy atlética y le __1__ (gustan/gusta) jugar al volibol y al básquetbol. A mí __2__ (me/te) gusta más navegar por Internet o ver películas. Me __3__ (gusta/gustan) las películas románticas. A Maribel __4__ (le/me) gustan las películas románticas también. Me gusta ir al cine con __5__ (ella/usted). Pero a nuestras amigas Ana y Rita no __6__ (les/le) gusta ir al cine. Ellas __7__ (quiero/quieren) alquilar videos o ver televisión.

3 Vocabulario 2
- talking about everyday activities
- saying how often you do things

pp. 94-97

3 Complete the sentences with logical answers. 1B

1. Me gustan los deportes. Los sábados me gusta _____.
2. Soy introvertida. Después de clases me gusta _____.
3. Me gusta la música. Me gusta _____ el piano.
4. ¿Te gusta _____ por teléfono con amigos todos los días?
5. Cuando hace mal tiempo nos gusta _____.
6. Me gustan las películas. No me gusta ir al cine. Me gusta _____ videos.

Visit Holt Online
go.hrw.com
KEYWORD: EXP1 CH3
Chapter Self-test

4 Complete the paragraph with the correct verb forms. 1B

Yo ___1___ (jugar) al fútbol con amigos los domingos. Me gusta jugar cuando ___2___ (hacer) sol. Después, ellos y yo ___3___ (pasear) y con frecuencia ___4___ (ir) a la piscina. A mí me gusta el cine, y los sábados ___5___ (ir) al cine con mi amigo Bernardo. A él le gusta la música. Él ___6___ (tocar) el piano y ___7___ (cantar). Cuando ___8___ (hacer) mal tiempo, mis amigos y yo ___9___ (jugar) al básquetbol. Yo ___10___ (descansar) los lunes y los martes ___11___ (ir) al entrenamiento de fútbol.

5 Answer the following questions. 2A, 4B

1. How can Latin American students participate in sports?
2. When do parents and teenagers expect to meet each other? Is this true for you and your parents too?
3. Who pays the bill when friends go out **a la americana?**

6 Marta is interviewing students for an article for her journalism class. Listen to her interview with Paco. List the days of the week and write what Paco does during the week. 1B

7 Use the drawings to describe what is happening or to tell a story about Miguel and Pepe. 1C

4 Gramática 2
- regular **-ar** verbs
- **ir** and **jugar**
- weather expressions

pp. 98–103

5 Cultura
- **Comparaciones** pp. 92–93
- **Notas culturales** pp. 84, 90, 96
- **Geocultura** pp. 76–79

TEKS Focus
2A Demonstrate understanding of practices (what people do) and how they relate to perspectives (how people perceive things) of the cultures studied

Gramática 1
- **gustar** with infinitives **pp. 86–87**
- pronouns after prepositions **pp. 88–89**
- **querer** with infinitives **pp. 90–91**

Repaso de Gramática 1

Use **gustar** with an **infinitive** to say what you and others like to do.

A mí **me gusta hablar** por teléfono contigo.
Use these pronouns after the prepositions **a, de, en,** and **con.**

mí	(conmigo)	nosotros(as)
ti	(contigo)	vosotros(as)
usted, él, ella		ustedes, ellos, ellas

Use **querer** with an **infinitive** to say what you and others want to do.

qu**ie**ro	queremos
qu**ie**res	queréis
qu**ie**re	qu**ie**ren

Queremos ir a la playa.

Gramática 2
- regular **-ar** verbs **pp. 98–99**
- **ir** and **jugar** **pp. 100–101**
- weather expressions **pp. 102–103**

Repaso de Gramática 2

hablar	
habl**o**	habl**amos**
habl**as**	habl**áis**
habl**a**	habl**an**

ir	
voy	vamos
vas	vais
va	van

jugar	
juego	jugamos
juegas	jugáis
juega	**jue**gan

Use the verb **hacer** to ask about the weather.

¿Qué tiempo **hace**?
Hace buen/mal tiempo.
Hace frío. **Hace** calor.
Hace sol. **Hace** fresco.
Hace viento. Llueve. Nieva.

TEKS Focus
1B Demonstrate understanding of simple, clearly spoken, and written language when dealing with familiar topics

Letra y sonido h j g

Las letras h, j, g

- The letter **h** in Spanish is silent. It is not pronounced: **h**ola, **h**ora, **h**ablar, **h**acer, **h**oy.
- The letter **j** is pronounced much like the English *h,* though sometimes it sounds harsher, a little like the *h* in *hue.* The letter **g** before the vowels **e** and **i** **(ge, gi)** has the same pronunciation: **j**ugar, **j**ueves, **J**osé, **g**eografía, **g**imnasio, e**j**ercicio, pelirro**j**a, intelig**e**nte, a**g**itar.

Trabalenguas

El hipopótamo Hipo
está con hipo.
Me trajo Tajo tres trajes,
tres trajes me trajo Tajo.

Dictado 1B

Escribe las oraciones de la grabación.

Repaso de Vocabulario 1

Talking about what you and others like to do

A ellos/ellas les gusta...	*They like to . . .*
alquilar videos	*to rent videos*
el básquetbol	*basketball*
el béisbol	*baseball*
cantar	*to sing*
el centro comercial	*mall*
el cine	*movie theater*
comer	*to eat*
correr	*to run*
dibujar	*to draw*
escribir cartas	*to write letters*
escuchar música	*to listen to music*
el fútbol	*soccer*
el fútbol americano	*football*
hacer ejercicio	*to exercise*
hacer la tarea	*to do homework*
ir a la/al...	*to go to the . . .*
ir de compras	*to go shopping*
los juegos de mesa	*board games*
jugar (ue)	*to play*
leer	*to read*
Me gusta...	*I like to . . .*
montar en bicicleta	*to ride a bike*
nadar	*to swim*
navegar por Internet	*to surf the Internet*
las novelas	*novels*
pasar el rato solo(a)	*to spend time alone*
pasear	*to go for a walk*
patinar	*to skate*
¿Qué te gusta hacer?	*What do you like to do?*
las revistas	*magazines*
salir	*to go out*
el tenis	*tennis*
ver televisión	*to watch television*
el volibol	*volleyball*

Talking about what you want to do

con mis amigos(as)	*with my friends*
con mi familia	*with my family*
conmigo	*with me*
contigo	*with you*
Está bien.	*All right.*
Ni idea.	*I have no idea.*
¿Qué quieres hacer hoy?	*What do you want to do today?*
querer (ie)	*to want to*
Quiero ir...	*I want to go . . .*

Pronouns after prepositions . . . . . *See p. 88.*

Repaso de Vocabulario 2

Talking about everyday activities

¿adónde?	*where (to)?*
bailar	*to dance*
el baile	*dance*
la casa de...	*. . . 's house*
el colegio	*school*
...cuando hace buen/mal tiempo...	*. . . when the weather is good/bad . . .*
descansar	*to rest*
el ensayo	*rehearsal*
el entrenamiento	*practice*
estudiar	*to study*
el gimnasio	*gym*
hablar por teléfono	*to talk on the phone*
la iglesia	*church*
Le gusta...	*He/She likes . . .*
No va a ninguna parte.	*He/She doesn't go anywhere.*
el parque	*park*
la piscina	*pool*
la playa	*beach*
practicar deportes	*to play sports*
¿Qué hace...?	*What does . . . do?*
¿Qué haces...?	*What do you do . . .?*
la reunión	*meeting*
tocar el piano	*to play the piano*
trabajar	*to work*
el trabajo	*work*

Weather expressions . . . . . *See p. 102.*

Saying how often

a veces	*sometimes*
(casi) nunca	*(almost) never*
(casi) siempre	*(almost) always*
¿Con qué frecuencia vas...?	*How often do you go . . . ?*
después de clases	*after class*
los fines de semana	*weekends*
salir con amigos	*to go out with friends*
todos los días	*every day*

Saying when you do something . . . . . *See p. 97.*

Integración

capítulos 1-3

1 Listen to each conversation and match it with the appropriate picture. 1B

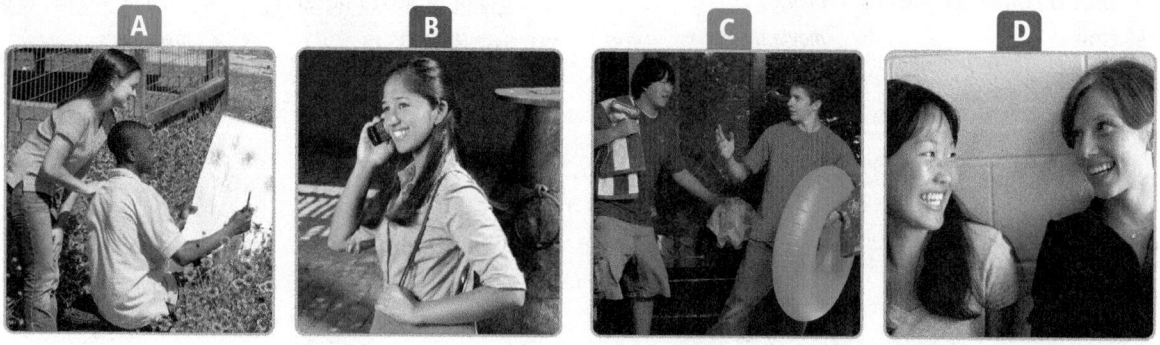

2 Marisol wants to find an e-mail pen pal. Read her e-mail and then answer the questions. 1B, 1C

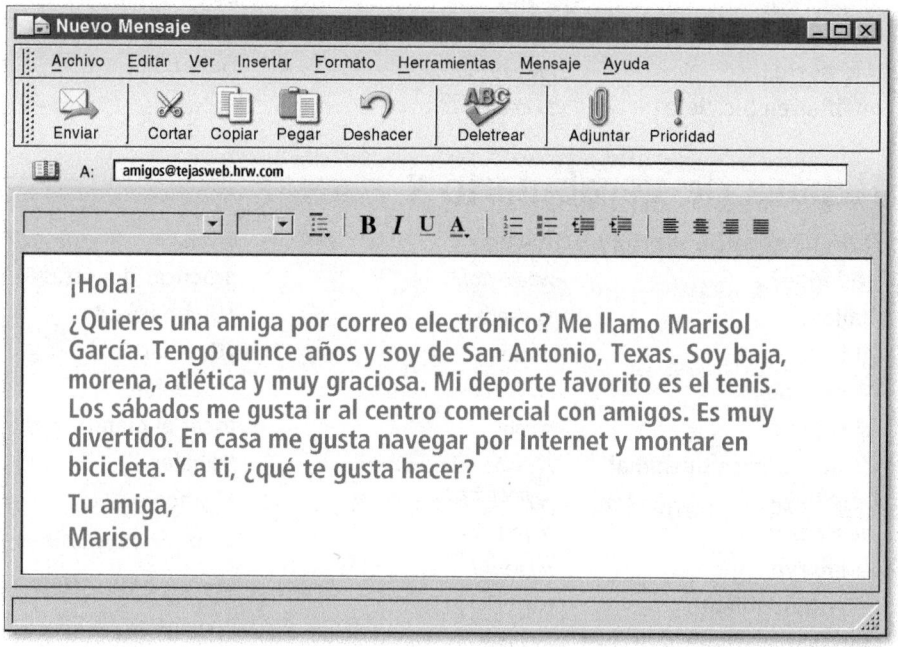

1. ¿Cuántos años tiene Marisol y de dónde es?
2. ¿Cómo es Marisol?
3. ¿Qué deporte le gusta más?
4. ¿Cuándo le gusta salir con amigos? ¿Adónde van?
5. ¿Qué le gusta hacer a Marisol cuando pasa el rato sola?

Visit Holt Online
go.hrw.com
KEYWORD: EXP1 CH3
Cumulative Self-test

3 Your Spanish teacher asks you to work with a new student. Greet each other and exchange names. Ask your partner what he or she likes to do. Your partner responds, telling you what he or she likes to do when the weather is good and when it's bad. Mention what you like to do. 1A

4 On a separate sheet of paper, choose five characters from the painting and make speech bubbles for them. Have them introduce themselves, say where they're from and how old they are, and then say what they like to do. One of the characters should talk about the weather they're having for the fair. 1C

© Carmen Lomas Garza, Collection of the artist, photo credit: Wolfgang Dietze

La feria en Reynosa, de Carmen Lomas Garza (n. 1948)

5 The Spanish Club wants to start a buddy system with the Latino Students Association at your school. Prepare a survey for students so the two clubs can match buddies. Write six questions you would ask students to find out what they're like and what they do in their free time. 1B

TEKS Focus
1A Engage in oral and written exchanges of learned material to socialize and to provide and obtain information

6 1A

Situación

The members of the Spanish Club and the Latino Students Association are getting together to choose their buddies. Using the surveys you wrote in Activity 5, interview three people. Find one person whose answers to your questions are closest to the answers you would give. When you've found your buddy, introduce him or her to a different group of buddies.

GeoVisión

Geocultura

Costa Rica

▲ **El volcán Arenal,** que se formó en 1968, es el volcán más activo de Costa Rica. Se encuentra cerca de la Laguna Arenal.

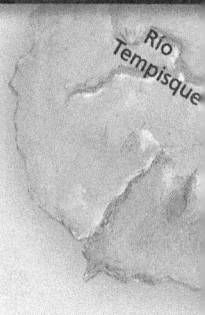

▼ **San José,** la capital de Costa Rica, se encuentra en el Valle Central, que es la región más poblada del país. El valle está rodeado por volcanes.

Almanaque

Población
3,8 millones

Capital
San José

Gobierno
república democrática

Idioma oficial
español

Moneda
colón

Código Internet
www.[ ].cr

¿Sabías que...?

Even though Costa Rica is less than one-tenth the size of Texas in area, it has more bird species than the United States and Canada combined.

◀ **Los payasos** son disfraces populares en mascaradas costarricenses.

▶ **El perezoso de tres dedos** se caracteriza por ser lento en su movimiento. Pasa la mayoría del tiempo en las copas de los árboles.

▲ **El café** es el cultivo principal del Valle Central.

▲ **El Parque Nacional Tortuguero,** en la costa caribeña de Costa Rica, es hogar de muchas plantas y animales como la tortuga verde, el jaguar y el mono congo.

◀ **El Parque Nacional Corcovado,** en la península de Osa, contiene bosques húmedos que reciben casi 6 metros de lluvia por año.

3B

¿Qué tanto sabes?

How is Costa Rica protecting the country's natural resources?

A conocer Costa Rica

Las celebraciones

▲ **Las fiestas patronales** Durante las fiestas en honor al Santo patrono es muy común ver a los jóvenes disfrazados de payasos bailando con la música de la banda.

► **El Día de Juan Santamaría** conmemora la muerte valerosa del héroe nacional, un muchacho que luchó en la batalla contra el invasor William Walker en 1856.

▲ **El Día del Boyero,** en San Antonio de Escazú, se celebra el segundo domingo de marzo, con un colorido desfile de carretas.

El arte

► **Jorge Jiménez Deredia** (1954–) es famoso por todo el mundo por sus esculturas de mármol y bronce. Esta escultura se encuentra en San José.

▲ **Teodorico Quirós** (1897–1977) fue uno de los más importantes artistas y arquitectos de Costa Rica. *Calle de Santo Domingo* es un ejemplo de su obra del paisaje costarricense.

La comida

Interactive TUTOR

Visit Holt Online
go.hrw.com
KEYWORD: EXP1 CH4
Photo Tour

▲ **El gallo pinto,** arroz con frijoles, es un plato popular en el desayuno del tico.

► **Olla de carne** es una sopa con carne y verduras como camote, chayote, maíz y papas.

¿Sabías que...?

One third of the men on Columbus's fourth voyage, during which he reached today's Limón in Costa Rica, were between the ages of 13 and 18.

TEKS Focus

3B Use the language to obtain, reinforce, or expand knowledge of other subject areas

Los animales

► **El perro de los naranjos,** una mariposa muy común, se ve mucho entre marzo y abril.

► **El mono congo** es fácil de localizar en el bosque por sus fuertes bramidos.

▼ **La lapa roja** se puede observar en la península de Osa.

▲ **Las reservas** son centros de investigación de insectos, aves y mamíferos.

Conexión Ciencias naturales

Reserva Biológica del Bosque Nuboso de Monteverde
Monteverde Cloud Forest is a natural preserve home to 400 species of birds, 490 species of butterflies, 2500 species of plants, and 100 species of mammals. Many of these species are in danger of extinction. Look at the previous four pages and say what the Costa Rican government is doing to protect endangered species. Compare this to similar efforts in the United States. **3B, 4B**

► **El quetzal** vive en los bosques nubosos.

Capítulo 4

La vida escolar

OBJETIVOS

In this chapter you will learn to

- say what you have and need
- talk about classes
- talk about plans
- invite someone to do something

And you will use

- indefinite articles, **¿cuánto?, mucho,** and **poco**
- **tener** and some **tener** idioms
- **venir** and **a la/las** with time
- **ir a** with infinitives
- regular and irregular **-er** and **-ir** verbs
- tag questions

¿Qué ves en la foto?

- ¿Cómo son los estudiantes?
- ¿Les gusta pasar el rato con amigos?
- ¿Qué hora es?

Texas

TEKS Look for the ★ next to each activity to learn how it can help you achieve the goals of the **Texas Essential Knowledge and Skills,** found on page xxiii.

Visit Holt Online
go.hrw.com
KEYWORD: EXP1 CH4
Online Edition

Colegio de Santa Ana, San José

Objetivos
Saying what you have and what you need, talking about classes
Vocabulario en acción 1
Video/DVD
ExpresaVisión
Tengo muchas cosas, pero...
todavía necesito unos útiles escolares.
unos cuadernos
unos lápices (un lápiz, sing.)
una regla
papel (m.)
una mochila
También necesito...
unas carpetas
unos bolígrafos
un diccionario
una computadora
zapatos (m.)
un reloj (unos relojes, pl.)
ropa (f.)

Visit Holt Online
go.hrw.com
KEYWORD: EXP1 CH4
Vocabulario 1 practice

CENTRO EDUCATIVO NUEVA ESPERANZA
400 mts Oeste del Beneficio La Meseta,
San Juan de Santa Barbara Heredia,
Telfax (Primaria) 506.265.5393
Tel (Secundaria) 506.265.7934

Horas	Clases
8:00	*matemáticas*
8:50	*arte*
9:40	*biología*
10:30	*español*
11:20	*educación física*
12:10	*almuerzo*
13:00	*historia*
13:50	*inglés*

Más vocabulario...

las materias	***school subjects***
el alemán	*German*
las ciencias	*science*
la computación	*computer science*
el francés	*French*
la química	*chemistry*
el taller	*shop, workshop*

Texas También se puede decir...

In Spain, a computer is called **un ordenador,** while in Colombia, the word is **un computador.**

In Latin America and Texas, many speakers say **una pluma, un lapicero,** or **un boli** instead of **un bolígrafo.** In Spain and Mexico, **un lapicero** is a pencil case.

¡Exprésate!

To ask what others have or need	To respond
¿Necesitas algo para el colegio? *Do you need anything for school?*	**Sí, necesito muchas cosas.** *Yes, I need a lot of things.*
¿Necesitas algo para la clase de arte? *Do you need anything for art class?*	**No, no necesito nada.** *No, I don't need anything.*
¿Necesitas una calculadora? *Do you need a calculator?*	**Sí, necesito una calculadora.** *Yes, I need a calculator.*
¿Tienes carpetas? *Do you have folders?*	**Sí, tengo un montón./No, no tengo.** *Yes, I have a ton of them./ No, I don't have any.*

Interactive TUTOR

Online
Vocabulario y gramática, pp. 37–39

▶ **Vocabulario adicional** — Materias, p. R7

1 ¿Qué necesitas y qué tienes? 1B

Escuchemos Listen as Óscar and his mom talk about what school supplies he needs and already has. Choose the picture that shows what they're going to buy.

a.

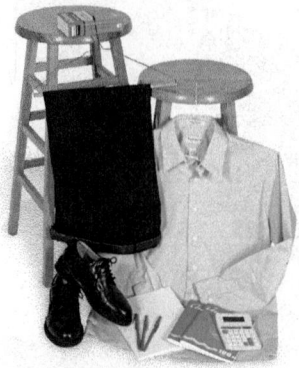

b.

TEKS Focus

2A Demonstrate understanding of practices (what people do) and how they relate to perspectives (how people perceive things) of the cultures studied

Nota cultural

The beginning of the school year varies from country to country. Spain, Mexico, and countries in the Spanish-speaking Caribbean generally have a similar calendar to the United States, whereas in Costa Rica school begins around March 1 and ends in December. Students in Costa Rica have three weeks of vacation in July. Why do you think the school year begins in the fall in the United States?

2A, 2B

2 Necesito mucho para las clases 1B, 1C

Escribamos/Hablemos Use the model and one word from each box to make logical sentences.

MODELO **Para la clase de arte, necesito unos lápices. No necesito una calculadora.**

matemáticas	inglés	un diccionario	una computadora
español	computación	unos lápices	unas carpetas
arte	historia	papel	una calculadora

3 Necesito muchas cosas 1C

Hablemos Di *(Say)* cuatro cosas que tienes y cuatro cosas que necesitas.

MODELO **Tengo una mochila. Necesito ropa.**

¡Exprésate!

To ask about classes	To respond
¿Qué clases tienes esta tarde/después del almuerzo? *What classes do you have this afternoon/ after lunch?*	**Primero tengo español y después tengo computación.** *First I have Spanish and afterwards I have computer science.*
¿Cuál es tu materia preferida? *What's your favorite subject?*	**Mi materia preferida es matemáticas. Es fácil. No me gusta la clase de inglés porque es difícil.** *My favorite subject is math. It's easy. I don't like English because it's hard.*

Interactive TUTOR

Online
Vocabulario y gramática, pp. 37–39

4 Muchas materias 1B, 1C

Leamos/Hablemos Imagine this is your class schedule. Answer the questions that follow.

Día	lunes	martes	miércoles	jue
Horario				
8:45	*historia*	*biología*	*historia*	*bio*
9:40	*matemáticas*	*computación*	*matemáticas*	*con*
10:35	*ed. física*	*arte*	*ed. física*	*arte*
11:30	*español*	*ciencias*	*español*	*cie*
12:25	*almuerzo*	*almuerzo*	*almuerzo*	*alm*
12:55	*química*	*inglés*	*química*	*ing*
1:50	*taller*	*francés*	*taller*	*fra*

1. ¿Qué clases tienes los lunes por la mañana?
2. ¿Qué tienes primero los martes?
3. ¿Qué días tienes educación física?
4. ¿Qué clase tienes después de química los miércoles?
5. ¿Qué clases tienes por la tarde los martes?

Nota cultural

Students in public schools in some Spanish-speaking countries have fewer elective classes than students in the United States. In Costa Rica, high school students take the same classes for the first three years. In their third year, they take a national exam to see if they continue a college preparatory program, or spend their last two years in a technical or vocational program. How is this different from your school? 4B

5 Mis clases 1B

Leamos/Escribamos Completa el párrafo, describiendo tu propio horario *(your own schedule)*.

Por la mañana tengo __1__ clases. Primero, tengo la clase de __2__. Después, tengo __3__ y __4__. Me gusta la clase de __5__ porque es __6__. Después de __7__ tengo el almuerzo. Por la tarde tengo la clase de __8__. El profesor (La profesora) es __9__. Para la clase de español, necesito __10__ y para la clase de matemáticas, necesito __11__. Mi materia preferida es __12__.

Comunicación

6 ¿Qué clases tienes? 1A

Escribamos/Hablemos Create your own class schedule, using the one from Activity 4 as a model. With a partner, talk about your classes, using the schedules you've created. Mention at least three classes and say why you like or dislike them.

MODELO **—¿Qué clase tienes primero los jueves?**
—Primero, tengo la clase de... Me gusta porque...

Objetivos

Using indefinite articles, **¿cuánto?, mucho** and **poco, tener** and some **tener** idioms, **venir** and **a la/las** with time

Gramática en acción 1

GramaVisión

Indefinite articles; ¿cuánto?, mucho, and poco

1 The **indefinite articles un** and **una** are used to say *a* or *an* before a singular noun, while **unos** and **unas** are used to say *some* before a plural noun. The indefinite articles can sometimes be left out, especially when the noun is plural.

Necesito **un** diccionario. *I need a dictionary.*

¿Tienes (**unos**) lápices? *Do you have (some) pencils?*

2 The indefinite articles agree with the noun in gender and number.

	Masculine	Feminine
SINGULAR	**un** libr**o**	**una** mochil**a**
PLURAL	un**os** libr**os**	un**as** mochil**as**

3 To talk about amounts of things, use the following adjectives. These words also agree with the noun they describe in gender and number.

SINGULAR	¿cuánto(a)? how much?	mucho(a) a lot of, much	poco(a) little, not much
PLURAL	¿cuántos(as)? how many?	muchos(as) a lot of, many	pocos(as) few, not many

—¿Cuánta tare**a** tienes? *How much homework do you have?*

—Tengo mucha. *I have a lot.*

Online

Vocabulario y gramática, pp. 40–42 | Actividades, pp. 31–33

En inglés

In English, adjectives go before the nouns they modify.

It's an awful book.

In Spanish, adjectives like **¿cuánto?, mucho** and **poco** go before the noun.

¿Cuánta tarea tienes?

Tengo muchas carpetas.

Hay poca tarea hoy.

However, most other adjectives follow the noun they modify.

Es un libro pésimo.

7 ¿Tienes o necesitas? 1B

Hablemos Give the correct indefinite article for the following nouns. Then say whether you need these items or whether you already have them.

MODELO una regla

Necesito una regla. (Tengo una regla.)

1. ____ cuaderno
2. ____ calculadora
3. ____ lápices
4. ____ bolígrafos
5. ____ carpetas
6. ____ mochila
7. ____ diccionario
8. ____ computadora
9. ____ reloj

Visit Holt Online
go.hrw.com
KEYWORD: EXP1 CH4
Gramática 1 practice

8 ¿Cuánto? 1B

Hablemos How would you ask a friend how many of these items he or she has? Use **cuánto, cuántos, cuánta,** or **cuántas.**

MODELO **—¿Cuántas mochilas tienes?**

1. ¿_____ ropa tienes?
2. ¿_____ lápices tienes?
3. ¿_____ relojes tienes?
4. ¿_____ reglas tienes?
5. ¿_____ cuadernos tienes?
6. ¿_____ carpetas tienes?
7. ¿_____ papel tienes?
8. ¿_____ libros tienes?

9 ¿Mucho o poco? 1C

TEKS Focus
1C Present information using familiar words, phrases, and sentences

Escribamos/Hablemos Now answer the questions from Activity 8, using the correct forms of **mucho** and **poco.**

MODELO **—Tengo muchas (pocas) mochilas.**

10 Útiles escolares 1B

Escuchemos Gabi is helping her younger sister, Verónica, figure out what school supplies she still needs. Look at the picture and decide if what she says is **cierto** or **falso.**

Comunicación

11 ¿Qué necesitamos? 1A

Hablemos You and your partner need to prepare a report that includes pictures, graphs, and mathematical calculations. Talk about the supplies you have and make a list of the supplies you need.

MODELO **—Necesitamos papel.**
—Tengo mucho papel pero *(but)* **necesitamos revistas.**

Present tense of tener and some tener idioms

Interactive TUTOR

1 Use the verb **tener** to tell what someone *has.* To conjugate the **yo** form, drop the **-er** ending and add **-go**. To conjugate all the other forms except for **nosotros(as)** and **vosotros(as),** change the **-e** to **-ie.**

yo	ten**go**	nosotros(as)	tenemos
tú	t**ie**nes	vosotros(as)	tenéis
Ud., él, ella	t**ie**ne	Uds., ellos, ellas	t**ie**nen

—¿T**ie**nes un bolígrafo? *Do you have a pen?*
—No. Ten**go** un lápiz. *No. I have a pencil.*

2 **Tener** is also used in these common expressions.

tener que + infinitive	*to have to do something*
tener ganas de + infinitive	*to feel like doing something*
tener prisa	*to be in a hurry*
tener (mucha) hambre	*to be (very) hungry*
tener (mucha) sed	*to be (very) thirsty*

Tengo ganas de descansar, ¿y tú?
I feel like resting, and you?

Tengo prisa. Tengo que ir a un ensayo.
I'm in a hurry. I have to go to a rehearsal.

¿Tienes hambre? *Are you hungry?*

Online
Vocabulario y gramática, pp. 40–42 | Actividades, pp. 31–33

En inglés

In English, we use the verb *to be* to say how old we are, or to say we're hungry or thirsty.

I am 15 years old.

We are hungry and thirsty.

In Spanish, you use a form of **tener** *(to have)* with a noun in those expressions.

Tengo 15 años.

Tenemos hambre y sed.

12 ¿De quién habla? ←1B

Escuchemos Listen as Ana Mari talks about some of her friends. Match each picture to each statement she makes.

a.

b.

c.

d.

13 ¿Qué planes tienes? 1B

TEKS Focus
1B Demonstrate understanding of simple, clearly spoken, and written language when dealing with familiar topics

Leamos Complete the conversation between Elena and her friend with the correct forms of **tener** and **tener que.**

—Elena, necesito un favor. ¿ __1__ un diccionario?

—No, pero la señora López __2__ muchos diccionarios en el salón de clase.

—Buena idea. __3__ irme. ¿Nos vemos por la tarde?

—¿Hoy? ¿Qué __4__ hacer (tú)?

—Nosotras __5__ un examen de alemán mañana y __6__ estudiar.

—¡Ay! Sí, está bien. Nos vemos a las 4:00.

14 Rompecabezas 1B

Hablemos/Escribamos Use the correct form of **tener** and a phrase from each puzzle piece to form six logical sentences.

1	2	3
Quiero salir. ¿(Tú)...?	tener	pasear conmigo
Son las 8:10 y el profesor...	tener que	hoy por la tarde
Hace calor. (Yo)...	tener ganas de	mucha prisa
Y ustedes, ¿qué clases...?		nadar
		sed
		los lunes
		bailar

Comunicación

15 Planes 1A

Hablemos Look at the pictures. With a partner, take turns asking each other if you either want to or have to do these things today.

MODELO **—¿Tienes ganas de ir al baile hoy por la noche?**
—Sí, tengo ganas de bailar.

The verb venir and a + time

Interactive TUTOR

1 The verb **venir** means *to come.* In the present tense its endings are like those of **tener,** except for the **nosotros** and **vosotros** forms.

yo ven**go**		nosotros(as)	venimos
tú v**ie**nes		vosotros(as)	venís
Ud., él, ella v**ie**ne		Uds., ellos, ellas	v**ie**nen

2 To say at what time something happens, put the preposition **a** before the **time.**

¿A qué hora vienes al colegio?
At what time do you come to school?

Vengo **a las ocho en punto.**
I come at eight o'clock.

¿A qué hora es la clase de álgebra?
At what time is algebra class?

Es **a la una de la tarde.**
It's at one in the afternoon.

Online
Vocabulario y gramática, pp. 40–42 | Actividades, pp. 31–33

16 Mi fiesta 1B

Escuchemos Listen as Marta plays the messages on her answering machine. On a sheet of paper, write down at what time Marta's friends are coming to her party tonight.

1. Jorge
2. Juliana
3. Anabel
4. Valentín
5. Marisol y Chema
6. Gabi

17 ¿Vienes conmigo? 1B

Escribamos/Hablemos Write sentences or questions using words from each of the word boxes below. Remember to use the correct form of the verb.

MODELO (tú) ¿Vienes a la clase de español los miércoles?

yo tú nosotros el profesor (la profesora) ustedes usted	(no) venir	a la clase de español al colegio a la clase de... a la reunión de...	los fines de semana los lunes y... los... a veces todos los días

Unos amigos llegan a una fiesta de cumpleaños, San José.

18 ¿A qué hora viene el autobús? 3A

Escribamos/Hablemos Given the situations below, use the bus schedule to find the earliest bus that goes to Chirripó National Forest. Follow the model.

MODELO **Son las once y veinte. Roberto está en San Isidro.**
El autobús cincuenta y seis viene a las once y media.

1. Es mediodía. Juan está en San Isidro.
2. Son las nueve en punto. Ángela está en Cartago.
3. Es la una y cuarto. Mónica está en San Isidro.
4. Son las ocho y diez. Antonio está en San José.
5. Son las diez y cinco. Carlos está en Cartago.
6. Son las once menos cuarto. Jorge está en Cartago.
7. Son las nueve y treinta y cinco. Amalia está en San José.
8. Son las nueve y veinticinco. Raúl está en San José.

Autobuses, San José

San José-Chirripó

PRESTACIONES	56	77	91
ORIGEN			
San José	8:30	9:30	10:30
Cartago	9:15	10:15	11:15
San Isidro	11:30	12:30	1:30
Chirripó	12:20	1:20	2:20

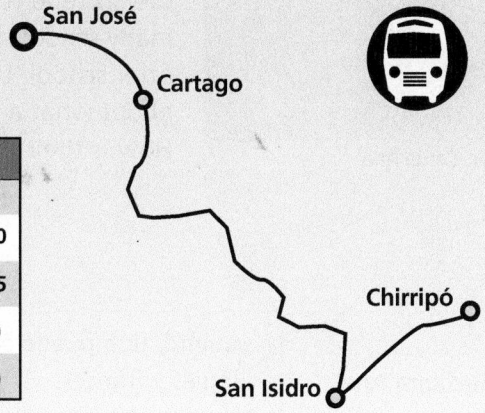

TEKS Focus
3A Use resources in the language and cultures being studied to gain access to information

Comunicación

19 En el colegio 1A

Hablemos Ask your classmate when he or she comes to school, what classes he or she has, and at what time. Then switch roles.

MODELO **—¿A qué hora vienes al colegio?**
—Vengo a las ocho y media.
—¿Qué clases tienes?
—Tengo español, matemáticas, historia...
—¿A qué hora es la clase de...?
—Es a...

Cultura

VideoCultura

Comparaciones

El comienzo del día en el Colegio de Santa Ana

¿Cómo es un día típico en tu colegio? 2A, 4B

Students in the United States usually have certain classes they must take, as well as a few elective classes such as choir, drama, shop, and so on. Most schools have after-school activities as well, such as sports or band. In Spain and Latin America, all classes tend to be obligatory, and there aren't many school-sponsored clubs or teams that meet after school. Listen as the following speakers talk about what a typical day is like at their schools. How is their day similar to or different from yours?

Julio

San José, Costa Rica

¿A qué colegio asistes?

Yo asisto al colegio de Santa Ana.

¿Cómo es un día típico en tu colegio?

Un día típico es entrar a las siete de la mañana, salir a las once y veinte de la mañana, ir a almorzar, regresar de nuevo a las doce y de ahí hasta las cuatro y veinte de la tarde. Luego ya retorna uno a la casa de uno.

¿Qué materias tienes?

A nosotros nos dan matemáticas, inglés, francés, español, estudios sociales.

¿Son materias obligatorias u opcionales?

Hasta el tercer año inglés y francés son obligatorias y de cuarto a quinto, uno puede escoger entre inglés y francés.

¿Cuál es tu materia favorita y por qué?

Mi materia favorita es matemáticas. Es más fácil para mí desarrollarla.

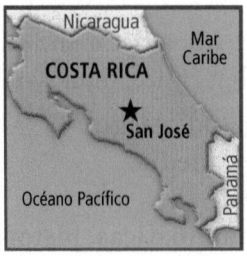

Jasna
Santiago, Chile

¿A qué colegio asistes?

Asisto al Colegio Carmen Macfi.

¿Cómo es un día típico en tu colegio?

Bueno, entro en la mañana, ocho y media, y bueno, tenemos distintas materias durante los días y tenemos recreo, luego el almuerzo y después salgo a las tres. Y me voy a mi casa y estudio.

¿Qué materias tienes?

Tengo castellano, historia, matemáticas, inglés, los electivos y ciencias que es química, física y biología.

¿Son materias obligatorias u opcionales?

Los electivos son opcionales. Yo en mi caso tomé ciudad contemporánea y problemas del conocimiento. Y cuando estás en cuarto medio, con ciencias, puedes eliminar una que, en mi caso, yo eliminé física.

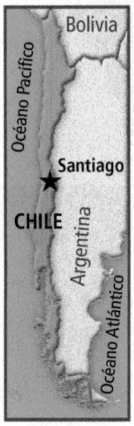

Para comprender 1B

1. ¿A qué hora va Julio al colegio?
2. ¿Estudia Julio ciencias?
3. ¿Qué hace Jasna después de ir a casa?
4. ¿Jasna estudia ciencias?
5. ¿Te gusta más el día escolar de Julio o Jasna? ¿Por qué?

Para pensar y hablar 2A, 4B

Make a list of three classes that Julio and Jasna have in common. Do you also have these classes? Why or why not? Both Julio and Jasna are required to study English as a foreign language. Does your school require you to study a foreign language, or is it an elective? Do you think requiring a foreign language is a good idea? Why or why not?

Cuaderno para hispanohablantes, pp. 29–36

Texas

Comunidad

Spanish Club in the Community 5A

Does your school have a Spanish Club? Spanish Club activities help you learn your new language and have fun. Your club can host Spanish-language films and invite community members to talk about the Spanish-speaking world. Your Spanish Club could host meals with foods from Spanish-speaking countries and invite cooks from your own city or town! Texas communities often have a wealth of opportunities for learning Spanish. Find out what resources are available by looking in the phone book or on the Internet.

Spanish Club and sponsor trying new foods

Objetivos

Talking about plans, inviting someone to do something

Vocabulario en acción 2

ExpresaVisión

un partido

un concierto

una clase de baile

Más vocabulario...

esta semana	*this week*
este fin de semana	*this weekend*
mañana	*tomorrow*
pasado mañana	*day after tomorrow*
la próxima semana	*next week*

Visit Holt Online
go.hrw.com
KEYWORD: EXP1 CH4
Vocabulario 2 practice

En el colegio

la biblioteca

el auditorio

el estadio

la cafetería

el salón de clase

También se puede decir...

In Mexico, **escuela** refers to a public school, while **colegio** means private school. In Colombia and Costa Rica, **escuela** is an elementary school while **colegio** is a high school.

In Texas and Mexico, **una reunión** can also be called **una junta.**

¡Exprésate!

Interactive TUTOR

To talk about plans	To respond
¿Vas a ir a... el lunes por la noche? *Are you going to go to . . . Monday night?*	**No. Tengo una reunión del club de español.** *No. I have a Spanish Club meeting.*
¿Qué vas a hacer el viernes próximo? *What are you going to do next Friday?*	**Voy a presentar el examen de inglés, y después... Luego regreso a casa.** *I'm going to take an English test, and afterwards . . . Then I'm going back home.*
¿A qué hora vas a llegar al partido? *What time are you going to get to the game?*	**Voy a llegar temprano (a tiempo). No me gusta llegar tarde.** *I'm going to arrive early (on time). I don't like to be late.*

Online
Vocabulario y gramática, pp. 43–45

Nota cultural

In Costa Rica, if a student fails a course it must be made up during vacation. If a student fails two classes and also fails the exams offered at the end of vacation, he or she must repeat the whole semester. How does this compare to the grading system and to state exams in the United States? 2A, 4B

VALORACIÓN DE LOS APRENDIZAJES Y DE LA CONDUCTA

ASIGNATURAS / PERÍODOS	I	II	III	PROMEDIO ANUAL	CONDICIÓN
Estudios Sociales	80	84	86	83	Aprobado
Cívica					
Matemática	83	75[6]	72	77	Aprobado
Español	89	84	93	90	Aprobado
Biología	86	74	88	83	Aprobado
Química	79	89	88	85	Aprobado
Física					
Inglés	82	80	74	80	Aprobado
Educación Física	78	85	93	85	Aprobado
Educación Musical	80	96	100	92	Aprobado
Psicología Ética Profesional	65	85	81	77	Aprobado
Educación Religiosa	100	95	98	97[60]	Aprobado
Conducta	91[89]	98	99	97	Aprobado

ESPECIALIDAD: Secretariado

Sub área*	I	II	III	PROMEDIO ANUAL	CONDICIÓN
Ad. de la Of. Sum	89	94	95	94	Aprobado
Ice - Excusión					
Ad. de un Pco. S.C.	96	93	100	96	Aprobado
Automa. Ofimática	79	89[14]	87	83	Aprobado

* Consignar el nombre de cada sub área

20 ¿Dónde están? 1B

Escuchemos Escucha las conversaciones. Para cada conversación decide dónde están las personas.

a. en el salón de clase
b. en la biblioteca
c. en la cafetería
d. en el auditorio
e. en el estadio
f. en el club de computación

21 Tengo que hacer muchas cosas 1B

Leamos Usa las palabras del cuadro para completar el párrafo.

luego	partido	tarde	club
presentar	auditorio	regresar	pasado

Esta semana voy a hacer muchas cosas. Hoy por la __1__, a las 2:30, voy a __2__ el examen de química y __3__ voy a ir a la reunión del __4__ de alemán. Mañana a las 5:00 tengo un __5__ de béisbol. __6__ mañana voy a ir al ensayo de piano en el __7__ del colegio. Voy a __8__ a casa tarde.

22 ¿Qué haces? 1B

Hablemos Use **hay** *(there is, there are)* and a word from the box to say where the following things are at your school.

los salones de clase	el auditorio	la cafetería
el estadio	la biblioteca	la clase de...

MODELO **partidos de fútbol**
Hay partidos de fútbol en el estadio.

1. muchos libros
2. conciertos
3. comida
4. bailes
5. una reunión
6. revistas
7. diccionarios
8. partidos de béisbol
9. un piano

¡Exprésate!

To invite someone to do something	To respond
¿Qué tal si vamos al partido de fútbol? *How about if we go to the soccer game?*	**No sé. ¿Sabes qué? No tengo ganas.** *I don't know. You know what? I don't feel like it.*
Vienes conmigo a la cafetería, ¿no? *You're coming with me to the cafeteria, aren't you?*	**¡Claro que sí! Tengo mucha hambre.** *Yes, of course! I'm very hungry.*
Hay un concierto... Vas a ir, ¿verdad? *There's a concert . . . You're going to go, right?*	**No, no voy a ir. Tengo que estudiar.** *No, I'm not going to go. I have to study.*

Interactive TUTOR

Online
Vocabulario y gramática, pp. 43–45

23 Invitaciones 1B

Escuchemos/Escribamos Listen to the conversations. On a separate piece of paper, write down what each person is invited to do, then tell whether the invitation is accepted or not.

1. Raquel **2.** Andrés **3.** Silvia **4.** Marta

24 ¿Qué tal si...? 1B

Hablemos/Escribamos Usa las expresiones en los cuadros para invitar a un(a) amigo(a) a ir a cada evento *(each event)*.

MODELO **¿Qué tal si vamos al gimnasio el martes por la tarde?**

¿Qué tal si vamos...?	al gimnasio	el martes por la tarde
¿Quieres ir conmigo...?	a la cafetería	el sábado próximo
¿Vas a ir...?	al concierto de piano	pasado mañana a las 4:30
¿Vienes conmigo...?	al baile del colegio	el viernes por la noche
	al partido de volibol	el miércoles a las 12:00
	a la reunión del club de alemán	el lunes próximo por la mañana

25 ¿Sabes qué? 1B

Hablemos Now turn down your friend's invitations from Activity 24 by saying you have to do what is pictured.

MODELO **No. Tengo que ir a un partido de fútbol.**

A

B

C

D

Comunicación

26 ¿Vienes conmigo? 1A

Hablemos Choose three school events you'd like to attend, then invite three different classmates to each of them. They will accept or turn down the invitation.

MODELO **—Hay un baile el viernes por la noche en el colegio. ¿Quieres ir conmigo?**

—¡Claro que sí! Me gustan los bailes.

TEKS Focus

1A Engage in oral and written exchanges of learned material to socialize and to provide and obtain information

Objetivos

Using **ir a** with infinitives, **-er** and **-ir** verbs, tag questions, and **-er** and **-ir** verbs with irregular **yo** forms

Gramática en acción 2

GramaVisión

Ir a with infinitives

1 To talk about what someone is or isn't going to do, use the present tense of **ir** with **a** followed by an **infinitive**.

—¿**Vas a estudiar**?
Are you going to study?

—No, **voy a descansar**.
No, I'm going to rest.

—¿**Van a salir**?
Are you going to go out?

—Sí, **vamos a comer**.
Yes, we're going to eat.

2 To say that you are going to do something on a certain day of a particular week, use **el** before the **weekday**.

El sábado voy a ir de compras.
On Saturday I'm going to go shopping.

Online
Vocabulario y gramática, pp. 46–48 | Actividades, pp. 35–37

¿Te acuerdas?

Use **los** and a plural form of the day of the week to say you do something on that day every week.

¿Qué haces **los sábados**?
What do you (usually) do on Saturdays?

27 Planes diferentes ◆1B

Escuchemos Say whether Roberto and Nora are talking about **a**) plans for the weekend or **b**) things they do every weekend.

28 ¿Qué van a hacer? ◆1B

Leamos/Escribamos Complete the sentences with the correct form of **(no) ir a** based on the cues.

MODELO **Yo ═══ descansar el sábado. Tengo que trabajar.**
Yo no voy a descansar el sábado.

1. Mi mejor amigo casi siempre quiere pasar el rato conmigo. Él ═══ comer conmigo este fin de semana.
2. Mis amigos y yo ═══ salir el viernes por la noche. Nos gusta salir.
3. Mi familia y yo ═══ ir al cine el domingo. Tenemos que ir a una reunión el domingo.
4. Yo ═══ comer en la cafetería hoy. No tengo hambre.
5. Los estudiantes de la clase de español ═══ estudiar mucho esta tarde. Van a presentar un examen mañana.
6. Mi mejor amiga ═══ ir de compras el domingo. Siempre va de compras los sábados.

Visit Holt Online
go.hrw.com
KEYWORD: EXP1 CH4
Gramática 2 practice

29 ¿Cuándo vas a...? 1B, 1C

Hablemos Say what these people are going to do and when. Then say whether or not you're going to do the same things and when.

MODELO **Sara va a estudiar mañana. Yo no. Voy a estudiar pasado mañana.**

Sara/mañana

Lucía
el sábado próximo

Enrique
el domingo

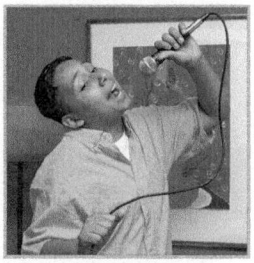
Andrés
el viernes próximo

Mario y Lola
el lunes

30 ¿Sabes qué van a hacer? 1B

Escribamos/Hablemos Say whether the following people are going to do the activities listed. For items 4 and 5, guess what another student and your teacher are going to do.

TEKS Focus
1B Demonstrate understanding of simple, clearly spoken, and written language when dealing with familiar topics

MODELO **yo (salir con amigos esta noche, ver televisión)**
No voy a salir con amigos esta noche.
Voy a ver televisión.

1. yo (hacer ejercicio hoy, tocar el piano después de clases)
2. mis amigos y yo (salir este fin de semana, ir al cine el sábado)
3. mi mejor amigo(a) (pasar el fin de semana conmigo, jugar al básquetbol esta semana)
4. tú (llegar temprano al colegio mañana, ir a una reunión hoy)
5. usted (venir al colegio mañana, alquilar un video esta noche)

Comunicación

31 ¡Cuántos planes! 1A

Hablemos Ask your classmate what he or she is going to do on Friday, Saturday, and Sunday. After he or she invites you along, say whether you want to go or do something else. Switch roles.

MODELO **—¿Qué vas a hacer el viernes por la noche?**
—El viernes por la noche voy a bailar. ¿Quieres venir conmigo?
—Sí. Me gusta bailar. (—No. El viernes voy a nadar.)

The present tense of -er and -ir verbs and tag questions

Interactive TUTOR

1 To conjugate a regular **-er** or **-ir** verb in the present tense, drop the **-er** or **-ir** of the infinitive and add **these endings**.

	comer *to eat*	**escribir** *to write*
yo	como	escrib**o**
tú	com**es**	escrib**es**
Ud., él, ella	com**e**	escrib**e**
nosotros(as)	com**emos**	escrib**imos**
vosotros(as)	com**éis**	escrib**ís**
Uds., ellos, ellas	com**en**	escrib**en**

2 Some **-er** and **-ir** verbs are **beber** *(to drink)*, **asistir (a)** *(to attend)*, **abrir** *(to open)*, and **interrumpir** *(to interrupt)*. To say that someone drinks something, use **beber algo.**

3 A **tag question** is attached to the end of a sentence to make it a question. If you expect someone to answer *yes*, use **¿no?** or **¿verdad?** When the expected answer is *no*, use **¿verdad?**

—¿Vienes a la fiesta, **¿no? (¿verdad?)** —**Sí**, voy a ir.
You're coming . . . aren't you? *Yes, I'm going to go.*

—¿No vas al partido, **¿verdad?** —**No**, no voy.
You're not going . . . right? *No, I'm not going.*

Online
Vocabulario y gramática, pp. 46–48 | Actividades, pp. 35–37

Nota cultural

Private schools in Costa Rica start in the morning and run until early afternoon, similar to what happens in U.S. schools. On the other hand, some public schools in Costa Rica have three sessions: **el turno matutino** is four hours of classes in the morning, **el turno vespertino** is four hours in the afternoon, and **el turno nocturno** is four hours in the evening. How would your life be different if you had classes in the evenings? 2A, 4B

32 ¿Cierto o falso? 1B

Leamos/Escribamos Completa las oraciones con los verbos correctos del cuadro.

comen	**asistimos**	**lee**	**escriben**	**corro**
escribimos	**bebes**	**beber**	**abre**	**corres**

1. Mis amigas y yo ____ al colegio en julio.
2. Mis compañeros de clase ____ muchas cartas en español.
3. Yo casi nunca ____ en la clase de educación física.
4. Mis amigos ____ conmigo en la cafetería.
5. El(La) profesor(a) ____ revistas interesantes en clase.
6. Tú a veces ____ algo en la clase.
7. La biblioteca ____ a las 9:00 de la mañana.

33 En la clase de español 1C

TEKS Focus
1C Present information using familiar words, phrases, and sentences

Escribamos/Hablemos Using the words from each word box, say whether or not these things happen in your school. Remember to conjugate the verbs.

MODELO **Muchos estudiantes leen muchas cartas en español.**

muchos (pocos) estudiantes	comer	muchas (pocas) cartas en español
el profesor (la profesora)	beber	algo (nada) en clase
yo	interrumpir	temprano (tarde) los viernes
nosotros	(no) leer	pocas (muchas) revistas
tú	escribir	al colegio en diciembre
ustedes	asistir	a los estudiantes/al profesor/a la profesora
la cafetería (la biblioteca)	abrir	en la cafetería

34 Un día típico en el colegio 1C

Leamos/Escribamos Complete the sentences with an activity pictured below.

MODELO **A veces los profesores comen en la cafetería.**

1. Yo nunca...
2. Con frecuencia el (la) profesor(a)...
3. Mis compañeros de clase y yo...
4. Todos los días mi mejor amigo(a)...
5. La biblioteca siempre...
6. Cuando tienen educación física, los estudiantes...

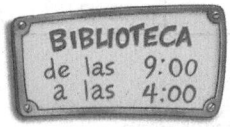

Comunicación

35 En nuestra escuela 1A

Hablemos Create questions using the pictures in Activity 34 and tag questions. Have your partner answer the questions. Switch roles.

MODELO **—La biblioteca del colegio abre a las 10:00, ¿verdad?**
—No, la biblioteca abre a las 9:00.

Some -er/-ir verbs with irregular yo forms

Interactive TUTOR

1 The following **-er** and **-ir** verbs have irregular **yo** forms.

	hacer *to do, to make*	**poner** *to put*	**traer** *to bring*
yo	ha**go**	pon**go**	trai**go**
tú	haces	pones	traes
Ud., él, ella	hace	pone	trae
nosotros(as)	hacemos	ponemos	traemos
vosotros(as)	hacéis	ponéis	traéis
Uds., ellos, ellas	hacen	ponen	traen
	saber *to know information*	**ver** *to see*	**salir** *to go out*
yo	**sé**	**veo**	sal**go**
tú	sabes	ves	sales
Ud., él, ella	sabe	ve	sale
nosotros(as)	sabemos	vemos	salimos
vosotros(as)	sabéis	veis	salís
Uds., ellos, ellas	saben	ven	salen

2 The preposition **de** is used after **salir** to talk about leaving a place. It is used after **saber** to say how much someone knows about something.

Salgo de mi casa a las siete.	*I leave my house at seven.*
No **sé** mucho **de** arte.	*I don't know much about art.*

Online
Vocabulario y gramática, pp. 46–48 | Actividades, pp. 35–37

Texas Nota cultural

Many Texas high schools have Mexican folk-dancing or **ballet folklórico** clubs, as well as traditional music groups, such as **mariachis.** These clubs offer opportunities for Mexican American teens to speak—and sing—in Spanish. Do research at your library or on the Internet to find out if music and dance clubs exist in high schools in Latin American countries.

5B 36 Y tú, ¿qué haces? 1B

Leamos Complete these sentences with the correct verb.

1. ¿Tú ____ del colegio a las 5:30?
   a. hago **b.** sales **c.** salgo
2. Yo ____ mis papeles en mi mochila.
   a. pongo **b.** vemos **c.** salgo
3. Mi amigo ____ su tarea por la noche.
   a. ponen **b.** pone **c.** hace
4. A veces mis amigas ____ su almuerzo de casa.
   a. traigo **b.** ponen **c.** traen
5. Nosotros nunca ____ películas en la cafetería.
   a. sé **b.** sabemos **c.** vemos
6. Yo no ____ mucho de computadoras.
   a. salgo **b.** sé **c.** hace

37 Un amigo de Internet ✦1B

Leamos/Escribamos Rogelio posts this e-mail on a pen pal Web site. Read the e-mail and decide if the statements that follow are true or false. Then write Rogelio and tell him about your interests.

1. Rogelio sale con amigos los fines de semana.
2. Rogelio lee libros de misterio.
3. Rogelio hace ejercicio a veces.
4. A Rogelio no le gusta el Internet.
5. A veces, Rogelio tiene conciertos.
6. A Rogelio le gusta ir al cine.

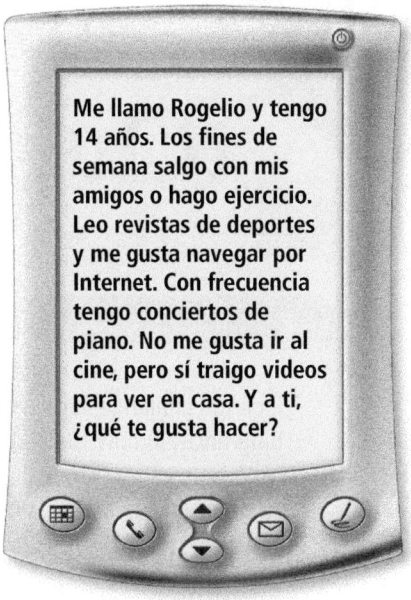

38 Las fiestas ✦1B, 1C

Hablemos/Escribamos Answer these questions about what you do with your friends on weekends.

1. ¿Sales con amigos los fines de semana?
2. ¿Vas a la casa de amigos?
3. ¿Qué hacen ustedes? ¿Escuchan música o ven videos?
4. ¿Traen comida? ¿Salen a comer? ¿Qué les gusta comer?
5. ¿Les gusta ir al cine? Cuando van al cine, ¿a qué hora salen?
6. ¿Qué más haces con ellos?

TEKS Focus
1C Present information using familiar words, phrases, and sentences

Comunicación

39 Después de clases ✦1C

Hablemos/Escribamos With a partner, take turns describing this student's day after school. Include as many details as possible.

Novela en vídeo

¿Quién será?

Episodio 4

ESTRATEGIA

Comparing and Contrasting When you compare and contrast two or more things, you look for similarities and differences. For example, you can look for similarities or differences in how the students in Mexico and those in Puerto Rico dress and behave. You can also compare and contrast the Puerto Rican and Mexican students with yourself and students in your school. What are some similarities and differences you notice as you watch the video? 3B

En Puerto Rico

Marcos is trying to gather information on Nicolás. Nicolás is completely unaware.

1

2

Mateo Oye, Nicolás, ¿a qué hora es tu clase de matemáticas?

Nicolás Tengo matemáticas a la una de la tarde. ¿Por qué?

Mateo Porque yo tengo matemáticas ahora y necesito muchas cosas.

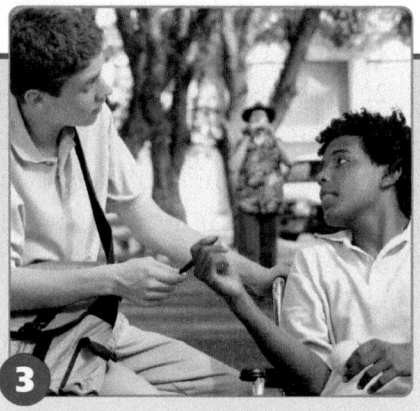

3

Nicolás ¿Qué necesitas?

Mateo Necesito un lápiz... una regla... y papel.

4

Mateo ¿Qué tal si vamos al partido de béisbol después de clases?

Julia Claro que sí.

Nicolás No, no tengo ganas.

Mateo ¿No tienes ganas? ¿Qué vas a hacer?

Nicolás Voy a... voy a... voy a...

5

Julia ¿Vas a qué? ¿Vas a hacer ejercicio?

Nicolás No, nunca hago ejercicio los lunes, ¿sabes? Los lunes son para...

Mateo ¿Para qué? ¿Qué vas a hacer?

Nicolás Voy a ver televisión. Mi programa favorito... esta noche...

Julia ¿Cuál es tu programa preferido?

6

Mateo ¿Y mañana? ¿Vas al concierto en el gimnasio?

Julia ¿Y pasado mañana?

Visit Holt Online
go.hrw.com
KEYWORD: EXP1 CH4
Online Edition

After school, Mateo and Julia decide to follow Nicolás to see where he's going.

7

Mateo ¿Quieres ver adónde va Nicolás?
Julia Sí, pero, ¿el partido de béisbol?
Mateo No importa, vamos.

8

Mateo ¿Qué hace Nicolás?
Julia No sé. Pero...

9

Julia *...¿Qué hace ese señor?*

En España

The professor tells Marcos about her next candidate and his next trip.

10

La profesora Ahora tengo un candidato de Costa Rica, Marcos. Sí, sí, después de Puerto Rico vas a El Paso y después de El Paso, a San José.

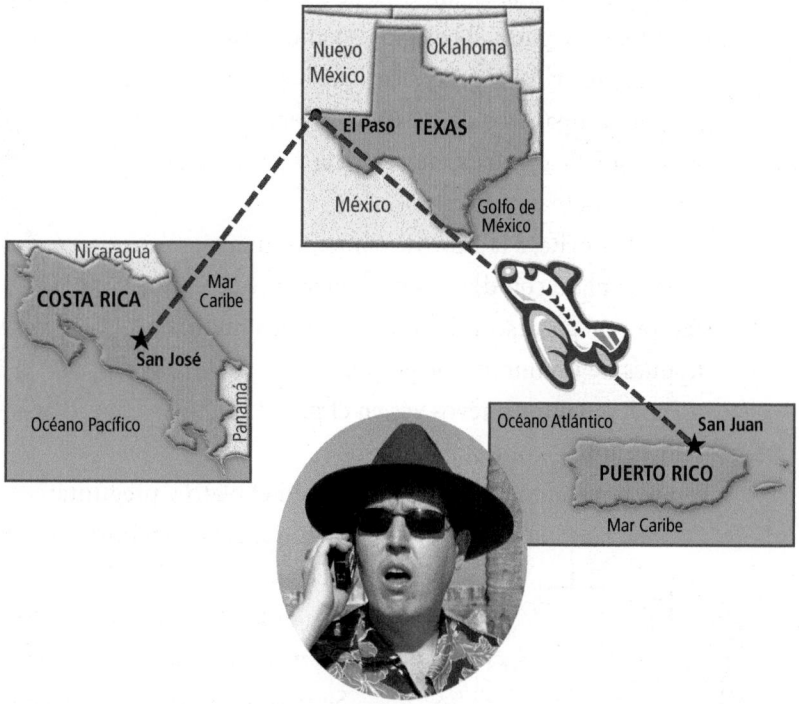

¿COMPRENDES?

1. Contrast Nicolás's preparation for geometry class with Mateo's.
2. Where does Mateo want to go after school? How does Nicolás feel about that plan?
3. Does Nicolás answer his friends truthfully? How can you tell?
4. Can Mateo and Julia tell what Nicolás is doing? Who else is there? What is he doing?
5. Compare and contrast how Sofía acts in **Episodio 3** with how Nicolás acts in this episode. What about how their friends act?
1B, 3A

Próximo episodio:
Can you predict what Marcos will do in Costa Rica?
PÁGINAS 180–181

Leamos y escribamos

ESTRATEGIA

para leer To improve your comprehension as you read a story, stop after each paragraph or section and ask yourself the ***who, what, where, when,*** and ***why*** of the story. Focusing on these questions as you read will not only help you check your comprehension, but also make reading in Spanish more fun.

A Antes de leer ✦1B, 3A, 3B

Read the title and the first paragraph of the story. Can you answer at least one of each of the questions in the Estrategia para leer?

Pepito, el niño precoz

Pepito es un niño gracioso, inteligente y precoz[1]. Tiene siete años y hoy es su primer día de colegio. Cuando viene a casa por la tarde, los padres de Pepito tienen muchas preguntas: ¿te gusta el colegio?, ¿cómo es tu profesora?, ¿cuál es tu materia preferida? Pepito dice[2] que le gusta mucho el colegio: sus compañeros de clase son divertidos, la profesora es simpática y no es muy estricta y su materia preferida es matemáticas.

Por la noche, a la hora de comer, su mamá pone un plato con dos huevos[3] en la mesa. Pepito, siempre precoz, esconde[4] uno de los dos huevos y después de un minuto pregunta:

—Papá, ¿cuántos huevos ves en el plato?

—Pues, uno—contesta[5] el padre.

Pepito pone entonces el otro huevo en el plato y pregunta:

—Y ahora, papá, ¿cuántos huevos ves?

—Dos—contesta el padre.

—¡Magnífico!—exclama Pepito—los dos huevos que ves ahora y el otro huevo de antes[6], son tres huevos, ¿verdad?

Su papá está un poco confundido[7]. Sólo ve dos huevos en el plato y no tres. Pero la mamá de Pepito, que escucha todo esto y que también es muy inteligente y graciosa dice:

—¡Claro que sí, Pepito! Hay tres huevos. El primero es para mí, el segundo[8] es para tu papá, y el tercero[9] es para ti.

1 precocious **2** says **3** eggs **4** hides **5** answers **6** from before **7** confused **8** second **9** third

Visit Holt Online
go.hrw.com
KEYWORD: EXP1 CH4
Online Edition

B Comprensión 1B, 1C

Contesta las siguientes preguntas.

1. ¿Cuántos años tiene Pepito y cómo es?
2. ¿Cuál es la materia preferida de Pepito?
3. ¿Cómo es la profesora de Pepito? ¿Y los compañeros de clase?
4. ¿Qué pone la mamá en la mesa y qué hace el niño?
5. ¿Qué le pregunta Pepito a su papá? ¿Qué dice él?
6. ¿Qué dice la mamá de Pepito?

C Después de leer 3A

What is Pepito like? Which sentences in the story give you clues about his personality? What about his parents? What are they like? Do they have a sense of humor? Explain.

TEKS Focus
3A Use resources in the language and cultures being studied to gain access to information

Taller del escritor

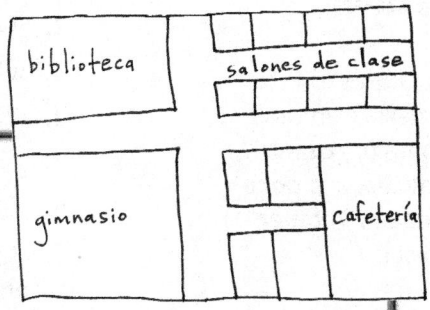

ESTRATEGIA

para escribir Using drawings can help organize your writing. If you can picture the setting in which the events occur, your writing may be clearer to your readers.

Un recorrido con nuevos estudiantes 1C

Imagine you're helping with orientation at your school and you're taking two new students on a tour. Create a conversation based on your first meeting with them. Explain what classes they will take and when, and include questions new students might ask. Invite them to attend a club meeting, play, or another school activity.

1 Antes de escribir

Sketch the layout of your school, labeling the places you would show new students. You may wish to draw arrows to show the route you plan to take.

2 Escribir un borrador

Begin your dialog based on the route you drew. The places you go should be based on the new students' questions and your explanations. End the dialog with an invitation and the students' responses.

3 Revisar

Make sure the dialog is logical by reading over the questions, explanations, and answers. Check for correct use of grammar, spelling, and punctuation.

4 Publicar

Display your dialog and sketch on the bulletin board. You may wish to act out your dialogs in groups of three.

Cuaderno para hispanohablantes, pp. 29–36

Prepárate para el examen

Repaso capítulo 4

Interactive TUTOR

1 Vocabulario 1
- saying what you have and what you need
- naming school supplies
- talking about classes

pp. 120–123

2 Gramática 1
- indefinite articles
- forms of **¿cuánto?, mucho,** and **poco**
- **tener** and **tener** idioms
- **venir**
- **a** with time

pp. 124–129

3 Vocabulario 2
- talking about plans
- inviting someone to do something

pp. 132–135

1 Completa el diálogo de manera lógica. **1B**

—¿Qué clases tienes esta tarde?

—Tengo __1__, __2__ y __3__.

—¿Cuál es tu materia preferida?

—Bueno, me gusta __4__ porque es __5__. Y tú, ¿cuál es tu materia preferida?

—Es __6__. Bueno, ¿qué necesitas para la clase de inglés?

—Necesito __7__ y __8__.

1B, 1C

2 Answer the following questions about you and your friends.

1. ¿A qué hora vienen ustedes al colegio por las mañanas?
2. ¿Generalmente tienen prisa ustedes cuando vienen al colegio?
3. ¿Cuántas clases tienes en un día?
4. ¿Necesitas muchas cosas para las clases?
5. ¿Qué cosas necesitas para la clase de español?
6. ¿Qué tienes que hacer después de clases?
7. ¿Qué tienes ganas de hacer este fin de semana? ¿y tu mejor amigo(a)?

3 Invite your partner to each of the events pictured. Your partner will accept or turn down each invitation. **1A, 1B**

A

B

C

D

Visit Holt Online
go.hrw.com
KEYWORD: EXP1 CH4
Chapter Self-test

4 Answer these questions about your weekend plans. 1B, 1C

1. ¿Vas a ir a un concierto este fin de semana?
2. ¿Ves televisión los sábados?
3. ¿Va a venir un amigo a tu casa el domingo?
4. ¿Van a hacer la tarea en casa tú y tu amigo?
5. ¿Vas a ir a un partido de béisbol el sábado?
6. ¿Sales mucho con amigos los viernes?
7. ¿Sales a comer comida china los domingos?

5 Answer the following questions. 4B

1. How are programs of study in Latin America similar to or different from those in the United States?
2. What advantages or disadvantages do you think there are in having students repeat a semester if they fail two classes and the final exam?
3. What are the three class sessions in Costa Rican public schools called? When do they begin?

6 Escucha las preguntas y escribe las respuestas en tu papel. 1B

7 Use the drawings to describe what happens to this student who is always running late. 1C

4 Gramática 2
- **ir a** with infinitives
- **-er** and **-ir** verbs and tag questions
- **-er** and **-ir** verbs with irregular **yo** forms
pp. 136–141

5 Cultura
- **Comparaciones**
pp. 130–131
- **Notas culturales**
pp. 122, 123, 134, 138
- **Geocultura**
pp. 114–117

TEKS Focus
4B Demonstrate understanding of the concept of culture through comparisons

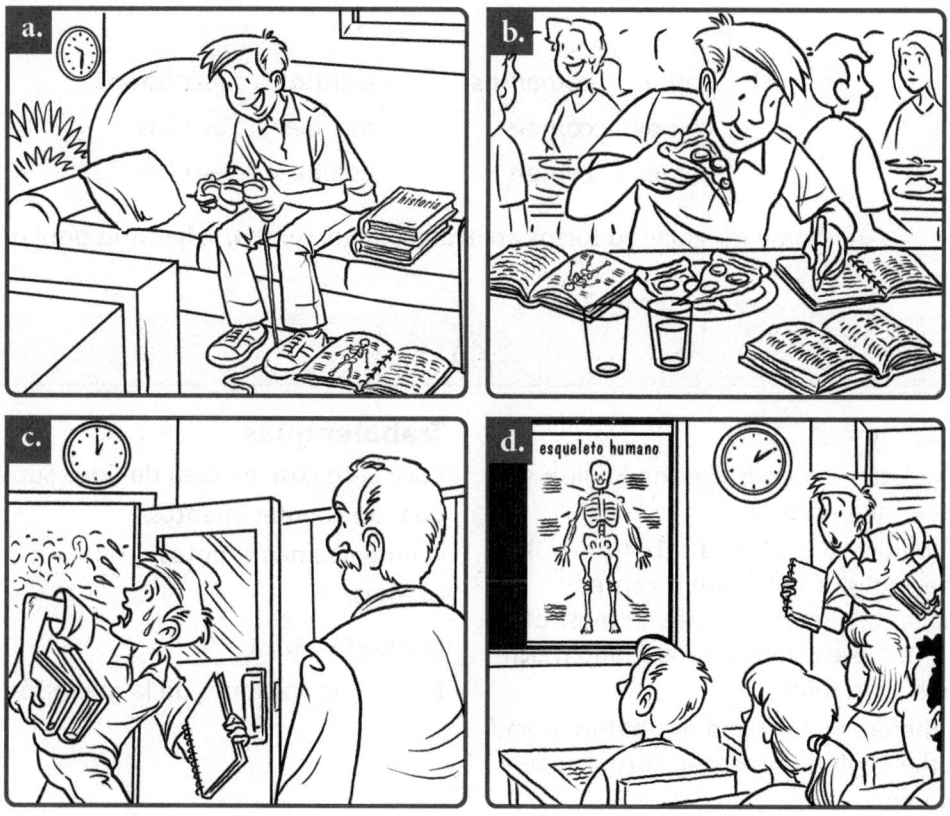

Gramática 1
- indefinite articles; **¿cuánto?, mucho, poco** **pp. 124–125**
- present tense of **tener** and some **tener idioms** **pp. 126–127**
- **venir** and **a** + time **pp. 128–129**

Repaso de Gramática 1

	Masculine		Feminine	
SINGULAR	un cuánto	mucho poco	una cuánta	mucha poca
PLURAL	unos cuántos	muchos pocos	unas cuántas	muchas pocas

ten**go**	tenemos
tienes	tenéis
tiene	tienen

ven**go**	venimos
vienes	venís
viene	vienen

The preposition a followed by the time tells at what time something happens.
—¿Vienes a mi casa a **las 8:15**? —Sí. Tenemos clase a **las 9 en punto**.

Gramática 2
- **ir a** + infinitive **pp. 136–137**
- present tense of **-er** and **-ir** verbs and tag questions **pp. 138–139**
- **-er** and **-ir** verbs with irregular **yo** forms **pp. 140–141**

TEKS Focus
1B Demonstrate understanding of simple, clearly spoken, and written language when dealing with familiar topics

Repaso de Gramática 2

The verb ir followed by **a** and an infinitive tells what is going to happen in the near future. Tag questions such as ¿no? and ¿verdad? ask the person listening to agree with the person speaking.

Vas a bailar en la fiesta, ¿no?

Sí, también **voy a cantar**.

comer	
como	comemos
comes	coméis
come	comen

escribir	
escribo	escribimos
escribes	escribís
escribe	escriben

Some irregular **yo** forms are **traigo, hago, sé, veo, salgo,** and **pongo.**

Letra y sonido s z c qu

Las letras s, z, c y qu

- In Spanish, the letter s sounds like the English *s* in *sun:* salsa, seso, silla, solo, sus
- The letters z (before a, o, u), and c (before e, i) sound like the English *c* in the word *center:* zapatos, zona, azul, centro, ciencias. In most of Spain, z and c in these combinations sound much like the English *th* in *think.*
- The letters c (before a, o, u) and qu (before e and i) sound like the English *k:* carpeta, coro, cuaderno, querer, quién

Trabalenguas

Cuca Seco cose en casa de Coco Suca.
Cuando cuentes cuentos,
cuenta cuántos cuentos
cuentas.

Dictado 1B

Escribe las oraciones de la grabación.

Repaso de Vocabulario 1

Saying what you have and need

el bolígrafo	*pen*
la calculadora	*calculator*
la carpeta	*folder*
la computadora	*computer*
el cuaderno	*notebook*
el diccionario	*dictionary*
el lápiz/los lápices	*pencil/pencils*
la mochila	*backpack*
mucho(a)	*a lot of, much*
muchos(as)	*a lot of, many*
¿Necesitas algo para el colegio/la clase de arte?	*Do you need anything for school/art class?*
No, no necesito nada.	*No, I don't need anything.*
el papel	*paper*
poco(a)	*little, not much*
pocos(as)	*few, not many*
la regla	*ruler*
el reloj/los relojes	*clock, watch/clocks, watches*
la ropa	*clothes*
Sí, necesito muchas cosas.	*Yes, I need a lot of things.*
Sí, tengo un montón.	*Yes, I have a ton of them.*
¿Tienes...?	*Do you have . . . ?*
un/una	*a/an*
unos/unas	*some*
los útiles escolares	*school supplies*
los zapatos	*shoes*

Talking about classes

el alemán	*German*
el almuerzo	*lunch*
el arte, las artes	*art, the arts*
la biología	*biology*
las ciencias	*science*
la computación	*computer science*
¿Cuál es tu materia preferida?	*What's your favorite subject?*
la educación física	*physical education*
Es fácil/difícil.	*It's easy/hard.*
el español	*Spanish*
el francés	*French*
la historia	*history*
el inglés	*English*
las matemáticas	*mathematics*
las materias	*school subjects*
Mi materia preferida es...	*My favorite subject is . . .*
Primero tengo... y después tengo...	*First I have . . . and afterwards I have . . .*
por la mañana/tarde	*in the morning/afternoon*
¿Qué clases tienes esta tarde?	*What classes do you have this afternoon?*
la química	*chemistry*
el taller	*shop, workshop*
tener	*to have*
venir	*to come*

Some tener idioms . . . . . *See p. 126.*

Repaso de Vocabulario 2

Talking about plans . . . . . *See p. 133.*

el auditorio	*auditorium*
la biblioteca	*library*
la cafetería	*cafeteria*
la clase de baile	*dance class*
el concierto	*concert*
el estadio	*stadium*
esta semana	*this week*
este fin de semana	*this weekend*
hacer	*to do, to make*
hay	*there is, there are*
mañana	*tomorrow*
el partido de...	*. . . game*
pasado mañana	*day after tomorrow*
poner	*to put*
la próxima semana	*next week*
saber (de)	*to know information, to know about*
salir (de)	*to go out, to leave*
el salón de clase	*classroom*
traer	*to bring*
ver	*to see, to watch*
el viernes próximo	*next Friday*

Inviting others to do something . . . . . *See p. 134.*
Other -er and -ir verbs . . . . . *See p. 138.*

Integración

capítulos 1-4

1 Match each picture to the statements that best describe Lorenzo's busy day. 1B

a.

b.

c.

d.

2 Manuel has been accepted as an exchange student in the United States. Read his e-mail to his host parents and then tell whether each statement is **cierto** or **falso.** Correct the false statements. 1B

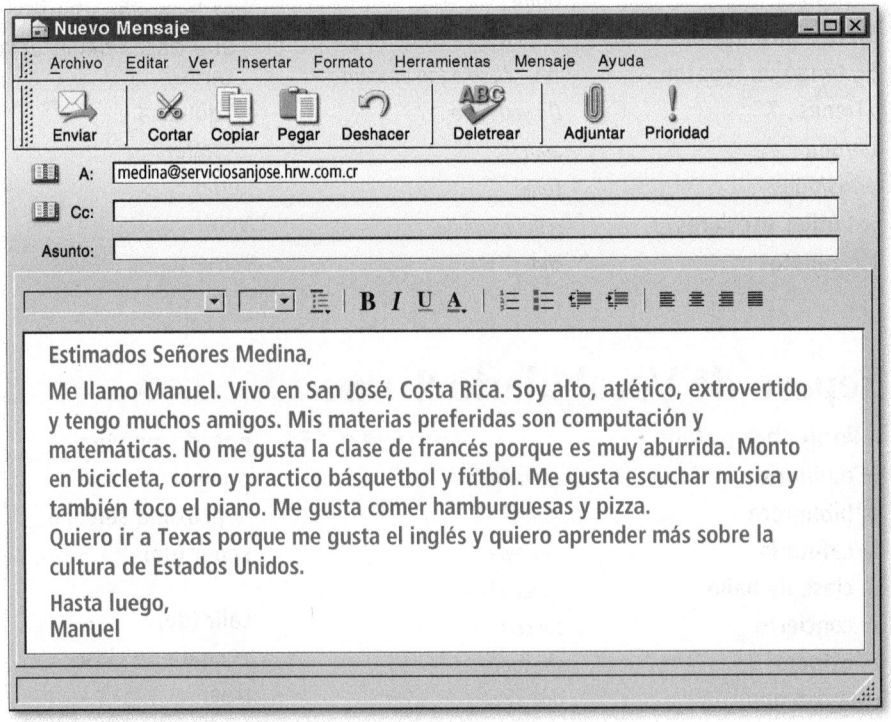

1. Manuel es alto, atlético y tiene pocos amigos.
2. Las clases que más le gustan a Manuel son computación y matemáticas.
3. A Manuel no le gusta la clase de francés porque es difícil.
4. Manuel quiere ir a Costa Rica.
5. Manuel tiene ganas de visitar Estados Unidos.

Visit Holt Online
go.hrw.com
KEYWORD: EXP1 CH4
Cumulative Self-test

3 Work in groups of four to welcome an exchange student from Costa Rica. Start with a greeting and introductions. Describe a typical day at your school. Tell when the school day starts and ends, what after-school activities are offered and what you and your friends like to do after school and on weekends. **1C**

4 Where do you think these people are going? What plans have they made for the afternoon? Pick two people from the painting and write a conversation in Spanish between them. Include either what they want or have to do, and their plans. Read your finished conversation to the class, and have your classmates identify the characters you've chosen. **1B, 1C**

Víctor Hugo Fernández, Gráficos del Globo, S.A., Costa Rica

Domingueando, **de Tomás Povedano de Arcos (1847–1943)**

5 Write a conversation in which you invite a classmate to eat lunch in the cafeteria. He or she agrees and then invites you to the soccer game this Friday night at the school stadium. Agree to go and ask him or her what time to arrive. He or she tells you, and you both say goodbye. **1A, 1C**

6 **Situación**

Create an information center where some students serve as peer counselors for new students. The new students have questions about classes, teachers, supplies, location of different areas of the school, after-school activities and school events. Use vocabulary and grammar you have learned to present your situation. **1A**

GeoVisión

Geocultura
Chile

▲ **La costa pacífica** A pesar de tener sólo 180 kilómetros de ancho, Chile tiene más de 6.000 kilómetros de costa pacífica. Aquí se ve la playa de Viña del Mar.

▼ **Cerca de 600 estatuas de piedra,** conocidas como moais y creadas entre los siglos XII y XVII, se encuentran en la Isla de Pascua, o Rapa Nui.

▼ **Santiago,** la capital de Chile, fue fundada en 1541 por el explorador español Pedro de Valdivia. Hoy día es una ciudad muy moderna.

Almanaque

Población
15.498.930

Capital
Santiago de Chile

Gobierno
república

Moneda
peso chileno

Idioma oficial
español

Código Internet
www.[ ].cl

◀ **La cueca** es el baile nacional de Chile. Representa el cortejo entre el gallo y la gallina.

¿Sabías que...?
The flags of Texas and Chile are very similar in design and color.

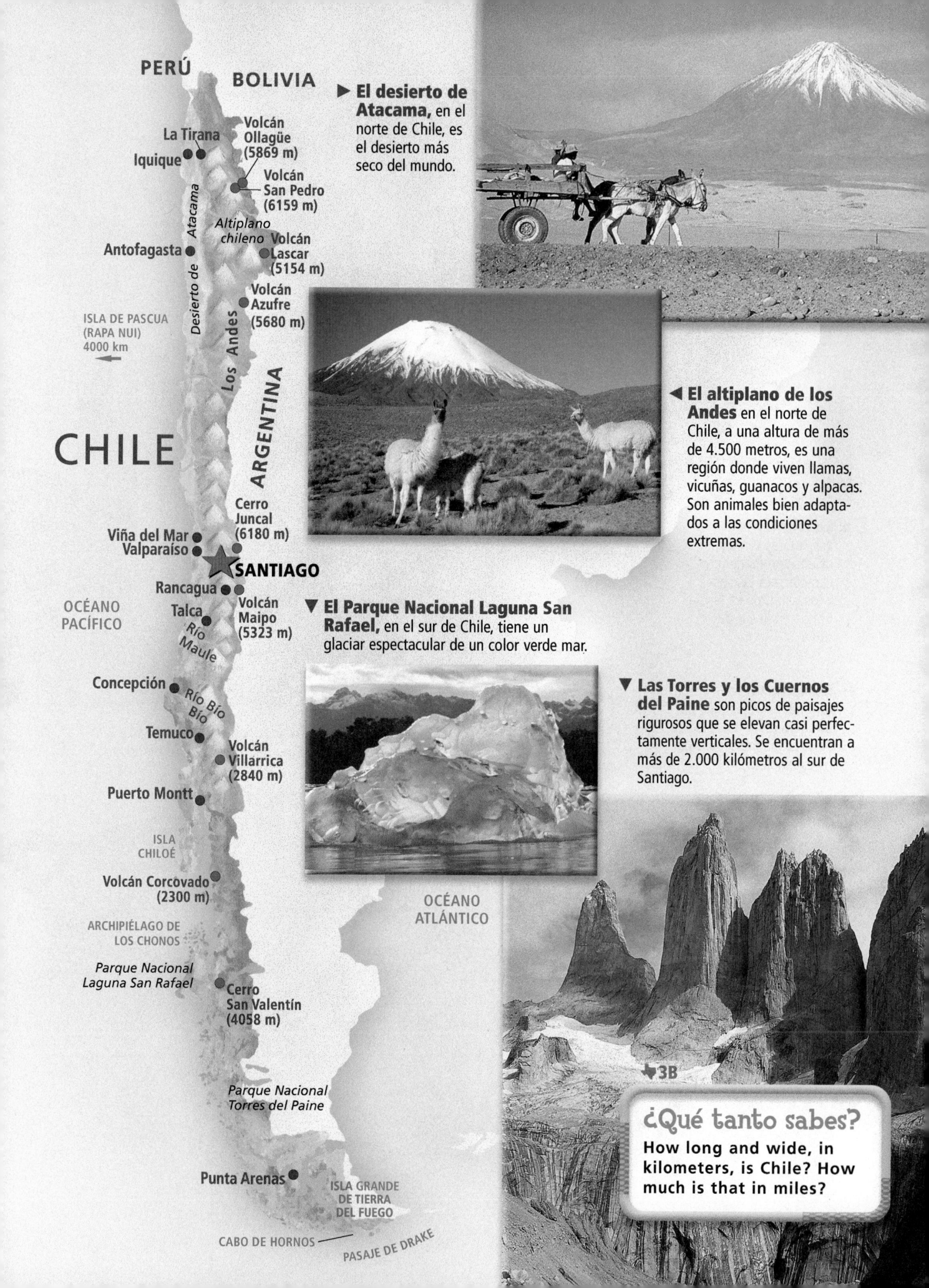

▶ **El desierto de Atacama,** en el norte de Chile, es el desierto más seco del mundo.

◀ **El altiplano de los Andes** en el norte de Chile, a una altura de más de 4.500 metros, es una región donde viven llamas, vicuñas, guanacos y alpacas. Son animales bien adaptados a las condiciones extremas.

▼ **El Parque Nacional Laguna San Rafael,** en el sur de Chile, tiene un glaciar espectacular de un color verde mar.

▼ **Las Torres y los Cuernos del Paine** son picos de paisajes rigurosos que se elevan casi perfectamente verticales. Se encuentran a más de 2.000 kilómetros al sur de Santiago.

¿Qué tanto sabes?

How long and wide, in kilometers, is Chile? How much is that in miles?

A conocer Chile

La arquitectura

▲ **La isla Chiloé** Los colores vivos y los diseños en madera caracterizan las casas y los palafitos en la isla Chiloé en el sur de Chile.

► **En Iquique,** en la costa norteña, hay ejemplos de la arquitectura mudéjar, un estilo árabe importado por los españoles.

▲ **Lo moderno y lo antiguo** se mezclan en Santiago, creando un ambiente casi europeo.

La comida

► **Platos con mariscos** como el curanto son muy comunes en Chile debido a la gran extensión de su costa.

► **El pastel de choclo** es un plato típico que se prepara con carne y maíz.

Las celebraciones

Interactive TUTOR

Visit Holt Online
go.hrw.com
KEYWORD: EXP1 CH5
Photo Tour

▲ **La Fiesta de La Tirana** se celebra con bailes que tienen sus raíces en los ritmos de ceremonias incaicas, el carnaval chino y las fiestas diabladas de España.

◀ **Los mapuches,** habitantes indígenas de Chile, conservan sus costumbres a través de los festivales, la música, la artesanía y los trajes tradicionales.

¿Sabías que...?

The Mapuches of middle Chile successfully stopped the southern expansion of the Inca Empire at the Río Maule. They are also known for their bravery in the struggle against Spanish and Chilean forces from the early 1500s to the 1880s.

Las bellas artes

▲ **Pablo Neruda (1904-1973) y Gabriela Mistral (1889-1957)** son dos famosos poetas chilenos. Ambos ganaron el Premio Nóbel de literatura.

▶ **Pedro Lira (1845-1912)** ganó fama internacional cuando recibió una medalla en la Exposición Universal de París con su retrato *La fundación de Santiago.*

Conexión Música

TEKS Focus
4B Demonstrate understanding of the concept of culture through comparisons

On September 11, 1973, the Chilean army under Augusto Pinochet toppled the elected government of Salvador Allende. Chile was ruled by a dictatorship until 1990. The politically inspired music known as ***la nueva canción chilena*** lost one of its best known representatives, Víctor Jara, in the repression following the coup. This mural in Santiago is about Jara's music. In your library or on the Internet, try to find a Víctor Jara song. How does it compare to political songs in the United States? **2B, 4B**

Capítulo 5

En casa con la familia

OBJETIVOS

In this chapter you will learn to

- describe people and family relationships
- talk about where you and others live
- talk about your responsibilities

And you will use

- possessive adjectives
- stem-changing verbs: **almorzar, dormir, volver, merendar, entender,** and **empezar**
- **estar** with prepositions
- negation with **nunca, tampoco, nada,** and **nadie**
- **tocar** and **parecer**

¿Qué ves en la foto?

- ¿Qué hacen los muchachos en el parque?
- ¿Qué le gusta hacer a la muchacha?
- ¿Tienen hambre? ¿Tienen prisa?

Texas

TEKS Look for the ✦ next to each activity to learn how it can help you achieve the goals of the **Texas Essential Knowledge and Skills,** found on page xxiii.

Visit Holt Online
go.hrw.com
KEYWORD: EXP1 CH5
Online Edition

Una familia chilena en Santiago, Chile

Objetivos
Describing people and family relationships

Vocabulario en acción 1

ExpresaVisión

La familia Pérez

Hola. Soy Julia Pérez. Ésta es mi familia.

el/la perro(a)

mis abuelos

mi abuelo Augusto

mi abuela Rosa

el/la gato(a)

mis padres

mis tíos

mi padre (papá) Rigoberto

mi madre (mamá) María, la hija de Augusto y Rosa

mi tío Arturo, el hijo de Augusto y Rosa

mi tía Delia

mis hermanos y yo

mis primos

yo, Julia, la nieta de Augusto y Rosa

mi hermano mayor Juan, el nieto de Augusto y Rosa

mi hermana menor Orieta, la nieta de Augusto y Rosa

mi primo José, el sobrino de mis padres

mi prima Mari, la sobrina de mis padres

▶ **Vocabulario adicional** — La familia, p. R9

Visit Holt Online
go.hrw.com
KEYWORD: EXP1 CH5
Vocabulario 1 practice

Tiene los ojos...

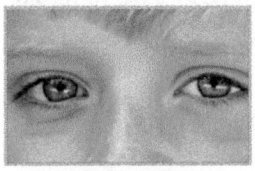
azules

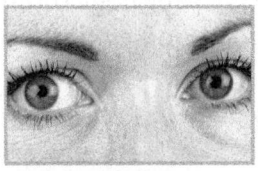
verdes

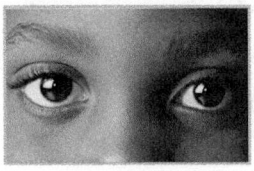
negros

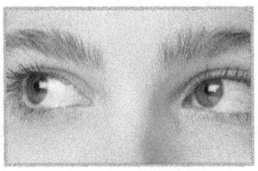
de color café

Tiene el pelo...

castaño

canoso

negro

largo

corto

Más vocabulario...

¿Cómo es?

ciego(a)	*blind*	**sordo(a)**	*deaf*
gordo(a)	*fat*	**travieso(a)**	*mischievous*
joven	*young*	**viejo(a)**	*old*

Texas También se puede decir...

In Spain, there are several words for *eyeglasses:* **los lentes, los anteojos, los espejuelos,** and **las gafas.**

Some Spanish speakers say **ojos marrones** instead of **ojos de color café,** and in Texas they say **ojos cafés.** In Texas and Mexico, **ojos borrados** are hazel eyes.

¡Exprésate!

To ask about people and family relationships	To respond
¿Cuántas personas hay en tu familia? *How many people are in your family?*	**En mi familia somos cuatro personas.** *There are four people in my family.*
¿Cómo es tu familia? *What is your family like?*	**Somos delgados y tenemos el pelo rubio. Todos usamos lentes. Mi hermana María está en una silla de ruedas.** *We are thin and have blond hair. We all wear glasses. My sister María is in a wheelchair.*
¿Cómo es tu tía? *What is your aunt like?*	**Es profesora. Es una persona callada. Ella y mi tío tienen dos hijos pero no tienen nietos.** *She's a teacher. She's a quiet person. She and my uncle have two children, but they don't have any grandchildren.*

Interactive TUTOR

Online
Vocabulario y gramática, pp. 49–51

▶ **Vocabulario adicional** — Profesiones, p. R10

Nota cultural

The system of Hispanic surnames **(apellidos)** gives information about both parents' families. In most Latin American countries, people use both their parents' names, as in the name María Baraona Uribe, in which Baraona is the father's last name and Uribe is the mother's maiden name. Notice that, in this case, María uses her father's name as her first last name. In the United States, the custom is to use only the father's last name, and Hispanics in the U.S. sometimes use their mother's maiden name as their middle name. Compare María's name to yours. 4B

1 ¿Cierto o falso? 1B

Escuchemos Mira el árbol genealógico *(family tree)* y escucha las oraciones. Indica si cada oración es **cierta** o **falsa.**

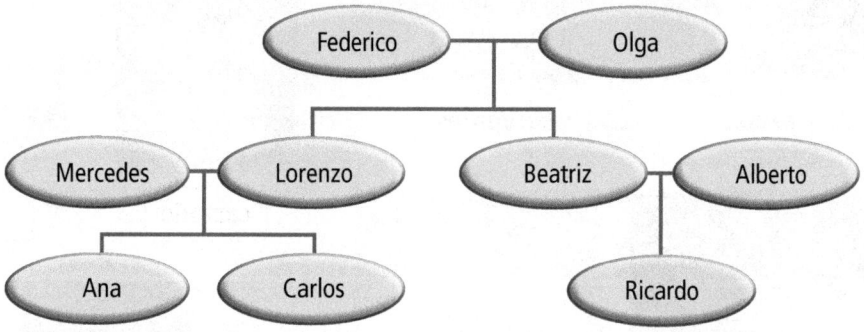

2 ¿Quién es quién? 1B

Leamos/Escribamos Contesta las preguntas con base en el árbol genealógico de la Actividad 1.

1. ¿Quién es la hermana de Lorenzo?
2. ¿Cómo se llama el tío de Ricardo?
3. ¿Cómo se llama la abuela de Ana?
4. ¿Quién es la madre de Carlos?
5. ¿Cuántos nietos tienen Federico y Olga?
6. ¿Cómo se llama el padre de Ricardo?
7. ¿Cuántos hijos tienen Mercedes y Lorenzo?
8. ¿Quién es el primo de Carlos?

3 Descripciones 1B

Leamos/Escribamos Completa la descripción de cada foto con una respuesta lógica.

1. Mi abuelo es _____. Tiene el pelo _____ y _____.
2. Mi tío es _____. Tiene un _____ inteligente.
3. Mi papá es _____. Usa _____.
4. Mi _____ se llama Barrigón. Es muy _____, ¿no?

1. mi abuelo

2. mi tío

3. mi papá

4. Barrigón

4 ¿Cómo son? 1C

TEKS Focus
1C Present information using familiar words, phrases, and sentences

Escribamos Use words from each list to write at least three sentences about yourself and your family members.

MODELO **Mi hermano tiene doce años. Es bajo y tiene el pelo rubio. Es travieso.**

yo	tener	____ años	delgado(a)
mi hermano(a)	(no) usar	los ojos	gordo(a)
mi abuelo(a)	ser	el pelo	travieso(a)
mi padre		lentes	serio(a)
mi madre		alto(a)	joven
mi perro		bajo(a)	viejo(a)
mi gato		ciego(a)	trabajador(a)
		sordo(a)	perezoso(a)

5 La familia Herrera 1C

Escribamos Imagine that you are an exchange student in Chile. This is a photograph of your host family. Write a letter to your best friend describing each family member.

MODELO **En la familia Herrera hay seis personas...**

Comunicación

6 Entrevista 1A, 1C

Hablemos Ask three classmates the following questions. Based on their answers, who is most like you? Report your findings to the class.

¿Se te olvidó? The preposition **de,** p. 64

1. ¿Cuántas personas hay en tu familia?
2. ¿Con quién de tu familia te gusta más pasar el rato? ¿Cómo es?
3. ¿Cuántos hermanos mayores tienes? ¿Cuántos menores? ¿Cómo son?
4. ¿Tienes un perro o un gato? ¿Cómo se llama(n)?

Objetivos
Possessive adjectives, stem-changing verbs

Gramática en acción 1

GramaVisión

Possessive adjectives

1 **Possessive adjectives** show ownership or relationships between people. They are placed before the noun.

Owner		Owner	
yo	**mi** libro **mis** libros	nosotros(as)	**nuestro** libro/**nuestra** casa **nuestros** libros/**nuestras** casas
tú	**tu** libro **tus** libros	vosotros(as)	**vuestro** libro/**vuestra** casa **vuestros** libros/**vuestras** casas
usted él ella	**su** libro **sus** libros	ustedes ellos ellas	**su** libro **sus** libros

2 While possessive adjectives refer to the owner, their form agrees in gender and number with the noun that comes after them.

refers to *agrees grammatically*

Martín vive con **sus** abuelos.

Carlos y yo vivimos con **nuestra** abuela.

3 **Su** and **sus** can take the place of a phrase with **de + person**.

¿De dónde es la madre **de Juan**? **Su** madre es de Puebla.

Online
Vocabulario y gramática, pp. 52–54 | Actividades, pp. 41–43

En inglés

In English, the possessive adjectives *his, her,* and *their* tell whether something belongs to a male, a female, or more than one person.

In Spanish, the possessive adjective **su** has many possible meanings *(his, her, its, your, their).* Context usually makes the meaning clear.

7 Nuestras cosas ➜1B

Leamos Complete the sentences to say that each person is looking for his or her own belongings.

1. Busco (mi/su) libro de español.
2. Buscamos (sus/nuestros) cuadernos.
3. Ellos buscan (tus/sus) mochilas.
4. Mi hermana menor busca (mis/sus) lentes.
5. Buscas (tus/vuestros) lápices.
6. Mamá busca (su/tu) reloj.

Visit Holt Online
go.hrw.com
KEYWORD: EXP1 CH5
Gramática 1 practice

8 ¿De Carolina o de Marta? 1B

Escuchemos Listen to the following sentences. Then, based on the photos, decide whether each sentence refers to Carolina's family or Marta's family.

la familia de Carolina

la familia de Marta

9 En mi familia 1B, 1C

Leamos/Escribamos Juan is talking about his family with a friend. Fill in the blanks in the conversation and then tell the class about Juan's family.

— Juan, ¿cuántas personas hay en __1__ familia?

— Somos cinco en mi familia: __2__ padres, __3__ hermana mayor, __4__ hermano menor y yo.

— ¿Dónde trabajan __5__ padres?

— __6__ madre es profesora. __7__ trabajo es muy interesante. __8__ padre trabaja con __9__ padre, mi abuelo. A mis padres les gusta mucho __10__ trabajo.

— Ustedes tienen una casa verde, ¿verdad?

— No, __11__ casa no es verde pero __12__ carro es verde.

Nota cultural

When many Spanish speakers talk about **la familia,** they are referring to not only their immediate family, but also their grandparents, aunts and uncles, and cousins. The members of the extended family often get together on a regular basis for meals or to go on outings. It is also common for grandparents or elderly relatives to live with younger family members. Throughout the Spanish-speaking world, elderly members of the family hold a place of honor and respect.

Comunicación

10 La familia de mi amigo 1A

Hablemos Interview a classmate about someone from his or her extended family. Find out the family member's name, what he or she is like, and what your classmate and he or she like to do together.

MODELO **—¿Cómo se llama tu primo?**
—Se llama Robert Miller.

TEKS Focus
1A Engage in oral and written exchanges of learned material to socialize and to provide and obtain information

Stem-changing verbs: o → ue

Interactive TUTOR

1 Verbs with vowel variations in their stems are called **stem-changing verbs.** You have already learned **jugar** where the **u** changes to **ue.** In the verb **dormir** *(to sleep)*, the **o** of the stem changes to **ue** in all forms except **nosotros(as)** and **vosotros(as).**

yo	d**ue**rmo	nosotros(as)	dormimos
tú	d**ue**rmes	vosotros(as)	dormís
Ud., él, ella	d**ue**rme	Uds., ellos, ellas	d**ue**rmen

El perro **duerme** mucho. *The dog sleeps a lot.*

2 Other verbs that follow this pattern are **almorzar** *(to have lunch)*, **volver** *(to go back or come back)*, and **llover** *(to rain).*

Cuando **llueve**, **vuelvo** a casa en el autobús.
When it rains, I come home on the bus.

3 Use **dormir hasta** to say you *sleep until* a certain time.

Los domingos **dormimos hasta** las once.

Online
Vocabulario y gramática, pp. 52–54 | Actividades, pp. 41–43

¿Te acuerdas?

In Spanish, regular verbs have **regular stems** and regular endings.

hablar

hablo	**habl**amos
hablas	**habl**áis
habla	**habl**an

comer

como	**com**emos
comes	**com**éis
come	**com**en

escribir

escribo	**escrib**imos
escribes	**escrib**ís
escribe	**escrib**en

11 Su rutina diaria 1B

Leamos Lee el mensaje que Bernardo le escribe a su abuela. Completa el párrafo con los verbos lógicos. Usa cada verbo sólo una vez.

duermo	almuerzo	vuelvo	almorzamos
duerme	almuerza	vuelve	volvemos
jugamos	dormimos		

Nuevo Mensaje

Archivo Editar Ver Insertar Formato Herramientas Mensaje Ayuda

Enviar Cortar Copiar Pegar Deshacer Deletrear Adjuntar Prioridad

Nosotros casi siempre ____1____ en la cafetería. Mi hermano ____2____ a las once y media y yo ____3____ a la una. Siempre tengo mucha hambre. Mi hermano ____4____ a casa en su bicicleta a las dos y media y yo ____5____ a las tres. A veces nosotros ____6____ a videojuegos después de volver y a veces yo ____7____ un poco en el sofá. A las cuatro y media vamos al parque por una hora. Nosotros ____8____ del parque a las cinco y media. Después de cenar hacemos nuestra tarea. Los sábados nosotros ____9____ hasta tarde. El perro siempre ____10____ conmigo.

12 Un fin de semana típico 1B

Leamos/Escribamos Complete each sentence with the correct form of the underlined verb. Sometimes the sentence requires a conjugated form and sometimes an infinitive.

1. Cuando llueve no tengo ganas de salir, pero no va a ____ mañana.
2. Voy a almorzar en el centro comercial. Yo siempre ____ con mis primos en el centro comercial los sábados.
3. Luego mi prima Juana viene a mi casa y jugamos al tenis. A ella le gusta ____ conmigo.
4. Después Juana y yo ____ al centro comercial. Nos gusta ir de compras. Pero nuestros amigos no vuelven.
5. Luego yo ____ a mi casa y Juana vuelve a su casa.
6. Cuando vuelvo a casa por la tarde siempre quiero dormir un poco. Yo ____ mucho por la tarde los sábados.
7. Por la noche mis hermanos ____ a videojuegos. No juego con ellos porque no me gustan los videojuegos.
8. Los domingos, mi hermana mayor y yo no ____ hasta tarde porque nos gusta correr en el parque por la mañana. Mi hermano sí duerme hasta muy tarde porque es muy perezoso.

In Texas, many Mexican-American extended families get together often. **Abuelitos** and **abuelitas** often live with their children and grandchildren. When many people speak of their **familia,** they have in mind their **tíos, tías, primos,** and **primas** as well as their immediate family. A first cousin has almost the same status in the family as a sibling. How does this compare to other families you know? 4B

Comunicación

13 ¿Quién de tu familia...? 1A

Hablemos Interview your partner using the photos and question words as a guide. Your partner should talk about what he or she and at least two other family members do. Then switch roles.

MODELO **—¿Con qué frecuencia juegas al básquetbol?**
—Mi hermano y yo a veces jugamos al básquetbol. Mi madre nunca juega al básquetbol.

¿con qué frecuencia?

a. ¿dónde?

b. ¿con qué frecuencia?

c. ¿mucho? ¿poco?

d. ¿a qué hora?

Stem-changing verbs: e → ie

Interactive TUTOR

1 Some verbs show a vowel stem change from **e** to **ie**, such as **empezar** *(to begin, to start)*, **merendar** *(to have a snack)*, **entender** *(to understand)* and **querer** *(to want)*. The **e** changes to **ie** in all but the **nosotros(as)** and **vosotros(as)** forms.

yo	emp**ie**zo	nosotros(as)	empezamos
tú	emp**ie**zas	vosotros(as)	empezáis
Ud., él, ella	emp**ie**za	Uds., ellos, ellas	emp**ie**zan

—¿A qué hora **empieza** la película? —**Empieza** a las siete.
What time does the movie start? *It starts at seven o'clock.*

Tengo que estudiar más. No **entiendo** nada en la clase de francés.

2 You can also use **empezar a** followed by an **infinitive** to say what you or others start to do.

—¿A qué hora **empiezan a trabajar** tus padres?

—**Empiezan a trabajar** a las ocho de la mañana.

Online
Vocabulario y gramática, pp. 52–54 | Actividades, pp. 41–43

¿Te acuerdas?

The verb **tener** is also an **e → ie** stem-changing verb. It is irregular in the **yo** form.

tengo	tenemos
t**ie**nes	tenéis
t**ie**ne	t**ie**nen

14 Después de clases ➜1B

Leamos/Hablemos Complete the conversation using the correct verbs from the box. One verb will be used twice.

jugamos quieres merendamos tengo tienes empieza entiendo

—Hola, Guillermo.
—Hola, Fernando. ¿Cómo estás?
—Más o menos. Esta tarde __1__ mucha hambre.
—Sí, yo también. ¿Qué tal si __2__ algo? Hay fruta en la mesa.
—Sí, buena idea. Y después de comer, ¿(tú) __3__ ir al cine conmigo? La película "El perro invisible" __4__ a las cinco.
—No, no __5__ ganas de ver una película.
—Si no __6__ ganas de ir al cine, ¿quieres jugar al básquetbol? Tengo un partido mañana y necesito practicar.
—Sí, está bien. ¿Qué tal si __7__ una hora? Luego tengo que estudiar.
—¿Por qué tienes que estudiar esta tarde?
—Porque mañana hay un examen en la clase de historia y yo no __8__ nada. Es una clase difícil.

15 ¿A qué hora? 1B

6:30 A.M.

Leamos/Hablemos Mira las fotos y contesta las siguientes preguntas. *¿Se te olvidó?* a + time, p. 128

MODELO **¿Hasta qué hora duerme Gabi los lunes? Los lunes Gabi duerme hasta las seis y media de la mañana.**

1. ¿A qué hora merienda?
2. ¿A qué hora empieza a hacer su tarea?
3. ¿A qué hora tiene su ensayo de banda?
4. ¿A qué hora empieza la primera clase de Gabi?
5. ¿A qué hora almuerza?
6. ¿Qué quiere hacer Gabi después de hacer su tarea?

8:10 A.M.

11:45 A.M.

3:00 P.M.

4:20 P.M.

7:00 P.M.

8:30 P.M.

Comunicación

16 Entrevista 1A, 1C

Hablemos Use the questions from Activity 15 to ask your partner about his or her daily routine. Then report to the class what you found out.

MODELO **—¿Hasta qué hora duermes los lunes?**
—Los lunes duermo hasta las seis y media.

TEKS Focus
1A Engage in oral and written exchanges of learned material to socialize and to provide and obtain information

Cultura

VideoCultura

Comparaciones

Una familia unida

¿Quiénes son los miembros de tu familia y cómo son? 2A

In Spain and in Latin America, it is not uncommon to see extended families sharing a house or an apartment. Young adults often continue to live at home with their parents even after graduating from college. One reason for this is the cost of housing relative to income in Spain and Latin America. Many young people simply don't make enough money to live in their own homes or apartments. What advantages and disadvantages do you see to having a large extended family living together? Think about this question as you listen to several Spanish speakers talk about their families.

Amaru
Santiago, Chile

¿Quiénes son los miembros de tu familia?

Bueno, está mi papá, mi mamá y tengo dos hermanos y una hermana.

¿Cómo son ellos?

Bueno, mi mamá es muy trabajadora. Ella es pequeña y es muy linda. Mi hermano pequeño es muy grande, muy simpático, pero un poco travieso.

¿Tienes mascotas?

Tengo dos gatos y dos perros.

¿Con qué frecuencia ves a tus tíos y a tus primos?

Bueno, los veo más o menos un domingo al mes.

¿Se llevan bien ustedes?

Bueno, no nos vemos mucho pero nos llevamos bien.

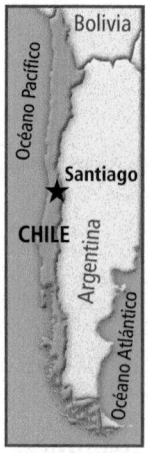

Cristian
Buenos Aires, Argentina

¿Quiénes son los miembros de tu familia?

Bueno, los miembros de mi familia son mi papá, mi mamá y mi hermana mayor. Después estoy yo. Me llamo Cristian. Y después está mi hermanito más chiquito.

¿Cómo son ellos?

Te puedo describir, por ejemplo, a mi papá. Es un hombre alto. Tiene el pelo negro, los ojos marrones y es un poco gordo. Y después te puedo también describir a mi hermana. Es una chica linda. Tiene los ojitos claros, tiene pecas, tiene el pelo castaño, y es un poquito más baja que yo.

¿Tienes mascotas?

Sí. Dos perros.

¿Con qué frecuencia ves a tus tíos y a tus primos?

Los veo una vez por mes, dos veces.

Para comprender 1B

1. ¿Quién es travieso de la familia de Amaru?
2. ¿Cuántas mascotas tiene Amaru?
3. ¿Cómo es el papá de Cristian?
4. ¿Cómo es la hermana de Cristian?
5. ¿Quién tiene la familia más grande? ¿Amaru o Cristian?
6. ¿Quién ve más a sus tíos y a sus primos? ¿Amaru o Cristian?

Para pensar y hablar 4B

Do you think Amaru's and Cristian's families are large or small? Are families in your community typically larger or smaller than theirs? Name two advantages to having a large family (six or more) and two advantages to having a small family (three or four).

Cuaderno para hispanohablantes, pp. 37–44

Texas

Comunidad

Surnames and Family Trees 3A, 3B

Genealogy is a fascinating way to learn more about Spanish-speaking cultures. Research the background of a Hispanic family—maybe your own, or that of a famous Hispanic Texan, like Juan Nepomuceno Seguín. Check out the Spanish American Genealogical Society in Corpus Christi; it is a great source of information. To do this research, you need to know that many Hispanic Texans changed their surnames when they came to the United States. Can you find an example of how a family's name changed? Does the new name reflect the family's Spanish-speaking roots?

The Seguín family crest

Objetivos

Talking about where you and others live, talking about responsibilities

Vocabulario en acción 2

ExpresaVisión

En casa

Visit Holt Online
go.hrw.com
KEYWORD: EXP1 CH5
Vocabulario 2 practice

¿Dónde vives?

en la ciudad

en el pueblo

en las afueras

en el campo

Texas También se puede decir...

The word for *bedroom* has many regional variations: **la alcoba, la recámara, el dormitorio, la pieza.** In Texas, **el cuarto** means both *room* and *bedroom.*

In Mexico, **el departamento** is the preferred word for *apartment.*

¡Exprésate!

To ask about where someone lives	To respond
¿Dónde viven ustedes? *Where do you live?*	**Vivimos en un apartamento pequeño. Está en un edificio de diez pisos.** *We live in a small apartment. It's in a ten-story building.*
¿Cuál es tu dirección? *What's your address?*	**Es calle Valdivia, número 56.** *It's 56 Valdivia Street.*
¿Cómo es tu casa? *What's your house like?*	**Es bastante grande. Tiene cuatro habitaciones, y un patio y jardín muy bonitos.** *It's quite large. It has four bedrooms, and a very pretty patio and garden.*

Interactive TUTOR

Online
Vocabulario y gramática, pp. 55–57

Más vocabulario...

cocinar
to cook

cortar el césped
to cut the grass

hacer la cama
to make the bed

hacer los quehaceres
to do the chores

limpiar
to clean

sacar la basura
to take out the trash

17 ¿Dónde? 1B

Leamos/Hablemos Complete each sentence with a logical place.

1. El carro y las bicicletas están en ____.
   a. el garaje **b.** la sala
2. Almorzamos en ____.
   a. el baño **b.** el comedor
3. Hay muchas plantas en las ventanas ____.
   a. de la sala **b.** del baño
4. Descanso y veo películas en ____.
   a. la sala **b.** el garaje
5. Preparamos la comida en ____.
   a. la cocina **b.** la habitación
6. Hay dos habitaciones en ____.
   a. la sala **b.** la casa
7. Hay un escritorio y una cama en ____.
   a. el jardín **b.** la habitación

18 Donde vivo 1C

Escribamos Complete the paragraph so that it's true for you.

MODELO **Vivo en las afueras. Mi dirección es calle Mercado, número 3232.**

Vivo en ____. Mi dirección es ____. Mi ____ es bastante ____. Es de ____ piso(s) y tiene ____ habitaciones. Tiene ____ baños. Casi siempre comemos en ____. Me gusta estudiar en ____. Mi familia ve televisión en ____.

¡Exprésate!

To ask about responsibilities	To respond
¿Qué te parece tener que ayudar en casa? *What do you think about having to help out at home?*	**A veces tengo que cuidar a mis hermanos, pero me parece bien. No es gran cosa.** *Sometimes I have to take care of my brothers and sisters, but it's all right with me. It's no big deal.* **A mí siempre me toca pasar la aspiradora en la sala. ¡Qué lata!** *I always have to vacuum the living room. What a pain!*
¿Qué te toca hacer a ti? *What do you have to do?*	**A menudo tengo que arreglar mi cuarto.** *I often have to pick up my room.*
¿Y a Juan? *And Juan?*	**A Juan nunca le toca lavar los platos. Me parece injusto.** *Juan never has to do the dishes. It seems unfair to me.*

Interactive TUTOR

19 En la casa 1B

Escuchemos Match each sentence you hear with the picture to which it corresponds. Not every sentence will have a matching picture.

a.

b.

c.

d.

20 Los quehaceres 1C

TEKS Focus
1C Present information using familiar words, phrases, and sentences

Hablemos/Escribamos Indica quién en tu familia hace los siguientes quehaceres y con qué frecuencia: **casi siempre, a veces, casi nunca** o **nunca.**

MODELO **Mi padre casi siempre corta el césped.**

1. cortar el césped
2. pasar la aspiradora
3. limpiar el baño
4. lavar los platos
5. cocinar
6. hacer las camas
7. arreglar la sala
8. sacar la basura
9. cuidar a los hermanos
10. limpiar la cocina

21 Reacciones 1C

Leamos/Hablemos Use the expressions from the word box to react to your list of chores from the previous activity.

MODELO **Mi mamá nunca cocina. Me parece injusto.**

Me parece (muy) bien.	¡Qué lata!	Me parece injusto.	No es gran cosa.

Comunicación

22 La casa ideal 1A

Hablemos Have your partner describe his or her ideal home. Ask whether it is in the city or the country, whether he or she wants to live in a house or an apartment, how many stories it has, and how many bedrooms it has. Then switch roles.

MODELO **—¿Dónde está tu casa ideal?**
—Mi casa ideal está en el campo.

Objetivos

Using estar with prepositions, negation with nunca, tampoco, nadie, and nada; using tocar and parecer

Gramática en acción 2

GramaVisión

Estar with prepositions

1 You've already used some forms of the verb **estar** to talk about how someone is feeling. **Estar** is irregular in the present tense.

yo	**estoy**	nosotros(as)	**estamos**
tú	**estás**	vosotros(as)	**estáis**
Ud., él, ella	**está**	Uds., ellos, ellas	**están**

2 The verb **estar** is also used with some **prepositions** to say where someone or something is in relation to someone or something else. Some prepositions are made up of more than one word.

detrás de	*behind*	**delante de**	*in front of*
cerca de	*close to, near*	**lejos de**	*far from*
debajo de	*underneath*	**encima de**	*on top of, above*
al lado de	*next to*		

—¿Dónde **está** tu apartamento?
—**Está detrás de** un edificio grande.

Online

Vocabulario y gramática, pp. 58–60 | Actividades, pp. 45–47

Nota cultural

Climate and ethnic traditions influence housing styles throughout the world. For instance, a home in southern Chile may show the influence of German or British immigrants, as well as the need for protection against the cold winters. Homes in the Amazon basin, on the other hand, may be built high off the ground and have good ventilation, providing comfort and safety from high water and hot weather. How do the homes in your area reflect its history and climate? 2B, 4B

23 Un día escolar 1B

Leamos/Escribamos Complete the conversation with the correct forms of **estar.** Then rewrite the conversation, answering the questions about yourself.

—¿Con quiénes almuerzas en el colegio?
—Almuerzo con mis amigos Raquel y Joel.
—¿A qué hora ___1___ ustedes en la cafetería?
—___2___ en la cafetería a las doce y media.
—¿Dónde ___3___ (tú) a las dos de la tarde?
—___4___ en mi clase de matemáticas.
—¿Y después de clases? ¿___5___ (tú) en casa o en el colegio?
—___6___ en el entrenamiento de volibol. Vuelvo a la casa a las cinco.
—¿Tu casa ___7___ cerca del colegio?
—No, ___8___ bastante lejos.

Visit Holt Online
go.hrw.com
KEYWORD: EXP1 CH5
Gramática 2 practice

24 ¿Dónde están? 1B

Hablemos/Escribamos Mira el dibujo e indica dónde está la primera cosa con relación a *(in relation to)* la segunda.

MODELO **la mochila/el bolígrafo**
La mochila está lejos del bolígrafo.

1. la computadora/el escritorio
2. la mochila/el perro
3. la silla/el escritorio
4. la planta/la ventana
5. el gato/la planta
6. los lentes/las revistas
7. la computadora/el bolígrafo
8. el perro/la silla
9. el diccionario/las revistas
10. las revistas/los lentes

25 En nuestra familia 1B, 1C

Hablemos/Escribamos Tell where you and your family members are at the following times.

MODELO **Los lunes a las diez de la mañana, mi padre está en su trabajo.**

1. Los viernes a las ocho de la noche, yo...
2. Los sábados a las seis de la mañana, mi madre...
3. Los miércoles a la una de la tarde, yo...
4. Los lunes a las diez de la mañana, mis hermanos...
5. Los martes a las dos de la mañana, mi familia y yo...
6. Los domingos a las tres de la tarde, mi padre...
7. Los jueves a las seis de la tarde, mis padres...
8. Los sábados a las diez de la noche, yo...

TEKS Focus
1C Present information using familiar words, phrases, and sentences

Comunicación

26 ¿Qué es? 1A

Hablemos Pick five things in the classroom. Tell your partner where they are, using a preposition. Your partner guesses what you're talking about. Switch roles.

MODELO **—Está cerca de la ventana.**
—¿Es el escritorio del profesor?

Negation with nunca, tampoco, nadie, and nada

Interactive TUTOR

1 **Nunca** *(never)* and **tampoco** *(neither, not either)* can take the place of **no**, or they can be added toward the end of a sentence that already has **no**.

No voy a la playa.	*I don't go to the beach.*
Nunca voy a la playa.	*I never go to the beach.*
No voy a la playa **nunca**.	*I never go to the beach.*
Tampoco voy a la piscina.	*I don't go to the pool either.*
No voy a la piscina **tampoco**.	*I don't go to the pool either.*

2 The word **nada** means *nothing* when it is the subject of a sentence and *not anything* or *nothing* when it goes after the verb. When **nada** is after the verb, **no** must be placed before the verb.

Nada es fácil.	*Nothing is easy.*
No quiero **nada** hoy.	*I don't want anything today.*

3 Use **nadie** to say *nobody* or *not anybody.* When **nadie** is after the verb, **no** must be placed before the verb.

Nadie quiere lavar los platos. Todos quieren ir al cine.
Nobody wants to wash the dishes. Everybody wants to go to the movies.

No hay **nadie** aquí. *There isn't anybody here.*

Online

Vocabulario y gramática, pp. 58–60 | Actividades, pp. 45–47

¿Te acuerdas?

The word **no** can mean *not, do not,* or *don't.* It goes before the verb or before the pronouns that go with **gustar**.

No soy de Madrid.

No quiero ir al cine.

A mí **no** me gusta la pizza.

27 Después de cenar 1B

Escuchemos Escucha las oraciones y decide si son **ciertas** o **falsas** según *(according to)* las fotos.

la hija

el hijo

la madre

28 No queremos hacer nada 1B

Leamos/Hablemos Completa las oraciones.

1. Mis primos no van a la playa. No voy a la playa (también/tampoco).
2. No quiero hacer (nada/nunca) hoy.
3. Mis padres, mis hermanos y yo tenemos el pelo castaño. (Siempre/Nadie) en mi familia tiene el pelo rubio.
4. Cuando llueve y hace frío, mi perro no quiere salir. A mí (tampoco/nada) me gusta salir cuando hace mal tiempo.
5. Siempre preparamos la cena en la cocina. (Nunca/Tampoco) cocinamos en el patio.
6. Después de cenar, me toca lavar los platos. (Tampoco/Nadie) me ayuda.

Un cine en Viña del Mar, Chile

29 ¿Vas a ir al cine hoy? 1B

Leamos Complete the conversation with your friend about this weekend using words from the box.

tampoco	siempre	también
nada	nunca	algo

—¿Vas a hacer __1__ el sábado?
—No, no voy a hacer __2__. ¿Y tú?
—Casi __3__ voy al cine los sábados. ¿Quieres ir conmigo?
—Sí, yo __4__ quiero ir al cine. ¿Sales mucho los sábados?
—Sí. Casi __5__ paso los fines de semana en casa.
—Yo __6__ paso los fines de semana en casa. Siempre salgo con mis amigos y mis primos.

Comunicación

30 ¿Y tú? 1A

Hablemos Entrevista a un(a) compañero(a) de clase sobre lo que hace.

1. ¿Qué días siempre tienes mucho que hacer?
2. ¿Qué quehaceres casi siempre te toca hacer en casa?
3. ¿Quiénes ayudan con los quehaceres?
4. ¿Qué haces cuando no tienes tarea?
5. ¿Qué haces cuando no tienes nada que hacer?

TEKS Focus
1A Engage in oral and written exchanges of learned material to socialize and to provide and obtain information

Tocar and parecer

1 To say what you have to do, what your duties are, or whose turn it is to do something, use the verb **tocar** followed by an **infinitive**. **Tocar** may be used like **gustar.**

me	toca(n)	**nos**	toca(n)
te	toca(n)	**os**	toca(n)
le	toca(n)	**les**	toca(n)

—A ti **te toca sacar** la basura hoy.
It's your turn to take out the trash today.

—¿A mí? No. Hoy **le toca** a Fernando.
My turn? No. It's Fernando's turn today.

2 The verb **parecer** means *to seem* and may also be used like **gustar.** It's very common to use this verb when asking for and giving opinions.

me	parece(n)	**nos**	parece(n)
te	parece(n)	**os**	parece(n)
le	parece(n)	**les**	parece(n)

Siempre me toca a mí lavar los platos. **Me parece** injusto.
I always have to wash the dishes. It seems unfair to me.

A mi hermano **le parece** una lata **cortar** el césped pero a mí me gusta mucho.
My brother thinks cutting the grass is a pain, but I like it a lot.

Online
Vocabulario y gramática, pp. 58–60 | Actividades, pp. 45–47

¿Te acuerdas?

The verb **gustar** uses these **pronouns** for the person who likes something. The verb agrees with what is liked.

me	gusta(n)	**nos**	gusta(n)
te	gusta(n)	**os**	gusta(n)
le	gusta(n)	**les**	gusta(n)

31 ¡Qué lata! ◆1B

Escuchemos For each picture, you'll hear two sentences. Tell whether they are **cierto** or **falso.**

mi hermana

mi hermano

mi papá y mi hermano menor

mi mamá y yo

32 ¿A quién le toca? 1B

Hablemos/Escribamos Tell your sister it's her turn to do the chores and your turn to have fun.

MODELO **A ti te toca limpiar el baño. A mí me toca jugar.**

1. descansar/cortar el césped
2. lavar los platos/ir de compras
3. cocinar/ver televisión
4. jugar/hacer la cama
5. leer/limpiar la casa
6. limpiar el baño/cantar

33 ¿Qué les parece? 1C

TEKS Focus
1C Present information using familiar words, phrases, and sentences

Hablemos/Escribamos Say how the following activities seem to you. Then name someone you know who has a different opinion.

MODELO **A mí me parece divertido ir de compras pero a mi padre le parece aburrido.**

divertido	fácil	muy bien	interesante
difícil	aburrido	fenomenal	pésimo

1. trabajar en el jardín
2. vivir en el campo
3. jugar con los perros
4. ir al centro comercial
5. jugar a videojuegos
6. hablar por teléfono
7. bailar
8. hacer ejercicio

Comunicación

34 Mi familia 1C

Hablemos Take turns with a partner. Imagine that one of you is the girl in the art below. Ask and answer questions about her house and family.

Novela en video

¿Quién será?

Episodio 5

ESTRATEGIA

Understanding Humor Understanding humor is an important part of enjoying a story on video. Sometimes humor can be created by contrasting what a character is actually experiencing with what a character *feels* like he or she is experiencing. As you watch or read, compare Sofía's and Nicolás's real household chores with how they see those chores. Does the comparison make you laugh? Do you feel the same way about household chores? 3B

En México

Es sábado, un día que a veces no le gusta mucho a Sofía.

Sofía Hoy es sábado. Los sábados mi familia y yo hacemos el quehacer.

Sofía ¿Ves a esa señora de pelo negro y ojos de color café? Ella es mi madre. Le gusta tener la casa muy, pero muy limpia.

Sofía ¿Ves a ese señor canoso con los lentes y la sonrisa graciosa? Es mi padre. No le gusta lavar los platos.

Sofía ¿Ves a ese niño travieso? Es Quique, mi hermano. A Quique no le toca hacer los quehaceres. ¡Me parece injusto!

Sofía ¡Qué lata! Nunca puedo descansar.

Visit Holt Online
go.hrw.com
KEYWORD: EXP1 CH5
Online Edition

En Puerto Rico

Es sábado en la casa de Nicolás, en San Juan...

6

Nicolás Hoy es sábado. Quiero salir de casa antes de que…

7

Nicolás ¡El césped! ¡Ay, no! Mi abuela es muy exigente. ¡Quiere todo perfecto!

8

Nicolás Mi papá es mecánico. ¡Está loco por los carros! Le gusta tener el garaje muy organizado.

9

Nicolás Un sábado bonito ¡arruinado! Y ¿para qué? ¡Para hacer labores! ¡Me parece injusto!

En Chile

As Marcos learns more about the Chilean candidate, he gets a call from the Professor telling him to go to Mexico next.

10

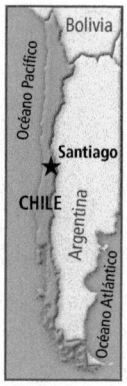

¿COMPRENDES?

1. Which statement by Sofía tells you something about her mother's personality?
2. Why does Sofía think her father doesn't like to wash dishes?
3. Why does Sofía call her little brother **ese niño travieso**?
4. Do you think Sofía is being treated unjustly?
5. How does Nicolás end up spending his Saturday?
6. Why are the attitudes of Sofía and Nicolás amusing?

1B, 3A

Próximo episodio

Can you guess who Marcos will investigate in Mexico?

PÁGINAS 218–219

Leamos y escribamos

TEKS Focus
3A Use resources in the language and cultures being studied to gain access to information

ESTRATEGIA

para leer Scanning for specific information means reading to find a particular fact—a price, a feature, or a location, for example. When that is your purpose, you do not have to read or understand every word. Simply scan the text until you find what you are looking for.

A Antes de leer 3A

Scan the following ads. What can you find about the prices and the locations of the properties?

CASAS Y APARTAMENTOS

AGENCIA INMOBILIARIA[1]

Zamora + Asociados
Calle Loma Linda 546
Tel: 5-55-69-32
www.vivienda[2]enlínea.hrw.com

A. Se vende[3] casa, estilo chalet, en pueblo tranquilo. 5 dormitorios, 3 baños, gran sala/comedor, sala de juegos, oficina, cocina moderna, garaje doble y piscina. ¡Precio incomparable!

B. Se alquila[4] apartamento remodelado. Av. Providencia 3192. 2 dormitorios, 2 baños, sala, cocina/comedor y garaje. A sólo tres cuadras[5] de la universidad. ¡Un sitio ideal!

C. Se vende casa en las afueras de la ciudad. El Rosal, calle Margarita 89. Aire y calefacción[6] central. 2 dormitorios, 1 baño, sala, comedor, cocina, garaje y magnífico jardín. Precio negociable.

D. Se alquila apartamento amueblado[7]. Nuevo edificio en el centro de la ciudad. Perfecto para hombre o mujer profesional. 1 habitación, 1 baño, sala, cocina y balcón con magnífica vista[8] de la ciudad. ¡Gran oportunidad!

E. Se vende pequeño condominio en zona residencial. Enfrente de un parque y cerca de la Escuela Primaria Salazar. 3 dormitorios, 2 baños, sala con chimenea, comedor, cocina y garaje. ¡Gran precio!

1 real estate company **2** properties **3** for sale **4** for rent **5** blocks **6** heating **7** furnished **8** view

Visit Holt Online
go.hrw.com
KEYWORD: EXP1 CH5
Online Edition

B Comprensión ✦1B

Based on each person's profile, match these prospective home buyers or tenants with the properties in the previous ads.

1. Una abuela que vive con su nieto de cuatro años y un gato.
2. Dos hermanos que empiezan sus estudios en la universidad.
3. Una mujer de negocios joven.
4. Una familia con tres hijos y dos perros grandes.
5. Una familia pequeña con dos hijos de siete y nueve años.

C Después de leer ✦1C

What kinds of things, other than size and cost, do people take into consideration when looking for a home to rent or buy? Describe the ideal home for your real family or an imaginary one. Explain why the features of your prospective home make it ideal.

Taller del escritor

ESTRATEGIA

para escribir Graphic organizers can help you remember details you may otherwise forget. You can draw bubbles containing the characteristics of the things you describe, then connect the bubbles to help you see your writing plan more clearly.

¿Qué les toca hacer? ✦1C

Write a paragraph describing your dream home. Say where it is, what it is like, who lives there with you, and the chores each person does, based on his or her likes and dislikes.

1 Antes de escribir

Draw bubbles with a description of your dream home, **(En mi casa ideal hay...)**; the likes and dislikes of the people who live there with you **(A mi papá le gusta cocinar.)**, and the chores each person does based on his or her likes and dislikes. **(A mi papá le toca cocinar.)**

2 Escribir un borrador

Start your paragraph with a detailed description of your dream home including where it is located and why that location is ideal. Then write about the people who live there with you, what each person likes and dislikes, and the chores that each person has to do.

3 Revisar

Read your draft at least twice. Check for spelling, punctuation, and correct grammar. Make sure you have included all the information requested.

4 Publicar

You may want to draw your dream home to display on a poster board with your paragraph. How does it compare to your classmates' dream homes?

Cuaderno para hispanohablantes, pp. 37–44

Prepárate para el examen

Repaso capítulo 5

Interactive TUTOR

1 Vocabulario 1
- describing people and family relationships

pp. 158–161

2 Gramática 1
- possessive adjectives
- stem-changing verbs

pp. 162–167

3 Vocabulario 2
- talking about where you and others live
- talking about your responsibilities

pp. 170–173

1 Imagine that these photos come from your family album. Describe the family members and tell how old they are. Write at least three sentences for each picture. 1B

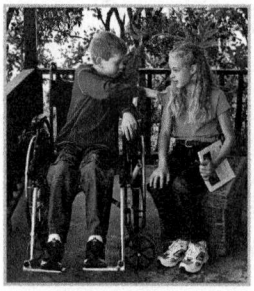
1. mis hermanos

2. mi abuelo

3. mis padres

4. mi gato

2 Pablo describe las actividades de él y de su familia los domingos. Completa su descripción con la forma correcta del verbo o del adjetivo posesivo. 1B

Los domingos, __1__ (mis/tus) hermanos y yo __2__ (empezar/volver) el día muy temprano. Mi hermano corre por el parque y después __3__ (empezar/volver) a casa y ayuda a __4__ (tus/mis) padres en el jardín. Vamos a la iglesia y __5__ (volver/dormir) a la una. A la una y media mi familia y yo __6__ (almorzar/merendar). Después de almorzar, los abuelos __7__ (volver/jugar) a juegos de mesa. Yo nunca __8__ (volver/jugar) con ellos. Me gusta más salir con __9__ (nuestro/mis) amigos. A mis amigos y a mí nos gusta __10__ (arreglar/merendar) a las tres y media.

3 Tell how often you have to do the following chores. If you never do them, say who does. 1B, 1C

1. hacer las camas
2. lavar los platos
3. sacar la basura
4. limpiar el baño
5. pasar la aspiradora
6. cocinar
7. cortar el césped
8. cuidar a mis hermanos

Visit Holt Online
go.hrw.com
KEYWORD: EXP1 CH5
Chapter Self-test

4 Completa las siguientes oraciones. 1B

1. A mí me ____ (tocar/parecer) hacer todo en casa.
2. Los libros de mi papá ____ (hacer/estar) encima del sofá.
3. A mi hermano le ____ (tocar/parecer) fenomenal salir con sus amigos.
4. El perro no quiere jugar ____ (siempre/nunca).
5. Mis amigos nunca hacen nada. Yo no hago nada ____ (también/tampoco).

5 Answer the following questions. 2A, 2B

1. What information do Latin American last names provide?
2. Does the term **familia** refer to a small or an extended family?
3. How do culture and climate influence homes?

6 Complete the paragraph based on what you hear. 1B

La casa de Sara está en __1__. En la familia hay __2__ personas. Hay __3__ habitaciones en la casa. A Sara le toca __4__. Le parece __5__. A su hermano nunca le toca __6__. A Sara le parece __7__.

7 Tell what José says about himself and his sister based on the drawings. 1C

4 Gramática 1
- using **estar** with prepositions
- negation
- **tocar** and **parecer**

pp. 174–179

5 Cultura
- **Comparaciones** **pp. 168–169**
- **Notas culturales** **pp. 160, 163, 174**
- **Geocultura** **pp. 152–155**

TEKS Focus
2A Demonstrate understanding of practices (what people do) and how they relate to perspectives (how people perceive things) of the cultures studied

Repaso

Gramática 1
- possessive adjectives **pp. 162–163**
- stem-changing verbs **pp. 164–167**

Repaso de Gramática 1

possessive adjectives	
mi/s	nuestro/a/os/as
tu/s	vuestro/a/os/as
su/s	su/s

Almorzar, dormir, llover and **volver** have **o** → **ue** stem-changes.
Empezar, entender, querer and **merendar** have **e** → **ie** stem-changes.

alm**ue**rzo	almorzamos
alm**ue**rzas	almorzáis
alm**ue**rza	alm**ue**rzan

emp**ie**zo	empezamos
emp**ie**zas	empezáis
emp**ie**za	emp**ie**zan

Gramática 2
- **estar** with prepositions **pp. 174–175**
- negation with **nunca, tampoco, nadie** and **nada** **pp. 176–177**
- **tocar** and **parecer** **pp. 178–179**

TEKS Focus
1B Demonstrate understanding of simple, clearly spoken, and written language when dealing with familiar topics

Repaso de Gramática 2

estar	
estoy	estamos
estás	estáis
está	están

prepositions of location		
al lado de	detrás de	encima de
cerca de	delante de	lejos de
debajo de		

Negation

nada	nunca	nadie	no	tampoco

tocar			
me	toca(n)	**nos**	toca(n)
te	toca(n)	**os**	toca(n)
le	toca(n)	**les**	toca(n)

parecer			
me	parece(n)	**nos**	parece(n)
te	parece(n)	**os**	parece(n)
le	parece(n)	**les**	parece(n)

Letra y sonido b v

Las letras b y v

The letters **b** and **v** follow these rules:

- At the beginning of a sentence, or after **m** or **n**, both are pronounced as *b* in the English word *boy:*
  Voy a casa., ¿**B**ailas mucho?, diciem**b**re, un **b**aile
- Everywhere else, their pronunciation is softer, with the lips barely touching:
  vi**v**ir, a**b**uelo, re**v**ista, a**b**urrido

Trabalenguas

El buen abuelo Vicente vende bonitas boinas baratas, baberos babosos, bolillos verdes, botas bellas y revistas aburridas.

Dictado 1B

Escribe las oraciones de la grabación.

Repaso de Vocabulario 1

Describing people and family relationships

el/la abuelo(a)	*grandfather (grandmother)*
los abuelos	*grandparents*
almorzar (ue)	*to have lunch*
callado(a)	*quiet*
canoso(a)	*gray-haired*
castaño(a)	*dark brown*
corto(a)	*short*
ciego(a)	*blind*
de color café	*brown*
delgado(a)	*thin*
dormir (ue)	*to sleep*
empezar (ie)	*to begin, to start*
En mi familia somos cuatro personas.	*There are four people in my family.*
entender (ie)	*to understand*
estar en una silla de ruedas	*to be in a wheelchair*
el/la gato(a)	*cat*
gordo(a)	*fat*
hasta	*until*
el/la hermano(a)	*brother (sister)*
los hermanos	*siblings*
el/la hijo(a)	*son (daughter)*
los hijos	*children, sons*
joven	*young*
largo(a)	*long*
la madre (mamá)	*mother (mom)*
mayor	*older*
menor	*younger*
merendar (ie)	*to have a snack*
negro(a)	*black*
los nietos	*grandsons, grandchildren*
el padre (papá)	*father (dad)*
los padres	*parents*
el pelo	*hair*
el/la perro(a)	*dog*
la persona	*person*
el/la primo(a)	*cousin*
los primos	*cousins*
el/la sobrino(a)	*nephew (niece)*
los sobrinos	*nieces and nephews*
sordo(a)	*deaf*
tener (ie) los ojos azules	*to have blue eyes*
el/la tío(a)	*uncle (aunt)*
los tíos	*uncles and aunts*
todos(as)	*everyone, all of us*
travieso(a)	*mischievous*
usar lentes	*to wear glasses*
verde	*green*
viejo(a)	*old*
volver (ue)	*to go back or come back*

Possessive adjectives . . . . . *See p. 162.*

Repaso de Vocabulario 2

Talking about where you and others live

las afueras	*outskirts*
el apartamento	*apartment*
el baño	*bathroom*
el campo	*countryside*
la casa	*house*
la cocina	*kitchen*
el comedor	*dining room*
la ciudad	*city*
la dirección	*address*
el edificio (de diez pisos)	*(ten-story) building*
el escritorio	*desk*
el garaje	*garage*
grande	*big, large*
la habitación	*bedroom*
el jardín	*garden*
la mesa	*table*
nadie	*nobody, not anybody*
el patio	*patio, yard*
pequeño(a)	*small*
las plantas	*plants*
el pueblo	*town, village*
la puerta	*door*
la sala	*living room*
la silla	*chair*
el sofá	*couch*
tampoco	*neither, not either*
la ventana	*window*
vivir	*to live*

Talking about your responsibilities . . . . . *See p. 172.*
Prepositions . . . . . *See p. 174.*

Integración

capítulos 1-5

1 Listen to Josefina talk about her family and then match her descriptions with the correct photo. 1B

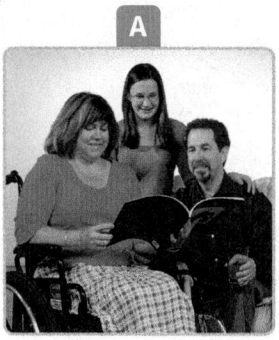

2 Esteban is writing to "Metida", an advice columnist. Read his letter and then answer the questions that follow. 1B

Querida Metida,

"Quiero salir más con mis amigos los fines de semana, pero no tengo tiempo. Los viernes por la tarde practico fútbol en el estadio. No llego a casa hasta las 8:00. Los sábados tengo un montón que hacer en casa. Arreglo mi cuarto y corto el césped. Ayudo a lavar los platos después de comer. Los domingos cuido a mi hermano menor porque mis padres juegan al tenis. Por la noche tengo que hacer la tarea. Me parece injusto pero, ¿qué puedo hacer?"

–Esteban

1. ¿Qué problema tiene Esteban?
2. ¿Por qué no sale los viernes?
3. ¿Qué le toca hacer a Esteban los sábados?
4. ¿Cuándo salen los padres de Esteban? ¿Qué hacen?
5. ¿Qué le toca a Esteban hacer cuando salen sus padres?
6. ¿Qué necesita hacer Esteban? En tu opinión, ¿qué consejos *(advice)* le va a escribir "Metida" a él para resolver *(solve)* su problema?

Visit Holt Online
go.hrw.com
KEYWORD: EXP1 CH5
Cumulative Self-test

3 In groups of four, create a conversation between a family and a real-estate agent. The family describes the ideal place to live and the real-estate agent suggests a house or apartment, based on what they want. 1A

4 What kind of information can you get from the painting by looking at it? Where are these people and what do you think they're doing? What do you think the painter wanted to capture? Write a paragraph in Spanish describing the scene. Include the weather, a description of the people, their ages, and what their relationship to each other is. 1C, 2B

Isidoro Molleda, Chilean painter. MarPau Art Gallery, Viña del Mar, Chile

Esperando a los pescadores, de Isidoro Molleda (n. 1930)

5 Complete the word web below about your favorite family member. Then, using the chart, write a paragraph describing this person. 1C

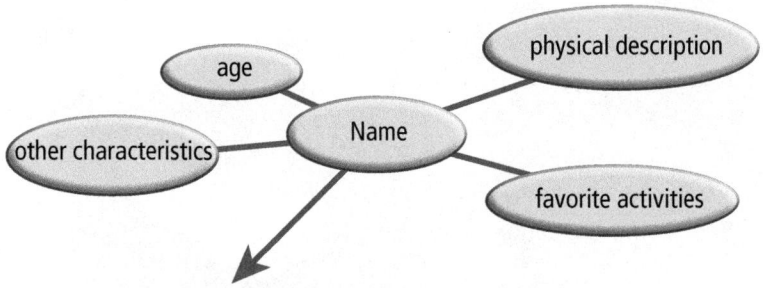

CONCLUSION: Why this is your favorite family member

6 **Situación**

You're having an outdoor birthday party for a relative at your house. Three of your friends volunteer to help you get ready. Decide who to invite, what chores you and your friends will do, what type of food people like, and what games you will have for good and/or bad weather. Act out your conversation for the class. 1A, 1C

TEKS Focus

1A Engage in oral and written exchanges of learned material to socialize and to provide and obtain information

GeoVisión

▲ **El volcán Popocatépetl** está en el valle central de México y es el segundo pico más alto del país con una altura de 5.465 metros.

Geocultura México

GOLFO DE CALIFO

Baja California

► **La Ciudad de México,** también conocida como el D.F., es la capital de México y se considera una de las ciudades más grandes del mundo.

Almanaque

Población
103.400.165

Capital
La Ciudad de México

Gobierno
república federal

Idioma oficial
español

Moneda
peso mexicano

Código Internet
www.[ ].mx

◄ **El jarabe tapatío,** el baile folclórico nacional, se caracteriza por ser muy alegre.

¿Sabías que...?

Antes de que Texas fuera una república o un estado, formaba parte de México.

◀ **La Barranca del Cobre,** una serie de cañones en la Sierra Madre Occidental, es más grande que el Gran Cañón en Arizona.

▲ **Agua Azul** Las aguas claras de Agua Azul en el estado de Chiapas forman una serie de bellas cascadas.

▲ **Tulum** Por toda la península de Yucatán se encuentran sitios arqueológicos de las antiguas civilizaciones mayas.

▼ **Teotihuacán** Las ruinas de la antigua ciudad de Teotihuacán reflejan la civilización que existía antes de la de los aztecas.

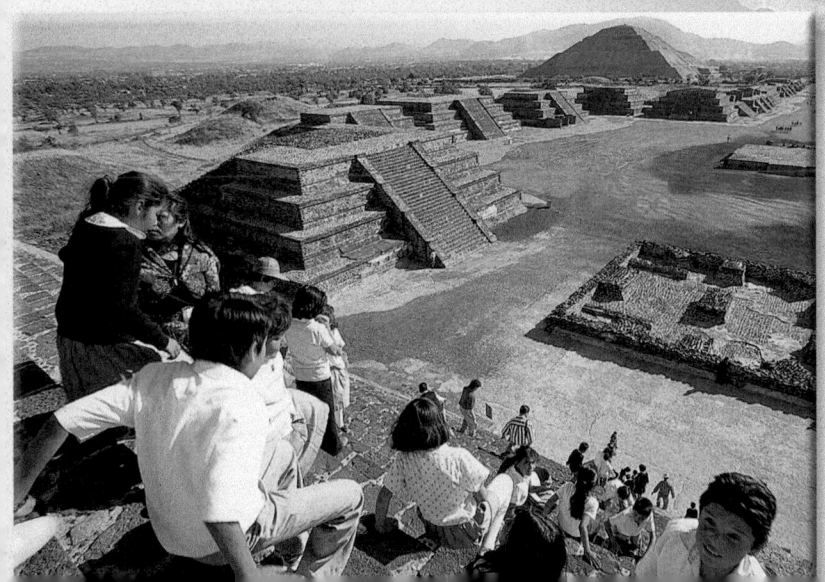

3B

¿Qué tanto sabes?

¿A qué estado mexicano vas para nadar en las aguas de Agua Azul?

A conocer México

El arte

▲ ***Vendedora de Alcatraces*** fue pintado por Diego Rivera (1886-1957). Rivera también es famoso por sus murales.

Rivera, Diego *Self-Portrait*, 1941, oil on canvas 60.96 X 42.8625 cm; painting photo source Smith College Museum of Art, Gift of Irene Rich Clifford; *Vendedora de Alcatraces*, photo © Archivo Iconografico, S.A./CORBIS; Diego Rivera paintings © 2004 Banco de México Diego Rivera & Frida Kahlo Museums Trust. Av. Cinco de Mayo No. 2, Col. Centro, Del. Cuauhtémoc 06059, Mexico, D.F.; Reproduction Authorized by the National Institute of Fine Arts and Literature, Mexico City.

▲ **Los antiguos murales mayas** de Bonampak, Chiapas, se encuentran en un templo antiguo.

▲ **Diego Rivera,** autorretrato

La arquitectura

▲ **La biblioteca de la Universidad Nacional Autónoma de México** en la Ciudad de México es la obra maestra de Juan O'Gorman. El mosaico cuenta la historia de México.

◀ **Casa-Estudio Diego Rivera y Frida Kahlo** La casa de los famosos pintores Diego Rivera y Frida Kahlo es un ejemplo del funcionalismo en México.

▼ **Taxco** La arquitectura colonial es testimonio de la llegada de los españoles al valle central del país en el siglo XVI.

Las celebraciones

Interactive TUTOR

Visit Holt Online
go.hrw.com
KEYWORD: EXP1 CH6
Photo Tour

▶ **El Festival Internacional Cervantino** en Guanajuato se dedica a Miguel de Cervantes. Se celebra con obras de teatro y danzas.

¿Sabías que...?

Casi un cuarto de la población mexicana vive en la región cerca de la Ciudad de México.

◀ **El Festival de La Guelaguetza,** o Lunes del Cerro, en Oaxaca reúne a comunidades distintas de todo el estado para bailar y celebrar sus raíces indígenas.

▶ **El Festival del 16 de Septiembre,** el día de la independencia de México de España, se festeja en todo el país.

La comida

▲ **El mole poblano** es un plato preparado con chocolate y chiles.

▼ **Las empanadas de flor de calabaza** son comida típica de Morelos.

▲ **Chiles en nogada** son parte de la comida típica de la Navidad.

Conexión Economía doméstica

Mucha de la comida que se come hoy en día en muchas partes del mundo tiene su origen en las Américas. Por ejemplo, las papas, el chile, el cacao, el maíz, los frijoles, la calabaza, el tomate y el pavo son de esta región. Así que los europeos no conocían el chocolate antes de que los exploradores lo llevaran a Europa. Piensa en una cena típica en tu casa y haz una lista de las comidas que originalmente vienen de las Américas. 3B, 4C

Capítulo 6

¡A comer!

OBJETIVOS

In this chapter you will learn to

- comment on food
- take an order and make polite requests
- talk about meals
- offer help and give instructions

And you will use

- **ser** and **estar**
- **pedir, servir, preferir, poder,** and **probar**
- direct objects and direct object pronouns
- affirmative informal commands with pronouns

¿Qué ves en la foto?

- ¿Dónde están los muchachos?
- ¿Cómo son?
- ¿Qué tiempo hace?

Texas

TEKS Look for the ★ next to each activity to learn how it can help you achieve the goals of the **Texas Essential Knowledge and Skills,** found on page xxiii.

Visit Holt Online
go.hrw.com
KEYWORD: EXP1 CH6
Online Edition

Una vendedora en el Parque Chapultepec, Ciudad de México

Objetivos

Commenting on food, taking orders and making polite requests

Vocabulario en acción 1

ExpresaVisión

¿Qué vas a pedir?

¿Qué prefieres pedir de almuerzo en este restaurante?

un sándwich de atún

una ensalada

una ensalada de frutas

la salsa

unas papas fritas

un sándwich de jamón con queso

Más vocabulario...

Está...

riquísimo(a)	*very good (tasty)*
salado(a)	*salty*
picante	*spicy*
frío(a)	*cold*
(muy) caliente	*(very) hot*

Texas También se puede decir...

There are a variety of words in Spanish to say *lunch.* In Texas and the Southwest **el lonche** is common, while **la comida** is used in Spain, Mexico, and much of South America.

A *sandwich* is called **un emparedado** in many Spanish-speaking countries. It is also called **un bocadillo** in Spain, or **una torta** in Mexico.

In Spain, **el jugo** is usually called **el zumo.**

Visit Holt Online
go.hrw.com
KEYWORD: EXP1 CH6
Vocabulario 1 practice

Para tomar, puedes pedir...

un jugo de naranja

el agua

un refresco

la leche

En la mesa hay...

un vaso
un plato hondo
un cuchillo
una servilleta
un plato
un tenedor
una cuchara

¡Exprésate!

To comment on food

Interactive TUTOR

¿Qué tal si pruebas un sándwich de atún? Son muy buenos aquí. *How about trying a tuna sandwich? They're very good here.*	**¡Ay no! Nunca pido atún. No me gusta.** *Oh no! I never order tuna. I don't like it.*
Aquí preparan muy bien (mal) la salsa picante. *They make very good (bad) hot sauce here.*	**(No) estoy de acuerdo.** *I (don't) agree.*
¡Qué ricas están las papas! *The potatoes are really good (tasty)!*	**Sí, me encantan.** *Yes, I love them.*
¿Qué tal está la sopa (de verduras)? *How's the (vegetable) soup?*	**Está un poco salada.** *It's a little salty.*

Online
Vocabulario y gramática, pp. 61–63

Nota cultural

The foods we eat often reflect our ethnic traditions and history. In Mexico, many foods trace their origins to pre-Columbian times. **Atole,** a drink first enjoyed by the Aztecs and the Mayas, combines corn meal, milk or water, and a flavoring such as chocolate, fruit, or even chile peppers. **Atole** is so popular that it even comes packaged like instant hot chocolate. What foods do we eat in the United States that were part of the Native American diet? ➤ 2B, 4C

TEKS Focus

4C Demonstrate understanding of the influence of one language and culture on another

1 Una dieta balanceada ➤1B

Leamos Escoge la comida más saludable *(healthful)*.

MODELO **la pizza/la ensalada**
la ensalada

1. las papas fritas/las verduras
2. el refresco/el agua
3. la sopa de verduras/el helado
4. la pizza/la ensalada de frutas
5. el sándwich de jamón/la ensalada
6. el sándwich de atún/la hamburguesa con queso
7. el refresco/la leche

2 ¿Qué tal está la comida? ➤1B

Escuchemos Con base en cada comentario, indica si preparan bien o mal la comida.

1. la sopa
2. las hamburguesas
3. el sándwich de jamón
4. la ensalada
5. el sándwich de atún
6. las papas fritas
7. la sopa de verduras
8. el helado

3 ¿Qué necesitas? ➤1C

Hablemos Indica qué necesitas para comer o servir estas cosas.

MODELO **un sándwich**
Necesito un plato y una servilleta.

1. agua
2. sopa
3. papas
4. helado
5. verduras
6. una ensalada
7. jamón
8. leche
9. una pizza

¡Exprésate!

To take someone's order	To request something
¿Qué desea usted? *What would you (formal) like?*	**Quisiera un sándwich de queso.** *I would like a cheese sandwich.*
¿Y para tomar? *And to drink?*	**Para tomar, quiero jugo de tomate.** *To drink, I want tomato juice.*
¿Desea algo de postre? *Would you like something for dessert?*	**Sí, ¿me trae un flan?** *Yes, could you bring me a flan?*
¿Algo más? *Anything else?*	**¿Nos trae la cuenta, por favor?** *Could you bring us the bill, please?*

Interactive TUTOR

Online
Vocabulario y gramática, pp. 61–63

4 En el restaurante 1B

Hablemos Pídele estas cosas al camarero *(waiter)* de una manera cortés *(polite)*.

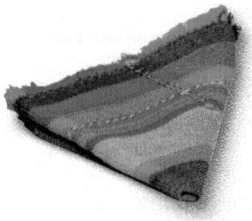

1.

2.

3.

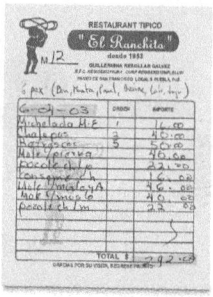

4.

5.

5 ¿Cómo se dice? 1C

Escribamos Estás en un restaurante con un(a) amigo(a). ¿Cómo dices lo siguiente en español?

MODELO **ask your friend how the ham sandwich is**
—¿Qué tal está el sándwich de jamón?

1. suggest that your friend try the fruit salad
2. tell the server you would like a flan
3. say that the soup is a little spicy
4. say that the French fries are delicious
5. say that they make very good desserts here
6. ask the server to bring the bill

Comunicación

6 ¿Qué desea usted? 1A

Hablemos Imagina que estás en un restaurante. Con un(a) compañero(a), túrnense para dramatizar una conversación entre un(a) camarero(a) y un cliente. Incluyan la siguiente información.

MODELO **—¿Qué desea usted?**
—Quisiera...

1. what you want to eat
2. what you want to drink
3. what you think of the food
4. whether you want dessert
5. whether there's anything else you need

TEKS Focus

1A Engage in oral and written exchanges of learned material to socialize and to provide and obtain information

Objetivos

Using **ser** and **estar**, **pedir** and **servir**, **preferir**, **poder**, and **probar**

Gramática en acción 1

GramaVisión

Ser and estar

1 Both **ser** and **estar** mean *to be*, but they have different uses. You use **estar** to say where someone is or where something is located, and to ask and say how people are doing.

La servilleta **está** en la mesa.
The napkin is on the table.

Estoy bien, gracias.
I'm fine, thanks.

2 You have used **ser** to identify people and things; to say where they are from; to describe what someone or something is like; and to give the day, date, and time.

Ricardo **es** mi amigo. **Es** de México. **Es** alto y simpático.

Es lunes. **Es** el 2 de marzo. **Son** las cuatro en punto.

3 Both **ser** and **estar** can be used to describe foods and drinks. Use **ser** to describe what foods and drinks are normally like.

—¿Cómo **es** el arroz con pollo?
What is chicken and rice like?

—**Es** riquísimo.
It's delicious.

To say how something looks, tastes, or feels at a particular moment, use **estar**.

—¿Cómo **está** tu sopa?
How is your soup?

—**Está** fría.
It's cold.

Online

Vocabulario y gramática, pp. 64–66 | Actividades, pp. 51–53

Nota cultural

Corn is a food staple in many Spanish-speaking countries, but Mexico claims it as its own. The first varieties of corn were grown near the present-day capital, Mexico City, and can be seen in the National Museum of Anthropology. In Nahuatl, the language of the Aztecs, one word for corn was **elotl** *(ey'-lotl)*, which became **elote** in Mexican Spanish. What traditional dishes in the United States use corn as a staple ingredient? 4C

7 ¿Cómo son? ¿Cómo están? 1B

Leamos Decide si las personas hablan **a**) de las características de un plato o **b**) del sabor *(taste)* en un momento específico.

1. La sopa de verduras es buena para ti.
2. ¡Ay! ¡Qué caliente está la sopa!
3. Me gusta el flan de la tía Elena. Está rico.
4. No me gusta el atún. Es muy salado.
5. Preparan muy bien la salsa aquí. Está deliciosa, ¿verdad?
6. No nos gusta la salsa. Es muy picante.
7. ¿Quieres probar mi sándwich? Está rico.

Visit Holt Online
go.hrw.com
KEYWORD: EXP1 CH6
Gramática 1 practice

8 ¿Ser o estar? 1B

Leamos/Escribamos Tu nueva amiga por correspondencia Carla, acaba de *(just)* escribirte. Completa el párrafo con el verbo correcto entre paréntesis. Luego di por qué se usa **ser** o **estar.**

Hola. ¿Cómo __1__ (eres/estás)? __2__ (Soy/Estoy) Carla. __3__ (Soy/Estoy) de Chicago. Y tú, ¿de dónde __4__ (eres/estás)? Hoy __5__ (es/está) lunes. __6__ (Son/Están) las diez de la mañana y mis compañeros y yo __7__ (somos/estamos) en la clase de español. La profesora __8__ (es/está) la señora Gómez. La clase de español __9__ (es/está) un poco difícil, pero me gusta.

9 ¿Cómo estás tú? 1C

Escribamos Ahora escríbele a Carla, contestando sus preguntas. También habla de tu horario, usando **ser** y **estar.**

10 ¿Qué tal está...? 1B, 1C

Hablemos Estás en un restaurante y el camarero te pregunta qué tal está todo. Contéstale.

MODELO **—¿Qué tal está el flan?**
—Está muy rico.

1.

2.

3.

4.

5.

6.

Comunicación

11 ¿Te gustan? 1A

Hablemos Escoge cinco comidas. Con un(a) compañero(a), túrnense para preguntar si les gusta cada una y decir por qué.

MODELO **—¿Te gustan los sándwiches de atún?**
—Sí, me gustan mucho. Son deliciosos.

TEKS Focus
1A Engage in oral and written exchanges of learned material to socialize and to provide and obtain information

Pedir and servir

Interactive TUTOR

1 In some **-ir** verbs with an **e** in the stem, this **e** changes to **i** in all the present-tense forms except those of **nosotros(as)** and **vosotros(as).** Two such verbs are **pedir** *(to ask for, to order)* and **servir** *(to serve).*

yo **pido**	nosotros(as) pedimos
tú **pides**	vosotros(as) pedís
él, ella, Ud. **pide**	ellos, ellas, Uds. **piden**

—¿Qué vas a **pedir**?
What are you going to order?

—Siempre **pido** una ensalada.
I always order a salad.

yo **sirvo**	nosotros(as) servimos
tú **sirves**	vosotros(as) servís
él, ella, Ud. **sirve**	ellos, ellas, Uds. **sirven**

—¿Qué **sirven** en la cafetería?
What do they serve in the cafeteria?

—**Sirven** muchas comidas diferentes.
They serve many different foods.

Online

Vocabulario y gramática, pp. 64–66 | Actividades, pp. 51–53

¿Te acuerdas?

Stem-changing verbs like **dormir** and **querer** do not change in the **nosotros(as)** and **vosotros(as)** forms.

d**ue**rmo	dormimos
d**ue**rmes	dormís
d**ue**rme	d**ue**rmen
qu**ie**ro	queremos
qu**ie**res	queréis
qu**ie**re	qu**ie**ren

12 ¿De quién habla? 1B

Escuchemos En cada oración, decide si la persona habla...

a) de ella misma *(herself)*
b) de otras personas y ella misma
c) de otras personas
d) de otra persona

13 ¿Qué pedimos? 1B

Escribamos ¿Qué piden estas personas en cada situación?

MODELO **Para beber cuando hace mucho frío**
(yo) Pido chocolate.

Para beber cuando hace mucho calor

1. yo
2. mis amigos
3. mi familia y yo
4. mi mejor amigo(a)

Para almorzar cuando todos tenemos mucha hambre

5. yo
6. mi mejor amigo(a)
7. mis padres
8. mis amigos y yo

14 ¿Qué servimos? 1C

Hablemos Carlos habla con un amigo de lo que sirven estas personas en las fiestas. ¿Qué dice? Usa la forma correcta de **servir** en tus respuestas.

MODELO **nosotros**
Siempre servimos helado.

nosotros

1. yo

2. tú

3. tus amigos y tú

4. mi hermano y yo

5. mis amigos

6. mi madre

15 ¿Servir o pedir? 1B

Escribamos/Hablemos Completa las preguntas con la forma correcta de **pedir** o **servir**.

1. En un restaurante, ¿ _____ (pedir/tú) una ensalada o un sándwich?
2. ¿Qué refresco generalmente _____ (pedir/tú)?
3. ¿Qué _____ (servir/ellos) en tu restaurante preferido?
4. ¿Qué _____ (servir/tú) en una fiesta?
5. ¿Qué _____ (pedir) tus padres en un restaurante mexicano?
6. ¿Quién _____ (servir) la cena *(dinner)* en tu casa?
7. ¿Qué tipo de sándwich siempre _____ (pedir) tu mejor amigo(a)?

Comunicación

16 Una entrevista 1A

Hablemos Usa las preguntas de la Actividad 15 para entrevistar a tu compañero(a).

TEKS Focus
1A Engage in oral and written exchanges of learned material to socialize and to provide and obtain information

Preferir, poder, and probar

Interactive TUTOR

1 The verb **preferir** has an **e → ie** stem change. It can be followed by a noun to say what someone *prefers* or by an **infinitive** to say what someone *would rather do* or *prefers to do.*

yo	pref**ie**ro	nosotros(as)	preferimos
tú	pref**ie**res	vosotros(as)	preferís
él, ella, Ud.	pref**ie**re	ellos, ellas, Uds.	pref**ie**ren

¿Prefieres jugo o leche? *Do you prefer juice or milk?*

¿Prefieres **salir** o **ver** televisión? *Would you rather go out or watch TV?*

2 The verbs **poder** and **probar** have an **o → ue** stem change. **Poder** is normally followed by an **infinitive** to say what someone *may, is able to,* or *can do.* **Probar** means *to try* something, as in *to taste.*

yo	p**ue**do	nosotros(as)	podemos
tú	p**ue**des	vosotros(as)	podéis
él, ella, Ud.	p**ue**de	ellos, ellas, Uds.	p**ue**den

¿Nos **puede traer** otra silla? *Can you bring us another chair?*

yo	pr**ue**bo	nosotros(as)	probamos
tú	pr**ue**bas	vosotros(as)	probáis
él, ella, Ud.	pr**ue**ba	ellos, ellas, Uds.	pr**ue**ban

¿Qué tal si **pruebas** la sopa? *How about trying the soup?*

Online

Vocabulario y gramática, pp. 64–66 | Actividades, pp. 51–53

¿Te acuerdas?

Tener and **dormir** are also stem-changing verbs.

Ella t**ie**ne 16 años.
Tú d**ue**rmes mucho.

The **nosotros** and **vosotros** forms do not have stem changes.

T**e**néis un perro bonito.
D**o**rmimos más los sábados.

17 Preferir, poder o probar 1B

Escribamos Completa las oraciones con la forma correcta del verbo entre paréntesis. Luego escribe una oración con el mismo verbo.

MODELO **Mi tío no _____ (poder) comer el flan. (nosotros)**
Mi tío no puede comer el flan.
No podemos comer las hamburguesas.

1. Analisa _____ (preferir) el flan más que el helado. (mis amigos)
2. Siempre _____ (probar) la sopa cuando comes en restaurantes. (mis amigos y yo)
3. Mi abuela no _____ (poder) comer salsa picante. (mis padres)
4. Nosotros _____ (preferir) almorzar en la cafetería. (usted)
5. Mis hermanas nunca _____ (probar) los postres. No les gustan. (yo)

TEKS Focus
1B Demonstrate understanding of simple, clearly spoken, and written language when dealing with familiar topics

18 ¿Qué prueban? ➜1C

Escribamos/Hablemos Basándote en los gustos de estas personas, di qué plato prueban cuando almuerzan en restaurantes nuevos.

MODELO **A Lucinda le gustan los postres. Ella... Ella siempre prueba el flan.**

1. A Andrés le gusta el atún. Él...
2. A ustedes les gusta el postre. Ustedes...
3. A Linda y a Jorge les gusta el jamón. Ellos...
4. A Elsa y a mí nos gustan las frutas. Nosotras...
5. Lucinda, a ti te gustan las verduras. Tú...
6. A mí me gustan el queso y la salsa de tomate. Yo...

Probando nuevos platos en un restaurante, Ciudad de México

19 Rompecabezas ➜1B, 1C

Escribamos Usa una palabra o expresión de cada columna para escribir seis oraciones.

MODELO **Prefiero tomar jugo.**

1	2	3
yo	preferir	la cuenta
mi mejor amigo(a)	servir	tomar jugo o leche
tú	pedir	una sopa de...
mis compañeros	querer	comida italiana
el (la) profesor(a)	probar	una ensalada de...
mis amigos y yo		algo de postre

Comunicación

20 ¿Qué prefieres hacer? ➜1A

Escribamos/Hablemos En una hoja de papel, escribe lo que te gusta hacer en las horas indicadas. Pregunta a tres compañeros(as) qué les gusta hacer a ellos(as). Trata de encontrar a alguien a quien le guste hacer las mismas cosas.

MODELO **—¿Qué prefieres hacer los viernes por la noche?**
—Prefiero... ¿Y tú?

1. los viernes por la noche
2. los sábados por la tarde
3. los sábados por la mañana
4. los domingos por la mañana

Cultura

VideoCultura

Comparaciones

Platos típicos mexicanos

¿Cuál es tu plato preferido y cómo es? 2B, 4B

«A buena hambre no hay mal pan» dice el refrán, y ¿qué mejor pan que un plato que nos encanta? Todos tenemos un plato preferido que no sólo es delicioso sino que muchas veces nos hace recordar a nuestra familia, nuestro país de origen y nuestras costumbres. En Estados Unidos, ¿qué platos son regionales o nacionales? ¿Son éstos algunos de tus platos preferidos? ¿Cuáles son algunos platos preferidos de los jóvenes en otros países?

Angélica
Ciudad de México, México

Dime, ¿cuáles son dos o tres platos típicos de México?

Bueno, está el mole, el pozole y los chiles en nogada.

¿Cuál es tu plato favorito?

Los chiles en nogada.

Dime cómo es.

[Los chiles] son muy ricos porque además de ser picantes, también son dulces.

¿Qué contienen?

Bueno, tienen el chile poblano, la carne molida, pasitas, acitrón, crema, nueces y un poquito de granada.

¿Es un plato típico de la región donde vives?

Claro, en el Distrito Federal se consume mucho.

Muchas gracias, Angélica.

No hay de qué, al contrario.

Visit Holt Online
go.hrw.com
KEYWORD: EXP1 CH6
Online Edition

Paula

Santo Domingo, República Dominicana

Dime, ¿cuáles son unos platos típicos en la República Dominicana?

El plato más típico de la República Dominicana es el arroz con habichuela y carne, que puede ser de res o de pollo.

¿Cuál es tu plato favorito?

El moro de guandules con pescado.

¿Me puedes decir cómo es?

El moro de guandules es una mezcla de guandules con arroz y un poco de salsa para el color. Y el pescado se hace con el limón y sal y ajo.

¿Es un plato típico de tu región?

Sí, es muy típico.

Muchas gracias, Paula.

Gracias a ti.

Para comprender 1B

1. ¿Qué plato se come mucho en el Distrito Federal?
2. ¿Cómo es el plato preferido de Paula?
3. ¿Cuáles son tres platos típicos de México?
4. ¿Cómo son los chiles en nogada?
5. ¿Qué se come con el arroz con habichuelas?
6. ¿Cuál es el plato más típico de la República Dominicana?

Para pensar y hablar 4B

Angélica and Paula tell us about their favorite dishes, both of which are typical of their countries. How are their favorite dishes different? Do they seem simple to make or do they seem rather complicated? Are there foods unique to where you live? What are they?

Cuaderno para hispanohablantes, pp. 45–52

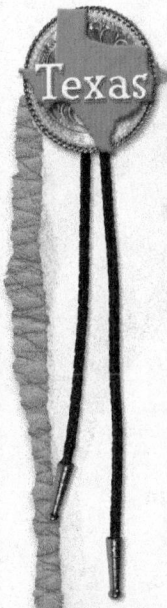

Comunidad

Regional Foods

All around Texas there are plenty of opportunities to eat Mexican and Tex-Mex food, but especially so in the open-air markets along the border. There you can ask for an **horchata mexicana,** a sweet drink made with rice, water, cinnamon, and sugar. Also all over Texas, many Mexicans and Mexican Americans make **tamales**—a traditional dish prepared with corn, a meat or bean filling, wrapped in corn husks, and then steamed. The preparation is quite a holiday event! Research some traditional foods from your city or area of Texas and find out what country they came from. 2B, 5B

Vendedor de frutas, Ciudad Juárez

Objetivos
Talking about meals, offering help, giving instructions

Vocabulario en acción 2

Video/DVD
ExpresaVisión

El desayuno en casa

Texas También se puede decir...

In Central and South America, as well as in Spain, **un melocotón** is used instead of **un durazno.**

In some parts of Texas, Mexico, and Central America, speakers refer to an egg as **un blanquillo.**

Nota cultural

In the United States, dinner is considered the main meal of the day, while lunch is a lighter meal. In Mexico and Spain, the biggest meal of the day, **la comida,** is served around 2:00 P.M. Family members come home from work and school to eat together. **La cena,** a light meal, ends the day around 9:00 P.M. Chileans and Colombians regard **la cena** as a formal evening meal for special occasions. Most days they eat a light supper early in the evening. How do your meal times compare? 2A

TEKS Focus

2A Demonstrate understanding of practices (what people do) and how they relate to perspectives (how people perceive things) of the cultures studied

21 Tengo mucha hambre 1B

Leamos Completa las oraciones con las palabras más lógicas.

1. ¿Qué hay de ____ ? Tengo mucha hambre.
   a. tomar **b.** cena **c.** pastel
2. Hoy vamos a almorzar ____.
   a. cereales **b.** pan dulce **c.** pollo
3. No me gustan los postres. Voy a comer ____.
   a. flan **b.** pastel **c.** un durazno
4. Ricardo siempre desayuna cereales con ____.
   a. leche **b.** zanahorias **c.** arroz
5. Me encantan las verduras. Siempre como muchas ____.
   a. naranjas **b.** espinacas **c.** manzanas
6. No me gusta el ____. Es muy salado.
   a. tocino **b.** pastel **c.** durazno

22 ¿Desayuno o cena? 1B

Hablemos ¿Cuáles de estos alimentos comes para el desayuno y cuáles para la cena?

MODELO **los huevos**
Como los huevos para el desayuno.

1. el tocino
2. el pescado
3. las espinacas
4. las zanahorias
5. el arroz con pollo
6. el pan tostado
7. el maíz
8. el bróculi
9. el café con leche
10. la carne con verduras

23 En el restaurante 1B

Leamos/Escribamos Sugiéreles algo del menú del Restaurante Don José a las siguientes personas.

MODELO **A Alicia le gustan los postres.**
Alicia, ¿qué tal si pruebas el pastel?

1. Alicia quiere probar comida mexicana.
2. De postre, Julio prefiere comer algo muy frío.
3. De tomar, Elena y su amigo quieren un jugo.
4. A Manolo y a mí nos gusta el pollo.
5. Carmen nunca pide carne.
6. A Julio le gusta el pescado.
7. Elena siempre pide algo de chocolate para el postre.

Restaurante Don José

PLATOS DEL DÍA
Ensalada de atún
Arroz con pollo
Tacos de pollo
Sopa de pescado
Tacos de verduras

BEBIDAS
Refrescos
Jugos
(de manzana, de naranja, de zanahoria)

POSTRES
Pastel de chocolate
Helado de mango

¡Exprésate!

To offer help	To give instructions
¿Necesitas ayuda? *Do you need help?*	**Sí, saca el pollo y ponlo en el horno (el microondas).** *Yes, get out the chicken and put it in the oven (the microwave).*
¿Puedo ayudar? *Can I help?*	**Saca el flan del refrigerador.** *Take the flan out of the refrigerator.* **¿Por qué no preparas los sándwiches?** *Why don't you make the sandwiches?*
¿Pongo la mesa? *Shall I set the table?*	**Sí, ponla, por favor.** *Yes, set it, please.*

Interactive TUTOR

Online
Vocabulario y gramática, pp. 67–69

24 ¿En qué puedo ayudar?

Escuchemos Mira las fotos y escucha la conversación entre Patricia y su madre. Decide qué parte del diálogo corresponde a cada foto.

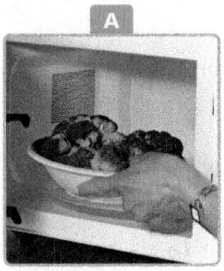
A

B

C

D

E

Comunicación

25 En tu opinión... 1A

Hablemos Con un(a) compañero(a), túrnense para contestar las siguientes preguntas. ¿Cuántas cosas tienen ustedes en común?

1. En tu opinión, ¿cuál es el desayuno perfecto?
2. ¿Desayunas en casa o en la cafetería?
3. Si no desayunas, ¿por qué no?
4. ¿Prefieres comprar el almuerzo en la cafetería o prepararlo en casa?
5. ¿Qué te gusta comprar en la cafetería? ¿Qué no te gusta?
6. ¿Dónde prefieres cenar cuando sales con amigos?
7. En casa, ¿qué haces para ayudar a preparar la cena?

Objetivos

Using direct objects, pronouns, and affirmative informal commands with pronouns

Gramática en acción 2

GramaVisión

Direct objects and direct object pronouns

1 Verbs can be followed by **direct objects**, the person or thing receiving the action of the verb.

Rafaela pone **la mesa**. Siempre pido **la sopa**.

2 A **direct object** can be a noun or a pronoun. Use **direct object pronouns** to avoid repeating nouns that have already been mentioned. These pronouns must agree with the nouns they stand for.

	Masculine	Feminine
SINGULAR	**lo** *him, it*	**la** *her, it*
PLURAL	**los** *them*	**las** *them*

—¿Quién va a pedir **el flan**? —Yo **lo** voy a pedir.

3 **Direct object pronouns** go before the conjugated verb. If there is an infinitive in the sentence, the pronouns go before the conjugated verb or are attached to the end of the infinitive.

—¿Quién prepara **los sándwiches**? —Yo **los** preparo.

—¿Quién va a preparar **la cena**? —Mi padre **la** va a preparar.

—Mi padre va a preparar**la**.

Online

Vocabulario y gramática, pp. 70–72 | Actividades, pp. 55–57

¡Te acuerdas?

Pronouns take the place of nouns. They have different forms depending on how they're being used in the sentence.

Ana es mi amiga. **Ella** es muy simpática. **La** llamo por teléfono todos los días.

26 ¿Qué comes? 1B

Leamos/Escribamos Contesta las preguntas con el pronombre correcto de complemento directo *(correct direct object pronoun)*.

1. —¿Comes huevos en el desayuno?
   —Sí, _____ como todos los días.
2. —¿Pides tocino con los huevos?
   —No, nunca _____ pido.
3. —¿Tomas leche en el desayuno?
   —No, nunca _____ tomo.
4. —¿Comes naranjas por la mañana?
   —Sí, siempre _____ como.

Visit Holt Online
go.hrw.com
KEYWORD: EXP1 CH6
Gramática 2 practice

27 ¿Qué van a traer? 1B

Escribamos Di quién va a traer las siguientes cosas a la fiesta de la clase de español.

MODELO **¿Quién va a traer el pastel?**
Yo lo voy a traer. (Yo voy a traerlo.)

yo

1. Miguel

2. Tomás y Raquel

3. Elsa y yo

4. Tú

28 ¿A quién le tocan los quehaceres? 1A, 1B

Hablemos ¿Quién hace los quehaceres en tu casa? Usa pronombres de complemento directo *(direct object pronouns)* en tus respuestas.

MODELO **¿Quién prepara la cena?**
Yo la preparo. (Mi hermano la prepara.)

1. ¿Quién limpia la casa?
2. ¿Quién pone la mesa?
3. ¿Quién corta el césped?
4. ¿Quién hace las camas?
5. ¿Quién sirve el desayuno?
6. ¿Quién arregla los cuartos?
7. ¿Quién saca la basura?
8. ¿Quién pasa la aspiradora?

Comunicación

29 ¿Cuándo lo hacemos? 1A

Hablemos/Escribamos ¿Con qué frecuencia hacen tus compañeros las siguientes cosas? Haz un cuadro como el siguiente, y con tres compañeros, túrnense para hacer y contestar las preguntas. Usen los pronombres de complemento directo en sus respuestas.

TEKS Focus
1A Engage in oral and written exchanges of learned material to socialize and to provide and obtain information

MODELO **preparar tu almuerzo**
—¿Con qué frecuencia preparas tu almuerzo?
—Lo preparo a veces.

1. preparar el desayuno
2. beber refrescos
3. comer pizza
4. traer el almuerzo al colegio
5. poner la mesa
6. almorzar hamburguesas y papas fritas

todos los días	a veces	nunca

Affirmative informal commands

Interactive TUTOR

1 To tell someone you address as **tú** to do something, use an **affirmative informal command**.

2 To form the affirmative informal command of regular or stem-changing verbs, just drop the final **s** off the end of the **tú** form of the verb.

(tú) hablas → **habla**	*you speak → speak*
(tú) comes → **come**	*you eat → eat*
(tú) pides → **pide**	*you ask (for) → ask (for)*

Pide un sándwich de pollo. *Order a chicken sandwich.*

Lava los platos. *Wash the dishes.*

3 Some verbs have irregular affirmative informal command forms.

tener → **ten** *(have)* ir → **ve** *(go)* hacer → **haz** *(do, make)*
venir → **ven** *(come)* ser → **sé** *(be)* salir → **sal** *(go out, leave)*
poner → **pon** *(put)*

4 Here are some verbs you might use to ask someone to help you in the kitchen. They all have regular command forms. Note that **calentar** is an **e** → **ie** stem-changing verb.

abrir *to open* calentar (ie) *to heat up* sacar *to take out*
cortar *to cut* mezclar *to mix* añadir *to add*

Corta las zanahorias, por favor. *Cut the carrots, please.*

Calienta el chocolate. *Heat up the chocolate.*

Online
Vocabulario y gramática, pp. 70–72 | Actividades, pp. 55–57

Nota cultural

In Mexico, many people buy snacks like cucumbers or roasted corn with chile powder, mango, pineapple, or watermelon from street vendors. For their afternoon snack, Argentines, Chileans, Uruguayans, and Colombians meet in tea-rooms to drink tea or coffee and eat sandwiches or pastries. Spaniards and Mexicans have a **merienda** around 6:00 P.M., a small snack such as **chocolate** and **churros** or **pan.** Compare your snacks to those in Spanish-speaking countries. Do you snack with your friends or family at a particular time? What do you eat? ➤2A, 4B

30 La ensalada de frutas ➤1B

Leamos/Escribamos Graciela ayuda a su hermano a preparar una ensalada de frutas. Completa sus oraciones con el mandato informal *(informal command)* correcto. Luego pon las oraciones en orden.

1. _____ (Servir) la ensalada fría.
2. _____ (Lavar) las frutas.
3. _____ (Probar) la ensalada para ver qué tal está.
4. _____ (Añadir) un poco de azúcar *(sugar)* a las frutas.
5. _____ (Cortar) las frutas en trozos *(pieces)* con el cuchillo.
6. _____ (Poner) los trozos en un plato hondo.
7. _____ (Tener) cuidado con el cuchillo.
8. _____ (Mezclar) las frutas con un poco de jugo de naranja.

31 ¡Sé buena estudiante! 1B

Escribamos/Hablemos Tu amiga quiere mejorar *(improve)* sus notas. Dile qué necesita hacer.

MODELO **estudiar mucho**
Estudia mucho.

1. hacer la tarea
2. ir a clase todos los días
3. salir temprano para el colegio
4. escuchar bien en clase
5. trabajar en clase
6. venir conmigo a la biblioteca
7. ser trabajadora
8. tener los útiles contigo

Comunicación

32 Necesito ayuda 1C

Hablemos Tus padres necesitan ayuda con los quehaceres. Con un(a) compañero(a), túrnense para decir qué deben hacer. Usa mandatos informales.

MODELO **Lava los platos.**

1.

2.

3.

4.

5.

6.

TEKS Focus
1C Present information using familiar words, phrases, and sentences

33 Te toca a ti 1C

Escribamos/Hablemos Escribe una lista de todos los quehaceres que te toca hacer en casa. Escoge tres que no te gustan para nada. Usando mandatos informales, dile a tu compañero(a) que le toca a él (ella) hacer esos tres quehaceres. Sigan el modelo y túrnense.

MODELO **—Lava el carro.**
—Saca la basura.

Affirmative informal commands with pronouns

Interactive TUTOR

1 You know that the **direct object pronoun** goes immediately before the conjugated verb. It can also be attached to the end of an infinitive.

—¿Siempre preparas **la cena**?

—No, no **la** preparo siempre, pero hoy sí voy a preparar **la**.

2 When you use a pronoun with an affirmative informal command, attach it to the end of the verb. Add an accent to the stressed vowel of the verb, unless the verb is only one syllable long.

—¿Preparo **la carne**? —Sí, prepára **la**.

—¿Pongo **los vasos** en la mesa? —Sí, pon **los** allí.

Online

Vocabulario y gramática, pp. 70–72 | Actividades, pp. 55–57

Barbecue (from the Taíno word *barbacuá*) is one of the most traditional foods of Texas. One way of preparing barbecue is to grill it outdoors over a fire made with chunks of mesquite or other aromatic wood. Mexican Americans normally serve **barbacoa** with jalapeños, salsa, beans, and tortillas. What other traditional foods are popular in Texas? **2B, 4C**

34 ¿De qué hablas? 1B

Leamos Identifica los pronombres de complemento directo en cada oración. Luego decide a qué cosa se refiere.

1. Ponlo en el refrigerador.
   a. el queso **b.** la leche **c.** el libro
2. Sácala del horno.
   a. la basura **b.** el tocino **c.** la pizza
3. Ábrelo otra vez.
   a. el durazno **b.** el refrigerador **c.** la aspiradora
4. Córtalas con el cuchillo.
   a. las zanahorias **b.** las servilletas **c.** la manzana
5. Sírvelos en el plato hondo.
   a. los cereales **b.** la sopa **c.** los refrescos
6. Mézclalo con el bróculi.
   a. el queso **b.** el flan **c.** las espinacas
7. Mézclalos en el plato hondo.
   a. los huevos **b.** las naranjas **c.** los tenedores

35 Ponlas aquí 1B

Hablemos Tu amigo te ayuda a mudar *(move)*. Dile dónde poner las siguientes cosas.

MODELO **el refrigerador**
Ponlo en la cocina.

1. la cama
2. las plantas
3. la comida
4. los vasos
5. el microondas
6. los libros
7. los videojuegos
8. las sillas
9. la mesa

36 ¿Qué hago? 1B

Escuchemos Escucha las preguntas de Nuria y escoge la respuesta más lógica.

a. Caliéntalo en el horno.
b. Sácalos del refrigerador y ponlos en la mesa.
c. No, todavía no. Ponla con las otras bebidas.
d. Sí, ponlas a calentar en el microondas.
e. Córtalas y mézclalas en un plato hondo.

37 El amigo desesperado 1B

Escribamos Tu amigo quiere preparar la cena para sus padres, pero no sabe cocinar. Contesta sus preguntas con un mandato informal y un pronombre de complemento directo.

1. ¿Caliento la sopa antes de preparar el pollo o después?
2. ¿Pongo las servilletas al lado de los platos o encima de ellos?
3. ¿Saco el flan del refrigerador antes de comer o después?
4. ¿Mezclo el café con leche o con agua?
5. ¿Preparo el pollo con zanahorias o con espinacas?
6. ¿Sirvo el helado con la comida o con el postre?
7. ¿Pruebo la ensalada antes de añadir el atún o después?

Comunicación

38 ¡Arregla la casa! 1A

Hablemos Con un(a) compañero(a), túrnense para decir cómo contesta el padre las preguntas de su hija. Usa mandatos informales.

MODELO **—¿Papá, qué hago con las frutas?**
—¡Ponlas en el refrigerador!

TEKS Focus
1A Engage in oral and written exchanges of learned material to socialize and to provide and obtain information

Novela en video

¿Quién será?

Episodio 6

ESTRATEGIA

Recognizing a Make-believe Situation In order to understand this episode, it is helpful to recognize that certain parts are make-believe. With the help of her little brother, the cooperation of her parents, and a little imagination, Sofía turns an ordinary event into a more interesting experience. As you watch the video, figure out which parts are make-believe and then see what problem Sofía's make-believe situation creates for her. 3B

En México

Sofía va a casa a preparar la cena. Marcos la mira para ver adónde va.

1

2

Quique Sofía, ¡es tarde! Mamá y papá están por llegar.

Sofía Ya sé, Quique.

Quique ¿Y la cena?

Sofía No te preocupes, Quique. No es tu problema. Yo la voy a preparar.

3

Quique ¿En qué puedo ayudar? ¿Pongo la mesa?

Sofía Sí, ponla.

Quique ¿Y el menú?

Sofía Ponlo en el comedor.

4

Sofía Señor y Señora Corona. Bienvenidos al **Restaurante Sofía.** Veo aquí que tienen una reservación para dos personas a las ocho en punto.

Sr. Corona Eh, sí, señorita.

5

Sra. Corona Señorita, ¿nos puede traer los menús, por favor?

Quique Aquí están los menús, señor, señora.

Sr. Corona ¿Qué tal están los tamales oaxaqueños hoy?

Sofía Riquísimos, señor, pero, malas noticias, no quedan tamales oaxaqueños.

6

Sra. Corona Óscar, a mí me apetece pollo con mole con arroz y tortillas de maíz azul. ¿Qué tal está el pollo con mole hoy, señorita?

Sofía No lo recomiendo. Está un poco salado.

Visit Holt Online
go.hrw.com
KEYWORD: EXP1 CH6
Online Edition

7

Sr. Corona ¿Y el bistec, señorita? Aquí dice que viene con puré de papa y zanahoria.

Sofía Sí, señor, buena elección, el bistec está delicioso, pero… hoy es viernes, y los viernes no sirvo bistecs.

8

Un poco más tarde...

9

Sra. Corona Pues, dígame, señorita, ¿cuál es la especialidad de la casa?

Sofía La especialidad de la casa son ¡LAS FLAUTAS! Y si no le importa, señor, aquí está la cuenta. ¿Me la puede pagar ahora?

En España

La profesora decide adónde va Marcos ahora.

10

¿COMPRENDES?

1. ¿Qué tiene que hacer Sofía? ¿Para quiénes? ¿Qué tiene que hacer Quique?
2. Cuando llegan los padres de Sofía, ¿cómo los saluda?
3. En realidad, ¿están en un restaurante? ¿Dónde están?
4. ¿Qué dice Sofía de los tamales oaxaqueños? ¿del pollo en mole? ¿de los bistecs?
5. ¿Cuál es la especialidad de la casa?
6. ¿Por qué crees que lo único que puede servir Sofía son las flautas?

1B, 3A

Próximo episodio:
Marcos sale para otro país. ¿Cuántos países más le toca visitar?
PÁGINAS 256–257

Leamos y escribamos

TEKS Focus
3A Use resources in the language and cultures being studied to gain access to information

ESTRATEGIA

para leer Consider the *genre* of a text before you read it. The *genre* tells you what kind of writing to expect. Some examples of different genres are short story, novel, poem, essay, and play. Knowing the genre of a text will help you predict what it's about.

A Antes de leer 3A, 3B

La siguiente lectura es una versión de una leyenda sobre Quetzalcóatl, dios[1] de las culturas maya, azteca y mexicana. Usando la **Estrategia para leer,** escribe una lista de las características que esperas encontrar en el texto.

La montaña del alimento[2]

Es una época muy difícil en la tierra[3]. Los hombres están desesperados porque no hay alimento y todos tienen mucha hambre. Van a hablar con Quetzalcóatl, la serpiente emplumada[4] y le explican que no tienen nada que comer.

Quetzalcóatl, dios compasivo, noble y generoso, decide ayudar a los hombres. Va a la montaña del alimento. Allí ve a un grupo de hormigas[5] gigantes que cuidan una fabulosa cantidad de maíz, la comida de los dioses. Quetzalcóatl les pide a las hormigas unos granos de maíz.

—¿Por qué quieres tú el maíz? —preguntan ellas.

—Mi gente tiene hambre —explica Quetzalcóatl.

—¿Son dioses tu gente? —dice una de las hormigas.

—No —responde Quetzalcóatl. —Son simplemente gente con hambre que vive sobre la tierra.

—Este maíz es sólo para los dioses —dicen las hormigas. —Busca[6] comida en otra parte.

Quetzalcóatl se va, pero no se da por vencido[7]. Vuelve a la montaña en la forma de una inmensa e imponente hormiga. Las hormigas le permiten entrar y el dios ve con admiración que hay granos de maíz de muchos colores. Les dice que nunca ha visto[8] granos rojos, amarillos, azules o morados y las hormigas, orgullosas[9] de su maíz, le dan un grano de cada color.

El dios vuelve rápidamente a la tierra y les enseña a todos a cultivar el maíz. Después de un tiempo hay mucho alimento y la gente de la tierra no vuelve a tener hambre nunca más.

1 god **2** food **3** earth **4** the feathered serpent **5** ants **6** Look for **7** doesn't give up **8** he has never seen **9** proud

Visit Holt Online
go.hrw.com
KEYWORD: EXP1 CH6
Online Edition

B Comprensión ✦3B

Contesta las siguientes preguntas con oraciones completas.

1. ¿Qué problema tienen los hombres de la tierra?
2. ¿Quién va a ayudar a los hombres? ¿Por qué?
3. ¿Qué les dice Quetzalcóatl a las hormigas y qué responden ellas?
4. ¿Qué pasa cuando Quetzalcóatl vuelve a la montaña?
5. ¿Qué hace el dios al regresar a la tierra?

C Después de leer ✦4B

Legends often reflect the values and beliefs of a culture. What values are reflected in this legend? Explain your choices. What are some similarities between this legend and other legends or stories you have read?

Taller del escritor

SALSA (para 4 personas)

4 tomates grandes
1 cebolla mediana
2 cucharadas de cilantro fresco
1 cucharada de vinagre
1 latita de chiles verdes

Corta el tomate, la cebolla y el cilantro. Añade sal al gusto. Mezcla todos los ingredientes. Sirve con tostadas.

ESTRATEGIA

para escribir Arranging your ideas in chronological order helps you map out a plan for your writing. When you give written instructions such as recipes, the ordering of elements becomes crucial.

¿Cómo lo preparas? ✦1C

You are invited to a potluck party where you are expected to exchange your favorite recipe with other guests. Write a simple recipe for a dish with clear instructions on how to prepare it.

1 Antes de escribir

List the foods you need to prepare your dish, then arrange them in the order you will need them. Write a command telling what needs to be done with each ingredient.

2 Escribir un borrador

After listing your ingredients, use command forms and adjectives to describe in detail the different steps in the preparation.

Para hacer una ensalada de frutas muy rica, usa muchas frutas diferentes.

3 Revisar

Exchange your recipe with a classmate to see if it sounds appetizing to him or her. Your classmate may suggest an addition to your dish. Check for spelling and punctuation as well as for logical order.

4 Publicar

You may want to illustrate your recipe and display it on a poster board in class or compile all of the recipes in a book. Consider testing a few in class or at home.

Cuaderno para hispanohablantes, pp. 57–68

Repaso capítulo 6

Interactive TUTOR

1 Vocabulario 1
- commenting on food
- making polite requests

pp. 196–199

1 Pide las siguientes cosas en un restaurante. ➤1B

1.

2.

3.

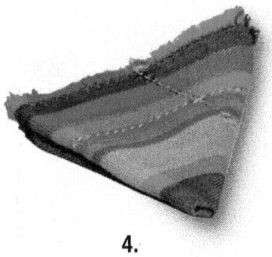
4.

5.

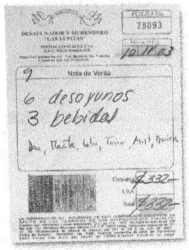

6.

2 Gramática 1
- **ser** and **estar**
- **pedir** and **servir**
- **preferir, poder,** and **probar**

pp. 200–205

2 Completa el párrafo con las formas correctas de los verbos del cuadro. ➤1B

poder	**estar**	**pedir**
ser	**preferir**	**servir**

Mis amigos y yo no ___1___ almorzar en casa porque siempre ___2___ en el colegio, y los fines de semana ___3___ cenar en el Restaurante Don Carlos. La comida ___4___ muy deliciosa allí. Yo siempre ___5___ una ensalada y me gusta también la sopa porque siempre ___6___ caliente. Mis amigos ___7___ el pescado porque les encanta. También ___8___ unos sándwiches riquísimos en el restaurante.

3 Vocabulario 2
- talking about meals
- offering help and giving instructions

pp. 208–211

3 Contesta las preguntas sobre lo que comes. ➤1C

1. ¿Qué desayunas?
2. ¿Qué vas a almorzar hoy? ¿Te gusta la comida de la cafetería?
3. ¿Qué quieres cenar esta noche?
4. ¿Qué te gusta pedir cuando vas a un restaurante?
5. ¿Qué prefieres, la carne o el pescado?
6. ¿Qué sirven Uds. de cena en casa los fines de semana?

Visit Holt Online
go.hrw.com
KEYWORD: EXP1 CH6
Chapter Self-test

4 Algunos amigos llegan temprano para ayudarte a preparar para una fiesta. Dile a cada uno qué hacer, usando mandatos informales y pronombres de complemento directo. ➜1B

1. ¿La sala? (limpiar)
2. ¿Las frutas? (poner)
3. ¿Los sándwiches? (hacer)
4. ¿Los refrescos? (sacar)
5. ¿La carne? (calentar)
6. ¿El cuarto? (arreglar)
7. ¿Las zanahorias? (cortar)
8. ¿El café? (servir)

5 Contesta las siguientes preguntas en español. ➜2A, 2B

1. What are some foods that reflect Mexico's indigenous heritage?
2. In most Spanish-speaking countries, when is the big meal of the day?
3. What are some popular snack foods in Mexico? In other Hispanic countries?

6 Verónica, Antonio y Carlos están en un restaurante. Escucha mientras hablan de lo que van a comer. Luego contesta las preguntas. ➜1B

1. ¿Quién tiene sed?
2. ¿Quién pide un refresco?
3. ¿Qué prefiere Carlos?
4. ¿Cómo es la sopa?
5. ¿Van a pedir unos sándwiches?

7 Usa los dibujos para decir qué pasa. ➜1C

4 Gramática 2
- direct objects and direct object pronouns
- affirmative informal commands with pronouns

pp. 212–217

5 Cultura
- **Comparaciones** pp. 206–207
- **Notas culturales** pp. 198, 200, 210, 214
- **Geocultura** pp. 190–193

TEKS Focus
2B Demonstrate understanding of products (what people create) and how they relate to perspectives (how people perceive things) of the cultures studied

Repaso

Gramática 1
- uses of **ser** and **estar** **pp. 200–201**
- **pedir** and **servir** **pp. 202–203**
- **preferir, poder** and **probar** **pp. 204–205**

Repaso de Gramática 1

Uses of **ser**	Uses of **estar**
• to say where someone is from • to identify people and things • to describe what someone or something is like • to tell the day, date, and time	• to say where someone or something is • to say how people are doing • to say how something looks, feels, or tastes at a given moment

pedir, servir e → i	
pido	pedimos
pides	pedís
pide	piden

poder, probar e → ue	
yo p**ue**do	nosotros podemos
preferir e → ie	
yo pref**ie**ro	nosotros preferimos

Gramática 2
- direct objects and direct object pronouns **pp. 212–213**
- affirmative informal commands **pp. 214–215**
- affirmative informal commands with pronouns **pp. 216–217**

TEKS Focus
1B Demonstrate understanding of simple, clearly spoken, and written language when dealing with familiar topics

Repaso de Gramática 2

Direct object pronouns		
	Masculine	**Feminine**
SINGULAR	**lo**	**la**
PLURAL	**los**	**las**

Affirmative informal commands			
Regular	**Irregular**		
habl**a**	**ten**	**sé**	**haz**
com**e**	**ven**	**ve**	**sal**
pid**e**	**pon**		

Attach direct object pronouns to the end of the affirmative commands.

Letra y sonido d

La letra d

- At the beginning of a phrase, or after **n** or **l**, the letter **d** is similar to the English *d* in *Daniel:* **d**elicioso, hon**d**o, an**d**ar, un **d**ía, el **d**eporte
- After other consonants and especially after a vowel, it is much like English *th* in *then:* na**d**ar, me**d**ia, cua**d**erno, ma**d**re, usted, aburri**d**o, tar**d**e, ver**d**e, la**d**o, a **d**ormir

Trabalenguas

Me han dicho
que has dicho un dicho,
un dicho que he dicho yo,
ese dicho que te han dicho
que yo he dicho, no lo he dicho;
y si yo lo hubiera dicho,
estaría muy bien dicho

Dictado 1B

Escribe las oraciones de la grabación.

Repaso de Vocabulario 1

Commenting on food

el agua *(f.)*	*water*
el atún	*tuna*
(muy) caliente	*(very) hot*
encantar	*to really like, to love*
la ensalada (de frutas)	*(fruit) salad*
(No) estoy de acuerdo.	*I (don't) agree.*
el flan	*flan, custard*
frío(a)	*cold*
el jamón	*ham*
el jugo de...	*. . . juice*
la leche	*milk*
las papas	*potatoes*
las papas fritas	*French fries*
pedir (i)	*to ask for, to order*
picante	*spicy*
preferir (ie)	*to prefer*
preparar	*to prepare, to make*
probar (ue)	*to try, to taste*
¿Qué tal está(n)...?	*How is (are) . . .?*
el queso	*cheese*
el refresco	*soft drink*
el restaurante	*restaurant*
riquísimo(a)	*delicious*
(un poco) salado(a)	*(a little) salty*
la salsa	*sauce, gravy*
el sándwich de...	*. . . sandwich*
servir (i)	*to serve*
la sopa (de verduras)	*(vegetable) soup*
el tomate	*tomato*

Making polite requests

la cuchara	*spoon*
el cuchillo	*knife*
la cuenta	*bill*
desear	*to want, to wish for, to desire*
el plato	*dish, plate*
el plato hondo	*bowl*
poder	*to be able to, can*
el postre	*dessert*
querer	*to want*
Quisiera...	*I would like . . .*
la servilleta	*napkin*
el tenedor	*fork*
tomar	*to drink, to take*
traer	*to bring*
el vaso	*glass*

Repaso de Vocabulario 2

Talking about meals

almorzar (ue)	*to eat lunch*
el arroz	*rice*
el bróculi	*broccoli*
el café (con leche)	*coffee (with milk)*
la carne	*meat*
la cena	*dinner*
cenar	*to eat dinner*
los cereales	*cereal*
el chocolate	*chocolate*
desayunar	*to eat breakfast*
el desayuno	*breakfast*
el durazno	*peach*
las espinacas	*spinach*
el huevo	*egg*
el maíz	*corn*
la manzana	*apple*
la naranja	*orange*
el pan	*bread*
el pan dulce	*pastries*
el pan tostado	*toast*
el pastel	*cake*
el pescado	*fish*
el pollo	*chicken*
el tocino	*bacon*
la zanahoria	*carrot*

Offering help

la ayuda	*help*
ayudar	*to help*
¿Puedo...?	*Can I . . .?*
el refrigerador	*refrigerator*

Useful verbs for cooking

añadir	*to add*
calentar (ie)	*to heat up*
cortar	*to cut*
mezclar	*to mix*

Integración

capítulos 1-6

1 Escucha los comentarios sobre la comida y escoge la foto correspondiente.

A

B

C

D

2 La señora Ramírez va a preparar la cena. Lee las recetas y contesta las preguntas que siguen. 3B

ENSALADA MIXTA

1 lechuga grande
4 tomates
1 taza de arroz cocido
100 g atún de lata
1/2 zanahoria rallada
1/2 cebolla picada

Se limpian las verduras y se cortan en trozos. Se mezcla todo junto y se sirve con aceite, vinagre, sal y pimienta.
Raciones 6–8
Tiempo–15 minutos

TORTILLA ESPAÑOLA

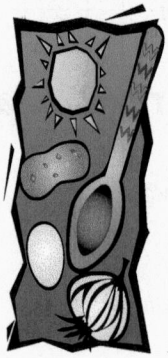

4 huevos
4 papas medianas
1/2 cebolla
sal y aceite de oliva

Corta las papas y la cebolla en pedacitos. Fríe con aceite en una sartén. Bate los huevos y mézclalos con las papas. Agrega la sal. Tapa con otra sartén y fríe al gusto. Dale la vuelta con la sartén superior y cocina el otro lado.
Raciones 6–8
Tiempo–30 minutos

1. ¿Qué ingredientes tienen en común las dos recetas?
2. ¿Cuáles son tres verduras que necesita la señora Ramírez?
3. ¿Qué tiene que cocinar antes de preparar la ensalada mixta?
4. ¿Para cuántas personas son las recetas?
5. ¿Cuánto tiempo necesita la señora Ramírez para cocinar la cena?

TEKS Focus

3B Use the language to obtain, reinforce, or expand knowledge of other subject areas

Visit Holt Online
go.hrw.com
KEYWORD: EXP1 CH6
Cumulative Self-test

3 En grupos de tres, hagan un menú para una fiesta latina. Incluyan varias comidas y bebidas, y hablen de las comidas que prefieren o que no les gustan. Presenten su menú a la clase y compárenlo con el de otros grupos. **1A, 1C**

4 Mira la pintura. ¿Quiénes son estas personas y qué hacen? ¿Qué tipo de comida ves? ¿Dónde crees que están las personas? Escribe un diálogo entre el señor y la mujer que está de rodillas *(kneeling)*. ¿Qué le trae ella a él? **1C, 3A**

Painting ©2003 Banco de México Diego Rivera & Frida Kahlo Museums Trust. Av. Cinco de Mayo No. 2, Col. Centro, Del. Cuauhtémoc 06059, México, D. F.; photo © Archivo Iconográfico, S.A./CORBIS; Reproduction Authorized by the National Institute of Fine Arts and Literature, Mexico City.

The Market of Cuernavaca in the Age of the Spanish Conquest,
de Diego Rivera (1886–1957)

5 Antes de ir al trabajo, tu madre te dejó *(left you)* una lista de cinco quehaceres. Estás muy ocupado(a) hoy, y no puedes hacer cada cosa. Escríbele un recado *(message)* y explícale por qué sólo puedes hacer algunos quehaceres. Dile que puedes hacer un quehacer extra este fin de semana. **1C**

6 **Situación**

Your Spanish class has decided to go out to dinner at a local Mexican restaurant. There are two servers waiting on your group. One is doing a great job, but the other is having problems. Order food and drinks, make polite requests, comment on the food served and ask for the bill. **1A**

GeoVisión

▲ **Buenos Aires,** la capital de Argentina, se encuentra en la boca del Río de la Plata en la costa del Océano Atlántico.

Geocultura Argentina

► **San Carlos de Bariloche,** al pie de los Andes y al borde del Lago Nahuel Huapí en la Patagonia, se conoce como la Suiza de los Andes debido a su geografía montañosa.

► **La Pampa,** la tierra de los gauchos y el corazón de la ganadería argentina, se caracteriza por ser casi plana.

OCÉA
PACÍF

Almanaque

Población
37.812.817

Capital
Buenos Aires

Gobierno
república

Idioma oficial
español

Moneda
peso argentino

Código Internet
www.[ ].ar

¿Sabías que...?

La imagen romántica del vaquero tejano, hombre independiente cabalgando con su ganado por llanuras interminables, se parece mucho a la imagen del gaucho argentino.

◄ **Los porteños** A la gente de Buenos Aires se le conoce como *porteños*. Aquí se ven dos jóvenes porteños en vestidos tradicionales.

▶**La Garganta del Diablo,** una de 275 cascadas en la frontera con Brasil, es la caída de agua más impresionante de las Cataratas del Iguazú.

▼ **El Parque Provincial Ischigualasto** es un área de extrañas formaciones geológicas, con fósiles del periodo triásico. El Eoraptor lunensis, uno de los dinosaurios más antiguos, fue descubierto en este lugar.

▼ **Los pingüinos de Magallanes** viven en grandes colonias en el extremo sur de Argentina.

▼ **Ushuaia,** en la Tierra del Fuego, es la ciudad más sureña del mundo. Durante el verano en diciembre y enero hay días que cuentan con veinte horas de luz.

¿Qué tanto sabes...?

¿A dónde vas si quieres encontrar fósiles? ¿Dónde hay días muy largos?

A conocer Argentina

La arquitectura

▼ **La arquitectura europea** de los Alpes en la ciudad de San Carlos de Bariloche refleja la herencia alemana de esta región andina.

▲ **Iglesia y Convento de San Francisco de Salta** se halla al extremo norte del país. La torre, diseñada por arquitectos españoles e italianos, es una de las más altas de Sudamérica. Mide 53 metros.

▲ **La Boca, Buenos Aires** Originalmente el hogar de los inmigrantes italianos, las calles pintorescas del barrio de La Boca son famosas por el colorido de sus casas y la música de tango que permea el ambiente.

El arte

▼ **En la Cueva de las Manos** en la Patagonia, la representación de manos negativas es obra de los cazadores prehistóricos que habitaron la región hace más de diez mil años.

▲ ***Vuel Villa*** (1936) es obra del maestro del arte argentino, Xul Solar (1887–1963). El artista, de herencia alemana, tuvo gran influencia en el desarrollo del arte moderno de su país.

Las celebraciones

Visit Holt Online
go.hrw.com
KEYWORD: EXP1 CH7
Photo Tour

Interactive TUTOR

▼ **La Fiesta de la Semana de la Tradición** se celebra en San Antonio de Areco. Es la mayor fiesta en Argentina dedicada al gaucho y sus costumbres.

▲ **El Festival del Tango** en Buenos Aires se dedica a la música y al baile de tango, una expresión puramente argentina, que se originó en los barrios de los inmigrantes durante el siglo XIX.

¿Sabías que...?

Entre 1857 y 1939 3,5 millones de personas inmigraron a Argentina de Italia, España, Alemania, Inglaterra, Suiza, Austria, Noruega, Siria y muchos países más. Para 1914, 30% de la población argentina había nacido fuera del país.

La comida

► **Las picadas** son restaurantes que sirven una gran variedad de tapas y bocaditos preparados con queso, carne, mariscos y nueces.

▲ **La parrillada** es una comida muy típica de Argentina. Se combinan varios tipos de carne y se sirven en grandes bandejas.

Conexión Ciencias sociales

El mate Cada día, entre las 4 y las 6 de la tarde, los argentinos toman un té fuerte que se llama mate. Se sirve en una calabacita con bombilla. En España se observa la siesta cada día y en Colombia se toman las onces. ¿Hay costumbres en tu familia o comunidad? Compara una costumbre tuya con una de Argentina. 3B, 4B

▼ **Calabacitas de mate con bombilla**

Capítulo 7

Cuerpo sano, mente sana

OBJETIVOS

In this chapter you will learn to

- talk about your daily routine
- talk about staying fit and healthy
- talk about how you feel
- give advice

And you will use

- verbs with reflexive pronouns
- infinitives
- stem-changing verbs
- **estar, sentirse,** and **tener**
- negative informal commands
- object and reflexive pronouns with commands

¿Qué ves en la foto?

- ¿Cómo son las personas de la foto?
- ¿Qué tiempo hace?
- ¿Qué deportes puedes practicar en el agua?

Texas

TEKS Look for the ✦ next to each activity to learn how it can help you achieve the goals of the **Texas Essential Knowledge and Skills,** found on page xxiii.

Visit Holt Online
go.hrw.com
KEYWORD: EXP1 CH7
Online Edition

El windsurf en el Río de la Plata, Buenos Aires

Objetivos
Talking about your daily routine, talking about staying fit and healthy

Vocabulario en acción 1

ExpresaVisión

Por la mañana, tengo que...

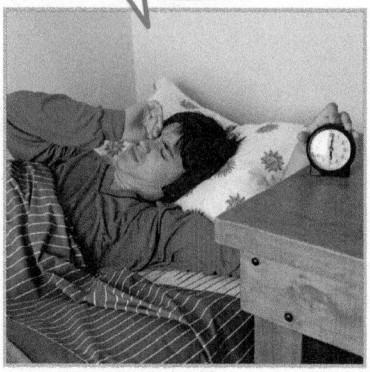

peinarme.

maquillarme.

afeitarme.

lavarme los dientes.

la nariz

la cara

los dientes

la boca

la toalla

el peine

la pasta de dientes

la navaja

el maquillaje

el jabón

el cepillo de dientes

Visit Holt Online
go.hrw.com
KEYWORD: EXP1 CH7
Vocabulario 1 practice

Por la tarde, después de clases, voy a...

Por la noche, necesito...

¡Exprésate!

To talk about your daily routine

Interactive TUTOR

¿Estás listo? ¿Qué te falta hacer?

Are you ready? What do you still have to do?

¡Ay, no! Acabo de levantarme. Tengo que lavarme la cara antes de desayunar.

Oh, no! I just got up. I have to wash my face before I eat breakfast.

¿Qué tienes que hacer para prepararte?

What do you have to do to get ready?

Tengo que secarme el pelo, pero no encuentro la secadora de pelo.

I have to dry my hair, but I can't find the hair dryer.

Online
Vocabulario y gramática, pp. 73–75

▶ **Vocabulario adicional** — Partes del cuerpo, p. R10

Nota cultural

Argentina boasts some of the finest ski resorts in the world. Argentina's city of Bariloche is well known for its July ski season. Each August, Bariloche celebrates the National Snow Party, a week of winter celebrations. Why do you think the ski season is in July and August in Argentina? 2A

1 ¿Qué te falta hacer? 1B

Leamos Completa las oraciones con la palabra más apropiada entre paréntesis.

1. Quiero lavarme (la cara/la nariz) antes de cenar.
2. Me gusta (acostarme/entrenarme) temprano por la mañana.
3. Tengo que estirarme (la boca/los brazos) antes de levantar pesas.
4. Voy a afeitarme (las piernas/el pelo) antes de ir a la piscina.
5. Necesito lavarme (los dientes/la nariz) después de comer.
6. ¿Dónde está (la navaja/la secadora)? Tengo que secarme el pelo.

2 ¿Qué vas a hacer primero? 1B

Hablemos ¿En qué orden vas a hacer las siguientes cosas?

MODELO **vestirme/bañarme**
Primero voy a bañarme y luego voy a vestirme.

1. bañarme/levantarme
2. secarme el pelo/bañarme
3. lavarme la cara/maquillarme
4. lavarme el pelo/peinarme
5. ponerme la ropa/bañarme
6. acostarme/ponerme el piyama
7. quitarme la ropa/ponerme el piyama
8. vestirme/salir para el colegio

3 ¿Estás listo? 1B

Escribamos/Hablemos Contesta la pregunta del modelo para cada foto.

MODELO **¿Qué tienes que hacer?**
Tengo que afeitarme,
pero no encuentro la navaja.

1.

2.

3.

4.

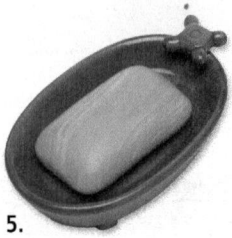
5.

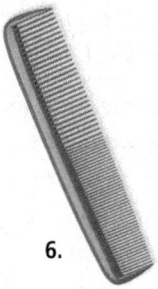
6.

7.

8.

¡Exprésate!

To talk about staying fit and healthy

Interactive TUTOR

¿Cómo te mantienes en forma? *How do you stay in shape?*	**Corro y levanto pesas. Entreno las piernas y los brazos.** *I run and lift weights. I work out my legs and my arms.*
¿Qué haces para relajarte? *What do you do to relax?*	**Me entreno. También duermo la siesta o escucho música.** *I work out. I also take a nap or listen to music.*

Online
Vocabulario y gramática, pp. 73–75

4 El sábado 1B

Escuchemos Escucha la conversación entre Juan y Laura sobre los planes de ella para el sábado. Luego completa las oraciones con las palabras correctas.

1. Voy a levantarme (temprano/tarde) este sábado.
2. (Corro/Levanto pesas/No me entreno) los sábados.
3. (Casi siempre/A veces/Nunca) almuerzo en casa los sábados.
4. Voy a bañarme (por la mañana/por la tarde) este sábado.
5. Quiero (relajarme/salir con mis amigos) este sábado por la tarde.
6. Para relajarme, prefiero (leer/escuchar música/ir de compras).
7. (Siempre/A veces/Nunca) duermo la siesta por la tarde los sábados.

Dos muchachas se estiran en Buenos Aires

5 Y tú, ¿te entrenas? 1B, 1C

Hablemos/Escribamos Completa las oraciones sobre tu propia rutina o la rutina de un atleta *(athlete)*.

1. Para mantenerme en forma, yo...
2. Cuando hago ejercicio, me gusta...
3. Cuando no tengo ganas de hacer ejercicio, me gusta...
4. A veces tengo que acostarme temprano porque...
5. Para relajarme, prefiero...

Comunicación

6 Tengo prisa 1A

Escribamos/Hablemos En parejas, dramaticen *(role-play)* la siguiente situación. Acabas de levantarte tarde, las clases empiezan en menos de una hora y no encuentras dos cosas que necesitas para prepararte.

TEKS Focus
1A Engage in oral and written exchanges of learned material to socialize and to provide and obtain information

Objetivos

Verbs with reflexive pronouns, infinitives, review of stem-changing verbs

Gramática en acción 1

GramaVisión

Verbs with reflexive pronouns

Interactive TUTOR

1 If the subject and object of a verb are the same, a **reflexive pronoun** can be used. The reflexive pronoun shows that the subject acts upon itself. When you conjugate a verb like **lavarse,** include the reflexive pronoun that agrees with the subject.

yo **me** lavo	nosotros(as) **nos** lavamos
tú **te** lavas	vosotros(as) **os** laváis
Ud., él, ella **se** lava	Uds., ellos(as) **se** lavan

2 **Reflexive pronouns** can go before a conjugated verb or can be joined to the end of an **infinitive**. After reflexive verbs, use **el, la, los** or **las** with parts of the body or clothing.

(Yo) **Me** voy a **lavar** la cara.
I'm going to wash my face.

(Yo) Voy a **lavarme** la cara.
I'm going to wash my face.

3 Verbs can be used with **reflexive pronouns** that refer to the subject or with direct objects that are different from the subject.

refers to the subject

Juan **se acuesta.**
Juan goes to bed.

different from the subject

Juan **acuesta** a los niños.
Juan puts the children to bed.

4 Here are some common verbs with **reflexive pronouns**.

afeitar**se**	levantar**se**	preparar**se**
bañar**se**	mantener**se** (ie)	quitar**se**
despertar**se** (ie)	maquillar**se**	relajar**se**
entrenar**se**	peinar**se**	secar**se**
estirar**se**	poner**se**	vestir**se** (i)

Online

Vocabulario y gramática, pp. 76–78 | Actividades, pp. 61–63

Texas

Nota cultural

Keeping in shape is easy for surfers along the 500 miles of Texas coastline. Good surfing spots include South Padre Island, Corpus Christi, Matagorda, Port Aransas, and Galveston. Surfers check weather reports, Internet bulletins, and live video from Web cameras because the surf changes quickly along the Texas coast. Why do you think hurricanes in the Gulf of Mexico attract surfers to Texas? 2A

7 ¿Qué hace Manuel? 1B

Escuchemos Escucha lo que dice Manuel. ¿Va al colegio o se acuesta?

Visit Holt Online
go.hrw.com
KEYWORD: EXP1 CH7
Gramática 1 practice

8 Por la mañana 1B

Leamos Una muchacha habla de su día típico. Lee el párrafo y decide si se necesita el pronombre reflexivo con cada verbo.

Mis padres **1.** (levantan/se levantan) a las seis todos los días. Mientras *(While)* mi padre **2.** (prepara/se prepara) para ir al trabajo, mi madre va a la cocina, **3.** (lava/se lava) las manos y **4.** (prepara/se prepara) el desayuno para la familia. Mi hermano menor y yo **5.** (levantamos/nos levantamos) a las siete. Mientras mamá y yo **6.** (vestimos/nos vestimos), papá **7.** (viste/se viste) a mi hermano. Después del desayuno, mamá **8.** (lava/se lava) los platos rápidamente mientras mi hermano y yo **9.** (lavamos/nos lavamos) los dientes antes de salir de la casa.

TEKS Focus
1B Demonstrate understanding of simple, clearly spoken, and written language when dealing with familiar topics

9 ¿Qué y cuándo? 1C

Escribamos Mira las fotos. Escribe una oración para cada foto.

MODELO **El señor Vargas se afeita por la mañana.**

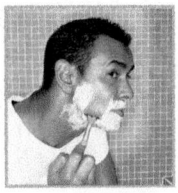

el señor Vargas
por la mañana

1. Laura
7:00 A.M.

2. ellas
por la tarde

3. nosotros
los fines de semana

4. tú
por la noche

Comunicación

10 Cuéntame de ti 1A

Hablemos En grupos pequeños, utilicen estas frases para preguntarles a sus compañeros qué hacen los sábados.

relajarse	entrenarse en el gimnasio
levantarse temprano	ponerse ropa vieja
maquillarse/afeitarse	salir con los amigos

Using infinitives

Interactive TUTOR

1 A **reflexive pronoun** can go at the end of an **infinitive** or before a conjugated verb. The meaning does not change.

Yo no quiero **afeitarme** hoy. = Yo no **me** quiero **afeitar** hoy.
I don't want to shave today.

2 To say what someone just did, use the present tense of **acabar de** followed by an **infinitive.**

Acabo de lavar el carro.
I just washed my car.

Los niños **acaban de acostarse.**
The children just went to bed.

3 Use the preposition **para** before an infinitive to explain your purpose for doing something. Verbs after prepositions and prepositional phrases such as **para**, **antes de** and **después de** are in the **infinitive.**

Tengo que levantarme temprano **para levantar** pesas con Ana en el gimnasio.
I have to get up early (in order) to . . .

Online

Vocabulario y gramática, pp. 76–78 | Actividades, pp. 61–63

En inglés

In English, you can say **in order to** or just **to** to explain your purpose for doing something.

I need to call John (**in order**) **to** see how he's doing.

In Spanish, use **para** followed by an infinitive to explain your purpose. If you're talking about going somewhere to do something, use **a** followed by an infinitive.

Necesito llamar a Juan **para** saber cómo está.

Necesito ir al gimnasio **a** levantar pesas.

Manteniéndose en forma en un gimnasio

11 ¿Qué sigue? ➤1B, 1C

Escribamos/Hablemos Completa las oraciones con los verbos correctos entre paréntesis. Luego di si cada oración es **cierta** o **falsa** para ti.

1. **(se levanta, se levantan, me levanto, levantarse, levantarme)**
   a. Mis padres ____ a las seis de la mañana.
   b. Mi padre ____ primero.
   c. (Yo) ____ temprano todos los días también, pero prefiero ____ a las nueve o diez.
2. **(se viste, me visto, vestirse, vestirme)**
   a. Mi madre desayuna antes de ____.
   b. (Yo) prefiero desayunar después de ____.
   c. (Yo) siempre ____ en el baño.
3. **(me lavo, nos lavamos, lavarme, lavarnos)**
   a. Después de desayunar voy al baño a ____ los dientes.
   b. (Yo) siempre ____ los dientes por la mañana.
   c. En el colegio no nos gusta ____ los dientes.
4. **(se acuesta, me acuesto, nos acostamos, acostarse)**
   a. Nosotros ____ tarde en mi familia.
   b. (Yo) ____ primero, a las once.
   c. Mi padre prefiere leer un poco antes de ____.

12 Antes de acostarte 1B, 1C

Hablemos Di cuándo vas a hacer las siguientes actividades.

MODELO **bañarme**
Me voy a bañar esta noche antes de acostarme.

1. levantarme
2. acostarme
3. ponerme el piyama
4. relajarme
5. entrenarme
6. vestirme

13 ¿Cuál es la situación? 1B

Escribamos/Hablemos Mira las fotos de las personas e indica qué acaban de hacer y qué van a hacer.

MODELO **Acabo de ponerme el piyama. Voy a acostarme.**

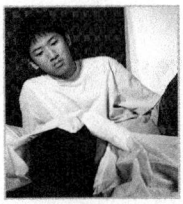

yo

1. ella

2. él

3. tú

4. Juan

Comunicación

14 ¿Cómo es tu rutina? 1A, 1C

Escribamos/Hablemos Prepara cinco preguntas para un(a) compañero(a) de clase usando palabras de cada grupo. Luego, contesta las preguntas de tu compañero(a).

MODELO **¿Vas a levantarte temprano mañana?**

TEKS Focus
1A Engage in oral and written exchanges of learned material to socialize and to provide and obtain information

ir a	levantarte	todos los días/los sábados
necesitar	acostarte	temprano/tarde
tener que	lavarte el pelo	por la mañana/por la noche/por la tarde
querer	afeitarte	esta noche/mañana/el sábado
poder	entrenarte	antes de desayunar/después de estudiar

15 Encuesta 1A

Hablemos En grupos, comparen sus respuestas a la Actividad 14. Basándose en lo que dice cada persona, ¿quién se cuida mejor la salud?

Stem-changing verbs

Interactive TUTOR

1 In the present tense, some verbs have a stem change in all but the **nosotros** and **vosotros** forms.

2 The verbs **despertarse** *(to wake up)* and **mantenerse en forma** *(to stay in shape)* have an **e → ie** stem change. **Acostarse** *(to go to bed)* and **encontrar** *(to find)* have an **o → ue** change, while **vestirse** *(to get dressed)* has an e → **i** stem change.

acostarse (o → ue)					
yo	me	ac**ue**sto	nosotros(as)	nos	acostamos
tú	te	ac**ue**stas	vosotros(as)	os	acostáis
Ud., él, ella	se	ac**ue**sta	Uds., ellos, ellas	se	ac**ue**stan

Mi hermana y yo nos **acostamos** a las diez.

vestirse (e → i)					
yo	me	v**i**sto	nosotros(as)	nos	vestimos
tú	te	v**i**stes	vosotros(as)	os	vestís
Ud., él, ella	se	v**i**ste	Uds., ellos, ellas	se	v**i**sten

Mi abuela se **viste** de ropa elegante.

Online

Vocabulario y gramática, pp. 76–78 | Actividades, pp. 61–63

¿Te acuerdas?

Here are some of the **stem-changing verbs** you have seen so far.

querer (**e → ie**)
poder (**o → ue**)
jugar (**u → ue**)
pedir (**e → i**)

16 Nuestra rutina 1B

Escuchemos Decide si estas oraciones son **ciertas** o **falsas.**

1. El papá de Camila se acuesta antes que su mamá.
2. Su hermano se acuesta después de jugar al ajedrez por Internet.
3. Su mamá sirve huevos, tocino, y pan tostado para el desayuno.
4. Por la mañana, Camila y su hermano se levantan tarde.
5. Después de desayunar, Camila se viste y se maquilla.

17 Lo que hacen todos 1C

Escribamos Di quién hace las siguientes cosas, cómo y cuándo.

MODELO **(no) jugar (mis abuelos/mi hermano)**
Mis abuelos no juegan a los videojuegos nunca.
Mi hermano juega al ajedrez conmigo a veces.

1. (no) acostarse (yo/mi mejor amigo)
2. (no) vestirse (mis padres/mi hermano(a) mayor)
3. (no) pedir verduras en restaurantes (yo/mis amigos)
4. (no) tener prisa (mi profesor(a)/mis padres)

TEKS Focus
1C Present information using familiar words, phrases, and sentences

18 La rutina familiar ➜1B

Leamos/Escribamos Completa las oraciones con las formas correctas de los verbos lógicos entre paréntesis.

Después del colegio mi hermana __1__ (servir/jugar) videojuegos pero yo __2__ (probar/empezar) mi tarea a las tres. Mi hermana y yo __3__ (servir/almorzar) la cena todos los días. Mis padres __4__ (acostar/preferir) cenar muy temprano. Mi padre siempre __5__ (querer/servir) leer un libro después de cenar pero mi madre __6__ (dormir/preferir) escuchar música. Mi padre siempre __7__ (levantarse/acostarse) antes de las nueve de la noche.

19 ¿Qué pasa en casa? ➜1B, 1C

Escribamos Utiliza las palabras de los cuadros para describir qué hacen las personas en cada dibujo.

1.

2.

jugar	llover
poder	querer

probar	servir
preferir	vestirse

Comunicación

20 Tu rutina diaria ➜1A, 1C

Hablemos Utiliza estas frases para entrevistar a tu compañero(a) sobre los días que va al colegio. Comparen sus respuestas.

despertarse temprano/tarde	vestirse en menos de veinte minutos
dormir mucho/poco	dormir la siesta
jugar a...	encontrar tu mochila/libro de español
volver a casa	empezar la tarea

Cultura

VideoCultura

Comparaciones

Parque Palermo, Argentina

¿Cómo te mantienes en forma? 1B, 2A, 4B

La necesidad de mantenerse en forma es universal. En Argentina los jóvenes prefieren mantenerse en forma practicando el esquí, el patinaje en hielo y el hockey, también el ciclismo, la natación, el windsurf, el taekwondo, el alpinismo y, desde luego, el fútbol. Muchos jóvenes se mantienen en forma con la práctica del fútbol todos los fines de semana. ¿Qué diferencia hay entre lo que hacen estos jóvenes y lo que haces tú para mantenerte en forma?

Miguel
Buenos Aires, Argentina

¿Crees que estás en forma ahora?

Eh, sí, creo que estoy en forma, me mantengo, trato siempre de salir a correr, cosas por el estilo, cosa de mantenerme siempre en forma.

¿Cómo te mantienes en forma?

Practico gimnasia acrobática desde hace nueve años. Este, salgo a correr, distintos tipos de deportes... me gusta un poquitito de todo, muy variado.

Para ti, ¿qué es lo difícil de mantenerte en forma?

Lo difícil de mantenerse en forma, yo creo que es mantener una constancia en un entrenamiento, fijarse objetivos y a partir de ahí, bueno, a ver qué pasa.

¿Qué haces para relajarte?

Me gusta leer. Me gusta escuchar música, especialmente leer porque como quien dice, este, en un cuerpo sano, mente sana.

Visit Holt Online
go.hrw.com
KEYWORD: EXP1 CH7
Online Edition

Ivania
San José, Costa Rica

¿Crees que estás en forma en este momento?

Sí, sí, creo que estoy en forma.

¿Cómo te mantienes en forma?

Yo, para mantenerme en forma, camino, corro o voy al gimnasio.

Para ti, ¿qué es lo difícil de mantenerte en forma?

Para mí, lo difícil de mantenerme en forma es poder evitar comer chocolate, picaditas o helados.

¿Qué haces para relajarte?

Yo para relajarme hago muchas cosas, leo poemas, hablo con mis amigos, salgo a pasear.

Para comprender 1B, 2A

1. ¿Qué hace Miguel para mantenerse en forma? ¿Qué deportes le gustan a Miguel?
2. ¿Por qué es difícil para Miguel mantenerse en forma?
3. ¿Cómo se mantiene en forma Ivania? ¿Qué le gusta comer a Ivania?
4. ¿Qué hacen Miguel e Ivania para relajarse? ¿Qué cosa hacen los dos? En tu opinión, ¿es cierto lo que dice Miguel, "en un cuerpo sano, mente sana"? ¿Por qué?

Para pensar y hablar 2A, 4B

Very often exercise involves going to the gym. But, simple things like walking or riding a bike to places can be enough exercise. Both Miguel and Ivania live in cities in their home countries where places are often within walking distance. Are places easy to walk to in your community, or are they spread out so you have to ride there in a car or bus? How can the way a city is built make it easy or hard for a person to get exercise?

Cuaderno para hispanohablantes, pp. 69–80

Texas

Comunidad

Popular Sports in Texas

Soccer is not only popular in all of Latin America, but also in many areas of Texas. There are programs to develop soccer players from young children to adults. In Dallas, you can attend a professional game and watch the Dallas Burn. If there is a league in your area, you might be able to interview a trainer or coach in Spanish because many of them are from Latin America. If you meet Claudio Reyna or Carlos Llamosa, members of the U.S. national soccer team, you can greet them in Spanish! What other sports are popular in both Latin America and your city or area of Texas? 4B, 5A

The Dallas Burn

Objetivos
Talking about how you feel, giving advice

Vocabulario en acción 2

ExpresaVisión

¿Te duele algo?

¿Qué te pasa?

Me duele...

la cabeza

el oído

la garganta

el estómago

la mano

el pie

¿Cómo se sienten?

Visit Holt Online
go.hrw.com
KEYWORD: EXP1 CH7
Vocabulario 2 practice

Está cansada.

Está aburrido.

Está nerviosa.

Está triste.

Para cuidarte la salud debes...

hacer yoga

caminar

seguir una dieta sana

Más vocabulario...

bajar de peso	*to lose weight*
buscar un pasatiempo	*to find a hobby*
dejar de fumar	*to stop smoking*
enojarse	*to get angry*
estar contento(a)	*to be happy*
subir de peso	*to gain weight*

¡Exprésate!

Interactive TUTOR

To ask how someone feels	To respond
Te veo mal. *You don't look well.*	**Es que estoy enferma. Tengo catarro.** *I'm sick. I have a cold.*
¿Qué te pasa? ¿Te duele algo? *What's wrong with you? Does something hurt?*	**Me siento (un poco) cansado y me duelen los pies (las manos).** *I feel (a little) tired and my feet (hands) hurt.*
¿Qué tiene Rosita? ¿Está enojada? *What's the matter with Rosita? Is she angry?*	**No. Le duele el cuello.** *No. Her neck hurts.*

Online
Vocabulario y gramática, pp. 79–81

▶ **Vocabulario adicional** — En el consultorio, p. R8

Nota cultural

Argentina is famous for its **parrilladas**—steaks and other grilled meats. Another important element in Argentine cooking is the influence of Spain and Italy. You might be surprised to find a **milanesa napolitana** served in Buenos Aires. How does Argentine food compare to your diet? 2A, 4B

21 Debes cuidarte mejor 1B

Leamos Lee lo que varios amigos te dicen sobre sus problemas. Escoge la mejor respuesta para cada situación.

1. Me duelen mucho los ojos.
2. Siempre estoy aburrido.
3. Me siento muy cansada.
4. Nunca como frutas ni verduras.
5. Siempre me duele la garganta.
6. Quiero bajar de peso.
7. Tengo catarro.
8. ¡Estoy enojada!
9. Me duelen los pies.

a. Debes dejar de fumar.
b. Necesitas seguir una dieta sana.
c. ¡Usa tus lentes!
d. ¿Qué tal si buscas un pasatiempo?
e. Debes comer menos y hacer ejercicio.
f. No debes correr sin zapatos.
g. Debes dormir lo suficiente.
h. Toma jugo de naranja y descansa.
i. Debes relajarte. ¿Por qué no haces yoga?

22 ¿Qué te duele? 1B, 1C

Hablemos Explica qué parte(s) del cuerpo te duele(n) si no puedes hacer las siguientes cosas.

MODELO **correr**
No puedo correr. Me duelen las piernas y los pies.

1. hablar
2. levantar pesas
3. comer
4. escribir
5. oír *(to hear)*
6. estudiar
7. bailar
8. leer
9. jugar al tenis
10. hacer yoga

TEKS Focus
1B Demonstrate understanding of simple, clearly spoken, and written language when dealing with familiar topics

¡Exprésate!

To give advice

Interactive TUTOR

¿Sabes qué? Comes muy mal. No debes comer tanto dulce ni grasa.
You know what? You eat very badly. You shouldn't eat so many sweets nor so much fat.

Para cuidarte mejor, debes dormir lo suficiente. ¿Por qué no te acuestas más temprano?
To take better care of yourself, you should get enough sleep. Why don't you go to bed earlier?

No debes ver demasiada televisión.
You shouldn't watch too much television.

Online
Vocabulario y gramática, pp. 79–81

23 ¿Qué te pasa? 1B

Escuchemos Escucha las conversaciones. Escoge el consejo *(advice)* apropiado.

a. Debes usar lentes.
b. Necesitas dormir lo suficiente.
c. ¿Qué tal si caminas o montas en bicicleta?
d. Tienes que relajarte. Debes hacer yoga.
e. ¡Hombre, debes seguir una dieta sana!
f. ¡Deja de fumar!
g. Debes estirarte antes de hacer ejercicios.

24 ¡Ponte en forma! 1B

Escribamos/Hablemos Dile a tu amigo(a) qué debe hacer para ponerse en forma y sentirse mejor. Usa mandatos informales.

1. acostarte temprano
2. hacer ejercicio
3. salir con los amigos
4. ser más activo(a)
5. aprender un deporte nuevo
6. comer bien
7. hacer yoga

Nota cultural

Mate is a popular South American drink made from an herb called **yerba mate.** The dried herb is placed in a gourd or metal cup, also called **mate,** and hot water is poured from a kettle called a **pava.** **Mate** is then sipped through a straw called a **bombilla.** What kinds of herbal teas do you know about? How are they prepared? 2A, 4B

Comunicación

25 ¿Cómo te sientes? 1A, 1C

Hablemos Crea una conversación con tu compañero(a) con base en las personas de los dibujos. ¿Cómo se sienten? ¿Qué deben hacer?

1.

2.

3.

Objetivos

Estar, sentirse, and **tener,** negative informal commands, object and reflexive pronouns with commands

Gramática en acción 2

GramaVisión

Estar, sentirse, and tener

1 You have used **ser** to tell what people and things are normally like. Use **estar** with adjectives describing mental or physical states or conditions.

Mi amigo **es** joven.
My friend is young.

Está muy cansado.
He's very tired.

2 Like **estar, sentirse** *(to feel)* can be used with adverbs **bien/mal** or with adjectives to describe mental or physical states.

sentirse (e → ie)	
yo me s**ie**nto	nosotros(as) nos sentimos
tú te s**ie**ntes	vosotros(as) os sentís
Ud., él, ella se s**ie**nte	Uds., ellos(as) se s**ie**nten

Nos sentimos cansados.
We feel tired.

No **se sienten** bien.
They don't feel well.

3 The following expressions use **tener** with a **noun** to describe a mental or physical state.

tener frío *to be cold*
tener calor *to be hot*
tener miedo *to be afraid*
tener sueño *to be sleepy*

Online

Vocabulario y gramática, pp. 82–84 | Actividades, pp. 65–67

TEKS Focus

1B Demonstrate understanding of simple, clearly spoken, and written language when dealing with familiar topics

26 ¿Cómo están? 1B

Escuchemos Escucha las oraciones y decide qué dibujo corresponde a cada oración. Algunos dibujos se usan más de una vez.

a.

b.

c.

d.

e.

Visit Holt Online
go.hrw.com
KEYWORD: EXP1 CH7
Gramática 2 practice

27 ¿Quién es? 1B

Escribamos ¿A quién describen las siguientes palabras? Mira las fotos y haz oraciones con **estar, sentirse** o **tener.**

1. Leti

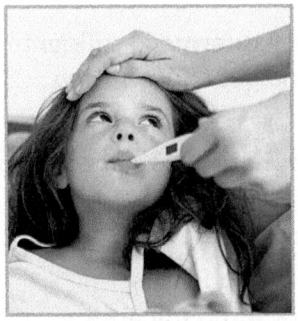
2. Marta

3. Ricardo

4. Vicente

1. aburrido(a)
2. enfermo(a)
3. sed
4. nervioso(a)
5. miedo
6. calor
7. bien
8. sueño

28 En el colegio 1B

Leamos/Escribamos Josefina habla de su colegio. Completa las oraciones con las formas correctas de **estar, sentirse** o **tener.** Luego cambia las oraciones para describir tu situación.

MODELO **A veces Luis está aburrido en la clase de matemáticas. Yo casi nunca estoy aburrido(a) en mis clases.**

1. Muchos estudiantes ____ miedo de los exámenes de inglés.
2. Joaquín y Mateo ____ nerviosos cuando presentan un examen.
3. Yo ____ calor cuando practico deportes en el gimnasio.
4. Mi amiga Matilde siempre ____ hambre antes del almuerzo.
5. A veces nosotros ____ sueño después de almorzar.
6. Mis profesores no ____ enojados casi nunca.

Comunicación

29 Un catarro 1A

Hablemos Dramatiza la siguiente situación con un(a) compañero(a). Tienes catarro y le dices a tu amigo(a) cómo te sientes. Él o ella te dice qué debes hacer para cuidarte. Usen las palabras del cuadro.

enfermo(a)	frío	calor	sed
cansado(a)	mal	sueño	me duele(n)

Negative informal commands

Interactive TUTOR

1 An **affirmative command** tells someone what to do. The **affirmative informal command** form of most verbs is the **tú** form without the final **s.**

Come bien y **duerme** lo suficiente.
Eat right and get enough sleep.

2 A **negative command** tells someone not to do something. To form the **negative informal command** of most **-ar** verbs, drop the final **o** of the **yo** form and add **-es**.

(yo) fum**o** → no fum**es**
(yo) trabaj**o** → no trabaj**es**

No trabajes tanto. *Don't work so much.*

3 To form the **negative informal command** of most **-er** and **-ir** verbs, drop the final **o** of the **yo** form and add **-as**.

(yo) veng**o** → no veng**as**
(yo) com**o** → no com**as**
(yo) duerm**o** → no duerm**as**

No duermas hasta tarde. *Don't sleep late.*

No pongas las frutas en la sopa. *Don't put . . .*

4 These verbs have irregular negative informal commands.

dar → **no des**
ir → **no vayas**
ser → **no seas**

Online
Vocabulario y gramática, pp. 82–84 | Actividades, pp. 65–67

¡Te acuerdas?

These verbs have irregular affirmative informal command forms.

hacer	**haz**
ir	**ve**
poner	**pon**
salir	**sal**
ser	**sé**
tener	**ten**
venir	**ven**

¡No corras, Lalo!

30 Consejos 1B

Leamos/Hablemos Por lo general, ¿qué le dicen los padres a su hijo?

1. (Come/No comas) verduras.
2. (Compra/No compres) muchos dulces.
3. (Sal/No salgas) tarde para el colegio.
4. (Haz/No hagas) tu tarea.
5. (Pon/No pongas) los pies en la mesa.
6. (Vuelve/No vuelvas) tarde a casa.
7. (Ve/No vayas) al colegio.
8. (Sé/No seas) bueno.
9. (Arregla/No arregles) tu cuarto.

31 ¿Qué deben hacer? 1B

Escribamos Usando mandatos *(commands)*, dile a un amigo si *(if)* debe hacer las cosas indicadas entre paréntesis o no.

MODELO **Si siempre estás enfermo... (fumar/dormir lo suficiente)**
No fumes. Duerme lo suficiente.

1. Si quieres cuidarte la salud... (comer verduras/hacer ejercicio/pasar el día delante de la televisión)
2. Si te duelen los pies... (correr/descansar/ir a bailar)
3. Si siempre estás aburrido... (dormir tanto/salir con los amigos/buscar un pasatiempo)
4. Si no entiendes algo en la clase de matemáticas... (estudiar más/hacer la tarea/ver tanta televisión)
5. Si siempre estás cansado... (volver tarde a casa/dormir más/salir con los amigos todas las noches)

32 En el colegio 1B

Escribamos Tu hermano menor va a ser estudiante en tu colegio el año que viene. Dale consejos sobre qué debe hacer y no hacer.

MODELO **comer en clase**
No comas en clase nunca.

1. correr en clase
2. participar en un deporte o club
3. interrumpir a los profesores
4. comprar el almuerzo en la cafetería
5. ser tímido
6. estudiar todos los días

Un colegio en Argentina

Comunicación

33 Nuestros problemas 1A, 1C

TEKS Focus
1C Present information using familiar words, phrases, and sentences

Escribamos/Hablemos Escribe en una hoja de papel un problema real o imaginario. Luego, dale la hoja a tu profesor(a) para que escriba *(so that he/she writes)* algunos de los problemas en la pizarra. Con un(a) compañero(a), prepara consejos para los problemas.

MODELO **Siempre tengo sueño en mi primera clase.**
¡Duerme más en casa!

Object and reflexive pronouns with commands

Interactive TUTOR

1 **Direct object pronouns** and **reflexive pronouns** are attached to the end of **affirmative commands**. A written accent mark goes over the stressed vowel of the verb, unless the verb is only one syllable long.

> **Levánta**te y **pon**te los zapatos.
> *Get up and put your shoes on.*
>
> ¿El jabón? **Busca**lo en el baño.
> *The soap? Look for it in the bathroom.*

2 **Direct object pronouns** and **reflexive pronouns** go in between **no** and the verb in **negative commands**.

> Este libro es pésimo. **No lo leas**.
> *This book is awful. Don't read it.*
>
> **No te levantes** muy tarde.
> *Don't get up too late.*

Online

Vocabulario y gramática, pp. 82–84 | Actividades, pp. 65–67

¿Te acuerdas?

Words ending in a **vowel**, **-n**, or **-s** are normally stressed on the next-to-last syllable. If another syllable is stressed, there must be a written accent on its vowel.

está	**esta**
teléfonos	**lentes**
jóvenes	**joven**

34 Más consejos 1B

Leamos/Hablemos Escoge el consejo apropiado.

1. ¿Tienes sueño?
   a. ¡Acuéstate! **b.** ¡No te acuestes!
2. ¿Te duelen los pies?
   a. ¡No te quites los zapatos! **b.** ¡Quítate los zapatos!
3. Vamos a comer.
   a. ¡Lávate las manos! **b.** ¡No te laves las manos!
4. Necesitas dormir más.
   a. ¡Levántate! **b.** ¡No te levantes!
5. ¿Tienes frío?
   a. ¡Vístete! **b.** ¡No te entrenes!
6. ¿Estás nervioso?
   a. ¡Relájate! **b.** ¡No te estires!
7. ¿Tienes catarro?
   a. ¡No te cuides! **b.** ¡Cuídate!
8. Los libros son muy aburridos.
   a. ¡No los leas! **b.** ¡Léelos!
9. A mi hermano no le tocan los quehaceres.
   a. ¡No te enojes! **b.** ¡Limpia el baño!
10. ¿Te gusta este escritorio?
    a. ¡Cómpralo! **b.** ¡No lo compres!

35 El hombre prehistórico 1B

Leamos/Escribamos Por un salto en el tiempo *(time warp)* un hombre prehistórico llega a tu casa y hace las siguientes cosas. Explícale cómo se hacen las cosas en el mundo moderno.

MODELO **Se baña en la cocina.**
¡No te bañes en la cocina! ¡Báñate en el baño!

1. Se pone el piyama para salir.
2. Se lava los dientes con una toalla.
3. Se levanta a las once de la noche.
4. Se lava con la pasta de dientes.
5. Se viste en el patio.
6. Se acuesta en la mesa.
7. Se peina con el jabón.
8. Se afeita con un cuchillo.

36 ¿Qué hago con esto? 1B

Escribamos/Hablemos Sigue el modelo para decirle al hombre prehistórico qué debe hacer y qué no debe hacer con las cosas.

MODELO **los platos (poner en el piso/poner en la mesa)**
¡No los pongas en el piso! ¡Ponlos en la mesa!

1. la ropa (lavar en la casa/lavar en el carro)
2. los lentes (usar para cortar/usar para leer)
3. las ventanas (limpiar con jugo/limpiar con agua y jabón)
4. la aspiradora (pasar en la sala/pasar en el césped)
5. la computadora (poner en el escritorio/poner en el microondas)
6. los sándwiches (hacer con papel/hacer con pan)
7. el arroz con pollo (comer con los pies/comer con un tenedor)

Comunicación

TEKS Focus
1A Engage in oral and written exchanges of learned material to socialize and to provide and obtain information

37 La madre cansada 1A

Hablemos Con un(a) compañero(a), dramatiza la conversación entre la madre y el hijo en los dibujos.

Novela en vídeo

¿Quién será?

Episodio 7

ESTRATEGIA

Understanding a Character's Motives To understand a character, you must first understand motives—why he or she is doing something or acting a certain way. To understand someone's motives, you must watch behavior. Nicolás has to get ready to go to his grandmother's birthday lunch. Can you tell from his actions whether he really wants to go? When he tells his grandmother he is sick, what is his motive? Watch what he does throughout the episode and decide what his motive is. 3B

En Puerto Rico

La mamá de Nicolás quiere hablar con él. Él tiene que alistarse para el almuerzo de cumpleaños de su abuela.

1

Sra. Ortega ¿Nicolás? ¿Hijo?

2

Sra. Ortega ¿Nicolás, estás listo? Hijo, ya sabes que hoy es el cumpleaños de tu abuela y tenemos que ir a almorzar con ella.

3

Sra. Ortega ¡Nicolás, por favor! ¡Levántate, hijo! Tienes que bañarte. Aquí está el jabón.

4

Sra. Ortega ¡Nicolás, por favor! ¡También tienes que lavarte el pelo! Aquí está el champú.

5

Sra. Ortega Nicolás, ¿no me oyes? Abre esta puerta, ¡ahora mismo! Sé que necesitas pasta de dientes… aquí está.

6

Visit Holt Online
go.hrw.com
KEYWORD: EXP1 CH7
Online Edition

7

Abuela Nicolás, te veo cansado.
Nicolás Sí, abuela, estoy un poco cansado. Tengo frío y me duele la cabeza.

8

Abuela Anda, vete, acuéstate un rato. Te despertamos cuando esté listo el almuerzo.
Nicolás Gracias, abuela.

9

Nicolás se acuesta pero no descansa.

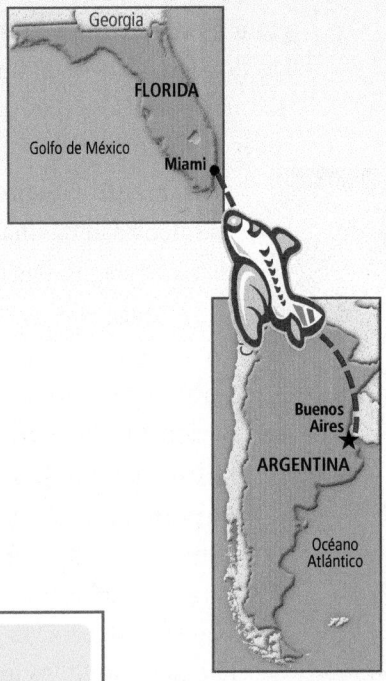

¿COMPRENDES?

1. Según su mamá, ¿qué necesita hacer Nicolás?
2. ¿Nicolás escucha a su mamá? ¿Qué motivo tiene para no escucharla?
3. ¿Qué necesita para bañarse? ¿Qué producto sale en la televisión?
4. ¿Qué necesita para lavarse el pelo? ¿Qué producto sale en la tele?
5. ¿Qué necesita para lavarse los dientes? ¿Qué producto sale en la tele?
6. ¿Está enfermo Nicolás? ¿Cómo lo sabes?
7. ¿Qué motivo tiene Nicolás para decir que está enfermo?

1B, 3A

Próximo episodio:
Ahora le toca a Marcos ir a Miami. ¿Qué piensas que va a hacer allí?
PÁGINAS 294–295

Leamos y escribamos

TEKS Focus
3A Use resources in the language and cultures being studied to gain access to information

ESTRATEGIA

para leer Background knowledge is the information you already know about a subject. Before you read something, take a moment to recall what you already know about the topic. Doing this will make it easier to guess the meaning of unfamiliar words or phrases.

A Antes de leer 1B, 3A

Piensa en lo que ya *(already)* sabes sobre la salud y la dieta. Ahora lee el artículo a continuación y deduce los significados de las palabras marcadas en el texto con un asterisco* rojo.

¡En buena salud!

Cecilia Mendoza, famosa entrenadora* y nutricionista argentina, contesta algunas preguntas sobre la salud y la dieta.

¿Qué es mejor para mantenerse en forma: levantar pesas o hacer aeróbicos?
Las dos actividades son buenas. Puedes hacer aeróbicos cuatro veces* por semana y levantar pesas dos veces por semana. Y recuerda[1], siempre debes estirarte después de hacer ejercicio.

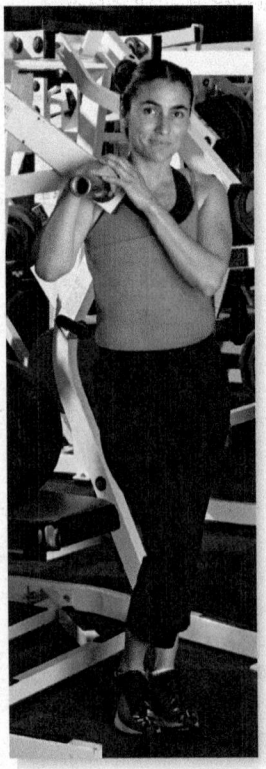

¿Por cuánto tiempo se debe hacer una actividad aeróbica?
La intensidad de una actividad determina su duración. Si la actividad requiere más energía, no hay que hacerla por mucho tiempo.

¿Qué dieta recomiendas para bajar de peso?
Lo más importante es comer comida sana y prestar atención[2] a la cantidad* de comida que comes. Si reduces el tamaño* de las porciones y sigues las recomendaciones de la pirámide alimenticia, vas a bajar de peso.

Sufro[3] mucho de estrés durante el año escolar. ¿Qué puedo hacer?
Para reducir[4] el estrés, haz lo siguiente: duerme lo suficiente, haz ejercicio todos los días, come una dieta sana, no tomes bebidas con cafeína[5], maneja* bien tu tiempo, toma las cosas con calma y siempre respira[6] profundamente*.

Pirámide alimenticia

1 remember 2 pay attention 3 I suffer 4 reduce 5 caffeinated beverages 6 breathe

Visit Holt Online
go.hrw.com
KEYWORD: EXP1 CH7
Online Edition

B Comprensión ✦1B

¿Son **ciertas** o **falsas** las siguientes oraciones? Corrige las oraciones falsas.

1. Cecilia Mendoza sólo *(only)* habla del ejercicio.
2. Para mantenerse en forma es necesario levantar pesas todos los días.
3. La intensidad de un ejercicio determina la cantidad de tiempo que debes hacerlo.
4. Para bajar de peso sólo es necesario seguir una dieta sana.
5. Para reducir el estrés es importante tener una vida sana.

C Después de leer ✦1B, 2B

Which of Cecilia's recommendations do you already follow? How difficult would it be for you to follow all of her recommendations? Which ones would be the most difficult to follow? Why?

Clínica Fierro

¿Te duele...?
- _____
- _____

¿Estás...?
- _____
- _____

Taller del escritor

ESTRATEGIA

para escribir Graphic organizers can help you organize your thoughts visually and are especially helpful in designing posters and charts. Consider bulleted charts or cluster bubbles as you sketch out your display.

El doctor te aconseja... ✦1C

You are a doctor who believes that patients should take a more active role in avoiding or curing their ailments. Design a chart for the patients' waiting room listing common symptoms followed by your suggestions on how to avoid or cure the problem.

1 Antes de escribir

List the symptoms in question form: **¿Te duele la garganta? ¿Estás cansado(a)?** Then think of one or more suggestions to solve each problem or illness. Write down your ideas.

2 Escribir un borrador

Use a graphic organizer to arrange the symptoms and their solutions on a poster board. Write out suggestions telling patients what to do. Use expressions for giving advice as well as affirmative and negative commands.

3 Revisar

Read your advice to a classmate, consider his/her input, and check for proper use of vocabulary, spelling, and punctuation.

4 Publicar

Illustrate your chart if you want and show it to the class. Share one piece of advice from your chart. Do other students suggest different solutions to the same health problems?

Cuaderno para hispanohablantes, pp. 69–80

Prepárate para el examen

Repaso capítulo 7

Interactive TUTOR

1 Vocabulario 1
- talking about your daily routine
- talking about staying fit and healthy

pp. 234-237

2 Gramática 1
- verbs with reflexive pronouns
- infinitives
- review of stem-changing verbs

pp. 238-243

3 Vocabulario 2
- talking about how you feel
- giving advice

pp. 246-249

1 Todos se preparan para salir. ¿Qué tiene que hacer cada persona para prepararse? 1B

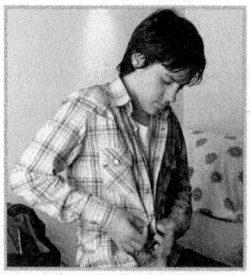
1. Miguelito

2. el señor Blanco

3. Elena

2 Completa el párrafo con los verbos lógicos y con la forma correcta de los verbos.

Por la mañana, mi madre __1__ (dormir/cuidarse) hasta las seis. Luego, ella __2__ (almorzar/levantarse) y __3__ (cenar/vestirse) antes de desayunar. Yo me levanto muy temprano para __4__ (entrenarse/dormir) antes de ir al colegio. Después de clases, mis hermanos y yo __5__ (poder/deber) ver un poco de televisión antes de __6__ (ver/empezar) la tarea. A veces mi hermana Maribel __7__ (jugar/ponerse) videojuegos. Por la noche, (yo) __8__ (desayunar/bañarse) y luego escucho música para __9__ (cuidarse/relajarse) un poco antes de acostarme.

3 Prepara una lista de consejos para un(a) amigo(a) usando las palabras de los cuadros. 1B

1	2	3
Debes	comer tanto dulce	si estás aburrido(a)
No debes	acostarte tarde	si siempre tienes catarro
	comer verduras	si no quieres subir de peso
	hacer yoga	si siempre tienes sueño
	buscar un pasatiempo	para mantenerte en forma
	entrenarte	para seguir una dieta sana
	cuidarte	para relajarte

Visit Holt Online
go.hrw.com
KEYWORD: EXP1 CH7
Chapter Self-test

4 Tu amigo tiene problemas. Escribe mandatos, usando los dos verbos entre paréntesis para darle tus consejos. 1B

1. No tengo nada que hacer después de clases. Estoy aburrido. (ser perezoso/buscar un pasatiempo)
2. Siempre me siento muy cansado en clase. (acostarse más temprano/dormir en clase)
3. Muchas veces tengo miedo de hablar en clase. (ser tímido/hablar)
4. Me duele el estómago después de comer en un restaurante. (comer comida sana/pedir muchos postres)
5. Me duelen los ojos y la cabeza. (ver tanta televisión/comprar lentes)

5 Answer the questions. 2A, 2B

1. What sport is practiced in July in Bariloche?
2. Name some foods that are popular in Argentina.
3. What is **mate**? How is it prepared?

6 Escucha la conversación entre Roberto y Laura. Luego di si las oraciones que siguen *(that follow)* son **ciertas** o **falsas.**

7 Escribe lo que dicen y lo que hacen los muchachos. 1C

4 Gramática 2
- **estar, sentirse,** and **tener**
- negative informal commands
- object and reflexive pronouns with commands

pp. 250–255

5 Cultura
- **Comparaciones** **pp. 244–245**
- **Notas culturales** **pp. 236, 248, 249**
- **Geocultura** **pp. 228–231**

TEKS Focus
1C Present information using familiar words, phrases, and sentences

Repaso

Gramática 1
- verbs with reflexive pronouns **pp. 238-239**
- using infinitives **pp. 240-241**
- review of stem-changing verbs **pp. 242-243**

Repaso de Gramática 1

Some verbs are used with **reflexive pronouns** if the subject and object of the verb are the same. For a list of such verbs, see p. 238.

lavarse			
me	lavo	**nos**	lavamos
te	lavas	**os**	laváis
se	lava	**se**	lavan

Use the **infinitive** of a verb after **acabar de, para, antes de, después de.**

Acabo de bañarme. Necesito una toalla **para secarme.**

For the forms of **acostarse** (**o** → **ue**) and **vestirse** (**e** → **i**), see page 242.

Gramática 2
- **estar, sentirse,** and **tener** **pp. 250-251**
- negative informal commands **pp. 252-253**
- object and reflexive pronouns with commands **pp. 254-255**

TEKS Focus
1B Demonstrate understanding of simple, clearly spoken, and written language when dealing with familiar topics

Repaso de Gramática 2

Use these expressions to describe mental or physical states.

estar bien/mal/*adjective*
sentirse bien/mal/*adjective*
tener frío/calor/miedo/sueño

To review negative commands, see p. 252. An **object** or **reflexive pronoun** goes just before the verb in **negative commands** and is attached to the end of an **affirmative command.**

fumar → **no fumes**
dormir → **no duermas**
levantarse → **no te levantes (levánta**te**)**
dar → **no des**
ir → **no vayas**
ser → **no seas**

Letra y sonido g gu

La letra g

- The letters **g** and **gu** sound like the "hard" *g* in *game* at the beginning of a phrase starting with **ga, gue, gui, go, gu, gr, gl** or when these follow **n:**
  gato, guerra, guitarra, tengo, un gusto, ¡Grita!
- The letters **g** and **gu** sound much softer than the *g* in *game* when **ga, gue, gui, go, gu, gr, gl** follow a vowel or a consonant other than **n:**
  mi gato, águila, algo, mucho gusto, negro

Trabalenguas

Tres tigres tragaban trigo en un trigal, y el más grande se puso a entigretar.

Contigo entró un tren con trigo
un tren con trigo contigo entró.

Dictado 1B

Escribe las oraciones de la grabación.

Repaso de Vocabulario 1

Talking about your daily routine

acabar de	*to just (have done something)*
acostarse (ue)	*to go to bed*
afeitarse	*to shave*
antes de	*before*
bañarse	*to bathe*
la boca	*mouth*
el brazo	*arm*
la cara	*face*
el cepillo de dientes	*toothbrush*
despertarse (ie)	*to wake up*
los dientes	*teeth*
encontrar (ue)	*to find*
entrenarse	*to work out*
la espalda	*back*
estar listo(a)	*to be ready*
estirarse	*to stretch*
los hombros	*shoulders*
el jabón	*soap*
lavarse	*to wash*
levantar pesas	*to lift weights*
levantarse	*to get up*
el maquillaje	*makeup*
maquillarse	*to put on makeup*
la nariz	*nose*
la navaja	*razor*
la pantorrilla	*calf*
la pasta de dientes	*toothpaste*
el pecho	*chest*
peinarse	*to comb your hair*
el peine	*comb*
la pierna	*leg*
el piyama	*pajamas*
ponerse	*to put on*
prepararse	*to get ready*
¿Qué te falta hacer?	*What do you still have to do?*
quitarse	*to take off*
la secadora de pelo	*hair dryer*
secarse	*to dry*
la toalla	*towel*
vestirse (i)	*to get dressed*

Talking about staying fit and healthy

mantenerse (ie) en forma	*to stay in shape*
¿Qué haces para relajarte?	*What do you do to relax?*

Repaso de Vocabulario 2

To talk about how you feel

bajar de peso	*to lose weight*
buscar un pasatiempo	*to find a hobby*
la cabeza	*head*
caminar	*to walk*
el cuello	*neck*
los dedos	*fingers*
dejar de fumar	*to stop smoking*
doler (ue)	*to hurt*
enojarse	*to get angry*
Es que...	*It's because/just that . . .*
estar aburrido(a)	*to be bored*
estar cansado(a)	*to be tired*
estar contento(a)	*to be happy*
estar enfermo(a)	*to be sick*
estar enojado(a)	*to be angry*
estar nervioso(a)	*to be nervous*
estar triste	*to be sad*
el estómago	*stomach*
la garganta	*throat*
hacer yoga	*to do yoga*
las manos	*hands*
Me duele(n)...	*My . . . hurt(s)*
el oído	*ear*
los pies	*feet*
¿Qué te pasa?	*What's wrong with you?*
¿Qué tiene...?	*What's the matter with . . . ?*
seguir (i) una dieta sana	*to eat a balanced diet*
sentirse (ie)	*to feel*
subir de peso	*to gain weight*
¿Te duele algo?	*Does something hurt?*
Te veo mal.	*You don't look well.*
tener catarro	*to have a cold*

To give advice

demasiado(a)	*too much*
dormir lo suficiente	*to get enough sleep*
ni	*neither*
No debes...	*You shouldn't . . .*
Para cuidarte la salud,	*To take care of your health,*
Para cuidarte mejor,	*To take better care of yourself,*
tanta grasa	*so much fat*
tanto dulce	*so many sweets*
tanto(a)	*so much*

Expressions with tener . . . . . *See p. 250*

Integración

capítulos 1-7

1 Escucha la descripción de una mañana típica en casa de los Muñoz. Escoge la foto correspondiente. 1B

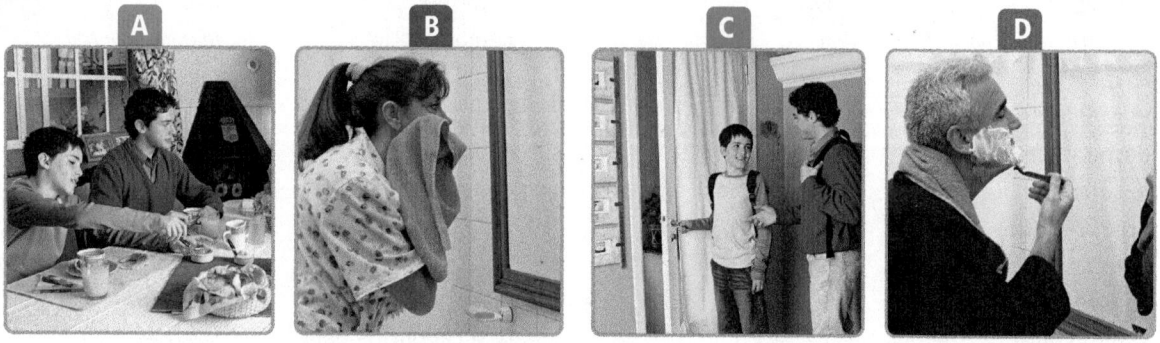

2 Lee los problemas y los consejos que se encuentran en esta revista para jóvenes. Luego contesta las preguntas. 1B, 1C

Querida DameEsperanza...

Querida DameEsperanza:
Necesito hacer más ejercicio, pero no me gusta levantar pesas. Quiero cambiar mi rutina, pero no sé qué hacer. ¿Me ayudas?
– Siempre cansado

Querido Cansado:
Para cuidarte mejor, tienes que hacer ejercicio por lo menos tres veces a la semana. ¿Qué te gusta hacer? Necesitas buscar una actividad divertida, como bailar, montar en bicicleta, nadar o caminar en el parque. Si no haces algo divertido, no vas a seguir con el ejercicio.

Querida DameEsperanza:
Tengo muchas clases difíciles y soy muy trabajadora. Mis amigos prefieren salir y no estudian. Quiero salir con ellos, pero no puedo porque tengo mucha tarea. ¿Qué debo hacer?
– Frustrada

Querida Frustrada:
Sí, debes estudiar, pero necesitas relajarte también. Puedes estudiar dos o tres horas cada noche. Entonces, los viernes y sábados puedes ir con tus amigos a un partido o al cine. ¡No necesitas pasar todas las noches en la biblioteca!

1. ¿Por qué le escribe Siempre cansado a DameEsperanza?
2. Según ella, ¿cuántas veces a la semana se debe hacer ejercicio?
3. ¿Qué tipo de ejercicio recomienda DameEsperanza?
4. ¿Qué problema tiene Frustrada?
5. ¿Qué consejos le da DameEsperanza a Frustrada? ¿Son buenos consejos, en tu opinión?

Visit Holt Online
go.hrw.com
KEYWORD: EXP1 CH7
Cumulative Self-test

3 Tu amigo(a) quiere ponerse en forma, pero no le gusta hacer ejercicio ni comer bien. Crea un diálogo en que tú le das consejos *(give advice)* y él/ella te dice que no le gusta la idea o que prefiere hacer otra cosa. **1A, 1B, 1C**

4 Mira la pintura. ¿Quiénes son las personas y cómo son? En otro papel, escribe una descripción breve de tres de las personas. Incluye una descripción física y cómo crees que es su personalidad. Con un(a) compañero(a), túrnense para leer las descripciones y adivinar *(guess)* a quién pertenecen. **1A, 1B, 1C**

by Prilidiano Pueyrredón, 1823-70, Argentinian; The Art Archive / Museo Nacional de Bellas Artes Buenos Aires / Dagli Orti

Un alto en el campo (detalle), **de Prilidiano Pueyrredón (1823–70)**

5 Estás en un campamento de verano *(summer camp)* con tu mejor amigo(a). Escríbeles una tarjeta postal a tus padres. Describe tu rutina diaria, tus actividades preferidas y la comida del campamento. **1B, 1C**

6

Situación

It's time for your school's annual health fair. The Spanish department is conducting a survey to find out what its students do to relax and stay in shape. Create a survey with five questions in Spanish about diet, exercise habits, and stress-reducing activities. Poll classmates to get their answers. Compile the results and write a final presentation to take to the fair. **1A, 1B, 1C**

GeoVisión

Geocultura Florida

▲ **Florida** es uno de los exportadores más grandes de cítricos del mundo. Los primeros naranjos llegaron a Florida con los exploradores españoles en el siglo XVI.

Panama City

▼ **Miami,** un paraíso multicultural con muchos hispanohablantes, se encuentra en la costa atlántica de Florida, a sólo 366 kilómetros de La Habana, Cuba.

Almanaque

Población
15.982.378

Capital
Tallahassee

Área
58.664 millas cuadradas
(151.939km²)

Moneda
dólar estadounidense

Economía
manufactura, turismo, productos de frutas cítricas, pesca comercial, electrónica, comercio con Latinoamérica

¿Sabías que...?

En los estados de Florida y Texas los hispanohablantes influyen en muchos aspectos de la vida diaria y la cultura. En Florida predominan las tradiciones cubanas y en Texas las mexicanas.

◄ **Muchos floridianos** pasan el tiempo libre en las playas de su estado.

▶ **El Parque de los Everglades** es el único lugar del mundo donde cohabitan los cocodrilos y los caimanes.

▲ **Cape Canaveral** El Centro Espacial Kennedy coexiste en armonía con el Refugio de Fauna de la Isla Merritt, donde hay más especies en peligro de extinción que en cualquier otra reserva de Estados Unidos.

▲ **La Pequeña Habana** es un distrito cubano en Miami.

▼ **Los Cayos de Florida** se conectan a través de 42 puentes incluso el famoso Puente de la Bahía Honda.

3B

¿Qué tanto sabes?

¿Cómo se conectan los Cayos de Florida? ¿Dónde cohabitan los cocodrilos y los caimanes?

A conocer Florida

La comida

▲ **Floribbean, o floribeño,** se llama una tradición culinaria que combina los sabores del Caribe y de Florida. Plátanos, yuca, hierbas finas, especias, mariscos y frutas tropicales como el mango son ingredientes típicos de la cocina floribeña.

▲ **Las croquetas y las empanadas** son bocadillos cubanos que se venden por todos lados de Miami. El sándwich cubano también es muy popular. El flan cubano es un postre dulce y muy típico en restaurantes de la Pequeña Habana, Miami.

El arte

► **Los seminoles** de Florida producen cestas de paja de los Everglades.

▲ ***Guantanameros,*** 1996, fue pintado por Xavier Cortada, un artista cubanoamericano que aporta mucho a la comunidad de Miami.

▲ ***Calle Ocho*** fue pintado por Mildrey Guillot. Nacida en La Habana, Cuba, esta artista se mudó a Miami en 1962.

◄ **Mildrey Guillot**

La arquitectura

Interactive TUTOR

Visit Holt Online
go.hrw.com
KEYWORD: EXP1 CH8
Photo Tour

▲ **St. Augustine** fue fundada en 1565 por los españoles. La arquitectura colonial da testimonio al legado español de la ciudad.

◀ **Tampa** En 1899 inmigrantes cubanos fundaron el Círculo Cubano. El edificio fue construido en 1917 al estilo neoclásico.

¿Sabías que...?

Juan Ponce de León, un explorador español, llegó a la costa de la península en 1513 y la llamó «la Florida».

Las celebraciones

◀ **Baila USA** Durante cuatro días se celebran las tradiciones artísticas de la comunidad latina con temas afrolatinos en Miami.

▶ **El Carnaval de Miami** en la Pequeña Habana acaba con el gran *Festival de la Calle Ocho* donde se celebra la cultura hispana de la ciudad.

Conexión Música

En marzo se da el *Festival de Jazz Latino*, el cual forma parte de las celebraciones del *Carnaval de Miami*. El jazz latino es una fusión del jazz con la sección rítmica afrocubana. Busca en un periódico o en Internet qué géneros de música son los preferidos de tu comunidad. Compara éstos con el jazz latino. 2B, 3B

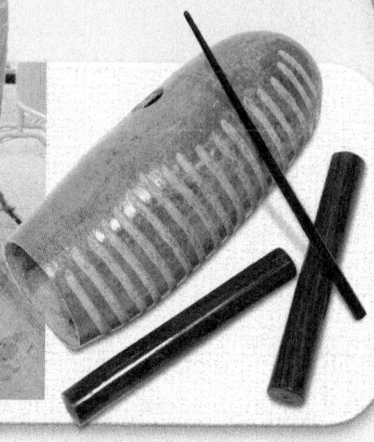

Capítulo 8

Vamos de compras

OBJETIVOS

In this chapter you will learn to

- ask for and give opinions
- ask for and offer help in a store
- say where you went and what you did
- talk on the phone

And you will use

- **costar** and numbers to one million
- demonstrative adjectives and comparisons
- **quedar**
- preterite of **-ar** verbs
- preterite of **ir**
- preterite of verbs with reflexive pronouns

¿Qué ves en la foto?

- ¿Cuántas personas hay? ¿Cómo están?
- ¿Qué toman?
- ¿Cómo es el edificio?

Texas

TEKS Look for the ★ next to each activity to learn how it can help you achieve the goals of the **Texas Essential Knowledge and Skills,** found on page xxiii.

Visit Holt Online
go.hrw.com
KEYWORD: EXP1 CH8
Online Edition

De compras en Miami

Objetivos

Asking for and giving opinions, asking for and offering help in a store

Vocabulario en acción 1

ExpresaVisión

En la tienda de ropa

¿Qué le parece esta camisa?

Muy bien. También me gustaría comprar un suéter.

el cliente (la cliente)

el dependiente (la dependiente)

un suéter

una chaqueta

un abrigo

un par de pantalones vaqueros

Más vocabulario...

Es...

de algodón	*made of cotton*
de lana	*made of wool*
de seda	*made of silk*
para hombres	*for men*
para mujeres	*for women*
para niños	*for children*

▶ **Vocabulario adicional** — Ropa, p. R10

Texas También se puede decir...

In Spain, you might hear **pantalones tejanos** as well as **vaqueros**. A sweater is called **un jersey** and tennis shoes are **zapatillas de tenis.**

Bluejeans are also known as **pantalones de mezclilla** and T-shirts are **playeras** in Mexico and Texas. Many Spanish speakers have borrowed the term **bluejeans** directly from English.

Visit Holt Online
go.hrw.com
KEYWORD: EXP1 CH8
Vocabulario 1 practice

¿Qué ropa llevas hoy?

Voy al gimnasio. Llevo...

un sombrero

una camiseta

unos pantalones cortos

unos zapatos de tenis

Voy a salir con amigos. Llevo...

un vestido

unas sandalias

Voy a clase. Llevo...

una blusa

una falda

unas botas

Voy a salir al teatro. Llevo...

una camisa

unos pantalones

unos calcetines

unos zapatos

¿Qué color te gusta más?

rojo · azul · verde · amarillo · morado · blanco · negro · anaranjado · gris · café

¡Exprésate!

To ask for an opinion	To give your opinion
¿Qué te parece el traje de baño anaranjado? *What do you think of the orange swimsuit?*	**Me parece feo y cuesta mucho. ¡Es un robo!** *It's ugly and costs a lot. It's a rip-off!*
¿Cómo me queda el saco? *How does the sport coat fit me?*	**Te queda muy bien. Y está a la (última) moda.** *It looks good on you. And it's in (the latest) style.*
¿Y el/la...? ¡Cuesta ochenta dólares! *What about this . . .? It costs $80.00!*	**¡Qué caro(a)! Además, está pasado(a) de moda.** *How expensive! Besides, it's out of style.*
La bolsa es una ganga, ¿verdad? *The purse is a bargain, isn't it?*	**Tienes razón. Es muy barata.** *You're right. It's very inexpensive.*

Interactive TUTOR

Online
Vocabulario y gramática, pp. 85–87

Nota cultural

Most Spanish-speaking countries use the metric system, so clothing and shoe sizes are different from sizes in the United States. The word for "size" also varies, depending on what you're buying. If you're looking for clothing, use **talla**. For shoes, use **número**. Look at the chart and compare the different sizes. What size shirt would you wear in Spain? What size shoes? 2B, 4B

Tallas para hombres	USA	EUR
Camisas	14	36
	15	38
	16	40
Zapatos	7	40
	8	41
	9	43

Tallas para mujeres	USA	EUR
Blusas	8	36
	10	38
	12	40
Zapatos	5	36
	6	37
	7	38

1 ¿Les gustan? 1B

Escuchemos Basándote en los comentarios, decide si a las personas les gusta o no les gusta la ropa de que hablan.

1. la camisa
2. la blusa
3. el saco
4. el vestido
5. las botas
6. la chaqueta
7. el sombrero
8. el traje de baño
9. los pantalones vaqueros
10. el abrigo

2 ¿Qué te parecen? 1B

Hablemos Describe la ropa en cada dibujo. No te olvides de usar las formas correctas de los verbos y los adjetivos.

MODELO **Son unos calcetines rojos. Son bastante caros.**

Es bonito.	**Es feo.**
Es bastante barato.	**Es bastante caro.**
¡Es una ganga!	**¡Es un robo!**
Está a la última moda.	**Está pasado de moda.**

1.

2.

3.

4.

5.

3 ¿Qué ropa llevas para...? 1B, 1C

Escribamos/Hablemos Di qué llevas en estas situaciones.

MODELO **Para ir a clase...**
Para ir a clase, llevo pantalones, una camisa...

1. Para pasear por el parque en junio...
2. Para ir a un concierto...
3. Para salir con amigos...
4. Cuando hace frío...
5. Para nadar...
6. Para ir a clase...
7. Para ir a la playa...
8. Para jugar al fútbol...

¡Exprésate!

To offer and ask for help in a store	
¿En qué le puedo servir? *How can I help you?*	**Busco una camisa de seda.** *I'm looking for a silk shirt.* **Nada más estoy mirando.** *I'm just looking.* **Quiero devolver esta falda. La necesito en otro color.** *I want to return this skirt. I need it in another color.*
¿Qué número/talla usa? *What shoe/clothing size do you wear?*	**Uso el/la 8.** *I wear a size 8 in shoes/clothes.*
¿Cómo le queda la camisa? *How does the shirt fit you?*	**Me queda bien/mal. Necesito una talla más grande/pequeña.** *It fits well/poorly. I need a bigger/smaller size.*
¿A qué hora cierra la tienda? *What time does the store close?*	**Cierra a las siete.** *It closes at 7:00.*

Interactive TUTOR

Online
Vocabulario y gramática, pp. 85–87

Comunicación

4 Hablando de ropa 1A

Hablemos Con un(a) compañero(a), túrnense para contestar las siguientes preguntas.

1. ¿Qué te parece la ropa de... *(famous designer)*? ¿Cómo te queda?
2. ¿Qué colores prefieres llevar?
3. ¿Qué ropa está a la última moda? ¿Qué está pasado(a) de moda?
4. ¿Qué ropa te gusta llevar a los bailes en el colegio?
5. ¿Qué ropa no te gusta?
6. ¿A qué hora cierran las tiendas donde te gusta ir de compras?
7. Si necesitas una talla más grande/pequeña, ¿te ayuda el(la) dependiente?

TEKS Focus
1A Engage in oral and written exchanges of learned material to socialize and to provide and obtain information

5 Busco... 1A

Hablemos Quieres comprar un vestido o un traje nuevo para una fiesta, y tienes $100.00. Tu compañero(a) es dependiente en una tienda de ropa y te puede ayudar a encontrar algo. Túrnense para crear una conversación.

MODELO **—Buenas tardes. ¿En qué le puedo servir?**
—Buenas tardes. Busco un...

Objetivos

costar and numbers to one million, demonstrative adjectives and comparisons, **quedar**

Gramática en acción 1

GramaVisión

Costar, numbers to one million

1 Use the verb **costar (o → ue)** to talk about what something costs. **Costar** is usually only used in the third person.

La blusa **cuesta** treinta dólares. Las botas **cuestan** setenta dólares.

2 To tell what something costs, you may need to use larger numbers.

100	cien	600	seiscientos(as)
101	ciento uno(a)	700	setecientos(as)
102	ciento dos	800	ochocientos(as)
200	doscientos(as)	900	novecientos(as)
300	trescientos(as)	1.000	mil
400	cuatrocientos(as)	2.000	dos mil
500	quinientos(as)	1.000.000	un millón (de)

TEKS Focus

1B Demonstrate understanding of simple, clearly spoken, and written language when dealing with familiar topics

3 Use **uno** when counting. **Uno** at the end of a number, changes to **un** before a masculine noun and **una** before a feminine noun: **veintiún dólares, veintiuna faldas.**

Tengo **ciento un** dólares. Tengo **veintiuna** bolsas.

4 **Cien(to)** is used with both masculine and feminine nouns, but 200, 300, and so on agree with the noun they modify. **Mil** does not change.

cien dólares **ciento** dos dólares **doscientos** dos dólares **mil** dólares

cien personas **ciento** dos personas **doscientas** dos personas **mil** personas

5 **Un millón** changes to **millones** in the plural. Use **de** after **millon(es)** when it is followed by a noun.

3.520.312 = tres **millones,** quinientos veinte mil, trescientos doce

un millón de dólares **dos millones de** personas

Un supermercado en Miami

Online

Vocabulario y gramática, pp. 88–90 | Actividades, pp. 71–73

6 ¡Qué caro! 1B

Escuchemos Escribe los números que corresponden a los precios.

Visit Holt Online
go.hrw.com
KEYWORD: EXP1 CH8
Gramática 1 practice

7 Tenemos que pagar 1C

Escribamos Escribe el valor de cada cifra *(number)*.

MODELO **$354**
trescientos cincuenta y cuatro dólares

1. $2.168
2. $1.319.672
3. $1.550
4. $213.434
5. $11.721
6. $1.946

8 El inventario 1C

Escribamos/Hablemos Tienes que hacer un inventario de los artículos de ropa en la tienda donde trabajas. Usa el cuadro para decir cuántas cosas tienen.

MODELO **botas 22.336**
Tenemos veintidós mil, trescientos treinta y seis pares de botas.

zapatos	367.555	**blusas**	3.689
faldas	19.324	**sombreros**	475
pantalones	150.743	**bolsas**	2.079
camisas	4.597	**camisetas**	78.521

Nota cultural

Shopping in small-town flea markets in Texas is a unique experience. You can find almost anything for sale, including crafts, antiques, food, clothing, and plants. In larger cities, the markets are in huge warehouse buildings, and shoppers enjoy snacks and the music of Tejano bands. Canton, Texas, located about 60 miles east of Dallas, has the world's largest flea market. Why do you think flea markets are so popular? 2A

Comunicación

9 ¡Vamos de compras! 1A

Hablemos Con un(a) compañero(a), crea una conversación entre un(a) cliente y un(a) dependiente sobre las cosas que el(la) cliente quiere comprar de un catálogo.

MODELO **—Quiero comprar el suéter rojo. ¿Cuánto cuesta?**
—Cuesta doscientos nueve dólares.
—¡Es un robo! No voy a comprarlo.
(—Bueno. Voy a comprarlo.)

Demonstrative adjectives and comparisons

Interactive TUTOR

1 **Demonstrative adjectives** point out things. Use forms of **este** for things close to you. Use forms of **ese** for things farther away.

		Masculine	Feminine
this	SINGULAR	**este**	**esta**
these	PLURAL	**estos**	**estas**
that	SINGULAR	**ese**	**esa**
those	PLURAL	**esos**	**esas**

—¿Te gusta **este** vestido? —Me gusta más **esa** falda.

2 Use these expressions with adjectives to compare things. The adjective agrees in gender and number with the object described.

más + *adjective* + que	*more . . . than*
tan + *adjective* + como	*as . . . as*
menos + *adjective* + que	*less . . . than*

Esta camiset**a** es **más bonit a que** esa camiseta.

Esta camiset**a** es **tan bonit a como** esa camiseta.

3 These adjectives have irregular comparative forms.

bueno(a)	*good*	malo(a)	*bad*
mejor(es)	*better*	**peor(es)**	*worse*
joven	*young*	viejo(a)	*old*
menor(es)	*younger*	**mayor(es)**	*older*

Este disco compacto es **malo,** pero ese disco es **peor.**

4 Use **más que, menos que,** and **tanto como** to say if someone does something *more than, less than* or *as much as* someone else.

Efraín compra **tanto como** Isabel.

Mis padres salen **menos que** mis abuelos.

Online

Vocabulario y gramática, pp. 88–90 | Actividades, pp. 71–73

Nota cultural

In Florida it is common to see men wearing **guayaberas**, embroidered short-sleeved cotton or linen shirts. These shirts originated in Cuba over 200 years ago. Ramón Puig, a Cuban immigrant in Miami, is famous for his guayabera shirts and has custom-made them for celebrities. What fashions were developed in the United States and exported to other countries? 4C

TEKS Focus

4C Demonstrate understanding of the influence of one language and culture on another

10 ¿De qué habla? 1B

Escuchemos Escucha mientras estas personas dicen qué cosa prefieren. Escribe lo que prefieren en otro papel. Si les gustan las dos cosas igualmente, escribe **las dos.**

11 Julio y Nidia 1B

Leamos Lee las descripciones de Julio y Nidia y completa las comparaciones con **más...que, menos...que** o **tan... como** y la forma correcta del adjetivo entre paréntesis.

Julio tiene 15 años. Es alto, guapo y muy simpático. Es bastante serio y estudia mucho. Le gusta ver películas de amor, pasar el rato solo y leer. No le gustan los deportes. Nidia tiene 17 años. Es baja, guapa y muy simpática. No le gusta estudiar. Es muy graciosa. Le gusta practicar deportes y salir con amigos.

MODELO **Julio es _____ (romántico) _____ Nidia.**
Julio es más romántico que Nidia.

1. Julio es _____ (alto) _____ Nidia.
2. Nidia es _____ (guapo) _____ Julio.
3. Nidia es _____ (simpático) _____ Julio.
4. Nidia es _____ (serio) _____ Julio.
5. Julio es _____ (gracioso) _____ Nidia.
6. Nidia es _____ (atlético) _____ Julio.
7. Nidia es _____ (extrovertido) _____ Julio.

Nidia y Julio

12 Comparaciones 1B, 1C

Escribamos/Hablemos Ahora compárate con los dos muchachos de la Actividad 11. *¿Se te olvidó?* Adjective agreement, p. 50

MODELO **Soy menor que Julio. Él es más serio que yo...**

Comunicación

13 Prefiero... 1A

Hablemos Con un(a) compañero(a), habla de estas cosas. Decide cuál de las dos prefieres y di por qué, comparando cada par de cosas.

MODELO **—¿Prefieres estos zapatos blancos o esos...?**
—Prefiero los zapatos blancos. Son menos caros...

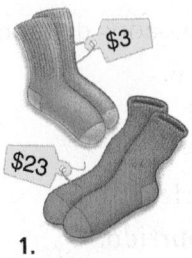

1.

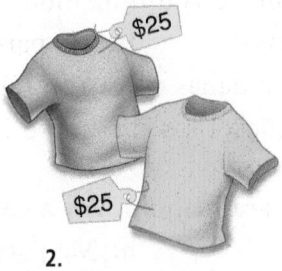

2.

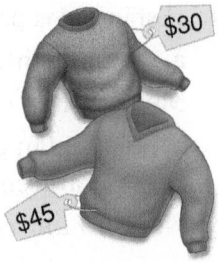

3.

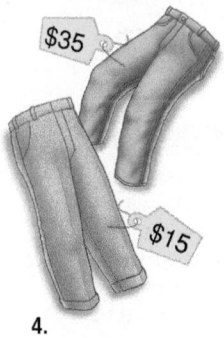

4.

Quedar

Interactive TUTOR

1 Use the verb **quedar** to say how something *fits* or *looks* on someone. **Quedar** works like **parecer** and **gustar.** Use **queda** when talking about one thing. Use **quedan** when talking about more than one thing.

(a mí)	me queda(n)	(a nosotros/as)	nos queda(n)
(a ti)	te queda(n)	(a vosotros/as)	os queda(n)
(a Ud., a él, a ella)	le queda(n)	(a Uds., a ellos, a ellas)	les queda(n)

one thing

Esa blusa te **queda** bien. *That blouse looks good on you.*

more than one thing

Estas botas me **quedan** grandes. *These boots are too big for me.*

2 Adjectives like **grande** and **pequeño(a)**, as well as adverbs like **bien** and **mal**, can follow **quedar.** All adjectives must agree, but the adverbs don't change form.

agrees

Esta falda me queda **pequeña**. Me queda **mal**.
This skirt is too small for me. It fits me badly.

agrees

Estas botas me quedan **grandes**. No me quedan **bien**.
These boots are too big for me. They don't fit me well.

Online

Vocabulario y gramática, pp. 88–90 | Actividades, pp. 71–73

¿Te acuerdas?

The verb **parecer** *(to seem)* can be used like **gustar**.

Esa falda me **parece** fea.

¿Cómo te **parecen** estos pantalones?

TEKS Focus

1B Demonstrate understanding of simple, clearly spoken, and written language when dealing with familiar topics

14 Comentarios 1B

Leamos Graciela y Leonora están de compras. Lee los comentarios de Graciela e indica las respuestas de Leonora.

1. Me gustan esos zapatos. ¿Vas a comprarlos?
   a. No, me quedan grandes. **b.** Sí, te quedan muy bien.
2. Esa blusa es una ganga, ¿no te parece?
   a. Me parece muy cara. **b.** Le queda pequeña.
3. Prefiero los pantalones vaqueros a los pantalones cortos.
   a. Les gustan los pantalones vaqueros.
   b. Te quedan mejor que los pantalones cortos.
4. ¿Están estos pantalones a la última moda?
   a. Te quedan pequeños. **b.** Me parecen pasados de moda.
5. Me encantan estas sandalias rojas. Son número 6.
   a. Te quedan pequeñas. Usas el número 7, ¿no?
   b. Les parecen bonitas.
6. Necesito un regalo para Joaquín. Voy a comprarle un libro.
   a. Le queda bien. **b.** Me parece aburrido.

15 ¿Cómo le queda? 1B

Escuchemos Escucha mientras varias personas hablan de ropa en una tienda. Para cada comentario, indica si el artículo de ropa **a**) le queda bien o **b**) le queda mal a la persona.

16 ¿Es bonita la ropa? 1B

Leamos/Escribamos Completa la conversación entre Daniela y su madre con la forma correcta de **quedar** o **parecer** y el pronombre correspondiente. *¿Se te olvidó?* Parecer, p. 178

MODELO **A mí *me queda* grande esta falda. Además, *me parece* fea.**

—Mamá, me gusta ese vestido. A ti ___1___ muy bien.

—Gracias, pero necesito otra talla. ___2___ pequeño. ¿Qué ___3___ esta blusa? Es bonita, ¿no?

—¡Uy!, ___4___ fea. Además, cuesta una fortuna.

—Daniela, ¿qué ___5___ estas botas? ¿Debo comprarlas para Raquel?

—Pero mamá, mira esas botas negras. No cuestan mucho y son muy bonitas. De verdad, ___6___ feas las botas amarillas. No me gusta ese color.

—Bueno, a nosotras no ___7___ bien nuestros zapatos viejos. ¿Quieres comprar unos nuevos?

—¡Ay, sí! Por ejemplo, estos zapatos negros ___8___ super bonitos.

Comunicación

17 ¿Qué te parece? 1A

Hablemos En parejas, den sus opiniones sobre la ropa de Luisa y Tomás. ¿Les gusta? ¿Cómo es; bonita, fea, cara? ¿Cómo les queda a ellos? Túrnense para hacer comentarios.

MODELO **El sombrero de Luisa no me gusta. Es feo y caro. Le queda grande.**

Cultura

VideoCultura

Comparaciones

Interactive TUTOR

De compras en la Pequeña Habana

¿Qué te gusta comprar cuando vas de compras? 4B

Sin duda, vas de compras y tienes un lugar donde te encanta ir. ¿Qué diferencias hay entre un centro comercial, un almacén y un mercado al aire libre? En los países de habla hispana, la gente puede ir a grandes almacenes para comprar de todo. También es posible ir a tiendas pequeñas donde venden sólo un tipo de producto. De todos modos, parece que los jóvenes hispanohablantes van de compras con frecuencia. Estas personas nos dicen qué les gusta comprar y adónde van cuando tienen ganas de comprar algo nuevo. ¿Compras las mismas cosas?

Dayana
Miami, Florida

¿Qué te gusta comprar cuando vas de compras?

Cuando voy de compras, me gusta comprar CDs, zapatos, blusas, pantalones. Cosas así.

¿Adónde fuiste de compras la última vez?

La última vez que fui de compras fui a un centro comercial aquí en Miami.

¿Qué clase de tienda es?

El centro comercial es... hay varias tiendas. Hay tiendas de discos, tiendas de películas, tiendas de zapatos, de todo tipo de ropa, vestidos. Cosas así.

¿Qué compraste?

Cuando fui de compras, compré unos discos, una película, unos aretes. Compré unos zapatos, unos pantalones y un vestido.

¿Qué más hiciste allí?

Después de terminar las compras, fui a almorzar y después me compré un helado. Después me encontré con una de mis amigas y charlamos.

Visit Holt Online
go.hrw.com
KEYWORD: EXP1 CH8
Online Edition

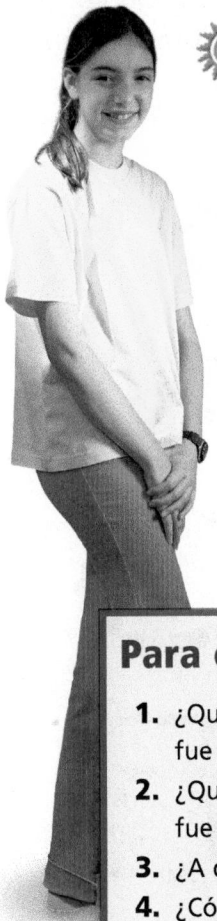

Miriam
Madrid, España

¿Qué te gusta comprar cuando vas de compras?

Pues, me gusta comprar pantalones ajustados, pantalones anchos, camisetas de colores y deportivas.

¿Adónde fuiste la última vez que fuiste de compras?

A «Tres Aguas», un centro comercial.

¿Qué clase de tienda es?

Pues, es de aire libre... muchas tiendas y mucho ocio.

¿Qué compraste?

Compré unos pantalones, una camiseta y unas deportivas.

¿Qué más hiciste allí?

Pues, después me fui con mis amigas al cine y a tomar una hamburguesa.

Para comprender 1B

1. ¿Qué compró Dayana la última vez que fue de compras?
2. ¿Qué compró Miriam la última vez que fue de compras?
3. ¿A quién le gusta comprar zapatos?
4. ¿Cómo es el centro comercial «Tres Aguas»?
5. ¿Quién fue a comer algo después de ir de compras?

Para pensar y hablar 4B

Dayana and Miriam both enjoy shopping for clothes, among other things. When you go shopping, what do you like to buy? For both girls, a shopping trip means spending time with friends. With whom do you normally go shopping? Where do you go? What do you like or not like about shopping?

Cuaderno para hispanohablantes, pp. 81–92

Texas

Comunidad

Where Do You Shop?

If you ever visit the towns of El Paso, Texas and Juarez, Mexico, you'll probably notice a steady stream of traffic in both directions. Shoppers travel from one country to another to look for bargains or hard-to-find items. In the stores of Juarez, you'll find authentic Mexican items as well as lots of delicious Mexican food. In El Paso, there are stores that cater to the residents of Juarez. Are there stores owned by Hispanics in your city? You can go to their store to buy something and practice your Spanish with them. Ask the owners where they are from and how long they've lived in your city. 5B

Colorful ceramic masks from Mexico

Objetivos
Saying where you went and what you did, talking on the phone

Vocabulario en acción 2

ExpresaVisión

un anillo

unos aretes

una pulsera

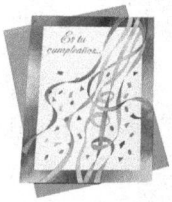
unas tarjetas

unas revistas de tiras cómicas

al almacén

unos DVDs

unos audífonos

un disco compacto (en blanco)

▶ **Vocabulario adicional** — De compras, p. R7

Visit Holt Online
go.hrw.com
KEYWORD: EXP1 CH8
Vocabulario 2 practice

Cuando voy de compras, me gusta...

ir a la zapatería

unos juguetes

ir a la juguetería

mirar las vitrinas

ir a la plaza de comida

Más vocabulario...

ahorrar	*to save money*
el dinero	*money*
gastar	*to spend*
vender (de todo)	*to sell (everything)*

¡Exprésate!

To ask where someone went and what someone did	To respond
¿Adónde fuiste anoche/ayer/anteayer? *Where did you go last night/yesterday/the day before yesterday?*	**Fui a la heladería a tomar un batido.** *I went to the ice cream shop to have a milkshake.*
¿Qué hiciste el fin de semana pasado? *What did you do last weekend?*	**Fui al centro comercial y compré unos zapatos. Pagué una fortuna.** *I went to the mall and bought some shoes. I paid a fortune.*

Interactive TUTOR

Online
Vocabulario y gramática, pp. 91–93

Nota cultural

Spanish speakers in the United States have amazing buying power. Retailers everywhere, but particularly in Florida and California, are marketing more to Spanish speakers. This group spends as much as or more than other Americans on food, clothing, telephone services, electronics, personal care products, public transportation, housing, and cleaning supplies. What products have you seen advertised in Spanish? 2B

18 ¿Adónde fuiste? 1B

Leamos Ricardo fue *(went)* al centro comercial anoche. Completa lo que dice con las palabras apropiadas del cuadro.

una tarjeta	la joyería	la zapatería
una heladería	unas revistas de tiras cómicas	unos audífonos
la plaza de comida	unos DVDs	unos juguetes

Anoche fui al centro comercial a buscar varias cosas. El cumpleaños de mi hermano es el sábado, así que *(so)* fui a la librería a comprarle __1__. También compré __2__ para leer. Después fui a __3__ a comprarle unos aretes a mi madre. Vi *(I saw)* a mi amiga Tere y fuimos *(we went)* a comer algo en __4__. Hay __5__ que me gusta, así que tomamos un batido de chocolate allí. A Tere le encantan las sandalias y ella fue a __6__ a ver los nuevos estilos *(styles)*. Al final, pagué una fortuna por __7__ en la tienda de música.

19 ¿Dónde están? 1B

Escuchemos Escucha las conversaciones y determina dónde tiene lugar *(takes place)* cada una.

20 Fui de compras 1B

Hablemos/Escribamos Di adónde fuiste y qué compraste *(you bought)*.

MODELO **Fui a la tienda de música esta semana. Compré unos discos compactos.**

1.

2.

3.

4.

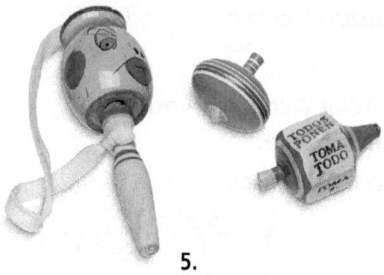

5.

6.

7.

8.

¡Exprésate!

To talk on the phone

Aló/Bueno/Diga.
Hello.

¿De parte de quién?
Who's calling?

Espera un momento, ya te lo (la) paso.
Hold on a moment. I'll get him (her).

Lo siento, no está. ¿Quieres dejarle un recado?
I'm sorry. He's not here. Would you like to leave a message?

Hola. ¿Está Andrés?
Hi. Is Andrés there?

Habla Felipe.
Felipe speaking.

Gracias, señor(a) León.
Thanks, Mr.(Mrs.) León.

No, gracias. Llamo más tarde.
No, thanks. I'll call back later.

Sí, por favor, que me llame después.
Yes, please ask him to call me later.

Online
Vocabulario y gramática, pp. 91–93

21 La llamada 1B

Leamos Vanesa habla por teléfono con la madre de Emilio. Pon las siguientes oraciones en orden lógico para crear su conversación.

- Lo siento, no está. ¿Quieres dejarle un recado?
- Habla Vanesa.
- No gracias. Llamo más tarde.
- Diga.
- ¿De parte de quién?
- Hola. ¿Está Emilio?

TEKS Focus
1B Demonstrate understanding of simple, clearly spoken, and written language when dealing with familiar topics

Comunicación

22 Por teléfono 1A

Hablemos Con dos compañeros(as), túrnense para crear una conversación. Llamas a un(a) amigo(a). Su padre(madre) contesta y le pasa el teléfono. Dile a tu amigo(a) que fuiste al centro comercial ayer. Dile qué compraste allí *(Tell him or her what you bought there)*. Luego, cambien de papel *(switch roles)*.

MODELO **—¿Aló?**
—Buenos días. Habla... ¿Está...?
—Un momento...

Objetivos

Preterite of **-ar** verbs, preterite of **ir**, preterite of verbs with reflexive pronouns

Gramática en acción 2

GramaVisión

Preterite of -ar verbs

Interactive TUTOR

1 Use the **preterite** tense to talk about what happened or what someone did at a specific point in the past. To form the **preterite** of **-ar** verbs, like **comprar,** add these endings to the verb's stem.

yo	compr**é**	nosotros(as)	compr**amos**
tú	compr**aste**	vosotros(as)	compr**asteis**
Ud., él, ella	compr**ó**	Uds., ellos, ellas	compr**aron**

Compré un DVD ayer. *I bought a DVD yesterday.*

2 Note that, in the preterite, the **nosotros** form of **-ar** verbs looks exactly like the present tense form. You will have to use context to decide whether the speaker is talking about the present or the past.

Isa y yo **gastamos** mucho ayer. Casi nunca gastamos tanto.

3 The stem-changing **-ar** verbs do not have stem changes in the **preterite**.

Encontré una camisa bonita y la compré.

Online

Vocabulario y gramática, pp. 94–96 | Actividades, pp. 75–77

Nota cultural

In most Spanish-speaking countries people often shop at open-air markets. Unlike department stores or malls, customers are expected to **regatear,** or bargain with vendors. Bargaining is an art form in these markets and successful shoppers may bring the price of an item down considerably. Are there any open-air markets where you live? Do you bargain with the vendors? 4B

TEKS Focus

1C Present information using familiar words, phrases, and sentences

23 ¿Pasado o presente? 1B

Escuchemos Escucha lo que dice Alicia y decide si habla **a)** del presente o **b)** del pasado.

24 Hicimos mucho este fin de semana 1C

Escribamos Combina una palabra o frase de cada cuadro para hacer seis oraciones. Usa el pretérito de los verbos.

Yo	hablar por teléfono	en el centro comercial
Mi familia y yo	mirar vitrinas	en la tienda de__?__
Mis amigos	escuchar música	en casa
Mi hermano(a)	comprar __?__	en la biblioteca
Mis amigos y yo	bailar	en una fiesta
Mis padres	estudiar	en la plaza de comida
	tomar un refresco	en la juguetería

25 Hablando del pasado 1B, 1C

Escribamos/Hablemos Di lo que hizo *(did)* cada persona. Luego di si hiciste lo mismo.

MODELO **Tomás cortó el césped ayer. Yo también corté el césped.**

Tomás

1. tú/anteayer

2. ellos/el sábado pasado

3. tus amigas y tú/ayer

4. Pablo y Mila/anoche

5. Carmela/ el martes pasado

6. Luis/ayer por la tarde

Comunicación

26 Ayer por la noche 1A

Hablemos En grupos de cuatro personas, pregunta quién hizo las siguientes cosas anoche.

MODELO **—Miguel, ¿alquilaste un video anoche?**
—Sí, alquilé uno.

alquilar un video *Miguel*	mirar televisión	estudiar
escuchar música	cenar con amigos	comprar ropa *Allison*
caminar	ayudar en casa	descansar

Preterite of ir

Interactive TUTOR

1 To say where someone went at a certain time in the past, use **ir** *(to go)* in the **preterite**. Its preterite forms are irregular.

yo	**fui**	nosotros(as)	**fuimos**
tú	**fuiste**	vosotros(as)	**fuisteis**
Ud., él, ella	**fue**	Uds., ellos, ellas	**fueron**

2 Remember to use **adónde** to ask where someone went.

—¿**Adónde fuiste** ayer? *Where did you go yesterday?*
—**Fui** al cine. *I went to the movies.*

3 Use **a + infinitive** after **ir** to say why someone went somewhere.

Fuimos a la librería **a comprar** libros.
We went to the bookstore to buy books.

Online
Vocabulario y gramática, pp. 94–96 | Actividades, pp. 75–77

En el Festival de la Calle Ocho, Miami

27 De tienda en tienda ←1B

Leamos Escoge la palabra correcta entre paréntesis para completar el párrafo.

Ayer (**1.** fui/fuimos) con mi familia al centro comercial. Mi hermana Delia (**2.** fuiste/fue) al almacén a comprar pantalones. Mis padres (**3.** fuimos/fueron) a la librería y mi hermano (**4.** fue/fuiste) a la juguetería. Por fin todos (**5.** fuimos/fuiste) a la heladería a tomar un batido.

28 ¿Fuiste al Festival este año? ←1B, 1C

Escribamos Combina una palabra o frase de cada cuadro para hacer seis oraciones. Di adónde fueron estas personas y qué hicieron.

MODELO **Fui al cine a ver una película.**

1	2	3	4
yo	ir	al cine	a comprar
tú		al parque	a leer
mi familia y yo		al estadio	a comer
mi mejor amigo(a)		al almacén	a ver
mis padres		al restaurante	a jugar
		a la biblioteca	a estudiar

29 ¿Adónde fueron? ¿Qué compraron? 1B

Escribamos/Hablemos María le cuenta a su madre adónde fueron todos de compras y qué compraron. Basándote en las fotos, completa sus oraciones.

MODELO **Carlos y Carmen fueron a la juguetería. Compraron videojuegos.**

Carlos y Carmen

1. nosotros

2. papá

3. mis amigas

4. yo

5. Gabi y Rebeca

Comunicación

30 Tiendas y compras 1A

Hablemos En secreto, escribe tres tiendas adonde fuiste de compras y tres cosas que compraste. Tu compañero(a) debe adivinar *(guess)* las tiendas y las cosas en tu lista. Túrnense para adivinar y contestar.

TEKS Focus
1A Engage in oral and written exchanges of learned material to socialize and to provide and obtain information

MODELO **—¿Fuiste a la tienda de música?**
—Sí, fui a la tienda de música.
—¿Compraste un disco compacto?
—No.
—¿Compraste un DVD?
—No, compré unos audífonos.

Tiendas	Cosas que compré
Muy de Moda	falda
Ropa y Más	sandalias
Joyería Sánchez	pulsera

Repaso Preterite of -ar verbs with reflexive pronouns

Interactive TUTOR

1 Use the **preterite** to talk about what happened at a particular point in the past and to narrate a sequence of events in the past.

Ayer **fui** al cine con mis amigos, **regresé** tarde a casa y **me acosté**.

2 Remember to use the correct form of the **reflexive pronoun** when necessary.

levantarse

yo	**me** levanté	nosotros(as)	**nos** levantamos
tú	**te** levantaste	vosotros(as)	**os** levantasteis
Ud., él, ella	**se** levantó	Uds., ellos, ellas	**se** levantaron

Me levanté y **me bañé**. *I got up and took a bath.*

Online

Vocabulario y gramática, pp. 94–96 | Actividades, pp. 75–77

31 ¡Qué día más ocupado! ◆1B

Escuchemos Escucha lo que hicieron Enrique y Lupita ayer. Según *(according to)* lo que oyes, pon los dibujos en orden cronológico *(chronological order)*.

a.

b.

c.

d.

e.

f.

g.

h.

32 La familia de Cristóbal 1B

Leamos/Escribamos Cristóbal y su familia hicieron las cosas de manera distinta *(did things differently)* esta semana. Completa las oraciones con el presente o el pretérito de los verbos.

1. Papá ____ por la mañana, pero ayer no ____. (afeitarse)
2. Siempre ____ a las 8:00, pero el miércoles yo ____ a las seis para estudiar. (despertarse)
3. Patricia y yo ____ del colegio a las 3:30, pero anteayer ____ a las 5:00. (regresar)
4. Papá y mamá ____ la cena juntos, pero mamá trabajó tarde así que solamente la ____ juntos el jueves y el viernes. (preparar)
5. Patricia, tú ____ temprano por lo general, pero anoche ____ después de la medianoche. (acostarse)

33 En mi familia 1C

TEKS Focus
1C Present information using familiar words, phrases, and sentences

Escribamos Di qué hacen tu familia y tú por lo general, y qué hicieron de manera distinta esta semana. Usa las palabras del cuadro.

MODELO **Generalmente me levanto a las 7:00, pero hoy me levanté a las 8:00.**

levantarse	desayunar	ir a	cenar
hablar	bañarse	alquilar videos	acostarse

Comunicación

34 ¿Qué pasó? 1C

Hablemos Con un(a) compañero(a), mira los dibujos y di adónde fueron Felipe y Cristina y qué hicieron.

Novela en video

¿Quién será?

Episodio 8

ESTRATEGIA

Recognizing Different Points of View When the same story is told from different points of view, it is important to keep track of who is telling what. The same events can be interpreted in a completely different way by everyone who experienced them. The truth probably lies somewhere between the different versions. Watch or read the episode and keep track of whose view is being expressed, Sofía's or Celeste's. What do you think really happened? 3B

En México

Celeste habla con Sofía. Celeste quiere ir de compras a buscar ropa y zapatos para la fiesta del sábado.

1

Celeste Hola, Sofía. Necesito comprar una falda, una blusa y unos zapatos para la fiesta del sábado.

Sofía Está bien.

Celeste Perfecto. ¿Por qué no nos encontramos en Kulte a las diez y media?

La versión de Sofía

Fui con Celeste a Kulte, una tienda de ropa.

Celeste ¿Qué te parece esta falda azul?

Sofía No te queda nada bien. Te debes probar otra.

Celeste ¡Qué bueno que estás de acuerdo! Es muy bonita.

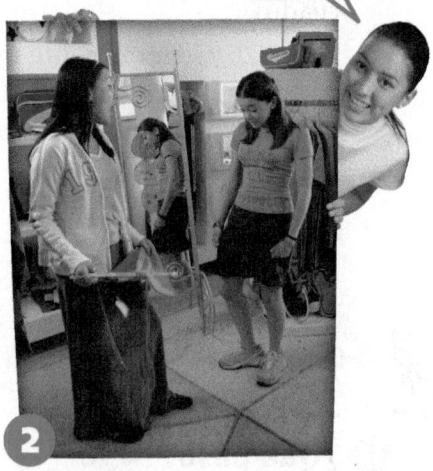

2

No me hizo caso. Compró una falda horrible. Luego, se probó una blusa morada.

3

Celeste ¿Te gusta esta blusa morada? ¿Me queda bien?

Sofía No. ¡Está pasada de moda! Y debes probarte otra talla.

Celeste ¡Me queda perfecta! Y está a la última moda, ¿no crees?

Traté de convencerla. Pero nada. Gastó su dinero en una blusa fea. Luego fuimos a la sección de zapatos.

Celeste ¿Qué piensas de estos zapatos? ¿Van bien con la blusa y la falda?

Sofía ¿Sabes qué? ¡Estás más loca que un zapato!

Celeste ¡Perfecto! Me voy a llevar estos zapatos. Ahora estoy lista para la fiesta del sábado. ¡Voy a estar a la última moda!

4

Visit Holt Online
go.hrw.com
KEYWORD: EXP1 CH8
Online Edition

La versión de Celeste

Celeste ¿Qué te parece esta falda azul?

Sofía ¡Te queda muy bien! ¡Muy bonita! Definitivamente debes comprarla.

Celeste ¿Estás segura? No sé.

Sofía ¡Te lo juro! ¡Te ves increíble!

Celeste ¿Te gusta esta blusa morada? ¿Me queda bien?

Sofía ¡Claro que sí! ¡Está a la última moda! Y es una ganga. ¡Mira el precio!

Celeste Pues, sí, tienes razón. Es muy barata. Pero...

Sofía ¿Pero qué? Hazme caso. Debes comprarla.

Celeste ¿Qué piensas de estos zapatos? ¿Van bien con la blusa y la falda?

Sofía ¡Amiga! ¡Estos zapatos son más bonitos que todos los zapatos en todo el mundo!

Celeste ¿De veras? Bueno, si te gustan a ti, los voy a comprar.

Celeste Sofía, tengo que regresar a Kulte. Tengo que devolver la falda, la blusa y los zapatos. ¿Vas conmigo?

Sofía Sí, pero, ¿por qué tienes que devolver todo?

Celeste Mamá dice que me veo horrible en esa falda y esa blusa y que los zapatos son más horribles que la ropa. No sé por qué me dejaste comprarlos.

¿COMPRENDES?

1. ¿Adónde van Sofía y Celeste? ¿Para qué?
2. En la versión de Sofía, ¿qué piensan las dos chicas de la falda azul y la blusa morada? ¿Qué piensan ellas en la versión de Celeste?
3. ¿Qué piensa Sofía de su amiga? ¿Qué decide comprar Celeste?
4. ¿Qué dice Celeste que tiene que hacer con sus compras? ¿A quién le echa la culpa? *(Whom does she blame?)* ¿Cómo se siente Sofía? **1B, 3A**

Próximo episodio:
Marcos sale para otro país. ¿Adónde va? ¿Qué piensas tú?
PÁGINAS 332–333

Leamos y escribamos

ESTRATEGIA

para leer Visualizing what you read in a story will help you better understand it. As you read, create pictures in your mind of each scene or event. This will help you connect what you know to what you are reading as well as help you summarize the main events of the story.

A Antes de leer 1B, 3B

Lee el primer párrafo del texto. Dibuja la imagen que tienes en la mente de esta escena. ¿Qué información te da esta imagen sobre el señor y su sirviente? Sigue leyendo el cuento y después de cada escena, dibuja la imagen que te imaginas.

Una moneda[1] de ¡Ay!

En un pueblo, como muchos otros pueblos, vive un gran señor con muchos sirvientes. Pedro, el sirviente más nuevo, es un muchacho que al señor le parece un poco tonto. Para burlarse de él[2], lo llama, le da dos monedas y le dice:

—Pedro, vete al mercado y cómprame una moneda de uvas y otra de ¡Ay!

El pobre Pedro va al mercado y compra las uvas, pero cada vez que pregunta por la moneda de ¡Ay!, todos los vendedores se ríen de él[3].

Finalmente Pedro se da cuenta[4] que el señor quiere burlarse de él. Entonces decide poner las uvas en una bolsa[5] y sobre las uvas pone un manojo de espinos[6].

Cuando regresa a casa el señor le pregunta:

—¿Fuiste al mercado?

—Sí, señor.

—¿Y lo traes todo?

—Sí, señor. Todo está en la bolsa.

El señor parece sorprendido. Rápidamente mete la mano[7] en la bolsa y al tocar los espinos, exclama:

—¡Ay!

—Y debajo están las uvas— le dice Pedro.

1 coin **2** to make fun of him **3** the vendors laugh at him **4** he realizes **5** a bag **6** handful of thorns **7** puts his hand in

B Comprensión 1B

Contesta las siguientes preguntas con oraciones completas.

1. ¿Quién es Pedro?
2. ¿Qué debe comprar Pedro en el mercado?
3. ¿Por qué se ríen los vendedores de Pedro?
4. ¿Qué hay en la bolsa que Pedro le da al señor?
5. ¿Cómo reacciona el señor cuando Pedro le dice que trae todo?
6. ¿Qué hace el señor cuando mete la mano en la bolsa?

C Después de leer 1B, 3B

Summarize the story using the drawings you made while reading it. Explain how you visualized each scene. What did each scene reveal about the characters? Did you find the ending of the story humorous? Why?

TEKS Focus
3B Use the language to obtain, reinforce, or expand knowledge of other subject areas

Taller del escritor

ESTRATEGIA

para escribir When you write about differing opinions it helps to choose terms that show sharp, clear contrasts. Using charts can help you visualize and contrast differing perspectives.

A mí me parece perfecto... 1C

Imagine that you are shopping for clothes with a friend. However, you and your friend can't agree about anything today! If you think something looks good and fits well, your friend says it looks awful. Write five items that you and your friend have different opinions about.

1 Antes de escribir

In a column, list at least five pieces of clothing. In the next column write what you like or don't like about each item. In a third column, write the contrasting opinions your friend has.

Ropa	Lo que (no) me gusta	Lo que (no) le gusta a mi amigo(a)

2 Escribir un borrador

Using your chart, write about your shopping trip. Include your and your friend's opinions about the clothes: how they fit, if they look good, or if they are in style. Include details to back up each opinion.

3 Revisar

Read your draft at least two times, comparing it with your chart. Are the contrasting opinions clear? Check spelling and punctuation.

4 Publicar

Share your paragraph with the class. Ask your classmates to respond by giving their opinions or preferences regarding the clothing.

Cuaderno para hispanohablantes, pp. 61–68

Prepárate para el examen

Repaso capítulo 8

Interactive TUTOR

1 Vocabulario 1
- asking for and giving opinions
- asking for and offering help in a store

pp. 272–275

2 Gramática 1
- **costar,** numbers to one million
- demonstrative adjectives and comparisons
- **quedar**

pp. 276–281

3 Vocabulario 2
- saying where you went and what you did
- talking on the phone

pp. 284–287

1 Buscas algunos regalos. Di qué quieres comprar. Luego di qué talla/número necesitas y qué color quieres. **1B, 1C**

2 Estás en un centro comercial. Compara lo que ves con las cosas que tienes en casa. Comienza con los precios y la forma correcta de **este.** Di cuánto cuestan. **1B**

1. mesa de plástico, $125/mi mesa
2. sofá de seda, $1.199/mi sofá
3. cama grande, $1.831/mi cama
4. plantas de seda, $45/mis plantas
5. refrigerador negro, ultra moderno, $2.057/mi refrigerador
6. teléfonos azules y verdes, $62 cada uno/mis teléfonos

3 Escoge la respuesta apropiada. **1B**

1. ¿Adónde fuiste el lunes por la noche?
2. Hola. ¿Está Andrés?
3. Compré aretes y un anillo.
4. Lo siento, no está. ¿Quieres dejarle un recado?
5. ¿Qué hiciste en la tienda de música?

a. Espera un momento. Ya te lo paso.
b. ¿Fuiste a una joyería o a un almacén?
c. Fui a la biblioteca a estudiar.
d. Escuché muchos discos compactos.
e. Sí, por favor, que me llame después.

Visit Holt Online
go.hrw.com
KEYWORD: EXP1 CH8
Chapter Self-test

4 Completa la conversación entre Carolina y su mamá usando el pretérito del verbo entre paréntesis. 1B

—Caro, te __1__ (llamar) Luisa. Quiere ir de compras.
—¡Qué lástima! Ya __2__ (ir) de compras.
—¿Ah, sí? ¿Con quién? ¿__3__ (comprar) algo?
—Sí, Maite y yo __4__ (comprar) toda la joyería.
—Carolina, sé buena...
—Ay, mami, no __5__ (gastar) nada de dinero. Maite nos __6__ (comprar) batidos y __7__ (mirar) vitrinas por dos horas.

5 Contesta las siguientes preguntas. 2A, 2B

1. How do you refer to clothing and shoe sizes in Spanish-speaking countries?
2. What are **guayaberas** and where did they originate?
3. Where would you likely see customers bargaining with vendors? Where wouldn't you?

6 Escucha y escribe qué cosas te comprarías *(would buy)* y en qué tienda. 1B

7 Describe lo que ves en los dibujos. En oraciones completas, di qué dicen Felipe y Cristina, y qué compraron. 1C

4 Gramática 2
- preterite of **-ar** verbs
- preterite of **ir**
- preterite of verbs with reflexive pronouns
pp. 288–293

5 Cultura
- **Comparaciones** **pp. 282–283**
- **Notas culturales** **pp. 274, 278, 286, 288**
- **Geocultura** **pp. 266–269**

TEKS Focus
2A Demonstrate understanding of practices (what people do) and how they relate to perspectives (how people perceive things) of the cultures studied

Repaso

Gramática 1
- **costar** and numbers to one million **pp. 276–277**
- demonstrative adjectives and comparisons **pp. 278–279**
- **quedar** **pp. 280–281**

Repaso de Gramática 1

100	cien	600	seiscientos(as)
101	ciento uno(un)	700	setecientos(as)
102	ciento dos	800	ochocientos(as)
200	doscientos(as)	900	novecientos(as)
300	trescientos(as)	1.000	mil
400	cuatrocientos(as)	2.000	dos mil
500	quinientos(as)	1.000.000	un millón (de+*noun*)

sing. subj. *pl. subj.*

La bolsa cuest**a** cien dólares. Las botas cuest**an** ciento veintiún dólares.

este/ese saco	**más**+*adj.*+**que**	**mejor(es)/peor(es) que**
estos/esos sacos	**tan**+*adj.*+**como**	
esta/esa blusa	**menos**+*adj.*+**que**	**mayor(es)/menor(es) que**
estas/esas blusas		

The verb **quedar** is used to say how something fits and is conjugated like **gustar**: **me/te/le/nos/os/les queda(n)**+*adjective/adverb.*

Gramática 2
- preterite of regular **-ar** verbs **pp. 288–289**
- preterite of **ir** **pp. 290–291**
- preterite verbs with reflexive pronouns **pp. 292–293**

TEKS Focus
1B Demonstrate understanding of simple, clearly spoken, and written language when dealing with familiar topics

Repaso de Gramática 2

The verb **comprar** has regular preterite forms; the verb **ir** is irregular.

compr**é**	compr**amos**
compr**aste**	compr**asteis**
compr**ó**	compr**aron**

fui	**fuimos**
fuiste	**fuisteis**
fue	**fueron**

The preterite is used to say what happened at a specific point in the past and to narrate a sequence of events.

Ayer **fui** al cine con mis amigos, **regresé** tarde a casa y **me acosté.**

Letra y sonido

El acento ortográfico

- Words ending in a vowel, **-n,** or **-s** are usually stressed on the next-to-last syllable. Exceptions have an accent mark over the stressed vowel:
  niño, joven, compras, semáforo, almacén, jóvenes
- Words ending in a consonant other than **-n,** or **-s** are usually stressed on the last syllable. Exceptions have an accent mark over the stressed vowel:
  papel, ciudad, repetir, ángel, lápiz, Héctor

Trabalenguas

El célebre cerebelo del cerebro celebrará con celeridad una celebérrima celebración.

Dictado 1B

Escribe las oraciones de la grabación.

Repaso de Vocabulario 1

Asking for and giving opinions

a la (última) moda	*in (the latest) style*
además	*besides*
barato(a)	*inexpensive*
caro(a)	*expensive*
costar (ue)	*to cost*
¡Es un robo!	*It's a rip-off!*
ese(a)	*that*
este(a)	*this*
feo(a)	*ugly*
la ganga	*bargain*
pasado(a) de moda	*out of style*
pequeño(a)	*small*
quedar bien/mal	*to fit well/badly*
tener razón	*to be right*

Colors . . . . . .*See p. 273.*

Asking for and offering help in a store

el abrigo	*(over)coat*
la blusa	*blouse*
la bolsa	*purse*
las botas	*boots*
los calcetines	*socks*
la camisa	*shirt*
la camiseta	*T-shirt*
cerrar (ie)	*to close*
la chaqueta	*jacket*
el/la cliente	*client, customer*
de algodón/lana/seda	*(made of) cotton/wool/silk*
el/la dependiente	*salesclerk*
devolver (ue)	*to return something*
¿En qué le puedo servir?	*How can I help you?*
la falda	*skirt*
llevar	*to wear*
Me gustaría...	*I would like . . .*
Nada más estoy mirando.	*I'm just looking.*
el número	*(shoe) size*
los pantalones (cortos/vaqueros)	*pants (shorts/jeans)*
un par de...	*a pair of . . .*
para hombres/mujeres/niños	*for men/women/children*
el saco	*jacket, sport coat*
las sandalias	*sandals*
el sombrero	*hat*
el suéter	*sweater*
la talla	*(clothing) size*
la tienda de ropa	*clothing store*
el traje de baño	*swimsuit*
usar	*to use, to wear*
el vestido	*dress*
los zapatos (de tenis)	*(tennis) shoes*

Numbers to one million . . . . . .*See p. 276.*

Demonstrative adjectives and comparisons . . . . . .*See p. 278.*

Repaso de Vocabulario 2

Saying where you went and what you did

ahorrar	*to save money*
el almacén	*department store*
el anillo	*ring*
anoche	*last night*
anteayer	*day before yesterday*
los aretes	*earrings*
los audífonos	*headphones*
ayer	*yesterday*
comprar	*to buy*
el dinero	*money*
el disco compacto (en blanco)	*(blank) CD*
el DVD	*DVD*
gastar	*to spend*
la heladería	*ice cream shop*
la joyería	*jewelry store*
la juguetería	*toy store*
los juguetes	*toys*
la librería	*bookstore*
mirar las vitrinas	*to window-shop*
pagar (una fortuna)	*to pay (a fortune)*
la plaza de comida	*food court in a mall*
la pulsera	*bracelet*
la revista de tiras cómicas	*comic book*
la tarjeta (de cumpleaños)	*greeting card (birthday card)*
la tienda de...	*. . . store*
tomar un batido	*to have a milkshake*
vender (de todo)	*to sell (everything)*
la zapatería	*shoe store*

Talking on the phone . . . . . .*See p. 287.*

Integración

capítulos 1-8

1 Escucha el anuncio y escoge la respuesta más apropiada. 1B

1. Los audífonos son _____.
   a. de la más alta calidad **b.** muy caros
2. Esta tienda vende _____.
   a. pocos videos **b.** muchos videos
3. Casa Electrónica tiene _____.
   a. muchas cosas caras **b.** pocas cosas caras
4. Casa Electrónica nunca _____.
   a. tiene descuentos **b.** cierra
5. Según el anuncio, vas a _____.
   a. ahorrar dinero **b.** pagar mucho

2 Con base en el anuncio, haz comparaciones entre las siguientes cosas, usando **más...que, menos...que** y **tan...como.** 1B, 3A

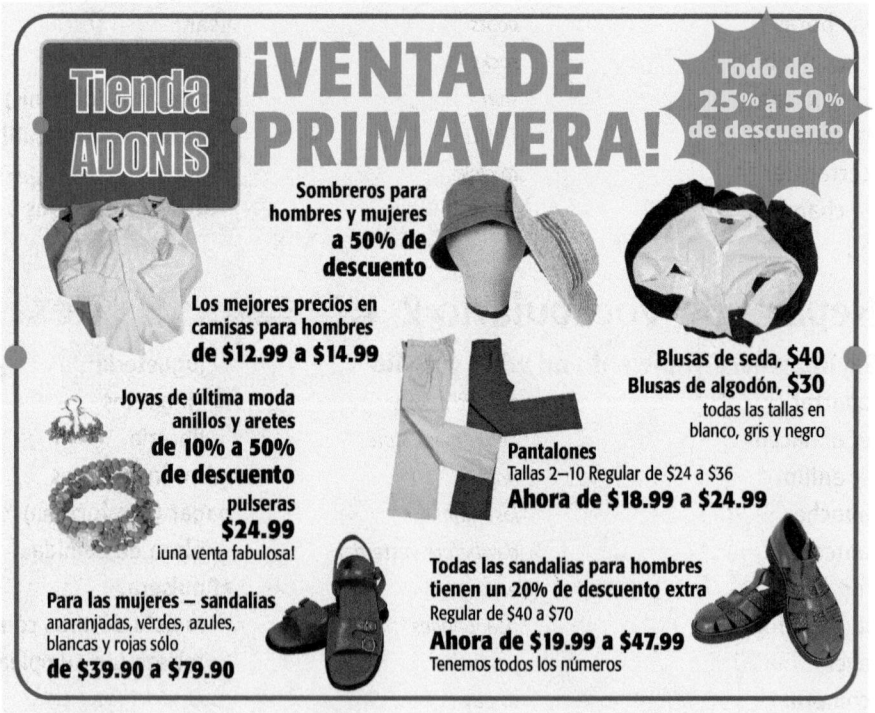

1. sandalias para mujeres/sandalias para hombres
2. blusas de seda/blusas de algodón
3. sombreros para hombres/sombreros para mujeres
4. pulseras/anillos y aretes
5. blusas para mujeres/camisas para hombres

Visit Holt Online
go.hrw.com
KEYWORD: EXP1 CH8
Cumulative Self-test

Integración

3 Entrevista a tres o cuatro amigos para saber cuál es su ropa favorita, de qué color es, dónde la compraron, cuánto costó y para qué ocasión la llevan. 1A

4 Imagina que estás en el mercado de la pintura. Contesta las preguntas. 1C, 2B

1. ¿Qué frutas hay en el mercado hoy? ¿Cuánto crees que cuesta cada fruta?
2. ¿Qué ropa lleva la mujer? ¿el hombre?
3. ¿Qué crees que compró la mujer? ¿Cuánto crees que pagó?
4. Compara este mercado con un mercado en tu comunidad.

Dra. Dominica Alcántara © 2003

Mercado caribeño, de la Dra. Dominica Alcántara

5 Eres un(a) estudiante de intercambio en Costa Rica. Escríbeles a tus padres para describirles tu primera semana allí. Diles tres o cuatro cosas que hiciste. Puedes hablar de las clases, los amigos, los profesores, tu rutina diaria y la comida. 1C

6 **Situación** Create a classroom department store. Make signs for different departments, announcing prices, items, and sales. Include clothing, accessories, furniture, school supplies, and personal items like shampoo and soap. Role-play clerks and shoppers who buy and sell merchandise. 1A

GeoVisión

► **Concurso anual en Cabarete** Aquí en las aguas de Cabarete se celebra un concurso anual de windsurf.

Geocultura

La República Dominicana

H I

HAITÍ

▼ **Santo Domingo** La capital de la República Dominicana está en la costa sur del país.

Almanaque

Población
8.581.477

Capital
Santo Domingo

Gobierno
democracia representativa

Idioma oficial
español

Moneda
peso dominicano

Código Internet
www.[ ].do

La güira y la tambora son instrumentos típicos dominicanos.

¿Sabías que...?

Sammy Sosa nació en San Pedro de Macorís. Empezó su carrera de béisbol en Estados Unidos con el equipo de los Texas Rangers.

◄ **El Parque Nacional de los Haitises** Para ver las colinas, o mogotes, en este parque, tienes que ir en bote.

► **El Pico Duarte** fue nombrado en honor a Juan Pablo Duarte, un revolucionario del siglo XIX.

▲ **Altos de Chavón** En los altos del Río Chavón, en La Romana, está la majestuosa villa de artistas, Altos de Chavón.

REPÚBLICA DOMINICANA

▼ **El Lago Enriquillo** es el lago de agua salada más grande de las Antillas y está a 40 metros bajo el nivel del mar.

▲ **Las iguanas y los cocodrilos** En la Isla Cabritos en el lago Enriquillo hay cocodrilos americanos y varias especies de iguanas.

3B

¿Qué tanto sabes?

¿Qué deporte se practica en Cabarete? ¿Cuál es el lago de agua salada más grande de las Antillas?

A conocer la República Dominicana

La arquitectura

▲ **Casas de madera** Es común ver en la República Dominicana casas de madera de colores brillantes con techo de zinc.

▲ **La Basílica de Higüey** Esta iglesia al estilo moderno tiene un arco de cemento de 75m de altura.

▲ **El Palacio Nacional** en Santo Domingo fue diseñado al estilo neoclásico.

El arte

▲ ***El Once*** fue creado por Ramón Oviedo. El pintor Ramón Oviedo (1924–) es uno de los pintores más famosos del país.

◀ **Cándido Bidó** La pintura dominicana tiene en Bidó (1936–) uno de sus representantes principales.

▼ **Este mural en cerámica** fue creado por Said Musa (1956–). Los colores brillantes caracterizan los murales de este artista.

Las celebraciones

Interactive TUTOR

Visit Holt Online
go.hrw.com
KEYWORD: EXP1 CH9
Photo Tour

► **El Carnaval de Santo Domingo** Siempre hay carrozas y disfraces en el carnaval dominicano.

▼ **El Festival del Merengue** El merengue es el baile y la música nacional de la República Dominicana.

¿Sabías que...?

El deporte nacional de la República Dominicana es el béisbol, también llamado pelota.

◄ **El Festival de Jazz** Este festival se celebra cada año en Sosúa con la participación de músicos internacionales y dominicanos.

La comida

▲ **El sancocho** es uno de los platos típicos del país.

▲ **El moro** es un plato tradicional donde se combina el arroz con las habichuelas.

▲ **Puesto de yaniqueque** El yaniqueque es una comida parecida al pan que se vende en los kioskos de las playas.

Conexión Ciencias naturales

Casabe dominicano
En la República Dominicana se prepara un alimento llamado casabe. Investiga de qué planta se hace el casabe. ¿Qué otros nombres tiene y en qué países crece esta planta? ¿Cuáles son sus características?
3B

Capítulo 9

¡Festejemos!

OBJETIVOS

In this chapter you will learn to

- talk about plans
- talk about past holidays
- talk about preparing for a party
- greet, introduce others, and say goodbye

And you will use

- preterite of **-ar, -er,** and **-ir** verbs
- **pensar que** and **pensar** with infinitives
- direct object pronouns
- **conocer** and personal **a**
- present progressive

¿Qué ves en la foto?

- ¿Qué hacen estas personas?
- ¿Dónde están?
- ¿Qué ropa llevan estas chicas?

Texas

TEKS Look for the ✦ next to each activity to learn how it can help you achieve the goals of the **Texas Essential Knowledge and Skills,** found on page xxiii.

Visit Holt Online
go.hrw.com
KEYWORD: EXP1 CH9
Online Edition

Festejando el Día de la Independencia en Santo Domingo

Objetivos
Talking about plans, talking about past holidays

Vocabulario en acción 1

ExpresaVisión

Los días festivos

el Día de la Independencia

la Semana Santa

el Día de la Madre

el Día de los Enamorados

el Día del Padre

el Hanukah

la Navidad

la Nochevieja

el Día de Acción de Gracias

▶ **Vocabulario adicional** — Celebraciones, p. R7

Visit Holt Online
go.hrw.com
KEYWORD: EXP1 CH9
Vocabulario 1 practice

recibir regalos

ver fuegos artificiales

abrir regalos

reunirse con (toda) la familia

mandar unas tarjetas

Más vocabulario...

el Año Nuevo	*New Year's Day*
celebrar	*to celebrate*
decorar la casa	*to decorate the house*
invitar	*to invite*
ir...	
a misa	*to Mass*
a la sinagoga	*to the synagogue*
al templo	*to the temple*

¡Exprésate!

Interactive TUTOR

To ask about plans	To respond
¿Qué vas a hacer el Día de la Independencia? *What are you going to do on Independence Day?*	**Pienso hacer una fiesta o tener un picnic.** *I plan to throw a party or have a picnic.*
¿Qué planes tienen para la Nochebuena? *What plans do you have for Christmas Eve?*	**Pensamos pasarla con mis abuelos, como siempre.** *We plan to spend it with my grandparents, as always.*

Online
Vocabulario y gramática, pp. 97–99

Celebrando un día festivo en Santo Domingo

1 Días festivos ✦1B

Leamos/Hablemos Lee las siguientes oraciones y decide qué día festivo le corresponde a cada una.

1. Papá Noel trae muchos regalos.
2. Decoramos con los colores azul, blanco y rojo.
3. Muchas personas salen para una cena romántica.
4. Compramos algo especial para nuestra madre.
5. Muchas personas van a la sinagoga.
6. La gente va a misa a la medianoche.
7. Nos reunimos con la familia en noviembre para una comida especial.
8. Hacemos algo para nuestro papá.
9. La gente sale a ver fuegos artificiales.
10. Festejamos el fin de año con una fiesta.

2 Celebraciones ✦1B, 1C

Escribamos Con base en las fotos, describe cómo estas personas van a pasar los días festivos. Escribe por los menos dos oraciones para cada foto.

1. mis padres

2. mi familia y yo

3. mis hermanas

4. mis amigos

¡Exprésate!

To ask about past holidays	To respond
¿Dónde pasaron la Navidad el año pasado? *Where did you spend Christmas last year?*	**La pasamos en casa de mis tíos.** *We spent it at my aunt and uncle's house.*
¿Qué tal estuvo? *How was it?*	**Estuvo a todo dar. Nos reunimos a comer.** *It was great. We got together to eat.*

Interactive TUTOR

Online
Vocabulario y gramática, pp. 97–99

3 Entre amigos 1B

Leamos Pon en orden las oraciones de la siguiente conversación entre Lourdes y Manuel.

—¿Qué tal estuvo?

—¿Qué planes tienes para el Año Nuevo?

—Hola, Lourdes, ¿cómo estás? ¿Cómo pasaste la Navidad?

—Pues, la pasé con mi familia en casa de los abuelos.

—¡Hola, Manuel!

—No sé, pero creo que lo voy a pasar con mis primos.

—Estuvo bien. Nos reunimos a decorar la casa, comer y abrir regalos.

4 ¿Pasado o futuro? 1B

Escuchemos Escucha la conversación entre Luis y Rosa. Indica si cada cosa ya *(already)* ocurrió el Día de Acción de Gracias o va a ocurrir el día de la Navidad.

	ya ocurrió	va a ocurrir
1. ir a casa de los abuelos		
2. almorzar en un restaurante		
3. ir al cine		
4. pasar la noche en casa		
5. decorar la casa		
6. ir a misa		
7. comer y abrir regalos		
8. dormir en casa de los abuelos		

5 Mi día festivo preferido 1C

Escribamos Escribe un pequeño párrafo sobre tu día festivo preferido. Explica cómo y con quiénes celebras el día.

TEKS Focus
1C Present information using familiar words, phrases, and sentences

Nota cultural

On February 27th, Independence Day, Dominicans celebrate **Carnaval.** In Santo Domingo, children and adults gather to watch a parade along **El malecón,** one of the main streets. The parade includes floats, marching bands, dancers, and **diablos cojuelos.** These figures wear brightly-colored, horned masks and costumes covered with toys, mirrors, and shiny objects. What celebrations in the United States or in other countries are similar to the Dominican Carnaval? 2A, 4B

Comunicación

6 ¿Cómo lo van a pasar? 1A, 1B

Hablemos Pregúntale a un(a) compañero(a) cuál es su día festivo preferido, cómo celebra el día y qué planes tiene para este año. Luego le toca a él o a ella hacerte preguntas.

MODELO **—¿Cuál es tu día festivo preferido?**
—Es la Nochevieja. Festejamos en casa con música y comida.

Objetivos

Using the preterite of **-ar, -er,** and **-ir** verbs; **pensar** with **que** and **pensar** with infinitives

Gramática en acción 1

GramaVisión

Preterite of -er and -ir verbs

1 The **preterite** is used to talk about what happened at a specific point in the past. To form the **preterite** of **-er** and **-ir** verbs, add these endings to the verb's stem.

volver		escribir	
yo	volv**í**	yo	escrib**í**
tú	volv**iste**	tú	escrib**iste**
usted, él, ella	volv**ió**	usted, él, ella	escrib**ió**
nosotros(as)	volv**imos**	nosotros(as)	escrib**imos**
vosotros(as)	volv**isteis**	vosotros(as)	escrib**isteis**
ustedes, ellos, ellas	volv**ieron**	ustedes, ellos, ellas	escrib**ieron**

—¿**Recibieron** la tarjeta? —Sí, la **recibimos** ayer. Gracias.

2 Regular **-er** and **-ir** verbs have the same endings in the **preterite**. Stem-changing **-er** verbs don't have a stem change in the preterite.

3 The verb **ver** has regular **preterite** endings but without written accents.

yo	v**i**	nosotros(as)	v**imos**
tú	v**iste**	vosotros(as)	v**isteis**
usted, él, ella	v**io**	ustedes, ellos, ellas	v**ieron**

Online

Vocabulario y gramática, pp. 100–102 | Actividades, pp. 81–83

¿Te acuerdas?

To form the **preterite** of a regular **-ar** verb, add these endings to the verb's stem.

merend**é** merend**amos**
merend**aste** merend**asteis**
merend**ó** merend**aron**

No **-ar** verbs have stem changes in the preterite.

7 La Navidad de Pablo 1B

Leamos Escoge el verbo correcto entre paréntesis.

Pablo y sus padres __1__ (salimos/salieron) muy temprano para la casa de sus abuelos el día de Navidad, donde __2__ (se reunieron/me reuní) con toda la familia. Pablo __3__ (vimos/vio) a unos tíos que viven lejos. Primero todos __4__ (comí/comieron) y Pablo __5__ (bebiste/bebió) tres vasos de limonada. Después de la comida ellos __6__ (abrimos/abrieron) los regalos. A las cuatro __7__ (fuimos/fueron) a misa. Cuando __8__ (volvieron/volviste), Pablo __9__ (decidí/decidió) dormir un rato.

Visit Holt Online
go.hrw.com
KEYWORD: EXP1 CH9
Gramática 1 practice

8 Ahora, ¿qué dice Pablo? 1C

Escribamos Vuelve a escribir el párrafo de la Actividad 7 desde el punto de vista *(point of view)* de Pablo. ¿Qué dice él?

9 El Año Nuevo 1B, 1C

Escribamos/Hablemos Mira las fotos. Di quiénes hicieron estas cosas para celebrar el Año Nuevo según *(according to)* Marcos.

MODELO **comer en un restaurante**
Mis padres comieron en un restaurante.

mi hermano y yo

mi abuela

mis padres

1. beber muchos refrescos
2. salir a un restaurante
3. beber café
4. comer pastel de chocolate
5. asistir a una fiesta
6. comer pizza
7. ver televisión
8. reunirse con la familia

Comunicación

10 La semana pasada 1A

Hablemos Pregúntale a un(a) compañero(a) si hizo las cosas de la Actividad 9 la semana pasada.

MODELO **—¿Comiste en un restaurante?**
—Sí, comí en un restaurante la semana pasada.

TEKS Focus
1A Engage in oral and written exchanges of learned material to socialize and to provide and obtain information

11 ¿Qué hiciste? 1A

Hablemos Usa las frases del cuadro para hacer cuatro preguntas sobre lo que hizo tu compañero(a) el año pasado para festejar algunos días festivos. Túrnense para contestar.

escribir tarjetas	reunirse con la familia	salir a comer
ver fuegos artificiales	recibir regalos	asistir a una fiesta

Repaso The preterite

Interactive TUTOR

1 Compare the preterite forms of regular **-ar**, **-er**, and **-ir** verbs and the irregular verb **ir**.

	invitar	**comer**	**salir**	**ir**
yo	invit**é**	com**í**	sal**í**	**fui**
tú	invist**aste**	com**iste**	sal**iste**	**fuiste**
usted, él, ella	invit**ó**	com**ió**	sal**ió**	**fue**
nosotros(as)	invit**amos**	com**imos**	sal**imos**	**fuimos**
vosotros(as)	invit**asteis**	com**isteis**	sal**isteis**	**fuisteis**
ustedes, ellos, ellas	invit**aron**	com**ieron**	sal**ieron**	**fueron**

—¿**Saliste** con tus amigos?
Did you go out with your friends?

—Sí, **fuimos** a una fiesta.
Yes, we went to a party.

—¿A quiénes **invitaron** a la fiesta?
Whom did they invite to the party?

—A todos. **Comimos** y **bailamos** mucho.
Everyone. We ate and danced a lot.

Online
Vocabulario y gramática, pp. 100–102 | Actividades, pp. 81–83

¿Te acuerdas?

Stem-changing **-ar** and **-er** verbs have no stem changes in the preterite.

El regalo **co**stó veinte dólares.

No **vo**lvimos hasta *(until)* las once.

12 ¿Cuándo? 1B

Escuchemos Escucha las oraciones y decide si la joven habla de **a)** lo que su familia siempre hace o de **b)** lo que hizo.

13 ¿Qué tal estuvo? 1B, 1C

Escribamos Indica qué hicieron las siguientes personas en varias fiestas. Luego di qué tal estuvo cada fiesta—a todo dar o aburrida.

MODELO **nosotros (no salir hasta muy tarde)**
No salimos hasta muy tarde.
La fiesta estuvo a todo dar.

1. su tía (cantar ópera)
2. yo (bailar toda la noche)
3. nosotros (comer muy bien)
4. sólo *(only)* cuatro personas (ir a la fiesta)
5. Laura y José (jugar al ajedrez)
6. muchas personas interesantes (hablar conmigo)
7. nosotros (pasar una noche fenomenal)
8. todos (salir temprano de la fiesta)
9. yo (ver a muchos de mis amigos)
10. mis primos (contar chistes)

14 Padres especiales 1C

TEKS Focus
1C Present information using familiar words, phrases, and sentences

Escribamos Escribe tres oraciones para cada foto y di cómo festejó cada familia el Día del Padre y el Día de la Madre.

MODELO **Pasaron el Día de la Madre con la abuela.**

el Día de la Madre

el Día del Padre

15 El calendario de Arturo 1B, 1C

Leamos/Escribamos Usa la información del calendario para escribir por lo menos siete oraciones sobre lo que hizo Arturo para cada día festivo. Después compara sus actividades con las tuyas.

MODELO **El 14 de febrero Arturo mandó tarjetas.**
No mandé tarjetas, pero sí comí chocolates.

14 de febrero	4 de julio	25 de diciembre	31 de diciembre
mandar tarjetas	ir a la playa	abrir regalos	ir a una fiesta
abrir regalos	ver fuegos artificiales	reunirse con la familia	bailar
comer chocolates	comer en el parque	ir a la iglesia	reunirse con amigos

Comunicación

16 ¿Y tú? 1A

Hablemos Pregúntale a tu compañero(a) cómo celebró los días festivos de la Actividad 15.

MODELO **—¿Recibiste muchas tarjetas para el Día de los Enamorados?**
—Recibí muchas tarjetas y unos regalos también.

Pensar que and pensar with infinitives

Interactive TUTOR

1 The **e** → **ie** stem-changing verb **pensar** means *to think.* When it's followed by **que,** it means *to think that . . .*

yo	pienso	nosotros(as)	pensamos
tu	piensas	vosotros(as)	pensáis
Ud., él, ella	piensa	Uds., ellos(as)	piensan

Pienso que los invitados van a hablar y bailar toda la noche. Va a ser una fiesta muy divertida.
I think that the guests are going to . . .

2 **Pensar** can also be followed by an **infinitive** to say what *someone plans* to do or *intends* to do.

—¿Qué **piensan hacer** para celebrar el Año Nuevo?
What do you plan to do to celebrate New Year's Eve?

—**Pensamos ir** a esquiar.
We plan to go skiing.

Online
Vocabulario y gramática, pp. 100–102 | Actividades, pp. 81–83

TEKS Focus
4B Demonstrate understanding of the concept of culture through comparisons

Nota cultural

Celebrations call for special foods. In the Dominican Republic, a food served during the Christmas season is **pasteles en hoja.** This dish is prepared by boiling and mashing green plantains. The mashed plantains are then spread onto plantain leaves. Next, the leaves are stuffed with ground beef or chicken. Finally, the stuffed leaves are folded, tied with string, and placed in a pot of boiling water. Which other cultures have dishes similar to this? 4B

17 Este año pienso... 1B

Leamos/Escribamos Completa cada resolución de Año Nuevo *(New Year's resolution)* de manera lógica. Usa el verbo **pensar** en tus respuestas.

relajarse más	**seguir una dieta más sana**
gastar menos en regalos	**tomar una clase de francés**
volver a la universidad	**hacer más ejercicio**
ir a la casa de los abuelos	**pasar más tiempo en casa**

MODELO **Voy a comer más verduras.**
Pienso seguir una dieta más sana.

1. Mi madre va a estudiar mucho.
2. Mi hermano y yo vamos a mantenernos en mejor forma.
3. Mi padre va a tomar menos café y no va a trabajar hasta tarde.
4. Vamos a reunirnos con todos mis tíos para la Navidad.
5. Mi madre va a estudiar francés.
6. Mis padres van a ahorrar dinero este año.
7. No voy a salir con mis amigos todos los sábados.

18 El Día de la Independencia ➤1A, 1B

Escribamos/Hablemos Mira los dibujos e indica cómo piensan pasar estas personas el 4 de julio. Luego usa **pienso que** para dar tu opinión sobre los planes.

MODELO **Pienso ir a la playa con mis amigos.**
Pienso que va a ser muy divertido.
(Pienso que me voy a divertir mucho.)

yo

1. mis amigos y yo

2. unos amigos

3. mis padres

4. mi hermana

5. por la noche, mis padres y yo

6. mis abuelos

Comunicación

19 ¡Ven a mi fiesta! ➤1A

Hablemos Con un(a) compañero(a), habla de una fiesta que piensas hacer. Menciona el motivo de la fiesta, dónde va a ser, los invitados, la música y la comida. Tu compañero(a) puede usar las frases del cuadro para hacerte preguntas y reaccionar a tus respuestas.

Pienso que...	(No) estoy de acuerdo.	Prefiero...
fenomenal	pésimo(a)	divertido(a)
(No) me gusta(n).	¡Buena idea!	delicioso(a)

Cultura

VideoCultura

Comparaciones

Interactive TUTOR

2A, 4B

Carnaval en la República Dominicana

¿Qué días festivos se celebran en tu país?

En los países hispanohablantes, los días festivos y los festivales son muy importantes. A veces los festivales son religiosos, y a veces son de sabor nacional o regional. De todos modos, toda la comunidad participa, y es común cerrar los colegios, tiendas y otros negocios para celebrar. Estas personas hablan de los días festivos en su país y de la manera en que se celebran. ¿Son días festivos que celebras también? ¿Los celebras igual que ellos? Si son festivales que no celebras, ¿te acuerdas de otros que sí celebras?

Waldemar

Santo Domingo, la República Dominicana

¿Me puedes decir cuáles son dos o tres días festivos que se celebran en República Dominicana, y en qué fechas son?

Celebramos la Semana Santa, que es la segunda semana de abril. Celebramos el Día de la Madre, catorce de mayo. Y también celebramos las Navidades.

¿Cuál es tu día festivo favorito?

Me gusta mucho la Semana Santa.

¿Qué significa para ti la Semana Santa?

Es una semana muy espiritual.

¿Cómo pasaste la Semana Santa el año pasado?

Muy común. Como todo el mundo, fuimos a la iglesia mucho. Pasé mucho tiempo con mi familia.

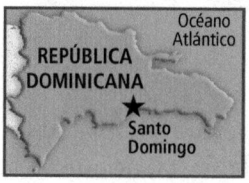

Visit Holt Online
go.hrw.com
KEYWORD: EXP1 CH9
Online Edition

Diana
El Paso, Texas

¿Me puedes decir dos o tres días festivos que se celebran aquí en El Paso?

Claro, aquí en El Paso festejamos el Día de la Independencia de Estados Unidos, que es el cuatro de julio. También festejamos la Navidad, que es el veinticinco de diciembre, y el Día de Gracias, que es el último jueves de noviembre.

¿Qué día festivo es tu favorito?

Mi día festivo favorito es la Navidad.

¿Cómo pasaste la Navidad el año pasado?

Toda mi familia nos sentamos en la casa de los abuelos, y comimos pavo.

Para comprender 1B

1. ¿Cuáles son tres días festivos que se celebran en la República Dominicana?
2. ¿Quién pasó su día festivo favorito con su familia?
3. ¿En qué día se celebra el Día de Acción de Gracias en Estados Unidos?
4. ¿Adónde fue Waldemar durante la Semana Santa?

Para pensar y hablar 2A

Waldemar and Diana say that their favorite holidays are *Semana Santa* and *la Navidad.* Why do you think they chose those holidays as their favorites? What similarity is there in the way they spent the holidays? What are your favorite holidays? Why are those days important to you?

Cuaderno para hispanohablantes, pp. 93–104

Comunidad

What Mexican holidays do you celebrate?

Two Mexican holidays celebrated in Texas are **Cinco de Mayo** and **El 16 de Septiembre,** Mexican Independence Day. There are also festivals that celebrate the Mexican roots of many Texans. For example, in Brownsville, Texas and Matamoros, Tamaulipas, people celebrate **Charro Days** every year. Mexic-Arte, a museum in Austin, presents eighty programs about Mexican holidays a year. What Mexican holidays does your community celebrate? To find out how people in your community take part in such festivities, interview in Spanish someone who helps organize them. Try to attend a festival. How are the Texan and Mexican cultures represented? 4B, 5A

Charro Days in Brownsville, Texas

Objetivos

Talking about preparing for a party, greeting, introducing others, and saying goodbye

Vocabulario en acción 2

ExpresaVisión

mandar invitaciones

colgar (ue) decoraciones, decorar

Entremeses

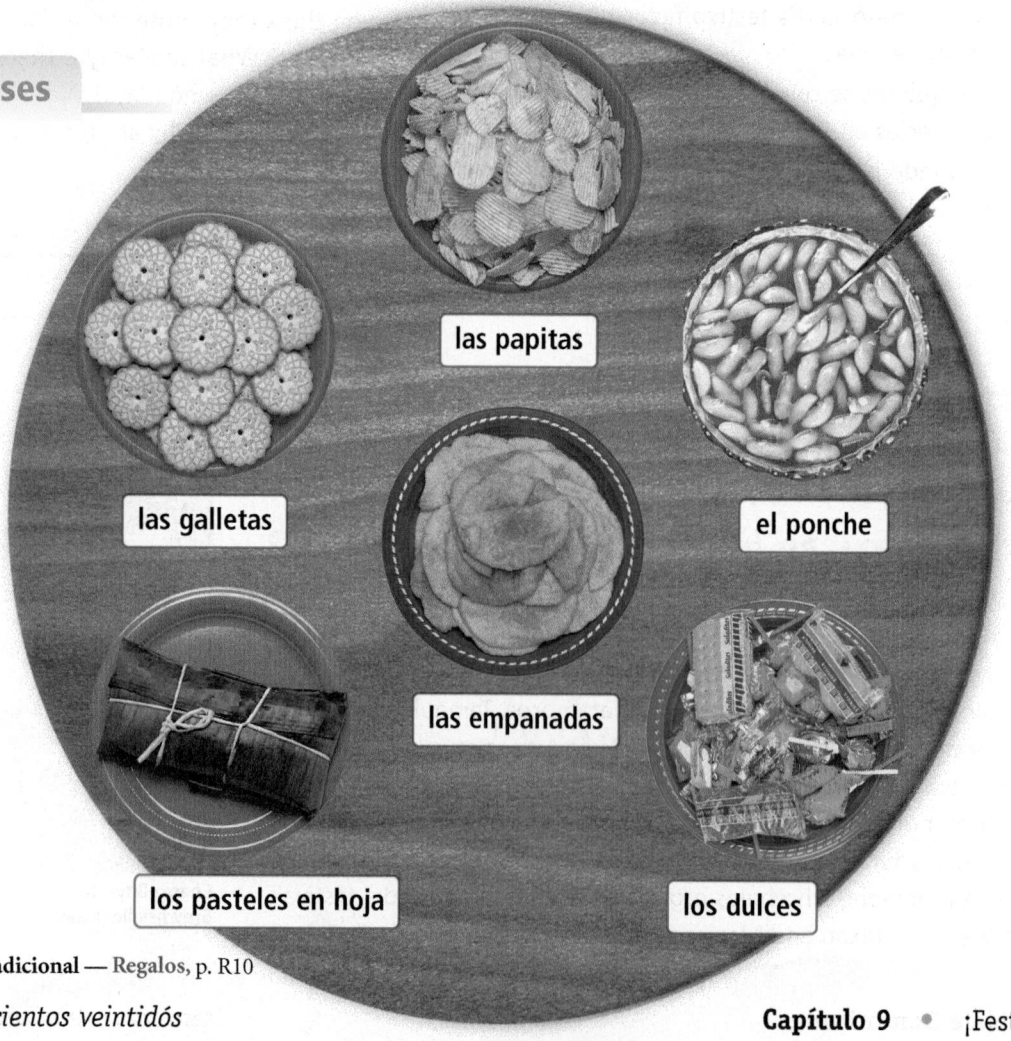

▶ **Vocabulario adicional** — Regalos, p. R10

Visit Holt Online
go.hrw.com
KEYWORD: EXP1 CH9
Vocabulario 2 practice

Los invitados van a...

Más vocabulario...

Las fiestas

el aniversario	*anniversary*
la boda	*wedding*
el cumpleaños	*birthday*
el día de tu santo	*your saint's day*
la fiesta sorpresa	*surprise party*
la graduación	*graduation*
la quinceañera	*girl's fifteenth birthday*

También se puede decir...

In the Dominican Republic, finger foods are called **bocadillos** or **picaderas,** but they may also be called **tapas** in Spain, **botanas** in Mexico, **pasapalos** in Venezuela, **bocas** in Costa Rica and El Salvador, or **apetitos** in Texas.

¡Exprésate!

To ask about preparing for a party	To respond
¿Está todo listo para la fiesta? ¿Ya terminaste con los preparativos? *Is everything ready for the party? Did you already finish the preparations?*	**Sí. Anoche compré las flores y preparé el ponche.** *Yes. Last night I bought the flowers and made the punch.*
¿Qué están haciendo los jóvenes ahora? *What are the young people doing now?*	**Están colgando la piñata.** *They are hanging the piñata.*

Interactive TUTOR

Nota cultural

In many Spanish-speaking countries, a girl's fifteenth birthday is recognized with a special celebration. In some countries, this party is called a **quinceañera.** However, in the Dominican Republic, the word refers to the girl herself and not just the party. While the idea behind the custom has changed over time, **quinceañera** parties are still common in the United States among Spanish-speaking families, as well as in other countries. What coming-of-age parties or celebrations have you heard of? 4B

20 ¡Vamos a festejar! 1B

Leamos/Hablemos Completa las oraciones con la(s) palabra(s) apropiada(s).

decoraciones	**ponche**	**está listo**	**invitados**	**fiesta sorpresa**
empanadas	**piñata**	**chistes**	**cumpleaños**	**pasteles en hoja**

1. Hoy es el _____ de mi primo Paco.
2. Esta noche hay una _____. Va a ser muy divertida.
3. Todo _____ para la fiesta.
4. Anteayer mi mamá, mis hermanos y yo preparamos los _____.
5. Esta mañana limpiamos la casa y luego colgamos las _____.
6. Ahora mi papá está colgando la _____ en el patio.
7. En unas horas, los _____ van a llegar a nuestra casa.
8. En la fiesta, vamos a beber _____ y comer muchas _____.
9. Voy a contar muchos _____ también.

21 La fiesta de Mila 1B, 1C

Escribamos/Hablemos Contesta las siguientes preguntas con base en el dibujo.

1. ¿Qué ocasión especial festejaron?
2. ¿Qué preparativos hicieron *(did they make)* para la fiesta?
3. ¿Qué tal estuvo la fiesta?
4. ¿Qué pasó en la fiesta?

¡Exprésate!

To greet, introduce others, and say goodbye

Interactive TUTOR

¡Qué gusto verte! *It's great to see you!*	**¡Tanto tiempo sin verte!** *Long time, no see!*
¿Qué hay de nuevo? *What's new?*	**Lo de siempre.** *Same as usual.*
Te presento a mis padres. *I'd like you to meet my parents.*	**Tanto gusto. ¡Feliz aniversario!** *So nice to meet you. Happy anniversary!*
Chao, te llamo más tarde. *Bye, I'll call you later.*	**Vale. Que te vaya bien.** *Okay. Hope things go well for you.*
	Cuídate. *Take care.*

22 Saludos, despedidas y presentaciones 1B

Escuchemos Indica si cada expresión es **a)** un saludo *(a greeting)*, **b)** una despedida *(a farewell)*, o **c)** una presentación *(an introduction)*.

23 ¿Qué dices? 1B

Leamos/Hablemos Decide qué expresiones de **¡Exprésate!** puedes usar en estas situaciones.

1. Ves a un amigo después de tres años.
2. Acaban de presentarte a dos amigos.
3. Estás con tus padres y ves a un amigo que no los conoce.
4. Vas a hablar por teléfono con un amigo más tarde.
5. Un amigo va a la República Dominicana por dos años.
6. Estás muy contento(a) de ver a un amigo.
7. Un amigo quiere saber qué hiciste el fin de semana, pero no hiciste nada nuevo.

Comunicación

24 Una reunión 1A, 1C

Escribamos/Hablemos En grupos de tres, dramaticen la siguiente situación. Diez años después de tu graduación del colegio regresas con tu esposo(a) *(spouse)* para una reunión de tu clase. Preséntales tu esposo(a) a tus compañeros de clase. Luego hablen de sus familias, de dónde viven y de qué hicieron después de graduarse.

TEKS Focus
1A Engage in oral and written exchanges of learned material to socialize and to provide and obtain information

Objetivos

Using direct object pronouns, **conocer** and personal **a**, the present progressive

Gramática en acción 2

GramaVisión

Repaso Direct object pronouns

Interactive TUTOR

1 Direct objects are people or things that receive the action of a verb. To avoid repetition, the **direct object pronouns** can take their place.

Subject	Direct Object	Subject	Direct Object
yo	**me** *me*	nosotros(as)	**nos** *us*
tú	**te** *you*	vosotros(as)	**os** *you*
usted (m.)	**lo** *you*	ustedes (m.)	**los** *you*
usted (f.)	**la** *you*	ustedes (f.)	**las** *you*
él	**lo** *him*	ellos	**los** *them*
ella	**la** *her*	ellas	**las** *them*

la stands for Paula

—¿Invitaste a **Paula**? —Sí, **la** invité. Ella viene.
Did you invite Paula? *Yes, I invited her. She's coming.*

2 When answering a question, remember to change the **direct object pronoun**, if necessary.

object me changes to te

—¿**Me** vas a llamar? —Sí, **te** llamo más tarde.
Are you going to call me? *Yes, I'll call you later.*

Online

Vocabulario y gramática, pp. 106–108 | Actividades, pp. 85–87

¿Te acuerdas?

The direct object pronouns **lo** *(him, it)*, **la** *(her, it)*, **los** *(them)* and **las** *(them)* can stand for things as well as people.

—¿Ya compraste **las flores?**

—Sí, ya **las** compré.

25 Invitaciones 1B, 1C

Escribamos Indica a qué celebración invitaste a las siguientes personas. Sigue el modelo.

MODELO **La invité a la quinceañera.**

Ana

1. a mis abuelos

2. a mi profesora

3. a mis amigas

4. a mi primo

Visit Holt Online
go.hrw.com
KEYWORD: EXP1 CH9
Gramática 1 practice

26 Una fiesta sorpresa 1B

Escribamos/Hablemos Una amiga te ayuda con una fiesta para tu hermano José. Contesta las preguntas con un pronombre de complemento directo *(direct object pronoun)*.

¿Se te olvidó? Pronoun placement, p. 212

MODELO **Vas a llevar *a tu hermano* a la fiesta, ¿verdad? (sí)**
Sí, voy a llevarlo. (Sí, lo voy a llevar.)

1. ¿*Me* vas a llamar antes de la fiesta, ¿verdad? (sí)
2. José no debe ver *a los invitados* antes de entrar, ¿verdad? (no)
3. ¿Debo poner *los regalos* en la mesa del patio? (sí)
4. ¿Invitaste *a los estudiantes de su clase?* (sí)
5. ¿Él no vio *las decoraciones?* (no)
6. ¿Tus padres *te* ayudaron a preparar todo? (sí)
7. ¿*Me* necesitas para mañana? (no)

27 ¡No nos fastidies! 1B

Escribamos/Hablemos Usando un pronombre de complemento directo con el imperativo, dile a cada persona qué debe o no debe hacer.

¿Se te olvidó? Object pronouns and informal commands, p. 254

MODELO **Hablas con tus amigos y tu hermano los interrumpe.**
—¡No nos interrumpas!

1. Un amigo que habla español nunca te ayuda a estudiar.
2. Hablas de algo secreto con un amigo y tu hermano los escucha.
3. El hermano menor de un amigo es antipático y tu amigo siempre lo trae cuando ustedes salen.
4. Tu mejor amigo no te llama.
5. Quieres comprar un regalo de cumpleaños para tu hermana y tu amigo la invita a ir de compras con ustedes.

Nota cultural

In most Spanish-speaking countries, including the Dominican Republic, dancing is an important part of any party. All kinds of music are played, food is served, and parties often do not end until the early morning hours. Spanish-speaking and Latin American countries have given us some of the most popular dances, including **merengue, salsa, samba, cha-cha-chá, tango, rumba,** and **cumbia.** Are these dances popular where you live? 2A, 4C

Comunicación

28 Planes para una fiesta 1A

Hablemos En parejas, hablen de los planes para una fiesta. ¿Cuándo quieren hacerla? Di quiénes te van a ayudar con los preparativos. ¿Qué van a servir? ¿Qué van a necesitar y dónde van a poner todo?

MODELO **—¿Cuándo quieres hacer tu fiesta de cumpleaños?**
—Quiero hacerla en dos semanas.

Conocer and personal a

Interactive TUTOR

Texas Nota cultural

Texas is rich in cultural heritages, including Mexican, German, Polish, Scottish, and Czech. Ethnic celebrations like Cinco de Mayo, Wurstfest in New Braunfels, and the Czech festival in Praha, feature traditional food, music, and dance. The University of Texas Institute of Texan Cultures in San Antonio annually hosts the Texas Folklife Festival. Is there a cultural festival in your area? 2A, 4B

1 The verb **conocer** is used to say you know or meet people, or that you are familiar with a place or a thing. It is irregular in the **yo** form.

yo	cono**zco**	nosotros(as)	conocemos
tú	conoces	vosotros(as)	conocéis
Ud., él, ella	conoce	Uds., ellos, ellas	conocen

—Aquí viene mi prima Claudia. ¿Quieres conocerla?
—Ya la **conozco**.

—¿Conocen las obras de Calderón de la Barca?
—No, no las conocemos.

2 When a name or noun referring to a person is the **direct object** of **conocer** or other verbs, the word **a** comes before it. This **a** has no translation.

—¿**Conoces a mi hermano**?
—Sí, **conozco a toda tu familia**.

The preposition **a** combines with the definite article **el** to form the contraction **al.**

Online
Vocabulario y gramática, pp. 106–108 | Actividades, pp. 85–87

29 ¿Conoces estas obras? 1B, 2B

Escribamos Indica si conoces o no las obras *(works)* de estos hispanos famosos. Usa un pronombre de complemento directo.

MODELO **Sí, la conozco.**
(No, no la conozco.)

la música de Andrés Segovia

las películas de Antonio Banderas

los libros de Isabel Allende

las canciones de Shakira

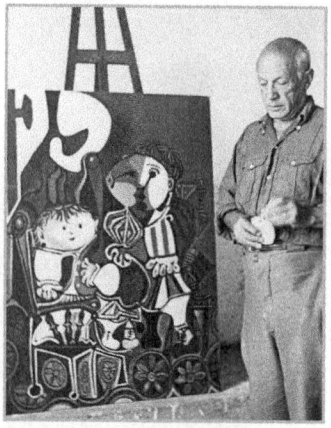

el arte de Pablo Picasso

30 Presentaciones 1B

Leamos Completa la siguiente conversación con las formas correctas de **conocer,** los pronombres de complemento directo o la palabra **a.**

SONIA Mario y Daniel, ¡qué gusto verlos! ¿ __1__ a mi hermano Carlos?

DANIEL No, no lo __2__.

SONIA Carlos, te presento __3__ mis amigos Mario y Daniel. Mario y Daniel, les presento __4__ mi hermano Carlos.

CARLOS Mario, ¿no eres el primo de Alberto Martínez?

MARIO Sí, soy su primo. ¿ __5__ conoces?

CARLOS Sí, lo __6__ muy bien. Está en mi clase de historia y a veces jugamos al tenis después de clases.

Un supermercado de la República Dominicana

31 ¿Se conocen? 1B

Leamos/Escribamos Lee cada oración. Indica si estas personas conocen a las personas o las cosas entre paréntesis. Repite la respuesta usando un pronombre de complemento directo.

TEKS Focus
1B Demonstrate understanding of simple, clearly spoken, and written language when dealing with familiar topics

MODELO **Mis padres siempre invitan a mi mejor amigo a nuestra casa. (mi mejor amigo)**
Mis padres conocen bien a mi mejor amigo.
Mis padres lo conocen bien.

1. Juan habla con Sara todos los días. (Sara)
2. Mi tía sabe dónde están las tiendas, los restaurantes, el colegio, el correo y el cine. (la ciudad)
3. Mis abuelos quieren venir a mi colegio pero no saben dónde está. (el pueblo)
4. Mi mejor amigo viene a mi casa los fines de semana. (mi casa)
5. Mi madre quiere hablar con mi profesor de español pero no sabe cómo se llama. (mi profesor de español)
6. Lola está en mi clase de inglés. Me parece muy simpática. (Lola)

Comunicación

32 Un encuentro 1A, 1C

Hablemos Imaginen que están en una fiesta. En grupos de cuatro, túrnense para presentar a dos de sus compañeros a la otra persona. Luego hablen de sus pasatiempos. Pueden usar la Actividad 31 de modelo.

Present progressive

Interactive TUTOR

1 To say what is happening right now, use the present progressive. To form the present progressive, combine a present tense form of **estar** with the present participle. Form the present participle by replacing **-ar** with **-ando** and **-er** or **-ir** with **-iendo**.

cantar → cant**ando**

Rosa **está** cant**ando**. *Rosa is singing.*

comer → com**iendo**

Estamos com**iendo**. *We are eating.*

2 When the stem of an **-er** or **-ir** verb ends in a vowel, form the present participle by changing the **i** of -iendo to **-y** (-yendo).

leer → le**y**endo

¿**Estás** le**y**endo? *Are you reading?*

3 The participles of stem-changing **-ir** verbs like **pedir, dormir,** and **servir** change **o** → **u** and **e** → **i**. There are no stem changes for **-ar** and **-er** verbs.

dormir → d**u**rmiendo servir → s**i**rviendo

4 The verbs **ir** and **venir** are not usually used in the present progressive. Use the simple present tense instead.

—¿**Vienes** a la fiesta? *Are you coming to the party?*

—No, **voy** a la biblioteca. *No, I'm going to the library.*

5 **Direct object** and **reflexive pronouns** can go before the conjugated form of **estar** or can be attached to the end of the present participle. When you attach the direct object or reflexive pronoun to the end of the present participle, place an accent mark on the stressed vowel.

¿La tarea? **La** estoy haciendo. (Estoy haciéndo**la**)

¿Mis hijos? **Se** están bañando. (Están bañándo**se**.)

Online

Vocabulario y gramática, pp. 106–108 | Actividades, pp. 85–87

En inglés

In English, the present progressive can mean that something is happening right now, is going on regularly, or is going to happen.

Everyone *is celebrating* in the living room.

We *are spending* a lot of time together.

I *am leaving* tomorrow.

In Spanish, the present progressive can mean that something is happening right now or is going on regularly in the present. It is not used for what is going to happen. Instead, the simple present is used.

Todos **están celebrando** en la sala.

Estamos pasando mucho tiempo juntos.

Salgo mañana.

33 ¿Qué están haciendo? 1B

Escuchemos Escucha las oraciones sobre la fiesta de Patricia y Roberto. Escoge las preguntas que le correspondan según el contexto.

a. ¿Qué están haciendo ustedes?

b. ¿Qué están haciendo los invitados?

c. ¿Qué está haciendo tu madre?

34 ¿Dónde están? 1B, 1C

Escribamos/Hablemos Indica qué están haciendo las siguientes personas según el contexto. Menciona varias posibilidades.

MODELO **Consuelo está en su cuarto.**
Está durmiendo. Está estudiando.

1. Lupe está en la clase.
2. Juan y Carlos están en el parque.
3. Laura y José están en una fiesta de cumpleaños.
4. Mi hermana y yo estamos en la cocina.
5. Estás en una tienda.
6. Tu primo y tú están en un restaurante.

Comunicación

35 Pantomimas 1C

Hablemos Cada estudiante va a representar una de las siguientes acciones sin hablar y la clase va a adivinar *(guess)* qué está haciendo.

hablar por teléfono	abrir un regalo	escribir una tarjeta
lavarse los dientes	secarse el pelo	maquillarse
peinarse	servir comida	acostarse

36 Una fiesta 1A, 1C

TEKS Focus
1C Present information using familiar words, phrases, and sentences

Hablemos Con un(a) compañero(a), describe la fiesta que hizo Paco con su familia. Usa el primer dibujo para hablar de lo que pasó antes de la fiesta, el segundo para hablar de lo que está pasando, y el tercero para decir lo que las personas piensan hacer después.

Novela en video

¿Quién será?

Episodio 9

ESTRATEGIA

Predicting When you plan an event, many things can go wrong. Before you watch the video, write a list of things that need to be done before a party. Write them in a logical sequence, then think about one or two things on your list that could go wrong. Compare your list with things mentioned in this episode. Based on the photos, predict what you think might go wrong in this episode. Watch the video and see how close your prediction was. 3B

En Puerto Rico

Nicolás hace los preparativos para la fiesta de cumpleaños de Mateo. Le pide ayuda a su hermana, Irene.

Nicolás ¿Qué estás haciendo, Irene?

Irene Estoy decorando la terraza. ¿Qué crees?

Nicolás Yo hago eso. Si quieres ayudar, ve a la cocina. Abre la lata de atún y prepara el dip. ¿De acuerdo?

Irene Bien, Nicolás.

Mamá Oye Irene, me parece que Picasso tiene hambre. ¿Quieres ponerle comida?

Irene Está bien, mamá.

Julia Hola, Nicolás, ¿cómo te va? ¿Tú conoces a Mari?

Nicolás Claro que te conozco. ¿Qué tal, Mari? Esperen un momento. Voy a traer la comida.

Nicolás Bueno, por fin llegaste Mateo, el invitado de honor. Feliz cumpleaños. Este año va a ser una fiesta muy buena.

Mateo Mejor que la del año pasado.

Nicolás ¿Qué pasó el año pasado?

Mateo Julia mandó las invitaciones a todos, pero en la invitación no escribió en la casa de Nicolás. Escribió en la casa de Julia.

Nicolás Julia, Mateo y yo nos reunimos aquí, pero todos los invitados se reunieron en la casa de Julia.

COMIDA DE GATO

Visit Holt Online
go.hrw.com
KEYWORD: EXP1 CH9
Online Edition

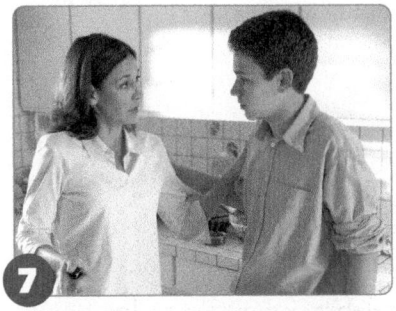

7

Mamá Nicolás, ¿cómo va todo?

Nicolás Muy bien, mamá. Todos están en la terraza. Están hablando. Acabo de poner la comida.

Mamá Muy bien. Voy a la casa de los abuelos por un rato. Te llamo más tarde, ¿eh?

Nicolás Gracias, mamá.

8

Nicolás No puede ser. Ya la están comiendo.

9

Mateo Nicolás, ¿qué estás haciendo?

Nicolás Nada. ¿Por qué me lo preguntas?

10

Nicolás ¡¡¿Le pusiste comida de gato al dip?!!

Irene ¿Qué dices? No, saqué una lata de atún del gabinete.

Nicolás Pensé que le pusiste comida de gato.

En España

La profesora considera a los candidatos.

11

Profesora Nueve candidatos. Sólo falta uno y luego puedo tomar mi decisión final.

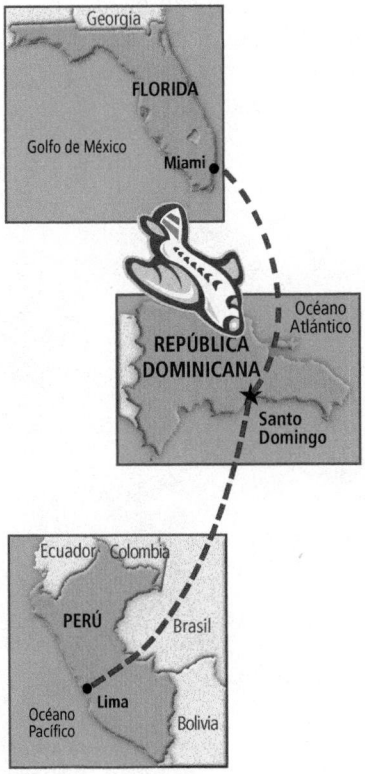

¿COMPRENDES?

1. ¿Qué tiene que hacer Irene para Nicolás? ¿Para su mamá?
2. ¿Qué pasó el año pasado en la fiesta de Mateo?
3. ¿Cuándo pudiste *(were you able)* predecir el problema?
4. ¿Qué piensa Nicolás cuando ve la lata de comida de gato?
5. ¿Puso Irene comida de gato al dip?
6. Según la profesora, ¿cuántos candidatos faltan? ¿Sabes para qué son candidatos? Trata de adivinar.

1B, 3A

Próximo episodio:
¿Puedes adivinar qué va a pasar en el último episodio?
PÁGINAS 370–371

Leamos y escribamos

TEKS Focus
3A Use resources in the language and cultures being studied to gain access to information

ESTRATEGIA

para leer You can guess the meaning of many words by looking for context and grammatical clues. Look for the words you understand around an unknown word to determine its meaning. Also try to guess the meaning of the word by determining what part of speech it is (noun, verb, adjective, etc.) and by looking at its root, prefix, and suffix.

A Antes de leer 3A

Usa las pistas del contexto para determinar el significado de las palabras en negrilla *(bold)* en las siguientes dos canciones.

Las serenatas son parte de muchas celebraciones. Estas dos canciones, la primera de México y la segunda de la República Dominicana, se cantan para celebrar los cumpleaños.

Las mañanitas

Éstas son las mañanitas
que **cantaba** el Rey David;
a las muchachas bonitas
se las cantamos aquí.

Despierta mi bien despierta,
mira que ya **amaneció**.
Ya los pajaritos cantan,
la luna ya se metió[1].

Qué linda está la mañana
en que vengo a saludarte,
venimos todos con gusto
y placer[2] a **felicitarte**.

Canción de cumpleaños

Celebro tu cumpleaños
tan pronto veo **asomar** el sol
y en este día glorioso
pido tu dicha[3] al Señor,
porque lo he considerado[4]
como el regalo mejor.

Toma mi abrazo[5] que yo te doy,
y mucha felicidad.

1 already set **2** pleasure **3** happiness
4 I have regarded it **5** hug

B Comprensión ➜1B

Contesta las siguientes preguntas con oraciones completas.

1. ¿Qué se celebra con estas dos canciones?
2. ¿Qué hace en este momento la persona a quién se le dedican *Las mañanitas?*
3. ¿Cómo se describe el día de la celebración en las dos canciones?
4. ¿Por qué vienen las personas a cantar la serenata?
5. En la segunda canción, ¿qué se considera el "regalo mejor"?

C Después de leer ➜2A, 4B

What other occasions might be celebrated with a serenade? How do these songs compare to others used to celebrate birthdays?

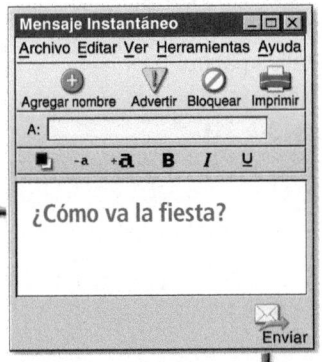

Taller del escritor

ESTRATEGIA

para escribir Descriptions with interesting details can improve your writing. Choose a topic, then brainstorm adjectives and adverbs that will liven up the description.

¡Huy, qué desastre! ➜1C

Last year you and your brothers planned a surprise party for your parents' anniversary. This year you decided to do it again, but things aren't going well. Someone forgot the punch, so the guests are all thirsty, and the dog is eating food from people's plates. Your brother got sick and couldn't come, but he's just sent you an instant message asking for a report. Tell what's happening, comparing it to how things went last year.

1 Antes de escribir

What were the highlights of last year's party? Which disasters from this year's party are you going to mention? Brainstorm some details about each, and then organize them, using a cluster diagram.

2 Escribir un borrador

Use your cluster diagram to compare and contrast this year's party with last year's. Give your brother the details listed in the diagram, and organize the comparison so that it's clear which party you're talking about. Conclude by asking your brother for advice.

3 Revisar

Read your draft twice, comparing it with your diagrams. Check spelling, punctuation, and verb usage. Have you used past-tense verbs to describe last year's party? Are you using the present progressive to talk about what's going on now? Exchange papers with a classmate for a peer edit.

4 Publicar

Read the description of the party to the class. Have the other students pretend to be your brother and give you advice to save this year's party.

Cuaderno para hispanohablantes, pp. 93–104

Repaso capítulo 9

Interactive TUTOR

1 Vocabulario 1
- talking about plans
- talking about past holidays

pp. 310–313

2 Gramática 1
- preterite of **-ar, -er,** and **-ir** verbs
- **pensar que** and **pensar** with infinitives

pp. 314–319

3 Vocabulario 2
- talking about preparing for a party
- greetings, introductions, and goodbyes

pp. 322–325

1 Mira las fotos y decide qué día festivo representa cada foto. Luego di cómo se celebra el día donde vives y qué planes tienes. 1B

1.

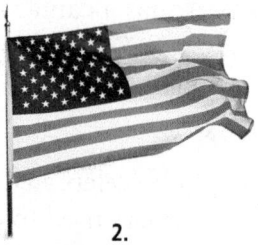
2.

3.

4.

5.

6.

2 Completa las oraciones con el verbo correcto en el pretérito. 1B

—Hola, Vero. ¿Cómo estás? ¿Qué hiciste ayer?

—Bueno, como sabes ayer fue el Día de la Madre. Por la mañana, yo __1__ (preparar/colgar) el desayuno para mi mamá. José y Beto __2__ (empezar/limpiar) y __3__ (decorar/comer) la sala. Por la tarde, nosotros __4__ (volver/ir) al parque para tener un picnic. Y tú, ¿cómo __5__ (pasar/mandar) el día?

—Yo __6__ (ir/invitar) a la iglesia con mi familia. Cuando (nosotros) __7__ (volver/merendar) a casa, mi mamá __8__ (pensar/abrir) sus regalos.

3 Completa las oraciones con las palabras apropiadas. 1B

1. Hoy es la _____ de Pablo y Carla. Es en la iglesia San Juan.
2. Hay más de cien _____ porque _____ muchas invitaciones.
3. Después de la ceremonia hay una _____.
4. Vamos a comer pastel y beber mucho _____.
5. En un año, ellos van a festejar su primer _____.
6. Ellos nos van a enseñar _____ de la ceremonia.

Visit Holt Online
go.hrw.com
KEYWORD: EXP1 CH9
Chapter Self-test

4 Completa la siguiente conversación. ✦1B

—¿Conoces ___1___ Juan Antonio Machado?

—No, no lo ___2___. ¿Quién es?

—Es mi primo. Muchas veces él ___3___ ayuda con mi tarea de historia. ___4___ puede ayudar a ti también si quieres.

—Buena idea, gracias.

—¿Qué ___5___ estudiando ustedes ahora en historia?

— ___6___ estudiando la Guerra Civil.

—Pues, no te preocupes. Juan ___7___ va a ayudar (a nosotros).

5 Answer the following questions. ✦2A, 2B, 4B

1. Name some celebrations in the Spanish-speaking world.
2. What are **pasteles en hoja**? When are they eaten?
3. What is a **quinceañera**? Is there a similar event in the United States?

6 Escucha mientras *(while)* Rita habla de una fiesta. Luego contesta las preguntas. ✦1B, 1C

7 Mira los dibujos. Escribe por los menos seis oraciones describiendo lo que le pasa a Paco. ✦1B, 1C

4 Gramática 2
- direct object pronouns
- **conocer** and personal **a**
- present progressive

pp. 326–331

5 Cultura
- **Comparaciones** **pp. 320–321**
- **Notas culturales** **pp. 313, 318, 324, 327**
- **Geocultura** **pp. 304–307**

TEKS Focus
2A Demonstrate understanding of practices (what people do) and how they relate to perspectives (how people perceive things) of the cultures studied

Repaso

Gramática 1
- preterite of **-ar, -er,** and **-ir** verbs
  pp. 314–317
- **pensar que** and **pensar** with infinitives
  pp. 318–319

Repaso de Gramática 1

invitar		**comer**		**salir**	
invit**é**	invit**amos**	com**í**	com**imos**	sal**í**	sal**imos**
invit**aste**	invit**asteis**	com**iste**	com**isteis**	sal**iste**	sal**isteis**
invit**ó**	invit**aron**	com**ió**	com**ieron**	sal**ió**	sal**ieron**

The verb **ver** has regular **-er** endings but without written accents.

The verb pensar followed by **que** means *to think.* When it's followed by an **infinitive,** it means *to plan* or *to intend.*

Pienso **que** debes comprar un regalo.
Pienso **comprar** un regalo.

Gramática 2
- direct object pronouns
  pp. 326–327
- **conocer** and personal **a**
  pp. 328–329
- present progressive
  pp. 330–331

Repaso de Gramática 2

me	me	**nos**	us
te	you (familiar)	**os**	you (familiar)
lo	him, you (formal), it	**los**	them, you (formal)
la	her, you (formal), it	**las**	them, you (formal)

When the direct object of a verb like conocer *(to meet, to know, to be familiar with)* is a person, use the personal **a**.

No conozco **a** Juan.

TEKS Focus
1B Demonstrate understanding of simple, clearly spoken, and written language when dealing with familiar topics

The present progressive tense is formed by using a form of the verb **estar** and a present participle ending in either **-ando** for **-ar** verbs or **-iendo** for **-er** and **-ir** verbs.

Estamos celebrando el cumpleaños de mi hermano.

Raquel **está escribiendo** una carta.

Letra y sonido a e i o u

Vocales fuertes (a, e, o) y débiles (i, u)

- Two **vocales fuertes** form two syllables:
  Rafael, teatro, traer, video, toalla
- One **vocal fuerte** and one accented **vocal débil** also form two syllables:
  día, tío, grúa, maíz
- One **vocal fuerte** and one unaccented **vocal débil** form one syllable called a *diphthong*, where i sounds like *y* and u sounds like *w*.
  piano, salió, cuando, nuevo, bailar, auto, seis

Trabalenguas

Cómo quieres que te quiera
Si el que quiero que me quiera
No me quiere como quiero que me quiera.

Dictado 1B

Escribe las oraciones de la grabación.

Repaso de Vocabulario 1

To talk about plans

el Año Nuevo	*New Year's Day*
celebrar	*to celebrate*
como siempre	*as always*
decorar la casa	*to decorate the house*
el Día de Acción de Gracias	*Thanksgiving Day*
el Día de la Independencia	*Independence Day*
el Día de la Madre	*Mother's Day*
el Día de los Enamorados	*Valentine's Day*
el Día del Padre	*Father's Day*
hacer una fiesta	*to have a party*
Hanukah	*Hanukkah*
invitar	*to invite*
la Navidad	*Christmas*
la Nochebuena	*Christmas Eve*
la Nochevieja	*New Year's Eve*
Pensamos...	*We plan to . . .*
¿Qué planes tienen para...?	*What plans do you have for . . .?*
la Semana Santa	*Holy Week*
tener un picnic	*to have a picnic*

To talk about past holidays

abrir regalos	*to open gifts*
el año pasado	*last year*
los días festivos	*holidays*
Estuvo a todo dar.	*It was great.*
festejar	*to celebrate*
La pasamos en casa de...	*We spent it at . . .'s house.*
mandar tarjetas	*to send cards*
la misa	*Mass*
pasar	*to spend*
¿Qué tal estuvo?	*How was it?*
recibir regalos	*to receive gifts*
reunirse con (toda) la familia	*to get together with the (whole) family*
la sinagoga	*synagogue*
el templo	*temple*
ver fuegos artificiales	*to see fireworks*

Repaso de Vocabulario 2

To talk about preparing for a party

ahora	*now*
el aniversario	*anniversary*
anoche	*last night*
la boda	*wedding*
charlar	*to talk, to chat*
colgar (ue)	*to hang (up)*
contar (ue) chistes	*to tell jokes*
el cumpleaños	*birthday*
las decoraciones	*decorations*
el día de tu santo	*your saint's day*
los dulces	*candy, sweets*
las empanadas	*turnover-like pastries*
enseñar fotos	*to show photos*
los entremeses	*appetizers*
¿Está todo listo para...?	*Is everything ready for . . .?*
la fiesta sorpresa	*surprise party*
las flores	*flowers*
las galletas	*cookies*
la graduación	*graduation*
las invitaciones	*invitations*
los invitados	*guests*
los jóvenes	*young people*
mandar	*to send*
las papitas	*potato chips*
los pasteles en hoja	*Dominican tamales*
la piñata	*piñata*
el ponche	*punch*
los preparativos	*preparations*
¿Qué están haciendo?	*What are they doing?*
la quinceañera	*girl's fifteenth birthday*
terminar	*to finish*
ya	*already*

To greet, introduce others, and say goodbye

Chao, te llamo más tarde.	*Bye, I'll call you later.*
conocer	*to know, to meet, to be familiar with*
Cuídate.	*Take care.*
¡Feliz aniversario!	*Happy anniversary!*
Lo de siempre.	*Same as usual.*
¡Qué gusto verte!	*It's great to see you!*
¿Qué hay de nuevo?	*What's new?*
Tanto gusto.	*So nice to meet you.*
¡Tanto tiempo sin verte!	*Long time, no see!*
Te presento a...	*I'd like you to meet . . .*
Vale. Que te vaya bien.	*Okay. Hope things go well for you.*

Integración

capítulos 1-9

1 Escucha las descripciones y escoge la foto correspondiente. 1B

A

B

C

D

2 Lee el anuncio y luego di si las oraciones son **ciertas** o **falsas**. 1B, 3A

TEKS Focus

3A Use resources in the language and cultures being studied to gain access to information

1. La especialidad de Fiesta Lala es comida mexicana.
2. Fiesta Lala puede ayudar con tus celebraciones de lunes a domingo.
3. La señora Quiñones tiene poca experiencia.
4. Fiesta Lala puede organizar la boda de tu hermana.
5. Fiesta Lala sólo ayuda con las fiestas de cumpleaños.

Visit Holt Online
go.hrw.com
KEYWORD: EXP1 CH9
Cumulative Self-test

3 Tus amigos y tú quieren darle una fiesta sorpresa a su profesor(a) de español y llaman a Fiesta Lala. Escriban la conversación entre ustedes y la señora Quiñones sobre los preparativos. Presenten su conversación a la clase. ✦1A, 1B, 1C

4 Imagina que estás en esta fiesta. Escoge dos personas de la pintura y escribe un diálogo entre ellas. Primero se saludan y hablan de la fiesta y lo que hicieron antes de llegar. Luego hablan de lo que están haciendo allí. Presenta tu diálogo con un(a) compañero(a) a la clase para ver si todos pueden adivinar *(guess)* quiénes hablan. ✦1B, 1C

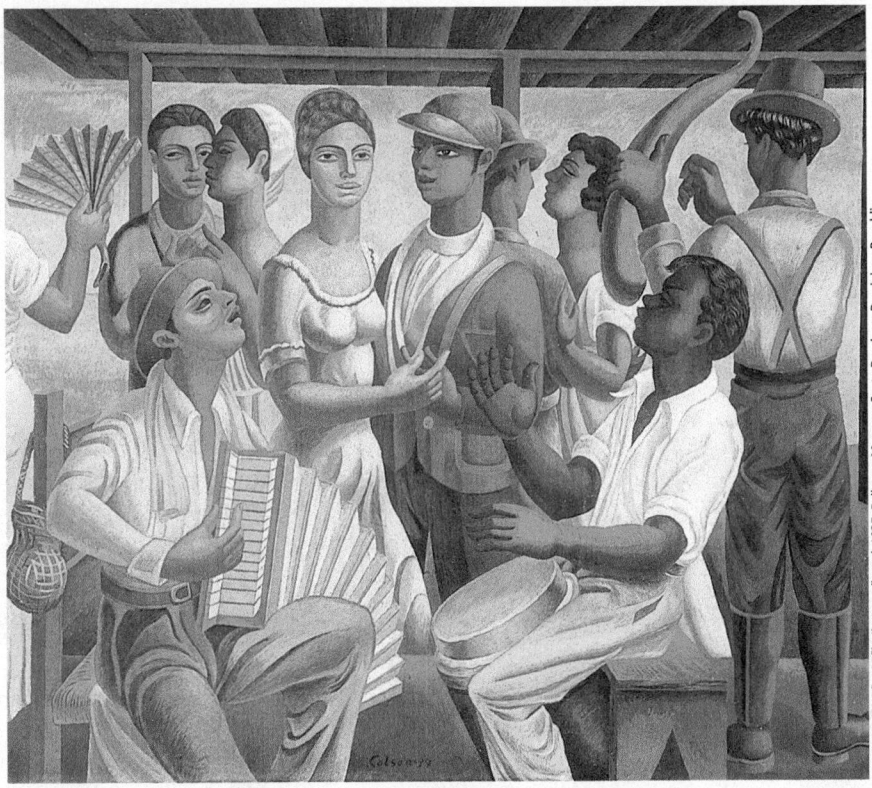

52 x 68cm (20.5" x 27") oil on cardboard, 1937; Bellapart Museum, Santo Domingo, Dominican Republic

***Merengue,* de Jaime Colson (1901–1975)**

5 Escribe un correo electrónico a tu amigo(a) en España en que le explicas cómo pasaste tu cumpleaños este año. Incluye una comparación con la celebración del año pasado. ✦1B, 1C

6 ✦1A, 2A, 2B

Situación

For your school's culture fair, the Spanish Club is making a booth **(puesto)** to recognize a holiday celebrated in a Spanish-speaking country. In small groups, discuss in Spanish what holiday you will present, and decide what food, decorations, music, and other customs associated with that holiday you will have at the booth.

GeoVisión

Geocultura Perú

▲ **El río Amazonas** empieza en los Andes peruanos, cruza la selva peruana y desemboca en el Océano Atlántico en Brasil.

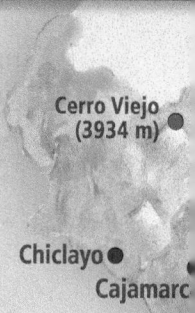

▼ **Lima,** la capital de Perú, fue fundada por Francisco Pizarro en 1535. Está en la costa, que es la región más árida del país. Aquí se ve Miraflores, el centro comercial de Lima.

Almanaque

Población
27.949.639

Capital
Lima

Gobierno
república constitucional

Idiomas
español, quechua, aymara

Moneda
nuevo sol

Código Internet
www.[ ].pe

▼ **Cuzco** Familias cuzqueñas celebran el Día de la Independencia vestidos con trajes tradicionales.

¿Sabías que...?

Perú es tres veces más grande que Texas, pero el número de habitantes por km² en Perú es menos de 50% de lo que es en Texas.

COLOMBIA

CUADOR

Río Tigre

Río Napo

Río Amazonas

Iquitos

Río Marañón

Río Ucayali

Cordillera Oriental

Los Andes

Pucallpa

rujillo

Nevado
scarán
768 m)

PERÚ

Cordillera Occidental

Río Urubamba

Parque Nacional del Manu

LIMA

Huancayo

Machu Picchu

Pisac

Cuzco

Cordillera Oriental

Nevado Coropuna (6613 m)

Líneas de Nazca

Nazca

Cordillera Occidental

Puno

Lago Titicaca

Altiplano Andino

Volcán Misti (5822 m)

Arequipa

OCÉANO PACÍFICO

BRASIL

BOLIVIA

CHILE

◀ **La cordillera de los Andes** constituye una gran parte de Perú. Los picos alcanzan alturas de más de 6.000 metros.

▶ **Pisac** La vida en los Andes es muy diferente de la vida en Lima. El mercado de Pisac, a 30 km de Cuzco, refleja las tradiciones incaicas.

▼ **El Parque Nacional del Manu,** en la selva tropical del sureste de Perú, contiene cientos de especies de aves, monos, felinos, reptiles, peces y plantas.

◀ **El lago Titicaca** es el lago navegable más alto del mundo, a 3.810 metros sobre el nivel del mar. Las balsas de totora se hacen de una planta que crece en las orillas del lago.

¿Qué tanto sabes?

¿Dónde está la zona más árida de Perú? ¿Dónde empieza el río Amazonas? 3B

A conocer Perú

La arquitectura

▲ **Machu Picchu,** la «ciudad perdida» de los incas, fue redescubierta en 1911. Demuestra lo avanzado de la cultura precolombina.

▲ **Cuzco** La combinación de los estilos colonial e incaico es notable en la Iglesia de Santo Domingo, construida encima del antiguo Templo del Sol del Inca, que también se conoce como Qoricancha.

▲ **Lima** La Catedral en la Plaza Mayor, el centro colonial de la capital, refleja la herencia española de la ciudad.

El arte

◀ **Los tejidos** de la región de los Andes son muy conocidos. Las campesinas quechuas son expertas tejedoras. Fabrican textiles preciosos de lana de alpaca.

▼ **Las famosas líneas de Nazca** se encuentran en el desierto de la costa del sur. Las formas talladas en la tierra se pueden observar solamente desde el aire.

▲ ***Danza*** fue pintado por el artista peruano Julio Quispe Virhues (1945–). El pintor, conocido como Quispejo, ha realizado exposiciones en muchos países, inclusive en Estados Unidos.

Las celebraciones

Interactive TUTOR

Visit Holt Online
go.hrw.com
KEYWORD: EXP1 CH10
Photo Tour

▼ **Durante la Semana del Andinismo** en la Cordillera Blanca se practican deportes como el alpinismo, esquí y kayaking.

▲ **El Concurso Nacional de Marinera,** celebrado en Trujillo a finales de enero, se dedica al baile nacional de Perú, la marinera.

¿Sabías que...?

Las paredes de los edificios incaicos están hechas de piedras talladas con extraordinaria precisión. Se cuenta que ni un cuchillo cabe entre las piedras.

► **En el Concurso Nacional del Caballo Peruano de Paso** se celebra el caballo nacional de Perú. Es una gran fiesta con elegantes desfiles que dura una semana.

La comida

▲ **El ají,** un pimiento picante, es un ingrediente típico de la cocina peruana.

◄ **El ceviche** es un plato de pescado crudo preparado con jugo de limón, cebolla, ají y maíz o camote. Se sirve en cevicherías, restaurantes muy típicos de Perú.

Conexión Geografía

Perú tiene tres distintas regiones geográficas—la costa, la selva y la sierra. La comida de cada región es diferente. Investiga la comida típica de cada región y explica cómo y por qué son diferentes. 3B

Capítulo 10

¡A viajar!

OBJETIVOS

In this chapter you will learn to

- ask for and give information
- remind and reassure others
- talk about a trip
- express hopes and wishes

And you will use

- preterite of regular verbs
- preterite of **-car, -gar, -zar** verbs
- preterite of **hacer**
- informal commands of spelling-change and irregular verbs
- direct object pronouns
- verbs followed by infinitives

¿Qué ves en la foto?

- ¿Cuántas personas hay en esta familia? ¿Cómo son?
- ¿Qué tiempo hace?
- ¿Qué ropa llevan estas personas?

Texas

TEKS Look for the ★ next to each activity to learn how it can help you achieve the goals of the **Texas Essential Knowledge and Skills,** found on page xxiii.

Visit Holt Online
go.hrw.com
KEYWORD: EXP1 CH10
Online Edition

De excursión en Machu Picchu, Perú

Objetivos
Asking for and giving information, reminding and reassuring

Vocabulario en acción 1

ExpresaVisión

En el aeropuerto

▶ **Vocabulario adicional** — Vacaciones, p. R11

Voy a abordar el avión ahora. Tengo todo. No quiero perder nada.

la billetera

la bolsa

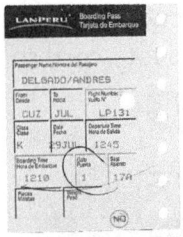

la tarjeta de embarque

el boleto de avión

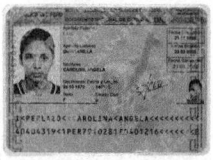

el carnet de identidad

el pasaporte

Visit Holt Online
go.hrw.com
KEYWORD: EXP1 CH10
Vocabulario 1 practice

Más vocabulario...

cambiar dinero	*to change money*
comenzar (ie) un viaje	*to begin a trip*
encontrarse (ue) con (alguien)	*to meet up with (someone)*
hacer un viaje	*to take a trip*
irse	*to leave*
la llegada	*arrival*
la salida	*departure*
sentarse (ie)	*to sit down*
los servicios	*restrooms*

Texas También se puede decir...

Some Latin American speakers say **la valija** instead of **la maleta.**

In Latin America you will hear **chequear el equipaje** instead of **facturar el equipaje.** In Texas, you may hear **checar el equipaje.**

El boleto is sometimes called **el billete, el ticket, la boleta, el tiquete,** or **el pasaje.**

¡Exprésate!

Interactive TUTOR

To ask for information	To give information
¿Me puede decir dónde está la oficina de cambio? *Can you tell me where the money exchange is?*	**Está a la vuelta.** *It's around the corner.*
¿Sabe Ud. a qué hora sale el vuelo 954? No quiero perderlo. *Do you know at what time Flight 954 leaves? I don't want to miss it.*	**Lo puede ver allí en esa pantalla.** *You can see it there on that monitor.* **Sí, sale a las cuatro en punto.** *Yes, it leaves at four on the dot.*
¿Dónde se puede conseguir un mapa? *Where can I get a map?*	**Lo siento, no sé.** *I'm sorry, (but) I don't know.*

Online
Vocabulario y gramática, pp. 109–111

1 ¿Dónde están? 1B

Escuchemos Mira las fotos y escucha las conversaciones. Decide qué foto corresponde a cada conversación.

A

B

C

D

2 Definiciones 1B

Leamos/Escribamos Completa las oraciones.

reclamo	cambio	vuelo	desembarcar
cola	seguridad	aeropuerto	abordar
embarque	avión	salida	perder

1. Un ____ es donde llegan y salen los aviones.
2. Una ____ es una línea de personas que esperan.
3. Necesitas una tarjeta de ____ para abordar un ____.
4. En la pantalla está el número del ____ y la hora de la ____.
5. El agente abre el equipaje en el control de ____.
6. Puedes cambiar dólares por soles en la oficina de ____.
7. Puedes recoger tus maletas en el ____ de equipaje.
8. Cuando un avión llega al aeropuerto, los pasajeros tienen que ____.
9. Si llegas tarde, vas a ____ el vuelo.
10. Antes de ____, los pasajeros se sientan en la sala de espera.

Nota cultural

The Uros Islands on Lake Titicaca are man-made and constructed of *totora*, a reed-like grass that grows on the lake's bed. Though walking on the surface is like walking on a water bed, there are reed houses, schools, churches, and even a post office. The Uros people also make reed boats to travel to the mainland. What do you think life is like on these islands? 2A, 2B

3 Conversaciones 1B

Leamos/Escribamos Completa las conversaciones con base en las fotos de la Actividad 1.

1. —¿Sabe Ud. dónde están ____?
   —Sí, cómo no. Están ____.
2. —¿Me puede decir a qué hora llega ____ 179?
   —Lo siento, ____. Pero lo puede ver allí en esa ____.
3. —¿Dónde puedo ____ el equipaje?
   —Tiene que ir a ese ____ y hacer ____.
4. —¿Sabe Ud. dónde ____ la aduana?
   —Lo ____, no sé.

TEKS Focus

2A Demonstrate understanding of practices (what people do) and how they relate to perspectives (how people perceive things) of the cultures studied

¡Exprésate!

To remind and reassure

Interactive TUTOR

¿Ya sacaste el dinero? *Did you already get the money?*	**Sí, ya lo saqué.** *Yes, I already got it.* **No, todavía no. Debo pasar por el cajero automático.** *No, not yet. I need to go by the automatic teller machine.*
¿Ya hiciste la maleta? *Did you already pack your suitcase?*	**No, todavía tengo que hacerla.** *No, I still have to pack it.*
¡Ay, dejé la cámara en casa! *Oh, I left the camera at home!*	**No te preocupes. Puedes comprar una cámara desechable en cualquier tienda.** *Don't worry. You can buy a disposable camera at any store.*

Online
Vocabulario y gramática, pp. 109–111

4 Preparativos para el viaje 1B

Leamos/Escribamos Joaquín planeó muchas cosas *(planned many things)* esta semana. Indica si ya hizo *(did)* las cosas o si todavía tiene que hacerlas.

MODELO **el lunes: Ya encontró el pasaporte.**
Todavía tiene que conseguir un mapa.

lunes	martes	miércoles	jueves	viernes
6 conseguir un mapa encontrar el pasaporte X	**7** lavar la ropa X sacar dinero	**8** ir a la oficina de cambio X limpiar el cuarto	**9** escribir cartas X hacer la maleta	**10** comprar una cámara desechable X llamar a tío Paco

Comunicación

5 ¿Ya lo hiciste? 1A

Hablemos Hablas con tu compañero(a) sobre un viaje. Contesta sus preguntas basándote en la lista.

MODELO **—¿Ya sacaste la tarjeta de embarque?**
—No, todavía no. Debo ir al mostrador.

Cosas por hacer:
- sacar la tarjeta de embarque
- √ encontrar el pasaporte
- √ sacar dinero
- √ comprar el boleto
- facturar el equipaje
- comprar revistas para el viaje

6 De viaje 1A

Hablemos Con un(a) compañero(a), dramatiza una conversación entre dos personas que hacen un viaje a Perú. Pregúntense acerca de los pasaportes, los boletos, el aeropuerto y otras cosas.

Objetivos

Review of the preterite; preterite of **-car, -gar, -zar** verbs; preterite of **hacer**

Gramática en acción 1

GramaVisión

Repaso The preterite

Interactive TUTOR

1 Use the preterite to talk about what happened at a specific point in the past and to narrate a sequence of events in the past.

Me levanté temprano, **me vestí** y **fui** al aeropuerto.

2 You know how to form the preterite of all regular verbs. Remember that **-ar** and **-er** verbs do not have stem changes in the preterite.

	esperar	**perder**	**abrir**
yo	esper**é**	perd**í**	abr**í**
tú	esper**aste**	perd**iste**	abr**iste**
Ud., él, ella	esper**ó**	perd**ió**	abr**ió**
nosotros(as)	esper**amos**	perd**imos**	abr**imos**
vosotros(as)	esper**asteis**	perd**isteis**	abr**isteis**
Uds., ellos, ellas	esper**aron**	perd**ieron**	abr**ieron**

Esperamos una hora. — *We waited an hour.*
Perdí mi boleto. — *I lost my ticket.*

Online

Vocabulario y gramática, pp. 112–114 | Actividades, pp. 120–121

¿Te acuerdas?

To say where someone *went,* use **ir** *(to go)* in the preterite.

fui	**fuimos**
fuiste	**fuisteis**
fue	**fueron**

7 ¡Qué viaje más difícil! ←1B

Escuchemos Jesse acaba de regresar de un viaje difícil. Escucha lo que dice y completa las oraciones con la respuesta correcta.

1. A las 8:00, Jesse _____.
   a. llegó al aeropuerto en taxi **b.** salió de la casa
2. Jesse regresó a casa porque _____.
   a. dejó el boleto allí **b.** olvidó sus lentes
3. Al llegar al aeropuerto, Jesse _____.
   a. compró un libro **b.** se encontró con sus amigos
4. En el control de seguridad, los agentes _____.
   a. facturaron el equipaje **b.** abrieron las maletas
5. Juan regresó al mostrador porque _____.
   a. recogió el equipaje **b.** perdió la tarjeta de embarque
6. Al fin, Carlos y Jesse _____.
   a. abordaron el avión **b.** perdieron el vuelo

Visit Holt Online
go.hrw.com
KEYWORD: EXP1 CH10
Gramática 1 practice

8 ¿Qué pasó? 1C

Escribamos/Hablemos Imagina que eres Daniela. Indica qué pasó el día en que ella y su familia comenzaron su viaje.

MODELO **(yo) Me levanté temprano.**

yo

1. nosotros

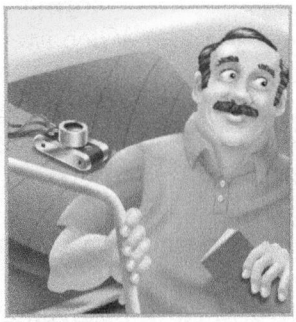

2. mi padre

3. mis padres

4. el agente

5. los agentes

6. yo

Comunicación

9 Un buen viaje 1A

Hablemos En grupos de tres, dramaticen esta situación. Un(a) estudiante de intercambio llama a sus padres para decirles que está en Lima. Sus padres hacen preguntas sobre el viaje y el (la) estudiante se las contesta.

TEKS Focus
1A Engage in oral and written exchanges of learned material to socialize and to provide and obtain information

MODELO **—¿Esperaste mucho tiempo antes de abordar?**
—No, no esperé mucho.

dejar	abordar	esperar	abrir
recoger	ir al mostrador	perder	encontrarse

Preterite of -car, -gar, -zar verbs

Interactive TUTOR

1 Verbs ending in **-car**, **-gar**, and **-zar** have spelling changes in the **yo** forms of the preterite.

In **-car** verbs, the **c** changes to **qu**.	In **-gar** verbs, the **g** changes to **gu**.	In **-zar** verbs, the **z** changes to **c**.
sa**qu**é	lle**gu**é	comen**c**é
sacaste	llegaste	comenzaste
sacó	llegó	comenzó
sacamos	llegamos	comenzamos
sacasteis	llegasteis	comenzasteis
sacaron	llegaron	comenzaron

Comencé mi viaje temprano. **Llegué** al aeropuerto y **saqué** dinero.
I started my trip early. I arrived at the airport and got money.

Online
Vocabulario y gramática, pp. 112–114 | Actividades, pp. 91–93

10 Cuando viajo... 1B

Escuchemos Indica si Carmen habla de **a)** lo que siempre hace cuando viaja *(travels)* o de **b)** lo que hizo *(did)* la última vez que viajó.

11 La tarjeta postal 1B

Leamos/Escribamos Completa la tarjeta postal que recibió Liliana con la forma correcta del pretérito de los verbos.

encontrar	**comenzar**	**buscar**	**llegar**	**almorzar**
comprar	**pagar**	**facturar**	**sacar**	**ir**

Hola Liliana,

Ya sabes que __1__ el día a las 7:00 y que __2__ al aeropuerto en taxi. Cuando __3__, fui directamente al mostrador donde __4__ el boleto y __5__ el equipaje. Después, __6__ un mapa en la librería y __7__ dinero del cajero automático. __8__ un sándwich y __9__ una tienda para comprarte un regalo, pero no __10__ nada. Voy a buscarte algo en Cuzco.

Con cariño,
Tía Juana

12 ¿Quién? 1C

Escribamos/Hablemos Escribe oraciones y di quién hizo las siguientes cosas.

MODELO **llegar al aeropuerto**
Olivia llegó al aeropuerto a las siete.

Olivia

TEKS Focus
1C Present information using familiar words, phrases, and sentences

llegar al aeropuerto	levantarse	sacar dinero
pagar el boleto	buscar los servicios	almorzar en un restaurante

1. Ana

2. Felipe

3. Maricela y yo

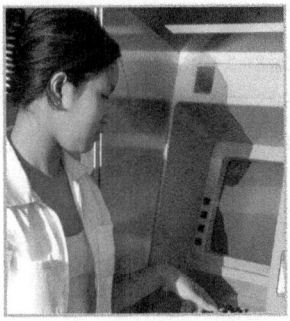

4. yo

5. Ricardo y Elena

6. yo

Comunicación

13 La fiesta de despedida 1A

Hablemos Anoche hubo *(there was)* una fiesta para un compañero que se va a Perú, pero no pudiste ir. Pregúntale qué pasó a un(a) compañero(a) de clase, usando las palabras del cuadro.

colgar decoraciones	comenzar la fiesta	llegar	jugar juegos de mesa
tocar instrumentos	contar chistes	bailar	preparar la comida

Preterite of hacer

Interactive TUTOR

1 The verb **hacer** *(to make, to do)* is irregular in the preterite. A question asked with **hacer** will often be answered using another verb.

yo	**hice**	nosotros(as)	**hicimos**
tú	**hiciste**	vosotros(as)	**hicisteis**
Ud., él, ella	**hizo**	Uds., ellos, ellas	**hicieron**

—¿Qué **hiciste** ayer? *What did you do yesterday?*
—**Fui** a la oficina de correo. *I went to the post office.*

2 To form the preterite of weather expressions with **hace**, replace **hace** with **hizo**. Use the preterite to say what the weather was like over a specific period or when telling how long conditions lasted. Use **nevó** for *it snowed* and **llovió** for *it rained.*

—¿Qué tiempo **hizo** ayer? —**Hizo** mal tiempo. **Llovió** todo el día.

El año pasado nunca **nevó**.

Online
Vocabulario y gramática, pp. 112–114 | Actividades, pp. 91–93

Nota cultural

The Incas called *quinoa* the Mother Grain. Every year the emperor planted the first seeds and on solstice, priests made quinoa offerings to Inti, the Sun. The Incan armies, which frequently marched for days at a time, ate war balls, a mix of quinoa and fat. Quinoa is still eaten in Peru and is imported to the United States for its high nutritional value. How do you think quinoa is used in recipes? 2B

TEKS Focus
2B Demonstrate understanding of products (what people create) and how they relate to perspectives (how people perceive things) of the cultures studied

14 Antes de comenzar el viaje 1B

Leamos Lee lo que dice Pablo e indica si **a**) habla de sí mismo *(himself)*, **b**) de sus padres, **c**) de él y sus amigos o **d**) del tiempo.

1. Antes de comenzar el viaje hicimos una fiesta en el Club Naval.
2. Hice planes para encontrarme con ellos al volver.
3. No hicieron las maletas hasta muy tarde.
4. Hice las maletas anteayer.
5. Hizo fresco e hizo sol.
6. Al llegar al aeropuerto, hicieron cola delante del mostrador.

15 ¿Qué hicieron ustedes? 1C

Escribamos Indica si estas cosas pasaron o no la última vez que hiciste un viaje con tu familia en carro.

MODELO **mi madre/hacer las maletas**
Mi madre (no) hizo las maletas.

1. (yo)/hacer la maleta
2. mi hermano/hacer las camas antes de irnos
3. mis amigos/hacer una fiesta antes del viaje
4. (yo)/hacer la tarea en el carro
5. mis padres/hacer sándwiches y nosotros/comer en el carro
6. hacer buen tiempo
7. hacer frío

Comunicación

16 De vacaciones ➜1A

Hablemos Roberto y su amiga están mirando las fotos de sus vacaciones. Con un(a) compañero(a), túrnense para preguntar y contestar qué tiempo hizo y qué hicieron estas personas.

MODELO **—¿Qué tiempo hizo el lunes?**
—Hizo calor y mucho sol.
—¿Qué hicieron Alicia y tú?
—Jugamos al tenis.

lunes/Alicia y yo

1. lunes/yo

2. martes/mis hermanas

3. miércoles/mis padres

4. jueves/mi padre

5. viernes/María y Jorge

6. sábado/mis amigos y yo

7. sábado/mi hermano

8. domingo/mi madre

17 El fin de semana pasado ➜1A

Hablemos En grupos de tres, túrnense para preguntar quién hizo las cosas de la lista el fin de semana pasado. Presenten los resultados del grupo a la clase.

MODELO **—¿Hiciste un viaje el fin de semana pasado?**
—Sí, hice un viaje./No, no hice ningún viaje.

hacer un viaje	hacer cola en una tienda
hacer planes para salir con amigos	hacer la tarea de español
hacer el almuerzo para llevar al colegio	hacer la cama

Cultura

VideoCultura

Comparaciones

Terminal de autobuses, Lima, Perú

¿Adónde fuiste y qué hiciste la última vez que viajaste? 1B, 4B

En Estados Unidos, la mayoría de la gente tiene carros, y es muy común viajar en coche. Si es un viaje de larga distancia, mucha gente va en avión. En Perú, es más común viajar en autobús, aunque *(although)* es posible ir en avión o en tren. Estas personas hablan de su último viaje y de lo que hicieron. ¿Cómo viajaron? ¿Qué hicieron al llegar a su destino *(destination)*? ¿Hacen las mismas cosas que tú haces cuando viajas? Compara sus viajes a tus propias experiencias.

Lisette
Lima, Perú

Cuando vas de vacaciones, ¿en qué medio de transporte viajas?

Bueno, cuando voy de vacaciones, a mí me encanta viajar en ómnibus porque en el camino veo los paisajes y los animales.

¿Qué haces cuando vas de vacaciones?

Cuando voy de vacaciones, voy [y] visito los lugares turísticos que me han recomendado.

¿Adónde fuiste de vacaciones la última vez?

Bueno, fui a Cajamarca.

¿Fuiste sola o fuiste con tu familia?

Fui con mi familia.

¿Qué hicieron allí?

Más que todo fuimos a visitar los lugares turísticos y a algunos familiares.

Visit Holt Online
go.hrw.com
KEYWORD: EXP1 CH10
Online Edition

Paola
Lima, Perú

Cuando vas de vacaciones, ¿en qué medio de transporte viajas?

Voy en bus mirando los paisajes.

¿Qué haces cuando vas de vacaciones?

Cuando voy de vacaciones, visito a mi familia, a mis amigos y los lugares turísticos.

¿Adónde fuiste de vacaciones la última vez?

Fui al departamento de Ica.

¿Fuiste sola o fuiste con tu familia?

Fui con mi familia.

¿Qué hicieron allí?

Visitamos a mi abuelita, primos, amigos y los lugares turísticos.

Para comprender 1B

1. ¿Cómo le gusta viajar a Lisette?
2. ¿Qué hizo Lisette en su último viaje?
3. ¿Con quién viajó Paola a Ica?
4. ¿Qué hicieron Paola y su familia en su último viaje?
5. ¿Qué hacen Lisette y Paola cuando viajan en bus?

Para pensar y hablar 1B, 4B

Both Lisette and Paola travel their country by bus. Do people in your community normally take the bus or other ground transportation when they travel somewhere? What other forms of transportation are common? What are two advantages of ground as opposed to air travel? What are two disadvantages?

Cuaderno para hispanohablantes, pp. 105–116

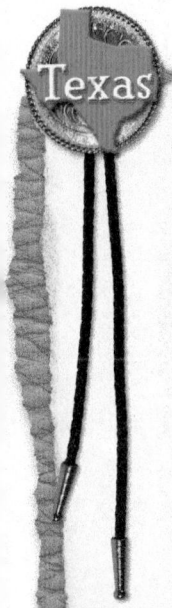

Comunidad

Spanish place names in Texas

When you look at a map of Texas, you'll see that many mountains, rivers, and towns have Spanish names. For example, in central Texas there is a river called **Pedernales** (**pedernal** means *flint*). In the western tip of the state is **El Paso,** so called because it was a place to ford the *big river*, or **Río Grande.** Other cities or towns with Spanish names include **San Antonio,** named after Saint Anthony, **Llano** or *plain,* and **Refugio** or *refuge.* Spanish names for rivers in Texas include the **Colorado** *(red),* and **Nueces** *(walnuts).* On a Texas map, find ten places or geographical features that have Spanish names. Look up these words in a dictionary to find out what they mean. 5B

Interstate highway signs in Texas

Objetivos
Talking about a trip, expressing hopes and wishes

Vocabulario en acción 2

ExpresaVisión

De vacaciones

acampar

pasear en canoa

esquiar en el agua

ir de excursión

ir de pesca

pasear en bote de vela en el lago

Lugares de interés

el museo

el centro

el zoológico

el parque de diversiones

▶ **Vocabulario adicional** — En las afueras y en la ciudad, p. R9

Visit Holt Online
go.hrw.com
KEYWORD: EXP1 CH10
Vocabulario 2 practice

Medios de transporte

el metro

el tren

el taxi

el autobús

el barco

Texas También se puede decir...

Mexicans and Texans call *the bus* **el camión**. In Puerto Rico and the Dominican Republic, they say **guagua.** You'll hear **colectivo** in Bolivia, Peru, and Ecuador.

Más vocabulario...

Expresiones

¡Ah, tuviste suerte!	*You were lucky!*
¡Qué bien!	*How great!*
¡Qué fantástico!	*How fantastic!*
¡Qué lástima!	*What a shame!*
¡Qué mala suerte!	*What bad luck!*

Actividades

quedarse en un hotel	*to stay in a hotel*
recorrer la ciudad/ el país/la isla	*to tour the city/ the country/ the island*
tomar el sol	*to sunbathe*

¡Exprésate!

To talk about a trip

Interactive TUTOR

¿Qué tal el viaje?
How was the trip?

¡Fue estupendo!/¡Fue horrible!
It was great!/It was horrible!

¿Adónde fueron?
Where did you go?

Fuimos al campo y subimos a la montaña El Misti.
We went to the countryside and went up Misti mountain.

¿Qué hicieron?
What did you do?

Conocimos las ruinas y sacamos muchas fotos.
We visited the ruins (for the first time) and took lots of pictures.

Luego pasamos por la oficina de correos y por fin regresamos al hotel.
Afterwards we stopped at the post office and finally we came back to the hotel.

Online
Vocabulario y gramática, pp. 115–117

Nota cultural

Starting in Cuzco, the train to Machu Picchu zigzags up the mountain to about 12,500 feet above sea level before starting its 7000-foot descent into the Urubamba Valley. In Peru, passengers can request oxygen because trains may climb above 15,000 feet. Though meals are served on some trains, most travelers carry food with them and purchase a drink on board. How does this compare to train travel where you live? 4B

TEKS Focus
4B Demonstrate understanding of the concept of culture through comparisons

18 ¿Qué dices? 1B

Escuchemos Escucha los comentarios y escoge la mejor respuesta.

1. **a.** ¡Qué lástima! **b.** ¡Qué bien!
2. **a.** ¡Qué mala suerte! **b.** ¡Ah, tuviste suerte!
3. **a.** ¡Qué lástima! **b.** ¡Qué divertido!
4. **a.** ¡Qué bien! **b.** ¡Qué lástima!
5. **a.** ¡Qué horrible! **b.** ¡Qué fantástico!
6. **a.** ¡Qué mala suerte! **b.** ¡Ah, tuviste suerte!

19 Analogías 1B

Leamos Completa las analogías con las palabras del cuadro.

fotos	**museo**	**montaña**	**estupendo**
campo	**autobús**	**oficina de cambio**	

1. hacer : maleta :: sacar : _____
2. esquiar : lago :: acampar : _____
3. animales : zoológico :: arte : _____
4. mal : bien :: horrible : _____
5. pasear : barco :: subir : _____
6. ir de pesca : lancha :: recorrer la ciudad : _____
7. correo : mandar cartas :: cambiar dinero: _____

20 El viaje de Carlos 1B

Leamos/Escribamos Lee la tarjeta de Carlos. Después pon en orden los elementos. Usa las expresiones **primero, luego** y **por fin.**

Querida Carla,
Aquí estoy en Perú. Es un país estupendo. Ayer me levanté temprano y desayuné en el hotel. Salí del hotel y fui al centro en autobús. Fui a una tienda para comprar una cámara y después recorrí el centro. Luego, almorcé en un restaurante. Después del almuerzo, tomé otro autobús y fui a las ruinas. Subí a la montaña y saqué muchas fotos. Regresé al hotel, cené en el restaurante de al lado y me acosté temprano. ¡Qué día tan magnífico!

Abrazos,
Carlos

MODELO **desayunar/salir/levantarse**
Primero, se levantó, luego desayunó y por fin salió.

1. ir al centro/comprar una cámara/ir a una tienda
2. recorrer el centro/almorzar/llegar al centro
3. sacar fotos/visitar las ruinas/tomar el autobús a las ruinas
4. acostarse/cenar en un restaurante/regresar al hotel

¡Exprésate!

To express hopes and wishes

Interactive TUTOR

Algún día me gustaría viajar a Perú.
One day I would like to travel to Peru.

Quiero conocer las ruinas de Machu Picchu.
I want to see the ruins at Machu Picchu.

Si tengo suerte, voy a visitar México.
If I'm lucky, I'm going to visit Mexico.

Espero ver las pirámides.
I hope to see the pyramids.

Online
Vocabulario y gramática, pp. 115–117

21 Espero... 1B

Escribamos Reacciona a estas actividades con una expresión de **¡Exprésate!**

MODELO **Me gustaría ir de excursión en las montañas. Espero ver algunos animales.**

Comunicación

22 ¿Qué te gustaría hacer para las vacaciones? 1A

Hablemos Pregúntale a tu compañero(a) qué le gustaría hacer para las vacaciones. Tu compañero(a) debe decir por lo menos tres cosas.

MODELO **—Dime tres cosas que te gustaría hacer en tus vacaciones.**
—Me gustaría ir al parque de diversiones, ir de pesca y nadar todos los días.
—¡Qué divertido!

23 El viaje de tus sueños 1A

Hablemos Entrevista a tu compañero(a). Pregúntale cuál es el viaje de sus sueños *(dream trip)*, y qué quiere hacer. Túrnense para responder.

Objetivos

Using informal commands, direct object pronouns, verbs followed by infinitives

Gramática en acción 2

GramaVisión

Informal commands of spelling-change and irregular verbs

Interactive TUTOR

1 Verbs ending in **-ger, -gir, -guir, -car, -gar,** and **-zar** have spelling changes in some command forms.

	affirmative	negative
	g changes to j	
-ger, -gir	reco**g**e	no reco**j**as
	gu changes to g	
-guir	si**gu**e	no si**g**as
	c changes to qu	
-car	bus**c**a	no bus**qu**es
	g changes to gu	
-gar	lle**g**a	no lle**gu**es
	z changes to c	
-zar	empie**z**a	no empie**c**es

Llega temprano al aeropuerto y **busca** a tus amigos. **No llegues** tarde.
Get to the airport early and look for your friends. Don't get there late.

2 Some verbs have irregular informal command forms.

	affirmative	negative
hacer	haz	no hagas
ir	ve	no vayas
poner	pon	no pongas
salir	sal	no salgas
ser	sé	no seas
tener	ten	no tengas
venir	ven	no vengas

Ve al aeropuerto en taxi.
Go to the airport by taxi.

No dejes nada en el taxi.
Don't leave anything in the taxi.

Online

Vocabulario y gramática, pp. 118–120 | Actividades, pp. 95–97

¿Te acuerdas?

Do you remember how to form affirmative informal commands?

tú piensa~~s~~ → piensa
tú come~~s~~ → come
tú escribe~~s~~ → escribe

Here's how to form negative informal commands.

yo pienso → no pienses
yo como → no comas
yo escribo → no escribas
yo vengo → no vengas

Visit Holt Online
go.hrw.com
KEYWORD: EXP1 CH10
Gramática 2 practice

24 ¿Es lógico? 1B

Escuchemos Decide si los consejos que Enrique les da a sus amigos son lógicos o ilógicos.

25 Consejos para los compañeros de viaje 1B

Escribamos Estás de vacaciones y tus compañeros no saben qué hacer. Lee sus comentarios y dales recomendaciones, usando mandatos afirmativos y negativos.

MODELO **—Salimos para Perú en tres horas y no estoy lista.**
—¡Sal inmediatamente! No llegues tarde al aeropuerto.

desembarcar del avión sin nosotros	ir de excursión
ponerse el traje de baño	ser puntual *(punctual)*
buscar un café Internet	llegar tarde al aeropuerto
hacer cola en la aduana	salir inmediatamente
ir al centro	comenzar el viaje tarde
ir al zoológico	tener miedo

1. Por fin llegamos a Lima. ¿Qué hago ahora en el aeropuerto?
2. Quiero ver las ruinas mañana, pero el autobús sale muy temprano.
3. No quiero recorrer el centro. Hace calor y quiero tomar el sol.
4. Quiero fotos de los animales, pero me dan miedo *(they scare me)*.
5. Nuestros compañeros quieren leer correo electrónico, pero no tengo ganas. Prefiero acampar.

Las ruinas de Machu Picchu, Perú

Comunicación

26 ¡Ayúdame, por favor! 1A

Hablemos Basándose en las fotos, dramaticen la siguiente situación. Tu compañero(a) va de vacaciones por primera vez y no sabe qué hacer. Escucha sus preguntas y dale los consejos más apropiados.

MODELO **—¿Cuándo hago la maleta?**
—Hazla un día antes de viajar. No lleves mucha ropa.

Repaso Direct object pronouns

Interactive TUTOR

1 Direct object pronouns can go before the conjugated verb or be attached to the end of an infinitive.

—¿Ya conoces **la ciudad**?	*Do you already know the city?*
—No, todavía no **la** conozco.	*No, I don't know it yet.*
—¿Quieres recorrer **la** conmigo?	*Do you want to tour it with me?*

2 In affirmative commands, attach the pronoun to the end of the verb. Don't forget to add an accent mark when needed. In negative commands, place the pronoun before the conjugated verb.

Llámame después de tu viaje, pero no **me** llames muy tarde.
Call me after your trip, but don't call me very late.

Online

Vocabulario y gramática, pp. 118–120 | Actividades, pp. 95–97

¿Te acuerdas?

Use these pronouns in the place of direct object nouns.

me	nos
te	os
lo	los
la	las

27 Para el viaje 1B

Escuchemos Héctor habla de lo que va a hacer mientras está de vacaciones con su familia. Escucha las oraciones y decide de qué o de quién habla: **a**) su padre, **b**) su tarjeta de embarque, **c**) sus hermanas, **d**) sus libros de texto.

28 ¡Vamos al centro! 1B

Leamos/Escribamos Completa las oraciones de la conversación entre dos amigos que están viajando juntos.

me	te	lo	la	los	las

—Mañana voy a visitar la ciudad. Voy a recorrer ___1___ en autobús. Tengo ganas de visitar los museos del centro. ¿Quieres visitar ___2___ conmigo?
—Sí, pero necesito dinero para la visita.
—Sáca ___3___ del cajero automático aquí en el hotel.
—También tengo que mandar estas tarjetas. Puedo mandar ___4___ mañana de la oficina de correos del centro, ¿no?
—Pues, ¿por qué no ___5___ mandas desde el hotel? Oye, ¿tienes hambre? Me gustaría invitar ___6___ a cenar conmigo.
—¡Con mucho gusto! ¿Quieres comer en el restaurante del hotel? No ___7___ conozco.
—Es bueno, pero me gustaría probar la cocina regional. ¿Qué tal si ___8___ probamos en el restaurante al lado del hotel?

TEKS Focus
1B Demonstrate understanding of simple, clearly spoken, and written language when dealing with familiar topics

29 ¿Conoces tu ciudad? ➤1B

Hablemos Construye oraciones y di si conoces estos lugares.

MODELO **el centro**
Lo conozco (muy) bien.

1. el zoológico
2. los museos
3. el centro comercial más cerca de tu casa
4. la piscina más cerca de tu colegio
5. el lago más cerca de tu ciudad
6. las tiendas del centro

30 Manito, llévame contigo ➤1B

Hablemos Tu hermanito te hace muchas preguntas. Contesta las preguntas usando pronombres de complemento directo.

MODELO **—¿Piensas visitar las ruinas de Machu Picchu? (sí)**
—Sí, las voy a visitar. (Sí, voy a visitarlas.)

1. ¿Vas a visitar el Parque Nacional Manu? (sí)
2. ¿Me vas a llamar todos los días? (no)
3. ¿Vas a ver a los abuelos? (sí)
4. ¿Te puedo ayudar con las maletas? (sí)
5. ¿Vas a llevar tu cámara desechable? (sí)
6. Me vas a llevar contigo, ¿verdad? (no)

Nota cultural

Peru's Manu rainforest has more than 1,000 species of birds and 300 species of trees. Many indigenous tribes also live there. Today Manu is a Biosphere Reserve composed of three parts: the Manu National Park, protecting the natural flora and fauna; the Manu Reserve Zone, for research and tourism; and the Manu Cultural Zone, for human settlement. Research animal or plant life in the forest. ➤2A

Comunicación

31 Las vacaciones de Araceli ➤1A

Hablemos Pregúntale a tu compañero(a) sobre el viaje que va a hacer Araceli. Tu compañero(a) debe responder usando pronombres de complemento directo.

MODELO **—¿Cuándo va a hacer la maleta?**
—Ya la hizo anoche.

Repaso Verbs followed by infinitives

Interactive TUTOR

1 You can use certain verbs followed by **infinitives** to express what someone *wants, hopes, or plans to do.*

me (te, le...) gustaría + **infinitive**	*. . . would like to . . .*
me (te, le...) gustaría más + **infinitive**	*. . . would prefer to . . .*
querer (ie) + **infinitive**	*to want to . . .*
esperar + **infinitive**	*to hope to . . .*
pensar (ie) + **infinitive**	*to plan (intend) to . . .*

Me gustaría ir al lago.	*I'd like to go to the lake.*
Quiero pasear en bote.	*I want to go boating.*
Espero salir con amigos.	*I hope to go out with friends.*
Pienso hacer un viaje este año.	*I plan to take a trip this year.*

2 Remember to use **tener que** to talk about what someone *has* to do.

tener que + **infinitive** *to have to . . ., must . . .*

Me gustaría ir de vacaciones, pero **tengo que trabajar**.
I'd like to go on vacation, but I have to work.

Online
Vocabulario y gramática, pp. 118–120 | Actividades, pp. 95–97

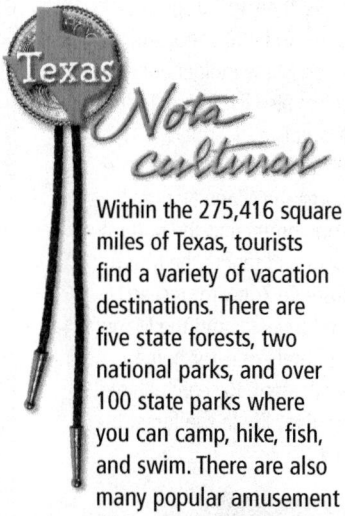

Within the 275,416 square miles of Texas, tourists find a variety of vacation destinations. There are five state forests, two national parks, and over 100 state parks where you can camp, hike, fish, and swim. There are also many popular amusement and water parks. What would you consider when planning a Texas vacation? What travel destinations in Texas have names in Spanish? 4C

TEKS Focus
4C Demonstrate understanding of the influence of one language and culture on another

32 Proyectos 1B

Escribamos/Hablemos Escribe oraciones e indica qué actividades Roberto quiere hacer y qué tiene que hacer.

MODELO **viajar a Perú/estudiar**
Quiere viajar a Perú. Tiene que estudiar.

1. acampar/trabajar
2. esquiar/limpiar el baño
3. hacer la tarea/ir al lago
4. tomar el sol/hacer la maleta
5. escribir cartas/salir con amigos

33 Lo que pensamos hacer es... 1B

Leamos/Escribamos Completa el párrafo con la forma correcta del verbo más apropiado entre paréntesis.

Mi hermana mayor y su esposo __1__ (pensar/le gustaría) ir a Alaska para las vacaciones. __2__ (Tener ganas/Esperar) de ir de pesca y acampar. A mi padre __3__ (querer/le gustaría) acompañarlos pero mi madre __4__ (le gustaría/querer) viajar a Chile. El problema es que ella __5__ (tener que/tener ganas) trabajar y no tiene tiempo para el viaje. Este año no es posible, pero algún día (yo) __6__ (tener que/esperar) hacer un viaje a España.

34 Planes ✦1B

Escribamos Rosalinda habla de sus planes. Combina palabras de cada cuadro para hacer seis oraciones.

mis padres y yo	querer	ver los animales	en el lago
yo	esperar	pasear en bote	en el zoológico
mi hermana mayor	pensar	ir de excursión	del correo
mis abuelos	tener que	quedarse	en las montañas
¿Y tú?		mandar tarjetas	en el centro
		visitar el museo	en el hotel

Comunicación

35 Un día ✦1A

Hablemos Con un(a) compañero(a), túrnense para contestar estas preguntas.

MODELO **—Un día me gustaría visitar Lima. ¿Y a ti?**
—A mí me gustaría más visitar Barcelona.

1. ¿Qué ciudad te gustaría visitar un día?
2. ¿Cómo quieres ir a esa ciudad?
3. ¿Con quién quieres hacer el viaje?
4. ¿Cuántos días quieres quedarte?
5. ¿Piensas acampar, quedarte en un hotel, o quedarte en la casa de un(a) amigo(a)?
6. ¿Qué piensas hacer en esa ciudad?

36 ¿Qué quieren hacer? ¿Qué deben hacer? ✦1A

Hablemos Con un(a) compañero(a), mira los dibujos y dramatiza la conversación entre Ana y Luis.

Novela en video

¿Quién será?

Episodio 10

ESTRATEGIA

Summarizing Before you watch the final episode of **¿Quién será?,** go back and summarize what has happened in the previous nine episodes. Pick only the most important moments that you think will help you understand the final episode. Write one or two sentences summarizing what happened in each episode. Do you see a pattern in your summary? Which characters appear the most often? Does summarizing in this way help you predict what might happen in the finale? 3B

En España

La profesora está lista para tomar la decisión. ¿Quién será?

1

Profesora Castillo Ahora sí, ya están los diez candidatos: Dos deben recibir la beca para venir a estudiar en Madrid. Voy a tener que pensarlo muy bien.

Más tarde...
Sofía y Nicolás reciben un e-mail.

2

Profesora Castillo Soy Aurelia Castillo Velasco. Soy la directora de la Fundación para Cultivar las Relaciones entre las Culturas de Habla Hispana. Mi asistente y yo identificamos a diez candidatos para las dos becas que vamos a otorgar este año.

En México

3

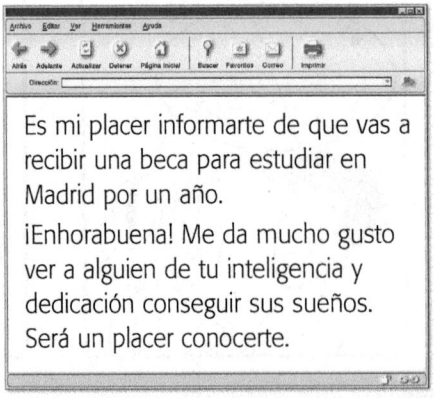

Es mi placer informarte de que vas a recibir una beca para estudiar en Madrid por un año.

¡Enhorabuena! Me da mucho gusto ver a alguien de tu inteligencia y dedicación conseguir sus sueños. Será un placer conocerte.

En Puerto Rico

4

Visit Holt Online
go.hrw.com
KEYWORD: EXP1 CH10
Online Edition

En Puerto Rico

5

Nicolás ¿Lo pueden creer? Yo, ¿estudiando dibujo en Madrid?

Sra. Ortega ¡Hijo! ¡Qué bien! ¡Estoy muy orgullosa de ti!

Nicolás Gracias, mamá. Van a venir a visitarme, ¿verdad?

Sr. Ortega Claro que sí, hijo. Me encantaría conocer Madrid.

En México

6

Sofía ¿Pueden creerlo? Yo, ¿estudiando danza en Madrid?

Sra. Corona ¡Hija! ¡Qué bien! ¡Estoy muy orgullosa de ti!

Sofía Gracias, mamá. Van a venir a visitarme, ¿verdad?

Sr. Corona Claro que sí, hija. Me encantaría conocer Madrid.

En España

7

Profesora Castillo Marcos, ¡buen trabajo! Debes tomar unas vacaciones, viajar a una isla, tomar el sol, descansar… ¡Diviértete! Yo te llamo cuando estemos listos para empezar la investigación para el año próximo.

En Perú

8

9

Después de investigar al candidato peruano, Marcos recibe el mensaje de la profesora. ¿Quiere trabajar en la investigación del año próximo?

¿COMPRENDES?

1. ¿Quién es la profesora?
2. ¿Qué va a recibir Sofía? ¿y Nicolás?
3. ¿Cómo reacciona Sofía a las noticias? ¿y Nicolás?
4. ¿Qué dicen los padres de Sofía y Nicolás sobre Madrid?
5. Según la profesora, ¿qué debe hacer Marcos?
6. Piensa en los 10 episodios. En algún momento, ¿pensaste que Sofía y Nicolás eran *(were)* los candidatos favoritos? ¿Por qué sí o por qué no?

1B, 3A

Episodio final:
Now that you know what the ten candidates were for, and which two of them won, can you understand the title of the video? Did the title ever help you predict what was going to happen?

Leamos y escribamos

TEKS Focus
3A Use resources in the language and cultures being studied to gain access to information

ESTRATEGIA

para leer When you read a brochure, it is important to read with a purpose. In other words, you need to decide beforehand what kind of information you want. If you want an overview, a quick, general reading may be all that is necessary. If you need specific information, however, a close reading will be required.

A Antes de leer 3A

Lee el título y los subtítulos del siguiente folleto. ¿Qué clase de información contiene? ¿Qué datos específicos esperas encontrar debajo de cada subtítulo?

¡Bienvenidos a la ciudad de Lima!
Aeropuerto Internacional Chávez

Transporte El servicio de transporte del aeropuerto a la ciudad y viceversa, se realiza por medio del[1] transporte público. Las compañías de taxis estacionan[2] sus vehículos en un área limitada, frente a la salida de las terminales nacional e internacional. La mayoría de hoteles cuentan con su propio[3] servicio de transporte.

Bancos

La moneda nacional de Perú es el nuevo sol. En los pasillos encontrará cajeros automáticos, los cuales aceptan tarjetas de crédito en moneda nacional y extranjera[4]. Las casas de cambio se encuentran en el pasillo principal[5] y en la zona de vuelos internacionales.

Información turística

En diversos lugares del aeropuerto encontrará módulos[6] con información sobre el arrendamiento[7] de coches, restaurantes, sitios turísticos de interés y una guía telefónica a los hoteles principales.

Otros servicios

En los pasillos encontrará teléfonos públicos que funcionan con monedas y tarjetas, las cuales se pueden conseguir en los diferentes quioscos[8] situados por todo el aeropuerto. Si necesita guardar[9] su equipaje por horas o por días, puede hacer uso del servicio de guardianía de equipajes, localizado en el pasillo principal.

1 by means of **2** park **3** have their own **4** foreign **5** main corridor **6** modules **7** rental **8** kiosk, stand **9** store

Visit Holt Online
go.hrw.com
KEYWORD: EXP1 CH10
Online Edition

B Comprensión ➤1B

Basándote en la lectura, decide si las oraciones son **ciertas** o **falsas.** Corrige las oraciones falsas.

1. Los cajeros automáticos no aceptan tarjetas de crédito.
2. Todas las casas de cambio están en la zona internacional.
3. Los taxis se encuentran en frente de las terminales nacionales e internacionales.
4. Hay información sobre los hoteles, las atracciones turísticas y el transporte público en los módulos de información.
5. Puedes dejar tu equipaje por un fin de semana en la guardianía de equipajes.

C Después de leer ➤2B, 4B

Which services in the brochure might travelers arriving in Peru use? Do you think these same services are available in airports in the United States and other countries?

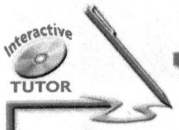

Taller del escritor

ESTRATEGIA

para escribir When narrating a series of events, using transitional phrases makes it easier to combine sentences and lends coherence to the text. Some phrases are **primero, luego,** and **por fin.**

Cartas del extranjero ➤1C

You are writing home to friends to tell them about your first few days traveling abroad. Tell where you went and include five or six events that made your trip interesting, narrating them in order. End by mentioning your plans for the next day.

1 Antes de escribir

Make a list of the events you will report. Then brainstorm some phrases that will link them together logically **(primero, luego, después).**

2 Escribir un borrador

Begin with a greeting, then tell about your trip, focusing mainly on actions and events. Work in the linking phrases, being careful not to lose any clarity.

3 Revisar

Exchange letters with a classmate. Read each other's letters checking for appropriate use of transitions and correct use of grammar, spelling, and punctuation.

4 Publicar

Write your letter on a large piece of paper or posterboard. On the other side illustrate one of the places you visited. Put your postcard up on the bulletin board. Which trip sounds most interesting to you?

Cuaderno para hispanohablantes, pp. 105–116

Repaso capítulo 10

Interactive TUTOR

1 Vocabulario 1
- asking for and giving information
- reminding and reassuring

pp. 348-351

2 Gramática 1
- review of the preterite
- preterite of **-car, -gar, -zar** verbs
- preterite of **hacer**

pp. 352-357

3 Vocabulario 2
- talking about a trip
- expressing hopes and wishes

pp. 360-363

1 Según las cosas o lugares dados *(given)*, di lo que tienes que hacer. 1B

1.

2.

3.

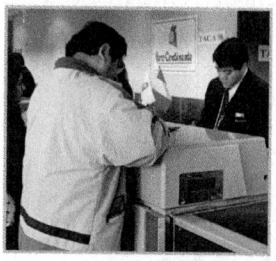

4.

5.

6.

2 Luis le escribe una carta a su prima Ana sobre su viaje. Complétala con los verbos correctos en el pretérito. 1B

Querida Ana,

Por fin estoy en Lima. ¡El viaje fue horrible! __1__ (Pasar/Ir) en taxi hasta el aeropuerto y __2__ (salir/llegar) allí temprano, a las seis de la tarde. __3__ (Hacer/Ir) cola en el mostrador. __4__ (Ver/Comprar) el boleto y la agente __5__ (facturar/hacer) la maleta. También __6__ (sacar/salir) la tarjeta de embarque. __7__ (Ir/Pasear) a la sala de espera. Entonces __8__ (comenzar/comprar) a nevar. ¡Por eso no __9__ (abordar/salir) el avión hasta las once. ¡Qué viaje más largo!

Escribe pronto.

Tu primo, Luis

3 Escoge la respuesta que mejor completa cada oración. 1B

1. Quiero ir de compras. Vamos al (correo/centro).
2. Fuimos a las ruinas, pero llovió. ¡Fue (estupendo/horrible)!
3. Quiero ir al lago. ¿Qué tal si (paseamos en lancha/vamos al centro)?
4. Perdí el autobús. ¡Qué (bien/mala suerte)!
5. Ana piensa ir a las islas Bermudas. Va en (barco/taxi).

Visit Holt Online
go.hrw.com
KEYWORD: EXP1 CH10
Chapter Self-test

4 Completa la siguiente conversación con un mandato informal, un pronombre de complemento directo o un infinitivo. **1B**

—¿Conoces al profesor Augustino?

—No, no __1__ conozco. ¿Cómo es?

—Es interesante, pero tenemos que __2__ (estudiar) mucho. Hoy tengo que __3__ (leer) tres capítulos.

—Bueno, __4__ (empezar) a __5__ (leer) los capítulos.

—No tengo ganas de leer __6__ ahora. Tengo sueño.

—Pues, __7__ (descansar) y __8__ (leer) más tarde.

5 Contesta las siguientes preguntas. **2A, 2B**

1. What material is used to build houses on the Uros Islands?
2. Name one unusual feature on trains in Peru.
3. How is the Manu rainforest in Peru preserved?

6 Escucha las siguientes oraciones. Decide si cada persona **a)** da un mandato, **b)** describe algo en el pasado o, **c)** busca información. **1B**

7 Crea *(Create)* una conversación entre Ana y Luis sobre lo que hicieron durante las vacaciones. **1A, 1C**

4 Gramática 2
- informal commands of spelling-change and irregular verbs
- review of direct object pronouns
- review of verbs followed by infinitives

pp. 364–369

5 Cultura
- **Comparaciones** **pp. 358–359**
- **Notas culturales** **pp. 350, 356, 362, 367**
- **Geocultura** **pp. 342–345**

Gramática 1
- review of the preterite **pp. 352–353**
- preterite of **-car, -gar, -zar** verbs **pp. 354–355**
- preterite of **hacer** **pp. 356–357**

Repaso de Gramática 1

For a review of the regular preterite forms of **-ar, -er,** and **-ir** verbs, see page 352.

Verbs ending in **-car, -gar, -zar** have spelling changes before the preterite ending **-é** of the **yo** form: **saqué, llegué, comencé.**

hacer			
yo	**hice**	nosotros(as)	**hicimos**
tú	**hiciste**	vosotros(as)	**hicisteis**
Ud., él, ella	**hizo**	Uds., ellos, ellas	**hicieron**

Gramática 2
- informal commands of spelling-change and irregular verbs **pp. 364–365**
- review of direct object pronouns **pp. 366–367**
- review of verbs followed by infinitives **pp. 368–369**

Repaso de Gramática 2

For a review of informal commands of irregular verbs, see page 364. Verbs ending in **-ger, -gir, -guir, -car, -gar,** and **-zar** have spelling changes in some informal command forms.

	affirmative	negative
-ger, -gir	reco**ge**	no reco**j**as
-guir	si**gue**	no si**g**as
-car	bus**ca**	no bus**qu**es
-gar	lle**ga**	no lle**gu**es
-zar	empie**za**	no empie**c**es

For a review of **direct object pronoun** placement with conjugated verbs, infinitives, and informal commands, see page 366.

Use these verbs followed by **infinitives** to say what someone *wants, hopes, plans,* or *has* to do.

me (te, le...) gustaría + infinitive
me (te, le...) gustaría más + infinitive
querer (ie) + infinitive
pensar (ie) + infinitive
esperar + infinitive
tener que + infinitive

TEKS Focus
1B Demonstrate understanding of simple, clearly spoken, and written language when dealing with familiar topics

Letra y sonido c p q t

Las consonantes c, p, q, t

- The letters **c, p, q, t** are not pronounced with a puff of air as in English *cat, pen, ten, quit:* **p**apa, **p**atinar, **p**arque, **c**arpeta, **q**ueso, **C**uzco
- The letter **t** is pronounced with the tip of the tongue right behind the teeth: **t**ía, **t**oalla, **t**riste, **t**raje, **t**engo, **t**arde

Trabalenguas

Pablito clavó un clavito. ¿Qué clavito clavó Pablito?

Dictado 1B

Escribe las oraciones de la grabación.

Repaso de Vocabulario 1

Asking for information

abordar	*to board*
la aduana	*customs*
el aeropuerto	*airport*
el (la) agente	*agent*
allí	*there*
el avión	*airplane*
la billetera	*wallet*
el boleto de avión	*plane ticket*
la bolsa	*travel bag, purse*
cambiar dinero	*to change money*
el carnet de identidad	*ID*
comenzar (ie) un viaje	*to begin a trip*
conseguir (i)	*to get*
el control de seguridad	*security checkpoint*
desembarcar	*to disembark, to deplane*
¿Dónde se puede...?	*Where can I . . . ?*
encontrarse (ue) con	*to meet up with*
esperar	*to wait*
Está a la vuelta.	*It's around the corner.*
facturar el equipaje	*to check luggage*
hacer cola	*to wait in line*
hacer un viaje	*to take a trip*
irse	*to leave*
la llegada	*arrival*
Lo siento, no sé.	*I'm sorry, (but) I don't know.*
la maleta	*suitcase*
el mapa	*map*
¿Me puede decir...?	*Can you tell me . . .?*
el mostrador	*counter*
la oficina de cambio	*money exchange*
la pantalla	*monitor, screen*
el (la) pasajero(a)	*passenger*
el pasaporte	*passport*
perder (ie)	*to miss, to lose*
la puerta	*gate*
el reclamo de equipaje	*baggage claim*
recoger	*to pick up*
la sala de espera	*waiting room*
la salida	*departure*
sentarse (ie)	*to sit down*
los servicios	*restrooms*
la tarjeta de embarque	*boarding pass*
el vuelo	*flight*

Reminding and reassuring . . . . . *See p. 351*

Repaso de Vocabulario 2

Talking about a trip

acampar	*to camp*
¡Ah, tuviste suerte!	*You were lucky!*
el autobús	*bus*
el barco	*boat*
la canoa	*canoe*
el centro	*downtown*
durante	*during*
esquiar en el agua	*to water-ski*
¡Fue estupendo!	*It was great!*
ir de excursión	*to go hiking*
ir de pesca	*to go fishing*
la isla	*island*
el lago	*lake*
la lancha	*motorboat*
los lugares de interés	*places of interest*
los medios de transporte	*types of transportation*
el metro	*subway*
el museo	*museum*
la oficina de correos	*post office*
el país	*country*
el parque de diversiones	*amusement park*
pasar por	*to stop at/by*
pasear en bote de vela	*to go out in a sailboat*
¡Qué bien!	*How great!*
¡Qué fantástico!	*How fantastic!*
¡Qué lástima!	*What a shame!*
¡Qué mala suerte!	*What bad luck!*
quedarse en...	*to stay in . . .*
recorrer	*to tour*
las ruinas	*ruins*
sacar fotos	*to take pictures*
subir a la montaña	*to go up a mountain*
el taxi	*taxi*
tomar el sol	*to sunbathe*
el tren	*train*
viajar	*to travel*
el viaje	*trip*
el zoológico	*zoo*

Expressing hopes and wishes . . . . . *See p. 363*

Integración

capítulos 1-10

1 Escucha las oraciones y escoge las fotos correspondientes. 1B

2 Hay cinco personas que buscan información sobre vuelos. Con base en la información de la pantalla, contesta las preguntas. 1B

LLEGADAS INTERNACIONALES

HORAS	AEROLÍNEA	VUELO	ORIGEN	DESTINO	PUERTA
9:00	IBERIA	350	DALLAS	CUZCO	7
18:00	MEXICANA	119	SAN ANTONIO	LIMA	9
15:00	DELTA	230	NUEVA YORK	LIMA	11

SALIDAS INTERNACIONALES

HORAS	AEROLÍNEA	VUELO	ORIGEN	DESTINO	PUERTA
12:00	IBERIA	112	LIMA	NUEVA YORK	2
13:00	MEXICANA	256	LIMA	CIUDAD DE MÉXICO	5
8:00	DELTA	987	CUZCO	MIAMI	10

1. Nora quiere saber el número del vuelo de su amiga que llega a las 3:00 de la tarde de Nueva York.
2. Riqui tiene que recoger a su mamá que llega de Dallas. ¿A qué puerta va?
3. Susana viaja a Cuzco. ¿En qué aerolínea y vuelo viaja?
4. Tomás quiere saber a qué hora sale el vuelo para Nueva York.
5. Rosa pregunta cuántos vuelos hay entre Lima y Estados Unidos.

Visit Holt Online
go.hrw.com
KEYWORD: EXP1 CH10
Cumulative Self-test

3 Unos amigos regresaron de un viaje a Perú. Escribe un diálogo entre tú y ellos, en que les haces preguntas sobre el viaje y ellos te explican qué hicieron. Usa el pretérito de cinco verbos diferentes. Después, preséntenle su diálogo a la clase. **1A**

4 Estás de viaje en Cuzco y sacaste esta foto. Escribe un párrafo y describe qué está pasando, qué hacen las personas y qué piensan hacer esta noche. **1B, 1C**

28h x 36w, oil; Columbine Galleries, Loveland CO

La vendedora de anticuchos, **de Juan de la Cruz Machicado**

5 Un(a) amigo(a) que nunca ha viajado *(has never traveled)* quiere acompañarte a Perú. Usando mandatos afirmativos y negativos, escríbele una lista de las cosas que (no) debe hacer. Incluye información sobre la ropa, los preparativos antes del viaje, instrucciones para el aeropuerto y las cosas que (no) puede hacer en Perú. **1C**

6 **Situación**

Set up two tourist agencies in your classroom, with two travel agents in each one. Make signs and posters for different places to visit. Role-play tourists who want to travel to different destinations. Ask and answer questions about prices, necessary travel documents, transportation arrangements, schedules, baggage restrictions, etc. **1A**

Literatura y variedades

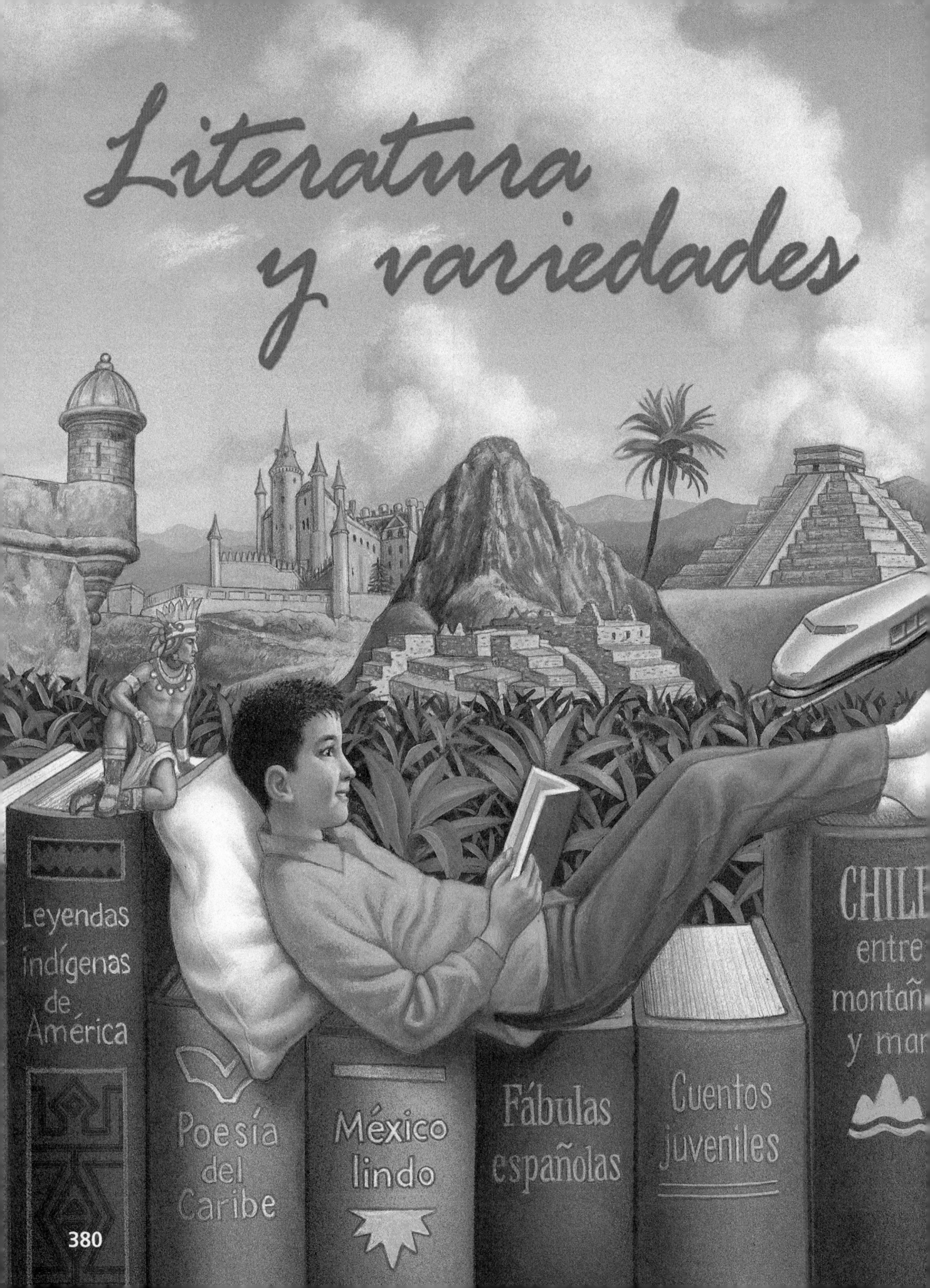

Visit Holt Online
go.hrw.com
Online Edition

Capítulo 1 • España **382–383**
El Museo del Prado (folleto)

Capítulo 2 • Puerto Rico **384–385**
El coquí (artículo)

Capítulo 3 • Texas **386–387**
Obras de Carmen Lomas Garza (comentarios)

Capítulo 4 • Costa Rica **388–389**
La artesanía chorotega (entrevista)

Capítulo 5 • Chile **390–391**
Las novelas de Isabel Allende (comentario y fragmento)

Capítulo 6 • México **392–393**
La comida de dos continentes (artículo)

Capítulo 7 • Argentina **394–395**
Juegos de palabras (adivinanzas)

Capítulo 8 • Florida **396–397**
El amor a la poesía (poemas)

Capítulo 9 • La República Dominicana **398–399**
El regalo de cumpleaños (cuento)

Capítulo 10 • Perú **400–401**
Ollantaytambo (leyenda)

España

El Museo del Prado

The Prado Museum, in downtown Madrid, Spain, is one of the largest and best-known art museums in the world. It houses over 9,000 works of art. The collection is so vast that only a tenth of it can be displayed at any one time. Although most of its paintings and sculptures are by European artists, it holds works by artists from around the world and reveals centuries of history through art. Read the following information in the visitor brochure and the descriptions of the paintings by three famous Spanish artists to learn more about the Prado and its collection.

ESTRATEGIA

Look for cognates (words with similar meanings and spellings in English and Spanish) to help you understand some of the words you do not know.

Información General:
Dirección:
Ruiz de Alarcón, 23, 28014 Madrid
Teléfono:
34 913 30 28 00
Correo electrónico:
museo.nacional@prado.mcu.es
Internet:
http://museoprado.mcu.es

Horas:
martes a domingo:
9.00-19.00 h
24 y 31 de diciembre:
9.00-14.00 h
Cerrado[1]:
los lunes; 1 de enero; Viernes Santo, 1 de mayo y 25 de diciembre

Precio de Entrada:[2]
Público general:
3,01 Euros
Menores[3] de 18 años:
gratuito[4]

1 closed **2** admission **3** younger **4** free

Cesto Con Flores[1]

Juan de Arellano, famoso pintor español, se especializó en la pintura[2] de flores. Esta obra es una de muchas obras que pintó con ese tema[3]. Como puedes ver, es una composición magnífica. Las flores están iluminadas en el centro para acentuar[4] los colores y la belleza[5].

1 Basket with Flowers **2** painting **3** theme **4** to highlight **5** beauty

La Familia de Carlos IV

Esta obra es de Francisco de Goya y Lucientes, uno de los artistas más famosos y el artista oficial de la Corte[1] de España. Es de la Familia Real y se llama *La Familia del Rey Carlos IV*. Los colores en esta pintura son extraordinarios. Hay muchas obras de Goya en el Prado.

1 court

El Caballero[1]

Esta pintura es de El Greco, uno de los más famosos pintores[2] españoles. En realidad, el verdadero nombre de El Greco es Doménikos Theotokópoulos. La mayoría de los temas de sus pinturas son religiosos y los colores en estas pinturas son vívidos y vibrantes. También son importantes sus retratos[3], como éste de un caballero.

1 knight **2** painters **3** portraits

Después de leer

3A, 3B

1. What time does the Prado generally close?
2. How much is admission to the museum?
3. What is the subject of many of Arellano's paintings?
4. Who are the people in Goya's painting?
5. What is El Greco's real name?
6. What are his paintings like?

Puerto Rico

El coquí

Puerto Rico's Yunque rainforest covers 28,000 acres and is one of the oldest reserves in the Western Hemisphere. It is the only rainforest in the U.S. National Forest System. The rainforest averages 240 inches of rain a year. The Yunque is home to 13 species of a tiny frog called the **coquí**. These frogs are considered a national symbol for the island. Read the following article to learn more about this unique amphibian.

ESTRATEGIA

Background knowledge is the information you already know about a subject. Before you read, take a minute to recall what you know about the topic.

Estruendo[1] musical

La voz[2] más famosa de Puerto Rico es la de una pequeña especie de rana que se llama coquí. Hay dieciséis especies de coquíes en Puerto Rico y trece de ellas viven en el Parque Nacional del Yunque. Se llama coquí porque por la noche miles de estas ranas salen y emiten un coro de cantos[3], "co-quí". El estruendo es muy fuerte porque una sola rana puede emitir hasta 100 decibeles, igual que una guitarra eléctrica. ¡Imagina un concierto de miles de guitarras eléctricas en tu vecindario[4] cada noche! El canto del coquí se oye por toda la isla de Puerto Rico.

1 racket 2 voice 3 calls, songs 4 neighborhood

No soy renacuajo[1]

El coquí es una especie de rana muy interesante porque nunca pasa por una etapa[2] de renacuajo. La madre, o hembra[3], pone aproximadamente 28 huevos[4]. El padre, o macho[5], cuida de[6] los huevos. Después salen los coquíes bebés, ¡ya en forma de rana!

De muchos colores

Algunas personas, aun los puertorriqueños, piensan que el coquí es solamente[7] verde. La verdad[8] es que hay coquíes de muchos colores: marrones, grises, amarillos, azules, verdes o anaranjados, como el coquí dorado en esta foto. El coquí es muy importante en Puerto Rico porque come gran cantidad de insectos como mosquitos. Es un símbolo nacional y su música resuena[9] por toda la isla.

1 tadpole **2** stage **3** female **4** eggs **5** male
6 takes care of **7** only **8** the truth **9** resonates

Después de leer ✦3A, 3B

1. What is **El Yunque**?
2. How did the **coquí** get its name?
3. Given the tiny size of the **coquí,** what is surprising about its call?
4. In what way are **coquíes** different from other frogs?
5. What color is the **coquí**?
6. Why is the **coquí** important in Puerto Rico?

Obras de Carmen Lomas Garza

Carmen Lomas Garza is one of the best-known Mexican American painters. In 1990 she published her first children's book, ***Cuadros de familia***, in which she combines her paintings with her own warm writing style. She uses the book to explain her work and describe her childhood in Kingsville, Texas, near the border with Mexico. In her second book, ***En mi familia***, 1996, Lomas Garza once again shares her memories of growing up in a traditional Mexican American community and family.

Read the following excerpts from these two books to experience a slice of life on the Texas border.

ESTRATEGIA

Actively picture in your mind what you are reading—the setting, the way the characters look and are dressed, their actions and speech. Visualization helps you create a context for what you are reading.

La tamalada de *Cuadros de familia*

Ésta es una escena de la cocina de mis padres. Todos están haciendo tamales. Mi abuelo tiene puesto rancheros[1] azules y camisa azul. Yo estoy al lado de él, con mi hermana Margie. Estamos ayudando a remojar[2] las hojas secas[3] del maíz[4]. Mi mamá está esparciendo la masa[5] de maíz sobre las hojas, y mis tíos están esparciendo la carne[6] sobre la masa. Mi abuelita está ordenando los tamales que ya están enrollados, cubiertos y listos[7] para cocer[8]. En algunas familias sólo las mujeres preparan tamales, pero en mi familia todos ayudan.

▲ ***Tamalada*** (1990)

1 overalls 2 soak 3 dry leaves 4 corn 5 spreading the dough 6 meat 7 rolled, covered, and ready 8 to cook

▲ ***El Baile en el Jardín*** (1995)

Baile en el Jardín de *En mi familia*

Ésta es una noche de sábado en El Jardín, un restaurante familiar de mi pueblo natal[1]. Es verano y hace tanto calor que la gente baila afuera[2]. Un conjunto[3] toca con tambora[4], acordeón, guitarra y bajo[5]. Ésta es la música con la que crecí[6]. Todos bailan formando un gran círculo: las parejas[7] jóvenes, las parejas más grandes[8], y los viejitos bailan con adolescentes o criaturas[9]. Hasta los bebés se ponen a bailar.

Para mí, el baile representa fiesta, celebración. Aquí está la música, los hermosos vestidos, y todos los miembros de la familia bailan juntos. Es como el cielo. Es la gloria.

---

1 hometown
2 outside
3 band
4 drum
5 bass
6 I grew up with
7 couples
8 older
9 little ones

Después de leer ✦1B, 2A

1. Name the four steps to making tamales that the author mentions.
2. In Lomas Garza's family, who makes the tamales?
3. In ***El Baile en el Jardín***, what is the weather like?
4. What instruments are in the band?
5. Who is dancing in El Jardín?
6. Why does Lomas Garza like the dance?

Costa Rica

La artesanía chorotega

The small village of Guaitil is one of the centers of Costa Rican folk art. Nearly the entire town is dedicated to making pottery using the methods, tools, and designs that their ancestors, the Chorotegas, used hundreds of years ago. The craftsmen of Guaitil use natural paints and basic colors like red, black, white, and brown to decorate their pottery with traditional symbols of nature and daily life. Learn more about Chorotega artistry in the following interview with Gustavo, who is one of the youngest and most famous potters in the village.

ESTRATEGIA

Many words can be understood based on how they are used in the sentence or paragraph. When you come to an unknown word, try to guess its meaning based on context (the other words around it).

Gustavo

¿Desde cuándo ayudas a tus padres en el taller[1] de cerámica?

Siempre me ha gustado ayudar a mi madre, Luz Marina; pero cuando era[2] pequeño lo que más me gustaba era modelar, hacer figuritas.

¿Y ahora?

Ahora pintar y decorar las piezas.

¿De dónde sacas estas ideas?

Bueno, los dibujos[3] que yo hago son aquellos que están en los libros antiguos[4] pero hay veces que invento otros dibujos para cambiar[5] y esos los saco de la mente[6], sólo de la mente.

¿Se te ocurren cuando estás pintándolas, o las pintas antes en un papel?

No, las pinto directamente sobre la tinaja[7].

1 workshop 2 I was 3 drawings 4 old 5 to change 6 mind 7 ceramic jar

¿Hay algún sitio donde enseñan esta artesanía[1]?
Sí, la cooperativa de artesanos[2] del pueblo tiene una escuela y ahí se enseñan los diseños[3] que hacían nuestros antepasados[4] chorotegas.

¿Tienes en casa libros de dibujos precolombinos?
No, yo los diseños los tengo grabados[5] en la mente.

¿Cuánto tardas en pintar una tinaja grande?
Normalmente media hora, o tal vez un poco más.

¿Cuántas horas dedicas a esto?
Bueno, a veces mis padres tienen mucho trabajo y todos tenemos que colaborar[6]. Entonces puedo hacer hasta 20 vasijas medianas en un día. Pero cuando hay menos trabajo, pinto en mis ratos libres.

¿Te quieres dedicar exclusivamente a esto?
Ahora estoy empezando y me gusta mucho. Es posible que siga[7] con el taller de mis padres.

---

1 folk art
2 craftmen's cooperative
3 designs
4 ancestors
5 etched
6 to help out
7 that I may continue

Después de leer

1B, 2B

1. What did Gustavo like to do when he was a small child?
2. What does he do now?
3. Does Gustavo draw his designs on paper first?
4. Where does Gustavo get his ideas for his designs?
5. How long does it take him to paint a piece of pottery?

Las novelas de Isabel Allende

Isabel Allende is from Peru, but she was raised in Chile. She is one of the most famous modern Latin American writers. Her novels and stories are read throughout the world. Her family is the theme of many of her stories and often her relatives are the inspiration for the characters in her novels. Today, Isabel Allende lives with her husband and family in California. Read the following commentary and the excerpt from one of her novels to learn more about her work and life in Chile.

ESTRATEGIA

Look at the title, the photos, and the important words in the text. Then read the first sentence of each paragraph. Skimming helps you understand the main ideas.

En 1981, Isabel Allende empezó[1] a escribir una carta a su abuelo en Chile. Un año más tarde esta carta de 500 páginas se convirtió[2] en su primera novela, *La casa de los espíritus (The House of the Spirits,* 1982).

Su novela *Paula* (1994) es la historia de su vida. Es dedicada a su hija, Paula, quien murió[3] a la edad[4] de 24 años, después de estar en el hospital por un año.

Vas a leer un fragmento de su libro *Mi país inventado*, en el que escribe sobre su familia y la historia de Chile. A través de[5] sus propios parientes[6] ilustra el carácter de los chilenos.

1 began **2** became **3** died **4** age
5 by means of **6** her own relatives

Por encima de[1] los clanes está la familia, inviolable y sagrada,[2] nadie escapa a sus deberes[3] con ella. Por ejemplo, el tío Ramón suele llamarme por teléfono a California, donde vivo, para comunicarme que murió un tío en tercer grado,[4] a quien no conocí,[5] y dejó[6] una hija en mala situación. La joven quiere estudiar enfermería,[7] pero no tiene medios[8] para hacerlo. Al tío Ramón, como el miembro de más edad del clan, le corresponde ponerse en contacto con cualquiera que tenga lazos de sangre con el difunto,[9] desde los parientes cercanos hasta los más remotos, para financiar los estudios de la futura enfermera. Negarse sería un acto vil,[10] que sería recordado[11] por varias generaciones.

1 at the top of 2 sacred 3 obligations 4 distant 5 hadn't met 6 left 7 nursing 8 means 9 whomever is related to the deceased 10 would be despicable 11 would be remembered

Después de leer

1B, 2A

1. What is the theme of Isabel Allende's novels?
2. How did her first novel begin?
3. Who is Paula?
4. To whom do Chileans have obligations?
5. What does the daughter of Allende's uncle want to study?
6. Who helps her?

México

La comida de dos continentes

Much of the food that is consumed around the world today is made from ingredients that came originally from the Americas. Tomatoes, chocolate, corn, chile peppers, vanilla, pears, and potatoes are some of the foods that the Spanish conquistadors presented to the kings of Europe. Read the following article in order to learn more about the history of four of these foods.

ESTRATEGIA

When reading a text, look first for the main idea of each paragraph. After that, read carefully all the details that support the main idea. This will help you better understand the text.

El tomate

El tomate es originalmente de México. Cuentan[1] que cuando los exploradores llevan el tomate a Europa en el siglo XVI, ¡nadie lo quiere comer! Por su color rojo tan fuerte, todos piensan que es una fruta venenosa. Los exploradores aseguran que lo pueden comer sin problema y la gente poco a poco empieza a probarlo[2].

En la actualidad[3], el tomate es un ingrediente básico en la preparación de platos[4] alrededor del mundo.

El chocolate: ¿para beber o comerciar?

El chocolate es original de América Central. En México, los aztecas lo usaban *(used)* con varios propósitos[5]. Antes del trabajo, los hombres lo tomaban *(would drink it)* por la mañana, hervido[6] con miel, agua y vainilla, y otra vez, por la tarde, después de la comida. Para el Gran Moctezuma, líder de los aztecas, el chocolate era *(was)* su bebida diaria y además, un elemento importante en los ritos, en las ceremonias y para comerciar[7].

1 They say 2 to taste it 3 today 4 dishes 5 purposes 6 boiled 7 to trade

El maíz: sustancia del hombre

Se dice que el maíz empieza a cultivarse[1] en América desde hace 10,000 años. Todos los miembros de la cultura maya comen maíz, desde el esclavo[2] hasta el rey. El *Popol Vuh*, libro religioso de los mayas, cuenta que el hombre mismo[3] se hace de[4] maíz. Cuando los exploradores españoles vienen a México prueban el maíz por primera vez en forma de tortillas y tamales.

Hoy en día, el maíz constituye un 20% de las calorías consumidas mundialmente[5]. En Estados Unidos se produce el 45% del maíz del mundo (mucho de éste destinado al ganado[6]) y en el continente de África el maíz es el grano que más se cultiva.

Los chiles: el picante del mundo[7]

Los chiles, sin duda, son el ingrediente más representativo de la comida mexicana en el mundo. En México hay más de cien variedades de chiles con nombres y sabores[8] diferentes. Algunos de los chiles más típicos son el serrano, el chipotle, el guajillo y el habanero, nativo de Yucatán y ¡muy picante!

Los grupos indígenas usan el chile para añadir sabor a los frijoles, las salsas, los arroces[9] y los moles.[10] Aunque el uso del chile no es tan popular entre los europeos, la llegada de éste a Asia cambia la cocina de la región para siempre. Hoy día se consumen más chiles en Tailandia que en cualquier otro país del mundo.

---

1 to grow **2** slave **3** man himself **4** is made of **5** worldwide **6** livestock
7 world's hot spice **8** tastes **9** rice dishes **10** sauces

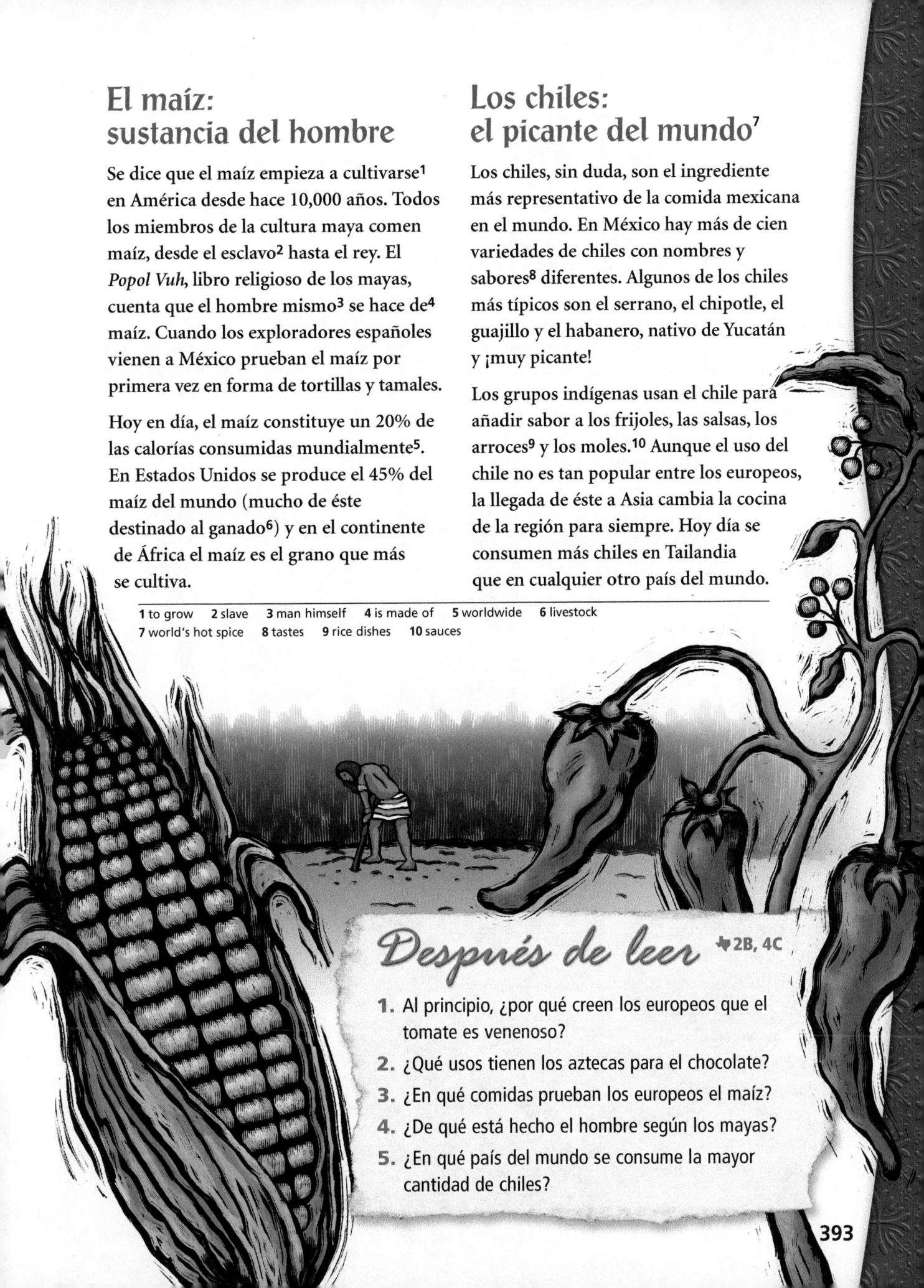

Después de leer

2B, 4C

1. Al principio, ¿por qué creen los europeos que el tomate es venenoso?
2. ¿Qué usos tienen los aztecas para el chocolate?
3. ¿En qué comidas prueban los europeos el maíz?
4. ¿De qué está hecho el hombre según los mayas?
5. ¿En qué país del mundo se consume la mayor cantidad de chiles?

Argentina

Juegos de palabras

In Argentina, as in many places, word games are one of the favorite types of entertainment among children and adults. Here, two Argentinian authors present four easy riddles about common, everyday things. The first one and the last one are from the book ***Adivinanzas*** *(Riddles)* by Carlos Silveyra, teacher and author. The other two are riddles from the book ***Los rimaqué*** by Ruth Kaufman, who is also a teacher. See if you can guess the riddles.

ESTRATEGIA

Read the riddles aloud and think about the images that occur to you. Creating visual images in your mind will help you understand the text.

1 Dos buenas piernas tenemos
y no podemos andar,
pero el hombre sin nosotros
no se puede presentar.

2 Poquitos rincones[1]
encuentro en los mapas
que no haya tocado[2]
mi cuerpo de plata[3].
Bajo con las lluvias
acaricio el suelo[4]
y en pocas semanas
¡de nuevo en el cielo[5]!
A un solo lugar
jamás he llegado[6]
por más que mil veces
lo haya intentado[7].
Le ruego[8] a las nubes
le suplico[9] al viento
¿por qué nadie quiere
llevarme al desierto?

1 corners
2 has not touched
3 silver
4 I touch the ground
5 sky
6 have never arrived
7 have tried
8 I beg
9 I implore

3 Se ponen las nubes
redondas y negras
de la tierra[1] sube
olor a tormenta[2].
Un fuerte estallido[3]
y volamos los dos:
hermanos mellizos[4]
relámpago[5] y yo.
Si juntos salimos
a andar por el mundo
¿por qué llego yo
siempre segundo?

1 earth **2** storm **3** crackling
4 twins **5** lightning

4 Siempre quietas[6],
siempre inquietas[7],
dormidas de día,
de noche despiertas[8].

6 still **7** restless **8** awake

Después de leer

1B, 1C, 3B

1. En la primera adivinanza, ¿qué necesita el hombre?
2. ¿Adónde vuelven las lluvias que bajan a la tierra según la segunda adivinanza?
3. La segunda adivinanza habla de poca agua en un lugar. ¿Cuál es?
4. En la tercera, ¿cuál es el compañero del relámpago?
5. En la cuarta, ¿qué dice sobre el día y la noche?

Florida

El amor a la poesía

Maricel Mayor Marsán was born in Cuba but has spent most of her life living in exile in the United States. She studied history and political science at the International University of Florida and discovered that she wanted to dedicate herself to writing. Even though she writes short stories and theatrical works, her true passion is poetry. She has published five books of poetry, including ***Un corazón dividido*** (1998), where she speaks of being bilingual and the difficulties of belonging to two cultures. Marsán lives in Miami.

ESTRATEGIA

In order to understand the main idea of a text, it is important to examine in detail each part. In poetry, for example, it is necessary to read and understand each stanza before deciding what the main idea of the poem is.

Apuntes° de un hogar° posmoderno

Yo como a las siete,
tú comes a las ocho,
el niño come a las seis
y la niña come a las nueve.
5 Queremos ser felices a toda costa°,
todos vemos televisión separados
en nuestras respectivas
habitaciones
siempre a la misma hora,
siempre a las diez.

Title: Notes
home
5 no matter what

Un corazón dividido

El mío es un corazón de dudas°,
esfuerzos° que luchan entre el aquí y el allá.
Es el grito° continuo de mi ser interior.
Es "estar aquí" en sustancia°
5 pero el "estar allá" siguiéndote° a todas partes.
Es como una canción sin ritmo definido
que se va contigo sin terminar la tonada°.

Es ser una y otra a la vez.
Es ser una queriendo ser la otra
10 y la otra deseando ser la primera.
Es saber muy poco acerca
de aquellas cosas en las cuales crees.
Es saber menos acerca
de otras cosas que quieres expresar
15 pero tienes miedo reclamar°.
Es la transpiración de mi olor° caribeño
encima de la superficie de mi gel° norteamericano.

Es solamente mi corazón que late°
rápido e incesante
20 como las corrientes constantes del Golfo de México.

Es mi corazón dividido
secando° los finales del tiempo
como el agua de esas corrientes
sobre el Estrecho de la Florida.

---

1 doubts
2 efforts
3 scream
4 physically
5 following you
7 tune
15 to demand
16 *fig.* my soul
17 *fig.* my shell
18 beats
22 drying

Después de leer

1B, 2B, 3B

1. En el primer poema, ¿qué es lo que más quieren los miembros de la familia?
2. En el segundo poema, ¿dónde crees que está el "allá" referido en las líneas dos y cinco?
3. ¿Quién crees que es "la una" y "la otra"?
4. ¿Por qué crees que su corazón está dividido? Explica tu respuesta.

La República Dominicana

El regalo de cumpleaños

Diógenes Valdez is a Dominican author who has written many acclaimed novels and short stories. In this story, the mother of David, a young Dominican, has spent years working in New York. In a letter to his mother, David tells her that everyone thinks that he should have more fun, that it is not good to be so sad, and that he must learn to smile. Read his mother's response and discover what the best gift is that she can give him.

ESTRATEGIA

In order to better understand a story, think about the culture that it represents. What do you know about the Dominican culture that can help you?

Querida mamá:

La abuela me ha dicho[1] que vendrás[2] pronto. Sé que dice esto para verme feliz, porque me paso mucho rato mirando tu fotografía y a veces los ojos se me llenan de lágrimas[3]. Comprendo que te fuiste a Nueva York a trabajar porque aquí cuesta mucho conseguir[4] un empleo.

En casa todos estamos bien, únicamente me preocupa[5] la abuela. Se pasa todo el día diciéndome que me divierta, que salga con los amigos, pero yo no siento deseos de hacerlo. Ha llegado a decirme que hace tiempo que no me ve sonreír[6], que parezco un niño viejo.

Sé que Nueva York es una gran ciudad y que allá se consigue de todo. Quiero que me traigas una sonrisa[7]. Estoy cansado de que me digan que no parezco feliz, sólo porque no sé sonreír.

Te quiere, tu hijo
David

Querido hijo:

Creo que tengo buenas noticias para ti. Voy a regresar pronto y aunque me pides algo que es difícil de conseguir[8], voy a hacer todo lo posible para complacerte[9]. Sé que costará mucho el conseguir esa sonrisa, pero puedes estar tranquilo. Espero estar contigo el mismo día de tu cumpleaños.

Tu madre que no te olvida,
Rebeca

1 has told me
2 you will come
3 tears
4 to get
5 I worry about
6 to smile
7 a smile
8 to get
9 to make you happy

Hoy es sábado 15 de agosto. Es el día del cumpleaños de David. En el aeropuerto, el niño mira los aviones[1] que despegan o aterrizan[2]. No se siente nervioso, ni emocionado. Contempla a su madre y tiene la esperanza de que en la cartera[3], envuelta primorosamente[4], venga esa sonrisa. La ve salir y un nudo[5] se le forma en la garganta. Ella corre a abrazarlo[6] y por un momento David se olvida de todo.

¡Mamá!—exclama David.

¡Hijo mío! —responde la madre.

¿Has traído[7] mi sonrisa? —se atreve a preguntarle.

Ella abre la cartera y le entrega un paquetito primorosamente envuelto.

¡Aquí está!—le dice—¡Ábrelo!

David lo toma entre sus manos temblorosas[8] y con los ojos llenos de lágrimas, responde:

¡Tengo miedo de hacerlo!

David comienza a abrir el pequeño paquete. Las manos le tiemblan cuando le quita la envoltura[9]. Abre la cajita, pero dentro tan sólo hay un papelito cuidadosamente doblado. Lo abre y lee:

"Querido hijo:

Mamá ha venido a quedarse definitivamente. Ya nunca más volverá a marcharse[10]."

Entonces David abrió los ojos y abrazó a su madre nuevamente. Sin darse cuenta comenzó[11] a sonreír.

1 airplanes
2 take off or land
3 purse
4 carefully wrapped
5 knot
6 to hug him
7 Have you brought
8 shaking
9 takes off the wrapping
10 She'll never go away again
11 he began

Después de leer ✦3A

1. ¿Por qué se fue a Nueva York la madre de David?
2. Según la abuela, ¿por qué debe divertirse David más? ¿Qué parece David, en su opinión?
3. ¿Qué le pide David a su madre?
4. En su carta, ¿cuándo dice que va a venir la madre de David?
5. ¿Cuál es el regalo que la madre le trae? Explica.

Perú

Ollantaytambo

The Incan warrior Ollanta was made immortal thanks to the famous Peruvian writer Juan Espinoza Medrano, who wrote the drama *Ollantay* during the colonial period. Many years later, in 1780, the story was presented to the public with great success. Read about the Incan people and this famous warrior for whom the legend is named.

ESTRATEGIA

Making predictions helps prepare you to read a passage. Read the first four lines of the text and, thinking about other legends that you know, try to guess what is going to happen in this Inca legend.

Ollantay es el mejor guerrero[1] del imperio inca. Conquista regiones de la selva y lleva riquezas[2] al Inca Pachacútec.

Su casco de oro[3] le distingue como el más valiente. Todos lo admiran pero su corazón es de la princesa Cusi Coyllur.

Cuando Pachacútec se entera del amor entre el guerrero y la princesa se pone rojo de ira[4]. Castiga[5] a Ollantay y encierra a la princesa en una cueva[6].

Un día Ollantay se escapa y se convierte en jefe de los pueblos de los Andes. Gana todos los combates contra Rumiñahui, el general de Pachacútec.

Rumiñahui busca venganza[7]. Durante una fiesta emborracha[8] a los hombres de Ollantay y los hace prisioneros. El guerrero está ahora en manos del malvado Rumiñahui.

Pero en Cuzco hay un nuevo Inca, Tupac Yupanqui. Tupac es bueno y justo. Cusi Coyllur y Ollantay se casan al fin y viven en Tambo, una magnífica ciudad de piedra[9], levantada[10] al pie de la selva.

---

1 warrior **2** riches **3** golden helmet **4** hatred **5** He punishes **6** cave **7** revenge **8** he intoxicates **9** rock **10** raised

Datos geográficos

Ollantaytambo es un pueblo de la provincia de Urubamba, muy cerca de las famosas ruinas de Machu Picchu, al sur de Perú. En este pueblo todo ha permanecido[1] intacto y en sus casas siguen viviendo[2] los descendientes de sus primeros ocupantes. Allí se encuentra una antigua fortaleza inca, uno de los mejores ejemplos de la asombrosa[3] arquitectura de esta civilización. Muchas de las piedras en su construcción, de más de 96 toneladas[4], fueron transportadas desde lugares lejanos, pero aún no se sabe cómo.

1 has remained **2** continue to live **3** astonishing **4** tons

Después de leer

1B, 3A, 3B

1. ¿De quién está enamorado Ollantay?
2. ¿Qué hace el Inca Pachacútec al saber de ese amor?
3. ¿Qué hace Ollantay cuando se escapa de Pachacútec?
4. ¿Cómo se salva Ollantay del malvado Rumiñahui?
5. ¿Por qué es famoso hoy en día el pueblo Ollantaytambo?
6. ¿Cuál es el misterio de su construcción?

La Península Ibérica

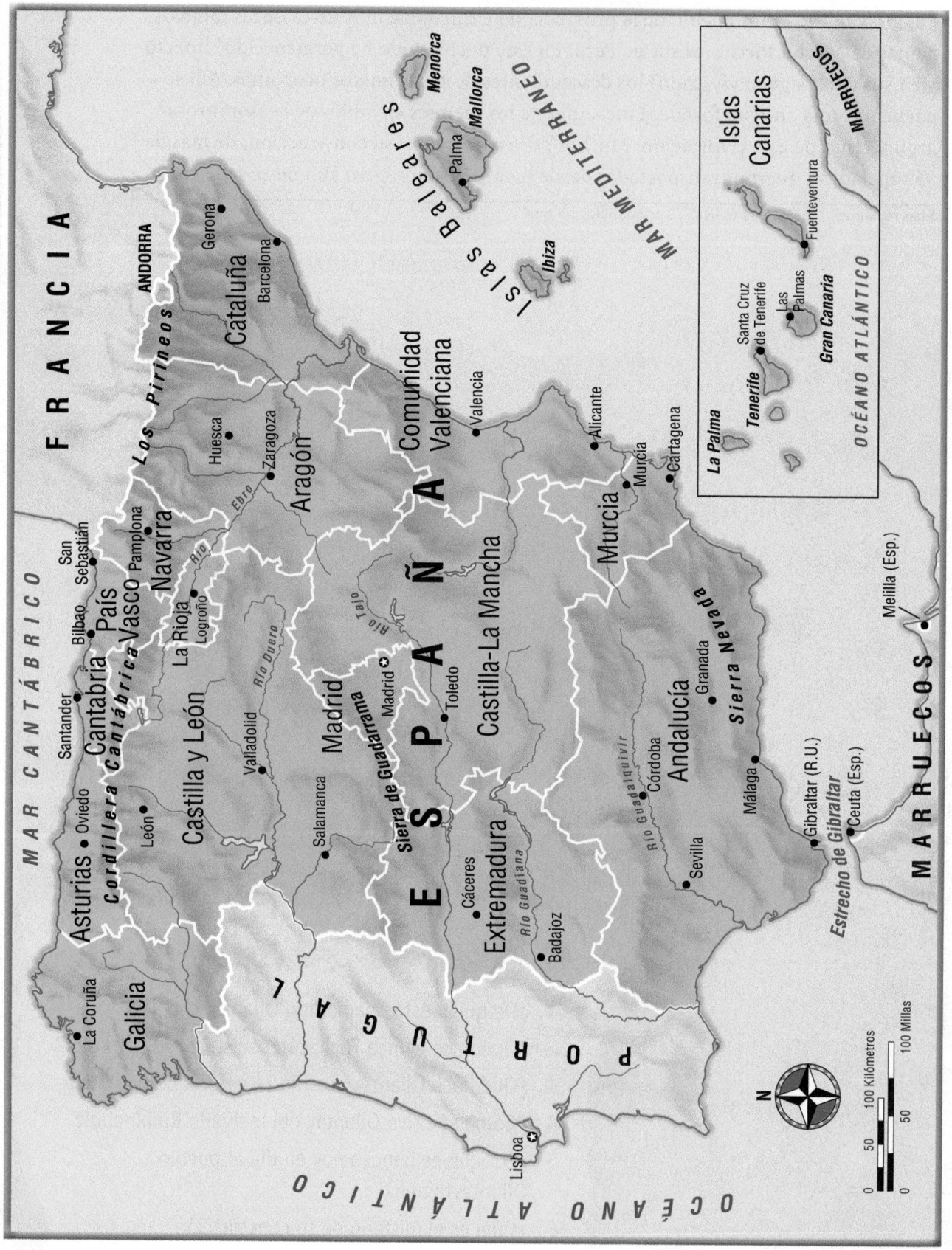

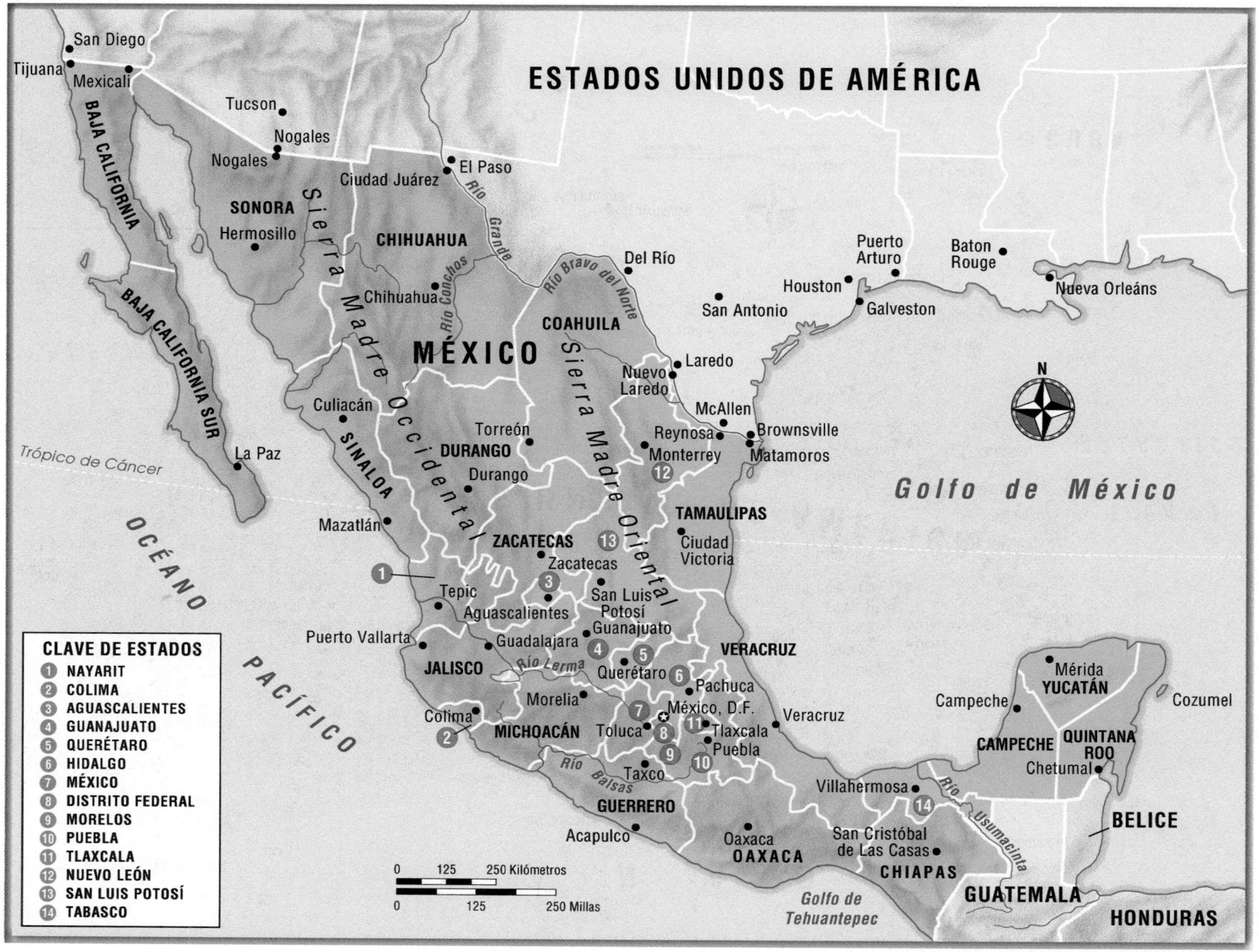
ESTADOS UNIDOS DE AMÉRICA
MÉXICO
San Diego
Tijuana
Mexicali
BAJA CALIFORNIA
BAJA CALIFORNIA SUR
La Paz
Tucson
Nogales
Nogales
SONORA
Hermosillo
Ciudad Juárez
El Paso
Río Grande
CHIHUAHUA
Chihuahua
Río Conchos
Sierra Madre Occidental
Sierra Madre Oriental
Río Bravo del Norte
Del Río
COAHUILA
Laredo
Nuevo Laredo
San Antonio
Houston
Puerto Arturo
Galveston
Baton Rouge
Nueva Orleáns
N
Golfo de México
Culiacán
SINALOA
Mazatlán
Torreón
DURANGO
Durango
Reynosa
Monterrey
McAllen
Brownsville
Matamoros
TAMAULIPAS
Ciudad Victoria
Trópico de Cáncer
OCÉANO PACÍFICO
ZACATECAS
Zacatecas
Tepic
Aguascalientes
San Luis Potosí
Guanajuato
Puerto Vallarta
Guadalajara
JALISCO
Río Lerma
Querétaro
Pachuca
VERACRUZ
Morelia
Colima
MICHOACÁN
Toluca
México, D.F.
Tlaxcala
Puebla
Veracruz
Río Balsas
Taxco
GUERRERO
Acapulco
Oaxaca
OAXACA
Villahermosa
Río Usumacinta
San Cristóbal de Las Casas
CHIAPAS
Golfo de Tehuantepec
Mérida
YUCATÁN
Campeche
CAMPECHE
QUINTANA ROO
Cozumel
Chetumal
BELICE
GUATEMALA
HONDURAS
CLAVE DE ESTADOS
1 NAYARIT
2 COLIMA
3 AGUASCALIENTES
4 GUANAJUATO
5 QUERÉTARO
6 HIDALGO
7 MÉXICO
8 DISTRITO FEDERAL
9 MORELOS
10 PUEBLA
11 TLAXCALA
12 NUEVO LEÓN
13 SAN LUIS POTOSÍ
14 TABASCO
0 125 250 Kilómetros
0 125 250 Millas

México

Estados Unidos de América

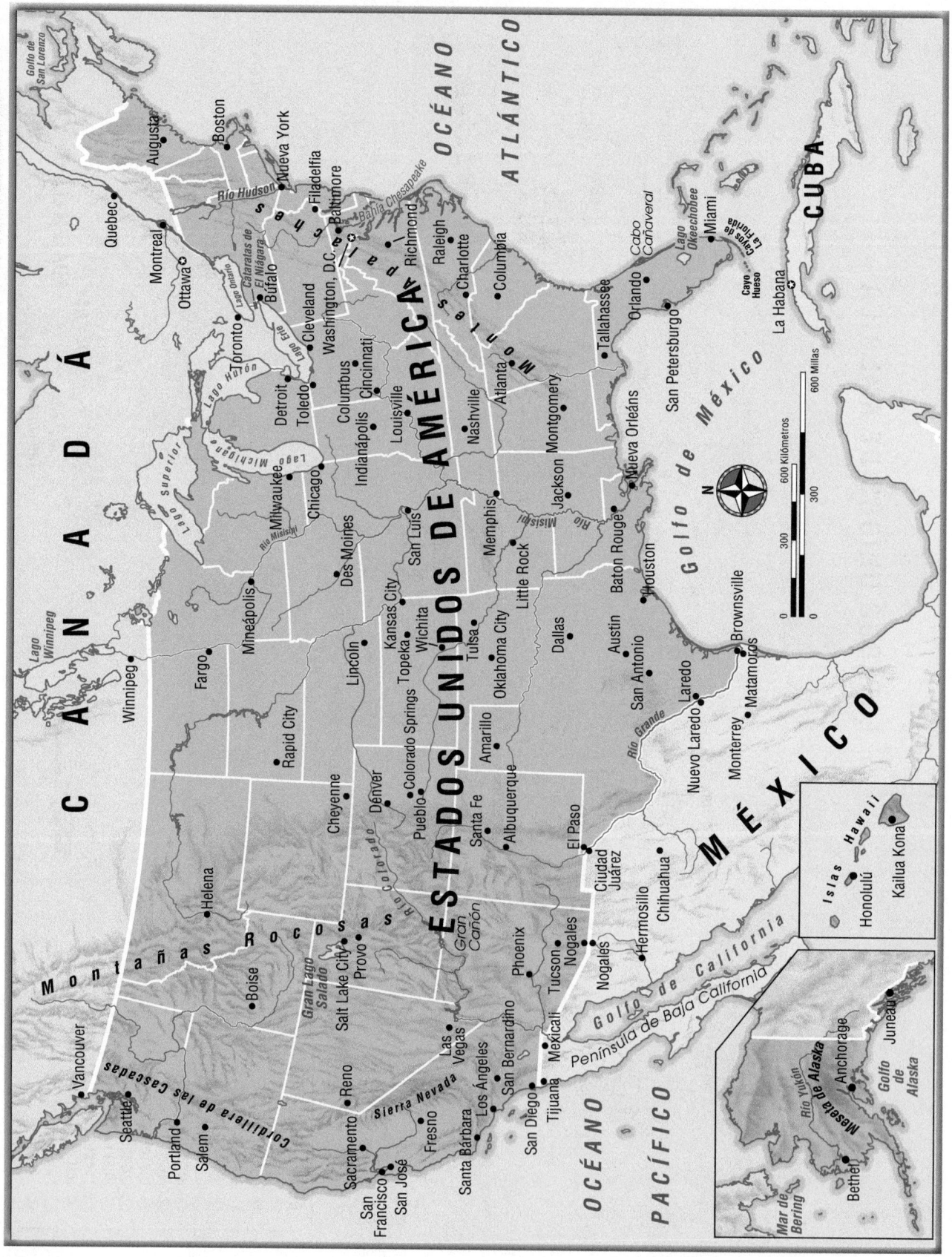

América Central y las Antillas

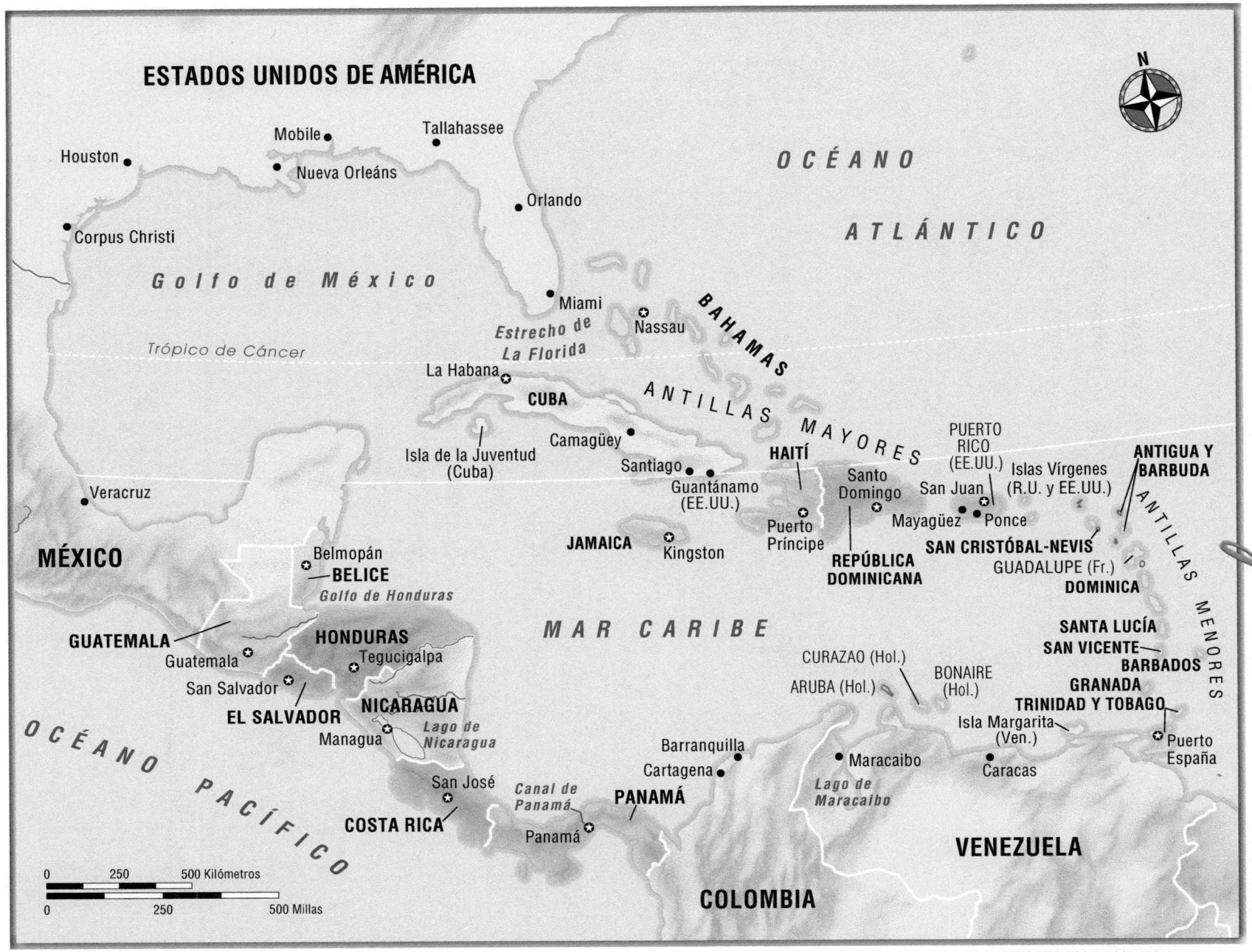

América del Sur

Vocabulario adicional

This list includes additional vocabulary that you may want to use to personalize activities. If you can't find a word you need here, try the Spanish-English and English-Spanish vocabulary sections, beginning on page R24.

Materias *(School Subjects)*

el álgebra	*algebra*
el cálculo	*calculus*
la contabilidad	*accounting*
la física	*physics*
la geometría	*geometry*
el italiano	*Italian*
el japonés	*Japanese*
el latín	*Latin*
la literatura	*literature*
el ruso	*Russian*

Celebraciones *(Celebrations)*

el bautizo	*baptism*
la canción	*song*
El Día de los Reyes	*Three Kings Day*
la Pascua Florida	*Easter*
las Pascuas	*Christmas*
el Ramadán	*Ramadan*
Rosh Hashaná	*Rosh Hashanah*

Comida *(Food)*

el ají picante (el chile)	*hot pepper*
el aguacate	*avocado*
las arvejas	*peas*
el azúcar	*sugar*
la banana (el guineo)	*banana*
el batido	*milkshake*
la cereza	*cherry*
la coliflor	*cauliflower*
el champiñón (el hongo)	*mushroom*
los condimentos	*seasonings*
los fideos	*noodles*
el filete de pescado	*fish fillet*
la lechuga	*lettuce*
la mayonesa	*mayonnaise*
el melón	*cantaloupe*
la mostaza	*mustard*
la pimienta	*pepper*
la piña	*pineapple*
el plátano	*plantain*
la sal	*salt*
el yogur	*yogurt*

Computadoras *(Computers)*

arrastrar	*to drag*
la búsqueda	*search*
buscar	*to search*
comenzar la sesión	*to log on*
la contraseña, el código	*password*
el disco duro	*hard drive*
en línea	*online*
grabar	*to save*
hacer clic	*to click*
la impresora	*printer*
imprimir	*to print*
el marcapáginas, el separador	*bookmark*
el ordenador	*computer*
la página Web inicial	*homepage*
el ratón	*mouse*
la Red	*the Net*
la tecla de aceptación	*return key*
la tecla de borrar, la tecla correctora	*delete key*
el teclado	*keyboard*
terminar la sesión	*to log off*
la unidad de CD-ROM	*CD-ROM drive*
el Web, la Telaraña Mundial	*World Wide Web*

De compras *(Shopping)*

cobrar	*to charge*
el dinero en efectivo	*cash*
el descuento	*discount*
en venta	*for sale*
la rebaja	*sale, sale price*
regatear	*to bargain*
la tarjeta de crédito	*credit card*
el (la) vendedor, -ora	*salesperson*

Deportes y pasatiempos *(Sports and Hobbies)*

el anuario	*yearbook*
las artes marciales	*martial arts*
la astronomía	*astronomy*
el ballet	*ballet*
el boxeo	*boxing*
coleccionar sellos (monedas, muñecas)	*to collect stamps (coins, dolls)*
coser	*to sew*
el drama	*drama*
la fotografía	*photography*
la gimnasia	*gymnastics*
jugar a las cartas	*to play cards*
jugar a las damas	*to play checkers*
la orquesta	*orchestra*
el patinaje en línea, (sobre hielo)	*inline (ice) skating*

En el cine o el teatro *(At the Movies or Theater)*

el actor	*actor*
actuar	*to act*
la actriz	*actress*
aplaudir	*to applaud*
la butaca	*box seat*
la escena	*scene*
el escenario	*stage*
el espectáculo	*performance, show*
la estrella	*star*
la pantalla	*screen*
el telón	*curtain*

En el consultorio *(At the Clinic)*

la alergia	*allergy*
el antibiótico	*antibiotic*
ponerle a alguien una inyección	*to give someone a shot*
el dolor	*pain*
los escalofríos	*chills*
estornudar	*to sneeze*
la gripe	*flu*
la medicina	*medicine*
las pastillas, las píldoras	*pills, tablets*
el síntoma	*symptom*
la tos	*cough*
toser	*to cough*

En el zoológico *(At the Zoo)*

el ave, las aves	*bird, birds*
el canguro	*kangaroo*
la cebra	*zebra*
el cocodrilo	*crocodile*
el delfín	*dolphin*
el elefante	*elephant*
el gorila	*gorilla*
el hipopótamo	*hippopotamus*
la jirafa	*giraffe*
el león	*lion*
la foca	*seal*
el mono, el chango	*monkey*
el oso	*bear*
el oso polar	*polar bear*
el pingüino	*penguin*
la serpiente	*snake*
el tigre	*tiger*

En la casa *(Around the House)*

la alfombra	*rug, carpet*
el ático	*attic*
el balcón	*balcony*
las cortinas	*curtains*
el despertador	*alarm clock*
las escaleras	*stairs*
el espejo	*mirror*
el estante	*bookcase*
el fregadero	*kitchen sink*
la galería	*porch*
la lámpara	*lamp*
el lavamanos	*bathroom sink*
la lavadora	*washing machine*
la mesita de noche	*nightstand*
los muebles	*furniture*
la secadora	*dryer*

el sillón	*easy chair*
el sótano	*basement*
el timbre	*doorbell*
el tocador	*dresser*

En las afueras y en la ciudad
(Places around Town)

la autopista	*highway*
el banco	*bank*
la esquina	*street corner*
la estación de autobuses (trenes)	*bus (train) station*
la fábrica	*factory*
la ferretería	*hardware store*
la farmacia	*drugstore*
la gasolinera	*gas station*
el hospital	*hospital*
la mezquita	*mosque*
el mercado	*market*
la oficina	*office*
la parada de autobuses	*bus stop*
la peluquería	*barbershop*
el puente	*bridge*
el rascacielos	*skyscraper*
el salón de belleza	*beauty salon*
el semáforo	*traffic light*
el supermercado	*supermarket*

Instrumentos musicales
(Musical Instruments)

el acordeón	*accordion*
el arpa	*harp*
la armónica	*harmonica*
el bajo	*bass*
la batería	*drum set*
el clarinete	*clarinet*
la flauta dulce	*recorder*
la flauta	*flute*
la guitarra	*guitar*
la mandolina	*mandolin*
las maracas	*maracas*
el oboe	*oboe*
el saxofón	*saxophone*
el sintetizador	*synthesizer*
el tambor	*drum*
el trombón	*trombone*
la trompeta	*trumpet*
la tuba	*tuba*
la tumbadora	*conga drum*
la viola	*viola*
el violín	*violin*

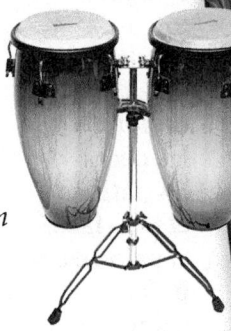

La familia *(Family)*

el (la) ahijado(a)	*godson, goddaughter*
el (la) bisabuelo(a)	*great-grandfather, great-grandmother*
el (la) biznieto(a)	*great-grandson, great-granddaughter*
el (la) cuñado(a)	*brother-in-law, sister-in-law*
el (la) hijastro(a)	*stepson, stepdaughter*
la madrina	*godmother*
la madrastra	*stepmother*
la nuera	*daughter-in-law*
el padrino	*godfather*
el padrastro	*stepfather*
el (la) suegro(a)	*father-in-law, mother-in-law*
el yerno	*son-in-law*

Palabras descriptivas *(Descriptive Words)*

amistoso(a)	*friendly*
la barba	*beard*
bien educado(a)	*well-mannered*
el bigote	*mustache*
calvo(a)	*bald*
la estatura	*height*
flaco(a)	*skinny*
lindo(a)	*pretty*
las pecas	*freckles*
las patillas	*sideburns*
el pelo lacio	*straight hair*
el pelo rizado	*curly hair*
pesar	*to weigh*
tranquilo(a)	*quiet*

Partes del cuerpo *(Parts of the Body)*

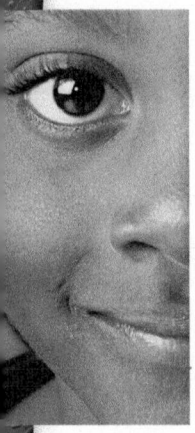

la barbilla	*chin*
las cejas	*eyebrows*
la cintura	*waist*
el codo	*elbow*
la frente	*forehead*
los labios	*lips*
la muñeca	*wrist*
el muslo	*thigh*
las pestañas	*eyelashes*
la rodilla	*knee*
la sien	*temple*
el tobillo	*ankle*
la uña	*nail*

Profesiones *(Professions)*

el (la) abogado(a)	*lawyer*
el (la) arquitecto(a)	*architect*
el (la) bombero(a)	*firefighter*
el (la) cartero(a)	*mail carrier*
el (la) cocinero(a)	*cook*
el (la) conductor, -ora	*driver*
el (la) constructor, -ora	*builder*
el (la) decorador, -ora	*interior decorator*
el (la) dentista	*dentist*
el (la) detective	*detective*
el (la) enfermero(a)	*nurse*
el (la) escritor, -ora	*writer*
el hombre (la mujer) de negocios	*businessman, businesswoman*
el (la) ingeniero(a)	*engineer*
el (la) médico(a)	*doctor*
el (la) piloto(a)	*pilot*
el (la) (mujer) policía	*police officer*
el (la) secretario(a)	*secretary*

Regalos *(Gifts)*

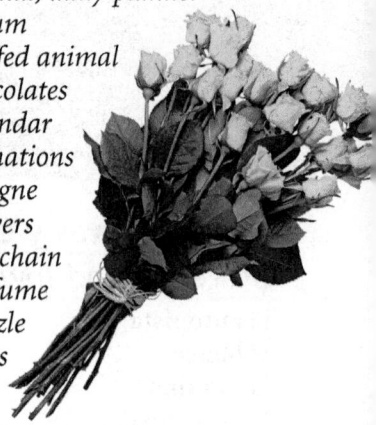

la agenda	*agenda, daily planner*
el álbum	*album*
el animal de peluche	*stuffed animal*
los bombones	*chocolates*
el calendario	*calendar*
los claveles	*carnations*
la colonia	*cologne*
las flores	*flowers*
el llavero	*key chain*
el perfume	*perfume*
el rompecabezas	*puzzle*
las rosas	*roses*

Ropa *(Clothes)*

la bata	*robe*
la bufanda	*scarf*
el chaleco	*vest*
las chancletas	*flip-flops*
la corbata	*tie*
los guantes	*gloves*
las medias	*socks, stockings, hose*
las pantuflas, las zapatillas	*slippers*
el pañuelo	*handkerchief*
el paraguas	*umbrella*
la ropa interior	*underwear*
los tacones, los zapatos de tacón	*high heels*

Temas de actualidad *(Current Issues)*

el bosque tropical	*rain forest*
la contaminación	*pollution*
el crimen	*crime*
los derechos humanos	*human rights*
la economía	*economy*
la educación	*education*
la guerra	*war*

el medio ambiente	*environment*
el mundo	*world*
las noticias	*news*
la paz	*peace*
la política	*politics*
la tecnología	*technology*
la violencia	*violence*

Vacaciones *(Vacation)*

la agencia de viajes	*travel agency*
el andén	*train platform*
el asiento	*seat*
los cheques de viajero	*traveler's checks*
hacer una reservación	*to make a reservation*
el horario	*schedule, timetable*
el mar	*sea*

la parada	*stop*
el pasillo	*aisle*
reservado(a)	*reserved*
la ventanilla	*window*
la visa	*visa*
visitar los lugares de interés	*to sightsee*
volar	*to fly*

Refranes *(Proverbs)*

Más vale pájaro en mano que cien volando.
A bird in the hand is worth two in the bush.

Hijo no tenemos y nombre le ponemos.
Don't count your chickens before they're hatched.

Quien primero viene, primero tiene.
The early bird catches the worm.

Más vale tarde que nunca.
Better late than never.

El hábito no hace al monje.
Clothes don't make the man.

Más ven cuatro ojos que dos.
Two heads are better than one.

Querer es poder.
Where there's a will, there's a way.

Ojos que no ven, corazón que no siente.
Out of sight, out of mind.

No todo lo que brilla es oro.
All that glitters is not gold.

Caras vemos, corazones no sabemos.
You can't judge a book by its cover.

Donde una puerta se cierra, otra se abre.
Every cloud has a silver lining.

En boca cerrada no entran moscas.
Silence is golden.

Dime con quién andas y te diré quién eres.
Birds of a feather flock together.

Al mal tiempo buena cara.
When life gives you lemons, make lemonade.

Antes que te cases mira lo que haces.
Look before you leap.

Expresiones de ¡Exprésate!

Functions are the ways in which you use a language for particular purposes. In specific situations, such as in a restaurant, in a grocery store, or at school, you will want to communicate with those around you. In order to do that, you have to "function" in Spanish: you place an order, make a purchase, or talk about your class schedule.

Here is a list of the functions presented in this book along with the Spanish expressions you'll need to communicate in a wide range of situations. Following each function is the chapter and page number from the book where it is introduced.

Socializing

Greetings
Ch. 1, p. 8

Buenos días, señor.
Buenas noches, señora.
Buenas tardes, señorita.

Saying Goodbye
Ch. 1, p. 8

Adiós.
Tengo que irme.
Hasta luego.
Buenas noches.
Hasta mañana.
Nos vemos.
Hasta pronto.

Asking how someone is and saying how you are
Ch. 1, p. 8

Hola, ¿cómo estás?
¿Cómo está usted?
¿Qué tal?
Estoy bien/regular/mal.
Más o menos.

Introducing people
Ch. 1, p. 10

Éste(a) es... Es un(a) compañero(a) de clase.
Ésta es... (Ella) es mi profesora de...
Encantado(a).
Mucho gusto.
Igualmente.
Éste es... (Él) es mi profesor de...

Inviting others to do something
Ch. 4, p. 134

¿Qué tal si vamos a...?
No sé. ¿Sabes qué? No tengo ganas.
Vienes conmigo a..., ¿no?
¡Claro que sí! Tengo mucha hambre.
Hay un concierto...
Vas a ir, ¿verdad?
No, no voy a ir. Tengo que...

Talking on the phone
Ch. 8, p. 287

Aló/Bueno/Diga.
Hola. ¿Está...?
¿De parte de quién?
Habla...
Espera un momento, ya te lo (la) paso.
Lo siento, no está. ¿Quieres dejarle un recado?
No, gracias. Llamo más tarde.
Sí, por favor, que me llame después.

Greetings, introducing others, and saying goodbye
Ch. 9, p. 325

¡Qué gusto verte!
¿Qué hay de nuevo?
Te presento a...
¡Feliz...!
Cuídate.
¡Tanto tiempo sin verte!
Lo de siempre.
Tanto gusto.
Chao, te llamo más tarde.
Vale. Que te vaya bien.

Exchanging Information

Asking and giving names
Ch. 1, p. 6

¿Cómo te llamas?
¿Cómo se llama usted?
Me llamo...
Soy...
¿Quién es...?
Él (Ella) es...
¿Cómo se llama (él/ella)?
(Él/Ella) se llama...

Saying where you and others are from
Ch. 1, p. 11

¿De dónde eres?
Soy de...
Es de...
¿De dónde es usted?
¿De dónde es...?

Asking and giving phone numbers
Ch. 1, p. 19
¿Cuál es tu teléfono?
Es tres-dos-cinco-uno-dos-tres-uno.
¿Cuál es el teléfono de...?
Es...

Saying what time it is
Ch. 1, p. 20
¿Qué hora es?
Son las... y cuarto de la mañana.
Es la una en punto.
Son las... y trece de la tarde.
Son las... y media de la tarde.
Son las... menos cuarto.
Son las... menos diez de la noche.
Es mediodía.
Es medianoche.

Asking and giving the date and the day
Ch. 1, p. 21
¿Qué fecha es hoy?
Es el primero (dos, tres...) de enero.
¿Qué día es hoy?
Hoy es...

Asking how words are spelled and giving e-mail addresses
Ch. 1, p. 23
¿Cómo se escribe...?
Se escribe...
¿Cuál es tu correo electrónico?
Es...
¿Cuál es el correo electrónico de...?
Es eme punto ge-o-ene-zeta-a-ele-o arroba ere-e-de punto a-ere.

Describing people
Ch. 2, p. 45
¿Cómo es...?
... es moreno(a). También es... y un poco...
¿Cómo eres? ¿Eres cómico(a)?
Sí, soy bastante cómico(a).

Asking and saying how old someone is
Ch. 2, p. 47
¿Cuántos años tienes?
Tengo ... años.
¿Cuántos años tiene...?
... tiene ... años.
¿Cuándo es tu cumpleaños?
Es el 6 de mayo.
¿Cuándo es el cumpleaños de...?
Es el...

Describing things
Ch. 2, p. 58
¿Cómo es...?
Es (muy)...
Es bastante...
Es...
Es algo...

Talking about what you and others want to do
Ch. 3, p. 85
¿Qué quieres hacer hoy?
Ni idea.
¿Quieres ir a... conmigo?
Está bien.
No, gracias. No quiero ir a... hoy.

Talking about everyday activities
Ch. 3, p. 95
¿Qué haces los fines de semana?
Los sábados, cuando hace buen tiempo, voy...
¿Qué hace... cuando hace mal tiempo?
Le gusta...
No va a ninguna parte.

Asking and saying how often
Ch. 3, p. 96
¿Con qué frecuencia vas a...?
Casi nunca. No me gusta...
¿Te gusta...?
Sí. Después de clases, casi siempre vamos a...
A veces vamos también a...

Talking about what you and others have or need
Ch. 4, p. 121
¿Necesitas algo para el colegio?
Sí, necesito muchas cosas.
No, no necesito nada.
¿Necesitas...?
Sí, necesito...
¿Tienes...?
Sí, tengo un montón.
No, no tengo.

Talking about classes
Ch. 4, p. 122
¿Qué clases tienes...?
Primero tengo... y después tengo...
¿Cuál es tu materia preferida?
Mi materia preferida es... Es fácil.
No me gusta la clase de... porque es difícil.

Talking about plans
Ch. 4, p. 133
¿Vas a ir a... el... por la...?
No. Tengo...
¿Qué vas a hacer el... próximo?
Voy a..., y después...
Luego regreso a...

¿A qué hora vas a llegar a...?
Voy a llegar temprano (a tiempo).
No me gusta llegar tarde.

Describing people and family relationships
Ch. 5, p. 159

¿Cuántas personas hay en tu familia?
En mi familia somos... personas.
¿Cómo es tu familia?
Somos... y tenemos... Todos usamos lentes.
Mi... está en una silla de ruedas.
¿Cómo es tu...?
Es... Es una persona... (Él/Ella) y mi...
tienen... hijos pero no tienen...

Describing where someone lives
Ch. 5, p. 171

¿Dónde viven ustedes?
Vivimos en un apartamento. Está en un
edificio... de... pisos.
¿Cuál es tu dirección?
Es calle..., número...
¿Cómo es tu casa?
Es bastante... Tiene... habitaciones,...

Talking about your responsibilities
Ch. 5, p. 172

¿Qué te parece tener que ayudar en casa?
A veces tengo que..., pero me parece bien.
No es gran cosa.
A mí siempre me toca... ¡Qué lata!
¿Qué te toca hacer a ti?
A menudo tengo que...
A... nunca le toca... Me parece injusto.

Commenting on food
Ch. 6, p. 197

¿Qué tal si pruebas...? Son muy buenos(as)
aquí.
¡Ay, no! Nunca pido... No me gusta.
Aquí preparan muy bien (mal)...
(No) estoy de acuerdo.
¡Qué ricos(as) están...!
Sí, me encantan.
¿Qué tal está(n)...?
Está(n) un poco...

Talking about meals
Ch. 6, p. 209

¿Qué desayunas?
Siempre desayuno...
¿Qué quieres hoy de almuerzo?
¿Qué tal si almorzamos...?
¿Qué hay de cena? Tengo mucha hambre.
Vamos a cenar...

Talking about your daily routine
Ch. 7, p. 235

¿Estás listo(a)? ¿Qué te falta hacer?
¡Ay, no! Acabo de levantarme. Tengo que... antes
de...
¿Qué tienes que hacer para prepararte?
Tengo que..., pero no encuentro...

Talking about staying fit and healthy
Ch. 7, p. 237

¿Cómo te mantienes en forma?
... y... Entreno...
¿Qué haces para relajarte?
... También... o...

Offering and asking for help in a store
Ch. 8, p. 275

¿En qué le puedo servir?
Busco...
Nada más estoy mirando.
Quiero devolver... Lo/La necesito en otro(a)...
¿Qué número/talla usa?
Uso el/la...
¿Cómo le queda(n)...?
Me queda(n) bien/mal.
Necesito una talla más grande/pequeña.
¿A qué hora cierra la tienda?
Cierra a las...

Saying where you went and what you did
Ch. 8, p. 285

¿Adónde fuiste anoche/ayer/anteayer?
Fui a... a...
¿Qué hiciste el fin de semana pasado?
Pagué una fortuna.

Talking about your plans
Ch. 9, p. 311

¿Qué vas a hacer...?
Pienso... o...
¿Qué planes tienen para...?
Pensamos pasarlo(la) con..., como siempre.

Talking about past holidays
Ch. 9, p. 312

¿Dónde pasaron... el año pasado?
Lo (La) pasamos en casa de...
¿Qué tal estuvo?
Estuvo a todo dar. Nos reunimos a...

Preparing for a party
Ch. 9, p. 323

¿Está todo listo para la fiesta?
¿Ya terminaste con los preparativos?
Sí. Anoche compré... y preparé...
¿Qué están haciendo...?
Están colgando...

Asking for and giving information
Ch. 10, p. 349

¿Me puede decir dónde está(n)...?
Está(n) a la vuelta.
¿Sabe Ud. a qué hora sale el vuelo...? No quiero perderlo.
Lo puede ver allí en esa pantalla.
Sí, sale/llega a las...
¿Dónde se puede conseguir...?
Lo siento, no sé.

Reminding and reassuring
Ch. 10, p. 351

¿Ya sacaste el dinero?
Sí, ya lo saqué.
No, todavía no. Debo pasar por el cajero automático.
¿Ya hiciste la maleta?
No, todavía tengo que hacerla.
¡Ay, dejé... en casa!
No te preocupes. Puedes comprar... en cualquier tienda.

Talking about a trip
Ch. 10, p. 361

¿Qué tal el viaje?
¡Fue estupendo!
¡Fue horrible!
¿Adónde fueron?
Fuimos a...
¿Qué hicieron?
Conocimos... y sacamos muchas fotos.
Luego pasamos por... y por fin...

Expressing Attitudes and Opinions

Talking about what you and others like
Ch. 2, p. 57

¿Te gusta(n)...? Sí, me gusta(n) mucho.
No, no me gusta(n). ¿Te gusta(n) más... o...?
Me gusta(n) más... Me da igual.

Talking about what you and others like to do
Ch. 3, p. 83

¿Qué te gusta hacer? A mí me gusta...
¿A... les gusta...? Sí, porque les gusta...

Asking for and giving opinions
Ch. 8, p. 273

¿Qué te parece el (la)...?
Me parece... y cuesta mucho. ¡Es un robo!
¿Cómo me queda el (la)...?
Te queda muy bien. Y está a la (última) moda.
¿Y el (la)...? Cuesta... dólares.
¡Qué caro(a)! Además, está pasado(a) de moda.
El (La)... es una ganga, ¿verdad?
Tienes razón. Es muy barato(a).

Expressing hopes and wishes
Ch. 10, p. 363

Algún día me gustaría...
Si tengo suerte, voy a...
Quiero conocer...
Espero ver...

Expressing Feelings and Emotions

Talking about how you feel
Ch. 7, p. 247

Te veo mal.
Es que estoy enfermo(a). Tengo catarro.
¿Qué te pasa? ¿Te duele algo?
Me siento (un poco)... y me duele...
¿Qué tiene...? ¿Está...?
Le duele...

Persuading

Taking someone's order and requesting something
Ch. 6, p. 198

¿Qué desea (usted)?
Quisiera...
¿Y para tomar?
Para tomar, quiero...
¿Desea algo de postre?
Sí, ¿me trae...?
¿Algo más?
¿Nos trae..., por favor?

Offering help and giving instructions
Ch. 6, p. 211

¿Necesitas ayuda?
Sí, saca... y ponlo(a) en el horno (el microondas).
¿Puedo ayudar?
Saca... del refrigerador.
¿Por qué no preparas...?
¿Pongo la mesa?
Sí, ponla, por favor.

Giving advice
Ch. 7, p. 248

¿Sabes qué? Comes muy mal. No debes comer tanto dulce ni grasa.
Para cuidarte mejor, debes... ¿Por qué no... más temprano?
No debes...

Síntesis gramatical

NOUNS AND ARTICLES

Gender of Nouns

In Spanish, nouns (words that name a person, place, or thing) are grouped into two classes or genders: masculine and feminine. All nouns, both persons and objects, fall into one of these groups. Most nouns that end in **-o** are masculine, and most nouns that end in **-a, -ción, -tad,** and **-dad** are feminine. Some nouns, such as **estudiante** and **cliente,** can be either masculine or feminine.

Masculine Nouns	Feminine Nouns
libro	casa
chico	universidad
cuaderno	situación
bolígrafo	mesa
vestido	libertad

FORMATION OF PLURAL NOUNS

	Add **-s** to nouns that end in a vowel.		Add **-es** to nouns that end in a consonant.		With nouns that end in **-z,** the **-z** changes to a **-c.**	
SINGULAR	libro	casa	profesor	papel	vez	lápiz
PLURAL	libro**s**	casa**s**	profesor**es**	papel**es**	ve**ces**	lápi**ces**

Definite Articles

There are words that signal the gender of the noun. One of these is the *definite article.* In English, there is one definite article: *the.* In Spanish, there are four: **el, la, los, las.**

SUMMARY OF DEFINITE ARTICLES

	Masculine	Feminine
SINGULAR	**el** chico	**la** chica
PLURAL	**los** chicos	**las** chicas

CONTRACTIONS

a + el → **al**
de + el → **del**

Indefinite Articles

Another group of words that are used with nouns are the *indefinite articles:* **un, una,** (*a* or *an*) and **unos, unas** (*some* or *a few*).

	Masculine	Feminine
SINGULAR	**un** chico	**una** chica
PLURAL	**unos** chicos	**unas** chicas

Pronouns

Subject Pronouns	Direct Object Pronouns	Indirect Object Pronouns	Objects of Prepositions	Reflexive Pronouns
yo	**me**	**me**	**mí**	**me**
tú	**te**	**te**	**ti**	**te**
él, ella, usted	**lo, la**	**le**	**él, ella, usted**	**se**
nosotros, nosotras	**nos**	**nos**	**nosotros, nosotras**	**nos**
vosotros, vosotras	**os**	**os**	**vosotros, vosotras**	**os**
ellos, ellas, ustedes	**los, las**	**les**	**ellos, ellas, ustedes**	**se**

ADJECTIVES

Adjectives are words that describe nouns. The adjective must agree in gender (masculine or feminine) and number (singular or plural) with the noun it modifies. Adjectives that end in **-e** or a consonant only agree in number.

		Masculine	Feminine
Adjectives that end in **-o** or **-a**	**SINGULAR** **PLURAL**	chico alt**o** chicos alt**os**	chica alt**a** chicas alt**as**
Adjectives that end in **-e**	**SINGULAR** **PLURAL**	chico inteligent**e** chicos inteligent**es**	chica inteligent**e** chicas inteligent**es**
Adjectives that end in a consonant	**SINGULAR** **PLURAL**	examen difícil exámenes difíci**les**	clase difícil clases difíci**les**

Demonstrative Adjectives

	Masculine	Feminine		Masculine	Feminine
SINGULAR **PLURAL**	**este** chico **estos** chicos	**esta** chica **estas** chicas	**SINGULAR** **PLURAL**	**ese** chico **esos** chicos	**esa** chica **esas** chicas

When demonstratives are used as pronouns, they match the gender and number of the noun they replace and are written with an accent mark: **éste, éstos, ésta, éstas, ése, ésos, ésa, ésas.**

Possessive Adjectives

These words also modify nouns and show ownership or relationships between people (*my* car, *his* book, *her* mother).

Singular		Plural	
Masculine	Feminine	Masculine	Feminine
mi libro	**mi** casa	**mis** libros	**mis** casas
tu libro	**tu** casa	**tus** libros	**tus** casas
su libro	**su** casa	**sus** libros	**sus** casas
nuestro libro	**nuestra** casa	**nuestros** libros	**nuestras** casas
vuestro libro	**vuestra** casa	**vuestros** libros	**vuestras** casas

Comparatives

Comparatives are used to compare people or things. With comparisons of inequality, the same structure is used with adjectives, adverbs, or nouns. With comparisons of equality, **tan** is used with adjectives and adverbs, and **tanto/a/os/as** with nouns.

COMPARISONS OF INEQUALITY

más / **menos**	+	adjective / adverb / noun	+ **que**	**más** / **menos**	+ **de** + number

COMPARISONS OF EQUALITY

tan + adjective or adverb + **como**
tanto/a/os/as + noun + **como**

These adjectives have irregular comparative forms.

bueno(a) *good*	malo(a) *bad*	joven *young*	viejo(a) *old*
mejor(es) *better*	**peor(es)** *worse*	**menor(es)** *younger*	**mayor(es)** *older*

Ordinal Numbers

Ordinal numbers are used to express ordered sequences. They agree in number and gender with the noun they modify. The ordinal numbers **primero** and **tercero** drop the final **o** before a singular, masculine noun. Ordinal numbers are seldom used after 10. Cardinal numbers are used instead: **Alfonso XIII, Alfonso Trece.**

1st	**primero/a**	**5th**	**quinto/a**	**9th**	**noveno/a**
2nd	**segundo/a**	**6th**	**sexto/a**	**10th**	**décimo/a**
3rd	**tercero/a**	**7th**	**séptimo/a**		
4th	**cuarto/a**	**8th**	**octavo/a**		

Affirmative and Negative Expressions

Affirmative	Negative
algo	**nada**
alguien	**nadie**
alguno (algún), -a	**ninguno (ningún), -a**
o ... o	**ni ... ni**
siempre	**nunca**

Interrogative words

¿Adónde?	**¿Cuándo?**	**¿De dónde?**	**¿Qué?**
¿Cómo?	**¿Cuánto(a)?**	**¿Dónde?**	**¿Quién(es)?**
¿Cuál(es)?	**¿Cuántos(as)?**	**¿Por qué?**	

Adverbs

Adverbs make the meaning of a verb, an adjective, or another adverb more definite. These are some common adverbs of frequency.

siempre	*always*	**casi nunca**	*almost never*
nunca	*never*	**a veces**	*sometimes*
todos los días	*every day*		

Prepositions

Prepositions are words that show the relationship of a noun or pronoun to another word. These are common prepositions in Spanish.

a	*to*	**debajo de**	*under*	**hacia**	*toward*
al lado de	*next to*	**delante**	*before*	**hasta**	*until*
antes de	*before*	**desde**	*from*	**para**	*for, in order to*
arriba	*over, above*	**detrás de**	*behind*	**por**	*for, by*
con	*with*	**en**	*in, on*	**sin**	*without*
de	*of, from*	**encima de**	*over, on top of*		

VERBS

Present Tense of Regular Verbs

In Spanish, we use a formula to conjugate regular verbs. The endings change in each person, but the stem of the verb remains the same.

Infinitive	habl**ar**		com**er**		escrib**ir**	
Present	habl**o**	habl**amos**	com**o**	com**emos**	escrib**o**	escrib**imos**
	habl**as**	habl**áis**	com**es**	com**éis**	escrib**es**	escrib**ís**
	habl**a**	habl**an**	com**e**	com**en**	escrib**e**	escrib**en**

Verbs with Irregular *yo* Forms

hacer		poner		saber		salir		traer	
hago	hacemos	**pongo**	ponemos	**sé**	sabemos	**salgo**	salimos	**traigo**	traemos
haces	hacéis	pones	ponéis	sabes	sabéis	sales	salís	traes	traéis
hace	hacen	pone	ponen	sabe	saben	sale	salen	trae	traen

tener		venir		ver		conocer	
tengo	tenemos	**vengo**	venimos	**veo**	vemos	**conozco**	conocemos
tienes	tenéis	vienes	venís	ves	veis	conoces	conocéis
tiene	tienen	viene	vienen	ve	ven	conoce	conocen

Verbs with Irregular Forms

ser		estar		ir	
soy	somos	estoy	estamos	voy	vamos
eres	sois	estás	estáis	vas	vais
es	son	está	están	va	van

Present Progressive

The present progressive in English is formed by using the verb *to be* plus the *-ing* form of another verb. In Spanish, the present progressive is formed by using the verb **estar** plus the **-ndo** form of another verb.

-ar verbs	**-er** and **-ir** verbs
hablar → estoy habl**ando** trabajar → está trabaj**ando**	comer → estamos com**iendo** escribir → estás escrib**iendo**

For **-er** and **-ir** verbs with a stem that ends in a vowel, the **-iendo** changes to **-yendo:**
leer → están le**yendo**

Stem-Changing Verbs

In Spanish, some verbs have an irregular stem in the present tense. The final vowel of the stem changes from **e → ie, o → ue, u → ue,** and **e → i** in all forms except **nosotros** and **vosotros**.

e → ie		**o → ue**		**u → ue**		**e → i**	
preferir		**poder**		**jugar**		**pedir**	
pref**ie**ro	preferimos	p**ue**do	podemos	j**ue**go	jugamos	p**i**do	pedimos
pref**ie**res	preferís	p**ue**des	podéis	j**ue**gas	jugáis	p**i**des	pedís
pref**ie**re	pref**ie**ren	p**ue**de	p**ue**den	j**ue**ga	j**ue**gan	p**i**de	p**i**den

Some **e → ie** stem-changing verbs are:		Some **o → ue** stem-changing verbs are:		Some **e → i** stem-changing verbs are:
empezar	**venir**	**almorzar**	**dormir**	**vestirse**
pensar	**merendar**	**llover**	**probar**	**servir**
querer	**calentar**	**encontrar**	**acostarse**	
nevar	**tener**	**volver**	**costar**	

The Verbs *gustar* and *encantar*

The verb endings for **gustar** and **encantar** always agree with what is liked or loved. The indirect object pronouns always precede the verb forms.

gustar (to like)		encantar (to really like or love)	
one thing:	more than one:	one thing:	more than one:
me **te** **le** } **gusta** **nos** **os** **les**	**me** **te** **le** } **gustan** **nos** **os** **les**	**me** **te** **le** } **encanta** **nos** **os** **les**	**me** **te** **le** } **encantan** **nos** **os** **les**

Verbs with Reflexive Pronouns

If the subject and object of a verb are the same, include the reflexive pronoun with the verb.

lavarse		ponerse		vestirse	
me lavo	**nos** lavamos	**me** pongo	**nos** ponemos	**me** visto	**nos** vestimos
te lavas	**os** laváis	**te** pones	**os** ponéis	**te** vistes	**os** vestís
se lava	**se** lavan	**se** pone	**se** ponen	**se** viste	**se** visten

Here are other verbs with reflexive pronouns.

acostarse	**bañarse**	**maquillarse**	**secarse**
afeitarse	**levantarse**	**peinarse**	**sentirse**

Preterite of Regular and Irregular Verbs

The preterite is used to talk about what happened at a specific point in time.

Infinitive	Preterite of Regular Verbs	
habl**ar**	habl**é**	habl**amos**
	habl**aste**	habl**asteis**
	habl**ó**	habl**aron**
com**er**	com**í**	com**imos**
	com**iste**	com**isteis**
	com**ió**	com**ieron**
escrib**ir**	escrib**í**	escrib**imos**
	escrib**iste**	escrib**isteis**
	escrib**ió**	escrib**ieron**

hacer	ir	ser	ver
hice	fui	fui	vi
hiciste	fuiste	fuiste	viste
hizo	fue	fue	vio
hicimos	fuimos	fuimos	vimos
hicisteis	fuisteis	fuisteis	visteis
hicieron	fueron	fueron	vieron

sacar	llegar	comenzar
saqué	llegué	comencé
sacaste	llegaste	comenzaste
sacó	llegó	comenzó
sacamos	llegamos	comenzamos
sacasteis	llegasteis	comenzasteis
sacaron	llegaron	comenzaron

Imperative Mood

The imperative is used to tell people to do things. Its forms are sometimes referred to as *commands*. Regular affirmative commands are formed by dropping the **s** from the end of the **tú** form of the verb. For negative commands, switch the **-as** ending to **-es** and the **-es** ending to **-as.**

(tú) hablas → habla (no hables)	you speak → speak (don't speak)
(tú) escribes → escribe (no escribas)	you write → write (don't write)
(tú) pides → pide (no pidas)	you ask for → ask for (don't ask for)

Some verbs have irregular **tú** imperative forms.

tener → ten (no tengas)	ser → sé (no seas)
venir → ven (no vengas)	hacer → haz (no hagas)
poner → pon (no pongas)	salir → sal (no salgas)
ir → ve (no vayas)	decir → di (no digas)

The Verbs *ser* and *estar*

Both **ser** and **estar** mean *to be*, but they differ in their uses.

Use **ser:**

1. with nouns to identify and define the subject
   La mejor estudiante de la clase es Katia.
2. with **de** to indicate place of origin, ownership, or material
   Carmen es de Venezuela.
   Este libro es de mi abuela.
   La blusa es de algodón.
3. to describe identifying characteristics, such as physical and personality traits, nationality, religion, and profession
   Mi tío es profesor. Es simpático e inteligente.
4. to express the time, date, season, or where an event is taking place
   Hoy es sábado y la fiesta es a las ocho.

Use **estar:**

1. to indicate location or position of the subject (but not events)
   Lima está en Perú.
2. to describe a condition that is subject to change
   Maricarmen está triste.
3. with the present participle (**-ndo** form) to describe an action in progress
   Mario está escribiendo un poema.
4. to convey the idea of *to look, to feel, to seem, to taste*
   Tu hermano está muy guapo hoy.
   La sopa está deliciosa.

Common Expressions

EXPRESSIONS WITH *TENER*

tener ... años	*to be . . . years old*	**tener (mucha) prisa**	*to be in a (big) hurry*
tener mucho calor	*to be very hot*	**tener que**	*to have to*
tener ganas de...	*to feel like . . .*	**tener (la) razón**	*to be right*
tener mucho frío	*to be very cold*	**tener mucha sed**	*to be very thirsty*
tener mucha hambre	*to be very hungry*	**tener mucho sueño**	*to be very sleepy*
tener mucho miedo	*to be very afraid*	**tener mucha suerte**	*to be very lucky*

EXPRESSIONS OF TIME

To ask how long someone has been doing something, use:
¿Cuánto tiempo hace que + present tense?

To say how long someone has been doing something, use:
Hace + quantity of time + **que** + present tense.
Hace **seis meses** que **vivo en Los Ángeles.**
You can also use:
present tense + **desde hace** + quantity of time
Vivo en Los Ángeles desde hace **seis meses.**

WEATHER EXPRESSIONS

Hace muy buen tiempo.	*The weather is very nice.*
Hace mucho calor.	*It's very hot.*
Hace fresco.	*It's cool.*
Hace mucho frío.	*It's very cold.*
Hace muy mal tiempo.	*The weather is very bad.*
Hace mucho sol.	*It's very sunny.*
Hace mucho viento.	*It's very windy.*
But:	
Está lloviendo mucho.	*It's raining a lot.*
Hay mucha neblina.	*It's very foggy.*
Está nevando.	*It's snowing.*
Está nublado.	*It's overcast.*

Vocabulario español-inglés

This vocabulary includes almost all words in the textbook, both active (for production) and passive (for recognition only). An entry in **boldface** type indicates that the word or phrase is active. Active words and phrases are practiced in the chapter and are listed on the **Repaso de gramática** and **Repaso de vocabulario** pages at the end of each chapter. You are expected to know and be able to use active vocabulary.

All other words are for recognition only. These words are found in exercises, in optional and visual material, in **Instrucciones** on page xxii, in **Geocultura,** which is referenced by chapter (1G), **Comparaciones, Leamos y escribamos, También se puede decir,** and **Literatura y variedades.** You can usually understand the meaning of these words and phrases from the context or you can look them up in this vocabulary index. Many words have more than one definition; the definitions given here correspond to the way the words are used in ***¡Exprésate!.***

Nouns are listed with definite articles and plural forms when the plural forms aren't formed according to general rules. The number after each entry refers to the chapter where the word or phrase first appears or where it becomes an active vocabulary word. This vocabulary index follows the rules of the **Real Academia,** with **ch** and **ll** in the same sequence as in the English alphabet.

Stem changes are indicated in parentheses after the verb: **poder (ue).**

a *to,* 3; *on,* 4; *at,* 8; a base de *based on,* 6; a continuación *that follows,* 7; a finales *at the end,* 10G; **a la (última) moda** *in the (latest) style,* 8; a la vez *at the same time,* 8; **a la vuelta** *around the corner,* 10; **A ...les gusta...** *They like to . . .,* 3; **a menudo** *often,* 5; **¿A qué hora vas a...?** *What time are you going to . . .?,* 4; **a tiempo** *on time,* 4; **a todo dar** *great,* 9; **Estuvo a todo dar.** *It was great.,* 9; a través de *through,* 5G; **a veces** *sometimes,* 3
abordar *to board,* 10
abrazar *to hug,* 9
el abrazo *hug,* 9
el abrigo (over)*coat,* 8
abril *April,* 1
abrir *to open,* 4; **abrir regalos** *to open gifts,* 9
la abuela *grandmother,* 5
el abuelo *grandfather,* 5
los abuelos *grandparents,* 5
aburrido(a) *boring,* 2; **estar aburrido(a)** *to be bored,* 7
acabar de *to just have done something,* 7
acampar *to camp,* 10
acariciar *to caress,* 7
la acción *action,* 2
el aceite de oliva *olive oil,* 1G
el acento *accent,* 1; el acento ortográfico *written accent,* 8
acerca de *about,* 8
acompañar *to go with,* 6; *to accompany,* 1G; estar acompañada *to be accompanied,* 3
acordarse (ue) *to remember,* 9
acostarse (ue) *to go to bed,* 7
la actividad *activity,* 3
activo(a) *active,* 2
la actualidad *present time,* 6
el acuerdo *agreement;* **Estoy de acuerdo.** *I agree.,* 6; **No estoy de acuerdo.** *I disagree.,* 6
adaptado(a) *adapted,* 5G
además *besides,* 8
Adiós. *Goodbye.,* 1
adivinar *to guess,* 2
el adjetivo *adjective,* 5
la admiración *admiration,* 1
admirar *to admire,* 10
el adolescente *adolescent,* 3
¿adónde? *where?,* 8; **Adónde fuiste?** *Where did you go?,* 8; **¿Adónde vas...?** *Where do you go . . .?,* 3
la aduana *customs,* 10
el adulto *adult,* 7
los aeróbicos *aerobics,* 7; hacer aeróbicos *to do aerobics,* 7
el aeropuerto *airport,* 10
afeitarse *to shave,* 7
afuera *outside,* 3
las afueras *suburbs,* 5
la agencia inmobiliaria *real estate agency,* 5
el agente, la agente *agent,* 10
agitar *to shake,* 3
agosto *August,* 1
el agua *water,* 6
el águila *eagle,* 7
ahí *there,* 4
ahora *now,* 9
ahorrar *to save money,* 8
el aire *air,* 3; el aire central *central air conditioning,* 5; el aire libre *open air,* 8
el ajedrez *chess,* 2
el ají *hot pepper,* 10G
el ajo *garlic,* 6
ajustado(a) *tight-fitting,* 8
al (a + el) *to, to the,* 3; *upon,* 6; al fin *finally,* 10; **al lado de** *next to,* 5
la alberca *swimming pool,* 3
alcanzar *to reach,* 7G
la alcoba *bedroom,* 5
alegre *happy,* 2
el alemán *German,* 4
el alfabeto *alphabet,* 1
algo *something, anything,* 4; **algo** + adjective *kind of* + adjective, 2
el algodón *cotton,* 8; **de algodón** *made of cotton,* 8
algún día *one day,* 10
algunas *some,* 2
el alimento *food,* 6
alistarse *to get ready,* 7

allá *there,* 8
allí *there,* 10
el almacén *department store,* 8
el almanaque *almanac,* 1G
almorzar (ue) *to have lunch,* 5
el almuerzo *lunch,* 4
Aló *Hello. (telephone greeting),* 8
el alpinismo *mountain climbing,* 7
alquilar *to rent,* 3; **alquilar videos** *to rent videos,* 3
alrededor *around,* 6
el altiplano *high plateau,* 10G
alto(a) *tall,* 2
la altura *height,* 6G
amanecer *to dawn,* 9
el amarillo *yellow,* 1G
amarillo(a) *yellow,* 8
el ambiente *atmosphere,* 5G
ambos *both,* 5G
amigable *friendly,* 2
el amigo(a) *friend,* 1; **mi mejor amigo(a)** *my best friend,* 1
el amor *love,* 8; **de amor** *romance,* 2
amueblado(a) *furnished,* 5
analítico(a) *analytical,* 2
anaranjado(a) *orange,* 8
ancho *width,* 5G; *wide,* 8
andar *to walk, to go,* 2; andar en bicicleta *to ride a bike,* 3; dime con quien andas y te diré quien eres *a person is known by the company he/she keeps,* 2
andino(a) *of the Andes,* 7G
el anfibio *amphibian,* 2G
la anguila *eel,* 7
el ángulo *angle,* 7
el anillo *ring,* 8
el animal *animal,* 2
el aniversario *anniversary,* 9
el año year, 2; **el Año Nuevo** *New Year,* 9; **el año pasado** *last year,* 9; **¿Cuántos años tiene...?** *How old is . . .?,* 2; **¿Cuántos años tienes?** *How old are you?,* 2
anoche *last night,* 8
anteayer *day before yesterday,* 8
anterior *previous,* 9
antes *before,* 1; **antes de** *before,* 7; de antes *from before,* 4
antiguo(a) *old,* 6G
antipático(a) *unfriendly,* 2
añadir *to add,* 6
aparecer *to appear,* 6
el apartamento *apartment,* 5
apasionado(a) *passionate,* 2
apellido *last name,* 2
apetecer *to appeal,* 6
aplicar *to apply,* 2
aportar *to contribute,* 8G
aprender *to learn,* 1
apropiado(a) *appropriate,* 7
aproximadamente *approximately,* 2
los apuntes *notes,* 8
aquella *that,* 6
aquello *that,* 4
aquí *here,* 6
árabe *Arab,* 5G
el árbol *tree,* 1; la copa del árbol *top of the tree,* 4G
los aretes *earrings,* 8
la argamasa *mortar,* 10G
argentino(a) *Argentine,* 7
árido(a) *dry,* 10G
la armonía *harmony,* 2
armonizar *to harmonize,* 7G
el arquitecto *architect,* 3G
arquitectónico(a) *architectural,* 10G
la arquitectura *architecture,* 2G
arreglar *to pick up,* 5; **arreglar el cuarto** *to pick up the room,* 5
el arrendamiento *rental,* 10
la arroba *@,* 1
el arroz *rice,* 6
el arte *art,* 4; las artes plásticas *sculpture,* 2
la artesanía *crafts,* 4
el artista, la artista *artist,* 1
artístico(a) *artistic,* 2
asegurar *to reassure,* 6
el asentamiento *colony, settlement,* 8G
el aseo *restroom,* 10
así *like this;* así que *so,* 8; Así es, *That's how it is.,* 2
asistente *assistant,* 10
asistir(a) *to attend,* 4
asomar *to peek out,* 9
el asterisco *asterisk,* 7
atlético(a) *athletic,* 2
el atole *Mexican drink made of cornmeal, milk or water, and flavoring,* 6
atraer *to attract,* 1G
atravesar *to cross,* 10G
atreverse *to dare,* 9
el atún *tuna,* 6
los audífonos *headphones,* 8
el auditorio *auditorium,* 4
aun *even,* 2
aún *still,* 10
aunque *even though,* 6
el autobús *bus,* 10
el autor *author,* 7
el autorretrato *self-portrait,* 6G
avanzado(a) *advanced,* 10G
el ave (pl. las aves) *bird,* 4G
la aventura *adventure,* 2
averiguar *to find out,* 10
el avión *airplane,* 10; por avión *by plane,* 10
¡Ay no! *Oh, no!,* 6
¡ay! *ouch!,* 8
ayer *yesterday,* 8
el aymara *indigenous language in Peru,* 10G
la ayuda *help,* 6
ayudar *to help,* 5; **ayudar en casa** *to help out at home,* 5; estamos ayudando *we are helping,* 3
el azúcar *sugar,* 6
el azul *blue,* 1G
azul *blue,* 5

la bahía *bay,* 8G
bailar *to dance,* 3; bailando *dancing,* 1; ponerse a bailar *to start dancing,* 3
la bailarina *dancer (fem.),* 3
el baile *dance,* 3
bajar de peso *to lose weight,* 7
bajo(a) *short,* 2
balanceado(a) *balanced,* 6
el balcón *balcony,* 5
el ballet *ballet,* 1
el baloncesto *basketball,* 3
bañarse *to bathe,* 7
la bandeja *platter,* 7G
la bandera *banner,* 9
el baño *bathroom,* 5; *restroom,* 10
barato(a) *inexpensive,* 8
la barbacoa *barbecue,* 3G
el barco *boat,* 10; el barquito *little boat,* 5
la barranca *cliff,* 6G
el barrio *neighborhood,* 7G
básico(a) *basic,* 6
el básquetbol *basketball,* 3
basta *it's enough,* 5
bastante + adjective *quite, pretty* + adjective, 2
la basura *trash,* 5; **sacar la basura** *to take out the trash,* 5
la batalla *battle,* 3G
el batido *milkshake,* 8
el bebé, la bebé *baby,* 1
beber *to drink,* 4; **beber algo** *to drink something,* 4
la bebida *drink,* 6
la beca *scholarship,* 10
el béisbol *baseball,* 3
bello(a) *beautiful,* 2G
la biblioteca *library,* 4
la bicicleta *bike,* 3; **montar en bicicleta** *to ride a bike,* 3
bien *all right, fine,* 1; *really,* 2; bien dicho *well said,* 6; **está bien** *it's okay,* 3; **Estoy bien.** *I'm fine.,* 1; **me parece bien** *it's all right/seems fine to me,* 5; **quedar bien** *to fit well,* 8; **Que te vaya bien.** *Hope things go well for you.,* 9
bienvenido *welcome,* 10
el billete *ticket,* 10
la billetera *wallet,* 10

la biología *biology,* 4
blanco(a) *white,* 8; **en blanco** *blank,* 8
el blanquillo *egg,* 6
la blusa *blouse,* 8
la boca *mouth,* 7
el bocadillo *sandwich* (Spain), 6, *finger food* (Dom. Rep.), 9
el bocadito *small servings of food,* 7G
las bocas *finger food* (Costa Rica), 9
la boda *wedding,* 9
la boleta *ticket,* 10
el boleto de avión *plane ticket,* 10
el bolígrafo *pen,* 4
la bolsa *purse,* 8; *bag,* 8; *travel bag,* 10
la bomba *music and dance style,* 2G
la bombilla *straw used for sipping* ***mate,*** 7
bonito(a) *pretty,* 2
el borde *edge,* 7G
el borrador *rough draft,* 1
el bosque *forest,* 2G; el bosque húmedo *rain forest,* 4G
la botana *finger food* (Mex.), 9
botar *to throw out,* 5
las botas *boots,* 8
el bote *boat,* 9G; **el bote de vela** *sailboat,* 10; **pasear en bote de vela** *to go out in a sailboat,* 10
el brazo *arm,* 7
brillar *to shine,* 7
brindar *to offer,* 5
el bróculi *broccoli,* 6
bueno(a) *good,* 2; **Buenas noches.** *Good evening., Good night.,* 1; **Buenas tardes.** *Good afternoon.,* 1; **Buenos días.** *Good morning.,* 1
Bueno. *Hello. (telephone greeting),* 8
burlarse de *to make fun of,* 8
el burro *donkey,* 1
buscar *to look for,* 7; **buscar un pasatiempo** *to find a hobby,* 7; búsquenme *look for me,* 3

el caballo de paso *horse with high-stepping gait,* 10G
caber *to fit,* 10G
la cabeza *head,* 7
el cacao *cocoa,* 6G
cada *each,* xxii; cada uno(a) *each one,* 6; cada vez *each time,* 8
el café *coffee,* 6; **el café (con leche)** *coffee (with milk),* 6; *brown,* 1G; **de color café** *brown,* 5
la cafetería *cafeteria,* 4; *coffee shop,* 6
la caída de agua *waterfall,* 7G
el caimán *caiman (reptile),* 7G
la caja *box,* 9
el cajero automático *automatic teller machine,* 10
la calabaza *squash, pumpkin,* 6G; la calabacita *gourd used for* ***mate*** *tea,* 7G
los calcetines *socks,* 8; **un par de calcetines** *a pair of socks,* 8
la calculadora *calculator,* 4
la calefacción *heating,* 5; la calefacción central *central heating,* 5
el calendario *calendar,* 1
calentar (ie) *to heat up,* 6
caliente *hot,* 6
callado(a) *quiet,* 5
la calle *street,* 5
el calor *heat,* 3; **Hace calor.** *It's hot.,* 3; **tener calor** *to be hot,* 7
la caloría *calorie,* 6
la cama *bed,* 5; **hacer la cama** *to make the bed,* 5
la cámara *camera,* 10; **la cámara desechable** *disposable camera,* 10
el camarero *waiter,* 6
cambiar *to change,* 4
cambiar dinero *to change money,* 10
el cambio *change,* 9
caminar *to walk,* 7
el camino *path,* 10G
el camión *bus (Mex.),* 10
la camisa *shirt,* 8
la camiseta *T-shirt,* 8; la camiseta deportiva *sport shirt,* 8
el camote *sweet potato,* 4G
el campo *countryside,* 5
la canción *song,* 8
candidato(a) *candidate,* 4
la canoa *canoe,* 10
el cañón *canyon,* 6G
canoso(a) *gray-haired,* 5
cansado(a) *tired,* 7; **estar cansado(a)** *to be tired,* 7
cantar *to sing,* 3; cantaba *he sang,* 9
el cantar *singing,* 2
la cantidad *amount,* 2; *quantity,* 6; las cantidades *large numbers,* 6
el canto *song,* 1G
la capilla *chapel,* 3G
la capital *capital,* 1G
el capítulo *chapter,* 1
la cara *face,* 7; cara de tortilla *tortilla face,* 1
el carácter *character,* 5
la característica *characteristic,* 6
caracterizar *to characterize,* 5G
la cárcel *jail,* 8
caribeño(a) *Caribbean,* 4G
el cariño *affection; (addressing someone) dear, 3;* con cariño *affectionately,* 10
la carne *meat, beef,* 6; la carne de res *beef,* 6; la carne molida *ground beef,* 6
el carnet de identidad *ID,* 10
caro(a) *expensive,* 8
la carpeta *folder,* 4
la carreta *cart,* 4G
el carro *car,* 2
la carroza *float,* 9G
la carta *letter,* 3
la casa *house,* 5; **ayudar en casa** *to help out at home,* 5; **la casa de...** *. . .'s house,* 3; **decorar la casa** *to decorate the house,* 9
el casabe *flat, dry bread made from manioc,* 9G
casarse *to get married,* 10
la cascada *waterfall,* 2G
la cáscara *shell,* 2G
casi *almost,* 3; **casi nunca** *almost never,* 3; **casi siempre** *almost always,* 3
el caso *case,* 2
castaño(a) *dark brown,* 5
las castañuelas *castanets,* 1G
el castellano *Spanish,* 1G
el castillo *castle,* 2G
el catalán *language from Catalonia, Spain,* 1G
el catálogo *catalog,* 8
la catarata *cataract, waterfall,* 7G
la catedral *cathedral,* 1G
catorce *fourteen,* 1
el cayo *key (island),* 8G
el cazador *hunter,* 7G
la cebolla *onion,* 10G
celebérrimo(a) *most famous,* 8
la celebración *celebration,* 1
celebrar *to celebrate,* 9; celebrará *will celebrate,* 8; se celebra *is celebrated,* 2G
célebre *famous,* 8
celeridad *speed,* 8
celta *Celtic,* 1G
la cena *dinner,* 6
cenar *to eat dinner,* 6
el centro *downtown,* 10; *center,* 3G
el centro comercial *mall,* 3
el cepillo de dientes *toothbrush,* 7
la cerámica *pottery,* 4
cerca de *close to, near,* 5
cercano(a) *close,* 5
los cereales *cereal,* 6
el cerebelo *cerebellum,* 8
el cerebro *brain,* 8
la ceremonia *ceremony,* 6
cero *zero,* 1
cerrado(a) *closed,* 1
cerrar (ie) *to close,* 8
el césped *grass,* 5
la cesta de paja *straw basket,* 8G
el ceviche *dish made with seafood, lemon, and seasonings,* 10G
chao *Bye,* 9
la chaqueta *jacket,* 8

charlar *to talk, chat,* 9
el chayote *type of squash,* 4G
la chica *girl,* 8
chicano(a) *Mexican that has emigrated to the United States,* 3G
el chile *pepper,* chile en nogada *peppers in walnut and spice sauce,* 6
el chileno *Chilean,* 5
la chimenea *fireplace,* 5
el chiste *joke,* 9
el choclo *corn on the cob,* 5G
el chocolate *chocolate,* 6; *hot chocolate,* 6
el churro *sugar-coated fritter,* 6
el ciclismo *cycling,* 1
ciego(a) *blind,* 5
el cielo *heaven,* 3
cien *one hundred,* 2
la ciencia ficción *science fiction,* 2
las ciencias *science,* 4; **...de ciencias** *science . . .,*1
el científico *scientist,* 6
ciento un(o) *one hundred one,* 8
cierto(a) *true,* xxii
la cifra *number,* 8
la cima *mountain top,* 7G
cinco *five,* 1
cincuenta *fifty,* 2
el cine *movie theater,* 3
el cinturón *belt,* 8
el círculo *circle,* 3
el citrón *lemon,* 6
la ciudad *city,* 5
¡Claro que sí! *Of course!,* 4
claro(a) *clear,* 6G
la clase *class,* 3; **después de clases** *after class,* 3
clasificar *to classify,* 6
clavar *to nail,* 10
el clavo *nail,* 10
el cliente, la cliente *client,* 8
el club de... *the . . . club,* 4
el cobre *copper,* 6G
cocer *to cook,* 3
el coche *car,* 10
la cocina *kitchen,* 5; *cooking,* 3G
cocinar *to cook,* 5
el coco *coconut,* 2G
el cocodrilo *crocodile,* 8G
el código *code,* 2G
cohabitar *to live together,* 8G
la cola: **hacer cola** *to wait in line,* 10
el colectivo *bus* (Bol., Perú, Ecuador), 10
el colegio *school,* 3
colgar (ue) *to hang,* 9
la colina *hill,* 9G
la colonia *colony,* 7G
el colonizador *colonist,* 6G
el color *color,* 5
el colorido *coloring,* 7G
colorido(a) *colorful,* 4G
la columna *column,* xxii
los combates *battles,* 10
la combinación *combination,* 1
combinar *to combine,* 5G
el comedor *dining room,* 5
comenzar (ie) *to start,* 10; **comenzar un viaje** *to begin a trip,* 10; comiencen *begin,* 8
comer *to eat,* 3; se comen *are eaten,* 2G
el comercio *commerce,* 3G
el comestible *food,* 3
cómico(a) *funny,* 2
la comida *food,* 2, *lunch,* 6; **la comida china (italiana, mexicana)** *Chinese (Italian, Mexican) food,* 2; la comida típica *traditional food,* 6
como *like,* 2; as, 9; **como siempre** *as always,* 9
¿cómo? *how?, what?,* 1; **¿Cómo eres?** *What are you like?,* 2; **¿Cómo es...?** *What is . . . like?,* 2; **¿Cómo está(s)?** *How are you?,* 1; **¿Cómo me queda(n)...?** *How does . . . look?,* 8; **¿Cómo se escribe...?** *How do you spell . . .?,* 1; **¿Cómo se llama?** *What's his (her/your) name?,* 1; **¿Cómo te llamas?** *What's your name? (fam.),* 1
la compañera de clase *classmate (female),* 1; **una compañera de clase** *a (female) classmate,* 1
el compañero de clase *classmate (male),* 1; **un compañero de clase** *a (male) classmate,* 1
la comparación *comparison,* 1
comparar *to compare,* 8
compasivo(a) *compassionate,* 6
el complemento directo *direct object,* 6
completar *to complete,* xxii
completo *complete,* 6; por completo *completely,* 6
comprar *to buy,* 8; comprarías *you would buy,* 8
las compras *shopping,* 2; estar de compras *to be on a shopping trip,* 8; **ir de compras** *to go shopping,* 3
la comprensión *comprehension,* 10
comprender *to understand,* 2; nos comprendemos *we understand each other,* 2
la computación *computer science,* 4
la computadora *computer,* 4
común *common,* 9
comunicar *to communicate,* 5
la comunidad *community,* 1
con *with,* 3; con base en *based on,* xxii; **con mis amigos** *with my friends,* 3; **con mi familia** *with my family,* 3; con motivo de *on the occasion of,* 9; **¿Con qué frecuencia vas...?** *How often do you go . . .?,* 3; con relación a *in relation to,* 5
el concierto *concert,* 4
el concurso *competition,* 9G
el condominio *condominium,* 5
conectar *to connect,* 8G
confundido(a) *confused,* 4
confundir *to confuse,* 10
el conjunto *musical group,* 3G
conmemorar *commemorate,* 3G
conmigo *with me,* 3
conocer *to know, to meet, to be familiar with,* 9; **conocimos...** *we visited . . .,* 10; **quiero conocer...** *I want to see . . .,* 10; se conoce *is known,* 2G
conocido(a) *known,* 2G
el conocimiento *knowledge,* 7
conquistar *to conquer,* 10
conseguir (i, i) *to get,* 10
el consejo *advice,* 7
conservar *to preserve,* 2G
considerar *to consider,* 2; *to regard,* 9
constituir *to make up,* 6
construir *to build,* 3G; construye *construct,* 10; fue construido *was built,* 3G
el consultorio médico *doctor's office,* 7
consumir *to consume,* 6; se consumen *are consumed,* 6
el consumo *consumption,* 6
contar (ue) *to count,* 1; *to tell,* 4; contando *counting,* 1; **contar chistes** *to tell jokes,* 9; contar con *to count on,* 10; cuenta *tells,* 6; cuentan *it is told,* 6
contemplar *to contemplate,* 9
contemporáneo *contemporary,* 1G
contener (ie) *to contain,* 10G; que contengan *that contain,* 10
contento(a) *happy,* 7; **estar contento(a)** *to be happy,* 7
contestar *to answer,* xxii
contigo *with you,* 3
el continente *continent,* 6
continuo *continual,* 8
contra *against,* 10
al contrario *to the contrary,* 6
la contribución *contribution,* 2G
contribuir *to contribute,* 8G
el control de seguridad *security checkpoint,* 10
controlar *to control,* 3G
el convento *convent,* 3G
la conversación *conversation,* xxii
convertirse (ie) *to become,* 10
la copa *treetop,* 4G
el coquí *small tree frog,* 2G
el corazón *heart,* 7G
la cordillera *mountain range,* 2G
el coro *chorus,* 2
correcto(a) *right, correct,* xxii
corregir *to correct,* xxii
el correo electrónico *e-mail address,* 1; **¿Cuál es el correo electrónico**

de...? *What is . . .'s e-mail address?,* 1; **¿Cuál es tu correo electrónico?** *What's your e-mail address?,* 1
correr *to run,* 3
la correspondencia *correspondence,* 1
corresponder *to correspond,* xxii; le corresponde *it falls to him,* 5; que le correspondan *that correspond to it,* 9
correspondiente *corresponding,* 8
la corriente *current,* 8
cortar *to cut,* 5; **cortar el césped** *to cut the grass,* 5
la Corte Suprema *Supreme Court,* 6
corto(a) *short,* 5
la cosa *thing,* 4; **Necesito muchas cosas.** *I need lots of things.,* 4; **no es gran cosa** *it's not a big deal,* 5
coser *to sew,* 4
la costa *coast,* 3G
costar (ue) *to cost,* 8; costará *will cost,* 9
costeño(a) *coastal,* 10G
la costumbre *custom,* 5G
la creación *creation,* 3
crear *to create,* 7; creado por *created by,* 7G; fue creado *was created,* 3G
la creatividad *creativity,* 6G
creativo(a) *creative,* 2
crecer *to grow,* 9G; crecí *I grew up,* 3
creer *to believe,* 6; *to think,* 9
la crema *cream,* 6
la criatura *child,* 3
crudo(a) *raw,* 10G
el cuaderno *notebook,* 4
la cuadra *block,* 5
cual: los cuales *which,* 10
el cuadro *box, chart,* xxii; *painting,* 1
¿cuál? *what?, which?,* 4; **¿Cuál es el correo electrónico de...?** *What is . . .'s e-mail address?,* 1; **¿Cuál es el teléfono de...?** *What is . . .'s telephone number?,* 1; **¿Cuál es tu correo electrónico?** *What's your e-mail address?,* 1; **¿Cuál es tu materia preferida?** *What's your favorite subject?,* 4; **¿Cuál es tu teléfono?** *What's your telephone number?,* 1
cualquier *any,* 10
cualquiera *whichever,* 6G
cuando *when,* 3
¿cuándo? *when?,* 2; **¿Cuándo es el cumpleaños de...?** *When is . . .'s birthday?,* 2; **¿Cuándo es tu cumpleaños?** *When is your birthday?,* 2
¿cuánto(a)? *how much?,* 4
¡cuántos! *so many!,* 4
¿cuántos(as)? *How many . . .?,* 2; **¿Cuántos años tiene...?** *How old is . . .?,* 2; **¿Cuántos años tienes?** *How old are you?,* 2
cuarenta *forty,* 2
cuarto *quarter,* 4; **menos cuarto** *a quarter to (the hour),* 1; **y cuarto** *quarter past,* 1
el cuarto *room,* 5; **arreglar el cuarto** *to pick up the room,* 5
cuatro *four,* 1
cuatrocientos *four hundred,* 8
cubierto(a) *covered,* 3
la cuchara *spoon,* 6
el cuchillo *knife,* 6
el cuello *neck,* 7
la cuenta *bill,* 6
el cuento *story,* 4
el cuerno *horn,* 2G
el cuerpo *body,* 7
el cuerpo de bomberos *fire department,* 2G
cuesta(n)... *cost(s) . . .,* 8
la cueva *cave,* 1G
el cuidado *care, 1*; ten cuidado *take care,* 6
cuidadosamente *carefully,* 9
cuidar *to take care of,* 5; **cuidar a mis hermanos** *take care of my brothers and sisters,* 5
cuidarse *to take care of oneself,* 7; **cuidarse la salud** *to take care of one's health,* 7; **para cuidarte la salud debes...** *to take care of your health, you should . . .,* 7; **Para cuidarte mejor, debes...** *To take better care of yourself, you should . . .,* 7; **Cuídate.** *Take care.,* 9
culinario(a) *culinary,* 6
cultivar *to cultivate,* 6
el cultivo *crop,* 4G
la cultura *culture,* 1
el cumpleaños *birthday,* 9; **¿Cuándo es el cumpleaños de...?** *When is . . .'s birthday?,* 2; **¿Cuándo es tu cumpleaños?** *When is your birthday?,* 2; **el cumpleaños de...** *birthday of . . .,* 2; **la tarjeta de cumpleaños** *birthday card,* 8
curioso(a) *odd, unusual,* 1
la curva *curve,* 3G

dado(a) *given,* 7
la danza *dance,* 1G
dar *to give,* 7; le dan *they give,* 7; **no des** *don't give,* 7; se da *is held,* 8G
darse cuenta *to realize,* 8
el dato *fact,* 10
de *of, from, in, by,* 1; *made of,* 8; **...de ciencias** *science . . .,* 1; **de color café** *brown,* 5; **¿De dónde eres?** *Where are you from? (fam.),* 1; **¿De dónde es usted?** *Where are you from? (formal),* 1; **¿De dónde es...?** *Where is . . . from?,* 1; de...en... *from . . . to . . .,* 8; **... de español** *Spanish . . .,* 1; **de la mañana** *in the morning,* 1; **de la noche** *at night,* 1; **de la tarde** *in the afternoon, evening,* 1; de nuevo *again,* 7; de nada *you're welcome*; **¿De parte de quién?** *Who's calling?,* 8; ¿de quién? *about whom?,* 1; de todo *everything,* 8; de todo tipo *all kinds,* 8; de todos modos *in any event,* 8; de veras *really,* 8
debajo *underneath,* 8; **debajo de** *underneath,* 5
deber *should,* 6; ¿Debo...? *Should I . . .?,* 8; **No debes...** *You shouldn't . . .,* 7; se debe hacer *should be done,* 6
los deberes *chores,* 5; *responsibilities,* 5
debido a *due to,* 7G
el decibel *decibel,* 2
decidir *to decide,* xxii
decir *to say,* 3; bien dicho *well said,* 6; di *say,* 4; dice *says,* 3; diciéndome *telling me,* 9; me han dicho *they have told me,* 6; se dicen adiós *they say goodbye,* 3; si lo hubiera dicho *if I had said it,* 6; te diré *I'll tell you,* 2; yo he dicho *I have said,* 6
declarar *to declare,* 6
la decoración *decoration,* 9
decorar *to decorate,* 9; **decorar la casa** *to decorate the house,* 9
dedicado(a) a *dedicated to,* 2G
dedicar *to dedicate,* 4; es dedicada *is dedicated,* 5; dedicación *dedication,* 10; se dedica *is dedicated,* 2G
el dedo *finger,* 7; **el dedo del pie** *toe,* 4G
deducir *to deduce,* 7
la definición *definition,* 10
definido(a) *defined,* 8
definitivamente *definitely,* 8; *permanently,* 9
dejar *to allow,* 3; *to leave,* 10; **dejar un recado** *to leave a message,* 8
dejar de + infinitive *to stop doing something,* 7; **dejar de fumar** *to stop smoking,* 7
del (de + el) *of the,* 2
delante de *in front of,* 5
delgado(a) *thin,* 5
delicioso(a) *delicious,* 2
demasiado(a) *too much,* 7
demostrar (ue) *to show,* 10G

dentro *inside,* 9
el departamento *apartment (Mexico),* 5; *district (Peru),* 10
el dependiente, la dependiente *salesclerk,* 8
los deportes *sports,* 2
deportivo(a) (adj.) *sports,* 8
la derecha *right,* 1
el desarrollo *development,* 7G
desarrollar *to develop,* 4
el desastre *disaster,* 9
desayunar *to eat breakfast,* 6
el desayuno *breakfast,* 6
descansar *to rest,* 3
el descendiente *descendant,* 10
describir *to describe,* 5
descubrir *to discover,* 8; fue descubierto *was discovered,* 7G
desde *since,* 4; *from,* 10; ¿desde cuándo? *since when?,* 4; desde hace *since,* 6; desde joven *since her youth,* 8; desde luego *of course,* 7
desear *to want, to wish for, to desire,* 6; deseando *wanting to,* 8
desembarcar *to disembark, to deplane,* 10
desembocar *to flow,* 10G
el deseo *desire,* 9
desesperado(a) *desperate,* 6
el desfile *parade, procession,* 4G
el desierto *desert,* 5G
la despedida *farewell,* 9; la fiesta de despedida *goodbye party,* 10
despertarse (ie) *to wake up,* 7
despierto(a) *awake,* 7
después *after,* 3; *afterwards,* 4; **después de** *after,* 7; **después de clases** *after class,* 3
destinado(a) *destined,* 6
el destino *destination,* 10
el detalle *detail,* 7
determinar *to determine,* 7
detrás de *behind,* 5
devolver (ue) *to return something,* 8
di *say,* 8
el día *day,* 1; **algún día** *someday,* 10; **el Día de Acción de Gracias** *Thanksgiving Day,* 9; **el Día de la Independencia** *Independence Day,* 9; **el Día de la Madre** *Mother's Day,* 9; **el día de la semana** *day of the week,* 1; **el Día de los Enamorados** *Valentine's Day,* 9; **el Día del Padre** *Father's Day,* 9; **el día de tu santo** *your saint's day,* 9; **el día festivo** *holiday,* 9; **¿Qué día es hoy?** *What day is today?,* 1
diablado(a) *devilish,* 5G
el diablo *devil,* 7G
el diálogo *dialog,* xxii
diario(a) *daily,* 3G
dibujar *to draw,* 3
el dibujo *drawing,* xxii
el diccionario *dictionary,* 4
dice (inf. decir) *(he/she) says,* 4
la dicha *happiness,* 9
diciembre *December,* 1
el dictado *dictation,* 1
diecinueve *nineteen,* 1
dieciocho *eighteen,* 1
dieciséis *sixteen,* 1
diecisiete *seventeen,* 1
los dientes *teeth,* 7
la dieta *diet,* 7; **seguir una dieta sana** *to eat a balanced diet,* 7
diez *ten,* 1
diferente *different,* 2
difícil *difficult,* 4; **Es difícil.** *It's difficult.,* 4
Diga. *Hello. (telephone greeting),* 8
el dinero *money,* 8
el dinosaurio *dinosaur,* 1
el dios *god,* 6; gracias a Dios *thank goodness,* 6
la dirección *address,* 5; **Mi dirección es...** *My address is . . .,* 5
directamente *directly,* 4
director (-a) *director,* 10
el directorio de teléfono *phone book,* 1
disciplinado(a) *disciplined,* 2
el disco *record,* 8
el disco compacto (en blanco) *(blank) compact disc,* 8
diseñar *to design,* 3G; fue diseñado(a) *was designed,* 3G
el diseño *design,* 5G
el disfraz *costume,* 9G
disfrazar *to wear a costume,* 4G
disfrutar *to enjoy,* 2G
disponible *available,* 7
dispuesto(a) *willing,* 6G
la distancia *distance,* 10
distinguirse *to distinguish oneself,* 10
distinto(a) *different,* 6G
la diversión *fun,* 2
diverso(a) *diverse,* 6
divertido(a) *fun,* 2; **¡Qué divertido!** *What fun!,* 10
divertirse (ie) *to have fun,* 1; diviértanse *have a good time* (pl.), 1; que me divierta *to have fun,* 9
doblado(a) *folded,* 9
doble *double,* 5
doce *twelve,* 1
el documento *document,* 1
el dólar *dollar,* 8
doler (ue) *to hurt,* 7; **Me duele(n)...** *My . . . hurt(s).,* 7; **¿Te duele algo?** *Does something hurt?,* 7
el domingo *Sunday,* 1; **los domingos** *on Sundays,* 3
dominicano(a) *Dominican,* 9
donde *where,* 8; *to the house of,* 9
¿dónde? *where?,* 5; **¿Dónde se puede...?** *Where can I . . .?,* 10
dorado(a) *golden,* 2
dormido(a) *asleep,* 7
dormir (ue) *to sleep,* 5; **dormir lo suficiente** *to get enough sleep,* 7
el dormitorio *bedroom,* 5
dos *two,* 1
dos mil *two thousand,* 8
dos millones (de) *two million,* 8
doscientos *two hundred,* 8
dramatizar *to dramatize, to role-play,* xxii
la duda *doubt,* 6; sin duda *without a doubt,* 6
dulce *sweet,* 7
el dulce *candy,* 9
la duración *duration,* 7
durante *during,* 10; *throughout,* 6G
durar *to last,* 10G
el durazno *peach,* 6
el DVD *DVD,* 8

e *and,* 5
la economía *economy,* 3G; la economía doméstica *home economics,* 6G
la edad *age,* 2G; de más edad *the oldest,* 5
el edificio *building,* 5; **el edificio de... pisos** *. . . story building,* 5
la educación física *physical education,* 4
eficaz *efficient,* 10G
eficiente *efficient,* 2
el ejemplo *example,* 3G
el ejercicio *exercise,* 3; **hacer ejercicio** *to exercise,* 3
el *the* (masc.), 2
él he, 1; **Él es...** *He is . . .,* 1; **Él se llama...** *His name is . . .,* 1
el elefante *elephant,* 1
la elegancia *elegance,* 5G
elegante *elegant,* 2
el elemento *element,* 1
elevar *to raise,* 5G
la elite *elite,* 6
ella *she,* 1; **A ella le gusta** + infinitive *She likes to . . .,* 3; **Ella es...** *She is . . .,* 1; ella misma *herself,* 6; **Ella se llama...** *Her name is . . .,* 1
ellas *they (f.),* 1
ellos *they (m.),* 1
el elote *corn on the cob (Mexico),* 6
emitir *to emit,* 2
emocionado(a) *excited,* 9
la empanada *turnover-like pastry,* 9

el emparedado *sandwich,* 6
empezar (ie) *to start,* 5
el empleado, la empleada *employee,* 7
el empleo *job,* 9
emplumado(a) *feathered,* 6
en *on, in, at,* 1; en frente *in front,* 3G; **en blanco** *blank,* 8; en las cuales *about which,* 8; en negrilla *bold,* 9; **en punto** *on the dot,* 1; en que *in which,* 8; **¿En qué le puedo servir?** *How can I help you?,* 8
enamorado(a) *in love,* 10
Encantado(a). *Pleased to meet you., Nice to meet you.,* 1
encantar *to really like, to love,* 6
encerrar *to lock up,* 10
encima de *on top of, above,* 5
encontrar (ue) *to find,* 7; encontrará *will find,* 10; se encuentra *is/it's located* 1G; se encuentran *they can be found,* 6
encontrarse (ue) con alguien *to meet up with someone,* 10
energético(a) *energetic,* 2
la energía *energy,* 2
enero *January,* 1
la enfermera *nurse,* 5
enfermo(a) *sick,* 7
en frente *in front,* 10
enhorabuena *congratulations,* 10
enojado (a) *angry,* 7
enojarse *to get angry,* 7
enrollado(a) *rolled up,* 3
la ensalada *salad,* 6
el ensayo *rehearsal,* 3
enseñar *to show, to teach,* 4; **enseñar fotos** *to show photos,* 9
entender *to understand,* 5
enterarse *to find out,* 10
entonces *then,* 4
entrar *to enter,* 4
entre *between,* 2; *in, within,* 6; *among,* 7
entregar *to hand over,* 9
los entremeses *appetizers,* 9
la entrenadora *trainer,* 7
el entrenamiento *practice,* 3
entrenarse *to work out,* 7
la entrevista *interview,* 2
entrevistar *to interview,* 2
enviar *to send,* 1
la envoltura *wrapping,* 9
la época *era,* 6; la época colonial *Spanish colonial era,* 2G
el equipaje *luggage,* 10
el equipo *equipment,* 3G; *team,* 9G; el equipo de transporte *transportation equipment,* 3G
¿Eres...? *Are you . . .?,* 2
la erupción *eruption,* 6G
Es... *He (She, It) is . . .,* 2; **Es algo divertido.** *It's kind of fun.,* 2; **Es bastante bueno.** *It's pretty good.,* 2; **Es de...** *He (She) is from . . .,* 1; **Es delicioso.** *It's delicious.,* 2; **Es el... de...** *It's the . . . of . . .,* 2; **Es el primero (dos, tres) de...** *It's the first (second, third) of . . .,* 1; **Es la una.** *It is one o'clock.,* 1; **Es pésimo.** *It's awful.,* 2; **Es que...** *It's because; It's just that . . .,* 7; **¡Es un robo!** *It's a rip-off!,* 8
ese(a) *that,* 5
escapar *to escape,* 5
la escena *scene,* 3
escoger *to pick,* 9; *to choose,* 6
escolar *school (adj.),* 4
esconder *to hide,* 4
escribir *to write,* 1; **¿Cómo se escribe...?** *How do you spell . . .?,* 1; escribamos *let's write,* 1; **escribir cartas** *to write letters,* 3; **Se escribe...** *It's spelled . . .,* 1
el escritor, la escritora *writer,* 1
el escritorio *desk,* 5
escuchar *to listen,* 3; **escuchar música** *to listen to music,* 3; escuchemos *let's listen,* 1; has escuchado *have you heard,* 2; he escuchado *I have heard,* 2
la escuela *school,* 2; la escuela primaria *elementary school,* 5; la escuela secundaria *high school,* 9
el escultor *sculptor,* 4G
la escultura *sculpture,* 2G
ese(a) *that,* 8
eso *that,* 2
esos(as) *those,* 8
espacial *space,* 8G
la espalda *back,* 7
el español *Spanish,* 1
el español *Spaniard,* 6
esparcir *to spread,* 3; está esparciendo *is spreading,* 3
la especia *spice,* 8G
la especialidad *specialty,* 6
la especie *species,* 2G
específico(a) *specific,* 10
los espejuelos *glasses,* 5
la esperanza *hope,* 9
esperar *to wait,* 8; *to hope,* 10; *to expect,* 10; **Espera un momento.** *Hold on a moment.,* 8; **espero ver...** *I hope to see . . .,* 10
las espinacas *spinach,* 6
el espino *thorn,* 8
espiritual *spiritual,* 9
espontáneo(a) *spontaneous,* 2
la esposa *wife,* 9
el esposo *husband,* 5
esquiar *to ski,* 10; **esquiar en el agua** *to water-ski,* 10
Está a la vuelta. *It's around the corner.,* 10
ésta, éste *this* (pron.), 1; **Ésta es... la señora...** *This is . . . Mrs. . . .,* 1; **Éste es... el señor...** *This is . . . Mr. . . .,* 1
establecer *to establish,* 8G, fue establecido *was established,* 8G
el establecimiento *colony,* 8G
estacionar *to park,* 10
el estadio *stadium,* 4
el estado *state,* 2G
los Estados Unidos *United States,* 1
estadounidense *pertaining to the United States,* 7
estar *to be,* 1; **¿Cómo está(s)?** *How are you?,* 1; **¿Está...?** *Is . . . there?,* 8; **Está bien.** *All right.,* 3; **estar aburrido(a)** *to be bored,* 7; **estar bien** *to be (doing) fine,* 7; **estar cansado(a)** *to be tired,* 7; **estar contento(a)** *to be happy,* 7; **estar mal** *to be (doing) badly,* 7; **estar enfermo(a)** *to be sick,* 7; **estar enojado(a)** *to be angry,* 7; **estar en una silla de ruedas** *to be in a wheelchair,* 5; **estar listo(a)** *to be ready,* 7; **estar nervioso(a)** *to be nervous,* 7; **estar triste** *to be sad,* 7; **¿Está todo listo?** *Is everything ready?,* 9; **Estoy bien, gracias.** *I'm fine, thanks.,*1; **Estoy de acuerdo.** *I agree.,* 6; **Estoy mal.** *I'm not so good.,* 1; **Estoy regular.** *I'm all right.,* 1; **No está.** *He/She is not here.,* 8; **Estuvo a todo dar.** *It was great.,* 9; **No estoy de acuerdo.** *I disagree.,* 6
estas, estos *these (adj.),* 6
la estatua *statue,* 5G
éste *this (pron.),* 6
este(a) *this,* 8
el estilo *style,* 3G
estirarse *to stretch,* 7
el estómago *stomach,* 7
el Estrecho de la Florida *Strait of Florida,* 8
la estrella *star,* 5
el estrés *stress,* 7
estricto(a) *strict,* 4
el estruendo *noise,* 10
el estudiante, la estudiante *student,* 1; el estudiante de intercambio *exchange student,* 10
estudiar *to study,* 3
los estudios *studies,* 5; los estudios sociales *social studies,* 4
estupendo(a) *great,* 10; **Fue estupendo.** *It was great.,* 10
la etapa *stage,* 2
el europeo *European,* 6G
el evento deportivo *sporting event,* 1
el examen *test,* 4; **presentar el examen de...** *to take a . . . test,* 4
exclamar *to exclaim,* 9
exclusivamente *exclusively,* 4
la excursión: **ir de excursión** *to go on a hike,* 10

la excursión turística *to go on a trip,* 1
exigente *strict,* 5
existir *to exist,* 7
el éxito *success,* 10
la experiencia *experience,* 6
el explorador *explorer,* 5G
exponer *to display,* 4G
el exportador *exporter,* 8G
exportar *to export,* 1G
la exposición *exposition,* 5G; *exhibition,* 10G
expresar *to express,* 6G
la expresión *expression,* xxii; *saying,* 2
extender *to cover,* 3G; se extiende *it extends,* 5G
la extensión *length,* 10G
extranjero(a) *foreign,* 10
el extranjero *abroad,* 10
extraño(a) *strange,* 7G
extremo(a) *far,* 7G
extrovertido(a) *outgoing,* 2

fabuloso(a) *fabulous,* 6
fácil *easy,* 4; **Es fácil.** *It's easy.,* 4
facturar *to check,* 10; **facturar el equipaje** *to check luggage,* 10
la falda *skirt,* 8
falso(a) *false,* xxii
faltar *to be missing,* 1; nos faltan *we're missing,* 3
la fama *fame,* 5G
la familia *family,* 3; **En mi familia somos...** *There are . . . people in my family.,* 5; la Familia Real *Royal Family,* 1
familiar *pertaining to the family,* 7
famoso(a) *famous,* 2
fascinar *to love, to like very much,* 2
fastidiar *to annoy,* 9
favorito(a) *favorite,* 1
febrero *February,* 1
la fecha *date,* 1
la felicidad *happiness,* 9
felicitar *to congratulate,* 9
el felino *cat,* 10G
feliz (pl. felices) *happy,* 8; **¡Feliz...!** *Happy (Merry) . . .,* 9
fenomenal *awesome,* 2
feo(a) *ugly,* 8
festejar *to celebrate,* 9
festivo *holiday* (adj), 9
la fibra de vidrio *fiberglass,* 3G
la fiesta *party,* 2; la fiesta patria *national holiday,* 5G; la fiesta patronal *feast celebrating the patron saint,* 4G; **la fiesta sorpresa** *surprise party,* 9; **hacer una fiesta** *to have a party,* 9
la figurita *shape, figurine,* 4
fijarse *to notice,* 7
el fin *end,* 9; al fin *finally,* 10
el fin de semana *weekend,* 3; **este fin de semana** *this weekend,* 4; **los fines de semana** *weekends,* 3
finales: a finales *at the end,* 10G
finalmente *finally,* 8
financiar *to finance,* 5
fino(a) *fine,* 2G
el flan *flan, custard,* 6
las flautas *rolled tortillas that are stuffed and fried,* 9
la flor *flower,* 1
las flores *flowers,* 9
las fogatas *campfires,* 3
el folleto *pamphlet,* 7
la forma *form,* xxii
formaba *formed*
la formación geológica *geological formation,* 7G
formar *to form,* 3
formidable *great,* 2
la fortaleza *fortress,* 10
la fortuna *fortune,* 8
la foto *photo,* xxii; **enseñar fotos** *to show photos,* 9; **sacar fotos** *to take photos,* 10
la fotografía *photograph,* 8
el fragmento *excerpt,* 5
el francés *French,* 4
la frase *phrase,* 8; *sentence,* 9
la frecuencia *frequency,* 8; con frecuencia *often,* 8; **¿Con qué frecuencia vas...?** *How often do you go?,* 3
frecuentado(a) *visited,* 1G
frente *front;* al frente *to the front,* xxii; en frente *in front,* 3G
fresco(a) *cool,* 3; **Hace fresco.** *It's cool.,* 3
el frijol *bean,* 2G
frío(a) *cold,* 6; **Hace frío.** *It's cold.,* 3; **tener frío** *to be cold,* 7
la frontera *border,* 7G
la fruta *fruit,* 2; la fruta cítrica *citrus fruit,* 8G
el fuego *fire,* 3
¡Fue estupendo! *It was great!,* 10
los fuegos artificiales *fireworks,* 9; **ver fuegos artificiales** *to see fireworks,* 9
fuera *outside,* 7G
fuera (inf. ser) *was,* 6G
fuerte *loud,* 2; *strong,* 3G
fumar *to smoke,* 7; **dejar de fumar** *to stop smoking,* 7
el funcionalismo *functional architectural style,* 6G
funcionar *to work,* 10
fundado(a) *founded,* 2G
el fútbol *soccer,* 3
el fútbol americano *football,* 3
el futuro *future,* 3
futuro(a) *future,* 5

el gabinete *cabinet,* 9
las gafas *glasses,* 5
el gallego *romance language from Galicia, Spain,* 1G
la galleta *cookie,* 9
la gana *desire;* **tener ganas de** + infinitive *to feel like doing something,* 4
la ganadería *cattle raising,* 7G
el ganado *cattle,* 3G
ganar *to win,* 5G
la ganga *bargain,* 8
el garaje *garage,* 5
la garganta *throat,* 7
la garita *sentry box,* 2G
gastar *to spend,* 8
el gato, la gata *cat,* 5
el gazpacho *cold tomato soup*
la generación *generation,* 5
generalmente *generally,* 8
el género *genre,* 8G
generoso(a) *generous,* 6
la gente *people,* 3
la geografía *geography,* 1
geográfico(a) *geographical,* 10
geometría *geometry,* 4
gigante *giant,* 6
el gimnasio *gym,* 3
el glaciar *glacier,* 5G
la gloria *heaven,* 3
glorioso *glorious,* 9
el gobierno *government,* 1G
el Golfo de México *Gulf of Mexico,* 8G
gordo(a) *fat,* 5
la gorra *cap,* 7
gótico(a) *gothic,* 3G
la grabación *recording,* 1
gracias *thank you,* 1, **Estoy bien, gracias.** *I'm fine, thanks.,* 1; **no, gracias** *no thank you,* 8
gracioso(a) *witty,* 2
la graduación *graduation,* 9
gran *big,* 5; *great,* 5; *large,* 3
la granada *pomegranate,* 6
grande *big, large,* 5
el grano *grain,* 6
la grasa *fat,* 7
gratuito *free,* 1
gris *gray,* 8
gritar *to yell,* 7
la grúa *tow truck,* 9
el grupo *group,* 6

la guagua *bus (P.R., Dom. Rep.)*, 10
los guandules *pigeon peas*, 6
guapo(a) *good-looking*, 2
guardar *to store*, 10
la guayabera *man's short-sleeved shirt*, 8
la guerra *war*, 7
la guía telefónica *telephone directory*, 10
guiar *to guide*, 10; *to drive*, 10
la güira *percussive instrument played by scratching with a stick across a rough surface*, 9G
el guiso *stew*, 6
la guitarra: la guitarra eléctrica *electric guitar*, 2
gustar *to like*, 2; **A ellos/ellas les gusta...** *They like . . .*, 3; **le gusta...** *he/she likes . . .*, 3; **Me gusta(n)...** *I like . . .*, 2; **Me gusta(n)... mucho.** *I like . . . a lot.*, 2; me gustaba *I liked*, 4; **Me gusta(n) más...** *I like . . . more.*, 2; **Me gustaría...** *I would like . . .*, 8; **Me gustaría más...** *I would prefer . . .*, 10; Me ha gustado... *I have liked . . .*, 4; **No, no me gusta(n)...** *No, I don't like . . .*, 2; **¿Te gusta(n)...?** *Do you like . . .?*, 2; **¿Te gusta(n) más... o...?** *Do you like . . . or . . . more?*, 2
el gusto *pleasure*, 9
los gustos *likes*, 2

haber: hubo *there was*, 10
las habichuelas *beans*, 2G
la habitación *bedroom*, 5
habitar *to inhabit*, 7G
el habla *speech*, 8
hablar *to talk, to speak*, 3; **Habla...** *. . . speaking (on the telephone)*, 8; **hablar por teléfono** *to talk on the phone*, 3; Hablemos. *Let's talk.*, 1
hacer (-go) *to make, to do*, 4; **estamos haciendo** *we are making/doing*, 9; están haciendo *are making*, 3; **Hace buen (mal) tiempo.** *The weather is good (bad).*, 3; **Hace calor.** *It's hot.*, 3; **Hace fresco.** *It's cool.*, 3; **Hace frío.** *It's cold.*, 3; Hace más de... años *It's more than . . . years ago*, 7G; **Hace sol.** *It's sunny.*, 3; Hace tanto... que... *It's so . . . that . . .*, 3; Hace tiempo. *It's been a long time.*, 9; **Hace viento.** *It's windy.*, 3; **hacer cola** *to wait in line*, 10; **hacer ejercicio** *to exercise*, 3; **hacer la cama** *to make the bed*, 5; **hacer la maleta** *to pack your suitcase*, 10; **hacer la tarea** *to do homework*, 3; **hacer los quehaceres** *to do the chores*, 5; **hacer una fiesta** *to have a party*, 9; **hacer un viaje** *to take a trip*, 10; **hacer yoga** *to do yoga*, 7; hacían *they made*, 4; **haz** *make, do*, 6; hizo *he/she did*, 9; **no hagas** *don't do*, 10; **¿Qué están haciendo?** *What are they doing?*, 9; qué hicieron *what they did*, 9; **¿Qué hiciste?** *What did you do?*, 8; se hace *is made*, 6
hallar *to find*, 7G
el hambre *hunger*, 4; **tener hambre** *to be hungry*, 4
la hamburguesa *hamburger*, 2
el Hanukah *Hanukkah*, 9
hasta *until*, 5; *up to*, 5; **Hasta luego.** *See you later.*, 1; **Hasta mañana.** *See you tomorrow.*, 1; **Hasta pronto.** *See you soon.*, 1
hay (inf. **haber**) *there is, there are*, 4; **Hay un(a)...** *There's a . . .*, 4
haz *make, do*, 6; Hazme caso. *Pay attention to me.*, 8
hecho(a) *made*, 2G
la heladería *ice cream shop*, 8
el helado *ice cream*, 2
la hembra *female*, 2
el hemisferio *hemisphere*, 7G
la herencia inheritance; la herencia alemana *German cultural tradition*, 7G; la herencia española *Spanish cultural tradition*, 10G
la hermana *sister*, 5
el hermano *brother*, 5
los hermanos *brothers, brothers and sisters*, 5
el héroe *hero*, 4G
la hierba *grass*, 8G; la hierba fina *herb*, 8G
la hija *daughter*, 5
el hijo *son*, 5
los hijos *sons, children*, 5
el hipo *hiccup*, 3; estar con hipo *to have hiccups*, 3
el hipopótamo *hippopotamus*, 1
hispano(a) *Hispanic*, 1
hispanohablante *Spanish-speaking*, 6
la historia *history*, 4
el hogar *home*, 3G
las hojas de maíz *cornhusks*, 3
hola *hi, hello*, 1
el hombre *man*, 8; el hombre de negocios *businessman*, 5, los hombres *men, humans*, 6; **para hombres** *for men*, 8
el hombro *shoulder*, 7
el homenaje *tribute*, 1G
hondo(a) *deep*, 8G
el honor *honor*, 3
la hora *hour*, 1; **¿A qué hora vas a...?** *What time are you going to . . .?*, 4; **¿Qué hora es?** *What time is it?*, 1
el horario *schedule*, 3
la horchata mexicana *sweet rice drink*, 6
la hormiga *ant*, 6
el horno *oven*, 6; el horno microondas *microwave oven*, 6
horrible *horrible*, 2; **¡Fue horrible!** *It was horrible!*, 10
el hotel *hotel*, 10; **quedarse en un hotel** *to stay in a hotel*, 10
hoy *today*, 1; hoy en día *nowadays*, 6G; **Hoy es...** *Today is . . .*, 1; **¿Qué día es hoy?** *What day is today?*, 1
el huevo *egg*, 6
húmedo(a) *damp;* el bosque húmedo *rainforest*, 4G
el huracán *hurricane*, 3

la idea *idea*, 6; la idea principal *main idea*, 6
el idioma *language*, 1G; idioma oficial *official language*, 1G
identificar *to identify*, 10
la iglesia *church*, 3
igual que *same as*, 2
igualmente *equally*, 8
Igualmente. *Likewise.*, 1
la iguana *iguana*, 1
ilustrar *to illustrate*, 5
imaginar *to imagine*, 2
el imperativo *imperative*, 9
el imperio *empire*, 10G
imponente *imposing*, 6
importado(a) *imported*, 5G
la importancia *importance*, 6
impresionante *impressive*, 7G
incaico(a) *Incan*, 10G
incesante *without stopping*, 8
inclusive *including*, 8
incluso *including*, 8G
incomparable *incomparable*, 5
la independencia *independence*, 6G
independiente *independent*, 2
indicar *to indicate*, xxii
indígena *indigenous*, 6G
la Infanta *princess*, 10
la influencia *influence*, 1G
Inglaterra *England*, 7G
el inglés *English*, 4
injusto *unfair*, 5; **Me parece injusto.** *I don't think that's fair.; It seems unfair to me.*, 5
inmediato(a) *immediate*, 10G
inmenso(a) *immense*, 6
el inmigrante *immigrant*, 7G
inmigrar *to immigrate*, 7G
el insecto *insect*, 2

inseparable *inseparable,* 3
inspirar *to inspire,* 1G
el instrumento *instrument,* 8G
intacto(a) *intact,* 10
intelectual *intellectual,* 2
inteligente *intelligent,* 2
la intensidad *intensity,* 7
el interés *of interest,* 10
interesante *interesting,* 2
internacional *international,* 6
interrumpir *to interrupt,* 4
el invasor *invader,* 4G
inventar *to invent,* 4
el inventario *inventory,* 8
inventivo(a) *inventive,* 2
la investigación *research,* 4G
el invierno *winter,* 1
inviolable *inviolable,* 5
la invitación *invitation,* 9; **mandar invitaciones** *to send invitations,* 9
el invitado *guest,* 9; el invitado de honor *guest of honor,* 9
invitar *to invite,* 9
ir *to go,* 2; **¿Adónde fuiste?** *Where did you go?,* 8; fue *went,* 8; fuimos *we went,* 8; **ir a** + infinitive *to be going to (do something),* 4; **ir de compras** *to go shopping,* 3; **ir de excursión** *to go hiking,* 10; **ir de pesca** *to go fishing,* 10; **no vayas** *don't go,* 7; **quiero ir...** *I want to go . . .,* 2; se va *leaves,* 6; **¿Vas a...?** *Are you going to . . .?,* 4; **Vas a ir, ¿verdad?** *You're going to go, aren't you?,* 4; **ve** *go,* 6
irse *to leave,* 10
la isla *island,* 10
italiano(a) *Italian,* 6
la izquierda *left*

el jabón *soap,* 7
el jamón *ham,* 6
el jardín *garden,* 5
el jefe *chief,* 10
el jersey *sweater,* 8
la jirafa *giraffe,* 1
joven *young,* 5
el joven, la joven *young person,* 9; **los jóvenes** *young people,* 9
la joyería *jewelry store,* 8
el juego *game,* 3; **el juego de mesa** *board game,* 3; el juego de palabras *word game,* 7
el jueves *Thursday,* 1; **los jueves** *on Thursdays,* 3
el jugador *player,* 2G
jugar (ue) *to play,* 3
el jugo *juice,* 6; **el jugo de...** *. . . juice,* 6
el juguete *toy,* 8
la juguetería *toy store,* 8
el juicio *judgment,* 6
julio *July,* 1
junio *June,* 1
juntos(as) *together,* 1
justo(a) *fair, just,* 10

el karate *karate,* 1
el kilómetro *kilometer,* 3
el kiosko *stand or stall,* 9G

la *the* (fem. article), 2
la *you, it,* (pronoun), 6; *you,* 9
las labores *chores,* 5
el lado: por todos lados *everywhere,* 8G
el lago *lake,* 10
la lágrima *tear,* 9
la lana *wool,* 8; **de lana** *made of wool,* 8
la lancha *motorboat,* 10; **pasear en lancha** *to go out in a motorboat,* 10
el lápiz (pl. los lápices) *pencil,* 4
largo(a) *long,* 5
las *the* (pl. fem. article), 2
las *you, them* (pronoun), 6
la lástima *pity,* 8; **¡Qué lástima!** *What a shame!,* 10
la lata *can,* 9; **¡Qué lata!** *What a pain!,* 5
latinoamericano(a) *Latin American,* 1
lavar *to wash,* 5; **lavar los platos** *to do the dishes,* 5
lavarse *to wash,* 7
le *to/for him, her, you,* 2
la leche *milk,* 6
leer *to read,* 3; al leer *upon reading,* 6; antes de leer *before reading,* 1; leamos *let's read,* 1; leer en voz alta *to read aloud,* 6; se leen *are read,* 5
el legado *legacy,* 8G
lejano(a) *distant,* 10
lejos *far,* 9; **lejos de** *far from,* 5
la lengua *language,* 9
los lentes *glasses,* 5; **usar lentes** *to wear glasses,* 5
lento(a) *slow,* 4G
el león *lion,* 1
les *to/for you* (pl.), *them,* 2
levantar *to lift,* 7; **levantar pesas** *to lift weights,* 7
levantarse *to get up,* 7
la leyenda *legend,* 10
libre *free,* 6G
la librería *bookstore,* 8
el libro *book,* 2; **el libro de amor** *romance book,* 2; **el libro de aventuras** *adventure book,* 2
el líder, la líder *leader,* 2
el limón *lemon,* 6
limpiar *to clean,* 5; limpio(a) *clean,* 5
lindo(a) *beautiful, pretty,* 6
listo(a) *ready,* 7; **estar listo(a)** *to be ready,* 7; **¿Está todo listo?** *Is everything ready?,* 9
llamado(a) *called,* 9G
llamar *to call,* 9; **llamar por teléfono** *to make a phone call,* 8; **Llamo más tarde.** *I'll call back later.,* 8; **Te llamo más tarde.** *I'll call you later.,* 9
la llegada *arrival,* 10
llegar *to arrive, to get there,* 4; al llegar *upon arriving,* 6; ha llegado *she has come,* 9
llenar *to fill up,* 3
lleno(a) *full,* 9
llevar *to wear,* 8; *to take,* 6; lo llevó *took it,* 6G; lleva años trabajando *he has been working for years,* 9
llevarse *to get along,* 2
llover (ue) *to rain,* 3; **llueve (mucho)** *it rains (a lot),* 3
la lluvia *rain,* 4G
lo *him, it,* 6; *you,* 9; **lo siento** *I'm sorry,* 8
lo: lo de siempre *same as usual,* 9; lo que *what,* 6; lo que pasa *what is happening,* xxii
loco *crazy,* 5
lógico(a) *logical,* 2
el lonche *lunch (Southwest U.S.),* 6
los *the* (pl. masc.), 2
los *you, them* (pronoun), 6
luchar *to struggle,* 8; *to fight,* 4G
luego *then, later,* 4
el lugar *place,* 1G
los lugares de interés *places of interest,* 10
la luna *moon,* 9
lunes *Monday,* 1; **los lunes** *on Mondays,* 3
la luz *light,* 7G

el macho *male,* 2
la madera *wood,* 5G

la madre *mother,* 5
madrina *godmother,* 1
el maestro *master,* 7G
magnífico(a) *magnificent,* 4
el maíz *corn,* 6
majestuoso(a) *majestic,* 9G
mal *bad;* **Estoy mal.** *I'm not so good.,* 1; **Te veo mal.** *You don't look well.,* 7
la maleta *suitcase,* 10
malo(a) *bad,* 2
malvado(a) *evil,* 10
la mamá *mom,* 5
el mamífero *mammal,* 4G
la mañana *morning,* 4; **por la mañana** *in the morning,* 4
mañana *tomorrow,* 4; **Hasta mañana.** *See you tomorrow.,* 1
mandar *to send,* 9; **mandar invitaciones** *to send invitations,* 9; **mandar tarjetas** *to send cards,* 9
el mandato *command,* 6
manejar *to manage,* 7
la manera *way,* 9
la mano *hand,* 7
el manojo *bunch,* 8
mantener (ie) *to preserve, to keep,* 6
mantenerse (ie) *to maintain,* 7; **mantenerse (ie) en forma** *to stay in shape,* 7
la manzana *apple,* 6
el mapa *map,* 10
el maquillaje *makeup,* 7
maquillarse *to put on makeup,* 7
marcado(a) *marked,* 7
marcar *to set, to dial,* 1
marcharse *to leave,* 9
el marisco *shellfish,* 5G
marítimo(a) *maritime,* 3G
marrón *brown,* 2; los ojos marrones *brown eyes,* 5
el martes *Tuesday,* 1; **los martes** *on Tuesdays,* 3
marzo *March,* 1
más *more,* 2; **Más o menos.** *So-so.,* 1; **más que** *more than,* 8; **más... que** *more . . . than,* 8
la masa *dough,* 3
la máscara *mask,* 2G
la mascarada *masquerade,* 4G
la mascota *pet,* 5
el mate *Argentine and Paraguayan tea,* 7
las matemáticas *mathematics,* 3
la materia *subject,* 4; las materias obligatorias *required subjects,* 4; las materias opcionales *electives,* 4
matutino(a) *(in the) morning,* 4
mayo *May,* 1
mayor(es) *older,* 5; *greater,* 3G
la mayoría *majority,* 4G
la mazorca *corn on the cob,* 6
me *to/for me,* 2; **Me da igual.** *It's all the same to me.,* 2; **Me duele(n)...** *My . . . hurt(s),* 7; **Me gusta(n)...** *I like . . .,* 2; **Me gusta(n) más...** *I like . . . more.,* 2; **Me gusta(n)... mucho.** *I like . . . a lot.,* 2; **Me llamo...** *My name is . . .,* 1; **No, no me gusta(n)...** *No, I don't like . . .,* 2; **Me parece bien.** *It seems fine to me.,* 5; **Me parece injusto.** *It's not fair.,* 5
me *me,* 9
mecánico *mechanic,* 5
la medalla *medal,* 5G
mediano(a) *medium,* 4
la medianoche *midnight,* 1
médico(a) *medical,* 7
medio(a) *half,* 4; **y media** *half past,* 1
los medios de transporte *means of transportation,* 10
el mediodía *midday, noon,* 1
medir (i) *to measure,* 5G
mejor(es) *better, best,* 7
el melocotón *peach,* 6
menor(es) *younger,* 5
menos *less,* 8; **menos cuarto** *a quarter to . . .,* 1; **menos que** *less than,* 8; **menos... que** *less . . . than,* 8
el mensaje *message,* 7G
la mente *mind,* 4
el mercado *market,* 6; el mercado al aire libre *open-air market,* 8
merendar (ie) *to have a snack,* 5
el merengue *music and dance style,* 9G
la merienda *snack,* 6
la mesa *table,* 5; **poner la mesa** *to set the table,* 6
los meses del año *months of the year,* 1
meter *to put in,* 8
meterse *to set,* 9
metódico(a) *methodical,* 2
el metro *meter,* 1G
el metro *subway,* 10
mezclar *to mix,* 6; mezcla *mixture,* 6
la mezquita *mosque,* 1G
mí *me,* 5; **A mí me gusta** + infinitive *I like to . . .,* 3; **a mí me toca...** *I have to . . .,* 5
mi(s) *my,* 1; **mi mejor amigo(a)** *my best friend,* 1; **mi profesor(-a)** *my teacher,* 1
la miel *honey,* 6
el miembro *member,* 3
mientras *while,* 6
el miércoles *Wednesday,* 1; **los miércoles** *on Wednesdays,* 3
mil *one thousand,* 8; miles *thousands,* 2
la milla cuadrada *square mile,* 3
un millón (de) *one million,* 8; **dos millones (de)** *two million,* 8
mío *mine,* 8
mirar *to look,* 9; **Nada más estoy mirando.** *I'm just looking.,* 8; **mirar las vitrinas** *to window-shop,* 8
la misa *Mass,* 9
la misión *mission,* 3G
mismo(a) *same,* 6
el misterio *mystery,* 2
misterioso(a) *mysterious,* 2
la mitad *half,* 6G
la mochila *backpack,* 4
la moda *style, fashion,* 8; **a la última moda** *in the latest fashion,* 8; muy de moda *very fashionable,* 8; **pasado(a) de moda** *out of style,* 8
modelar *to shape,* 4
moderno(a) *modern,* 7
el módulo *module,* 10
el mogote *knoll,* 9G
el mole *sauce made with chiles and flavored with chocolate,* 6
el molino *windmill,* 1G
el momento *moment,* 6; **Espera un momento.** *Hold on a moment.,* 8
la monarquía parlamentaria *constitutional monarchy,* 1G
la moneda *currency,* 2; *coin,* 8
el mono *monkey,* 4G
la montaña *mountain,* 10; **subir a la montaña** *to go up a mountain,* 10
montañoso(a) *mountainous,* 7G
montar *to ride,* montar a caballo *to ride a horse,* 3G; **montar en bicicleta** *to ride a bike,* 3
un montón *a ton,* 4
el monumento *monument,* 1G
el morado *purple,* 1G
morado(a) *purple,* 8
moreno(a) *dark-haired; dark-skinned,* 2
morir (ue) *to die,* 5; murió *died,* 5
el moro *rice and beans,* 9G
el mosaico *mosaic,* 6G
el mosquito *mosquito,* 2
el mostrador *counter,* 10
mostrar (ue) *to show,* 1G
el movimiento *movement,* 4G
la muchacha *girl,* 1
el muchacho *boy,* 1
mucho *a lot (of),* 2; *much,* 4; **Mucho gusto.** *Pleased/Nice to meet you.,* 1
muchos(as) *a lot of, many,* 4
mudarse *to move,* 8G
mudéjar *Moslem,* 5G
la muerte *death,* 4G
la mujer *woman,* 8; **para mujeres** *for women,* 8
mundialmente *worldwide,* 6
el mundo *world,* 1G; todo el mundo *everybody,* 9
el mural *mural painting,* 6G
la muralla *wall, rampart,* 1G
el museo *museum,* 10

la música *music,* 2; **la música de...** *music of/by . . .,* 2; la música clásica *classical music,* 2G
el músico *musician,* 2
muy *very,* 2

N

nacer *to be born,* 7G; había nacido *had been born,* 7G; nacido(a) *born,* 8G
nacional *national,* 1
nada *nothing,* 4; *not anything,* 4
Nada más estoy mirando. *I'm just looking.,* 8
nadar *to swim,* 3
nadie *nobody, not anybody,* 5
la naranja *orange,* 6
el naranjo *orange tree,* 8G
la nariz *nose,* 7
la natación *swimming,* 7
nativo(a) *native,* 6
la naturaleza *nature,* 2
la navaja *razor,* 7
navegar *to sail,* 5; *to navigate,* 10; **navegar por Internet** *to surf the Internet,* 3
la Navidad *Christmas,* 9
la necesidad *necessity,* 7
necesitar *to need,* 4; **¿Necesitas algo?** *Do you need anything?,* 4; **Necesito muchas cosas.** *I need a lot of things.,* 4; **No, no necesito nada.** *No, I don't need anything.,* 4
negarse *to refuse,* 5
negociable *negotiable,* 5
el negocio *business,* 9
negro(a) *black,* 5
nervioso(a) *nervous,* 7
nevar (ie) *to snow,* 3
ni *neither, nor,* 7; **Ni idea.** *I have no idea.,* 3
el nido *nest,* 1
la nieta *granddaughter,* 5
el nieto *grandson,* 5
los nietos *grandsons, grandchildren,* 5
nieva *it snows,* 3
la niña *girl,* 1
ninguno(a) *no, none,* 10G; **ninguna parte** *nowhere,* 3; **no va a ninguna parte** *he/she doesn't go anywhere,* 3
el niño *male child,* 8
los niños *children,* 8
el nivel del mar *sea level,* 9G
no no, 3; *not, do not,* 5; **No debes...** *You shouldn't . . .,* 7; **No es gran cosa.** *It's not a big deal.,* 5; **No está.** *He/She is not here.,* 8; **No estoy de acuerdo.** *I disagree.,* 6; **no, gracias** *no thank you,* 8; **nomás** *just, only,* 8; **No sé.** *I don't know.,* 4; **No, no me gusta(n)...** *No, I don't like . . .,* 2; **No, no necesito nada.** *No, I do not need anything.,* 4; **No, no voy a ir.** *No, I'm not going to go.,* 4; **No seas...** *Don't be . . .,* 7; **no va a ninguna parte** *he/she doesn't go anywhere,* 3; **No vayas.** *Don't go.,* 7
¿no? *right?,* 4
la Nochebuena *Christmas Eve,* 9
la Nochevieja *New Year's Eve,* 9
nocturno(a) *(in the) evening,* 4
nombrado(a) *named,* 9G
el nombre *name,* 10
el noreste *northeast,* 2G
normalmente *normally,* 4
el noroeste *northwest,* 7G
el norte *north,* 5G
norteamericano(a) *North American,* 8
norteño(a) *northern,* 5G
Noruega *Norway,* 7G
nos *(to/for) us,* 2; **Nos vemos.** *See you.,* 1
nosotros(as) *we,* 1
la nota *grade,* 6
la noticia *news,* 9
novecientos *nine hundred,* 8
la novela *novel,* 3
noventa *ninety,* 2
noviembre *November,* 1
la nube *cloud,* 7
nuestro(a) *our,* 5
nuestros(as) *our,* 5
nuevamente *again,* 9
nueve *nine,* 1
nuevo(a) *new,* 2
la nuez (pl. las nueces) *nut(s),* 6
el número *number,* 1; *shoe size,* 8
numeroso(a) *numerous,* 2G
nunca *never,* 5; **casi nunca** *almost never,* 3; nunca más *never again,* 6
la nutricionista *nutritionist,* 7

O

o *or,* 2
oaxaqueño *from the Mexican state of Oaxaca,* 6
el objetivo *objective,* 1
el objeto *object,* 1
la obra *work,* 7G; la obra de teatro *play,* 6G; la obra maestra *masterpiece,* 6G
observar *to observe,* 1
la ocasión *occasion,* 9
occidental *western,* 7G
ochenta *eighty,* 2
ocho *eight,* 1
ochocientos *eight hundred,* 8
el ocio *leisure time,* 8
octubre *October,* 1
el ocupante *occupant,* 10
ocupar *to occupy,* 7G
ocurrir *to occur;* ¿Se te ocurren? *Do they occur to you?,* 4
la oficina *office,* 5
la oficina de cambio *money exchange,* 10
la oficina de correos *post office,* 10
ofrecer *to offer,* 6
el oído *ear,* 7
oír *to hear,* 2; oyes *(you) hear,* 2; se oye *is heard,* 2
los ojos *eyes,* 5; los ojos borrados *hazel eyes,* 5; los ojos cafés *brown eyes,* 5; **tener los ojos azules** *to have blue eyes,* 5
la ola *wave,* 2G
la olla *pot,* 4G
olor *smell,* 7
olvidar *to forget,* 9; No te olvides. *Don't forget.,* 8
once *eleven,* 1
la oportunidad *opportunity,* 5
la oración *sentence,* xxii
el orden *order,* 1; el orden cronológico *chronological order,* 8
ordenar *to organize,* 3; está ordenando *is organizing,* 3
organizado(a) *organized,* 2
organizar *to organize,* 10
orgulloso(a) *proud,* 6
oriental *eastern,* 10G
el origen *origin,* 6G
originalmente *originally,* 3G
os *(to/for) you* (pl.), 2
el oso *bear,* 1
el otoño *fall,* 1
otro(a) *other, another,* 8
otros(as) *other, others,* 8

P

el paciente *patient,* 7
el padre *father,* 5
los padres *parents,* 5; los padres peregrinos *pilgrims,* 8G
pagar *to pay,* 8; **pagar una fortuna** *to pay a fortune,* 8
la página *page,* xxii; la página Web *Web page,* 1
el país *country,* 6; el país de origen *native country,* 6
el paisaje *landscape,* 4G
el pájaro *bird,* 9
la palabra *word,* xxii; la palabra clave *key word,* 1
el palacio *palace,* 1

el pan *bread,* 6; **el pan dulce** *pastries,* 6; **el pan tostado** *toast,* 6
la pantalla *monitor, screen,* 10
los pantalones (vaqueros) *pants (jeans),* 8
los pantalones cortos *shorts,* 8
la pantomima *pantomime,* 9
la pantorrilla *calf,* 7
el papá *dad,* 5
el Papá Noel *Santa Claus,* 9
la papa *potato,* 6; **las papas fritas** *French fries,* 6
el papel *paper,* 4
las papitas *potato chips,* 9
el paquete *package,* 9
el par *pair,* 8
para *for,* 4; *to, in order to,* 7
el paraíso *paradise,* 8G
parecer *to seem,* 5; *to think,* 8; me parece *It seems to me,* 9; **Me parece bien.** *It's all right. It seems fine to me.,* 5; **Me parece injusto.** *I don't think that's fair.; It seems unfair to me.,* 5; no parezco *I don't seem to be.,* 9; **¿Qué te parece...?** *What do you think of . . .?,* 8
parecido(a) similar, 2
la pared *wall,* 10G
la pareja *pair*; en parejas *in pairs,* xxii, *couple,* 3
el paréntesis *parenthesis,* 8
el pareo *matching,* 1
el pariente *relative,* 5
el parque *park,* 3; **el parque de diversiones** *amusement park,* 10
el párrafo *paragraph,* xxii
la parrilla *barbecue,* 7
la parrillada *Argentine barbecue,* 7G
la parte *part,* 6
participar *to participate,* 1
particular *particular,* 6
el partido de... *the . . . game,* 4
la pasa *raisin,* 6
el pasado *past,* 8
pasado mañana *day after tomorrow,* 4
pasado(a) *last,* 8; **el año pasado** *last year,* 9
pasado(a) de moda *out of style,* 8
el pasaje *ticket,* 10
el pasajero, la pasajera *passenger,* 10
el pasapalo *finger food (Ven.),* 9
el pasaporte *passport,* 10
pasar *to spend (time, occasion),* 9; con quien tú te pasas *who you spend time with,* 2; **la pasamos en casa de...** *we spent it at . . .'s house,* 9; lo que pasa *what is happening,* 9; **pasar el rato solo(a)** *to spend time alone,* 3; **pasar la aspiradora** *to vacuum,* 5; **pasar por** *to stop at/by,* 10; *to go through,* 2; qué pasa *what's happening,* 6
pasártelo(la) *to get someone (for a telephone call),* 8
el pasatiempo *hobby,* 7; **buscar un pasatiempo** *to look for a hobby,* 7
pasear *to go for a walk,* 3; **pasear en bote de vela** *to go out in a sailboat,* 10; **pasear en lancha** *to go out in a motorboat,* 10
el pasillo *corridor,* 10
la pasta de dientes *toothpaste,* 7
el pastel *cake,* 6
el pastel en hoja *mashed plantain dough filled with meat and wrapped in plantain leaves,* 9
la patata *potato,* 1G; *sweet potato,* 6
el patinaje en hielo *ice skating,* 7
patinar *to skate,* 3
el patio *patio, yard,* 5
la patrona *patron,* 9G
la pava *kettle used to make* ***mate,*** 7
el pavo *turkey,* 6G
el payaso *clown,* 4G
las pecas *freckles,* 5
el pecho *chest,* 7
pedir (i) *to order,* 6
peinarse *to comb your hair,* 7
el peine *comb,* 7
la película *film, movie,* 2; **(de ciencia ficción, de terror, de misterio)** *(science fiction, horror, mystery),* 2
el peligro de extinción *danger of extinction,* 8G
pelirrojo(a) *red-headed,* 2
el pelo *hair,* 5
la pelota *ball,* 9G
pensar (ie) *to think,* 9; **pensar** + inf. *to plan,* 9; **Pensamos...** *We plan to . . .,* 9
peor(es) *worse,* 8
pequeño(a) *small,* 5
la pera *pear,* 1
perder (ie) *to lose,* 10; *to miss,* 10; **perder el vuelo** *miss the flight,* 10; si me pierden *if you lose me,* 3; perdido(a) *lost,* 10G
perdone *I'm sorry,* 1
el perezoso *sloth,* 4G
perezoso(a) *lazy,* 2
perfecto *perfect,* 8
el periódico *newspaper,* 8G
la perla *pearl,* 2G
permiso *excuse me,* 9
permitir *to allow,* 6
pero *but,* 5
el perro, la perra *dog,* 5
la persona *person,* 5
el personaje *character,* 1G; el personaje ficticio *fictional character,* 1G
la personalidad *personality,* 2
las pesas *weights,* 7; **levantar pesas** *to lift weights,* 7
la pesca *fishing,* 10; **ir de pesca** *to go fishing,* 10; la pesca comercial *commercial fishing,* 8G
el pescado *fish,* 6
pescar *to fish,* 10
pésimo(a) *very bad,* 2
el peso *weight,* 7
el pez *fish,* 1
la picadera *finger food (Dom. Rep.),* 9
el picante *spice,* 6
picante *spicy,* 6
el picnic *picnic,* 9; **tener un picnic** *to have a picnic,* 9
el pico *peak,* 1G
el pico de gallo *spicy relish made with tomatoes, hot peppers, and onions,* 3G
el pie *foot,* 7
la piedra *stone,* 5G
la pierna *leg,* 7
la pieza *bedroom,* 5; *piece,* 4
la pileta *swimming pool (Arg.),* 3
la piñata *piñata,* 9
el pingüino *penguin,* 7G
pintado(a) *painted,* 2G
pintar *to paint;* fue pintado *was painted,* 1
el pintor *painter,* 2G
pintoresco(a) *picturesque,* 7G
la pintura *painting,* 1; la pintura al óleo *oil painting,* 3G
la pirámide *pyramid,* 10; la pirámide alimenticia *food pyramid,* 7
la piscina *swimming pool,* 3
el piso *floor,* 5; **de... pisos** *. . .-story,* 5
el piyama *pajamas,* 7
la pizza *pizza,* 2
el placer *pleasure,* 9
planes *plans,* 9; **¿Qué planes tienen para...?** *What plans do you have for . . .?,* 9
plano(a) *flat,* 7G
las plantas *plants,* 5
el plátano *plantain,* 8G
platicar *to chat,* 3
el plato *dish, plate,* 6; **lavar los platos** *to do the dishes,* 5; **el plato hondo** *bowl,* 6; el plato típico *traditional dish,* 2
la playa *beach,* 3
la playera *T-shirt,* 8
la plaza de comida *food court in a mall,* 8
la plena *music and dance style,* 2
la población *population,* 1G
poblado(a) *populated,* 4G
pobre *poor,* 8
poco(a) *few, little, not much,* 4; poco a poco *little by little,* 4; **un poco** *a little,* 2
pocos(as) *not many,* 4
poder (ue) *to be able to, can,* 6
el poema *poem,* 8
la poesía *poetry,* 8

el poeta, la poeta *poet,* 5G
el pollo *chicken,* 6; el pollo frito *fried chicken,* 2G
el ponche *punch,* 9
poner (-go) *to put,* 4; **no pongas** *don't put,* 10; **pon** *put,* 6; poner en orden *to put in order,* xxii; poner huevos *to lay eggs,* 2; poner la comida *to set out the food,* 9; **poner la mesa** *to set the table,* 6; tener puesto(a) *to have on,* 8
ponerse *to put on,* 7, *to get,* 6; ponerse *to start,* 7; ponerse a bailar *to start dancing,* 3; ponerse en contacto *to get in contact,* 5; ponerse rojo *to flush, to turn red,* 10
por in, by, 4; por ejemplo *for example,* 6G; por eso *that's why,* 6; **por el estilo** *of that sort,* 7; **por favor** *please,* 6; por fin *at last,* 8; **por la mañana** *in the morning,* 4; por la noche *at night,* 2; **por la tarde** *in the afternoon,* 4; por lo general *generally,* 8; por lo menos *at least,* 9; por más que *no matter how much,* 7; por medio de *by means of,* 10
¿por qué? *why?,* 2
la porción *portion, serving,* 7
porque *because,* 2
posible *possible,* 4
el postre *dessert,* 6
el pozole *soup made with hominy, meat, and chile,* 6
practicando *practicing,* 7
practicar deportes *to play sports,* 3
el precio *price,* 1; el precio de entrada *entry fee,* 1
precolombino(a) *of the New World era before the arrival of Europeans,* 2G
precoz *precocious,* 4
la preferencia *preference,* 3
preferido(a) *favorite,* 4
preferir (ie) *to prefer,* 6
la pregunta *question,* xxii
preguntar *to ask,* xxii
prehistórico(a) *prehistoric,* 7G
preocuparse *to worry,* 10; **No te preocupes.** *Don't worry.,* 10
preparar *to prepare,* 6
prepararse *to get ready,* 7
los preparativos *preparations,* 9
la preposición *preposition,* 2
la presentación *introduction,* 9
presentar *to present,* 6; *to introduce,* 9; **presentar el examen** *to take a test,* 4; se presentó *was performed,* 10; **Te presento a...** *I'd like you to meet . . .,* 9
presentarse *to present oneself,* 6
el presente *present,* 9
prestar: prestar atención *to pay attention,* 7
el pretérito *preterite,* 8
la primavera *spring,* 1
el primero *first,* 1
primero(a) *first,* 4
el primo, la prima *cousin,* 5; el primo hermano, la prima hermana *first cousin,* 5
los primos *cousins,* 5
la princesa *princess,* 10
principal *main,* 4G; *primary,* 9G
la prisa: tener prisa *to be in a hurry,* 4
el prisionero *prisoner,* 10
probar (ue) *to try, to taste,* 6
producir *to produce,* 1
el producto *product,* 3G; los productos petroleros *petroleum products,* 3G; los productos químicos *chemicals,* 3G
el profesor *teacher (male),* 1; **mi profesor** *my teacher,* 1
la profesora *teacher (female),* 1; **mi profesora** *my teacher,* 1
prometer *to promise,* 8
el pronombre *pronoun,* 6; el pronombre de complemento directo *direct object pronoun,* 9; el pronombre reflexivo *reflexive pronoun,* 7
pronto *soon,* 1; **Hasta pronto.** *See you soon.,* 1; tan pronto *as soon,* 9
la propiedad *property,* 5
propio(a) *own,* 4
el propósito *purpose,* 6
el provecho *benefit;* Buen provecho. *Enjoy your meal.,* 6
la provincia *province,* 10
próximo(a) *next,* 4; **la próxima semana** *next week,* 4; **el** *(day of the week)* **próximo** *next (day of the week),* 4
el proyecto *project,* 1
publicar *to publish,* 1
el pueblo *town, village,* 5; el pueblo natal *hometown,* 3
¿Puedo...? *Can I . . .?,* 6
el puente *bridge,* 8G
la puerta *door,* 5; *gate,* 10
el puerto *port,* 3G
el puesto *stall,* 9G
la pulsera *bracelet,* 8
punto: en punto *on the dot,* 1
el punto de vista *point of view,* 9
puntual *punctual, on time,* 2
el puré de papas *mashed potatoes,* 6

que *that;* **que me llame después** *tell him/her to call me later,* 8; **Que te vaya bien.** *Hope things go well for you.,* 9
¡Qué...! *How . . .!,* 6; **¡Qué bien!** *How great!,* 10; **¡Qué fantástico!** *How fantastic!,* 10; **¡Qué gusto verte!** *It's great to see you!,* 9; **¡Qué lástima!** *What a shame!,* 10; **¡Qué lata!** *What a pain!,* 5; **¡Qué mala suerte!** *What bad luck!,* 10
¿qué? *what?,* 1; **¿Qué clases tienes ...?** *What classes do you have . . . ?,* 4; **¿Qué día es hoy?** *What day is today?,* 1; **¿Qué están haciendo?** *What are they doing?,* 9; **¿Qué fecha es hoy?** *What's today's date?,* 1; **¿Qué hace...?** *What does . . . do?,* 3; **¿Qué haces para ayudar en casa?** *What do you do to help out at home?,* 5; **¿Qué haces...?** *What do you do . . .?,* 3; **¿Qué haces para relajarte?** *What do you do to relax?,* 7; **¿Qué hay de nuevo?** *What's new?,* 9; **¿Qué hiciste?** *What did you do?,* 8; **¿Qué hora es?** *What time is it?,* 1; **¿Qué planes tienen para...?** *What plans do you have for . . .?,* 9; **¿Qué quieres hacer?** *What do you want to do?,* 3; **¿Qué tal?** *How's it going?,* 1; **¿Qué tal...?** *How is . . .?,* 6; **¿Qué tal estuvo?** *How was it?,* 9; **¿Qué tal si...?** *How about if. . .?,* 6; **¿Qué tal si vamos a...?** *How about if we go to . . .?,* 4; **¿Qué te falta hacer?** *What do you still have to do?,* 7; **¿Qué te gusta hacer?** *What do you like to do?,* 3; **¿Qué te pasa?** *What's wrong with you?,* 7; **¿Qué te toca hacer a ti?** *What do you have to do?,* 5; **¿Qué tiempo hace?** *What's the weather like?,* 3; **¿Qué tiene...?** *What's the matter with . . .?,* 7; **¿Qué tienes que hacer?** *What do you have to do?,* 7; **¿Qué vas a hacer?** *What are you going to do?,* 4
el quechua *indigenous language in Peru,* 10G
quedar *to fit, to look,* 8; *to remain,* 3G; **¿Cómo me queda...?** *How does it fit?,* 8; **quedar bien/mal** *to fit well/poorly,* 8
quedarse *to stay,* 9; **quedarse en...** *to stay in . . .,* 10
los quehaceres *household chores,* 5; **hacer los quehaceres** *to do chores,* 5
querer (ie) *to want to,* 3; *to love,* 9; **quiero conocer...** *I want to see . . .,* 10; **Quiero devolver...** *I want to return...,* 8; queriendo *wanting to,* 8; **Quiero ir...** *I want to go . . .,* 3
querido(a) *dear,* 9
la quesadilla *tortillas with melted*

cheese, 3G
el queso *cheese,* 6
¿quién? *who?,* 1; **¿De parte de quién?** *Who's calling?,* 8; **Quién es...?** *Who's. . .?,* 1; ¿de quién? *about whom?,* 1
¿quiénes? *who?* (pl.), 2
la química *chemistry,* 4
quince *fifteen,* 1
la quinceañera *girl's fifteenth birthday,* 9
quinientos *five hundred,* 8
el quiosco *stand,* 10
Quisiera... *I would like . . .,* 6
quitarse *to take off,* 7

las raciones *servings,* 6
la raíz (pl. las raíces) *root,* 1G
rallado(a) *grated,* 6
la rana *frog,* 2
los rancheros *overalls,* 3
rápidamente *quickly,* 6
rápido(a) *fast,* 8
raro *odd, strange,* 3
rato: pasar el rato... *to spend time . . .,* 3; el rato libre *free time,* 4
reaccionar *to react,* 10
el realismo *realism,* 1
realizar *to carry out,* 10, ha realizado *has carried out,* 10G
el recado *message,* 8
la recámara *bedroom,* 5
recibir *to receive,* 9; **recibir regalos** *to receive gifts,* 9
reclamar *to reclaim,* 6G
el reclamo de equipaje *baggage claim,* 10
recoger *to pick up,* 10
la recomendación *recommendation,* 7
reconocido(a) *well-known,* 1G
recordar (ue) *to remember,* 6
recorrer *to tour,* 10
el recorrido *tour,* 4
el recreo *recreation time,* 4
la red *network,* 10G
redondo(a) *round,* 7
reducir *to reduce,* 7
referir *to refer,* 3; se refiere *refers,* 3G
reflejar *to reflect,* 1G
el refrán *proverb, saying,* 6
el refresco *soft drink,* 6
el refrigerador *refrigerator,* 6
el refugio de fauna *wildlife refuge,* 8G
el regalo *gift,* 9; **abrir regalos** *to open gifts,* 9; **recibir regalos** *to receive gifts,* 9
regatear *to bargain,* 8
la región *region,* 3
regional *regional,* 6
la regla *ruler,* 4
regresar *to return, to go back,* 4
regular *all right,* 1; **Estoy regular.** *I'm all right.,* 1
regularidad: con regularidad *regularly,* 6
reírse *to laugh,* 8; ríe *he/she laughs,* 9; se ríen *they laugh,* 8
relajarse *to relax,* 7
religioso(a) *religious,* 1
el reloj *clock, watch,* 4
remodelado(a) *remodeled,* 5
remojar *to soak,* 3
remoto(a) *distant,* 5
el renacuajo *tadpole,* 2
el repaso *review,* 1
representar *to represent,* 3
representativo(a) *representative,* 6
la república *republic,* 5G
el res *beast, livestock;* la carne de res *beef,* 6
la reservación *reservation,* 6
requerir (ie) *to require,* 7
la resolución de Año Nuevo *New Year's resolution,* 9
resolver (ue) *to solve,* 7
respectivo(a) *respective,* 8
responder *to answer,* 9
la respuesta *answer,* xxii, 3
el restaurante familiar *family restaurant,* 3
el restaurante *restaurant,* 6
el retrato *portrait,* 1G
la reunión *meeting,* 3; *reunion,* 9
reunir *to bring together,* 1G
reunirse *to get together,* 9; **reunirse con (toda) la familia** *to get together with the (whole) family,* 9
revisar *to check, to revise, to correct,* 1
la revista *magazine,* 3; **la revista de tiras cómicas** *comic book,* 8
el revolucionario *revolutionary,* 9G
el rey *king,* 1
rico(a) *magnificent,* 9
ridículo(a) *ridiculous,* 8
riguroso(a) *harsh,* 5G
el río *river,* 3G
las riquezas *riches,* 10
riquísimo(a) *delicious,* 6
el ritmo *rhythm,* 5G; el ritmo del momento *the latest rhythm,* 1
el rito *ritual,* 6
el robo: ¡Es un robo! *It's a rip-off!,* 8
rodeado(a) *surrounded,* 1G
rodear *to surround,* 7G
el rodeo *rodeo,* 3G
rojo(a) *red,* 8
romántico(a) *romantic,* 2
el rompecabezas *puzzle,* 4
la ropa *clothes,* 4
rubio(a) *blond,* 2
las ruinas *ruins,* 10
la rutina *routine,* 2

el sábado *Saturday,* 1; **los sábados** *on Saturdays,* 3
saber *to know information,* 4; **saber de** *to know about,* 4; no sabe cómo *doesn't know how,* 9; **No sé.** *I don't know.,* 4; **¿Sabes qué?** *You know what?,* 4; Sé. *I know.,* 9
el sabor *flavor,* 8G
sacar *to take out,* 5; **sacar el dinero** *to get money,* 10; **sacar fotos** *to take photos,* 10; **sacar la basura** *to take out the trash,* 5; sacar una idea *to get an idea,* 4
el saco *jacket,* 8
sal *go out, leave,* 6
la sal *salt,* 6
la sala *living room,* 5; **la sala de espera** *waiting room,* 10; la sala de juegos *game room,* 5
salado(a) *salty,* 6
la salida *departure,* 10; *exit,* 10
salir (-go) *to go out,* 3; *to leave,* 4; **No salgas** *Don't leave,* 10; que salga *go out,* 9; **sal** *go out, leave,* 6; salir bien *to work out well,* 7; **salir con amigos** *to go out with friends,* 3
el salón *room,* 1; **el salón de clase** *classroom,* 4
la salsa *sauce, gravy,* 6; **la salsa picante** *hot sauce,* 6
el salto *waterfall,* 2G
el salto en el tiempo *time warp,* 7
la salud *health,* 7
saludable *healthy,* 6
saludar *to greet,* 1
el saludo *greeting,* 9
salvarse *to save oneself,* 10
el salvavidas *lifeguard,* 1
el sancocho *stew made with meat, root vegetables, and plantains,* 9G
las sandalias *sandals,* 8
el sándwich de... *. . . sandwich,* 6
los sanitarios *restrooms,* 10
sano(a) *healthy,* 7; **seguir una dieta sana** *to eat a balanced diet,* 7
el santo, la santa *saint,* 2G
la sartén *frying pan,* 6
sé *be,* 6
la secadora de pelo *hair dryer,* 7
secarse *to dry,* 7
la sección rítmica *rhythm section,* 8G
seco(a) *dry,* 2G
secreto(a) *secret,* 1

la sed *thirst,* 4; **tener sed** *to be thirsty,* 4
la seda *silk,* 8; **de seda** *made of silk,* 8
seguir (i) *to follow,* 10; **seguir (i) una dieta sana** *to eat a balanced diet,* 7; sigue el modelo *follow the model,* xxii; siguiéndote *following you,* 8
según *according to,* 2
el segundo *second,* 4
segundo(a) *second,* 6
seis *six,* 1
seiscientos *six hundred,* 8
la selección *selection,* 6
la selva *jungle,* 10
la semana *week,* 4; **el día de la semana** *day of the week,* 1; **esta semana** *this week,* 4; **la próxima semana** *next week,* 4
la Semana Santa *Holy Week,* 9
el señor *sir, Mr.,* 1; *gentleman,* 8
el Señor *the Lord,* 9
la señora *ma'am; Mrs.,* 1
la señorita *Miss,* 1
la sensación *feeling,* 1
sentarse (ie) *to sit down,* 10
sentir (ie) *to feel,* 9
sentirse (ie) *to feel,* 7
separados *separately,* 8
separar *to separate,* 1G
septiembre *September,* 1
ser *to be,* 1; **¿Cómo eres?** *What are you like?,* 2; **¿Cómo es...?** *What is . . . like?,* 2; No puede ser. *It can't be true.,* 9; **no seas** *don't be,* 7; **sé** *be,* 6; **será** *will be,* 10; **Soy...** *I'm . . .,* 2; **Soy de...** *I'm from . . .,* 1
el ser *being,* 8
la serenata *serenade,* 9
la serenidad *serenity,* 1
la serie *series,* 6G
serio(a) *serious,* 2
la serpiente *serpent,* 6
el servicio *restroom,* 10
la servilleta *napkin,* 6
servir (i) *to serve,* 6; **¿En qué le puedo servir?** *How can I help you?,* 8
sesenta *sixty,* 2
el seso *brain,* 4
setecientos *seven hundred,* 8
setenta *seventy,* 2
si *if,* 3; si no *otherwise,* 3
sí *yes,* 4
siempre *always,* 5; **casi siempre** *almost always,* 3; **como siempre** *as always,* 9; **Lo de siempre.** *Same as usual.,* 9
la sierra *mountain range,* 10G
siete *seven,* 1
el siglo *century,* 3G
el significado *meaning,* 7
significar *to mean,* 2
siguiente *following,* 5; **lo siguiente** *the following,* 6
la sílaba *syllable,* 2
la silla *chair,* 5; **la silla de ruedas** *wheelchair,* 5
el símbolo *symbol,* 2
simpático(a) *friendly,* 2
simplemente *simply,* 6
sin *without,* 6; sin embargo *however,* 6
la sinagoga *synagogue,* 9
sincero(a) *sincere,* 2
sino *but also,* 6
los sirvientes *servants,* 8
el sistema *system,* 10G
el sitio *place,* 3; *site,* 7
la situación *situation,* 5
sobre *over,* 3; *on,* 4; *about,* 2
la sobrina *niece,* 5
el sobrino *nephew,* 5
los sobrinos *nephews, nieces and nephews,* 5
sociable *social,* 2
el sofá *couch,* 5
el sol *sun,* 3; **Hace sol.** *It's sunny.,* 3
solamente *only,* 3G
el soldado *soldier,* 6G
soler (ue) *to usually do,* 5; suele *usually,* 5
sólido(a) *solid,* 6
solo(a) *alone,* 3; **pasar el rato solo(a)** *to spend time alone,* 3
sólo *only,* 7
el sombrero *hat,* 8
somos (inf. **ser**) *we are,* 5; **Somos... personas...** *There are . . . people . . .,* 5
Son las... *It's . . . o'clock.,* 1
el sonido *sound,* 2G
la sopa *soup,* 6; **la sopa (de verduras)** *(vegetable) soup,* 6
sordo(a) *deaf,* 5
sorprendido(a) *surprised,* 8
Soy... (inf. **ser**) *I'm . . .,* 2; **Soy de...** *I'm from . . .,* 1
su(s) *his, her, its, their, your,* 5
suave *soft,* 7
subir *to rise,* 7
subir a la montaña *to go up a mountain,* 10; **subir de peso** *to gain weight,* 7
el subtítulo *subtitle,* 10
sucio(a) *dirty,* 6
el sudeste *southeast,* 10G
Suele + inf. *He (She) usually* + verb, 10
el sueño *dream,* 1G
la suerte *luck,* 10; **si tengo suerte...** *if I'm lucky . . .,* 10; **tuviste suerte** *you were lucky,* 10
el suéter *sweater,* 8
suficiente *enough,* 7; **dormir lo suficiente** *to get enough sleep,* 7
la sugerencia *suggestion,* 7
sugerir (ie) *to suggest,* 6
Suiza *Switzerland,* 7G
la superficie *surface,* 8
el sur *south,* 2G
sureño(a) *southern,* 7G
el surf a vela *windsurfing,* 9G
la sustancia *substance,* 6
suyo(a) *his,* 4G

Tailandia *Thailand,* 6
taíno(a) *belonging to the Tainos, Native Americans dominant in early Puerto Rico,* 2G
tal *such,* 7; tal vez *perhaps,* 4
la talla *(clothing) size,* 8
tallado(a) *carved, cut,* 10G
los tallarines *noodles,* 7
el taller *shop, workshop,* 4
la tamalada *gathering to make tamales,* 3G
los tamales *tamales,* 9
el tamaño *size*
también *also,* 2
la tambora *drum,* 9G
tampoco *neither, not either,* 5
tan *so,* 10G
tan sólo *only,* 9
tan... como *as . . . as,* 8
tanto *so much,* 7; *as much,* 1G; tanto... como... *both . . . and . . .,* 3G; **Tanto gusto.** *So nice to meet you.,* 9; **¡Tanto tiempo sin verte!** *Long time, no see.,* 9
la tapa *small servings of food,* 7G
tardar *to take;* ¿Cuánto tardas? *How long do you take?,* 4
la tarde *afternoon,* 4; **esta tarde** *this afternoon,* 4; **por la tarde** *in the afternoon,* 4
tarde *late,* 4; **más tarde** *later,* 8
la tarea *homework,* 1; **hacer la tarea** *to do homework,* 3
la tarjeta *greeting card,* 8; *card,* 9; **mandar tarjetas** *to send cards,* 9; **la tarjeta de cumpleaños** *birthday card,* 8; la tarjeta de crédito *credit card,* 10; **la tarjeta de embarque** *boarding pass,* 10; la tarjeta postal *postcard,* 10
el tataranieto *great-great-grandson,* 10
el taxi *taxi,* 10
la taza *cup,* 6
te *(to/for) you,* 2; **¿Te duele algo?** *Does something hurt?,* 7; **¿Te gusta(n)...?** *Do you like . . .?,* 2; **¿Te gusta(n) más... o...?** *Do you like . . . or . . . more?,* 2; **Te llamo más tarde.** *I'll call you later.,* 9;

Te presento a... *I'd like you to meet . . .*, 9; **Te veo mal.** *You don't look well.*, 7
el teatro *theater*, 8
el techo de zinc *sheet-metal roof*, 9G
la tecnología *technology*, 4
tejano(a) *Texan*, 3G
el tejido *weaving*, 10G
la tele *TV*, 4
el teléfono *telephone number*, 1; *telephone*, 8; **¿Cuál es el teléfono de...?** *What's . . . 's telephone number?*, 1; **¿Cuál es tu teléfono?** *What's your telephone number?*, 1; **hablar por teléfono** *to talk on the phone*, 3; llamar por teléfono *to make a phone call*, 8; el teléfono público *pay phone*, 10
la televisión *television (TV)*, 3; **ver televisión** *to watch TV*, 3
el tema *theme*, 6
temblar *to shake*, 9
tembloroso(a) *trembling*, 9
la temperatura *temperature*, 2G
templado(a) *temperate*, 2G
el templo *temple*, 9
temprano *early*, 4
ten *have*, 6
el tenedor *fork*, 6
tener (-go, ie) *to have*, 4; **¿Cuántos años tiene...?** *How old is . . .?*, 2; **¿Cuántos años tienes?** *How old are you?*, 2; **Él (Ella) tiene... años.** *He's (She's) . . . years old.*, 2; **no tengas** *don't have*, 10; **ten** *have*, 6; tendrán que separarse *will have to separate*, 3; **tener calor** *to be hot*, 7; **tener catarro** *to have a cold*, 7; **tener frío** *to be cold*, 7; **tener ganas** *to feel like (doing something)*, 4; **tener ganas de** + infinitive *to feel like doing something*, 4; **tener hambre** *to be hungry*, 4; **tener los ojos azules** *to have blue eyes*, 5; **tener miedo** *to be afraid*, 7; **tener prisa** *to be in a hurry*, 4; tener puesto *to have on*, 3; **tener que** + infinitive *to have to do something*, 4; **tener razón** *to be right*, 8; **tener sed** *to be thirsty*, 4; **tener sueño** *to be sleepy*, 7; **tener suerte** *to be lucky*, 10; **tener un picnic** *to have a picnic*, 9; **Tengo que irme.** *I've got to go.*, 1; **Tengo... años.** *I am . . . years old.*, 2; **Tiene... años.** *He (She) is . . . years old.*, 2; tuvo *had*, 7G
el tenis *tennis*, 3
el tentempié *snack*, 3G
el tercero *third*, 4
terminar *to finish*, 9
el territorio *territory*, 6G
el terror *horror*, 2
el testimonio *testimony*, 6G
el texto *text*, 6
ti *you (emphatic)*, 3; a ti *to you*, 6; **A ti te gusta** + infinitive *You like . . .*, 3; para ti *for you*, 2
la tía *aunt*, 5
el tico *nickname for Costa Rican*, 4G
el tiempo *weather*, 3; *time*, 1G; **a tiempo** *on time*, 4; **cuando hace buen/mal tiempo** *when the weather's good/bad*, 3
la tienda de... *. . . store*, 8
tiene *he/she/it has*, 2; **¿Cuántos años tiene...?** *How old is . . .?*, 2; **Él (Ella) tiene... años.** *He's (She's) . . . years old.*, 2
tienes *you have*, 4; **¿Cuántos años tienes?** *How old are you?*, 2; **¿Tienes...?** *Do you have . . .?*, 4
la tierra *earth*, 6; *land*, 6G
el tigre *tiger*, 2
la tilde *wavy line above the ñ*, 1
tímido(a) *shy*, 2
la tinta *ink*, 10
el tío *uncle*, 5
los tíos *uncles, uncles and aunts*, 5
típico(a) *typical*, 2G
el tipo *type*; de todo tipo *all kinds*, 8; el título *title*, 5
la toalla *towel*, 7
tocar *to play*, 3; *to touch*, 8; **A mí siempre me toca...** *I always have to . . .*, 5; **A... nunca le toca...** *It's never . . .'s turn; . . . never has to . . .*, 5; Le toca a él. *It's his turn.*, 9; **¿Qué te toca hacer a ti?** *What do you have to do?*, 5, Te toca a ti. *It's your turn.*, 6; **tocar el piano** *to play the piano*, 3; tocar la puerta *to knock on the door*, 3
el tocino *bacon*, 6
todavía *yet*, 10; *still*, 1G; **todavía no** *not yet*, 10
todo(a) *all, every*, 2; *whole*, 9; todo el mundo *everybody*, 9; de todo *everything*, 8; de todo tipo *all kinds*, 8; **todos(as)** *everyone*, 5; **todos los días** *every day*, 3
tomar *to drink*, 6; *to eat*, 8; *to take*, 9; siguen tomándolo *keep drinking it*, 6; **tomar el sol** *to sunbathe*, 10; tomar las cosas con calma *to take things calmly*, 7; tomar una decisión *to make a decision*, 9; **tomar un batido** *to have a milkshake*, 8
el tomate *tomato*, 6
la tonelada *ton*, 10
tonto(a) *silly, foolish*, 2
el tornado *tornado*, 3
la toronja *grapefruit*, 3G
la torre *tower*, 9G
la torta *sandwich (Mexico)*, 6
la tortilla *Spanish omelet*, 1G; *pancake-like bread made from corn*, 6
la tortuga *turtle*, 1
el tostón *fried green plantain*, 2G
trabajador(a) *hard-working*, 2
trabajar *to work*, 3
el trabajo *job*, 3; *work*, 4
el trabalenguas *tongue twister*, 1
la tradición *tradition*, 2
tradicional *traditional*, 1G
traer (-igo) *to bring*, 4; me trajo *he/she brought me*, 4; quiero que me traigas *I want you to bring me*, 9
el tráfico *traffic*, 3G
tragar *to swallow*, 2
el traje *suit*, 3; *dress*, 1G
el traje de baño *swimsuit*, 8
tranquilo(a) *quiet*, 5; *calm*, 9
la transpiración *perspiration*, 8
transportar *to transport*, 10; fueron transportadas *were transported*, 10
el transporte *transportation*, 10
el trasto *utensil, piece of junk*, 2
tratar *to try*, 10
travieso(a) *mischievous*, 5
trece *thirteen*, 1
treinta *thirty*, 1
treinta y cinco *thirty-five*, 2
treinta y dos *thirty-two*, 2
treinta y uno *thirty-one*, 1
el tren *train*, 10
tres *three*, 1
trescientos *three hundred*, 8
el trigal *wheat field*, 2
el trigo *wheat*, 2
triste *sad*, 7; **estar triste** *to be sad*, 7
el trozo *piece*, 6
tú *you*, 1
tu(s) *your*, 5
el turismo *tourism*, 8G
el turista *tourist*, 1G
turnarse *to take turns*, xxii
el turno *shift*, 4
tutear *to speak to someone informally*, 10
los tuyos, las tuyas *yours*, 9

último(a) *latest*, 8; la última vez *last time*, 8
el último, la última *last one*, 3
un(a) *a, an*, 4; **un poco** *a little*, 2; **un montón** *a ton*, 4
únicamente *only*, 9

único(a) *only,* 4G
la unidad *unity,* 3G
la universidad *university,* 5
uno *one,* 1
unos(as) *some,* 4
urgente *urgent,* 1
usar *to use, to wear,* 8; **usar el/la...** *to wear size . . .,* 8; **usar lentes** *to wear glasses,* 5; **usando** *using,* xxii
el uso *use,* 6
usted *you* (formal), 1
ustedes *you* (pl.), 1
los útiles escolares *school supplies,* 4
utilizar *to use,* 7
la uva *grape,* 1
¡Uy! *Oh!,* 1

V

Vale. *Okay.,* 9
valeroso(a) *brave,* 4G
valiente *brave,* 5
la valija *suitcase,* 10
el valle *valley,* 3G
vamos *let's go, we go,* 3
el vaquero *cowboy,* 3G
vaquero(a) *referring to cowboys,* 3G
los vaqueros *jeans,* 8
variado(a) *varied,* 7
varias *various,* 6G
la variedad *variety,* 6
vas *you are going,* 4; **¿Vas al (a la)...?** *Are you going to the. . .?,* 4; **Vas a ir, ¿verdad?** *You're going to go, aren't you?,* 4
el vasco *language from Basque Provinces, Spain,* 1G
la vasija *pot,* 4
el vaso *glass,* 6
ve *go,* 6
veces *times,* 7; **a veces** *sometimes,* 3; hay veces *there are times,* 4
veinte *twenty,* 1
veintiún *twenty-one,* 1
ven *come,* 6
vencido(a) *defeated,* 6; no se da por vencido *doesn't give up,* 6
el vendedor *vendor,* 8
vender *to sell,* 8; se vende *for sale,* 5; se venden *are sold,* 8; **vender (de todo)** *to sell (everything),* 8
venir *to come,* 4; ha venido *has come,* 9; **no vengas** *don't come,* 10; **ven** *come,* 6; venga *will come,* 9; **vienes conmigo a...** *you're coming with me . . .,* 4
la ventana *window,* 5
el ventanal *large window,* 6G
la ventura *happiness,* 5
ver *to watch, to see,* 4; nunca ha visto *never has seen,* 6; **Te veo mal.** *You don't look well.,* 7; **ver televisión** *to watch television,* 3; vi *I saw,* 8
el verano *summer,* 1
el verbo *verb,* xxii
la verdad *truth,* 2
¿verdad? *right?,* 4
verde *green,* 5; verde mar *sea green,* 5G
las verduras *vegetables,* 2
vespertino(a) *(in the) afternoon,* 4
el vestido *dress,* 8
vestirse (i) *to get dressed,* 7
vete *go,* 7
vez *time,* 4; cada vez *each time,* 8; hay veces *there are times,* 4; la última vez *last time,* 8
viajar *to travel,* 10
el viaje *trip,* 10
el viajero *traveler,* 10
la vida *life,* 3G
el video *video,* 3; **alquilar videos** *to rent videos,* 3
los videojuegos *videogames,* 2
los viejitos *older folks,* 3
viejo(a) *old,* 5
el viento *wind,* 3; **Hace viento.** *It's windy.,* 3
el viernes *Friday,* 1; **los viernes** *on Fridays,* 3
el Viernes Santo *Good Friday,* 1
el violín *violin,* 1
visitar *to visit,* 6
la vista *view,* 5
la vitrina *shop window,* 8; **mirar las vitrinas** *to window-shop,* 8
vivir *to live,* 5
vivo(a) *bright,* 5G
el vocabulario *vocabulary,* xxii
volar (ue) *to fly,* 7
el volcán *volcano,* 4G
el volibol *volleyball,* 3
volver (ue) *to go or come back,* 5; nunca más volverá *never will do it again,* 9; se vuelve *it becomes,* 6
vosotros(as) *you* (plural; informal), 1
el vuelo *flight,* 10
vuestra(s) *your,* 5
vuestro(s) *your,* 5

W

el wáter *restroom,* 10
el windsurf *windsurfing,* 7

Y

y *and,* 1; **y cuarto** *a quarter past,* 1; **y media** *half past,* 1
ya *already,* 10
Ya te lo (la) paso. *I'll get him (her).,* 8
la yerba mate *herb used to make* ***mate,*** 7
yo *I,* 1
el yogur *yogurt,* 7
la yuca *yucca,* 8G

Z

la zanahoria *carrot,* 6
la zapatería *shoe store,* 8
las zapatillas de tenis *tennis shoes,* 8
los zapatos *shoes,* 4; **los zapatos de tenis** *tennis shoes,* 8
la zona *area,* 4; la zona residencial *residential area,* 5
el zoológico *zoo,* 10
el zumo *juice (Spain),* 6

Vocabulario inglés-español

This vocabulary includes all of the words presented in the **Vocabulario** sections of the chapters. These words are considered active—you are expected to know them and be able to use them. Expressions are listed under the English word you would be most likely to look up.

Spanish nouns are listed with the definite article and plural forms, when applicable. If a Spanish verb is stem-changing, the change is indicated in parentheses after the verb: **dormir (ue)**. The number after each entry refers to the chapter in which the word or phrase is introduced.

To be sure you are using Spanish words and phrases in their correct context, refer to the chapters listed. You may also want to look up Spanish phrases in **Expresiones de ¡Exprésate!**, pp. R12–R15.

A

a little *un poco,* 2
a lot *mucho,* 2
a lot of, many *muchos(as),* 4
a ton *un montón,* 4
a, an *un(a),* 4
active *activo(a),* 2
to add *añadir,* 6
address *la dirección,* 5; **My address is . . .** *Mi dirección es...,* 5; **e-mail address** *correo electrónico,* 1
adventure *la aventura,* 2; **adventure book** *el libro de aventuras,* 2
after *después,* 3; *después de,* 7; **after class** *después de clases,* 3
afternoon *la tarde,* 4; **this afternoon** *esta tarde,* 4; **in the afternoon** *por la tarde,* 4
afterwards *después,* 4
agent *el agente, la agente,* 10
agree: I agree. *Estoy de acuerdo.,* 6
airplane *el avión,* 10; **by plane** *por avión,* 10
airport *el aeropuerto,* 10
all *todas,* 1; *todo(a),* 2
all right *regular,* 1
to allow *dejar,* 3
almost *casi,* 3; **almost never** *casi nunca,* 3; **almost always** *casi siempre,* 3
alone *solo(a),* 3
alphabet *el alfabeto,* 1
already *ya,* 10
also *también,* 2
always *siempre,* 5; **almost always** *casi siempre,* 3; **as always** *como siempre,* 9
amusement park *el parque de diversiones,* 10
an *un, una,* 4
and *y,* 1
animal *el animal,* 2
anniversary *el aniversario,* 9
another *otro(a),* 8
any *cualquier,* 10
anything *algo,* 4
apartment *el apartamento,* 5
apple *la manzana,* 6
April *abril,* 1
Are you . . .? *¿Eres...?,* 2
arm *el brazo,* 7
around the corner *a la vuelta,* 10
arrival *la llegada,* 10
to arrive *llegar,* 4
art *el arte,* 4
as . . .as *tan...como,* 8
as always *como siempre,* 9
at *a(l),* 8; **@** *la arroba,* 1; *en,* 3
athletic *atlético(a),* 2
to attend *asistir a,* 4
auditorium *el auditorio,* 4
August *agosto,* 1
aunt *la tía,* 5
automatic teller machine *el cajero automático,* 10
awesome *fenomenal,* 2

B

back *la espalda,* 7, **I'll call back later** *Llamo más tarde.,* 8; **to go (come) back** *volver (ue),* 5
backpack *la mochila,* 4
bacon *el tocino,* 6
bad *malo(a),* 2
bag *bolsa,* 8
baggage *el equipaje,* 10; **baggage claim** *el reclamo de equipaje,* 10
bargain *la ganga,* 8
baseball *el béisbol,* 3
basketball *el básquetbol,* 3
to bathe *bañarse,* 7
bathroom *el baño,* 5
be sé, 6
to be able to *poder (ue),* 6
to be *estar,* 1; **How are you?** *¿Cómo está(s)?,* 1; **to be all right** *estar regular,* 1; **to be angry** *estar enojado(a),* 7; **to be bored** *estar aburrido(a),* 7; **to be familiar with** *conocer,* 9; **to be fine** *estar bien,* 1; **to be hungry** *tener hambre,* 4; **to be tired** *estar cansado(a),* 7; **to be happy** *estar contento(a),* 7; **to be sick** *estar enfermo(a),* 7; **to be in a hurry** *tener prisa,* 4; **to be in a wheelchair** *estar en una silla de ruedas,* 5; **to be ready** *estar listo(a),* 7; **to be nervous** *estar nervioso(a),* 7; **to be right** *tener razón,* 8; **to be sad** *estar triste,* 7; **to be scared** *tener miedo,* 7; **to be sleepy** *tener sueño,* 7; **to be lucky** *tener suerte,* 10; **to be thirsty** *tener sed,* 4
to be *ser,* 1; **don't be** *no seas,* 7
beach *la playa,* 3
because *porque,* 2
bed *la cama,* 5; **to make the bed** *hacer la cama,* 5; **to go to bed** *acostarse (ue),* 7
bedroom *la habitación,* 5
beef *la carne,* 6
before *antes de,* 7
behind *detrás de,* 5
besides *además,* 8
best *el/la/los/las mejor(es),* 1
better *mejor(es),* 7
big *grande,* 5
bike *la bicicleta,* 3; **to ride a bike** *montar en bicicleta,* 3
bill *la cuenta,* 6
biology *la biología,* 4
birthday *el cumpleaños,* 9; **When is . . .'s birthday?** *¿Cuándo es el*

cumpleaños de...?, 2; **When is your birthday?** *¿Cuándo es tu cumpleaños?*, 2; **birthday card** *la tarjeta de cumpleaños*, 8; **girl's fifteenth birthday** *la quinceañera*, 9
black *negro(a)*, 5
blank *en blanco*, 8
blind *ciego(a)*, 5
blond *rubio(a)*, 2
blouse *la blusa*, 8
blue *azul*, 5; **to have blue eyes** *tener los ojos azules*, 5
board game *el juego de mesa*, 3
to board *abordar*, 10
boarding pass *la tarjeta de embarque*, 10
boat *el barco*, 10
book *el libro*, 2; **adventure book** *el libro de aventuras*, 2; **comic book** *la revista de tiras comícas*, 8; **romance book** *el libro de amor*, 2
bookstore *la librería*, 8
boots *las botas*, 8
boring *aburrido(a)*, 2; **to be bored** *estar aburrido(a)*, 7
bowl *el plato hondo*, 6
boy *el muchacho*, 1
bracelet *la pulsera*, 8
bread *el pan*, 6
breakfast *el desayuno*, 6
to bring *traer (-igo)*, 4
broccoli *el bróculi*, 6
brother *el hermano*, 5
brothers, brothers and sisters *los hermanos*, 5
brown *castaño(a)*, 5; *de color café*, 5
building *el edificio*, 5; . . . **story building** *el edificio de... pisos*, 5
bus *el autobús*, 10
but *pero*, 2
to buy *comprar*, 8; **you would buy** *comprarías*, 8
Bye *chao*, 9

cafeteria *la cafetería*, 4
cake *el pastel*, 6
calculator *la calculadora*, 4
calf *la pantorrilla*, 7
to call *llamar*, 9; **I'll call back later.** *Llamo más tarde.*, 8
camera *la cámara*, 10; **disposable camera** *la cámara desechable*, 10
to camp *acampar*, 10
can *poder*, 6
Can I . . .? *¿Puedo...?*, 6; **How can I help you?** *¿En qué le puedo servir?*, 8
candy *el dulce*, 9
canoe *la canoa*, 10
car *el carro*, 2
card *la tarjeta*, 8
carrot *la zanahoria*, 5
cat *el gato, la gata*, 5
to celebrate *festejar*, 9; *celebrar*, 9
cereal *los cereales*, 6
chair *la silla*, 5; **wheelchair** *la silla de ruedas*, 5
to change money *cambiar dinero*, 10
to chat *charlar*, 9
to check *facturar*, 10; **to check luggage** *facturar el equipaje*, 10
checkpoint: security checkpoint *control de seguridad*, 10
cheese *el queso*, 6
chemistry *la química*, 4
chess *el ajedrez*, 2
chest *el pecho*, 7
chicken *el pollo*, 6
children *los hijos*, 5; *los ninos*, 8
chocolate *el chocolate*, 6
chores *los quehaceres*, 5
Christmas *la Navidad*, 9; **Christmas Eve** *la Nochebuena*, 9
church *la iglesia*, 3
city *la ciudad*, 5
class *la clase*, 3; **after class** *después de clases*, 3
classmate (female) *la (una) compañera de clase*, 1
classmate (male) *el (un) compañero de clase*, 1
to clean *limpiar*, 5
to clean the room *arreglar el cuarto*, 5
client *el cliente, la cliente*, 8
to climb *subir*, 10
clock *el reloj*, 4
close to *cerca de*, 5
to close *cerrar (ie)*, 8
clothes *la ropa*, 4
club *el club de...*, 4
coat *el abrigo*, 8
coffee *el café*, 6; **coffee with milk** *el café con leche*, 6, **coffee shop** *la cafetería*, 6
cold *frío(a)*, 6; **It's cold.** *Hace frío.*, 3; **to be cold** *tener frío*, 7; **to have a cold** *tener catarro*, 7
comb *el peine*, 7
to comb your hair *peinarse*, 7
to come *venir*, 4; **come** *ven*, 6; **don't come** *no vengas*, 10; **to come back** *volver*, 5; **you're coming with me to . . .** *vienes conmigo a...*, 4
comic book *la revista de tiras cómicas*, 8
compact disc *el disco compacto*, 8; **blank compact disc** *el disco compacto en blanco*, 8
computer *la computadora*, 4; **computer science** *la computación*, 4
concert *el concierto*, 4
to cook *cocinar*, 5
cookie *la galleta*, 9
cool *fresco*, 3; **It's cool.** *Hace fresco.*, 3
corn *el maíz*, 6
to cost *costar (ue)*, 8; **costs . . .** *cuesta(n)...*, 8
cotton *el algodón*, 8; **made of cotton** *de algodón*, 8
counter *el mostrador*, 10
country *el país*, 10
countryside *el campo*, 5
court: food court in a mall *la plaza de comida*, 8
cousin *el primo, la prima*, 5
custard *el flan*, 6
customs *la aduana*, 10
to cut *cortar*, 5; **to cut the grass** *cortar el césped*, 5

dad *el papá*, 5
dance *el baile*, 3
to dance *bailar*, 3
dark: dark-skinned; dark-haired *moreno(a)*, 2
date *la fecha*, 1
daughter *la hija*, 5
day *el día*, 1; **day after tomorrow** *pasado mañana*, 4; **day before yesterday** *anteayer*, 8; **day of the week** *el día de la semana*, 1; **Father's Day** *el Día del Padre*, 9; **holiday** *el día festivo*, 9; **Independence Day** *el Día de la Independencia*, 9; **Mother's Day** *el Día de la Madre*, 9; **Thanksgiving Day** *el Día de Acción de Gracias*, 9; **someday** *algún día*, 10; **Valentine's Day** *el Día de los Enamorados*, 9; **What day is today?** *¿Qué día es hoy?*, 1; **your saint's day** *el día de tu santo*, 9
deaf *sordo(a)*, 5
December *diciembre*, 1
to decorate *decorar*, 9; **to decorate the house** *decorar la casa*, 9
decoration *la decoración*, 9
delicious *delicioso(a)*, 2; *riquísimo(a)*, 6
to delight *encantar*, 6
department store *el almacén*, 8
departure *la salida*, 10
to desire *desear*, 6
desk *el escritorio*, 5

dessert *el postre,* 6
dictionary *el diccionario,* 4
diet *la dieta,* 7; **to eat a balanced diet** *seguir una dieta sana,* 7
difficult *difícil,* 4; **It's difficult.** *Es difícil.,* 4
dining room *el comedor,* 5
dinner *la cena,* 6
disc: compact disc *el disco compacto,* 8
dish, *el plato,* 6
disposable *desechable,* 10; **disposable camera** *la cámara desechable,* 10
Do you like . . .? *¿Te gusta(n)...?,* 2
to do *hacer,* 4; **we are doing** *estamos haciendo,* 9; **to do homework** *hacer la tarea,* 3; **to do chores** *hacer los quehaceres,* 5; **to do yoga** *hacer yoga,* 7; **do** *haz,* 6; **don't do** *no hagas,* 10; **What are they doing?** *¿Qué están haciendo?,* 9; **What did you do?** *¿Qué hiciste?* 8
dog *el perro, la perra,* 5
door *la puerta,* 5
dot: on the dot *en punto,* 1
downtown *el centro,* 10
to draw *dibujar,* 3
dress *el vestido,* 8
dressed: to get dressed, *vestirse (i),* 7
to drink *beber,* 4; **to drink something** *beber algo,* 4; *tomar,* 6
to dry *secarse,* 7
during *durante,* 10
DVD *el DVD,* 8

ear *el oído,* 7
early *temprano,* 4
earphones *los audífonos,* 8
earrings *los aretes,* 8
easy *fácil,* 4; **It's easy.** *Es fácil.,* 4
to eat a balanced diet *seguir una dieta sana,* 7; **to eat breakfast** *desayunar,* 6; **to eat dinner** *cenar,* 6; **to eat lunch** *almorzar (ue),* 5
to eat *comer,* 3; *tomar,* 8
egg *el huevo,* 6
eight *ocho,* 1
eight hundred *ochocientos,* 8
eighteen *dieciocho,* 1
eighty *ochenta,* 2
eleven *once,* 1
e-mail address *el correo electrónico,* 1; **What is . . .'s e-mail address?** *¿Cuál es el correo electrónico de...?* 1; **What's your e-mail address?** *¿Cuál es tu correo electrónico?,* 1
English *el inglés,* 4
enough *suficiente,* 7; **to get enough sleep** *dormir lo suficiente,* 7
evening *la tarde,* 1
everybody *todos(as),* 5
everyone *todos(as),* 5
everything *todo,* 8
to exercise *hacer ejercicio,* 3
to expect *esperar,* 9
expensive *caro(a),* 8
eyes *los ojos,* 5; **to have blue eyes** *tener los ojos azules,* 5

face *la cara,* 7
fall *el otoño,* 1
family *la familia,* 3; **There are . . . people in my family.** *En mi familia somos...,* 5
familiar: to be familiar *conocer,* 9
fantastic: How fantastic! *¡Qué fantástico!,* 10
fat (in food) *la grasa,* 7
fat (overweight) *gordo(a),* 5
father *el padre,* 5; **Father's Day** *el Día del Padre,* 9
favorite *preferido(a),* 4
flan *el flan,* 6
February *febrero,* 1
to feel *sentirse (ie),* 7; **to feel like doing something** *tener ganas de + infinitive,* 4
few *pocos(as),* 4
fifteen *quince,* 1
fifteenth: girl's fifteenth birthday *quinceañera,* 9
fifty *cincuenta,* 2
film *la película,* 2
to find *encontrar (ue),* 7
fine *bien,* 1; **I'm fine.** *Estoy bien.,* 1
finger *el dedo,* 7
to finish *terminar,* 9
fireworks *los fuegos artificiales,* 9
first *el primero,* 1
first (adj) *primero(a),* 4
fish *el pescado,* 6
to fish *pescar,* 10
fishing *la pesca,* 10; **to go fishing** *ir de pesca,* 10
to fit *quedar,* 8; **How does it fit?** *¿Cómo me queda?,* 8
five *cinco,* 1
five hundred *quinientos,* 8
flight *el vuelo,* 10
floor *el piso,* 5
folder *la carpeta,* 4
to follow *seguir (i),* 10
food *la comida,* 2; **Chinese (Italian, Mexican) food** *la comida china (italiana, mexicana),* 2, **food court in a mall** *la plaza de comida,* 8
foolish *tonto(a),* 2
foot *el pie,* 7
football *el fútbol americano,* 3
for *para,* 4
fork *el tenedor,* 7
fortune *la fortuna,* 8
forty *cuarenta,* 2
four *cuatro,* 1
four hundred *cuatrocientos,* 8
fourteen *catorce,* 1
French *el francés,* 4
French fries *las papas fritas,* 6
Friday *el viernes,* 1; **on Fridays** *los viernes,* 3
friend *el amigo* (male), *la amiga* (female), 1
from *de,* 1
fruit *la fruta,* 2
fun *divertido(a),* 2; **What fun!** *¡Qué divertido!,* 10

to gain weight *subir de peso,* 7
game: board game *el juego de mesa,* 3; **the . . . game** *el partido de...,* 4
garage *el garaje,* 5
garden *el jardín,* 5
German *el alemán,* 4
to get angry *enojarse,* 7
to get dressed *vestirse (i),* 7
to get off a plane *desembarcar,* 10
to get someone (for a telephone call), *pasártelo(la),* 8
to get together *reunirse,* 9
to get up *levantarse,* 7
to get *conseguir (i, i),* 10
gift *el regalo,* 9
girl *la muchacha,* 1
girl's fifteenth birthday *la quinceañera,* 9
to give *dar,* 7; **don't give** *no des,* 7
glass *el vaso,* 6
glasses *los lentes,* 5; **to wear glasses** *usar lentes,* 5
go *ve,* 6
to go *ir,* 2; **Where did you go?** *¿Adónde fuiste?,* 8; **to go shopping** *ir de compras,* 2; **to go hiking** *ir de excursión,* 10; **don't go** *no vayas,* 7; **I want to go. . .** *Quiero ir...,* 2; **Are you going to the . . .?** *¿Vas a...?,* 4; **You're going to go, aren't you?** *Vas a ir, ¿verdad?,* 4; **to go back** *regresar,* 4; *volver (ue),* 5
to go for a walk *pasear,* 3

go out *sal,* 6
to go out *salir,* 3; **to go out with friends** *salir con amigos,* 3; **to go out in a sailboat (motorboat)** *pasear en bote de vela (lancha),* 10
to go to bed *acostarse (ue),* 7
good *bueno(a),* 2; **Good evening., Good night.** *Buenas noches.,* 1; **Good afternoon.** *Buenas tardes.,* 1; **Good morning.** *Buenos días.,* 1
good-looking *guapo(a),* 2
Goodbye. *Adiós.,* 1
graduation *la graduación,* 9
grandchildren *los nietos,* 5
granddaughter *la nieta,* 5
grandfather *el abuelo,* 5
grandmother *la abuela,* 5
grandparents *los abuelos,* 5
grandson *el nieto,* 5
grandsons *los nietos,* 5
grass *el césped,* 5; **to cut the grass** *cortar el césped,* 5
gravy *salsa,* 6
gray *gris,* 8
gray-haired *canoso(a),* 5
great *formidable,* 2; *estupendo(a),* 10; *a todo dar,* 9; **it was great** *fue estupendo,* 10
green *verde,* 5
greeting card *la tarjeta,* 8
guest *el (la) invitado(a),* 9
gym *el gimnasio,* 3

hair *el pelo,* 5; **to comb your hair** *peinarse,* 7; **hair dryer** *la secadora de pelo,* 7
half *medio,* 1; **half past** *y media,* 1
ham *el jamón,* 6
hamburger *la hamburguesa,* 2
hand *la mano,* 7
to hang *colgar (ue),* 9
Hanukkah *el Hanukah,* 9
happy *contento(a),* 7; **to be happy** *estar contento(a),* 7
Happy (Merry) . . . *¡Feliz...!,* 9
hard *difícil,* 4
hard-working *trabajador(a),* 2
hat *el sombrero,* 8
to have *tener (-go, ie),* 4; **have** *ten,* 6; **don't have** *no tengas,* 10; **to have a cold** *tener catarro,* 7; **to have a milkshake** *tomar un batido,* 8; **to have a picnic** *tener un picnic,* 9; **to have blue eyes** *tener los ojos azules,* 5; **to have to do something** *tener que + infinitive,* 4; **I have to . . .** *A mí me toca...,* 5
to have a party *hacer una fiesta,* 9; **to have a snack** *merendar,* 5; **to have lunch** *almorzar,* 5
he *él,* 1; **He is . . .** *Él es...,* 1
head *la cabeza,* 7
health *la salud,* 7
to heat *calentar (ie),* 6
Hello. *Aló.,; Bueno.,; Diga.,* 8
help *la ayuda,* 6; **to help out at home** *ayudar en casa,* 5
here *aquí,* 6
hi, hello *hola,* 1
hike *la excursión,* 10; **to go on a hike** *ir de excursión,* 10
his *su(s),* 5
history *la historia,* 4
hobby *el pasatiempo,* 7; **to look for a hobby** *buscar un pasatiempo,* 7
holiday *el día festivo,* 9
Holy Week *la Semana Santa,* 9
homework *la tarea,* 3
Hope things go well for you. *Que te vaya bien.,* 9
horrible *horrible,* 2; **It was horrible!** *¡Fue horrible!,* 10
horror *el terror,* 2
hot *caliente,* 6; **hot sauce** *la salsa picante,* 6
hot chocolate *el chocolate,* 6
hotel *el hotel,* 10; **to stay in a hotel** *quedarse en un hotel,* 10
hour *la hora,* 1
house *casa,* 5; **. . . 's house** *la casa de...,* 3; **to decorate the house** *decorar la casa,* 9
household chores *los quehaceres,* 5
how *¿cómo?,* 1; **How are you?** *¿Cómo está(s)?,* 1; **How do you spell . . .?** *¿Cómo se escribe. . .?,* 1; **How does it fit?** *¿Cómo me queda?,* 8; **How fantastic!** *¡Qué fantástico!,* 10; **How great!** *¡Qué bien!,* 10; **How many . . .?** *¿cuántos(as)?,* 2; **how much?** *¿cuánto(a)?,* 4; **How often do you go . . .?** *¿Con qué frecuencia vas...?,* 3; **How old are you?** *¿Cuántos años tienes?,* 2
hunger *el hambre,* 4; **to be hungry** *tener hambre,* 4
to hurt *doler (ue),* 7; **My . . . hurt(s)** *Me duele(n)...* 7; **Does something hurt?** *¿Te duele algo?,* 7

ID *carnet de identidad,* 10
I *yo,* 1
I agree. *Estoy de acuerdo,* 6; **I don't agree.** *No estoy de acuerdo.,* 6
I have no idea. *Ni idea.,* 3
I want to see . . . *Quiero conocer...,* 10
I would like . . . *Quisiera...,* 6
I'd like you to meet . . . *Te presento a...,* 9
I'll get him (her). *Ya te lo (la) paso.,* 8
I'm fine. *Estoy bien.,* 1
I'm sorry. *Lo siento.,* 8
I'm . . . *Soy...,* 2; **I'm from . . .** *Soy de...,* 1
I'm just looking. *Nada más estoy mirando.,* 8
I'm not so good. *Estoy mal.,* 1
ice cream *el helado,* 2
ice cream shop *la heladería,* 8
Independence Day *El Día de la Independencia,* 9
in front of *delante de,* 5
in the (latest) fashion *a la (última) moda,* 8
in, by *por,* 4
inexpensive *barato(a),* 8
intellectual *intelectual,* 2
intelligent *inteligente,* 2
interest *el interés,* 10
interesting *interesante,* 2
to interrupt *interrumpir,* 4
to introduce *presentar,* 9
invitation *la invitación,* 9
to invite *invitar,* 9
island *la isla,* 10
It seems all right/fine to me. *Me parece bien.,* 5
it snows *nieva,* 3
It's a rip-off! *¡Es un robo!,* 8
It's all the same to me. *Me da igual.,* 2
It's awful. *Es pésimo.,* 2
It's cold. *Hace frío.,* 3
It's cool. *Hace fresco.,* 3
It's delicious. *Es delicioso.,* 2
It's hot. *Hace calor.,* 3
It's kind of fun. *Es algo divertido.,* 2
It's not a big deal. *No es gran cosa.,* 5
It's okay. *Está bien.,* 3
It's rather good. *Es bastante bueno.,* 2
It's sunny. *Hace sol.,* 3
It's windy. *Hace viento.,* 3

jacket *la chaqueta,* 8; *el saco,* 8
January *enero,* 1
jeans *los vaqueros,* 8
jewelry store *la joyería,* 8
job *el trabajo,* 3
joke *el chiste,* 9; **to tell jokes** *contar (ue) chistes,* 9
juice *el jugo,* 6
July *julio,* 1
June *junio,* 1
just: to just have done something *acabar de,* 7

K

kitchen *la cocina,* 5
knife *el cuchillo,* 6
to know (facts) *saber,* 4; **I don't know.** *No sé.,* 4; **to know people** *conocer,* 9

L

lake *el lago,* 10
large *grande,* 6
last *pasado(a),* 8; **last night** *anoche,* 8
late *tarde,* 4; **later** *más tarde,* 8; **latest** *último(a),* 8
lazy *perezoso(a),* 2
to leave *irse,* 10; *dejar,* 10; **leave** *salir, 3; sal,* 6; **to leave a message** *dejar un recado,* 8; **don't leave** *no salgas,* 10
leg *la pierna,* 7
letter *la carta,* 3
library *la biblioteca,* 4
to lift *levantar,* 7; **to lift weights** *levantar pesas,* 7
to like: I(you, . . .) like *me(te, ...) gusta(n),* 2; **I would like . . .,** *me gustaría,* 10
Likewise. *Igualmente.,* 1
line: to wait in line *hacer cola,* 10
to listen *escuchar,* 3; **to listen to music** *escuchar música,* 3
little (adv.) *poco,* 2; **a little** *un poco,* 2
to live *vivir,* 5
living room *la sala,* 5
long *largo(a),* 5; **Long time no see.** *¡Tanto tiempo sin verte!,* 9
to look *mirar,* 8
to look for *buscar,* 7;
to lose weight *bajar de peso,* 7
to lose *perder (ie),* 10
luck *la suerte,* 10
luggage *el equipaje,* 10
lunch *el almuerzo,* 4; *la comida,* 6; **to have lunch** *almorzar,* 5

M

ma'am; Mrs. *la señora,* 1
magazine *la revista,* 3
to maintain *mantenerse (ie),* 7; **to stay in shape** *mantenerse en forma,* 7
to make *hacer,* 4; **make** *haz,* 6; **to make the bed** *hacer la cama,* 5
makeup *el maquillaje,* 7
mall *el centro comercial,* 3
man *el hombre,* 6; **for men** *para hombres,* 8
many *muchos (as),* 4
map *el mapa,* 10
March *marzo,* 1
Mass *la misa,* 9
mathematics *las matemáticas,* 4
May *mayo,* 1
me *mí,* 5; *me,* 9
meat *la carne,* 6
to meet *encontrarse (ue),* 10
meeting *la reunión,* 3
Merry . . . *¡Feliz...!,* 9
message *el recado,* 8
microwave *el (horno) microondas,* 6
midday *el mediodía,* 1
midnight *la medianoche,* 1
milk *la leche,* 6
milkshake *el batido,* 8
million *un millón de,* 8
mischievous *travieso(a),* 5
Miss *la señorita,* 1
to miss *perder (ie),* 10
to mix *mezclar,* 6
mom *la mamá,* 5
moment *un momento,* 8
Monday *lunes,* 1; **on Mondays** *los lunes,* 3
money *el dinero,* 8
money exchange *la oficina de cambio,* 10
monitor, screen *la pantalla,* 10
months of the year *los meses del año,* 1
month *mes,* 1
more *más,* 2; **more than** *más que,* 8; **more . . . than** *más... que,* 8
morning *la mañana,* 1
mother *la madre,* 5; **Mother's Day** *El Día de la Madre,* 9
motorboat *la lancha,* 10; **to go out in a motorboat** *pasear en lancha,* 10
mountain *la montaña,* 10
mouth *la boca,* 7
movie *la película,* 2
movie theater *el cine,* 3
museum *el museo,* 10
music *la música,* 2; **music by . . .** *la música de...,* 2
my *mi(s),* 1
mystery *el misterio,* 2

N

napkin *la servilleta,* 6
neck *el cuello,* 7
to need *necesitar,* 4
neither, not either *tampoco,* 5; *ni,* 7
nephew *el sobrino,* 5
nervous *nervioso(a),* 7; **to be nervous** *estar nervioso(a),* 7
never *nunca,* 5; **almost never** *casi nunca,* 3
New Year's Eve *la Nochevieja,* 9
next *próximo(a),* 4; **next to** *al lado de,* 5
nice *simpático(a),* 2; **Nice to meet you.** *Encantado(a),* 1; *Mucho gusto.,* 1
niece *la sobrina,* 5
nine *nueve,* 1
nine hundred *novecientos,* 8
nineteen *diecinueve,* 1
ninety *noventa,* 2
no *no,* 3
nobody, not anybody *nadie,* 5
noon *el mediodía,* 1
nor *ni,* 7
nose *la nariz,* 7
not yet *todavía no,* 10
notebook *el cuaderno,* 4
nothing *nada,* 4
novel *la novela,* 2
November *noviembre,* 1
now *ahora,* 9
nowhere *ninguna parte,* 3
number *el número,* 1

O

October *octubre,* 1
Of course! *¡Claro que sí!,* 4
of the *del, de la, de las, de los,* 2
of *de,* 1
office: post office *oficina de correos,* 10
often *a menudo,* 5
Oh, no! *¡Ay, no!,* 6
Okay. *Vale.,* 9
old *viejo(a),* 5
older *mayor(es),* 5
on the dot *en punto,* 1
on time *a tiempo,* 4
on top of, above *encima de,* 5
one *uno,* 1
one hundred *cien,* 2
one hundred one *ciento uno,* 8
one million *millón (de),* 8
one thousand *mil,* 8
only *sólo,* 7; *nomás,* 8
to open *abrir,* 4; **to open gifts** *abrir regalos,* 9
or *o,* 2
orange *la naranja,* 6; *anaranjado(a),* 8
to order *pedir (i),* 6
to organize *organizar,* 10
our *nuestro(a)(s),* 5
out of style *pasado(a) de moda,* 8

outgoing *extrovertido(a)*, 2
oven *el horno*, 6
overcoat *el abrigo*, 8

to pack your suitcase *hacer la maleta*, 10
pain: What a pain! *¡Qué lata!*, 5
pair *el par*, 8
pajamas *el piyama*, 7
pants *los pantalones*, 7
paper *el papel*, 4
parents *los padres*, 5
park *el parque*, 3; **amusement park** *el parque de diversiones*, 10
party: to have a party *hacer una fiesta*, 9; **surprise party** *la fiesta sorpresa*, 9
pass: boarding pass *la tarjeta de embarque*, 10
passenger *el pasajero, la pasajera*, 10
passport *el pasaporte*, 10
pastry *el pan dulce*, 6
patio *el patio*, 5
to pay *pagar*, 8
peach *el durazno*, 6
pen *el bolígrafo*, 4
pencil *el lápiz (pl. los lápices)*, 4
person *la persona*, 5
photo *la foto*, 9; **to show photos** *enseñar fotos*, 9; **to take photos** *sacar fotos*, 10
physical education *la educación física*, 4
to pick up *recoger*, 10
picnic *el picnic*, 9
piñata *la piñata*, 9
pizza *la pizza*, 2
place *el lugar*, 10
plane ticket *el boleto de avión*, 10
plans *planes*, 9
plants *las plantas*, 5
plate *el plato*, 6
to play: to play an instrument *tocar*, 3; **to play the piano** *tocar el piano*, 3; **to play a game or sport** *jugar (ue)*, 3; **to play sports** *practicar deportes*, 3
please *por favor*, 6
Pleased to meet you. *Encantado(a)*., 1; *Mucho gusto*., 1
pool *la piscina*, 3
porch *el patio*, 5
post office *la oficina de correos*, 10
potato *la papa*, 6; **potato chips** *las papitas*, 9
practice *el entrenamiento*, 3
to prefer *preferir (ie)*, 6
preparations *los preparativos*, 9
to prepare *preparar*, 6
pretty *bonito(a)*, 2
punch *el ponche*, 9
purple *morado(a)*, 8
purse *la bolsa*, 8
to put *poner*, 4; **put** *pon*, 6; **don't put** *no pongas*, 10; **to put on makeup** *maquillarse*, 7; **to put on** *ponerse*, 7
pyramid *la pirámide, 10*

quarter past (the hour) *y cuarto*, 1
quarter to (the hour) *menos cuarto*, 1
quiet *callado(a)*, 5

to rain *llover (ue)*, 3; **it rains a lot** *llueve mucho*, 3
rather *bastante* + adjective, 2
razor *la navaja*, 7
to read *leer*, 3
ready *listo(a)*, 7; **to be ready** *estar listo(a)*, 7
to receive *recibir*, 9; **to receive gifts** *recibir regalos*, 9
red *rojo(a)*, 8
red-headed *pelirrojo(a)*, 2
refrigerator *el refrigerador*, 6
rehearsal *el ensayo*, 3
to relax *relajarse*, 7
to rent *alquilar*, 3; **to rent videos** *alquilar videos*, 3
to rest *descansar*, 3
restaurant *el restaurante*, 6
restroom *el baño*, 5; *el servicio*, 10
to return *regresar*, 4; *volver (ue)*, 5
rice *el arroz*, 6
to ride a bike *montar en bicicleta*, 3
right? *¿no?, 4; ¿verdad?*, 4; **to be right** *tener razón*, 8
ring *el anillo*, 8
rip-off: It's a rip-off! *¡Es un robo!*, 8
romance book *el libro de amor*, 2
romantic *romántico(a)*, 2
room *el cuarto*, 5
ruins *las ruinas*, 10
ruler *la regla*, 4
to run *correr*, 3

sad *triste*, 7
sailboat *el bote de vela*, 10; **to go out in a sailboat** *pasear en bote de vela*, 10
salad *la ensalada*, 6
salesclerk *el dependiente, la dependiente*, 8
salty *salado(a)*, 6
same as usual *lo de siempre*, 9
sandals *las sandalias*, 8
sandwich *el sándwich*, 6
Saturday *el sábado*, 1; **on Saturdays** *los sábados*, 3
sauce *la salsa*, 6; **hot sauce** *la salsa picante*, 6
to save money *ahorrar dinero*, 8
school *el colegio*, 3
school supplies *los útiles escolares*, 4
science *las ciencias*, 4; **science fiction** *la ciencia ficción*, 2; **computer science** *la computación*, 4
season *la estación*, 1
security checkpoint *el control de seguridad*, 10
to see *ver*, 4; **See you tomorrow.** *Hasta mañana.*, 1; **See you.** *Nos vemos.*, 1; **See you later.** *Hasta luego.*, 1; **See you soon.** *Hasta pronto.*, 1
to seem *parecer*, 5
to sell *vender*, 8
to send *mandar*, 9
September *septiembre*, 1
serious *serio(a)*, 2
to serve *servir (i)*, 6
to set *poner (-go)*, 6; **to set the table** *poner la mesa*, 6
seven *siete*, 1
seven hundred *setecientos*, 8
seventeen *diecisiete*, 1
seventy *setenta*, 2
to shave *afeitarse*, 7
shirt *la camisa*, 8
shoe store *la zapatería*, 8
shoes *los zapatos*, 4; **tennis shoes** *los zapatos de tenis*, 8
shop (class) *el taller*, 4
shop window *la vitrina*, 8; **to window-shop** *mirar las vitrinas*, 8; **to go shopping** *ir de compras*, 3
short (height) *bajo(a), 2;* (length) *corto(a)*, 5
shorts *los pantalones cortos*, 8
should *deber*, 6
shoulder *el hombro*, 7
to show *enseñar*, 4; **to show photos** *enseñar fotos*, 9
shy *tímido(a)*, 2
sick: to be *estar enfermo(a)*, 7
silk *la seda*, 8
silly *tonto(a)*, 2
to sing *cantar*, 3
sir *el señor*, 1
sister *la hermana*, 5

to sit down *sentarse (ie)*, 10
six *seis*, 1
six hundred *seiscientos*, 8
sixteen *dieciséis*, 1
sixty *sesenta*, 2
size, *la talla*, 8; **shoe size** *el número*, 8
to skate *patinar*, 3
to ski *esquiar*, 10; **to water-ski** *esquiar en el agua*, 10
skirt *la falda*, 8
to sleep *dormir (ue)*, 5; **to get enough sleep** *dormir lo suficiente*, 7
small *pequeño(a)*, 5
to smoke *fumar*, 7; **to stop smoking** *dejar de fumar*, 7
to snack *merendar (ie)*, 5
to snow *nevar (ie)*, 3
so-so *más o menos*, 1
so much *tanto*, 7
soap *el jabón*, 7
soccer *el fútbol*, 3
socks *los calcetines*, 8; **a pair of socks** *un par de calcetines*, 8
sofa *el sofá*, 5
soft drink *el refresco*, 6
some *unos(as)*, 4
someday *algún día*, 10
something *algo*, 4
sometimes *a veces*, 3
son *el hijo*, 5
soup *la sopa*, 6; **vegetable soup** *la sopa de verduras*, 6
Spanish *el español*, 1
to speak *hablar*, 3
to spend time alone *pasar el rato solo(a)*, 3
to spend (money) *gastar*, 8; (time) *pasar*, 9
spicy *picante*, 6
spinach *las espinacas*, 6
spoon *la cuchara*, 6
sports *los deportes*, 2
spring *la primavera*, 1
stadium *el estadio*, 4
to start *empezar (ie)*, 5; *comenzar (ie)*, 10; **to start a trip** *comenzar un viaje*, 10
to stay *quedarse*, 10; **to stay in shape** *mantenerse (ie) en forma*, 7
stomach *el estómago*, 7
to stop doing something *dejar de + infinitive*, 7
store *la tienda de...*, 8
story *el piso*, 5; **...story building** *el edificio de . . .pisos*, 5
to stretch *estirarse*, 7
student *el estudiante, la estudiante*, 1
to study *estudiar*, 3
style *la moda*, 8; **in the latest style** *a la última moda*, 8; **out of style** *pasado de moda*, 8
subject *la materia*, 4
suburbs *las afueras*, 5
subway *el metro*, 10
suitcase *la maleta*, 10
summer *el verano*, 1
to sunbathe *tomar el sol*, 10
Sunday *el domingo*, 1; **on Sundays** *los domingos*, 3
supplies: school supplies *los útiles escolares*, 4
to surf the Internet *navegar por Internet*, 1
surprise party *la fiesta sorpresa*, 9
sweater *el suéter*, 8
sweet *dulce*, 7
to swim *nadar*, 3
swimsuit *el traje de baño*, 8
synagogue *la sinagoga*, 9

table *la mesa*, 5
to take care of *cuidar*, 5; **to take care of oneself** *cuidarse*, 7; **Take care.** *Cuídate.*, 9
to take off *quitarse*, 7
to take out *sacar*, 6; **to take out the trash** *sacar la basura*, 5
to take *tomar*, 9; **to take photos** *sacar fotos*, 10; **to take a test** *presentar el examen*, 4
to talk *hablar*, 3; *charlar*, 10
tall *alto(a)*, 2
to taste *probar (ue)*, 6
taxi *el taxi*, 10
teacher *la profesora* **(female),** *el profesor* **(male),** 1
teeth *los dientes*, 7
telephone number *el teléfono*, 1
television *la televisión*, 3; **to watch TV** *mirar la televisión*, 3
to tell jokes *contar (ue) chistes*, 9
temple *el templo*, 9
ten *diez*, 1
tennis *el tenis*, 3; **tennis shoes** *los zapatos de tenis*, 8
test *el examen*, 4; **to take a . . . test** *presentar el examen de...*, 4
Thanksgiving Day *el Día de Acción de Gracias*, 9
thank you *gracias*, 1
that *ese(a)*, 8
the *el, la, los, las*, 2
their *su(s)*, 5
them *los, las*, 6
then *luego*, 4
there *allí*, 10
there is, there are *hay*, 4
these *estos, estas*, 8
they *ellas, ellos*, 1
They like to . . . *A ...les gusta...*, 3
thin *delgado(a)*, 5
thing *la cosa*, 4
to think *pensar (ie)*, 9
thirst *la sed*, 4
thirteen *trece*, 1
thirty *treinta*, 1
this *ésta, éste*, 1; **this** *este(a)*, 8
those *esos, esas*, 8
three *tres*, 1
three hundred *trescientos*, 8
throat *la garganta*, 7
Thursday *el jueves*, 1; **on Thursdays** *los jueves*, 3
ticket *el boleto*, 10; **plane ticket** *el boleto de avión*, 10
time *el rato*, 3
tired *cansado(a)*, 7; **to be tired** *estar cansado*, 7
to/for me *me*, 2; **you** *te*, 2; **us** *nos*, 2; **him, her, you, them** *le(s)*, 2
toast *el pan tostado*, 6
today *hoy*, 1
tomato *el tomate*, 6
tomorrow *mañana*, 4
ton: a ton of *un montón de*, 4
too much *demasiado(a)*, 7
toothbrush *el cepillo de dientes*, 7
toothpaste *la pasta de dientes*, 7
to tour *recorrer*, 10
towel *la toalla*, 7
toy *el juguete*, 8
toy store *la juguetería*, 8
train *el tren*, 10
trash *la basura*, 5
to travel *viajar*, 10
trip *el viaje*, 10
to try, taste *probar (ue)*, 6
T-shirt *la camiseta*, 8
Tuesday *el martes*, 1; **on Tuesdays** *los martes*, 3
tuna *el atún*, 6
turnover-like pastry *la empanada*, 9
twelve *doce*, 1
twenty *veinte*, 1
two *dos*, 1
two hundred *doscientos*, 8
two thousand *dos mil*, 8

ugly *feo(a)*, 8
uncle *el tío*, 5
under, underneath *debajo (de)*, 5
unfair *injusto*, 5
unfriendly *antipático(a)*, 2
until *hasta*, 5
up to *hasta*, 5
us *nos*, 2; *nosotros(as)*, 3
usual: the usual *lo de siempre*, 9

V

to vacuum *pasar la aspiradora,* 5
vacuum cleaner *aspiradora,* 5
Valentine's Day *el Día de los Enamorados,* 9
vegetables *las verduras,* 2
very *muy + adjective,* 2
very bad *pésimo(a),* 2
video *el video,* 3
video games *los videojuegos,* 2
volleyball *el volibol,* 3

W

to wait *esperar,* 8
waiting room *la sala de espera,* 10
to wake up *despertarse (ie),* 7
to walk *caminar,* 7; **to go for a walk** *pasear,* 3
wallet *la billetera,* 10
to want *querer (ie),* 3
to wash *lavar,* 5, *lavarse,* 7; **to wash the dishes** *lavar los platos,* 5
watch (clock) *el reloj,* 4
to watch *ver,* 4; **to watch television** *ver televisión,* 3
water *el agua (f.),* 6; **to water ski** *esquiar en el agua,* 10
we *nosotros(as),* 1
to wear *llevar,* 8; **to wear glasses** *usar lentes,* 5
weather *el tiempo,* 3; **The weather is nice (bad).** *Hace buen (mal) tiempo.,* 3
wedding *la boda,* 9
Wednesday *el miércoles,* 1; **on Wednesdays** *los miércoles,* 3
week *la semana,* 4
weekend *el fin de semana,* 3; **weekends** *los fines de semana,* 3
weight *el peso,* 7; **to gain weight** *subir de peso,* 7; **to lose weight** *bajar de peso,* 7
weights *las pesas,* 7; **to lift weights** *levantar pesas,* 7
What? *¿Cómo?, ¿Qué?,* 1; **What a pain!** *¡Qué lata!,* 5; **What a shame!** *¡Qué lástima!,* 10; **What bad luck!** *¡Qué mala suerte!,* 10; **What are you going to do?** *¿Qué vas a hacer?,* 7; **What fun!** *¡Qué divertido!,* 10; **What are you like?** *¿Cómo eres?,* 2; **What day is today?** *¿Qué día es hoy?,* 1; **What did you do?** *¿Qué hiciste?,* 8; **What do you do to help out at home?** *¿Qué haces para ayudar en casa?,* 5; **What do you do to relax?** *¿Qué haces para relajarte?,* 7; **What do you have to do?** *¿Qué tienes que hacer?,* 7; **What do you like to do?** *¿Qué te gusta hacer?,* 3; **What do you still have to do?** *¿Qué te falta hacer?,* 7; **What do you want to do?** *¿Qué quieres hacer?,* 3; **What does . . . do?** *¿Qué hace...?,* 3; **What is . . . like?** *¿Cómo es...?,* 2; **What plans do you have for . . .?** *¿Qué planes tienen para...?,* 9; **What time are you going to . . .?** *¿A qué hora vas a...?,* 4; **What time is it?** *¿Qué hora es?,* 3; **What is . . .'s e-mail address?** *¿Cuál es el correo electrónico de...?,* 1; **What is . . .'s telephone number?** *¿Cuál es el teléfono de...?,* 1; **what?, which?** *¿cuál?,* 4; **What's his (her, your) name?** *¿Cómo se llama?,* 1; **What's new?** *¿Qué hay de nuevo?,* 9; **What's the matter with . . .?** *¿Qué tiene...?,* 7; **What's the weather like?** *¿Qué tiempo hace?,* 3; **What's today's date?** *¿Qué fecha es hoy?,* 1; **What's wrong with you?** *¿Qué te pasa?,* 7; **What's your name?** *¿Cómo te llamas?,* 1
wheelchair *la silla de ruedas,* 5; **to be in a wheelchair** *estar en una silla de ruedas,* 5
when *cuando,* 3
when? *¿cuándo?,* 2
where? *¿dónde?,* 5; **Where can I . . .?** *¿Dónde se puede...?,* 10; **Where did you go?** *¿Adónde fuiste?,* 8; **from where** *de dónde,* 1
white *blanco(a),* 8
whole *todo(a),* 9
Who's calling? *¿De parte de quién?,* 8
Who's . . .? *¿Quién es...?,* 1
why? *¿por que?,* 2
window *la ventana,* 5; **to window-shop** *mirar las vitrinas,* 8
winter *el invierno,* 1
to wish for *desear,* 6
with *con,* 3
with me *conmigo,* 3
with you *contigo,* 3
witty *gracioso(a),* 2
woman *la mujer,* 8
wool *la lana,* 8; **made of wool** *de lana,* 8
work *trabajar,* 3; *el trabajo,* 4
to work out *entrenarse,* 7
workshop *el taller,* 4
to worry *preocuparse,* 10; **Don't worry.** *No te preocupes.,* 10
worse *peor(es),* 8
to write *escribir,* 1; **How do you spell . . .?** *¿Cómo se escribe...?,* 1; **It's spelled . . .** *Se escribe...,* 1

Y

yard *el patio,* 5
year *el año,* 2; **New Year's Day** *el Año Nuevo,* 9; **last year** *el año pasado,* 9
yellow *amarillo(a),* 8
yes *sí,* 4
yesterday *ayer,* 8
yoga: to do yoga *hacer yoga,* 7
you *usted, ustedes,* (formal), 1; *tú, vosotros(as),* (informal), 1; **You were lucky!** *Ah, ¡tuviste suerte!,* 10
young *joven,* 5
young people *los jóvenes,* 9
younger *menor(es),* 5
your *tu(s), su(s), vuestro(a)(s),* 5

Z

zero *cero,* 1
zoo *el zoológico,* 10

Índice gramatical

Page numbers in boldface type refer to the first presentation of the topic. Other page numbers refer to grammar structures presented in the **¡Exprésate!** features, subsequent references to the topic, or reviewed in **Repaso de Gramática.** Page numbers beginning with R refer to the **Síntesis gramatical** in this Reference Section (pages R16–R23).

A

a: for clarification **62,** 88; with pronouns **88,** 110; after **ir** or **jugar 100;** combined with **el** to form **al 100,** 328, R16; with time **128,** 148; with **empezar: 166;** with infinitives **136,** 148, 166, 290; personal **328,** 338
abrir: 138; all preterite tense forms **352,** R21; see also -ir verbs
acabar de: 240, 262
acostarse: all present tense forms **242**
accent marks: **26,** 34, 72, 254, 300, 330, 338
adjectives: function of **48,** 72; agreement with nouns–masculine and feminine **50,** 72, R17; singular and plural **50,** 72, R17; placement **124;** demonstrative adjectives all forms **278,** 300, R17; possessive adjectives all forms **162,** 186, R17; with sentirse **250;** irregular comparative forms **278,** 300, R17; with quedar **280,** 300
adónde: 100, 290, R18; see also question words
adverbs: adverbs of frequency **96,** R19; adverbs of sequence **122;** adverbs of time **20;** with **quedar 280,** 300
affirmative informal commands: see also informal commands
agreement of nouns and adjectives: **50,** 72, 162, R17; see also adjectives
agreement of nouns and definite articles **60,** 72, R16
agreement of nouns and indefinite articles **124,** R16
agreement of nouns and possessive adjectives **162,** R17
agreement of verbs and reflexive pronouns **238**
al: 100, 328
almorzar: 164, R20; all present tense froms **186**
-ando: 330, 338, R20
antes de: 240, 262, R19; see also prepositions
-ar verbs: regular present tense **98,** 110, 164, R19; regular preterite tense **288,** 292, R21; affirmative commands **214,** 216, 224, **252,** 254, R22; negative command forms **252,** 254, 262; see also verbs
articles: definite **el, la, los, las 60,** 62, 136, 238; indefinite **un, una, unos, unas 124,** 148
asistir: 138

B

beber: 138
because and why: 62
buscar: commands **364**

C

calendar expressions: dates, days of the week, months **21**
-car, -gar, -zar verbs: See also spelling-change verbs
cien(to) 276; see also numbers
comenzar: all preterite tense forms **354,** 376
comer: 86, 98; all present tense forms **138,** 148, 164; all preterite tense forms **314,** 316, 338
commands (imperatives): **214,** 216, 224, 252, 254, 262, 364, 366, R22; affirmative informal commands **214,** 216, 224, 252, 254, 262, 364, 366, R22; negative informal commands **252,** 254, 262, 364, 366, R22; irregular verbs **214,** 252, 262, 364, 376, R22; spelling-change verbs **-ger, -car, -gar, -zar, -guir 364,** R21; with pronouns **216,** 224, 254, 262, 326, 366
cómo: 52, 72, R18; see also question words
comparative adjectives **mayor, mejor, menor, peor 278,** 300
comparisons: with adjectives using **más... que, menos... que, tan... como 278,** 300, R18; **tanto (a)... como, tantos(as)... como 278,** 300, R18
comprar: all preterite tense forms **288**
con: with pronouns **88,** 110; see also prepositions
conjunctions: **porque 62**
conmigo: 88
conocer: all present tense forms **328;** with personal **a 328,** 338
contigo: 88
contractions: **al 100,** 328, R16; **del 64,** 100, R16
correr: 138
costar: 276, 300
cuál: 19, 23, R18; see also question words
cuándo: 52, 72, R18; see also question words
cuánto: agreement with nouns **124,** 148, R18; see also question words

D

dates (calendar): **21**
days of the week: **21,** 136
de: used in showing possession or ownership **64,** 72, 162; to indicate a type of thing **64;** to say where someone is from 12, **64;** with **el 64;** with pronouns **88;** used as a preposition **140;** with **salir** and **saber 140; de** + person **162;** see also prepositions
definite articles: **el, la, los, las 60,** 62, 72, 136, 238, R16
del: contraction of **de** + **el 64,** 100, R16
demonstrative adjectives: **278,** 300, R17
después de: 240, 262
direct objects: **212,** 326
direct object pronouns: **212,** 326, 338, 366, 376, R17; with commands **216,** 224, 254, 262, 326, 366; with present participles **330;** with infinitives **212,** 326, 366; see also pronouns
dormir: all present tense forms **164,** 202; 204; present participle 330
double negative: see also negation

E

e→i stem-changing verbs: **pedir 202,** 224, 242; **servir:** all

present tense forms **202,** 224, R20; **vestirse 238,** 242; present participle **330,** R20
e→ie stem-changing verbs: **166,** 242, R20; **querer 90,** 110, 166, 202, 242; **nevar 102; tener 126,** 148, 166, 204, 368; **venir 128,** 148, 330; **empezar 166,** 186; **merendar 166,** 314; **preferir 204; calentar 214; pensar 318; servir,** present participle **330,** R20; see also verbs
el: 60, 62, 72; 136, 238, R16; with weekdays **136;** see also definite articles
empezar: 166, 186; **empezar a** + infinitive **166;** commands **364;** see also verbs
en: with pronouns **88,** 110
encontrar: 242; see also verbs
-er verbs: regular **-er** and **-ir** all present tense forms **138,** R19; affirmative and negative command forms **252,** R22; all preterite tense forms **314,** R21; present participle form **330,** R20; see also verbs
escribir: all present tense forms **138,** 148, 164; all preterite tense forms **314**
esperar: all preterite tense forms **352,** 376
estar: all present tense forms **174,** 186; to ask how someone is and say how you are 8, **52,** 174, 224; to tell where people and things are located **174,** 224; with prepositions **174,** 186; to describe food and drinks **200,** 224; contrasted with **ser 200,** 224, 250, R22; to describe mental or physical states or conditions **250,** 262; negative informal commands **252,** 262; **estar** + present participle **330,** 338, R20
este, esta, estos, estas: 278, 300, R17; see also demonstrative adjectives
expressions with **tener 126**

frequency: adverbs of **siempre 97; nunca, todos los días 97; casi nunca 96; a veces 96,** R19
future plans: expressions in the present tense **ir a** + infinitive **136,** 148, 318; **pensar** + infinitive **318,** 338

gender of adjectives: **50,** 72, R17
gender of nouns: **50,** 60, 72, R16
gustar: likes and dislikes **62,** 72, 176, 178, 280, R21; telling what one would like **(gustaría) 368;** all present tense forms **62;** with infinitives **86,** 90, 110; with **a** + pronouns **88**

hablar: 98; all present tense forms 110, **164**
hacer: all present tense forms **140;** with weather **102,** 110, 356, R21; commands **214,** 224, 252, 364; all preterite tense forms **356,** 376
hasta: 164
hay: 134, 209, 325

idioms with **tener 126**
-iendo: 330, 338, R20
imperatives (commands): **214,** 216, 224, 252, 254, 262, 364, 366, R22; affirmative informal commands **214,** 216, 224, 252, 254, 262, 364, 366, R22; negative informal commands **252,** 254, 262, 364, 366, R22; irregular verbs **214,** 252, 262, 364, R22; spelling-change verbs **-ger, -car, -gar, -zar, -guir 364;** with pronouns **216,** 224, 254, 262, 326, 366
indefinite articles: **un, una, unos, unas 124,** 148, R16
indirect object pronouns: **me, te, le, nos, os, les 88,** 178, R17; with **a** for clarification **62**
infinitives: **86,** 90, 98, 110; with **gustar 86,** 90, 110; with **querer 90,** 110; with **tener 126;** with **ir 136,** 290; with **empezar 166;** with **tocar 178;** with **poder** and **preferir 204;** with direct object pronouns **212,** 216, 326, 366; with reflexive pronouns **240,** 262; with **acabar de 240,** 262; with **para, antes de, después de 240,** 262; with **pensar 318,** 338; verbs followed by infinitives **368**
informal commands: **214,** 216, 224, 252, 254, 262, 364, 366, R22; affirmative informal commands **214,** 216, 224, 252, 254, 262, 364, 366, R22; negative informal commands **252,** 254, 326, 364, 366, R22; irregular verbs **214,** 252, 262, 364, R22; spelling-change verbs **-ger, -car, -gar, -zar, -guir 364,** R21; with pronouns **216,** 224, 254, 262, 366
interrogatives (question words), R18; **cuál** 19, 23; **cómo 52; qué 52; quién(es) 52; cuándo 52; por qué 62; adónde 100**
interrumpir: 138
invitar: all preterite tense forms **316,** 338
-ir verbs: regular present tense **138,** 148, 164, R19; regular preterite tense all forms **314,** 316, 352, R19; see also verbs
ir: all present tense forms **100,** 110, R20; **ir a** + infinitive **136,** 148; all preterite tense forms **290,** 300, 316, 352, R21; commands **214,** 224, 252, 364, R22; with **pensar 318;** present instead of present progressive **330**
irregular verbs: **100,** 140, 148, 174, 214, 224, 252, 300, 316, 356, 364, R19–R21; see also verbs
irregular **yo** forms: **140**

jugar: all present tense forms **100,** 110, 164, 224

la: used as a definite article **60,** 62, 238, R16; used as a pronoun **212,** 216, 224, 326, 330, 366
la, los, las: 60, 62, 136, 238, R16; see also definite articles
lavarse: all present tense forms **238,** 262
leer: 138; present participle **330,** R20; see also verbs
le, les: 62, 88, 178, R17; see also pronouns, indirect object pronouns
levantarse: all preterite tense forms **292**
llamarse: 6
llegar: all preterite tense forms **354,** 376; commands **364;** see also verbs
llover: 102, 164, 314, 356; see also verbs
lo: 212, 224, 254, 326, 366, R17; see also pronouns, direct object pronouns

más... que: 278, 300, R18; see also comparisons
mayor: 278, 300, R18; see also comparative adjectives
me: 62, 86, 178, R17; see also pronouns, indirect object pronouns
mejor: 278, 300, R18; see also comparative adjectives
menor: 278, 300, R18; see also comparative adjectives
menos... que: 278, 300, R18; see also comparisons
merendar: 166; all preterite tense forms **314**
mucho(a), muchos(as): agreement with nouns **124,** 148

nada: 176, 186, R18
nadie: 176, 186, R18
necesitar: to express needs 121, 124
negation: with **no** 24, 48, 52, 62, 176, 254; **nada, nunca, nadie,** and **tampoco** (use of more than one negative word or expression) **176,** 186
negative expressions: **no 24,** 48, 52, 62, 176, 254, R18; **nada, nadie, nunca, tampoco 176,** 186, R18
negative informal commands: see also informal commands or imperatives
nevar: 102, 356
nos: indirect object pronoun **62,** 88, 178, R17; direct object pronoun **326,** R17
nouns: as subjects **12,** 24; replaced with pronouns **12;** masculine and feminine forms **60,** 72, R16; singular and plural forms **60,** 72, R16; with definite articles **60,** 72; used with **tener 126;** as direct objects **212**
number, singular and plural: 14, **50,** 60, 62, 72, 124, 162, 276, 278, 280, R16
numbers 0–31 **18;** 32–100 **47;** 100–1,000,000 **276,** 300; R18
nunca: 176, 186, R18; see also negative expressions or negation

o→ue stem-changing verbs: R20; **llover 102,** 164, 314, 356; **almorzar, volver 164,** 186; **dormir 164,** 202, 204, 212, 326, 330; **probar 204,** 224, 300; **poder 204,** 224, 242; **acostarse 238,** 242; **encontrar 242; costar 276,** 300; see also verbs
object pronouns: direct object pronouns **lo, la, los, las 212,** 216, 224, 262, 326, 330, 338, 366, 376, R17; with commands **254;** indirect object pronouns **me, te, le, nos, os, les 62,**178, R17; see also pronouns
objects of prepositions: **88,** R17; **conmigo, contigo 88;** see also prepositions
organizar: commands, **364**
os: indirect object pronoun 62, **88,** 178, R17; direct object pronoun **326,** R17

para: as "in order to" **240;** see also prepositions
parecer: all present tense forms **178,** 186, 280
past (preterite) tense: regular **-ar** verbs all forms **288,** 292, 314, 316, 352, R21; regular **-er** and **-ir** verbs all forms **314,** 316, 352, R21; **ir 290,** 292, 352, R21; **ver 314,** R21; of spelling-change verbs **-car, -gar, -zar 354;** irregular verbs **290,** 352, 356, R21; see also verbs
pedir: all present tense forms **202,** 224; 242
pensar: all present tense forms **318; pensar** + infinitive **318,** 338; see also stem-changing verbs
peor: 278, R18; see also comparative adjectives
perder: all preterite tense forms **352**
personal **a: 328,** 338
plural nouns: 50, **60,** R16
poco(a), pocos(as): agreement with nouns **124,** 148
poder: all present tense forms **204,** 224, 242; see also verbs and stem-changing verbs
poner: all present tense forms **140;** commands **214,** 224, 252, 364
porque: 62; see also conjunctions
por qué: 62, R18; see also question words
possessive adjectives: **162,** 186, R17
preferir: all present tense forms **204,** 224; see also verbs
prepositions: **a 62,** 88, 100, 128, 166, 290, 328, R19; **al** contractions of **a** + **el 100,** 328, R16; **antes de, después de 240; de** 12, **64,** 88, 122, 140, 162; **con, conmigo, contigo 88,** 110; **al lado de, cerca de, debajo de, delante de, detrás de, encima de, lejos de 174,** 186; **del:** contraction of **de** + **el 64,** 100, R16; **de** with **salir, saber 140; para** as "in order to" **240,** 262; **acabar de 240,** 262; **en 88; estar** with prepositions 186
present participle: **330,** 338, R20
present progressive: **330,** 338, R20
present tense: **98,** R19
preterite (past) tense: regular **-ar** verbs all forms **288,** 292, 300, 314, 316, 338, 352, R21; **ir 290,** 292, 300, 316, 352, R21; irregular verbs **290,** 300, 314, 316, 352, 356, R21; **ver 314,** R21; regular **-er** and **-ir** verbs all forms **314,** 316, 338, 352, R21; of spelling-change verbs **-car, -gar, -zar 354,** 376, R21; **hacer 356,** 376; see also verbs
probar: all present tense forms **204,** 224; all preterite tense forms **300;** see also verbs
pronouns: replacing nouns **12,** 88, 212; direct object pronouns **lo, la, los, las 212,** 216, 254, 326, 330, 338, 366, R17; **me, te, le, nos, os, les** with **gustar 62,** 88; with **tocar** and **parecer 178,** R17; subject pronouns 12, **14,** 34, 48, 88, 98, 128, R17; after prepositions **mí, ti, él, ella, usted(es), nosotros(as) 88,** 110, R17; with affirmative informal commands **216,** 254, 366; reflexive pronouns **238,** 254, 262, 330, R17; with present participles **330**
punctuation marks: **26,** 34

que: as "than", **más...que, menos... que 278,** R18
qué: 52, 62, 72, R18; with preposition **a 128;** see also question words
quedar: present tense forms with pronouns **280,** 300
querer: all present tense forms **90,** 166, 202 242; with infinitives **90,** 110; see also verbs
question formation: **52,** 62, 72, 128, 290
question words (interrogatives): R18; **cuál** 19, 23; **cómo 52,** 72; **cuándo 52,** 72; **de dónde** 11, **qué 52,** 62, 72; with the preposition **a 128; quién(es) 52,** 72; with the prepostion **a 62; por qué 62; adónde 100,** 290; **cuánto(a), cuántos(as) 124,** 148
quién: 52, 72, R18; with preposition **a 62;** see also question words

recoger: commands **364;** see also commands
regular verbs: regular **-ar** all present tense forms **98,** R19; all preterite tense forms **288,** R21; regular **-er** and **-ir** all present tense forms **138,** R19; all preterite tense forms **314,** R21; see also verbs
reflexive pronouns **238,** 254, 292, R17; with present participles **330**

saber: all present tense forms **140;** with **de 140**
sacar: all preterite tense forms **354,** 376; see also verbs

salir: all present tense forms **140;** commands **214,** 224, 252, 364; all preterite tense forms **316,** 338; with **de 140;** see also verbs
seguir: commands **364;** see also commands
sentirse: all present tense forms **250,** 262
ser: to say who someone is 6, 10, 12, **24,** 34, 200; to identify people and things **6,** 10, 12, 34, 200, 224; to say where people are from **11,** 12, 24, **34,** 200, 224; for telling day, date, and time **20,** 24, 34, 200, 224; to give phone numbers **24;** all present tense forms **24,** 34, 48; with adjectives **48,** 52, 72; to talk about what something is like **48,** 52, 200; to describe food and drinks **200;** contrasted with **estar** 52, **200,** 224, 250, R22; commands **214,** 224, 252, 364; see also verbs
servir: all present tense forms **202,** 224; present participle **330;** see also verbs
siempre: as an adverb of frequency **96,** R19
spelling change verbs: **-car, -gar, -zar** verbs **354,** 364; **-ger, -guir** verbs **364;** informal commands **364**
stem-changing (spelling-change) verbs **e→ie** stem-changing verbs: **166,** 186, 242, R20; **querer 90,** 166, 242; **nevar 102; tener 126,** 166, 204, 368; **venir 128,** 330, 368; **empezar 166,** 186; **merendar 166,** 186, 314; **preferir 204; calentar 214; pensar 318; servir** present participle **330; u→ue** stem-changing verbs: **jugar 100,** 164; R20; **o→ue: llover 102,** 164; **almorzar, volver, empezar 164,** 186; **dormir 164,** 186, 242, present participle **330; probar 204; poder 204,** 242; **acostarse 238,** 242; **encontrar 242; costar 276,** R20; **e→i: pedir 202,** 242; **vestirse 238,** 242; **servir,** present participle **330;** R20; **-ar** verbs in the preterite **288,** 314, 316, 352, R21; **-er, -ir** verbs in the preterite **314,** 316, 352, R21; **leer,** present participle **330,** R20; see also verbs
subjects in sentences: **12,** 24, 34
subject pronouns: 12, **14,** 34, 48, 88, 98, 128, R17; see also pronouns

tag questions: **¿no?, ¿verdad? 138,** 148
tampoco: 176
tan... como: 278, 300, R18; see also comparisons
tanto(a)... como, tantos (as) como: 278, R18; see also comparisons
te: indirect object pronoun 62, 88, 178, R17; direct object pronoun **326,** R17; see also pronouns
tener: present tense all forms **126,** 148, 166, 204; with age **47,** 126; idioms: **tener ganas de** + infinitive **126; tener prisa 126; tener sueño** 250, 262; **tener hambre 126,** 250; **tener sed 126,** 250; **tener que** + infinitive **126,** 368; **tener frío 250,** 262; **tener calor 250,** 262; **tener miedo 250,** 262; R23; commands **214,** 224, 252, 364; see also verbs
tilde (~): 26
time: adverbs of, **de la mañana, de la tarde, de la noche 20;** at what time **128;** telling time **20;** see also adverbs
tocar: all present tense forms **178,** 186
traer: all present tense forms **140**
tú and **usted** contrasted **14,** 34; see also subject pronouns

u→ue stem-changing verbs: **jugar 100,** 110, 164, R20
un(o): 276; see also numbers
una, uno, unos, unas: 124, 148, R16; see also indefinite articles
ustedes and **vosotros** contrasted **14,** 34; see also subject pronouns

venir: all present tense forms **128,** 148, R19; commands 214, 224, 252, 364; present tense instead of present progressive tense 330; see also verbs
ver: all present tense forms **140,** R19; all preterite tense forms **314,** R21; see also verbs
verbs: in sentences **12,** 34; irregular verb **ser** 6,10, 11, 12, **24,** 34, 48, 52, 72, 200, 214, 250, 252, 364, R20, R22; regular **-ar** all present tense forms **98,** 110, R19; irregular verb **ir** all present tense forms **100,** 110, R20; **ir a** + infinitive **136,** 148; all preterite tense forms **290,** 300, 316, 352, R21; present instead of present progressive **330;** regular **-er** and **-ir** all present tense forms **138,** 148, 164, R19; irregular verb **ver** all present tense forms **140,** R19, all preterite tense forms **314,** R21; **e→ie** stem-changing verbs: **166,** 242, R20; **querer 90,** 110, 166, 202, 242; **nevar 102; tener 126,** 148, 166, 204, 368; **venir 128,** 330, 364; **empezar 166,** 186; **merendar 166,** 314; **preferir 204,** 224; **calentar 214; pensar 318; servir 202;** all present tense forms 224, R19; present participle **330,** R20; **u→ue** stem-changing verbs: R20; **jugar 100,** 110, 164, 224; **o→ue** stem-changing verbs: R20; **llover 102,** 164; **almorzar, volver 164; dormir 164,** 202, 204, 242; present participle **330,** R20; **probar 204,** 224, 300; **poder 204,** 224, 242; **acostarse 238,** 242; **encontrar 242; costar 276,** 300; verbs with irregular **yo** forms 148, R19; **tener 126,** 148, 166; **venir 128,** 148; **hacer 140,** 148; **poner 140,** 148; **salir 140,** 148; **traer 140,** 148; **ver 140,** 148; **saber 140,** 148; **conocer 328,** 338; irregular verb **estar** 8, 52, **174,** 200, 250, 330, 338, R22; **e→i** stem-changing verbs: R20; **pedir 202,** 224, 242; **servir 202,** 204; **vestirse 238,** 242; commands **214,** 216, 224, 252, 254, 364, 366, 376, R22; command forms of irregular verbs **214,** 224, 252, 262, 364, 376, R22; verbs with reflexive pronouns **afeitarse, bañarse, despertarse, entrenarse, estirarse, lavarse, levantarse, maquillarse, peinarse, ponerse, quitarse, relajarse, secarse 238; acostarse, vestirse 238,** 240, 242; all preterite tense forms of regular verbs **288,** 314, 316, 338, 352, 376, R21; regular **-ar** verbs all preterite tense forms **288,** 292, 300, 314, 316, 338, 352, 376, R21; preterite tense forms of spelling-change verbs **288,** 354, 376; regular **-er** and **-ir** verbs all preterite tense forms **314,** 316, 338, 352, 376, R21; present progressive tense **330,** 338, R20; preterite tense forms of **-car, -gar, -zar 354;** command forms of spelling-change verbs **-ger, -car, -gar, -zar, -guir 364,** R21; verbs followed by infinitives **166,** 178, 240, 368
vestirse: all present tense forms **242**

weather: with **hacer 102,** 356, R23; see also **hacer**
weekdays: **21,** 136
why and because: **62**

yes/no questions: **52**

Agradecimientos

STAFF CREDITS

Editorial
Priscilla Blanton, Barbara Kristof, Amber P. Nichols, Douglas Ward

Editorial Development Team
Marion Bermondy, Konnie Brown, Lynda Cortez, Janet Welsh Crossley, Zahydée González, Jean Miller, Beatriz Malo Pojman, Paul Provence, Jaishree Venkatesan, J. Elisabeth Wright

Editorial Staff
Sara Anbari, Hubert Bays, Yamilé Dewailly, Virginia Dosher, Milagros Escamilla, Rita Ricardo, Glenna Scott, Geraldine Touzeau-Patrick

Editorial Permissions
Ann B. Farrar, Yuri Muñoz

Book Design
Kay Selke, Marta Kimball, Marc Cooper, Robin Bouvette, José Garza, Sally Bess, Bruce Albrecht, Ed Diaz, Liann Lech

Image Acquisitions
Curtis Riker, Jeannie Taylor, Cindy Verheyden, Stephanie Friedman, Sam Dudgeon, Victoria Smith, Michelle Dike

Media Design
Richard Metzger, Chris Smith

Design New Media
Edwin Blake, Kimberly Cammerata

Production, Manufacturing, and Inventory
Beth Prevelige, Diana Rodriguez, Rose Degollado, Jevara Jackson, Rhonda Fariss, Jennifer Craycraft

New Media
Kenneth Whiteside, Lydia Doty, Jamie Lane, Chris Pittman, Cathy Kuhles, Nina Degollado

eLearning Systems
Beau Clark, Jim Bruno, Annette Saunders

ACKNOWLEDGMENTS

For permission to reprint copyrighted material, grateful acknowledgment is made to the following sources:

Agencia Literania Carmen Balcells: From "Una antigua casa encantada" from *Mi país inventado* by Isabel Allende. Copyright © 2003 by Isabel Allenda

Children's Book Press, San Francisco, CA: "Baile en el jardín" from *In My Family/En mi familia* by Carmen Lomas Garza, translated into Spanish by Francisco X. Alarcón. Text copyright © 1996 by Carmen Lomas Garza. "Tamalada" from *Family Pictures/Cuadros de familia* by Carmen Lomas Garza, translated into Spanish by Rosalma Zubizarreta. Text copyright © 1990 by Carmen Lomas Garza. "La Montaña del Alimento" from *The Legend of Food Mountain/La montaña del alimento,* adapted by Harriet Rohmer, translated into Spanish by Alma Flor Ada and Rosalma Zubizarreta. Copyright © 1982 by Children's Book Press.

Estate of Ángel Flores c/o The Permissions Company: From "El fracaso matemático de Pepito" from *First Spanish Reader: A Beginners Dual Language Book,* edited by ´´Ángel Flores. Copyright © 1988 by Ángel Flores.

Ediciones de la Fundación Corripio, Inc.: From "Regalo de cumpleaños" by Diógenes Valdez from *Cuentos dominicanos para Niños,* vol. V. Copyright © 2000 by Ediciones de la Fundación Corripio, Inc.

Editorial Fundación Ross: "Dos buenas piernas tenemos..." and "Siempre quietas,..." from *Adivinanzas para mirar en el espejo* by Carlos Silveyra. Copyright © 1985 by Editorial Fundacion Ross.

Editorial Sudamericana S.A.: "2" and "16" from *Los rimaqué* by Ruth Kaufman. Copyright © 2002 by Editorial Sudamericana S.A.

Francisco J. Briz Hidalgo, www.elhuevodechocolate.com: "Una moneda de ¡Ay!" by Juan de Timoneda from *El huevo de chocolate* Web site, accessed on September 10, 2003 at http://www.elhuevodechocolate.com. Copyright © by Francisco J. Briz Hidalgo.

Maricel Mayor Marsán: From "Un corazón dividido" from *Un corazón dividido/ A Split Heart* by Maricel Mayor Marsán. Copyright © 1998 by Maricel Mayor Marsán. From "Apuntes de un hogar postmoderno" from *Imprenta de los Rincones* by Maricel Mayor Marsán. Copyright © by Maricel Mayor Marsán.

Museum of New Mexico Press: "Los cuatro elementos" from *Cuentos: Tales from the Hispanic Southwest,* selected and adapted in Spanish by José Griego y Maestas. Copyright © 1980 by Museum of New Mexico Press.

Scholastic Inc.: From "Ollantaytambo" from *Ahora,* vol. 3, no. 2, September/October 1996. Copyright © 1996 by Scholastic Inc. From "Gustavo" from *Ahora,* vol. 4, no. 2, November/December 1997. Copyright © 1997 by Scholastic Inc.

PHOTOGRAPHY CREDITS

Abreviations used: c-center, b-bottom, t-top, l-left, r-right, bkgrd-background.

AUTHORS: Page iii (Smith) Courtney Baker, courtesy Stuart Smith; (McMinn) Courtney Baker, courtesy John McMinn; (Madrigal Velasco) courtesy Sylvia Madrigal; (Humbach) courtesy Nancy Humbach; (Chiquito) courtesy Ana B. Chiquito.

TABLE OF CONTENTS: Page vi (cr) Don Couch/HRW; (tr) ©Guido Alberto Rossi/Getty Images/The Image Bank; vii (cr) John Langford/HRW; (tr) ©Dennis Degnan/CORBIS; viii (cr) Gary Russ/HRW; (tr) ©Photo Researchers, Inc.; ix (cr) Don Couch/HRW; (tr) ©Buddy Mays/CORBIS; x (cr, tr) Don Couch/HRW; xi (cr) Don Couch/HRW; (tr) ©Robert Frerck/Odyssey/Chicago; xii (cr) Don Couch/HRW; (tr) Michael Everett/D. Donne Bryant Photography; xiii (cr, tr) Sam Dudgeon/HRW; xiv (cr, tr) John Langford/HRW; xv (cr) Don Couch/HRW; (tr) Digital Image copyright ©2006 PhotoDisc.

WHY STUDY SPANISH: Page xvi (Costa Rica) ©Buddy Mays/CORBIS; (Argentina) ©Jeremy Woodhouse, digitalvision; xvi (Dominican Republic) John Langford/HRW; (Mexico) Corbis Images; (Peru, Chile) Don Couch/HRW; (Spain) Corbis Images; xvii (br, cl) Don Couch/HRW; (bl, t) Álvaro Ortiz/HRW; xvii (tl) John Langford/HRW; xviii (b) Sam Dudgeon/HRW; (cl) ©Royalty-Free/CORBIS; (cr) Edward M. Pío Roda. ® & ©2003 CNN. An AOL Time Warner Co. All Rights Reserved; xix (br) Don Couch/HRW; (t) Alvaro Ortiz/HRW.

IN SPANISH CLASS: Page xx (bl) HRW; (cr) Victoria Smith/HRW.
COMMON NAMES: xxi (bkgrd) Álvaro Ortiz/HRW.
DIRECTIONS: xxii (br) Sam Dudgeon/HRW.

CHAPTER 1 All photos by Don Couch/HRW except: Page xxxiv (bc) ©Steve Vidler/SuperStock; (cl) ©S. Bavister/Robert Harding Picture Library Ltd./Alamy Photos; (cr) ©Nik Wheeler/CORBIS; (t) ©Stockphotos (Latin Stock) 1 (t) ©Robert Frerck/Getty Images; (bl) ©Guido Alberto Rossi/Getty Images/The Image Bank; (c) ©Stephen Saks/Lonely Planet Images; (cr) ©Larry Lee Photography/CORBIS; 2 (bl) ©Brand X Pictures; (br) Álvaro Ortiz/HRW; (tc) ©Chip & Rosa María de la Cueva Peterson; (c) Digital Image copyright ©2006 PhotoDisc; (tl) ©Robert

Frerck/Odyssey Productions; (tr) ©Isaac Hernández/Mercury Press International; 3 (bl) ©Christie's Images/CORBIS; (br) ©James A. Sugar/CORBIS; (cl) ©Robert Frerck/Getty Images/Stone; (cr) The Art Archive/Museo del Prado/Album/Joseph Martin; (tl) ©Chip & Rosa María de la Cueva Peterson; (tr) ©Guido Alberto Rossi/Getty Images/The Image Bank; (tc) Zefa Visual Media - Germany/Index Stock Imagery, Inc.; 4-5 (all) Álvaro Ortiz/HRW; 6 (bl, l) Álvaro Ortiz/HRW; 7-8 (all) Álvaro Ortiz/HRW; 10 (c) Álvaro Ortiz/HRW; 11 (c, cr, t) Marty Granger/Edge Video Productions/HRW; (cl) ©David H. Wells/CORBIS; (l) Christine Galida/HRW; (r) Peter Van Steen/HRW; 12 (bl) ©Pixtal; 13 (cl) ©Digital Vision; (cr) Marty Granger/Edge Video Productions/HRW; (l, r) Digital Image copyright ©2006 PhotoDisc; (tr) Álvaro Ortiz/HRW; 15 (bc) ©BananaStock; (bl) ©Digital Vision; (br, tl) Victoria Smith/HRW; (tc) Peter Van Steen/HRW; (tr) ©COMSTOCK, Inc.; 17 (br) Amy Graves – Fashion Wire Daily/AP Wide World Photos; 18 (all) Victoria Smith/HRW; 22 (a, b, e, h, m, p, q, z) Corbis Images; (c, ch, f, i, k, l, ll, n, o, r, rr, t, u) Digital Image copyright ©2006 PhotoDisc; (g, z, v) Sam Dudgeon/HRW; (j) ©Royalty Free/CORBIS; (w) Digital imagery® copyright 2003 PhotoDisc, Inc.; (x, y) Victoria Smith/HRW; 24 (l) John Langford/HRW; 25 (cl) Mark Antman/HRW; (cr, r) Marty Granger/Edge Video Productions/HRW; (l) ©Alison Wright/CORBIS; 30 (br) Corbis Images; (cl) Victoria Smith/HRW; (tr) Digital Image copyright ©2006 PhotoDisc; 32 (tc) ©A. Parada/Alamy Photos; (tl) ©Jimmy Dorantes/Latin Focus; (tr) Sam Dudgeon/HRW; 36 (A) Peter Van Steen/HRW; (B, C-girl) Dennis Fagan/HRW; (C-boy, D) Victoria Smith/HRW.

CHAPTER 2 All photos by John Langford/HRW except: Page 38 (b) ©Wally McNamee/CORBIS; (glove) Digital Image copyright ©2006 Artville; (c) ©Andrea Pistolesi/Getty Images/The Image Bank; (tr) ©Mark Bacon/Latin Focus; 39 (bl) ©Mark Bacon/Alamy Photos; (cr) ©Kevin Schafer/CORBIS; (tl) ©Steve Fitzpatrick/Latin Focus; (tr) ©Steve Bly/Getty Images/The Image Bank; 40 (bl) ©Christie's Images Inc., 1999; (cr) Victoria Smith/HRW; (tc) ©Townsend P. Dickinson/The Image Works; 41 (bl) ©Dennis Degnan/CORBIS; (br) Ricardo Alcaras/HRW; (cl) ©Michael Friang/Alamy Photos; (cr) ©Dave G. Houser/CORBIS; (t) Tony Arruza; (tc) ©Robert Fried/Robert Fried Photography; 45 (all) Victoria Smith/HRW; 46 (br, cl, l) Victoria Smith/HRW; (cr, tr) Sam Dudgeon/HRW; (tl) Randal Alhadeff/HRW; 49 (cl) ©John Kelly/Getty Images/The Image Bank; (cr, l, r) Victoria Smith/HRW; 55 (br) www.corbis.com/PhilipGould; (tl) Don Couch/HRW; 56 (bc) Sam Dudgeon/HRW; (bl, br, cr) Victoria Smith/HRW; (tc, tr) Corbis Images; (tl) Digital Image copyright ©2006 PhotoDisc; 57 (bc, bl, c, cl, cr, tr) Victoria Smith/HRW; (kangaroo, lion, zebra) Digital Image copyright ©2006 PhotoDisc; 58 (br) Scott Vallance/VIP Photo/HRW; (cl, l) Sam Dudgeon/HRW; (r) Victoria Smith/HRW; (tl) ©Reuters NewMedia Inc./CORBIS; 61 (bc, tc, tl, tr, bl) Victoria Smith/HRW; (7, 8-cat, 8-dog) Digital Image copyright ©2006 PhotoDisc; (t) ©Brand X Pictures; 62 (bl) Mari Biasco Photography; 63 (bc, br) Corbis Images; (bl) Digital Image copyright ©2006 PhotoDisc; (sports, pizza, cake) Victoria Smith/HRW; (cr) Scott Vallance/VIP Photo/HRW; 64 (bc, c, tr) Victoria Smith/HRW; (bl) ©Lisa Anne Auerbach/CORBIS; (br) Sam Dudgeon/HRW; (t) Digital Image copyright ©2006 PhotoDisc; (tl) Corbis Images; 68 (all) Victoria Smith/HRW; 70 (1, graciosa, romántica, tímida) Victoria Smith/HRW; (2) Digital Image copyright ©2006 PhotoDisc; (3) Corbis Images; (4) Sam Dudgeon/HRW; 74 (A, C) Victoria Smith/HRW.

CHAPTER 3 All photos by Gary Russ/HRW except: Page 76 (c) ©George H. H. Huey/CORBIS; (tr) Sam Dudgeon/HRW; 77 (bl) ©David Muench/CORBIS; (br) Courtesy of Houston Chamber of Commerce; (tl) Corbis Images; (tr) ©D. Donne Bryant Photography; 78 (bl) ©Carmen Lomas Garza, photo credit: Bob Hsiang; (cl) ©Carmen Lomas Garza, Collection of Paula Maciel-Benecke and Norbert Benecke Aptos, California, photo credit: M. Lee Fatherree; (tl) Courtesy of the San Antonio Public Library; Photographer: Clem Spalding; (tr) ©George H. H. Huey/CORBIS; 79 (c) ©Dave G. Houser/CORBIS; (cl) ©Scott Teven/photohouston.com; (cr) ©Jimmy Dorantes/Latin Focus; (tc, tl) Victoria Smith/HRW; 82 (all) Dennis Fagan/HRW; 83 (bc, tc, tl, tr) Peter Van Steen/HRW; (bl) Victoria Smith/HRW; (br) ©Getty Images/Stone; 84 (6, 8) Dennis Fagan/HRW; (5) ©Corbis Images/PictureQuest; (tr) Peter Van Steen/HRW; (2) ©Digital Vision; (1, 3) Victoria Smith/HRW; 87 (cl) Digital Image copyright ©2006 PhotoDisc; (cr) ©Peter M. Fisher/CORBIS; (l) CORBIS Images; (r) Dennis Fagan/HRW; 88 (l) John Langford/HRW; 89 (3, 5, tr) Victoria Smith/HRW; (2-ball, 2-racquet, 4) Digital Image copyright ©2006 PhotoDisc; (1) Sam Dudgeon/HRW; 90 (l) Martha Granger/Edge Video Productions/HRW; 91 (c) Victoria Smith/HRW; (cl, l) Corbis Images; (cr) Painet Inc.; (r) ©Nik Wheeler/CORBIS; 92 (tl) Scott Vallance/VIP Photographic Associates/HRW; 93 (br) Earl Nottingham/Texas Parks & Wildlife/AP/Wide World Photos; (tl) Don Couch/HRW; 94 (bc, bl-boy, br, cl, tc-boy, tl, tr) Dennis Fagan/HRW; (bl-piano) Corbis Images; (tc-glass) Victoria Smith/HRW; 95 (bc, tc) ©Jimmy Dorantes/Latin Focus; (br) ©Kevin Barry; (tl) Peter Van Steen/HRW; (tr) www.corbis.com/WilliamBoyce; 98 (bl) Bob Daemmrich/The Image Works; 100 (l) Don Couch/HRW; 101 (c, r, t) Digital Image copyright ©2006 PhotoDisc; (cl, cr) Victoria Smith/HRW; (l) Sam Dudgeon/HRW; 102 (bl) AP Photo/The Paris News, Bill Ridder; (cl) Harry Cabluck/AP/Wide World Photos; (cr) Donna McWilliam/AP/Wide World Photos; (l) Marty Granger/Edge Video Productions/HRW; 103 (tl) Henry Bargas/AP/Wide World Photos; (tr) Corbis Images; 108 (bc) Corbis Images; (bl, tc, tr) Dennis Fagan/HRW; (br, tl) Digital Image copyright ©2006 PhotoDisc; 112 (cr, l) Peter Van Steen/HRW; (r) Digital Image copyright ©2006 Artville; (tc) Victoria Smith/HRW.

CHAPTER 4 All photos by Don Couch/HRW except: Page 114 (c) ©Jimmy Dorantes/Latin Focus; (tr) Buddy Mays/CORBIS; 115 (bl, cr) Robin Karpan/D. Donne Bryant; (cl) ©Jimmy Dorantes/Latin Focus; (tr) Buddy Mays/CORBIS; 116 (bl) Víctor Hugo Fernández, Gráficos del Globo, S.A. Costa Rica; (tr) ©Dave G. Houser/CORBIS; 117 (bl, br) ©Kevin Schafer; (c) Robin Karpan/D. Donne Bryant; (cr) Alan Cave/D. Donne Bryant; 120 (all objects) Victoria Smith/HRW; 122 (tl, tr) Victoria Smith/HRW; 123 (r) Marty Granger/Edge Video Productions/HRW; 125 (c) Sam Dudgeon/HRW; 127 (c) ©Digital Vision; (cl) Victoria Smith/HRW; (cr) Peter Van Steen/HRW; (l) ©Stockbyte; (r) ©Royalty-Free/CORBIS; (t) Rubberball Productions®; 131 (br) Victoria Smith/HRW; 135 (cl) ©Royalty-Free/CORBIS; (cr) ©Comstock; (l) ©Stockbyte; (r) Sam Dudgeon/HRW; (tr) ©Danny Lehman/CORBIS; 137 (br, cl, cr, tr) Peter Van Steen/HRW; (l) Digital Image copyright ©2006 PhotoDisc; 140 (l) Gary Russ/HRW; 146 (bl) Reuters/CORBIS; (br) Victoria Smith/HRW; (tl) ©Chuck Savage/CORBIS; (tr) Corbis Images.

CHAPTER 5 All photos by Don Couch/HRW except: Page152 (cl) ©Fernando Paste/Latin Focus; (t) ©Daniel Rivadamar/Odyssey/Chicago; 153 (br, tr) D. Donne Bryant/D. Donne Bryant Photography; (parque) ©Wolfgang Kaehler/CORBIS; (altiplano) ©Graham Neden Ecoscene/CORBIS; 154 (bl) David Phillips / Words & Images; (cl) ©Hubert Stadler/CORBIS; (tl) D. Donne Bryant Photography; 155 (c) ©Bettmann/CORBIS; (cl) ©Conde Nast Archive/CORBIS; (cr) Fundacion de Santiago by Pedro Lira (tl) Roberto Candia/AP/Wide World Photos; (tr) ©Reuters NewMedia Inc./CORBIS; 158 (cat) John Langford/HRW; 159 (negro) ©Stockbyte; (corto) Sam Dudgeon/HRW; (largo) Peter Van Steen/HRW; (castaño) ©Rubberball Productions; (canoso) ©Image Source Ltd./Alamy Photos; (azules) Corbis Images; (verdes) ©CORBIS; (negros) ©RubberBall/Alamy Photos; (café) Digital Image copyright ©2006 PhotoDisc; 160 (cl) Mark Richards/PhotoEdit; (cr) ©Comstock; (l) ©John Foxx/Alamy Photos; (r) ©plainpicture/Alamy Photos; 163 (tl, tl-inset) Victoria Smith/HRW; (tr, tr-inset) Peter Van Steen/HRW; 165 (cr) ©Digital Vision; (l) ©Comstock; (r) Peter Van Steen/HRW; (t) Digital Image copyright ©2006 PhotoDisc; 166 (l) John Langford/HRW; 167 (11:45, 3:00, 7:00, 8:10, 8:30) Dennis Fagan/HRW; (6:30) Sam Dudgeon/HRW; 169 (br) Family Crests Store; 174 (l) Chris Sharp/D. Donne Bryant Photography; 176 (all) Victoria Smith/HRW; 177 (r) David Phillips/HRW; 178 (cl) Dennis Fagan/HRW; (cr) Digital Image copyright ©2006 EyeWire; (l) ©Comstock, Inc.; (r) Peter Van Steen/HRW; 184 (bl) Dennis Fagan/HRW; (br) ©Corel; (tc) Victoria Smith/HRW; (tr) Digital Image copyright ©2006 PhotoDisc; 188 (all) Dennis Fagan/HRW.

CHAPTER 6 All photos by Don Couch/HRW except: Page 190 (c) ©Danny Lehman/CORBIS; (tr) ©Getty Images/The Image Bank;

191 (bc, cr, tl) ©Robert Frerck/Odyssey/Chicago; (tr) Mark Newman/Bruce Coleman, Inc.; 192 (b) ©Royalty-Free/CORBIS; (tr) ©Charles & Josette Lenars/CORBIS; 193 (16 de septiembre) George H. H. Huey; (b) Sam Dudgeon/HRW; (Guelaguetza) Charlene E. Friesen/D. Donne Bryant Photography; (t) ©Danny Lehman/CORBIS; 197 (refresco) Victoria Smith/HRW; 199 (3) Michelle Bridwell/HRW; (4) Victoria Smith/HRW; (5) Sam Dudgeon/HRW; 200 (bl) Victoria Smith/HRW; 201 (4, tr) Michelle Bridwell/HRW; 203 (all) Victoria Smith/HRW; 205 (br) Sam Dudgeon/HRW; (tr) ©Robert Frerck/Odyssey/Chicago; 206 (tl) Victoria Smith/HRW; 207 (br) Gary Russ/HRW; (tl) John Langford/HRW; 209 (cl) Corbis Images; 213 (1) Digital Image copyright ©2006 PhotoDisc; (2) Victoria Smith/HRW; (3) ©Royalty-Free/CORBIS; (4) Judd Pilossof/FoodPix; 216 (l) Victoria Smith/HRW; 222 (6) Victoria Smith/HRW; 226 (bl, C) Victoria Smith/HRW; (D) Digital Image copyright ©2006 PhotoDisc.

CHAPTER 7 All photos by Don Couch/HRW except: Page 228 (Bariloche) Jean Lee/AP/Wide World Photos; 228 (La Pampa) Peter Lang/D. Donne Bryant Photography; 228 (t) ©Tony West/PICIMPACT/CORBIS; 229 (bl) Luis Martin/D. Donne Bryant Photography; 229 (br) ©Alissa Crandall/CORBIS; 229 (cr) ©Hubert Stadler/CORBIS; 229 (tr) Michael Everett/D. Donne Bryant Photography; 230 (bl) ©Hubert Stadler/CORBIS; 230 (br) Museo Xul Solar; 230 (tc) Peter Lang/D. Donne Bryant Photography; (tl) ©Robert Fried/Robert Fried Photography; 231 (tl) ©Russell Gordon/Odyssey/Chicago; (tr) Victoria Smith/HRW; 236 (1, 3, 4, 5, 6, 7) Sam Dudgeon/HRW; (2, tr) Digital Image copyright ©2006 PhotoDisc; (8) Victoria Smith/HRW; (tl) Jean Lee/AP/Wide World Photos; 238 (bl) Elizabeth Grivs/TxDOT; 239 (1) John Langford/HRW; (2) ©John Foxx/Alamy Photos; (3) Bob Daemmrich/The Image Works; (4) Image Source/elektraVision/PictureQuest; (tr) Stockbyte/PictureQuest; 240 (bl) David Phillips/HRW; 241 (1, 2) Peter Van Steen/HRW; (3) ©Jose Luis Pelaez, Inc./CORBIS; (4, yo) Dennis Fagan/HRW; 245 (br) Isaac Menashe/Icon SMI/NewsCom; 251 (1, 3) Peter Van Steen/HRW; (2) ©Image Source; (4) ©RubberBall Productions; 252 (bl) John Langford/HRW; 258 (bl) Peter Van Steen/HRW; 260 (c) Dennis Fagan/HRW; (r) Peter Van Steen/HRW.

CHAPTER 8 All photos by Sam Dudgeon/HRW except: Page 266 (tr) ©Owaki - Kulla/CORBIS; 267 (bl) Werner Bertsch/Bruce Coleman, Inc.; (cr) ©Richard Bickel/CORBIS; (tc) Masa Ushioda/Bruce Coleman, Inc.; (tr) Kennedy Space Center/NASA; 268 (bc, cr) ©Mildrey Guillot; (bl) Xavier Cortada; (tl) ©Tony Arruza/CORBIS; 269 (cl) Ife-Ile, Inc.; (cr) ©Latin Focus; (tc) ©Steven Ferry/Words & Images/HRW; (tl) ©Robert Frerck/Odyssey/Chicago; 279 (tr) Victoria Smith/HRW; 283 (br) Corbis Images; (t) Don Couch/HRW; 284 (br, disco) Digital Image copyright ©2006 PhotoDisc; (icon) HRW; (tarjetas) Don Couch/HRW; (tr) Victoria Smith/HRW; 286 (2) Corbis Images; (4) Digital Image copyright ©2006 PhotoDisc; (5) Don Couch/HRW; (7, música) Victoria Smith/HRW; 287 (r) PhotoDisc/gettyimages; 289 (2, 3) Victoria Smith/HRW; (4) Image Source Ltd/Alamy; (5) Digital Image copyright ©2006 EyeWire; (6) Dennis Fagan/HRW; (Tomás) Bob Daemmrich/The Image Works; 290 (l) ©Latin Focus; 291 (1, 2, tr) Victoria Smith/HRW; (4) Digital Image copyright ©2006 PhotoDisc; 298 (2) Michael Newman/PhotoEdit; (3) David Young-Wolff/PhotoEdit; 302 (all) Victoria Smith/HRW.

CHAPTER 9 All photos by John Langford/HRW except: Page 304 (c) (c) Jeremy Horner/CORBIS; (tr) Martha Cooper/Viesti Collection, Inc.; 305 (bl) David Pou; (br) (c) Giraud Philippe/Corbis Sygma; (cr, tl) Suzanne Murphy-Larronde; (tr) Tom Bean; 306 (cl, cr, tc) David Pou; 307 (b, c, cl, t, tr) David Pou; (tl) age fotostock/Suzanne Murphy-Larronde, 2006; 310 (bkgrd) Victoria Smith/HRW; (bl, cl) Christine Galida/HRW; (br) Bob Daemmrich Photo, Inc.; (cr) Michael Matisse/Photodisc/PictureQuest; (hanukah) Pam Ostrow/Index Stock Imagery/PictureQuest; (tc) Andres Leighton/AP/Wide World Photos; 311 (abrir, recibir, tarjetas) Sam Dudgeon/HRW; (sobres) Victoria Smith/HRW; (tc) Corbis Images; 312 (cl) (c) ©Tom and Dee Ann McCarthy/Index Stock Imagery/PictureQuest; (cr) (c) Creatas/PictureQuest; (l, r) Peter Van Steen/HRW; 315 (c, l) Peter Van Steen/HRW; (r) Victoria Smith/HRW; 317 (tl) Victoria Smith/HRW; (tr) Sam Dudgeon/HRW; 318 (l) David Pou; 320 (br) Sam Dudgeon/HRW; 321 (br) Ric Vasquez/AP/Wide World Photos; (tl) Gary Russ/HRW; 322 (background table) Corbis Images; (buzón) Marta Kimball/HRW; (galletas, papitas, ponche) Victoria Smith/HRW; (icon) HRW; 324 (l) José Carrillo/PhotoEdit Inc.; 328 (cl) Eric Risberg/AP/Wide World Photos; (cr, l) The Kobal Collection; (l) J. Griffis Smith/TxDOT; (r) (c) ©Bettmann/CORBIS; (t) (c) ©Hulton-Deutsch Collection/CORBIS; 336 (1) (c) ©Brand X Pictures; (2, 5) Digital Image copyright (c) 006 PhotoDisc; (3-clock) (c) ©Comstock; (3-hats, 4, 6) Corbis Images; 340 (A) Christine Galida/HRW; (arroz) (c) ©Corel; (B, C, D, dulces, tostones) Victoria Smith/HRW; (bizcochos) Don Couch/HRW.

CHAPTER 10 All photos by Don Couch/HRW except: Page 342 (tr) ©Jack Fields/CORBIS; 343 (bl) Todd Wolf; (br) Erwin and Peggy Bauer/Animals Animals/Earth Scenes; (tr) ©Wolfgang Kaehler/CORBIS; 344 (br) painting by Julio Quispe Virhues; (cl) ©Diego Lezama Orezzoli/CORBIS; (tl) Digital Image copyright ©2006 PhotoDisc; 345 (cr) Ricardo Choy Kifox/AP/Wide World Photos; (tc) ©William Albert Allard/National Geographic Image Collection; (tl) Hector Scagnetti; 349 (billetera) Victoria Smith/HRW; 350 (bl) Robert Frerck/Woodfin Camp & Associates; 355 (1) Peter Van Steen/HRW; (2) Digital Image copyright ©2006 PhotoDisc; (4) Dean Berry/Index Stock Imagery, Inc.; 359 (br) Courtesy of Texas Highways Magazine; (tl) Sam Dudgeon/HRW; 360 (acampar) Corbis Images; (bote de vela, pesca) ©Corbis; (canoa) ©Tom Stewart/CORBIS; (esquiar) Ron Chapple/Thinkstock/PictureQuest; (excursión) ©Ken Chernus/Getty Images/Taxi; 361 (barco) ©Travel Ink/Alamy Photos; (metro) Digital Image copyright ©2006 PhotoDisc; 363 (A) ©Rick Doyle/CORBIS; (B) ©Index Stock; (C) ©William Sallaz/CORBIS; (D) ©Index Stock; 365 (br) Digital Image copyright ©2006 PhotoDisc; 367 (r) ©Michael & Patricia Fogden/CORBIS; 368 (l) Courtesy of Texas Highways Magazine; 374 (1) Digital Image copyright ©2006 PhotoDisc.

LITERATURA Y VARIEDADES: Page 382 (c, l) Museo del Prado, Madrid; (cr) Don Couch/HRW; 383 (bl, tr) Museo del Prado, Madrid, Spain ©Erich Lessing/Art Resource, NY; (tl) Noortman, Maastricht, Netherlands/Bridgeman Art Library; 384-385 (bkgrd) Digital Image copyright ©2006 PhotoDisc; 384 (bl) ©Wolfgang Kaehler/CORBIS; (l) ©Kevin Schafer/CORBIS; 385 (cr) Doug Wechsler; (t) ©Michael and Patricia Fogden/CORBIS; 386 (br) ©Carmen Lomas Garza, Collection of Paula Maciel-Benecke and Norbert Benecke Aptos, California, photo credit: M. Lee Fatherree; 387 (t) ©1995 Carmen Lomas Garza, photo credit: Adam Reich, Collection of Aaron & Marion Borenstein, Coral Gables, Florida; 388, 389 (all) Jorge Albán/HRW; 390-391 (bkgrd) ©Jeremy Woodhouse, digitalvision; 390 (cl) Book cover (Spanish edition) from La Casa de los Espíritus by Isabel Allende. Reprinted by permission of HarperCollins Publishers, Inc.; (cr) Book cover (Spanish edition) from Paula by Isabel Allende and trans. by Margaret Sayers Peden. ©1994 by Isabel Allende. Translation ©1995 by HarperCollins Publishers. Reprinted by permission of HarperCollins Publishers Inc.; 391 (tr) Marcia Lieberman Photography; 397 (tl) Courtesy of Maricel Mayor Marsán; 398 (cr) Victoria Smith/HRW; 399 (cr) Victoria Smith/HRW; (tr) ©William James Warren/CORBIS; 400-401 (all) ©Wolfgang Kaehler/CORBIS; 400 (r) ©Bettmann/CORBIS.

VOCABULARIO ADICIONAL: Page R7 (r) ©BananaStock; (bl) Digital Image copyright ©2006 PhotoDisc; (tl) Sam Dudgeon/HRW; R8 (cr) Don Couch/HRW; (t) Digital Image copyright ©2006 PhotoDisc; (cl) Álvaro Ortiz/HRW; R9 (tl) Sam Dudgeon/HRW; (bl) Don Couch/HRW; (tr,cr) Gary Russ/HRW; (br) Álvaro Ortiz/HRW; R10 (tl) ©Digital Vision; (cl) ©RubberBall/Alamy Photos; (bl) Corbis Images; (cr) Digital Image copyright ©2006 PhotoDisc; R11 (tl) ©Buddy Mays/CORBIS; (bl) Álvaro Ortiz/HRW; (br) ©Dennis Degnan/CORBIS.

NOVELA STILL PHOTOS: Spain - Don Couch/HRW; Puerto Rico – John Langford/HRW; Mexico, Costa Rica, Peru, Chile - Don Couch/HRW.

ICONS: (Cultura) Don Couch/HRW. Conexión Icons: (Arte, Geografía, Economía doméstica, Música) PhotoDisc/gettyimages; (Ciencias naturales, Historia) ©Royalty-Free/CORBIS; (Ciencias sociales) Wolfgang Kaehler Photography.

Texas Essential Knowledge and Skills for Languages Other Than English

Levels I and II—Novice Progress Checkpoint

Knowledge and skills

1. Communication The student communicates in a language other than English using the skills of listening, speaking, reading, and writing.

The student is expected to:

A. engage in oral and written exchanges of learned material to socialize and to provide and obtain information;

B. demonstrate understanding of simple, clearly spoken, and written language such as simple stories, high-frequency commands, and brief instructions when dealing with familiar topics; and

C. present information using familiar words, phrases, and sentences to listeners and readers.

2. Cultures The student gains knowledge and understanding of other cultures.

The student is expected to:

A. demonstrate an understanding of the practices (what people do) and how they are related to the perspectives (how people perceive things) of the cultures studied; and

B. demonstrate an understanding of the products (what people create) and how they are related to the perspectives (how people perceive things) of the cultures studied.

3. Connections The student uses the language to make connections with other subject areas and to acquire information.

The student is expected to:

A. use resources (that may include technology) in the language and cultures being studied to gain access to information; and

B. use the language to obtain, reinforce, or expand knowledge of other subject areas.

4. Comparisons The student develops insight into the nature of language and culture bycomparing the student's own language and culture to another.

The student is expected to:

A. demonstrate an understanding of the nature of language through comparisons of the student's own language and the language studied;

B. demonstrate an understanding of the concept of culture through comparisons of the student's own culture and the cultures studied; and

C. demonstrate an understanding of the influence of one language and culture on another.

5. Communities The student participates in communities at home and around the world by using languages other than English.

The student is expected to:

A. use the language both within and beyond the school setting through activities such as participating in cultural events and using technology to communicate; and

B. show evidence of becoming a lifelong learner by using the language for personal enrichment and career development.

Texas Education Agency from http://www.tea.state.tx.us/rules/tac/chapter114/ch114c.html